ARLIS

Alaska Resources
Library & Information Services
Anchorage, Alaska

HABITAT DIVISION — LIBRARY
ALASKA DEPARTMENT OF FISH & GAME
333 RASPBERRY ROAD
ANCHORAGE, ALASKA 99518 - 1599

RIVER CONSERVATION
AND MANAGEMENT

ARLIS

Alaska Resources
Library & Information Services
Anchorage, Alaska

RIVER CONSERVATION AND MANAGEMENT

Edited by

P. J. BOON
Nature Conservancy Council for Scotland,
Edinburgh, UK

P. CALOW
University of Sheffield, UK

and

G. E. PETTS
University of Technology,
Loughborough, UK

HABITAT DIVISION — LIBRARY
ALASKA DEPARTMENT OF FISH & GAME
333 RASPBERRY ROAD
ANCHORAGE, ALASKA 99518 - 1599

JOHN WILEY & SONS
Chichester · New York · Brisbane · Toronto · Singapore

Copyright © 1992 by John Wiley & Sons Ltd,
                     Baffins Lane, Chichester,
                     West Sussex PO19 1UD, England

All rights reserved.

No part of this book may be reproduced by any means,
or transmitted, or translated into a machine language
without the written permission of the publisher.

Other Wiley Editorial Offices

John Wiley & Sons, Inc., 605 Third Avenue,
New York, NY 10158-0012, USA

Jacaranda Wiley Ltd, G.P.O. Box 859, Brisbane,
Queensland 4001, Australia

John Wiley & Sons (Canada) Ltd, 5353 Dundas Road West,
Fourth Floor, Etobicoke, Ontario M9B 6H8, Canada

John Wiley & Sons (SEA) Pte Ltd, 37 Jalan Pemimpin #05-04
Block B, Union Industrial Building, Singapore 2057

Library of Congress Cataloging-in-Publication Data:

River conservation and management / edited by P. J. Boon, P. Calow, and
   G. E. Petts.
      p.   cm.
   Includes bibliographical references and index.
   ISBN 0-471-92946-8
   1. Stream conservation—Congresses.   I. Boon, P. J.   II. Calow.
Peter.   III. Petts, Geoffrey E.
QH75.A1R58   1991
628.1'12—dc20   91–2797
                                                        CIP

British Library Cataloguing in Publication Data:

A catalogue record for
this book is available from
the British Library.

ISBN 0-471-92946-8

Typeset in 10/12 pt Times by Acorn Bookwork, Salisbury, Wiltshire
Printed and bound in Great Britain by Courier International Ltd, East Kilbride

Contents

List of Contributors

P. L. Angermeier   Virginia Polytechnic Institute and State University, Blacksburg VA, USA

P. D. Armitage   Institute of Freshwater Ecology, Wareham, UK

A. Bailey   Tennessee Technological University, Cookeville, TN, USA

P. J. Barham   National Rivers Authority, Brampton, UK

L. A. Barmuta   University of Tasmania, Hobart, Australia

T. J. Beechie   University of Washington, Seattle, WA, USA

E. F. Benfield   Virginia Polytechnic Institute and State University, Blacksburg, VA, USA

R. M. Biette   Ontario Ministry of Natural Resources, Toronto, Canada

J. H. Blackburn   Institute of Freshwater Ecology, Wareham, UK

P. J. Boon   Nature Conservancy Council for Scotland, Edinburgh, UK

A. Brookes   National Rivers Authority, Reading, UK

A. E. Brown   Nature Conservancy Council for England, Peterborough, UK

P. Calow   University of Sheffield, UK

F. M. Chutter   Council for Scientific and Industrial Research, Pretoria, Republic of South Africa

L. Cole   Land Use Consultants, London, UK

K. J. Collier   Department of Conservation, Wellington, New Zealand

K. W. Cummins   University of Pittsburgh, PA, USA

F. C. de Moor   Albany Museum, Grahamstown, Republic of South Africa

D. P. Dodge   Ontario Ministry of Natural Resources, Toronto, Canada

M. T. Furse   Institute of Freshwater Ecology, Wareham, UK

J. L. Gardiner   National Rivers Authority, Reading, UK

A. Gasith   Tel-Aviv University, Israel

S. W. Golladay   University of Oklahoma Biological Station, Kingston, OK, USA

J. A. Gore   Austin Peay State University, Clarksville, TN, USA

C. H. Green   Flood Hazard Research Centre, Middlesex Polytechnic, UK

K. J. Gregory   University of Southampton, UK

D. M. Harper   University of Leicester, UK

D. L. Howell   Nature Conservancy Council for Scotland, Edinburgh, UK

E. Jutila   Finnish Game and Fisheries Institute, Helsinki, Finland

Z. Kajak   Polish Academy of Sciences, Lomianki, Poland

K. Kern   Universität Karlsruhe, Germany

J. L. Kershner   Utah State University, UT, USA

J. M. King   University of Cape Town Rondebosch, Republic of South Africa

J. Lacoursière   University of Lund, Sweden

P. S. Lake   Monash University, Clayton, Australia

J. B. Layzer   Tennessee Technical University, Cookeville, TN, USA

D. G. Lonzarich   University of Washington, Seattle, WA, USA

R. Marchant   Museum of Victoria, Abbotsford, Australia

R. H. S. McColl   Department of Conservation, Wellington, New Zealand

P. Mellquist   Norwegian Water Resources and Energy Administration, Oslo, Norway

J. L. Meyer   University of Georgia, Athens, GA, USA

R. J. Naiman   University of Washington, Seattle, WA, USA

M. D. Newson   University of Newcastle-upon-Tyne, UK

L. B.-M. Petersen   University of Lund, Sweden

R. C. Petersen   University of Lund, Sweden

G. E. Petts   University of Technology, Loughborough, UK

S. C. Ralph   University of Washington, Seattle, WA, USA

I. A. Russell   South African National Parks Board, Wilderness, Republic of South Africa

F. Schiemer   University of Vienna, Austria

B. H. Seghers   University of Oxford, UK

F. Sheldon   University of Adelaide, Australia

C. D. Smith   University of Leicester, UK

W. M. Snider   California Department of Fish and Game, Sacramento, CA, USA

W. T. Swank   Coweeta Hydrologic Laboratory, Otto, NC, USA

M. C. Thoms   University of Adelaide, Australia

S. M. Tunstall   Flood Hazard Research Centre, Middlesex Polytechnic, UK

H. Waidbacher   University of Agriculture, Vienna, Austria

K. F. Walker   University of Adelaide, Australia

J. B. Wallace   University of Georgia, Athens, GA, USA

J. R. Webster   Virginia Polytechnic Institute and State University, Blacksburg, VA, USA

R. L. Welcomme   Food and Agriculture Organization of the United Nations, Rome, Italy

D. F. Westlake   Institute of Freshwater Ecology, Wareham, UK

J. F. Wright   Institute of Freshwater Ecology, Wareham, UK

Preface

From a human perspective, wild rivers are hazards; water flowing to the sea is wasteful; shallows are obstructions to navigation. These traditional views are slowly being replaced by recognition of the ecological and landscape values of natural rivers. The dilemma is to reconcile our immediate practical needs with long-term sustainability in terms of an ecologically sound and aesthetically acceptable environment—something that can only be achieved by strategic planning and sensible management involving thorough ecological understanding.

This is the backdrop against which this book has been compiled. The content arose out of a three-day international conference held at the University of York in September 1990 sponsored by the Nature Conservancy Council of Great Britain. However, we hope that the book is more than just a "proceedings", in that the chapters do not necessarily faithfully reflect the papers at the meeting, and their order is far more concerned with the flow of the subject than with the original order of presentation. Also, each chapter has been subject to peer review and of the chapters submitted for consideration, 60% were accepted.

The case for conservation is made in Chapters 2–6; first generally and then more specifically in particular river systems around the world. The tension referred to in the first paragraph above means that not all rivers can be treated in the same way—and systems of classification are needed, to identify "natural states", to suggest where management and conservation effort should be invested, and to indicate the extent to which management and conservation goals have been achieved. These techniques, again roughly arranged from general to particular, are critically reviewed in Chapters 7–14.

Most of our rivers have suffered some form of human impact; yet all seem to have an innate capacity to recover, at least partially, after stress and disturbance. The extent to which rivers can recover with or without human intervention is considered in Chapters 15–23. These are all based on experience with particular systems, as case studies, but most draw general conclusions and suggest understanding in terms of broad principles.

Protection, conservation, and management will, of course, come to nought unless they are backed up by appropriate and effective legislative constraints and public support. These issues, largely from UK and North American experience, are addressed in Chapters 24–28.

Throughout the book there are some persistent and general themes—the need for a holistic, whole-catchment approach; the need for more development of automated and macro-scale observations (for example, through remote sensing); the need to take into account the naturally dynamic, metastable condition of river systems; the need for a more thorough and general understanding of river ecosystems—all of which are highlighted in the general introduction and summary chapters that sandwich the rest. We hope, therefore, that the book serves not only to convey current understanding but also as a signpost for future developments in this complex, multi-disciplinary area.

ACKNOWLEDGEMENTS

We would like to thank Patrick Armitage, Ed Darby, Nigel Holmes, Peter Maitland and Chris Spray for their contributions in planning the programme at York upon which this book has been based, and the Nature Conservancy Council for its advice, support, and interest throughout.

P. J. Boon
P. Calow
G. E. Petts

1

River Management—Objectives and Applications

P. MELLQUIST

Norwegian Water Resources and Energy Administration, Directorate of Water Resources, Middelthuns gate 29, PO Box 5091, Majorstua, 0301 Oslo 3, Norway

INTRODUCTION

In this introductory chapter I intend to start with an historical glance at river management, then take a closer look at the decision processes concerning management of water resources, and finally try to peer into the sometimes clouded crystal ball called the future. The management of resources in general and that of water resources and rivers are different aspects of the same matter, so I am taking the liberty of interchanging these concepts.

Access to water is a necessity of life, and our ancestors were not slow to introduce management of water resources after they had climbed down from the trees—first, by throwing stones or a half-gnawed thighbone at outsiders who came too close to their waterhole. Later, more advanced "methods" supported by knives, axes, and strategic marriages have been used to secure control of water resources. Even after thousands of years of linguistic duels, now mostly fought by lawyers, it seems that man still has ground to cover in the more theoretical aspects of resource management.

Management is one of many words that have never been, and never will be, particularly precise as far as their meaning is concerned. "River management" and "conservation" are no different.

We find the management of a river or river system in its simplest form when someone moves a few stones in a river bed in order to improve passage for himself, fish, or timber and *maintains* these changes over a period of time. Diverting water through a water wheel or into an irrigation canal is a more advanced expression of this. The other extreme is a completely radical change of the hydrological and ecological conditions. One example is the proposal to reverse the flow of several major Russian rivers to restore the water level in the Aral Sea, the surface area of which has been reduced by 30–40% in recent years because of water withdrawal for agricultural purposes. Within the range of such extremes we find all kinds of conceivable (and, unfortunately, a number of inconceivable) variations of river management. In this context we should also consider the *laissez-faire* attitude which certain countries hold as a kind of management. By *not*

River Conservation and Management. Edited by P. J. Boon, P. Calow, and G. E. Petts
© 1992 John Wiley & Sons Ltd

doing something, in reality a decision has been made with clear and often very unfortunate consequences.

RIVER MANAGEMENT—THE ART OF THE IMPOSSIBLE?

Not all forms of river management are necessarily good administration of the river system in question. Unfortunately, the opposite is often the case, resulting partly from cynicism and the profit motive, but perhaps more often because of ignorance and lack of understanding. However, special-interest bias and a short-term outlook are not limited to the government agencies dealing with water resource development. These phenomena can also be seen in other resource agencies in most countries of the world.

Ideally, the purpose and objectives of river management should be as follows:

- Balancing between users' interests;
- Optimization of the use of resources;
- Inclusion of environmental interests and those of the general public when exploiting water resources;
- Cleaning up after "old sins".

Balancing between users' interests

In many countries river management has been coloured by the fact that, historically, one or a handful of strong interests have exploited the water resources. These special interests have so dominated law and practice that one can in reality equate their needs with the way management of water resources has been applied.

Norway is an example of this. Norwegian water resource legislation was completely dominated by timber-floating interests until exploitation for electricity generation took over this role. Until a few decades ago, other interests were mostly considered to be secondary. If they did not lead to too much "bother" for timber floating and/or hydropower generation, these other interests were considered—otherwise not.

In the Netherlands we must assume that consideration of the water balance in the low-lying land areas and of canal traffic has been a strong guide for that country's river management. In parts of the world where there is little precipitation we know that access to water for consumption or irrigation is of vital significance, and has consequently coloured management practice.

When more than one party claims the right to use a limited resource it goes without saying that it must be apportioned. This is especially true when concern for "voiceless" qualities such as landscape, plants, animals, etc. has to be included. But this is easier said than done. A conservative bureaucracy, based on a legal foundation at least as conservative, can often stop broad-minded river management. There is reason to maintain that the ideal objective for river management, that is, "fair" distribution among the different interests, has hardly been attained in any country.

In most countries the responsibility for water use is divided among several public agencies. Everything one agency does affects many other agencies, yet each operates in isolation. Concern or responsibility for the whole are very seldom felt, but curiously enough, more often a great struggle between entities for the "ownership of the problems" takes place.

We can obviously speculate as to why this is so, but one answer may be that it is much easier to speak of "overall planning", "comprehensive view", and "integrated management" than to carry them out. In recent years a sum of close to £8 million has been spent in Norway by different agencies on planning the utilization of water resources without anyone being able to say that the results match the input. Politicians especially may be held up for criticism in this respect, since they can vote one day for a general rule with the best of intentions, while the next day they can "forget" it in favour of a single decision which well suits the party programme with regard to establishment of industry or district interests. We seem to be most consistent in our inconsistency!

Optimization of the use of resources

Water resource development has contributed greatly to the economic and social growth of many countries, and, as previously stated, this is one of the reasons why one or a few major interests often dominate the use and management of rivers. In Norway this development has been primarily aimed at promoting electricity production (99.8% of Norway's electricity is generated by hydro); in the western states of the USA, at promoting agricultural irrigation. As much as 80% of the total use of water in Utah and 90% in New Mexico has been directly linked to irrigation and not to consumption or other purposes.

It follows that optimization of the use of resources, in a more modern meaning of the concept, often implies limiting the rights of economically weighty and historically important interests. We are often confronted by an almost hopeless balancing between a user's interests, which can easily be calculated in money or a number of jobs, and those interests that cannot be measured at all or are difficult to compare. Again, these will often be the appearance of the landscape or concerns for plant and animal life of which even scientists themselves do not know the entire ecological significance.

The protection of water resources, either the whole river system or parts of it, is also a form of resource use and therefore a link in a total optimization process. The eternal question is, of course: what are we protecting and what are we protecting it from?

Since 1960 in Norway we have worked to protect watercourses from hydropower development. This came as a reaction to a very intensive period of such development which had left considerable scars on the Norwegian landscape. Today there are three watercourse protection plans in operation in Norway and a total of 195 watercourses or sections of watercourses are protected. This corresponds to a power potential of 21 terrawatt hours (i.e. approximately 12% of the technically and economically exploitable hydropower potential). At this time, work on protection plan 4 is in process, which is assumed to be the last stage of this undertaking. Approximately 200 additional watercourses are being evaluated and these have a power potential equal to that of the three previous plans combined.

There are many interesting aspects of these protection plans. In particular, they present a paradox that illustrates part of the difficulty in administering good ideas in an otherwise complicated world. Watercourses are protected *from* hydropower development *in favour* of plants, wildlife, cultural relics, "scientific evidence", public access to outdoor life, etc. However, the interests of other users affect the watercourses in such a manner that the intentions of protection can be undermined just as effectively as if the development of the watercourse for hydropower purposes had been permitted. This is the same situation that arises when a designated wilderness is made into a national park: the greatest problems of wear and tear are caused by hikers and others for whom this untouched pearl of nature is supposed to be preserved. Here lie administrative challenges of the first order.

We cannot escape the fact that most of the population in Norway live fairly close to water, and we also have to live with engineers and other manipulators of nature in the future. They are not something apart from us—they just respond to our demands! The problem, of course, is to find an acceptable balance between use and conservation of natural resources of all kinds.

Politicians and other decision makers are submitted to considerable pressures when they have to decide on how resources are to be used. From the viewpoint of business economics, financial profits within a relatively limited time-frame weigh much heavier than presumed ecological disturbances in a 50- to 100-year perspective.

Fortunately, this view is in the process of change in many countries. Not least, worries about the future of the ozone layer, the greenhouse effect, desertification, etc. have had significant effects. The concept of "sustainable development" is beginning to force its way in at all levels and, just as important, it is being understood.

I have a real fear, however, that the words "optimal use of resources" in the language and actions of many administrative bodies will be synonymous with short-term financial concerns for a long time to come. Large parts of the world are so poor that they are not in a financial position to pay heed to what will only bear fruit in a far-distant future. "Hand-to-mouth economy" is the ugly spectre of comprehensive resource management.

It is not only in the poor parts of the world that such things happen. The above-mentioned situation in the Aral Sea shows that giving a one-sided priority to water for irrigation has led to consequences which cannot be called either management or optimal use of resources. In California, which would hardly consider itself a developing country, more than 90% of the original wetlands or marshlands have been lost to drainage, urbanization, and levee-building. Permits to continue this development are still being issued. Indemnities (money) and compensatory measures are usually granted, but these seldom bring back the lost aquatic biotopes, nor do they have a noticeable effect on the catchment area and on the rivers downstream from the encroachments.

Concern for wildlife as such and for individual species of plants and animals in particular is weak when their direct financial significance cannot be demonstrated. This situation does not only apply to poor countries, as many people seem to think. According to Sigel (1989), at least 85% of the Pacific Northwest's old-growth forests have been eliminated, compared to 40% of the world's tropical rain forest and 15% of the Amazon's. Examples can be multiplied endlessly. Undoubtedly there are many who should sweep their own doorsteps!

Environmental concerns and encroachments in river systems

The purpose of resource management is to try to reach the ideal state: utilization of the resources without deterioration of the natural basis. This concept is also the general principle in the report in 1987 by the World Commission on Environment and Development (the Brundtland Report). The prescription is sustainable development based on controlled use of resources, cutting back consumption and intensive measures to lessen damage where necessary.

It can hardly be doubted, however, that even renewable resources are suffering from the impact of degradation in quality and limitations on renewability. All over the world, water is increasingly degraded by soil erosion, chemical wastes, irrigation salts, organic overloads, and years of too heavy withdrawals or bypasses from parts of the watersheds.

Of course, in many places a lot of money and technical know-how is devoted to eliminating the unwanted side-effects, but in general these efforts are concentrated on specific locations or parts of a river, and the hydrological and ecological systems as a whole are beyond the thinking or capabilities of most decision makers.

Various studies on the consequences of different encroachments are usually carried out, but relatively few (if any) are made on long-term effects caused by, for example, urbanization, clearing of wooded areas, or cultivation/change in agricultural use. It is difficult to obtain long-term financing for long-term scientific studies on untouched (or virtually untouched) river systems (of which there are still a few in Norway), despite the recognition of the importance of having such reference watercourses.

However, several countries in Europe have invested much time and effort in preparing and implementing laws in order to attain better and more environment-oriented water management. There is also reason for hope in that the harmonization of environmental policy currently in progress within the EC will direct attention to this special area and thus raise standards.

The new openness that we have, to our surprise, seen sweeping the Eastern bloc countries has undoubtedly provided completely new possibilities for co-operation across previously closed borders in the field of river management. It cannot help much to keep one's own section of a river in order when the neighbours upstream do not. But if the openings in the Iron Curtain have increased in number, they have also brought to light these countries' great environmental problems, of which pollution and river basin management are only a small part.

Cleaning up after old sins

Using rivers as recipients and means of transport of waste material from industry and urbanized areas is no longer acceptable, as pollution of the large European rivers and the coastal marine areas (the North Sea and the Mediterranean) has shown. An improvement in the situation can nevertheless be attained—without actually turning to river management—by simply preventing the pollutants from reaching the watercourses. A diffuse flow of pollutants from agriculture, industry, and natural sources is, on the other hand, a problem that in addition requires deliberate use of discharge and the rivers' self-cleansing abilities.

One of the main problems today is that watercourses have been altered over centuries into hydraulically optimal but ecologically catastrophic sterotyped canal systems, which are often eutrophic and organically enriched. The broad range of natural variations has disappeared and with it the abundance of species and necessary flexibility within the ecosystems. Also, we must introduce modern technology in order to optimize our water consumption. In many respects, we exploit water resources in a very primitive way and substantial amounts of water drawn for consumption or irrigation never reach their destinations. In Oslo it is estimated that approximately 40% of the withdrawals from lakes within and around the city disappears due to leaks in water pipes. For all of Norway, the losses are estimated to lie between 20% and 60%. Because of the high costs of rehabilitating the water supply piping, which is in part very old, the authorities responsible are very reluctant to adopt radical measures. This is not only a Norwegian characteristic!

If we continue with this policy, however, we will be faced with increasing problems and expenses. Sources of water are continuously exploited in a more intense manner with an increasing use per capita, with negative consequences for discharge and water quality downstream. New sources further away from the cities must be tapped or the drawing upon groundwater intensified, entailing consequences for the supply of water to rivers, the intrusion of salt in groundwater reservoirs, the settling of subsoil, etc. This is a vicious circle, which is rapidly reducing the number of "untouched" river systems.

THE BASIS OF DECISION MAKING IN RIVER MANAGEMENT

Through the ages, river management and most other forms of resource management have been based on everything from pure anecdotal and very inaccurate historical "facts" to the previous decades' more or less sophisticated computer programs. In the 1960s, many scientists and administrators struggled through a time-consuming registration and classification marathon, during which they did not really quite know why they were registering those parameters that were "in" at the time. To an even lesser degree, they were able to combine the collected data in such a way that they revealed enough information about the locality concerned that would be valid over a period of time. The application of the results in other localities was often even less successful.

In Norway, and in the rest of Scandinavia, we were in a phase where we apparently produced more paper than results. There was great activity in many research institutes that led to a general raising of competence, but both those preparing and those using the reports generally lacked the ability to see the whole picture and thus to put equal emphasis on every separate piece of the puzzle. We ended in a hopeless situation where everything was equally important!

The next logical step in processing the large amounts of data accumulated was to use computers. The first models were so primitive that they were in fact useless. However, progress has been great, and now relatively sophisticated mathematical modelling tools are to be found in many countries. We have until now probably only seen the beginning of this development, but since so many people are still easily impressed by computers, it is important to remember that the result is no better than the quality of the input!

Problems with computer-based analyses and evaluations in river management are mainly of three types:

- There is much left to do regarding the actual development of mathematical models.
- As of today, it is too expensive and time-consuming to carry out the field work that is necessary for inputs when small encroachments by parties poor in resources are to be evaluated.

- Qualified "universal geniuses" are still needed to interpret and correctly apply the results. This type of person is still scarce!

I have a distinct feeling that the people developing the models at this time are turning the same stones without really getting any closer to the answers. A critical study of the whole concept is needed.

RIVER MANAGEMENT IN THE FUTURE

The outstanding Danish humourist, P. Storm, once said "It is difficult to make predictions—especially about the future", which is the best way of describing the problem!

The world's rapidly increasing population is itself the greatest strain on the total resource capital. The pressure on water resources will in future increase at the same time as the availability and quality of such resources decrease. Since the link between resource management in general, water resource management and river management in particular is so strong, it seems obvious that the need for well-qualified river managers will increase in the years to come if we hope to avoid being worse off than we are today.

It cannot be emphasized too strongly that river problems will not be solved in the rivers alone, because these problems for the most part originate in the rivers' catchment areas. Nevertheless, a better understanding of what happens in and along the rivers should provide the relevant "dry land" agencies with the guiding signals necessary for better resource exploitation and activity strategies and thus indirectly be part of overall river management.

Will the authorities in individual countries be prepared to cope with these challenges? Some will, but I am afraid that the poorer parts of the world will not manage to give these matters the necessary priority. Without any form of political undertone, it can be said that we in the developed countries are obliged to share our wealth with the poor if we want them to be capable of making ecologically correct choices.

Furthermore, there is also a need for a broad understanding that a resource cannot be exploited according to technical/economic criteria alone, and we must aim at long-term sustainable development and use of resources. This is presupposing the knowledge that resources are limited and that nature has its levels of tolerance, even though the perspective may be long by the human scale. In other words, we must be willing to reduce financial profits in the short term compared to what has been usual within certain water-exploiting fields.

In addition, more importance must be attached to ecological evaluations in contrast to the traditional technical/economic calculations. It is true that added value is the lubricant that makes society's wheels go round, but so is the fact that the economist's time frame is far too short in relation to ecological response time and nature's levels of tolerance. A cash return in five to ten years combines poorly with the growth rate of the previously mentioned old forests in the US Pacific North-west.

We can hardly expect to attach such importance to ecological needs voluntarily. A good dose of coercion is necessary, in the form of legislation and a framework to constrain unchecked market forces. Many old and toothless laws must be discarded and more appropriate ones drawn up so that it will be possible to intervene ahead of the development and before the problems arise. There are far too many examples of authorities retaining impotent sets of rules that are hardly capable of sorting out problems later. Many administrative bodies must also be forced to act from an overall point of view rather than just tending their own patches.

A more uniform international view of environmental questions in general is necessary to understand that use and management of resources are global, and not regional matters. The World Commission on Environment and Development is, as mentioned above, a step in this direction. Common standards which can be achieved by agreement (for example, within the USA and the EC) are other, and perhaps just as important, catalysts. To be able to refer to what others are doing, when there is little understanding within one's own ranks, is always valuable. Common standards also provide an important framework for otherwise unruly market forces.

How shall we achieve the ideal goals of river management? We need politicians who *dare*, bureaucrats who *want*, and scientists/engineers who *can*. If there is not enough light at the end of the tunnel, it is our task to provide it!

REFERENCES

Brundtland, G. H. (1987). *Our Common Future*, Report of the World Commission on Environment and Development (Chairman: G. H. Brundtland), Oxford University Press, Oxford.
Sigel, M. (1989). The destruction of America's rain forests, *Christian Science Monitor*, 21 September, 19.

SECTION I

THE CASE FOR CONSERVATION

The Yallahs River in the Jamaican Blue Mountains. (Photograph P.J. Boon)

2

Essential Elements in the Case for River Conservation

P. J. BOON

*Research and Development, Nature Conservancy Council for Scotland,
2/5 Anderson Place, Edinburgh EH6 5NP, UK*

THE BACKGROUND TO THE CASE

The case for global ecosystem conservation has been forcefully made, and in many countries largely accepted—at least in principle. The reasons generally given for the importance of biological conservation are summarized in Table 2.1, and are embodied in the threefold aim of the World Conservation Strategy (International Union for Conservation of Nature and Natural Resources, 1980):

- To maintain essential ecological processes and life-support systems;
- To preserve genetic diversity;
- To ensure sustainable utilization of species and ecosystems.

This strategy is undeniably anthropocentric. However, as Boardman (1981) comments, arguing for nature conservation seems to imply the neglect of issues affecting human welfare, despite the fact that for many years conservation organizations have stressed the close relationship between human well-being and the state of man's natural environment.

Use and abuse

Rivers have been used by man more than any other type of ecosystem. They have been abstracted from, fished in, boated on, discharged into; their headwaters have been diverted, their middle reaches dammed, their floodplains developed. One of the main features which has made rivers uniquely attractive to man is the presence of unidirectional moving water—a continuously renewable resource, a rapid removal system for unwanted substances, and a valuable store of potential energy. This same feature is also vitally important to many of the aquatic plants and animals inhabiting rivers and streams, providing fresh supplies of food and oxygen, downstream transport of waste, and an efficient means of dispersal. Unfortunately, where economic gain is the main motivator, other interests get short shrift. For example, the Columbia is North America's fourth

River Conservation and Management. Edited by P. J. Boon, P. Calow, and G. E. Petts
© 1992 John Wiley & Sons Ltd

TABLE 2.1. Motives for conservation

1. Maintenance of earth's life-support systems
2. Practical value (e.g. erosion control, pharmaceutical potential,
        genetic pool for cultivated species)
3. Economic importance (e.g. minerals, tourism)
4. Scientific research
5. Education
6. Aesthetic and recreational value
7. Ethical considerations

largest river. Since the mid-nineteenth century it has become the world's largest generator of hydroelectricity, with 19 major dams and more than 60 smaller ones (Lee, 1989); as one writer put it, "a river that died and was reborn as money" (Worster, 1985). Pressures such as this have ensured that conservation, as an accepted aim of river management, has only entered the reckoning comparatively recently (Figure 2.1).

The case for conservation appears in many guises, each reflecting a particular geographic, economic, scientific, or cultural perspective. Moreover, the arguments for conservation continually shift in emphasis. Populations grow, nations industrialize, global water demand increases (Table 2.2), and thus the effects of man on rivers change in diversity, extent, rate, and permanence.

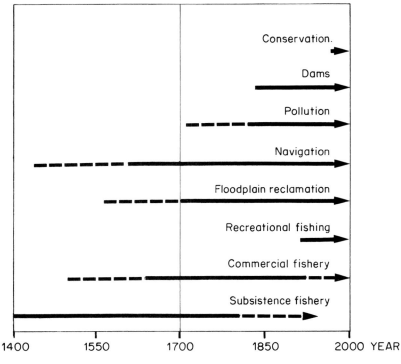

FIGURE 2.1. The historical sequence of river development in Europe (reproduced by permission from Petts, 1987)

TABLE 2.2. Trends in global water consumption by major category, $km^3 a^{-1}$

Water usage	1900	1950	1970	1990	2000	%
Agriculture	525	1130	1850	2680	3250	62.6
Industry	37	178	540	973	1280	24.7
Municipal needs	16	52	130	300	441	8.5
Reservoirs	<1	7	66	170	220	4.2
Total	579	1367	2586	4123	5191	

Source: Global Environment Monitoring System Global Freshwater Quality: A First Assessment, 1989. Meybeck, M., Chapman, D., and Helmer, R. Oxford: Basil Blackwell Ltd, pp. 306. Adapted by permission

The range of human activities potentially damaging to river systems is shown in Table 2.3. Of these, few are decreasing in intensity or even remaining stable. For example, construction of large dams in Britain has passed through several phases of rapid growth, but does now appear to be levelling off (Figure 2.2). In contrast, recorded incidents of river pollution in England and Wales showed a steady rise during the 1980s (Table 2.4). On a global scale, the most serious pollution problems are not found in highly industrialized regions, nor those with predominantly agricultural economies, but in rapidly developing countries such as Brazil and India (Meybeck et al, 1989). Here pollutants which gradually appeared in European rivers over the passage of a century or more are rapidly building up in the compressed time span of a few decades (Figure 2.3).

TABLE 2.3. Major anthropogenic activities affecting river systems

Supra-catchment effects
Acid deposition
Inter-basin transfers

Catchment land-use change
Afforestation and deforestation
Urbanization
Agricultural development
Land drainage/flood protection

Corridor engineering
Removal of riparian vegetation
Flow regulation—dams, channelization, weirs, etc.
Dredging and mining

Instream impacts
Organic and inorganic pollution
Thermal pollution
Abstraction
Navigation
Exploitation of native species
Introduction of alien species

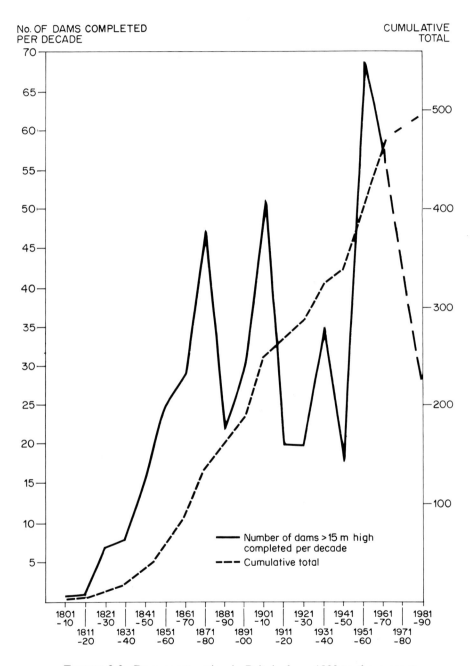

No. OF DAMS COMPLETED
PER DECADE

CUMULATIVE
TOTAL

Number of dams >15 m high
completed per decade
Cumulative total

FIGURE 2.2. Dam construction in Britain from 1800 to the present

TABLE 2.4. River pollution incidents in England
and Wales

Year	Total incidents	Agricultural incidents	Agricultural share (%)
1980	12 500	1671	13.4
1981	12 500	2367	18.9
1982	12 300	2428	19.7
1983	15 250	2795	18.3
1984	18 648	2828	15.2
1985	19 892	3510	17.6
1986	21 230	3427	16.1
1987	23 253	3890	16.7

(From Beck, 1989, *Journal of the Institution of Water
and Environmental Management*, **3**, 468. Reproduced
by permission)

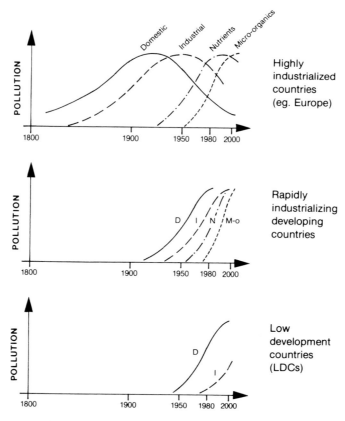

FIGURE 2.3. The successive appearance of pollution problems in countries according to their level and speed of development. Source: Global Environment Monitoring System Global Freshwater Quality: A First Assessment, 1989. Meybeck, M., Chapman D., and Helmer, R. Oxford: Basil Blackwell Ltd., pp. 306. Reproduced by permission

    Finally, the case for conservation must be set against a background of river engineering schemes which are of a magnitude and permanence hitherto unknown. Petts (1984) has estimated that on a worldwide scale large dams are completed at a rate of more than one per day, so that by the year 2000 two-thirds of the world's total stream flow will be controlled (Table 2.5). Although the rate of dam construction is slowing down, the trend now is for ever-larger structures, so that dams which once headed the league are rapidly slipping down the scale. There are now 28 large dams over 200 m high with 23 more planned or under construction. Projects such as the 300 m high Nurek Dam in the USSR now make earlier constructions, such as the 221 m Hoover Dam on the Colorado River, seem relatively insignificant (Petts, 1990).

TABLE 2.5. Number of dams constructed over 15 m high

	Before 1961	Between 1961 and 1980	After 1981 or under construction
World	7408	5556	1316
Africa	251	404	96
North and Central America	2258	993	64
South America	415	368	132
Asia	2235	2027	584
Europe	1993	1523	365
USSR	40	39	12
Oceania	216	202	63

Data from International Institute for Environment and Development and World Resources Institute, 1987

    As suitable sites for new reservoirs are becoming scarcer, inter-river transfer schemes are gaining popularity, some of them on a scale that defies imagination. The proposed redirection of 60 km^3 of water annually from the River Ob in Soviet Central Asia would reduce flows at the river's mouth by 25% (Petts, 1990). A project presently under construction in China will transfer 14 000 million m^3 of water 1150 km from Chang Jiang in the south-east to the North China Plain (Goldsmith and Hildyard, 1990). In some cases entire rivers are being sacrificed in the interests of power generation. For example, the Caroni River, a major tributary of the Orinoco in Venezuela, will have its entire basin impounded by nine dams by the year 2015 (Petts, 1990).
    The outlook is not all gloomy. There are many countries now where those who are the official stewards of our rivers have been given statutory conservation duties. In England and Wales, the setting up of a National Rivers Authority, whose responsibilities include the promotion of nature conservation, provides an excellent opportunity for improving river management. The time has come, then, to press for conservation strategies which encompass the river resource as a whole, so that the proponents of conservation are not continually forced to fight battles for individual systems—for the Danube, or the Loire, or the Rhine. This means better management now, sensitive planning in future, and undoing at least some of the damage of the past.

THE CHARACTER OF THE CASE

The practice of biological nature conservation may be viewed as a continuum, from that which is primarily cultural and frequently dependent upon scientific evaluation to that which is more obviously economic. In addition, the arguments for conservation range from those that are species oriented to those where habitats are the main focus. A sizeable part of the literature on river corridor conservation is directed at individual species or particular groups of species. From these references one might infer that a freshwater organism's best chance of survival is to be economically valuable (e.g. salmonid fish), large (e.g. crocodiles), or at least visually obvious and attractive (e.g. dragonflies), and preferably to have an enthusiastic public following (e.g. otters, birds). Such studies certainly constitute an important element in the case for river conservation, and national or international legislation has a major role to play in protecting rare or endangered species. Nevertheless, species conservation must always be seen in the wider context of functioning river systems.

The place of nature conservation within a wider framework

Making a case for river conservation based solely on scientific grounds requires three things: (1) survey, to identify the species and habitats of interest; (2) classification, to distinguish rivers of different types; and (3) assessment, to identify (in at least a semi-objective way) rivers which have greater conservation value than others. The extent to which these requirements have been met varies greatly from one country to another. In Britain two schemes have been devised over the past five to ten years, one classifying rivers according to their macrophytes (Holmes, 1983), the other based on invertebrate assemblages (Wright et al, 1989). The assessment of nature conservation value requires the use of criteria; those of Ratcliffe (1977) for sites of biological interest are perhaps the most widely accepted: size, diversity, naturalness, rarity, fragility, representativeness, recorded history, position in an ecological/geographical unit, potential value, and intrinsic appeal. Of these, "diversity", "naturalness", and "representativeness" are perhaps the most important in assessing rivers. However, the usefulness of "potential value" as a criterion should not be underestimated, especially in view of the progress being made in techniques of river rehabilitation.

It may not always be easy, of course, to disentangle a scientifically objective assessment of a river from its other values. Some watercourses may not meet standard nature conservation criteria but may be of great significance in a cultural, religious, or historical context. For example, the authors of a paper from Israel freely admit that it is difficult to present dispassionately the case for conserving the River Jordan, as for thousands of years it has occupied such a central position in the life of their nation (Dov Por and Ortal, 1985).

Several countries have adopted schemes for protecting river systems in which the case for nature conservation is merely part of a much broader framework. In the State of Washington, USA, the Wild and Scenic Rivers Program aims to protect "scenic values" which are defined as "wildlife habitat, historic character, archaeological sites, and the provision of public access and recreational enjoyment where possible" (Starlund, 1988).

Similar schemes are used in Canada (Parks Canada, 1984) and in New Zealand (Grindell and Guest, 1986).

In each of these programmes, visual attractiveness is considered to be a major contributor to conservation value. The system in New Zealand defines a "scenic" river as one "that makes an essential contribution to an outstanding scenic landscape", specifically mentioning features such as cascades, violent rapids, and waterfalls, and using such terms as "beauty", "grandeur", and "tranquil". In Britain the responsibilities for landscape and nature conservation are, for various historical reasons, kept clearly separate. It is the duty of the Countryside Commission (CC) "to protect the natural beauty of the countryside and to make it more accessible for public enjoyment" (Countryside Commission, 1986), whereas that of the Nature Conservancy Council (NCC) is restricted to "the conservation of wild flora and fauna, geological and physiographic features of Britain for their scientific, educational, recreational, aesthetic and inspirational value" (Nature Conservancy Council, 1984). This distinction ended in Wales on 1 April 1991, when NCC and CC combined to form the Countryside Council for Wales. A similar merger is scheduled to take place in Scotland on 1 April 1992.

There are two advantages in separating broader areas of recreation, access, and landscape from narrower nature conservation interests. First, there are times when the needs of wildlife are in conflict with other uses; second, it ensures that a scientifically important site, not outstanding for its natural beauty, is not undervalued.

The separatist approach to nature conservation has the disadvantage, however, of placing bodies such as the NCC in what is frequently an adversarial position, when the case for conservation then truly takes on a legal dimension. Most conservationists would argue that this is unsatisfactory, and that instead resources should be developed in an integrated way, with full weight given to the value of natural habitats and wildlife.

Five options for river conservation

Figure 2.4 illustrates a hypothetical gradient from rivers that are still essentially pristine through to those that are totally degraded. In this model the case for conservation then becomes one of five scenarios, with the point of transition from one to another varying according to local, regional, or national circumstances. At one end of the spectrum the case is for *preservation* of the few remaining examples of natural or semi-natural systems. The use of the term "preservation" has frequently been criticized as far too static, too museum-oriented, for a real world of dynamic interactions. Petersen (1990) has recently discussed the etymology of the words "conserve" and "preserve" in relation to rivers, emphasizing the need for conservation that allows rivers some flexibility for change. The challenge to conservationists is surely to distinguish between natural, acceptable change and anthropogenic, undesirable change. Lake (1980) states that for some Australian rivers, preservation is often the essential and only strategy as there are so few wild rivers left to conserve. This may necessitate some form of special management but might, in wilderness areas, simply be a "leave-alone" policy. It is interesting to note that the objective of the World Bank when funding dam-building projects is to site new dams on rivers already modified so that other rivers can be preserved in their natural state (Petts, 1990).

Most of the remainder of Figure 2.4 is concerned with conservation management to a

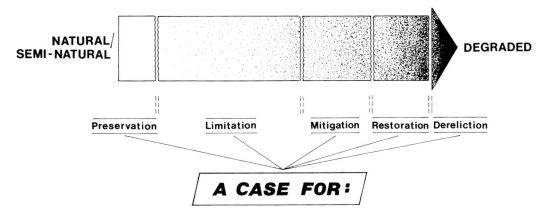

FIGURE 2.4 The case for conservation: a range of management options along a spectrum of decreasing conservation value

greater or lesser extent. Here the emphasis is really on integrated development, and thus the nature of the argument will vary geographically according to the needs of different societies, the environmental consequences of attempting to meet those needs, and the relative weighting given to cultural as opposed to economic aspects of nature conservation. In arid regions water shortage is the pivotal factor; in large areas of the tropics deforestation, catchment erosion, siltation, and waterborne diseases may feature prominently (Le Marquand, 1989) while in industrialized nations acidification, toxic wastes, and recreational demands may need to be addressed. The pressures and problems vary, but the overriding importance of the principle of catchment management remains the same. For rivers of higher quality the case is for *limitation* of catchment development. For rivers of lower quality the case essentially becomes one of *mitigation* (Ferrar et al, 1988), in which the need for river regulation, abstraction, or waste disposal is accepted, and where we try to salvage the best deal possible for aquatic habitats and organisms.

As we move further towards the degraded end of the spectrum, the emphasis now shifts towards river *restoration* in which attempts are made to enhance the process of recovery by manipulating some combination of water quality, hydrology, aquatic habitat structure, and riparian zones (Gore, 1985). Restoration projects have been attempted for everything from small streams to international rivers such as the Rhine, where both political will and massive investment are needed. One of the largest and most unusual river-restoration projects now under way is on the Kissimmee River in Florida, where a 1960s flood-protection scheme turned the 160 km meandering river into a concrete ditch, 78 km long, 60 m wide and 9 m deep. Populations of fish fell by 75%, waterfowl by 90%. Legislation to restore the river was passed in the 1970s, and work has now begun on reshaping the river channel and reflooding the adjacent marshland at an estimated cost of at least US $100 million (Glass, 1987; Pollock, 1989) (Figures 2.5 and 2.6).

This example introduces an economic perspective into the case for conservation. Attempts at producing an objective cost-benefit analysis for a project likely to be environmentally damaging will inevitably fail because there is no real way of attaching monetary value to nature. However, a pragmatic alternative is to discover whether

FIGURE 2.5. The river-floodplain of the Kissimmee River, Florida. Remnants of the old river meanders can be seen adjacent to the channel

FIGURE 2.6. A steel sheet-pile weir placed in the Kissimmee River, Florida, to block the channel partially and divert water to re-flood the adjacent floodplain

TABLE 2.6. The willingness of Norwegian households to pay an increase in yearly electricity rates, as a consequence of protecting 50 watercourses from hydroelectric power development

Groups	Percentage of total	Percentage with zero willingness to pay	Percentage willing to pay increase > 1000 NOK
Active nature conservationists	2.9	5.0	65.6
Concerned about nature conservation	23.9	12.6	53.5
Less concerned about nature conservation	44.3	13.4	31.1
Little concerned about nature conservation	18.9	37.0	11.5

Source: Royal Norwegian Council for Scientific and Industrial Research, 1988

people are prepared to pay for nature conservation. This was the purpose of a survey carried out by the Royal Norwegian Council for Scientific and Industrial Research in 1985. Their results nationwide (Table 2.6) showed a willingness to pay an increase of 500–1000 NOK in yearly electricity rates as a consequence of protecting 50 watercourses from hydropower development. This compared with only 100–450 NOK estimated for stream protection.

The end of the spectrum in Figure 2.4 marks the end of the road for river conservation. This represents rivers that have become so degraded for one reason or another that in the short and medium terms the only management option is to accept the status quo and direct resources towards restoration projects which have a fair chance of success. This, in short, is the case for *dereliction*.

THE DIMENSIONS OF THE CASE

Ward (1989a) has described flowing water ecosystems as four-dimensional, having longitudinal, lateral, vertical, and temporal components. This framework, together with an additional fifth dimension, is an appropriate way of describing what needs to be included in any case for river conservation (Figure 2.7).

The *conceptual* dimension addresses basic questions of philosophy, policy, and practice: "Why are we concerned about conservation?" "What are we trying to conserve?" "What priority should we give to the conservation of flora and fauna?" "How are we to assess the conservation potential of rivers?" The spatial and temporal dimensions are relevant to the practicalities of how we conserve rivers, and in particular they emphasize the importance of including more than just the channel in any conservation scheme.

River corridors are linear systems in which pronounced physical, chemical, and biological changes occur from source to mouth. Earlier studies of this *longitudinal* dimension gave rise to classification schemes in which rivers were divided into discrete zones (e.g. Shelford, 1911; Illies and Botosaneanu, 1963); later studies produced the River Continuum Concept (Vannote et al, 1980). This pictures a river as a continuum of biotic adjustments and organic matter processing along its length, in response to the continuous downstream gradient of physical conditions. Although this model has not

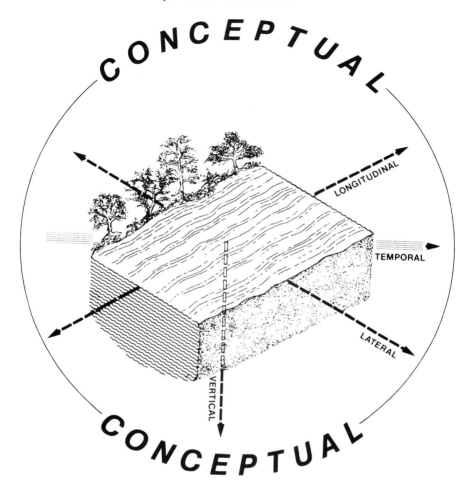

CONCEPTUAL

CONCEPTUAL

LONGITUDINAL

TEMPORAL

LATERAL

VERTICAL

FIGURE 2.7. A five-dimensional approach for considering river conservation (modified from Ward, 1989a)

been without its critics, it has proved useful in explaining a wide range of observations on the functioning of stream communities. The continuity of upstream and downstream reaches therefore becomes a vital concern for river conservation, especially as it is this continuity which can frequently be disrupted by the activities of man. For example, barriers to the migration of fish and invertebrates may be formed by reduced water flow due to over-abstraction, by a stretch of polluted water, or most notably by dam construction which may displace aquatic communities further along the river continuum (the serial discontinuity concept of Ward and Stanford, 1983).

Lateral connections between a river and its valley are equally important. The role of tropical floodplains in the functioning of river ecosystems has been recognized for many years, even if not always respected by governments and developers, but for many industrialized nations floodplain systems have been damaged irreversibly before their significance has been properly assessed. Floodplains fulfil many functions. Nutrients and organic matter transported from the river encourage the development of wetland plants, plankton, and benthic invertebrates, in turn providing a rich food source for fish. However, benefits are not all one-way. For some riverine invertebrates the seasonal flooding of adjacent land is essential for completing their life cycles (e.g. Hayden and Clifford, 1974). For others, organic matter such as detritus and plankton produced beyond the confines of the river channel re-enters it and acts as a valuable food supply.

There is an unusual example of this in South-east Asia, where irrigated rice fields alongside rivers effectively act as floodplain pools. Water is abstracted upstream, passes through an elaborate network of terraces, and then returns to the river at intervals downstream as a high-density source of plankton organisms (Figures 2.8 and 2.9). It was presumably this that was responsible for the very high numbers of filter-feeding Trichoptera and Lepidoptera larvae found in the Legi, a river in Central Java (Boon, unpublished data).

From the extensive floodplains of some of the great tropical rivers to the smaller areas of wet woodland or marsh found alongside temperate streams, riverine wetlands provide a diverse range of habitats and constitute an integral part of a river system. Despite this, many have been deliberately destroyed, sometimes by drainage or urbanization, often by flow regulation which isolates a river from its alluvial floodplain (Petts, 1987). It is crucial, therefore, that the case for conservation extends laterally to incorporate hydrologically contiguous areas.

Closer to the river, even a narrow riparian strip fulfils many functions, some of which have yet to be fully investigated. Bankside vegetation provides habitat and acts as a regulator of water temperature, light, seepage, erosion, and nutrient transfer. If the ultimate procedure for conserving rivers is the proper planning and control of complete catchments, then the management of riparian zones constitutes an important first step (Petersen et al, 1987). In some places, legislation already protects riparian strips, and this is not confined exclusively to first-world countries. In Sri Lanka, for instance, a Government Order stipulates that a specified width of land along either side of a stream should be retained as Crown Reserves whenever Crown land is sold or leased (Senanayake and Moyle, 1982), a move that has been particularly useful in helping to conserve the island's 15 endemic species of freshwater fish.

The *vertical* dimension of river interactions includes not only the hydrological and chemical effects of groundwater on stream flow but also the organisms living within the substratum. Compared with other fields of stream ecology, little work has been done on this so-called "hyporheic community". However, a recent and remarkable observation by Stanford and Ward (1988) has shed new light on the vertical dimension of river systems. They collected riverine invertebrates, particularly stoneflies, in their hundreds from 10 m deep wells located in the floodplain of the Flathead River, Montana, as far away as 2 km from the river channel. They concluded that the biomass in the hyporheic zone might well exceed the benthic biomass of the river. This introduces a whole new dimension into the functioning of river systems, and therefore into the case for river conservation.

Ward's final dimension is a *temporal* one. John Burns, a British politician in the late nineteenth/early twentieth century, once stood on the terrace of the House of Commons angered by some American visitors who belittled the size of the River Thames flowing beneath them. Pointing at it, he remarked, "The St Lawrence is water, and the Mississippi is muddy water, but that, sir, is liquid history". These words may have lacked scientific objectivity, but they were not entirely inappropriate. A river is, in many ways, "liquid history", as it both reflects the characteristics of the catchment in which it runs and itself helps to shape catchment topography.

The temporal dimension of river systems is significant for many reasons. Channel morphology may alter naturally over long periods of time; even the more abrupt and man-induced changes downstream from impoundments may take decades to become apparent (Petts, 1980); and within aquatic habitats organisms grow and develop in time spans from weeks to years, and aquatic communities evolve in time scales of millennia. The practical consequence of this is that river conservation should be planned from a long-term perspective, especially as the effects of a development scheme on biotic populations may not become noticeable for many generations. However, this is not always easy. As Lee (1989) points out in reference to the Columbia River, it is difficult to get very far with adaptive management when government officials are appointed for terms that are shorter than the life span of a salmon.

Case study of the River Spey, Scotland

The River Spey (Figure 2.10) provides a good example of this multi-dimensional approach to conservation. It is one of Britain's largest rivers, rising in the Scottish Highlands at an altitude of 1309 m, with a catchment area of 2655 km^2 and a mean flow of 55.9 m^3 s^{-1} (Maitland, 1985). The Spey was identified as a nationally important river in the Nature Conservation Review (Ratcliffe, 1977), and still remains largely unpolluted and relatively natural, despite some small-scale hydroelectric generation in its upper tributaries and a limited amount of land drainage and flood prevention management in parts of the catchment.

Its aquatic macrophyte communities are typical of oligotrophic conditions in the upper reaches and mesotrophic conditions further downstream, but the enriched communities often associated with the lower reaches of large rivers are not found in the Spey (Holmes, 1983). It has an invertebrate assemblage characteristic for a river of its type, with 18 species of mayflies, 19 species of stoneflies, and 32 species of caddis flies (Wright, pers. comm.), and is probably the best river in that part of Scotland for freshwater pearl mussels (*Margaritifera margaritifera*) (Young, pers. comm.), a species considered vulnerable worldwide (Wells et al, 1983). The river supports an excellent salmonid fishery, and is one of the best areas for otters (*Lutra lutra*) in Scotland (Green and Green, 1980).

The Spey is unusual in traversing an upland floodplain. This contains the internationally important Insh Marshes, the largest single tract of northern poor fen in Britain, a Site of Special Scientific Interest, and a site proposed for Ramsar designation (Fojt et al, 1987). Many stages of hydroseral succession are represented, including open-water communities in Loch Insh and other small lochans, tall reed beds, sedge communities, and semi-natural woodland. The list of plant species recorded includes many which are nationally scarce, such as pillwort (*Pilularia globulifera*), the water sedge (*Carex aquatilis*), and the least yellow water lily (*Nuphar pumila*). The site is renowned for its wetland birds such as goldeneye (*Bucephala clangula*), shoveler (*Anas clypeata*), and an

FIGURE 2.8. Flooded rice fields in Central Java

FIGURE 2.9. The River Legi, Central Java—part of a rice-field/river corridor

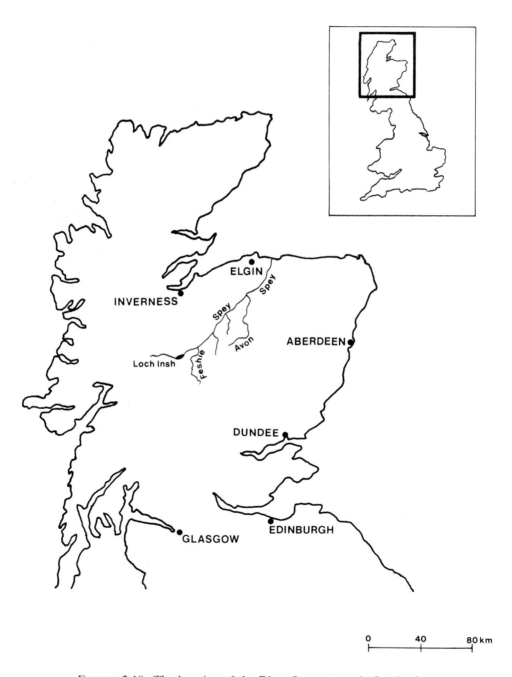

FIGURE 2.10. The location of the River Spey system in Scotland

internationally important over-wintering population of whooper swans (*Cygnus cygnus*) (Fojt et al, 1987).

The conservation of the Spey must therefore take account of both longitudinal (source to mouth) and lateral (river to floodplain) interactions. The temporal dimension needs addressing too, particularly with respect to an important geomorphological feature at the confluence of the Spey with the River Feshie. This is the best example of a forested alluvial fan with active braided river channels anywhere in Britain and one of the finest in the northern temperate zone of Western Europe (Petts, pers. comm.). It is the very fact that the system is dynamic with an actively migrating channel which gives this site its unique interest.

The Spey illustrates well a common problem for nature conservation. Those factors which are responsible for maintaining the interest of the site—in this case flooding, channel erosion, and sediment deposition—are also those which often conflict with other uses. Consequently, the nature conservation value of this whole region of the River Spey (incorporating the Insh Marshes and the Feshie confluence) may now be at risk. The owners of property and agricultural land are anxious to prevent a repeat of recent flooding, and pressure is mounting in the Spey for some form of engineering solution, either by channel excavation in the spey or by re-routing the Feshie. It is essential that the case for conservation be considered in a truly multi-dimensional framework.

STRENGTHENING THE CASE

How can the case for river conservation be made more effectively?

(1) *The application of theoretical ecology to river conservation*: Many concepts in stream ecology receive scant recognition from conservationists. The application of island biogeographic theory to stream colonization (Minshall and Petersen, 1985), nutrient spiralling in river channels, floodplains, and riparian zones (Ward, 1989b), the resilience of streams to outside disturbance (Webster et al, 1983), and studies of community structure (Calow et al, 1990) are examples of theoretical topics potentially beneficial to the practice of conservation.

(2) *Increased research effort*: This needs to be broad based, with less distinction made between "pure" and "applied" research, yet at the same time properly targeted at areas inadequately understood. The attitude prevalent in many countries that all environmental problems can be solved at a stroke by short-term, low-budget research projects requires changing fundamentally.

(3) *Studies on habitat requirements of riverine biota*: Conservation management is frequently ineffective because the requirements of important species or communities are not known. For example, the setting of "minimum ecological flows" downstream from dams or abstraction points is often arbitrary and has little or no ecological significance (Garcia de Jalon, 1987).

(4) *Taxonomic work*: River surveys, especially in the tropics and sub-tropics, are often hampered because the animals and plants collected cannot be properly identified. Despite their present lack of popularity, taxonomic studies are vital in underpinning ecology and conservation.

TABLE 2.7. A survey of papers published in scientific journals during the 1980s, in the areas of freshwater biology, applied ecology, and conservation

Journal	No. of papers examined	No. of papers on river conservation/ management	%
Hydrobiologia	1140	0	0.0
Archiv für Hydrobiologie	550	1	0.2
Freshwater Biology	571	2[a]	0.4
Journal of Applied Ecology	735	5	0.7
Environmental Conservation	1103	13	1.3
Biological Conservation	670	31	4.6
Environmental Management	580	30	5.2
Total	5249	82	1.6

[a]Plus 12 papers from a symposium on biology and conservation of brown trout

(5) *Scientific publication*: The case for conserving river habitats and their wildlife must be grounded in objective, ecological science, and the results of relevant research made widely available. An examination of seven mainstream, international journals in applied ecology, freshwater biology, and conservation (Table 2.7) showed that they contain very few papers focusing specifically on river conservation. Much of the work seems to disappear into unpublished reports from government departments, or into publications from university research institutes, and never reaches more than a tiny fraction of the potential readership.

(6) *National and international co-ordination*: Better liaison is needed between government and non-government research agencies nationally and internationally. The MAB project on land/water ecotones (Naiman et al, 1989; Naiman and Décamps, 1990) is a good example of fruitful co-operation in this field.

(7) *Improved procedures for Environmental Assessment*: Many countries have now passed laws requiring EAs to be carried out before development schemes are implemented. An EA provides an excellent opportunity for making the case for conservation, but only if the ecological component is of a uniformly high standard.

(8) *Adaptive management in river-modification schemes*: Even unwanted interference on rivers can be used to advantage if treated as ecological experimentation. There may then be scope for using the results to change the way in which schemes are managed (e.g. reservoir releases, river abstractions).

(9) *Long-term monitoring*: There are comparatively few examples of long-term studies in river ecology. More work needs to be done, for instance, on the natural variability of river systems if their conservation is to be effective (Calow et al, 1990). There are some encouraging signs. In the USA a network of 17 long-term ecological research sites, some of which contain flowing water, has been set up by the National Science Foundation, and in Britain the Natural Environment Research Council has recently discussed a programme for long-term monitoring of rivers and lakes.

(10) *Public education and participation*: River basins are rarely uninhabited. Where rivers are used by people, river conservation can only succeed with the involvement of people. Public education and participation are essential if the case for river conservation is to be persuasive.

ACKNOWLEDGEMENTS

I would like to thank M. Kent Loftin (South Florida Water Management District, West Palm Beach) for permission to reproduce photographs of the Kissimmee River (Figures 2.5 and 2.6).

REFERENCES

Beck, L. (1989). "A review of farm waste pollution", *Journal of the Institution of Water and Environmental Management*, **3**, 467–477.

Boardman, R. (1981). *International Organization and the Conservation of Nature*, Macmillan, London.

Calow, P., Armitage, P., Boon, P., Chave, P., Cox, E., Hildrew, A., Learner, M., Maltby, L., Morris, G., Seager, J., and Whitton, B. (1990). *River Water Quality*, Ecological Issues No. 1, British Ecological Society, London.

Countryside Commission (1986). *Your countryside our concern*, Cheltenham.

Dov Por, F. and Ortal, R. (1985). "River Jordan—the survival and future of a very special river", *Environmental Conservation*, **12**, 264–268.

Ferrar, A. A., O'Keeffe, J. H., and Davies, B. R. (1988). "The River Research Programme", *South African National Scientific Programmes Report No. 146*.

Fojt, W., Kirby, K., McLean, I., Palmer, M., and Pienkowski, M. (1987). "The national importance of the Insh Marshes", *Unpublished report*, Nature Conservancy Council, Peterborough.

Garcia de Jalon, D. (1987). "River regulation in Spain", *Regulated Rivers: Research and Management*, **1**, 343–348.

Glass, S. (1987). "Rebirth of a river", *Restoration and Management Notes*, **5**, 6–14.

Goldsmith, E., and Hildyard, N. (Eds) (1990). *The Earth Report 2: Monitoring the Battle for our Environment*, Mitchell Beazley, London.

Gore, J. A. (1985). *The Restoration of Rivers and Streams*, pp. vii–xii, Butterworth, Boston.

Green, J., and Green, R. (1980). *Otter Survey of Scotland 1977–79*, The Vincent Wildlife Trust, London.

Grindell, D. S., and Guest, P. A. (1986). "A list of rivers and lakes deserving inclusion in a Schedule of Protected Waters", *Report of the Protected Waters Assessment Committee, Water and Soil Miscellaneous Publication No. 97*, Wellington.

Hayden, W., and Clifford, H. F. (1974). "Seasonal movements of the mayfly *Leptophlebia cupida* (Say) in a brown-water stream of Alberta, Canada", *American Midland Naturalist*, **91**, 90–102.

Holmes, N. T. H. (1983). "Typing British rivers according to their flora", *Focus on Nature Conservation No. 4*, Nature Conservancy Council, Peterborough.

Illies, J., and Botosaneanu, L. (1963). "Problèmes et méthodes de la classification et de la zonation ecologique des eaux courantes, considerées surtout du point de vue faunistique", *Mitteilungen der Internationalen Vereinigung für theoretische und angewandte Limnologie*, **12**, 1–57.

International Institute for Environment and Development and World Resources Institute (1987). *World Resources 1987*, Basic Books, New York.

International Union for Conservation of Nature and Natural Resources (1980). *World Conservation Strategy*, Gland.

Lake, P. S. (1980). "Conservation", in *An Ecological Basis for Water Resource Management* (Ed. W. D. Williams), pp. 163–173, Australian National University Press, Canberra.

Lee, K. N. (1989). "The Columbia River Basin: Experimenting with sustainability", *Environment*, **31**, 6–11, 30–33.

Le Marquand, D. (1989). "Developing river and lake basins for sustained economic growth and social progress', *Natural Resources Forum*, **13**, 127–138.

Maitland, P. S. (1985). "The status of the River Dee in a national and international context", in *The Biology and Management of the River Dee* (Ed. D. Jenkins), pp. 142–148, Institute of Terrestrial Ecology, Monks Wood.

Meybeck, M., Chapman, D., and Helmer, R. (1989). *Global Freshwater Quality. A First Assessment*, Basil Blackwell, Oxford.

Minshall, G. W., and Petersen, R. C. (1985). "Towards a theory of macroinvertebrate community structure in stream ecosystems", *Archiv für Hydrobiologie*, **104**, 49–76.

Naiman, R. J., Décamps, H., and Fournier, F. (Eds) (1989). *Role of land/inland water ecotones in landscape management and restoration: a proposal for collaborative research*, MAB Digest 4, Unesco, Paris.

Naiman, R. J., and Décamps, H. (1990). *The Ecology and Management of Aquatic–Terrestrial Ecotones*, MAB Series, Volume 4, Unesco, Paris and Parthenon Publishing Group, New Jersey.

Nature Conservancy Council (1984). *Nature Conservation in Great Britain*, Peterborough.

Parks Canada (1984). *The Canadian Heritage Rivers System: Objectives, Principles and Procedures*, Ottawa, Ontario.

Petersen, R. C. (1990). "Comment on the term conservation", *Meanders* (Newsletter of the SIL Working Group on the Conservation and Management of Running Waters), **2**, 1.

Petersen, R. C., Madsen, B. L., Wilzbach, M. A., Magadza, C. H. D., Paarlberg, A., Kullberg, A., and Cummins, K. W. (1987). "Stream management: emerging global similarities", *Ambio*, **16**, 166–179.

Petts, G. E. (1980). "Long-term consequences of upstream impoundment", *Environmental Conservation*, **7**, 325–332.

Petts, G. E. (1984). *Impounded Rivers: Perspectives for Ecological Management*, John Wiley, Chichester.

Petts, G. E. (1987). "Ecological management of regulated rivers; a European perspective", *Regulated Rivers: Research and Management*, **1**, 358–363.

Petts, G. E. (1990). "Water, engineering and landscape: development, protection and restoration", in *Water, Engineering and Landscape. Water control and landscape transformation in the modern period* (Eds D. Cosgrove and G. E. Petts), pp. 188–208, Belhaven Press, London.

Pollock, S. (1989). "The Charge of the Brook Brigades", *Sierra Club Bulletin*, **74**, 24–28.

Ratcliffe, D. A. (Ed.) (1977). *A Nature Conservation Review*, Cambridge University Press, Cambridge.

Royal Norwegian Council for Scientific and Industrial Research (1988). "Methods for economic quantification of environmental impacts", in *Environmental Effects of Water Regulation Schemes (1982–1989), a Norwegian Research Programme*, Presented at the Fourth International Symposium on Regulated Streams, Loughborough.

Senanayake, F. R., and Moyle, P. B. (1982). "Conservation of freshwater fishes of Sri Lanka", *Biological Conservation*, **22**, 181–196.

Shelford, V. E. (1911). "Ecological succession I: Stream fishes and the method of physiographic analysis", *Biological Bulletin of the Marine Biological Laboratory, Woods Hole*, **21**, 9–35.

Stanford, J. A., and Ward, J. V. (1988). "The hyporheic habitat of river ecosystems", *Nature*, **335**, 64–66.

Starlund, S. (1988). "Washington's scenic rivers", *Washington State Parks and Recreation Commission*, Olympia, Washington.

Vannote, R. L., Minshall, G. W., Cummins, K. W., Sedell, J. R., and Cushing, C. E. (1980). "The river continuum concept", *Canadian Journal of Fisheries and Aquatic Sciences*, **37**, 130–137.

Ward, J. V. (1989a). "The four-dimensional nature of lotic ecosystems", *Journal of the North American Benthological Society*, **8**, 2–8.

Ward, J. V. (1989b). "Riverine–wetland interactions", in *Freshwater Wetlands and Wildlife, 1989, CONF-8603101, DOE Symposium Series No. 61* (Eds R. R. Sharitz and J. W. Gibbons), pp. 385–400, USDOE Office of Scientific and Technical Information, Oak Ridge, Tennessee.

Ward, J. V., and Stanford, J. A. (1983). "The serial discontinuity concept of lotic ecosystems", in

Dynamics of Lotic Ecosystems (Eds T. D. Fontaine and S. M. Bartell), pp. 29–42, Ann Arbor Science, Ann Arbor, Michigan.

Webster, J. R., Gurtz, M. E., Hains, J. J., Meyer, J. L., Swank, W. T., Waide, J. B., and Wallace, J. B. (1983). "Stability of stream ecosystems", in *Stream Ecology: Application and Testing of General Ecological Theory* (Eds J. R. Barnes and G. W. Minshall), pp. 355–395, Plenum Press, New York.

Wells, S. M., Pyle, R. M., and Collins, N. M. (1983). *The IUCN Invertebrate Red Data Book*, IUCN, Gland.

Worster, D. (1985). *Rivers of Empire: Water, Aridity and the Growth of the American West*, Pantheon, New York.

Wright, J. F., Armitage, P. D., Furse, M. T., and Moss, D. (1989). "Prediction of invertebrate communities using stream measurements", *Regulated Rivers: Research and Management*, **4**, 147–155.

3

The River Vistula and its Floodplain Valley (Poland): Its Ecology and Importance for Conservation

Z. KAJAK

Institute of Ecology, Polish Academy of Sciences, Dziekanow Lesny, near Warsaw, 05-092, Lomianki, Poland

GENERAL INFORMATION

The River Vistula is the largest Polish river; it is 1047 km long and 300–1000 m wide in its middle and lower reaches, with 194.4×10^3 km^2 of total drainage area (168.6×10^3 km^2 within Poland, draining 54% of the total area of Poland) (Figure 3.1). The river discharges, on average, 32 km^3 of water to the Baltic Sea annually and is the second largest river (after the Neva) in the Baltic Sea drainage area. It rises in the Beskidy Mountains (part of the Carpathian Mountains), at an elevation of 1100 m, and is composed of three very different reaches: the upper reach, from the source to the inflow of the River San; the middle reach, from the River San to the inflow of the River Narew; and the lower reach, from the River Narew to the Baltic Sea (Figure 3.1). The channel slope decreases through the three reaches from 0.4–0.3% to 0.26–0.20% to 0.18–0.10%.

There is usually one main period of high water (early spring snowmelt) and of low water (late summer) but additional floods of shorter duration can occur. The flow during the year is quite irregular, especially in the upper reach (Table 3.1). The river, particularly in its middle reach, is dynamic (Figure 3.2), with braided channels, permanent and temporary islands, and rich vegetation in the valley. Due to variable flow, longitudinal flood-protection dykes have been built along practically the whole length to protect neighbouring areas. Both the flow variability and the high erosion rate (16 t km^{-2} yr^{-1}) result from deforestation and extensive agricultural development (including potatoes, beets, and other crops whose fields are prone to soil erosion).

Of the total drainage area within Poland, arable land occupies 48.3%, meadows and pastures 14.0%, forests 26.5%, orchards 1.2%, water 2.5%, and other categories 7.4%. Soil erosion is especially severe in the upper mountainous and hilly part of the drainage basin (Klimek, 1983; Mikulski, 1990a). As is well known, forests play an important role in water retention, which results in more regular river flow. Deforestation, from the

River Conservation and Management. Edited by P. J. Boon, P. Calow, and G. E. Petts
© 1992 John Wiley & Sons Ltd

FIGURE 3.1. Map of Poland showing the Vistula drainage basin (dashed). Dotted lines—boundaries between drainage basins; triangles—reservoirs. Part of Vistula valley between the inflow of River San and the town of Plock—proposed Vistula Landscape Park

original almost complete forest cover, to the present state (about 27% forest) began as early as the fourteenth century (Bialkiewicz and Babinski, 1980; Falkowski, 1990). However, from the fifteenth to the seventeenth centuries important factors decreased the deleterious effect of deforestation: large areas of swamps, many water-retention features (weirs and other impoundments for water mills and other small industrial plants, fish ponds, etc.), and the lack of embankments enabled natural retention of water in the

TABLE 3.1. Flow of water in the three main reaches of the River Vistula (after Piskozub, 1982)

Reach of River Vistula	Flow ($m^3 s^{-1}$)			
	minimum[a]	mean	maximum[a]	maximum minimum
Upper	69	405	7440	108
Middle	110	541	7820	71
Lower	229	961	9130	40

[a]1% probability of occurrence
Data are from the downstream end of each reach; upper—just above the mouth of the River San; middle—above the mouth of the River Narev

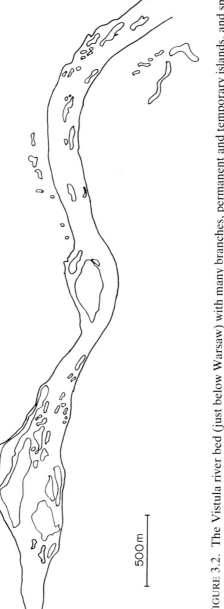

500 m

FIGURE 3.2. The Vistula river bed (just below Warsaw) with many branches, permanent and temporary islands, and small lakes of riverine origin showing the wilderness character of the river

broad floodplain valley during high flows. Since the eighteenth century this retention has gradually been reduced because of decreasing demand for hydroenergy (substituted by steam, oil, and electric energy), the building of lateral embankments, the drainage of wet areas, and also due to collectivization and the elimination of private enterprises after World War II. This has probably resulted in the loss of more than 90% of weirs and dams on rivers.

EUTROPHICATION AND POLLUTION

From the beginning of the Polish state, the River Vistula has played an essential role in the country's life, and most of the large towns, including the previous capital (Krakow) and the present one (Warsaw), are located along the river. To a great extent, this also applies to industry. Most of the water comes from the southern, mountainous part of Poland with a third of the water originating from one eighth of the country's area. Much of the heavy industry (coal and sulphur mines, forges, some nitrogen fertilizer plants, etc.) is also located in the drainage area of the upper Vistula, so the river becomes polluted almost from its source (Figure 3.3). The river serves as a source of drinking and industrial water for most of the towns and industry located along it, and at the same time it receives their sewage. The concentrations of pollutants are high, even at the mouth of the river, where they have been reduced by a long process of self-purification (Table 3.2, Figure 3.3; Dojlido and Taboryska, 1983). On average, about 70% of sewage is untreated, and much of the rest is treated unsatisfactorily (Dojlido and Woyciechowska, 1989). There are no sewage-treatment plants with phosphorus removal. There is a great

TABLE 3.2. Means and ranges for concentrations of selected chemical variables near the mouth of the River Vistula during 1987

	Mean	Range
BOD_5	4.6	0.8 – 10.0
Oxidability	11.5	7.8 – 16.9
COD	29.7	15.2 – 46.0
Cl	129.2	41.8 –204.0
SO_4	77.1	54.8 – 98.7
NH_4–N	0.75	0.12 – 3.43
NO_3–N	2.23	0.83 – 4.90
N_{tot}	4.19	2.44 – 8.03
PO_4–P	0.15	0.09 – 0.21
P_{tot}	0.21	0.13 – 0.31
Ca	89.0	55.0 –131.0
Fe	18.3	8.9 – 12.8
Cd	0.0004	0.0001– 0.001
Pb	0.005	0.001 – 0.013
Hg	1.39	0.12 – 6.67
Chlorophyll	52.1	3.0 –187.7

Chlorophyll and Hg are in $\mu\ l^{-1}$; all others are in mg l^{-1}; BOD, oxidability ($KMNO_4$) and COD ($K_2Cr_2O_7$) are in mg l^{-1} O_2

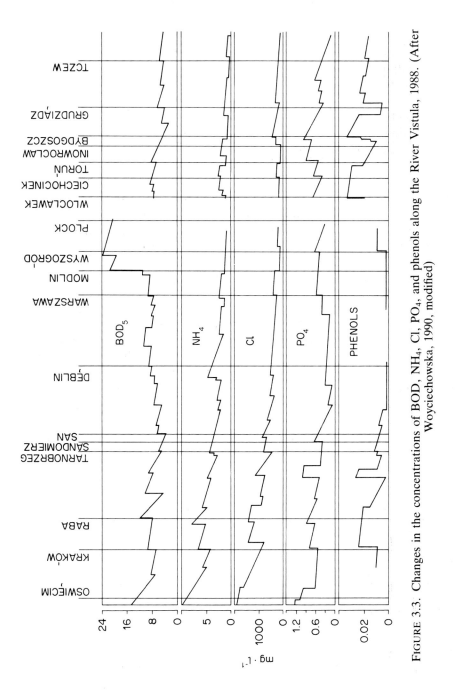

FIGURE 3.3. Changes in the concentrations of BOD, NH$_4$, Cl, PO$_4$, and phenols along the River Vistula, 1988. (After Woyciechowska, 1990, modified)

TABLE 3.3. Chemical loading to the Baltic Sea by
rivers from several countries in tonnes year^{-1}

	BOD_5	N_{tot}	P_{tot}
USSR	538	120	7
Finland	129	41	3
Sweden	—	98	4
Federal Republic of Germany	10	9	1
Poland	266	181	11
River Vistula	195	107	5

After Rybinski and Niemirycz, 1984. Data for the River
Vistula alone are included for comparison

need for pollution abatement in the River Vistula, in the interest not only of Poland but
also of the Baltic Sea and all Baltic countries, as the Vistula brings a fairly significant
proportion of the total riverine pollution load to the Baltic (Table 3.3).

The most important pollutants are nitrogen, phosphorus, phenols, NaCl, and SO_4.
NaCl comes mostly from coal and sulphur mines, and nitrogen and phosphorus from
sewage as well as from dispersed sources (mostly agriculture). Dispersed sources are
estimated to contribute about 50% of the nitrogen and phosphorus load brought into the
Baltic Sea by the river, although this fluctuates from year to year (between about 15%
and 70%, depending on water flow). This is, of course, a very rough estimate, and it may
be too high (Rybinski and Niemirycz, 1986). Very large increases in eutrophication and
organic pollution took place in the early 1960s (Figure 3.4). The rate of increase in water
pollution slowed in the 1980s, but nitrogen and phosphorus concentrations and loads are
still increasing (Figure 3.5). Salinity was increasing until recently (Figures 3.4, 3.5, and
Table 3.4). Increasing salinity does not harm the Baltic Sea, of course, but it does affect
metallic and concrete constructions, including water pipes; it is also harmful for soil,
when the water is used to irrigate agricultural areas. Phenols can be high and are
increasing (Table 3.2, Figure 3.3).

TABLE 3.4. Relative export of certain substances from the River Vistula to the Baltic
Sea between 1976 and 1984 compared with values for 1975

	1976	1977	1978	1979	1980	1981	1982	1983	1984
BOD_5	0.77	0.86	0.65	0.82	0.93	1.39	0.84	0.64	0.70
COD	0.86	1.39	1.18	1.24	1.67	1.36	0.88	0.78	0.72
Seston	0.57	1.12	0.54	0.80	1.28	1.12	0.90	1.41	0.68
Cl	0.97	1.06	1.00	1.25	1.72	1.59	1.44	1.47	1.39
SO_4	0.86	1.13	1.02	1.08	1.54	1.20	0.91	0.90	0.89
N_{tot}	0.74	0.91	1.00	1.11	1.16	0.82	0.43	0.64	0.76
P_{tot}	1.86	1.91	2.44	1.82	1.15	0.97	0.86	0.78	1.14
Water flow	0.78	0.95	0.97	1.12	1.37	1.16	0.85	0.78	0.61

(After Rybinski and Niemirycz, 1986). In 1975 the export in 10^3 tonnes year^{-1} was: BOD_5—215,
COD—936, Seston—1202, Cl—2305, SO_4—2139, N_{tot}—121, P_{tot}—5. The average water discharge in 1975 was 1300 m^3 s^{-1}

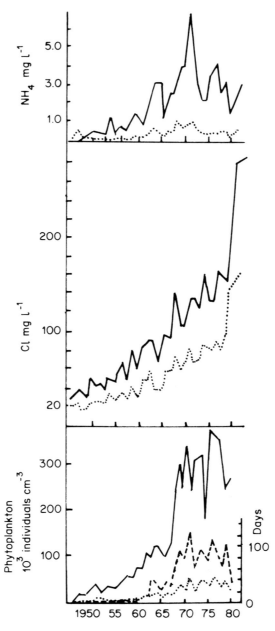

FIGURE 3.4. Annual average and maxima of NH₄, Cl, and phytoplankton in the middle Vistula (Warsaw) during 1946–1983 (based on data from Praszkiewicz et al, 1983; Dojlido and Woyciechowska, 1985). Dotted line—mean; unbroken line—maximum; broken line (for phytoplankton)—numbers of days with high abundance (> 50×10^3 individuals cm^{-3})

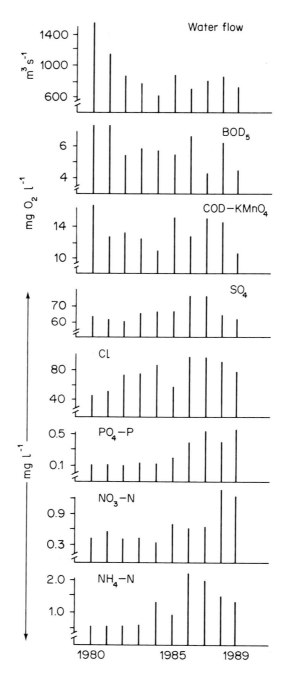

FIGURE 3.5. Changes in various parameters from 1980 to 1989 in the central part of Wloclawek impoundment (below Plock, lower Vistula). (After Zytkowicz et al, 1990)

Pesticides and heavy metals do not exceed allowed limits, and some of them (Pb, Cd) seem to have decreased, although levels are sometimes high (Taylor and Bogacka, 1979) and they can become concentrated to dangerous levels along the food chain (Rybinski and Niemirycz, 1986). Most of the upper reach of the river is acidified (Wrobel, 1989), caused by acid rain originating from areas of heavy industry in Germany, Czechoslovakia, and Poland.

RIVER ENGINEERING WORKS

Because of the high demand for water from the River Vistula (which is the largest source of water in Poland), and due to its very irregular flow, there is a great need for water retention, especially in southern Poland, where most of the Vistula's water originates. At present, there are only three small reservoirs on the Upper Vistula, near Krakow (with extremely dirty water—Kownacki, 1988), and a large, highly eutrophic one (Gizinski et al, 1989; Zytkowicz et al, 1990) on the lower Vistula (between Plock and Wloclawek), all with very short retention times (hours to a few days). There are also several reservoirs on Vistula tributaries (Figure 3.1). In the early 1970s there were plans to build a "Vistula cascade"—a series of more than 30 dams along the river for the purposes of hydroelectric generation, navigation, water supply, recreation, and flood prevention (Kajak, 1983). These plans, which were completely unrealistic, failed because of economic reasons.

Although both large and small reservoirs are necessary, the natural conditions for large-scale retention are poor because this would require large areas of land, as Poland is a lowland country. The prospect for small-scale retention is not very promising either; there is little economic motivation for it and with the recent tendency to decentralization, the local authorities seem to think they have more urgent needs than the conservation of water and aquatic life.

There was no management strategy for the whole of the Vistula during the nineteenth century, when most large European rivers were being regulated, mainly for navigation and transport purposes. The reason for this was the occupation of Poland by three countries for about 150 years. Until the end of World War I, the upper Vistula (approximately) belonged to Austria, the middle to Russia, and the lower to Germany. The free Poland developed a transport system composed mostly of railways and roads. Currently, the regulation of the middle reach of the River Vistula for navigation is unnecessary (Kloss and Stolarski, 1990; Mikulski, 1990a, b). The river is partly regulated in its upper and lower reaches, and there are plans for more regulation in these parts because of the demand for more transport in the southern, industrialized part of the country, and both the demand and feasibility for hydroelectricity and navigation in the lower reach. Many specialists have suggested that the middle (and wildest) reach of the river should be devoted to recreation and nature conservation (Kajak, 1990; Kloss and Stolarski, 1990; Mikulski, 1990a). The present engineering works consist mostly of improvements to embankments and the construction of some partial dams within the river bed to prevent shore erosion and to balance the transport of materials (Wierzbicki, 1990). The latter, although modest, are in conflict with bird protection, as they tend to result in losses of islands. In addition, the lateral embankments, although necessary to protect settlements and agriculture, increase the irregularity of water flow.

THE STATUS OF NATURE CONSERVATION

From the phytogeographical point of view, the Vistula floodplain contains a unique set of plant communities. Close to the river, in the lowest terraces where the subsoil consists mainly of coarse-grained, sandy-mud soils and flooding is frequent, is the zone of poplar–willow growth. Old river beds frequently occurred (and many still do) in this zone. They are more or less covered with plant growth in various stages of succession—from submerged vegetation through to rushes, swamp, and alder swamp forests. The communities on the lowest terrace (between embankments), although altered by human activity, are still governed to a large degree by natural processes. No settlements are located there because of the danger of flooding; agricultural activity consists mainly of extensive cattle grazing, since other forms of human activity are greatly restricted. Plant cover in this zone, which exhibits many characteristics of semi-natural vegetation, is an important element of the landscape. It is critical for animal life, especially for nesting and migrating birds, which are particularly abundant there. These sites are also very important for riverside recreation. Maximum protection should therefore be given to natural vegetation, especially the shrubs and trees.

Further from the river, behind the embankments where subsoil consists of fine-grained fen soil, and where flooding was originally rare, spreads the zone of ash–elm associations. Due to their very high fertility, these sites have been put into agricultural use, and there are now almost no forests left, except in some parks.

Old river terraces (of glacial age) border many sectors alongside the present Vistula floodplain, particularly where it lies on the old plain from glacial times. These terraces are usually sandy and often covered with dunes. They are much overgrown with pine and mixed forests which often stretch for long distances along the Vistula valley. Examples include the forest complex on the eastern bank of the Vistula between Pulawy and Warsaw, the Puszcza Kampinoska forests, a forest complex on the western bank of the river between Plock and Wloclawek, on the eastern bank between Wloclawek and Torun, and the Puszcza Bydgoska forest complex. In some places considerable areas of peat bogs occur on these terraces, usually away from the present river valley and mainly on alder swamp sites. They are now largely exploited as meadows. In places where the Vistula cuts through the highlands or hilly terrain, steep cliffs form an important element of the valley landscape, in spite of the relatively small area they occupy.

Specific soils (usually rich in calcium carbonate), but mainly specific microclimates, resulted in the formation of xerothermal plant communities. In southern (Sandomierz and Kazimierz regions), central (Plock, Wloclawek), and northern Poland (near Chelmno) there are some stretches of steppe with rare species worth protecting. Most such communities are included in nature reserves, but conservation of the remaining fragments of valley edge is necessary for protecting not only the plant associations but also the attractiveness and beauty of the local landscape. Within the National Nature Conservation Plan, worked out by the State Council for Nature Conservation, the Vistula river valley was highlighted as a particularly interesting and valuable ecological system. The river corridor of the Vistula consists of large forest complexes; Puszcza Niepolomicka, Puszcza Sandomierska, Puszcza Solecka, Puszcza Kozienicka, forests in regions of Garwolin, Otwock, Puszcza Kampinoska, Puszcza Bedkowska, Tuchola forests, many other smaller forest complexes and numerous aquatic ecosystems situated along the river, almost from its source to its mouth.

Most of the river still has very abundant phytoplankton and zooplankton populations although the number of species has decreased (Klimowicz, 1981, 1983; Praszkiewicz et al, 1983; Tyszka-Mackiewicz, 1983; Kowalczewski et al, 1985a–c; Simm, 1986). The rich plankton reflects the very high nutrient levels and good oxygen conditions, except in dammed areas which may have periodic or almost permanent oxygen deficits (Kownacki, 1988; Zytkowicz et al, 1990). Diatoms, such as *Cyclotella meneghiniana* (summer) and *Stephanodiscus hantzschii* (spring, autumn), are strongly dominant in the phytoplankton.

Benthos is also abundant, with Chironomidae, Tubificidae, and Mollusca being dominant, except in the dammed parts, where the water is extremely polluted (Mikulski and Tarwid, 1951; Szczepanski, 1953; Kajak, 1958, 1959; Kownacki, 1988; Gizinski et al, 1989; Zytkowicz et al, 1990).

Fish are still abundant (apart from extremely polluted parts), due to the river habitat diversity (Backiel, 1983). Angling is common, mainly for pleasure rather than for food, due to bad fish taste on long stretches of the river (Bontemps and Backiel, 1988). There is limited commercial fishing; the main species in catches are: bream (*Abramis brama*) (strongly dominant, >55%); roach (*Rutilus rutilus*) and white bream (*Blicca bjoerkna*) (each about 15%); and pike (*Esox lucius*), asp (*Aspius aspius*), and nase (*Chondrostoma nasus*) (each below 5%). Near banks and in shallows, bleak (*Alburnus alburnus*) (about 30%), roach (*Rutilus rutilus*), and gudgeon (*Gobio gobio*) are dominant (Backiel and Penczak, 1989). Sturgeon (*Acipenser sturio*) have disappeared completely; salmon (*Salmo salar*), sea trout (*Salmo trutta* m. *trutta*), and vimba (*Vimba vimba*) have also decreased very significantly both as a result of pollution and also the presence of dams making migration almost impossible (Backiel, 1985; Backiel Penczak, 1989). Brown trout (*Salmo trutta* m. *fario*) are extinct in the upper parts, (which was made a nature reserve especially for them!), due to acidification (Wrobel, 1989).

Birds are still flourishing although endangered by river regulation (especially by a tendency to lose sandy islands) and by pollution. About two-thirds of the Polish bird fauna (195 species) occur in the region of the middle Vistula (Sandomierz-Plock). The main nesting environments of birds associated with the Vistula are the islands (including sandy shoals), steep banks, and areas between embankments. Loss of the islands on the river would exterminate nesting populations of Common tern (*Sterna hirundo*), Little tern (*Sterna albifrons*), Little ringed plover (*Charadrius dubius*), Ringed plover (*Charadrius hiaticula*), Common gull (*Larus canus*), Black-headed gull (*Larus ridibundus*), Common sandpiper (*Tringa hypoleucos*), and Stone curlew (*Burhinus oedicnemus*). About 1500 pairs of *L. canus* (90% of the whole population in Poland), 650 pairs of *S. albifrons* (60% of the whole population in Poland), 2000 pairs of *S. hirundo*, 50 pairs of *C. hiaticula*, and 180 pairs of *C. dubius* nest in the wildest part of the middle Vistula valley (Pinowski and Wesolowski, 1983). The River Vistula forms a relatively undisturbed corridor connecting the Baltic Sea with the catchment areas of Dniester (through the River San) and the River Danube (through the Moravian Gate), and is therefore extremely important for migrating wetland birds. The winter fauna is very rich, particularly in species from Scandinavia. In fact, of the species which overwinter and migrate along the Vistula as many as 30 (almost 50%) are listed in the Polish Red Data Book of

Animals (Glowacinski, in press), which contains species seriously endangered with extinction. Areas below sewage outflows, which are abundant in food resources, attract many bird species, especially in winter (Pinowski and Wesolowski, 1983). However, there are also negative effects because these birds, especially the fish-eating ones, may suffer from toxic substances and oil, which can worsen their physical condition.

THE NEED FOR ENVIRONMENTAL PROTECTION

The River Vistula is a unique feature in Poland, and to a great extent also in Europe, as it is one of the last large rivers, and is almost wild for long stretches; it also forms an extremely important pathway for bird migration. The Vistula is important not only to Poland but to all Baltic countries, who have interests in the abatement of Baltic Sea pollution. Most of the Vistula pollution undoubtedly comes from industry and towns. More and more villages are now getting a centralized water supply; unfortunately they are not also provided with sewage-treatment plants. There is an urgent need for sewage purification and modern technology, but owing to the present economic situation in the country this can only come about by international help.

Diffuse pollution input is also important, and it is well known that this can be significantly diminished by vegetation belts along rivers. Fortunately, the Vistula has embankments up to hundreds of metres from the river along most of its length, with abundant vegetation cover between them and the river channel. This, together with the fertile soil, probably consumes most of the dispersed pollution flowing into the Vistula. Unfortunately, most of the tributaries do not have embankments; often agricultural areas adjoin the river banks. In addition, many small point sources from farms and villages enter the tributaries directly and finally reach the Vistula.

To improve this situation the following steps are necessary:

(1) Creation of riparian vegetation strips along all rivers and streams. This is not easy, not only because of the poor economic situation but also because of privately owned smallholdings and recent decentralization; decisions are in the hands of local authorities which feel that environmental protection is hardly their top priority.

(2) A programme of environmental education is needed covering areas such as the treatment and disposal of domestic and farm waste, the proper application of mineral fertilizers and manure, and methods of plant protection.

(3) Reducing the quantity and irregularity of surface run-off would help reduce pollution loading from dispersed sources to rivers. This could be done by constructing more retention reservoirs, increasing afforestation in agricultural territories (Bialkiewicz and Babinski, 1980), raising the percentage of organic matter in the soil, and stopping land drainage where it is not absolutely necessary.

(4) River engineering works, although modest, should be modified where they endanger water birds. At present, more than 20 species nesting on islands and two species nesting on steep shores are affected. All bird species nesting in the Vistula valley are protected by Polish law; thus conserving their habitats is obligatory.

(5) Periodic cutting of wood to facilitate flow at high water is also harmful for birds. This has recently been stopped, although it is not yet regulated by law.

(6) Keeping cattle on islands during nesting periods (April–July) results in destruction of nests. This problem must be tackled by negotiating with farmers.

(7) The most valuable fragments of the middle Vistula deserve to become nature reserves and to be designated under the international Ramsar convention. There are also proposals to make National Parks in some areas.

RECREATION AND TOURISM

The section of the Vistula from the mouth of the River San to Wloclawek (that is, the whole of the middle and part of the lower Vistula, excluding some fragments) has been included within the national programme of tourism development. This plan places other economic activities on an equal footing with tourism, but only where they do not endanger other environmental values important for tourism. For the population situated along the Vistula, especially in southern and central Poland where natural lakes do not occur, the river and its surroundings form an attractive region for recreational interests, including angling and water sports.

The settlements located in the Vistula valley are also important architecturally, with buildings representing a wide range in age from the early days of the State of Poland to contemporary times.

Thus the River Vistula is potentially a region of high recreational value. With appropriate environmental management it could become the fourth large tourist area— the other three being the coastline, mountains, and lakes. Furthermore, unlike the other three regions which are located at the peripheries of the country and run in an east–west direction, the Vistula occupies a central, north–south axis, which may help in solving the present problem of transport to recreational sites.

INTEGRATING NATURE CONSERVATION WITH RECREATION AND TOURISM

The need to conserve habitats and wildlife and to develop recreation and tourism led to the conception of a Vistula Landscape Park. This would be situated in the mostly natural, middle, and part of the lower reaches, from the town of Sandomierz to Plock, but excluding relatively small sections of regulated or modified river (Wesolowski and Nowicki, 1989; Kajak, 1990). This idea is now under active consideration.

Protected territories in the Vistula catchment should form a spatially continuous ecological corridor to ensure the exchange of species and the enrichment of gene pools. It is hoped that protected territories within the system—national parks, reserves, areas of protected landscape, and interconnecting corridors—will result in mutual protection, reinforcing resistance against the destructive processes associated with industrialization and urbanization. For these reasons, technical solutions and methods of river valley management should arise from, and be adjusted to, the local conditions and nature conservation needs in each particular area.

ACKNOWLEDGEMENTS

I am obliged to Dr J. Matuszkiewicz for information on plant cover in the Vistula valley, mgr J. Woyciechowska for new data on river pollution, mgr I. Kostrzewska-Szlakowska and mgr E.

Pietrzak for technical help in preparing the illustrations, and Mrs E. Owczarek for typing from my difficult handwriting, Dr P. Boon for language correction and general editorial assistance, and Mrs L. Boon for retyping the text.

REFERENCES

Backiel, T. (1983). "Rybactwo i ryby w Wisle", in *Ekologiczne podstawy zagospodarowania Wisly i jej dorzecza* (Ed. Z. Kajak), pp. 511–543, Panstwowe Wydawnictwo Naukowe, Warszawa–Lodz.

Backiel, T. (1985). "Fall of migratory fish population and changes in commercial fisheries in impounded rivers in Poland", in *Habitat Modification and Freshwater Fisheries* (Ed. J. S. Alabaster), pp. 28–41, Butterworth, London.

Backiel, T., and Penczak, T. (1989). "The fish and fisheries in the Vistula river and its tributary, the Pilica river", *Proceedings of the Large River Symposium. Special publication of the Canadian Journal of Fisheries and Aquatic Sciences*, **106**, 488–503.

Bialkiewicz, F. B., and Babinski, S. (1980). "Gospodarka lesna w ksztaltowaniu zasobow wodnych dorzecza Wisly", *Gospodarka Wodna*, **40**, 345–348.

Bontemps, S., and Backiel, T. (1988). "Ocena sensoryczna ryb z Wisly i jeziora Wloclawskiego w latach 1969–1970 i 1983–1984", *Roczniki naukowe Polskiego Zwiazku Wedkarskiego*, **1**, 191–211.

Dojlido, J., and Taboryska, B. (1983). "Mikrozanieczyszczenia wod Wisly i jej doplywow", in *Ekologiczne podstawy zagospodarowania Wisly i jej dorzecza* (Ed. Z. Kajak), pp. 327–353, Panstwowe Wydawnictwo Naukowe, Warszawa.

Dojlido, J., and Woyciechowska, J. (1985). "Zmiany jakosci wod powierzchniowych w Polsce w ciagu ostatniego pol wieku", *Gospodarka wodna*, **45**, 39–44.

Dojlido, J., and Woyciechowska, J. (1989). "Water quality classification of the Vistula river basin in 1987", *Ekologia Polska*, **37**, 405–417.

Falkowski, E. (1990). "Geologiczno inzynierskie aspekty ochrony srodowiska przyrodniczego na obszarach den dolinnych nizu Polskiego", in *Regulacja Wisly Srodkowej a ksztaltowanie i ochrona srodowiska przyrodniczego*, pp. 1–38, Materialy sympozjum Naczelnej Organizacji Technicznej, Warszawa.

Gizinski, A., Bledzki, L., Kentzer, A., Wisniewski, R., and Zytkowicz, R. (1989). "Hydrobiological characteristic of the lowland, rheolimnic Wloclawek reservoir on Vistula River", *Ekologia Polska*, **37**, 359–404.

Glowacinski, Z. (Ed.) (in press). "Polska czerwona ksiega zwierzat", *Panstwowe Wydawnictwo Rolnicze i Lesne*.

Kajak, Z. (1958). "Character of the numerical dynamics of benthic Tendipedidae in shallow parts of an old branch cut off from the river Vistula", *Bulletin de l'Academie Polonaise des Sciences*, **6**, 489–493, Serie des Sciences Biologique.

Kajak, Z. (1959). "Benthic Tendipedidae in river environments connected with the river in the central reaches of the Vistula", *Ekologia Polska*, seria A, **7**, 391–434.

Kajak, Z. (Ed.) (1983). *Ekologiczne Podstawy zagospodarowania Wisly i jej dorzecza*, Panstwowe Wydawnictwo Naukowe, Warszawa–Lodz.

Kajak, Z. (1990). "Walory przyrodnicze i rekreacyjne Wisly z punktu widzenia potrzeby utworzenia Nadwislanskiego Parku Narodowego", in *Regulacja Wisly Srodkowej a ksztaltowanie i ochrona srodowiska przyrodniczego*, pp. 51–56, Materialy sympozjum Naczelnej Organizacji Technicznej, Warszawa.

Klimek, K. (1983). "Erozja wglebna doplywow Wisly na przedpolu Karpat", in *Ekologiczne podstawy zagospodarowania Wisly i jej dorzecza* (Ed. Z. Kajak), pp. 97–108, Panstwowe Wydawnictwo Naukowe, Warszawa–Lodz.

Klimowicz, H. (1981). "Plankton rzeki Wisly w okolicach Warszawy w latach 1977–1979", *Acta Hydrobiologica*, **23**, 47–67.

Klimowicz, H. (1983). "Wplyw sciekow Warszawy na plankton Wisly", *Gaz, Woda i Techniko Sanitarna*, **57**, 188–190.

Kloss, A., and Stolarski, A. (1990). "Rola i znaczenie Wisly Srodkowej i Dolnej w gospodarce wodnej Polski w zaleznosci od hydrotechnicznego sposobu zagospodarowania koryta i doliny rzeki", in *Regulacja Wisly Srodkowej a ksztaltowanie i ochrona srodowiska przyrodniczego*, pp. 39–50, Materialy sympozjum Naczelnej Organizacji Technicznej, Warszawa.

Kowalczewski, A., Perlowska, M., and Przyluska, J. (1985a). "Seston of the Warsaw reach of the Vistula river in 1982 and 1983. I. Chlorophyll and environmental conditions", *Ekologia Polska*, **33**, 389–407.

Kowalczewski, A., Perlowska, M., and Przyluska, J. (1985b). "Seston of the Warsaw reach of the Vistula river in 1982 and 1983. II. Dry weight and organic carbon", *Ekologia Polska*, **33**, 407–422.

Kowalczewski, A., Perlowska, M., and Przyluska, J. (1985c). "Seston of the Warsaw reach of the Vistula river in 1982 and 1983. III. Phyto- and zooplankton", *Ekologia Polska*, **33**, 439–454.

Kownacki, A. (1988). "A regulated river ecosystem in a polluted section of the upper Vistula. 10 General considerations", *Acta Hydrobiologica*, **30**, 113–123.

Mikulski, Z. (1990a). "Hydrobiologiczne i ekologiczne przeslanki zagospodarowania Wisly", in *Regulacja Wisly Srodkowej a ksztaltowanie srodwiska przyrodniczego*, Materialy sympozjum, pp. 57–70, Naczelna Organizacja Techniczna, Warszawa.

Mikulski, Z. (1990b). "Water resources and management in Poland", in *Integrated Water Management. International experiences and perspectives* (Ed. B. Mitchell), pp. 172–187, Belhaven Press, London.

Mikulski, J., and Tarwid, K. (1951). "Prawdopodobny wplyw regulacji Wisly na niektore zerowiska ryb, zwiazane z bentosem", *Roczniki Nauk Rolniczych*, **51**, 179–204.

Pinowski, J., and Wesolowski, T. (1983). "Wplyw regulacji Wisly na avifaune", in *Ekologiczne podstawy zagospodarowania Wisly i jej dorzecza* (Ed. Z. Kajak), pp. 543–568, Panstwowe Wydawnictwo Naukowe, Warszawa–Lodz.

Piskozub, A. (Ed.) (1982). *Wisla–monografia rzeki*, Wydawnictwo Komunikacji i Lacznosci, Warszawa.

Praszkiewicz, A., Spodniewska, I., and Weglenska, T. (1983). "Seston Wisly i zbiornikow Kaskady Wisly na odcinku od ujscia Sanu do Wloclawka. Stan aktualny i przypuszczalne zmiany po zabudowie rzeki", in *Ekologiczne podstawy zagospodarowania Wisly i jej dorzecza* (Ed. Z. Kajak), pp. 417–434, Panstwowe Wydawnictwo Naukowe, Warszawa–Lodz.

Rybinski, J., and Niemirycz, E. (1984). "Rozwazania na temat splywu zanieczyszczen Wisla", *Materialy na 25 Konferencje Naczelnej Organizacji Technicznej w Katowicach*, 89–96.

Rybinski, J., and Niemirycz, E. (1986). "A Wisla plynie do Morza", *Aura*, **8**, 20–22.

Simm, A. T. (1986). "The phytoseston of the Vistula river between Gora Kalwaria and Nowy Dwor Mazowiecki in 1982", *Ekologia Polska*, **33**, 439–453.

Szczepanski, A. (1953). "Variations of the populations of the bottom living Oligochaeta in the Vistula", *Polskie Archiwum Hydrobiologii*, **1**, 249–268.

Taylor, R., and Bogacka, T. (1979). "Transport of pesticides to the sea by the Vistula river", *Oceanologia*, **11**, 129–138.

Tyszka-Mackiewicz, J. (1983). "Bioseston i peryfiton rzeki Wisly na odcinku od Pulaw do Warszawy", *Prace Komisji Biologicznej Poznanskiego Towarzystwa Przyjaciol Nauk*, **63**, 114, Panstwowe Wydawnictwo Naukowe, Warszawa–Poznan.

Wesolowski, T., and Nowicki, W. (1989). "Ptaki srodkowej Wisly", *Przyroda Polska*, **12**, 18–19.

Wierzbicki, J. (1990). "Regulacja rzek nizinnych a ochrona srodowiska", in *Regulacja Wisly srodkowej a ksztaltowanie i ochrona srodowiska przyrodniczego*, pp. 71–95, Materialy sympozjum Naczelnej Organizacji Technicznej, Warszawa.

Woyciechowska, J. (1990). *Atlas zanieczyszczenia rzek w Polsce. Dorzecza Wisly*, Instytut Meteorologii i Gospodarki Wodnej, Warszawa.

Wrobel, S. (Ed.) (1989). *Zanieczyszczenia atmosfery a degradacja wod*, Materialy sympozjum, Zaklad Ochrony Przyrody i Zasobow Naturalnych, Krakow.

Zytkowicz, R., Bledzki, L. A., Gizinski, A., Kentzer, A., Wisniewski, R., and Zbikowski, J. (1990). "Zbiornik Wloclawski Ekologiczna charakterystyka pierwszego zbiornika zaporowego planowanej kaskady doliny Wisly", *Wydawnictwo Szkoly Glownej Gospodarstwa Wiejskiego*, Warszawa.

4

Conservation and Management of the Coastal Streams of Israel: An Assessment of Stream Status and Prospects for Rehabilitation

A. GASITH

Institute for Nature Conservation Research, George S. Wise Faculty of Life Sciences, Tel-Aviv University, Ramat-Aviv 69978, Israel

INTRODUCTION

Prior to the establishment of the State of Israel (1948) many of its coastal streams had significant perennial lotic habitats. Today, two-thirds of the population, a large majority of the industries, and a considerable share of intensive agriculture activities are located in the Coastal Plain. Population increase and an ensuing rapid agricultural and urban development resulted in an augmented demand for water. This demophoric growth (Vallentyne, 1972) is also reflected in rapidly growing waste production, which takes a heavy toll on the environment, especially on aquatic habitats.

Adoption of the concept that "dilution is a feasible solution to pollution" was apparently behind the practice of using streams for wastewater removal. The outcome of this approach in Israel was a gradual transformation of rivers into conduits of waste. Many of the streams presently constitute a sanitary and aesthetic nuisance.

The following is an overview of the current status of the coastal streams in Israel, with special regard to the changes that have taken place in the last 30–50 years in their hydrology, water quality, and aquatic life. Stream conservation and the prospects for stream rehabilitation are discussed.

HYDROLOGY

The regional watershed divides Israel approximately into eastern and western catchments. The eastern catchment drains into the Jordan Valley. Israel's coastal streams drain the western catchment and flow into the Mediterranean (Figure 4.1).

Within the Coastal Plain, stream channels slope gently westward, forming slow-flowing habitats. Discharge from springs provides the base flow but run-off following winter storms contributes a considerable portion of the natural annual flow. The latter is

---

River Conservation and Management. Edited by P. J. Boon, P. Calow, and G. E. Petts
© 1992 John Wiley & Sons Ltd

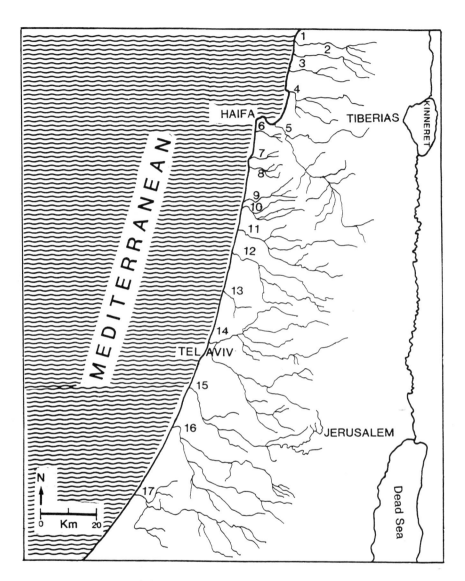

FIGURE 4.1. Map of the coastal streams of Israel (N.=*Nahal*). The streams are listed from north to south and the hydrological regime and relative state of pollution are indicated as follows: I=Intermittent, PP=partly perennial, P=perennial, UPL=unpolluted, SPL=slightly polluted, PLL=polluted, HPL=highly polluted. The respective BOD ranges are given in the text. 1 N. Bezet (PP; UPL); 2 N. Keziv (PP; UPL–SPL); 3 N. Ga'aton (I; HPL); 4 N. Na'aman (PP; PLL–HPL); 5 N, Qishon (P; PLL–HPL); 6 N. Gallim (I; PLL–HPL); 7 N. Oren (I; SPL); 8 N. Mearot (PP; SPL); 9 N. Daliyya (PP; UPL–PLL); 10 N. Tanninim (PP; UPL–SPL); 11 N. Hadera (PP; PLL–HPL); 12 N. Alexander (P; PLL–HPL); 13 N. Poleg (I; HPL); 14 N. Yarqon (PP; UPL–HPL); 15 N. Soreq (PP; HPL); 16 N. Lakhish (PP; HPL); 17 N. Shiqma (I; PLL)

particularly important since floods scour out accumulated sediments and debris and clear stream channels from invading riparian vegetation.

Spring discharge is influenced by the elevation of the underground water table, which in turn is strongly affected by the amount of rainfall. Spring flow diminishes following dry winters and peaks in rainy years.

For almost two decades the renewable water resource has been totally consumed (agriculture, 66%; domestic use, 27%; industry, 7%). In the absence of a consensus among decision makers and water specialists about the lowest permissible level of the underground water table, water exploitation in excess of the renewable volume continued almost without restraint. Since the summer of 1989, the estimated total water deficit in the main aquifers of Israel amounts to one year's consumption (>1500 MCM, million cubic metres). Over-pumping caused diminished stream flow and partial or complete drying up of streams. Thus at present, many coastal streams function practically as series of elongated reservoirs with short periods of winter flow. In addition, in the process of reclaiming agricultural land and combating malaria, floodplains have been completely eliminated.

The following examples illustrate the major hydrological changes in the Coastal Plain that have taken place during the last 40–50 years. Nahal Yarqon (*Nahal* is Hebrew for stream), the southernmost perennial stream in the Coastal Plain, once carried 50–60 MCM of water annually with peak discharges of three to four times that amount. This earned the Yarqon a reputation second only to the River Jordan (Avitsur, 1957). Diversion of the main springs (Rosh-Ha-Ayin) in the mid-1950s has reduced base flow to less than 10% of the average annual discharge. If not for the release of effluents and sewage into the stream channel, this former river would have turned into a mostly intermittent stream.

In another case, prior to the 1940s, the annual spring discharge into N. Na'aman exceeded 40 MCM. Increased regional water exploitation reduced spring discharge to no more than 10% of the natural inflow. Incidents of complete cessation of spring discharge were reported in the early 1960s (Paz, 1981) and have been observed since in dry years (Lahav, 1978; Gasith and Jennings, unpublished data). Most of the coastal streams are currently devoid of spring discharge except for short durations following periods of significant rainfall (Ben-Zvi, pers. comm.).

Reservoirs impounding effluents and storm water have been constructed and more are planned in the catchment basins of the coastal streams. These reservoirs function as supplemental sources of irrigation water, and while not totally excluding flood flow could influence the hydrograph by reducing total run-off and lowering peak flows.

Another activity which affects stream flow is exemplified by the Menashe Streams Water Works, which diverts 14–20 MCM of storm water annually for the purpose of recharging the aquifer (Ben-David, 1983). This efficient diversion of flood water from the catchment basin of N. Tanninim minimizes flood events in the streams.

Some of the coastal streams are used as operational reservoirs for irrigation water (e.g. N. Na'aman, N. Tanninim, N. Yarqon) or for aquaculture (e.g. N. Na'aman, N. Tanninim). N. Tanninim is an example of economic considerations superseding those of nature conservation (Figure 4.2). Local water demands severely decrease stream discharge each summer, and in dry years lower sections of the stream may dry up (Ben-David, 1987).

FIGURE 4.2. Typical view of a channelized, lowland coastal stream (N. Tanninim), with agricultural land on both sides, less than 10 m from the stream bank. The riparian vegetation (mostly *Phragmites australis* and *Rubus sanguineus*) is kept under control by routine cutting to prevent channel blocking. (Mount Carmel is in the background)

WATER QUALITY

Apart from a few northern coastal streams which are truly freshwater (Cl^- <250 mg l^{-1}), the rest of the coastal streams are partly or entirely oligohaline (Table 4.1) due to discharge from brackish springs and backflow from the sea. Salinity is usually lower in winter and increases downstream in summer. The streams are hard water (>300 mg l^{-1} calcium carbonate), naturally eutrophic ecosystems, which receive nutrient inputs from rich alluvial soils (Dan and Koyumdjinsky, 1963).

Until the early 1950s, the coastal streams remained relatively undisturbed. Thereafter, their condition rapidly deteriorated due to discharge of municipal and industrial wastes (Figure 4.3) (Whitman, 1988; Gabbay, 1989). The amounts of wastewater estimated to enter representative streams is shown in Table 4.2. Effluents of different quality comprise the bulk of the base flow in most of the streams. Water quality conditions vary significantly, both spatially and temporally (e.g. Gafny et al, 1989), depending on the quality of the effluent released, the metabolic response of the system (respiration, photosynthesis), and the capacity of flood water to wash away accumulated contaminants.

The poor water quality conditions of the coastal streams is reflected, for example, in high organic load (BOD), extreme levels of low and high oxygen saturation, high

TABLE 4.1. Selected water quality parameters[a] of representative streams in the Coastal Plain

No.	Stream	Chloride (mg l^{-1})	Oxygen saturation (%)	BOD (mg l^{-1})	Turbidity (JU)	Detergent ABS. (mg l^{-1})
1	Bezet[b]	39–43	90–96	< 5	< 2	0.1–0.3
2	Keziv[b]	38–59	95–106	< 5 (d)	< 2	—
3	Ga'aton[b]	35–48	90–101	< 5 (e)	< 2	0.2–0.5
4	Na'aman[c]	800–12 660	13–165	< 5–73	< 2–180	0.1–0.6
5	Qishon[c]	284–17 840	0–194	< 5–264	< 2–180	0.1–13
6	Galim[b]	348–493	7–39	50–380	70–155	2.5–8.3
7	Oren[b]	129–2500	25–107	< 5–30	17–2000	0–0.4
8	Mearot[b]	97–710	30–120	< 5–30	40–612	0–2.1
9	Dalliyya[c]	40–1240	42–146	< 5–18	< 2–80	0–0.7
10	Tanninim[c]	93–1460	21–147	< 5–60	—	0–0.6
11	Hadera[c]	120–1080	0–178	< 5–188	< 2–300	0–3.8
12	Alexander[c]	95–7800	0–176	< 5–500	10–320	0–3.6
13	Poleg[b]	66–890	2–95	6–71	12–80	1.4–5.0
14	Yarqon[c]	66–20 902	0–162	< 5–160	10–140	0–3.8
15	Soreq[c]	169–675	0–380	< 5–410	15–105	0–8.7
16	Lakhish[c]	44–420	0–35	< 5–182	15–225	0.7–5.8

Minimum and maximum values during the periods (i) 1974–1978[b] and (ii) 1982–1985[c] for the entire stream. Streams listed as in Figure 4.1
[a]For most cases represents analysis of one to three samples per season, taken in winter and summer at selected sites
[b]Eren et al. (1980)
[c]Gafny et al. (1989)
[d]Recent reports of effluent contamination
[e]Recent reports of sewage contamination

turbidity, and relatively high detergent levels carried in with effluents (Table 4.1). When considering BOD level as a measure of organic pollution, the current state of the coastal streams may be described as follows: unpolluted, BOD<5 mg l^{-1}; slightly polluted, BOD=5–10 mg l^{-1}; polluted, BOD=10–20 mg l^{-1}; highly polluted, BOD>20 mg l^{-1} (Figure 4.1). This classification is arbitrary but reflects the reality of naturally eutrophic waters at the lower scale and severe oxygen deficit and related lower water quality conditions observed in streams in Israel when the BOD level exceeds 20 mg l^{-1}.

Only a single stream (N. Bezet) may be considered almost entirely unpolluted. Four streams may rank as slightly polluted. Ten streams (60%) fall into polluted to highly polluted categories. The remaining two streams have polluted to highly polluted reaches as well as unpolluted sections. In general, the less polluted streams are located in the north while the more polluted ones are in the central and southern Coastal Plain, in accordance with population size and activities in the catchment basins. In two extreme cases, industrial pollution has completely annihilated stream biota in the main stream channels. In N. Qishon it is mostly caused by chemical contamination, while in N. Hadera the most damaging effluents originate from the paper industry. Fish mortality has been observed in some coastal streams following the first major flood in winter (e.g. N. Yarqon—Gasith, unpublished data). Low oxygen levels produced by high organic

FIGURE 4.3. Effluent from a nearby meat-processing factory entering N. Na'aman as white plume
(shown on the left of the photograph)

load, as well as toxic materials carried in from contaminated tributaries, could account
for this mortality.

In the light of the severe wastewater pollution in many of the streams the impact of
pesticide residues and fertilizers from agricultural drainage may be limited. Nonetheless,
incidents of fish mortality following accidental spraying over a stream have been
recorded (e.g. N. Tanninim—Goren, 1986). In relatively unpolluted sections of the
coastal streams, nutrient enrichment from agricultural drainage could be an important
source of contamination (Gafny, 1983).

AQUATIC BIOTA

Despite limited information on the state of the coastal streams 50 years ago, it is clear
that they were flowing and rich in plant and animal life (Avitsur, 1957). Since then, many
biotic changes have occurred in the coastal streams. These changes are summarized
below.

Macrophytes

Litav and Agami (1976) studied the distribution of hydrophytic (aquatic) and hygrophy-
tic (semi-aquatic) vegetation in the Alexander and Yarqon streams. The highest species

TABLE 4.2. Estimated amounts of effluent released into major streams in the Coastal Plain and their proportion with reference to total flow

No.	Stream	Volume of effluent[a] (10^3 m^3)	Effluent discharge relative to total flow[b] (%)
4	N. Na'aman	1 917	40–100
5	N. Qishon	30 923	> 90
10	N. Tanninim	751	< 5
11	N. Hadera	5 173	≈ 100
12	N. Alexander	4 274	≈ 100
14	N. Yarqon	9 321	≈ 70
15	N. Soreq	8 883	≈ 100

Streams numbered as in Figure 4.1
[a]MAWC (Ministry of Agriculture, Water Commission) (1983)
[b]100% = effluents only (no base flow)

diversity was recorded at unpolluted sites. Floating-leaved and submerged species, for example, were found exclusively in relatively clean water habitats. The yellow water lily (*Nuphar lutea*) was the only floating-leaved species which was found to tolerate temporary flushing of sewage effluent in otherwise clean habitats.

The effect of water quality on the survival and growth of seven aquatic macrophytes from clean sections in the above streams was examined. It was shown that only two species (*Cyperus papyrus* and *Lemna gibba*) survived unaffected the transplantation into polluted sites of the same streams (Agami et al, 1976). Agami et al also showed that detergents can inflict severe damage on aquatic plants, and suggested that high detergent levels, in combination with other factors, may account for the limited distribution of aquatic vegetation in polluted sections of these streams.

A recent survey of hydrophytes in the Yarqon stream (Figure 4.4) reveals that five out of seven species recorded 20 years ago have disappeared (Agami, 1990). Among these was the rare floating-leaved, blue water lily (*Nymphaea caerulea*) which was last seen in the Yarqon stream in 1975. The disappearance of these plants is attributed to repetitive application of herbicides on the stream banks, macrophyte consumption by coypu (*Myocastor coypu*, an exotic species in Israel), and reduction in stream flow (Agami, 1980).

In the Tanninim stream, ten submerged and floating-leaved plant species were recorded during 1967 to 1977. In a survey carried out eleven years later, eight species were recorded (Table 4.3). Only four species are common to the two reports, suggesting a recent change in species composition.

Five species of hydrophytes were recorded in the Na'aman stream 20 years ago (Lindheimer, 1967), including *Potamogeton nodosus*, *P. trichoides*, and the blue water lily (*Nymphaea caerulea*). The last, which apparently constituted a unique ecotype, has since vanished from its southern range of distribution (N. Yarqon, N. Na'aman—Agami, 1980). A rare filamentous alga (*Compsopogon sp.*) was recently discovered in the spring area of the Na'aman stream (Jennings and Gasith, unpublished data). Frequent cessation of spring discharge threatens the existence of this species.

FIGURE 4.4. A view of a stagnant reach of the N. Yarqon, within the limits of the city of Tel-Aviv. In the foreground, on the left, is a small remnant stand of *Phragmites australis*; in the background, *Eucalyptus*, an exotic tree which successfully replaces the native trees (mostly *Salix*) in most coastal streams

Little is known about past and present aquatic flora in other coastal streams, although occasional observations suggest that submerged and floating-leaved species are absent in polluted reaches. Riparian vegetation is routinely removed in most of the streams to prevent channel blocking or to allow access from the banks for mosquito control.

The far-reaching effect of habitat modification on the flora of the coastal streams and other wetlands in Israel is reflected in the fact that aquatic plants constitute no more than 10% of the flora of Israel but about 70% of the vanished plant species or those on the verge of extinction (Dafni and Agami, 1976; Agami, 1980).

Macroinvertebrates

Based on the literature and on collection records, Mienis (1977) concluded that over the last 120 years at least 22 species of freshwater molluscs were present in the Yarqon stream. According to Mienis, only 15 species were recorded between 1970 and 1977. All these species were collected in the relatively unpolluted upper reach of the stream. He attributes the disappearance of the molluscs to degradation in water quality over the last two to three decades. The author also notes the recent introduction of an exotic lymnaeid species (*Pseudosuccinea columella*) into N. Yarqon.

TABLE 4.3. Recent records of macrophytes from the
Tanninim stream[a,b]

Taxon	Taxon
Spirogyra[b]	*Nuphar luteum*[a,b]
Cladophora[b]	*Ruppia maritima*[b]
Vaucheria[b]	*Zannichellia palustris*[a]
Ceratophyllum demersum[a,b]	*Ludwigia stolonifera*[a]
Potamogeton nodosus[a,b]	*Ranunculus aquatilis*[a]
Potamogeton pectinatus[a]	*Lemna minor*[a,b]
Potamogeton crispus[a]	*Lemna gibba*[a]

[a]Berliner (1977)
[b]Lipkin (1986)

Herbst and Mienis (1985) conducted a survey of macroinvertebrates in N. Tanninim during 1978 to 1981. They recorded a total of 59 taxa, including those collected from a reach which flows intermittently. The richest taxonomic groups were malacostracan crustaceans, gastropods, and oligochaetes. Of the seven malacostracan species found, only three are known in other coastal streams. One species (*Cyathura carinata*), which formerly existed in both the Qishon and Tanninim streams, is presently known in the latter only. This is probably due to the severe pollution in N. Qishon. Of the molluscs collected in this study, several taxa were represented only by partly or completely fossilized shells. Presumably, these taxa became locally extinct as a result of draining the Kebara swamps in the 1930s. A noticeable feature of the macroinvertebrate fauna of the Tanninim stream is the relatively poor representation of aquatic insects, even in unpolluted sites (<25 taxa, most of which are restricted to intermittently flowing fresh water in the upper Tanninim). This may be associated with the oligohaline nature of the stream.

In a relatively unpolluted site of the Na'aman stream, 11 species of macroinvertebrates were recently collected on artificial substrates (Jennings and Gasith, 1989). The total number of macroinvertebrate taxa recorded in the stream was less than 20. Species richness was negatively correlated with the level of BOD; species number declined downstream as the level of pollution increased. Chironomid larvae and oligochaetes were the only taxa collected at heavily polluted sites. Mienis (1970) recorded 14 species of gastropods in the vicinity of the Na'aman springs whereas only three species were recently found by Jennings and Gasith (1989). It is interesting to note that, as recently as 1972, Lahav (1978) found the gastropods *Melanopsis praemorsa* and *Theodoxus macrii* in the spring area; however, 17 years later, these gastropods appeared only as broken shells. Frequent cessation of spring discharge and drying up of the spring pools could account for the recent disappearance of these species from the Na'aman stream.

Fish

Sixteen species of fish were recorded in the coastal streams in the 1950s and late 1960s (Goren, 1974, 1983). Since then, preferred habitats have been lost by recurrent drying up and pollution. Incidents of fish mortality in the coastal streams following release of

TABLE 4.4. Recent records of fishes from the Tanninim stream[a]

Family	Species (synonym)	Local name
Cyprinidae	*Capoeta damascina* (*Varicorhinus damascinus*)	Khafaf
	Garra rufa (*Discognathus rufus*)	Agleset
Clariidae	*Clarias gariepinus* (*C. lazera*)	Sfamnun
Anguillidae	*Anguilla anguilla*	Tzlofach
Cyprinodontidae	*Aphanius mento striptus* (*A. cypris.*)	Navit khula
Poeciliidae	*Gambusia affinis*	Gambusia
Mugilidae	*Mugil cephalus*	Kifon gdol–rosh
	Liza ramada (*Mugil capito*)	Kifon
Blenniidae	*Salaria fluviatilis* (*Blennius fluviatilis*)	Karnun hanakhalim
Cichlidae	*Tilapia zillii*	Amnun mazui
	Oreochromis aureus (*Tilapia aureus*)	Amnun yarden
	Sarotherodon galilaeus (*Tilapia galilaea*)	Amnun Galil

[a]Goren (1986)

wastewater were observed in the 1970s and 1980s (e.g. lower N. Tanninim, N. Alexander, N. Yarqon, N. Soreq—Gasith, unpublished data). Today, the coastal stream with the richest ichthyofauna is N. Tanninim, which contains 12 species (Table 4.4). According to Goren (pers. comm.), fish populations in other coastal streams were once as rich as in N. Tanninim. However, pollution and water exploitation decimated the fish fauna in these streams.

Species such as *Clarias gariepinus*, which is relatively tolerant to low-oxygen conditions, probably survive in most streams and small populations of other species may still persist in the few remaining clean water sections. Continuing deterioration of lotic habitats threatens the existence of at least one endemic cyprinid species Lavnun Hayarqon (*Acanthobrama telavivensis*), which was last recorded in the Yarqon stream (Goren, 1983). Populations of catadromus fish such as *Mugil cephalus* and *Liza ramada* have been strongly reduced due to pollution.

The proximity of some of the streams to fish ponds results in recurrent introductions of commercial species; mainly *Tilapia* hybrids and the common carp (*Cyprinus carpio*). Recently, the Japanese ornamental carp (koi) was observed in the Tanninim stream (Gasith, unpublished data).

Other vertebrates

The soft-shelled turtle (*Trionyx triunguis*) is presently the largest vertebrate in the coastal streams and Israel's largest reptile. It was once common in most coastal streams (Arbel, 1984), but according to Mendelssohn (1983) the habitat of this species was destroyed by drainage and pollution. It was suggested that initial organic enrichment improved the turtle's food supply of chironomid larvae and tubificid worms, but that increased levels of pollution, including chemical contamination, later reduced its food supply. Currently the only significant population of the soft-shelled turtle persists in the Alexander stream, which is highly polluted with domestic effluent. Supplemental feeding might be needed to maintain this population. A small reproducing population of this species exists in the Tanninim stream, and adult individuals are also occasionally seen in the Na'aman and Yarqon streams (Gasith, unpublished data).

The hard-shelled Caspian terrapin (*Mauremys caspica*) is common in all the coastal streams which maintain perennial reaches (Gasith and Sidis, 1983). Unlike its soft-shelled relative, it prospers in polluted water bodies (Gasith and Sidis, 1984). Thus, the distribution range of this species extends southwards to include perennial reaches formed by effluents in otherwise intermittent streams (e.g. N. Lakhish—Gasith and Sidis, 1983, 1984).

In the past, the water snake, *Natrix tesselatta*, was regularly observed in the water and on the banks of coastal streams but today it is rarely seen (Mendelssohn, pers. comm.).

The waterfowl fauna is poorly represented in most coastal streams. Moorhens (*Gallinula chloropus*), water rails (*Rallus aquaticus*), and European coots (*Fulica atra*) are occasionally seen in some of the streams. The restricted waterfowl fauna may be attributable to elimination of the floodplains by drainage and channelization, destruction of riparian vegetation, water exploitation, pollution, and direct human disturbance.

The declining diversity of the fauna and flora in the coastal streams reflects the continuing destruction of aquatic environments and the degradation in habitat quality of those few that still remain. At present, there are no reassuring signs of an end to (or reversal of) this trend. On the contrary, a plan to overcome a severe water shortage in the Haifa area, for example, calls for further exploitation of the N. Tanninim sources, risking the drying up of the last perennial stream in the Coastal Plain.

CONSERVATION AND REHABILITATION

The value of wetlands for recreation and nature conservation is recognized in Israel, as elsewhere. Nevertheless, in reality they are treated as systems of no economic value. Of the perennial coastal streams, only a small section of a few hundred metres in N. Tanninim is designated as a nature reserve. Even this status does not guarantee the integrity of this last "living museum". Less than 80 years ago, N. Tanninim hosted the Nile crocodile (*Crocodilus niloticus*) from which this stream derives its name (crocodiles =*tanninim* in Hebrew). Today, the remaining aquatic flora, macroinvertebrate, and fish fauna are threatened by pollution and unregulated water extraction. There is a pressing need to set criteria for assessment of streams in Israel, to designate the few remaining unpolluted reaches of the coastal streams as nature reserves and others for restoration as national parks. If steps in this direction are not immediately taken, remnants of the past fauna and flora (including endemic species) are likely to be lost for ever.

Under current conditions of severe water shortage, rehabilitation of the coastal streams seems almost a "mission impossible". Although removal of major pollution sources is feasible, such as by re-use of effluent in agricultural production, this step alone would dry up the streams. Sufficient water of reasonable quality is needed in order to maintain lotic conditions which can support plant and animal life and be amenable to recreation. The current legal position leaves the decision of water allocation to streams with the Water Commissioner, who may at any time change his decision. At present, N. Tanninim is the only major perennial stream in the Coastal Plain with a statement for water allocation from the Water Commissioner.

Considering that the entire freshwater potential of Israel is already being exploited, stream rehabilitation may need to rely, at least in part, on a supply of lower-quality water—namely, treated effluents. Even this, however, is easier said than done, as the use of any available water resource is expected to be in competition with irrigation demands. This may halt any realistic plans for stream rehabilitation. In March 1986, the government of Israel cut water allocation to agricultural and industrial sectors by 10% (200 MCM) and called for a five-year water-conservation programme with a 240 MCM yr^{-1} cutback (Whitman, 1988). More recently (1991), as a result of the worsening situation, the cutback was increased to 40–70%. Israel's National Sewerage Project aims at providing adequate sewage-treatment facilities which would reduce pollution and alleviate potential health hazards (Whitman, 1988). However, this project already trails behind existing sewerage needs due to lack of sufficient funding. In the wake of rising immigration to Israel, domestic water consumption and subsequent sewage return are expected to increase beyond the scope of current plans. Measures taken to cut water consumption and reduce water pollution may prove insufficient for stream restoration.

The Water Law 1959 is the principal legislation relating to fresh water in Israel. The law regulates, among other things, the flow of pollutants into the State's water arteries, many of which drain into the Mediterranean. The 1971 amendment to the law introduces a new provision concerning prevention of water pollution, under which every person must refrain from any act which directly or indirectly causes water pollution, either immediately or subsequently; it is immaterial whether or not the water resource was polluted prior to the Act. No person may throw, or cause to flow, into or near a water resource any liquid, solid, or gaseous substance, or deposit any such substance in or near a water resource. The Stream and Spring Authorities Law 1965 empowers the Minister of the Interior and the Minister of Agriculture, after consultation with the local authorities concerned, to establish an authority for a particular stream or part thereof, a spring, or any water source. Such authorities are termed "Stream Authorities". Their functions include the abatement of sanitary nuisances connected with pollution of the stream or water source for which they are responsible (Whitman, 1988).

This legal framework is the basis for the present efforts for stream restoration being made at national and local levels. A steering committee for stream rehabilitation appointed by the newly created Ministry of the Environment is currently working on a master plan for stream restoration and conservation in Israel. Meanwhile, municipal organizations such as Environmental Protection Units, The Association of Towns for Environmental Protection (e.g. Hadera, Haifa), The Asher Region Drainage Authority, and the Yarqon River Basin Authority have been given responsibility to take action to prevent water pollution. Their immediate goal is cleaning up the streams. Effluent discharge standards have been set and industries along the streams will be obliged to treat their wastewater accordingly prior to discharge into the streams (Whitman, 1988).

The Yarqon River Basin Authority, made up of all affected municipalities and local regional authorities, has been charged with responsibility for the implementation of rehabilitation plans for the Yarqon stream (Whitman, 1988). This runs through Israel's most populated area and is considered the best option for a metropolitan recreational park for the 1.5 million inhabitants of the Dan Metropolitan region (encompassing the city of Tel-Aviv). The first phase of restoration will involve cleaning up the accumulated debris from the stream channel and eliminating all wastewater discharges. At present, it is not clear what source of water will be used to restore lotic conditions. One option is to use high-quality effluent produced by filtration through the soil into an isolated aquifer (Y. Rosenblum, Yarqon River Basin Authority, pers. comm.).

The enhanced water crisis in the eastern Mediterranean calls for an urgent consideration of the future of natural wetland ecosystems. Hopefully, a growing public awareness of the state of the environment in Israel will influence decision makers to take more decisive action toward environmental protection and restoration. The status of the coastal streams illustrates the inherent difficulty of maintaining the integrity of aquatic environments under conditions of increasing demophoric growth and diminishing water resources.

ACKNOWLEDGEMENTS

I thank Dr M. Goren of the Zoology Department and Drs M. Agami and Y. Lipkin of the Botany Department (TAU) for providing valuable information. For reviewing the manuscript, I thank Professor H. Mendelssohn, J. Winkelman, and N. Paz of the Zoology department (TAU) and Z. Kuller of the Nature Reserves Authority. I wish to thank Y. Lakritz of the Association of Towns for Environmental Protection (Hadera) for providing material on the past and present state of Nahal Hadera.

REFERENCES

Agami, M. (1980). "The mysterious disappearance of the blue water lily", *Israel, Land and Nature*, **5**, 154–156.

Agami, M. (1990). "Changes in the flora of the eastern section of the Yarqon River during the last 20 years", *Israel Society for Ecology and Environmental Quality Sciences*, 21 Annual meeting, Ben Gurion University, June 1990 (abstract, in Hebrew).

Agami, M., Litav, M., and Waisel, Y. (1976). "The effect of various components of water pollution on the behavior of some aquatic macrophytes of the coastal rivers of Israel", *Aquatic Botany*, **2**, 203–213.

Arbel, A. (1984). "*Trionyx triunguis*", in *Plants and Animals of the Land of Israel* 5 (Ed. A. Arbel), pp. 41–42, Ministry of Defence/The Publishing House, Society for Protection of Nature, Israel (in Hebrew).

Avitsur, S. (1957). *The Yarkon, the River and its Environment*, Hakibbutz Hameuchad Publishing House Ltd (in Hebrew).

Ben-David, Z. (1983). *Nehaley Menashe Water Works*, The Yitzhak Noyfeld, Hof-Carmel Field School, Society for Nature Conservation, Report (in Hebrew).

Ben-David, Z. (1987). "Crocodile River: the last unpolluted stream in the Coastal Plain", *Israel, Land and Nature*, **12**, 143–147.

Berliner, R. (1977). "Wetland survey in the N. Tanninim catchment basin and its surroundings", in *Nature Conservation in Israel*, Nature Reserves Authority, **2**, 244–332 (in Hebrew).

Dafni, A., and Agami, M. (1976). "Extinct plants of Israel", *Biological Conservation*, **10**, 49–56.

Dan, J., and Koyumdjinsky, H. (1963). "The soils of Israel and their distribution", *Journal of Soil Science*, **14**, 12–20.

Eren, Y., Ortal, R., Gafny, G., Zack, Y., and Grinberg, S. (1980). *The Streams of Israel, 1974–1978*, Water Commission, Ministry of Agriculture and Nature Reserve Authority, Jerusalem, Report No. 1 (in Hebrew).

Gabbay, S. (1989). "Annual Environment Report", *Israel Environmental Bulletin, Ministry of the Environment*, **12**, 7–9.

Gafny, G. (1983). *Pollution of surface water by underground drainage from agricultural areas*, M.Sc. thesis, Hebrew University, Jerusalem, Faculty of Agriculture, Rehovot (in Hebrew, English summary).

Gafny, G., Ortal, R., Kuller, Z., Keshet, N., Glazman, H., Pergament, D., and Bachar, E. (1989). *The Streams of Israel, 1982–1987*, Water Commission, Ministry of Agriculture and Nature Reserve Authority, Jerusalem, Report No. 3 (in Hebrew).

Gasith, A., and Sidis, I. (1983). "The distribution and nature of the habitat of the Caspian terrapin, *Mauremys caspica rivulata* (Testudines, Emydidae) in Israel", *Israel Journal of Zoology*, **32**, 91–102.

Gasith, A., and Sidis, I. (1984). "Polluted water bodies, the main habitat of the Caspian terrapin (*Mauramys caspica rivulata*) in Israel", *Copeia*, 1984 (1), 216–219.

Goren, M. (1974). "The freshwater fishes of Israel", *Israel Journal of Zoology*, **23**, 67–118.

Goren, M. (1983). *Freshwater Fishes of Israel, Biology and Taxonomy*, Hakibbutz Hameuchad Publishing House Ltd.

Goren, M. (1986). "The presence of *Gara rufa* in the Tanninim stream (N. Tanninim)", *Teva ve-Aretz*, **28**, 28 (in Hebrew).

Herbst, G. N., and Mienis, H. K. (1985). "Aquatic invertebrate distribution in Nahal Tanninim, Israel", *Israel Journal of Zoology*, **33**, 51–62.

Jennings, J., and Gasith, A. (1989). "Use of artificial substrate for evaluation of the effect of water pollution on macroinvertebrates in the Na'aman stream", in *Environmental Quality and Ecosystem Stability* (Eds E. Spanier, Y. Steinberger, and M. Luria), 4/B, pp. 317–323, ISEEQS Pub., Jerusalem.

Lahav, H. (1978). *Effect of pollution in the Na'aman on populations of* Melanopsis *and* Theodoxus *(Gastropoda)*, Carmel Field School, Society for Nature Conservation, Report (in Hebrew).

Lindheimer, A. (1967). *The vegetation of the Kurdani springs*, Reali School Haifa, Report (in Hebrew).

Lipkin, Y. (1986). *Submerged macrophytes in N. Tanninim*, Report of the N. Tanninim Survey Expedition, April, September 1986, Botany Department, Tel-Aviv University (in Hebrew).

Litav, M., and Agami, M. (1976). "Relationship between water pollution and the flora of two coastal rivers in Israel", *Aquatic Botany*, **2**, 23–41.

MAWC (1983). *Survey of collection, treatment and use of effluents, 1989*, Ministry of Agriculture Water Commission (MAWC), Jerusalem, March (in Hebrew).

Mendelssohn, H. (1983). "Herpetological nature protection", *Israel, Land and Nature*, Fall, 21–27.

Mienis, H. K. (1970). "Some notes on freshwater mollusca from the marshes of Kurdani, Galilee", *Argamon*, **1**, 51–54.

Mienis, H. K. (1977). "The freshwater molluscs of the Yarqon, a polluted stream", *Levantina*, **8**, 81–82.

Paz, U. (1981). *Nature Reserves in Israel*, pp. 139–140, Massada Ltd—Israel (in Hebrew).

Vallentyne, J. R. (1972). "Freshwater supplies and pollution: effects of the demophoric explosion on water and man", in *The Environmental Future* (Ed. N. Polunin), pp. 181–211, Macmillan, London.

Whitman, J. (1988). *The Environment in Israel*, 4th edn, pp. 125–147, State of Israel Ministry of the Interior, Environmental Protection Service.

5

Degradation of Australian Streams and Progress towards Conservation and Management in Victoria

L. A. BARMUTA

Department of Zoology, University of Tasmania, Box 252C GPO, Hobart, Tasmania 7001, Australia

R. MARCHANT

Invertebrate Survey Department, Museum of Victoria, 71 Victoria Crescent, Abbotsford, Victoria 3170, Australia

and

P. S. LAKE

Department of Ecology and Evolutionary Biology, Monash University, Clayton, Victoria 3168, Australia

INTRODUCTION

Since European settlement, many of Australia's rivers and streams have been degraded by direct interference with their channels and flow regimes, discharges of pollutants, and modifications to their catchments (reviewed by Lake and Marchant, 1990). It is only comparatively recently that the extent of degradation has received official political recognition (Department of Resources and Energy, 1983; Standing Consultative Committee on River Improvement, 1983). Before this recognition, documentation of degradation was largely on a single-issue or case-by-case basis. In the last half of the 1980s, however, some efforts have been made to provide managers with more systematic data, although these have not been attempted in all States in Australia.

In this chapter we will briefly review the extent of the degradation of rivers and streams in Australia, and discuss the various approaches to conserving and rehabilitating them.

River Conservation and Management. Edited by P. J. Boon, P. Calow, and G. E. Petts
© 1992 John Wiley & Sons Ltd

FORMS OF DEGRADATION

Rapport et al (1985) divide human stresses on ecosystems into four categories: (1) harvesting of renewable resources, (2) discharge of pollutants, (3) physical modification and restructuring, and (4) introduction of exotic species. Australian streams have been exposed to all of these impacts. Most biological research has concentrated on permanent upland streams, although there is some work on the lowland sections of the Murray–Darling system (e.g. Hillman, 1986; Pressey, 1986; Walker, 1986), tropical streams (e.g. Smith and Pearson, 1987), and temperate temporary streams (Boulton and Suter, 1986).

Harvesting

As the driest inhabited continent, water harvesting has been pursued vigorously since European settlement. The ecological effects of dam construction and operation have been studied most intensively in Tasmania and Victoria, and have concentrated on the effects on benthic invertebrates and fish. Macroinvertebrates have been depleted in sections below dams with hypolimnial releases of water (e.g. Coleman, 1978; Blyth et al, 1984; Doeg, 1984), whereas some dams which discharge surface waters (Marchant, 1989) and those where erosion from construction has been minimized (Chessman et al, 1987) have not greatly depleted the downstream invertebrate biota. Many native river fish are migratory and there is no doubt that dams have depleted their stocks by preventing or greatly reducing their movements. Examples of such fish include the catadromous Australian Bass (Harris, 1986), the Australian Grayling (Bishop and Bell, 1978), and the potadromous Macquarie Perch and Golden Perch (Cadwallader, 1986; Harris, 1986).

The effects of river regulation on riparian and floodplain systems dependent on flood cycles have been extensive in the Murray–Darling basin, affecting germination and recruitment of the dominant tree species, *Eucalyptus camaldulensis* (River Red Gum) (Dexter, 1973, 1978) and the supply of water to billabongs and wetlands on the floodplain (Walker, 1979, 1986; Hillman, 1986). Similar effects probably prevail along other lowland rivers in Australia, but are largely undocumented in the published literature.

Pollutants

Rapport et al (1985) further divide stresses from pollutants into those due to excess organic matter (e.g. sewage) and those due to anthropogenic toxins to which organisms have no adaptive evolutionary history (e.g. PCBs, pesticides). Organic pollution from sewage outfalls has been documented in a number of case studies in both temperate (Jolly and Chapman, 1966; Campbell, 1978) and sub-tropical streams (Arthington et al, 1982; Cosser, 1988). Particularly in large urban areas, both point-source discharges and diffuse run-off are mixtures of both organic and inorganic pollutants, thus complicating the patterns of response of biotic communities and making predictions about the efficacy of abatement measures difficult (Arthington et al, 1982).

Australia's rich history of mining has left a legacy of environmental hazards for streams, some of which endure long after mining has ceased (e.g. Lake et al, 1977; Bycroft et al, 1982). Perhaps the best-known example is the long-term contamination of the Molonglo River near Canberra. The upper Molonglo has been contaminated by heavy metals (zinc, copper, lead, and cadmium) from mine workings at Captains Flat

(Weatherley et al, 1967). Mining ceased in 1962 and a survey in 1963 revealed reduced invertebrate and fish abundance for 40 km downstream of Captains Flat. The same pattern of distribution was found during 1974–1977 (Nicholas and Thomas, 1978). Even after specific engineering works to abate the pollution between 1974 and 1976, Norris (1986) found that the distribution of invertebrates in 1982 was similar to that reported in 1963 by Weatherley et al (1967). Consequently, it appears that such sources of pollution will pose long-term, perhaps intractable, effects on many streams and rivers in Australia.

Modifications

Streams have been modified as a result of changes in catchment land use as well as direct intervention with instream habitat. Extensive land clearance and subsequent cultivation have led to major soil erosion across many parts of the continent, with concomitant problems in rivers and streams (e.g. Smith and Finlayson, 1988). In some areas of Australia (e.g. south-west Western Australia), land clearance has contributed to rising saline water tables, resulting in extensive salinization of soils, wetlands, and streams. In other areas, intensive irrigation has interacted with shallow water tables, resulting in salinization (Peck et al, 1983; Smith and Finlayson, 1988).

In addition, diffuse run-off containing nutrients and pesticides from agricultural and urban areas contributes to declining water quality, while timber harvesting in forested catchments can increase sediment inputs to the detriment of water quality and instream biota (Richardson, 1985; Campbell and Doeg, 1989). Generally, however, the ecological effects on instream biota of these changes in land use and salinity remain poorly documented (Williams, 1987; Lake and Marchant, 1990).

Apart from the construction of dams and weirs, the major modifications to river channels have been connected with "river improvement". These activities have included re-alignment or channelization of streams, removal of debris dams and submerged timber, and engineering works to protect banks, bridges, and other cultural artefacts close to the stream. Hortle and Lake (1982, 1983) described some of the faunal changes resulting from such activities in the Bunyip River in Victoria, while the removal of cover for fish is often cited as a major factor in the decline of native fish stocks (e.g. Cadwallader, 1978).

Exotic taxa

Lowland waters have been affected by many more species of introduced aquatic plants and fish than upland streams (Arthington and Mitchell, 1986; Lake and Marchant, 1990). Although there have been some spectacular successes in the control of *Salvinia molesta* (Room, 1990), species such as *Eichhornia crassipes* and *Alternanthera philoxeroides* remain major pest plants in many lowland systems (Arthington and Mitchell, 1986). Among the fish, conclusive data about their deleterious effects on native species are patchy; the best-documented cases are for salmonids and mosquito fish (*Gambusia*) (Arthington, 1986; Fletcher, 1986).

The principal problems in temperate upland streams are modification of channel morphology and riparian habitat by willows (*Salix* spp.) and blackberries (*Rubus* spp.), and interactions between introduced salmonids and native fish and invertebrate communities (Fletcher, 1979, 1986; Jackson and Williams, 1980). Fletcher (1979, 1986) has carried out one of the few experimental tests of the effects of brown trout and found that they depleted populations of the native *Galaxias olidus* and altered the composition of macroinvertebrate benthos. There is a clear need for further studies of this nature to confirm or refute the largely anecdotal literature on the deleterious effects of introduced fish in Australian streams (Arthington, 1986). Nevertheless, the paucity of well-controlled experimental studies should not excuse the continued accidental or deliberate release or translocation of aquatic plants and animals.

ATTEMPTS AT CONSERVATION

While the extent of riverine degradation in Australia has been prominent in public perception in the last 20 years (Lake, 1978), and the scientific community was aware of the intensively studied examples cited above, little attempt was made to assess the degradation across broad geographic areas. In the mid-1980s, some government bodies recognized the need for systematic inventory in order to identify remaining pristine or near-pristine areas for preservation, to rank areas for restoration, and to discover those aspects of riverine issues that need research before further action could be taken. These approaches have been most extensively pursued in Victoria, and our discussion concentrates on that State.

Inventories

The Victorian Department of Water Resources Victoria (DWR) has published three important compilations of data. The first (Department of Water Resources Victoria, 1989a), a resource handbook, documents the quantity of water available from various sources; the second (Department of Water Resources Victoria, 1989b), an environmental handbook, details environmental and biological data for the major drainage basins; and the third (Mitchell, 1990) describes the results of a survey of the physical and vegetational characteristics of rivers at representative sites across the State. The resource handbook gives data on river discharge and historical changes to this, the volume of various water storages, the amount of groundwater and its potential for use (some is very saline), and information on water quality. This last item comprised data on salinity, turbidity, dissolved oxygen, nutrients, and general potability. The sites for which water quality data are available are not numerous, but exist for 27 of the 29 major drainage basins of Victoria.

The environmental handbook is the most useful for determining the extent of modification to Victorian rivers and streams. Extensive data are presented on maps of each drainage basin covering the following features: catchment vegetation and land use, land type, riparian tree cover and adjacent land use, stream management works, fish, and benthic invertebrates. Less detailed information is given on erosion hazards, flooding, and point sources of pollution.

The freshwater fish fauna of Victoria is well known and consists of 53 species, of which 11 are introduced (Department of Water Resources Victoria, 1989b). The distribution of fish in the Yarra basin (Figure 5.1) demonstrates the widespread distribution of introduced species: six of the 16 species present are introduced and at least one of these is present at all but four of the 21 sites surveyed. By contrast, the East Gippsland drainage basin, which is a collection of small catchments (Figure 5.2), has 25 species of fish of

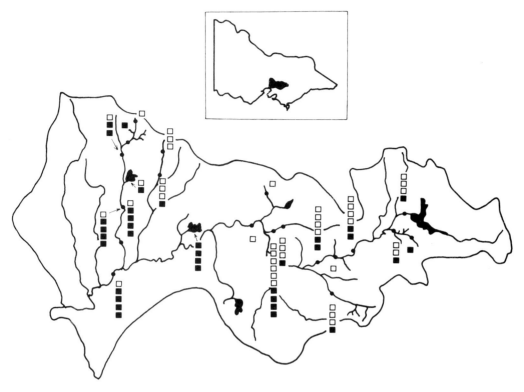

FIGURE 5.1. Records of fish species from the Yarra basin, Victoria. Each column of squares represents a surveyed site or reach; each square represents a fish species; open squares are native species; closed squares are introduced species. (Redrawn from Department of Water Resources Victoria, 1989b)

which only one is introduced. This basin is largely undeveloped and has the highest proportion of streams in the State with high environmental quality (Mitchell, 1990).

The distribution of benthic invertebrates is mapped at family level. This approach was taken because the studies on which the maps were based were undertaken by a variety of groups over a number of years with differing aims, methods, and levels of taxonomic expertise. It must be recognized that some of the major groups encountered (e.g. chironomid, coleopteran and trichopteran larvae, ephemeropteran nymphs, oligochaetes) are very poorly known taxonomically with few published descriptions or keys available. Despite these shortcomings, an attempt has been made to assign these families to various habitats (e.g. taxa found in cool, clear, well-oxygenated streams, intolerant of pollution) and to give an idea of seasonal variation in the fauna.

The third publication (Mitchell, 1990) provides important data on the environmental condition of Victorian streams based on physical and vegetational variables for 868 sites throughout the State. Physical features included streambed composition, flow velocity, and water depth; vegetational features comprised percentage cover of bank, verge, and underwater vegetation, cover for fish, and amount of organic debris. Each of these features was scored according to its suitability for aquatic life (Table 5.1). These scores were combined into an overall "environmental rating" for each site. The ratings were

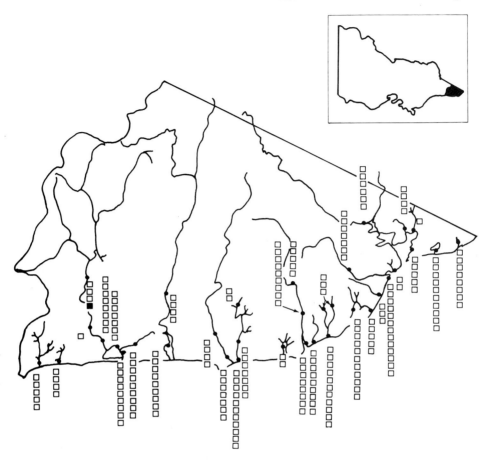

FIGURE 5.2. Records of fish species from the East Gippsland basin, Victoria. Each column of squares represents a surveyed site or reach; each square represents a fish species; open squares are native species; closed squares are introduced species. (Redrawn from Department of Water Resources Victoria, 1989b)

then checked with independent assessments from experienced, professional field biologists; only 5% of the ratings disagreed with the biologists' assessments. Sites were also classified into three stream categories: major streams, tributary streams, and minor streams. The length of stream in each category with a given environmental rating was then calculated. As might be expected, for the State as a whole the minor streams made up the greatest proportion (70%) of their total length in an excellent or good condition, while the major streams had the least (21%) in this condition. Only 5% of the length of streams running through cleared areas was in an excellent or good condition (Table 5.2).

Another government body in Victoria, the Office of the Commissioner for the Environment (1989), has produced the *State of the Environment Report*, largely based on data gathered for the above documents. This report makes the first attempt to interpret these data and assess comprehensively the environmental condition of the State's inland waters, including rivers. The report deals with many aspects of water use and water quality in Victorian rivers in addition to strictly biological matters, e.g. environmental flows, persistent contaminants, conservation measures, effects of roads, forestry, agriculture, mining, industry, and urbanization. It emphasizes biological indicators of environmental impact and the need to monitor long-term changes in the biota (macroinvertebrates, fish, and aquatic plants) if impact is to be assessed properly. Unfortunately, as the report is at pains to point out, there are generally insufficient data on lotic fish or macroinvertebrates to give a comprehensive picture for more than a few drainage basins or to delineate any temporal trends. The report recommends that statewide monitoring be undertaken for both fish and invertebrates, and that major improvements be made in gathering and analysing these data. There are more data available on the status of riparian vegetation; as might be expected, the most degraded riparian habitats are along lowland reaches of rivers.

Concurrent with the compilation of the above documents, other attempts were made to interpret and supplement this information to assess conservation status of rivers and streams in five regions in the State (Macmillan et al, 1987; Seymour, 1987; Meredith et al, 1989; Macmillan, 1990; Macmillan and Kunert, 1990a). Macmillan and Kunert (1990b) have developed methods for evaluating the conservation status of rivers and streams using four criteria: (1) the integrity of the stream and its surrounding catchment; (2) instream features (including physicochemical and biotic); (3) terrestrial riparian features; and (4) geological and geomorphic features. Macmillan and Kunert (1990b) acknowledge that data for these criteria are incomplete in many areas of Victoria. They call for more systematic information to be collected, especially to evaluate the meaningfulness of their assessments for instream biota. Nevertheless, their approach has resulted in useful recommendations for river conservation in Victoria, and represents a significant advance over previous attempts in Australia (cf. Helman, 1981).

All these activities, in concert with a reappraisal of routine chemical water quality monitoring across the State, have resulted in an attempt to link long-term physicochemical and biological monitoring in a network of fixed sites representative of the wide variety of riverine habitats in Victoria. Invertebrate samples will be collected using uniform, standardized methods from the same sites as the physicochemical data and should ultimately lead to more consistent and useful data sets as stressed in all of the inventories cited above. Presently, the network consists of 67 sites with plans to increase this to approximately 200 (G. Bennison and R. Butcher, Rural Water Commission, pers. comm.).

Predictive models

Inventories alone are limited in guiding management actions. Their scope is necessarily broad, and some of the assumptions made in assessing environmental quality or conservation value may not apply to all rivers at all times. Mitchell's (1990) environmental rating categories, for example, give high values to streams and rivers with fast water flowing over shingle or cobble beds. However, there are some pristine streams with sandy substrata or slow or intermittent flows.

Work is in progress to develop a more predictive approach similar to the River Communities Project in Britain (Furse et al, 1984; Wright et al, 1984). Ultimately, we hope to predict the composition of benthic invertebrates at any site within a drainage

TABLE 5.1. Criteria used by Mitchell (1990) to determine environmental ratings for 868 sites on rivers in Victoria

Stream size[a]	Environmental rating				
	Very Poor	Poor	Moderate	Good	Excellent
Bed composition					
Minor	All sand	Gravel, sand	Gravel, some cobbles, some sand	With at least 10% cobbles mainly shingle	Boulders/ cobbles/ shingles, small amount gravel or finer material
Tributary	N/A	All sand	Gravel, sand	Mainly shingle, gravel	Shingle, cobble gravel
Major	N/A	N/A	All sand	Shingle, gravel, sand	Shingle, cobbles present
Proportion of pools and riffles					
Minor	100% riffle or pool	90% riffle or pool	70–80% riffle or pool	60% riffle or pool	50% riffle or pool
Tributary	Intermittent pools	All pools	< 10% riffles	10–30% riffles	> 30% riffles
Major[b]	Intermittent pool or very shallow	N/A	100% pools	N/A	Some riffles
Bank vegetation					
All	Introduced ground cover with lots of bare ground, occasional tree	Introduced ground cover, little native overstorey or understorey or predominantly exotic cover (e.g. willows)	Moderate cover, mixed native/exotics, or one side cleared, other undisturbed	Minor clearing	Mainly undisturbed native vegetation
Verge vegetation					
All	Bare or pasture	Very narrow corridor of native vegetation or exotics	Wide corridor mixed native and exotics, or one side cleared, and other native and wide	Mainly undisturbed native, < 30m or some exotics or reduced cover of natives	Mainly undisturbed native vegetation, > 30 m wide

TABLE 5.1. (*continued*)

Stream size[a]	Environmental rating				
	Very Poor	Poor	Moderate	Good	Excellent
Cover for fish					
All	None	Poor	Moderate	Good	Abundant
Average flow velocity					
Minor	0	0.1–0.2 m s^{-1}	0.3–0.6 m s^{-1}	0.6–0.7 m s^{-1}	> 0.8 m s^{-1}
Tributary	0	0.1–0.2 m s^{-1}	0.3–0.6 m s^{-1}	0.6–0.7 m s^{-1}	> 0.8 m s^{-1}
Major	N/A	0	0.1 m s^{-1} (pools)	0.2 m s^{-1} (pools)	> 0.3 m s^{-1} (pools)
Water depth					
Minor	Dry or trickle	< 0.2 m	0.3–0.5 m	0.6–1 m	> 1.0 m
Tributary	Dry or trickle	< 0.2 m	0.3–0.5 m	0.6–1 m	> 1.0 m
Major	< 0.3 m	0.4 m	0.5–0.9 m	1.0–2.0 m	> 2.0 m
Underwater vegetation					
All	0 or > 80% cover	1–5% or 60–80% cover	5–20% cover	20–30% cover	30–60% cover
Organic debris					
All	0	0–10% cover	10–20% cover	20–40% cover	40% cover
Erosion/sedimentation					
All	Extensive	Significant	Moderate, affecting parts of reach	Only spot erosion	Stable no erosion/ sedimentation

[a]Major streams have a catchment area > 30 000 ha, tributary streams have a catchment area < 30 000 ha and > 5000 ha, minor streams have a catchment area < 5000 ha
[b]Only three rating categories were given for proportion of riffles and pools in major rivers

basin given its physicochemical conditions, and thus detect likely causes for deviations from the expected faunal composition in a similar fashion to Armitage et al (1987). At present, we are confined to using pre-existing data collected by a number of different agencies for differing purposes. Nevertheless, by restricting the data to replicated sampling programmes where both winter and summer samples have been collected for more than one year, and where all invertebrates have been identified to species level using a common voucher system, we have assembled data for sites across Victoria that are either essentially undisturbed or of the highest possible environmental quality within that basin or region.

A preliminary analysis of the first 34 sites in this database shows that there is a large degree of regional, inter-basin difference in the macroinvertebrate benthos across

TABLE 5.2. Percentage of stream length of Victoria's rivers in the different environmental rating categories of Mitchell (1990)

Type of stream	Rating category		
	Excellent or good (%)	Moderate (%)	Poor or very poor (%)
Major streams	21	51	28
Tributaries	35	20	45
Minor streams	70	7	23
All streams	60	13	27
All streams in cleared areas	5	30	65

Major streams have a catchment area > 30 000 ha, tributary streams have a catchment area < 30 000 ha and > 5000 ha, minor streams have a catchment area < 5000 ha

Victoria (Figure 5.3). The site from the Wimmera basin in the semi-arid west of the State (group A in Figure 5.3) showed a markedly different fauna from all the other sites from the wetter eastern basins. All of the sites from alpine and sub-alpine areas (group G) formed a discrete cluster most closely related to the upland rocky sites in the La Trobe and Thomson basins. Group C consisted of a polluted site on the Yarra in Melbourne and was included in the analysis as an "out-group". Although faunistically quite different from sites further upstream on the same river (group D), it was nevertheless more closely related to these and other sites in the same region than to anything else.

When the additional eight sites from East Gippsland are included, we hope to analyse these data at coarser taxonomic resolutions to determine the robustness of the patterns exemplified in Figure 5.3. If the results are sufficiently encouraging, then it may be possible to repeat the exercise for the 350 sites across the State for which family-level data are available.

ATTEMPTS AT RESTORATION

River restoration has had a chequered history in Australia, and has often concentrated on protecting soils and infrastructure on adjacent properties, rather than conserving instream values. Many of the engineering works carried out to "improve" rivers consisted of "hard" solutions such as large concrete drop structures, weirs, channelization, and stream clearing; revegetation of modified banks often involved using easily propagated exotic species such as willows (*Salix* spp.) (e.g. Strom, 1962). Sometimes works were carried out illegally without regard for downstream consequences, and some rivers in north-eastern Victoria have hundreds of recorded attempts at bank or channel stabilization (Department of Water Resources Victoria, 1989b).

Recently, there have been concerted efforts to manage whole catchments in Victoria, rather than attempt piecemeal restoration works. One of the most ambitious and thorough projects initiated recently is the rehabilitation and restoration of streams draining into Western Port Bay (Department of Water Resources and Rural Water

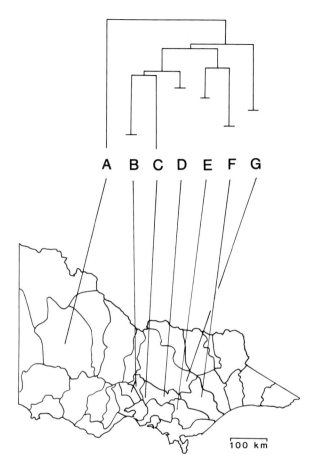

FIGURE 5.3. Classification of sites based on macroinvertebrate abundances from several drainage basins across Victoria. Group A: Wimmera River; Group B: Maribyrnong and Werribee Rivers; Group C: polluted site on lower Yarra River; Group D: upper Yarra River; Group E: upper La Trobe River system; Group F: Thomson River; Group G: alpine streams near Mount Stirling

Commission, 1987a,b). Extensive clearing and draining for agriculture over the last century has resulted in spectacular gully and head erosion in many of the streams, with some channels now several metres deeper than they were prior to European settlement (Bird, 1980; Seymour, 1987). It is estimated that, on average, 130 000 m^3 yr^{-1} of sediment is deposited in Western Port Bay, the majority of it derived from the increased erosion of these streams (Department of Water Resources and Rural Water Commission, 1987b).

The present plan focuses on "soft engineering" solutions to stabilize and reduce bed and bank erosion and hence improve the environmental quality of these streams. This is exemplified by the use of many smaller rock chute drop structures rather than a few large concrete barriers. Frequently, these "soft" solutions are not only aesthetically more pleasing but are more desirable environmentally, since the chutes are less of a barrier to fish migration and, once established, are less likely to be circumvented by subsequent erosion (e.g. Bird, 1982). In addition, such approaches are usually less expensive than the more spectacular structures characteristic of "hard engineering" solutions (Department of Water Resources and Rural Water Commission, 1987b).

However, instream engineering works also need to be complemented with careful planning and catchment management to ensure or improve the quality of the water in the streams. The activities that will need to be managed in the Western Port area range from timber harvesting in the upland reaches of some of the streams, through agricultural practices on the floodplains, to the pressures of increased urbanization resulting from the expansion of Melbourne (Seymour, 1987). Extensive negotiations with the Dandenong Valley Authority, local councils, and interested members of the public have resulted in the establishment of the new Dandenong Valley and Western Port Authority. The Authority should have the necessary finance and powers to implement this extensive programme of capital works over the next 15 years, and commitment to maintain these and implement planning controls into the future (P. Geraghty, Office of Water Resources Victoria, pers. comm.).

CONCLUSIONS

The degradation of rivers and streams across Australia since European settlement has been rampant and widespread. Some States now officially recognize this to the extent that they have characterized the amount of this degradation and assign priorities to remedial works. However, most of these efforts have concentrated on wet-temperate, permanent upland streams.

Lowland rivers have been subject to more extensive disturbances, and are complicated by their close association with floodplain wetland and billabong systems. The linkages between such rivers and their associated wetlands remains largely uninvestigated in Australia, and meaningful assessments of the conservation status of these rivers will be hard to make. Similarly, intermittent and ephemeral streams remain poorly known despite their ubiquity across Australia. Presumably, the methods developed for assessing the conservation status of permanent waters will need to be modified to accommodate such systems.

The scarcity of ecological knowledge about Australia's instream biota remains a major barrier to effective restoration or rehabilitation of rivers and streams. Although much effort is now being expended on catchment management and stream protection works, little is being done to assess the efficacy of such projects in benefiting the aquatic flora and fauna. Given the extent of the degradation of streams in Australia, it seems imperative that such monitoring be carried out so as to guide future attempts at restoration and rehabilitation.

ACKNOWLEDGEMENTS

We thank the following for discussions, for making unpublished material available, and for logistic and technical support: Scott Seymour and Pat Condina of the Dandenong Valley Authority, Trish Geraghty and Jane Doolan of the Office of Water Resources, Gary Bennison, Phil Mitchell, and Rhonda Butcher of the Rural Water Commission, Peter Lillywhite and Vasilay Ting of the Museum of Victoria, and Barry Hart of the Centre for Stream Ecology.

REFERENCES

Armitage, P. D., Gunn, R. J. M., Furse, M. T., Wright, J. F., and Moss, D. (1987). "The use of prediction to assess macroinvertebrate response to river regulation", *Hydrobiologia*, **144**, 25–32.

Arthington, A. H. (1986). "Introduced cichlid fish in Australian inland waters", in *Limnology in Australia* (Eds P. De Deckker and W. D. Williams), pp. 239–248, CSIRO and W. Junk, Melbourne and Dordrecht.

Arthington, A. H., and Mitchell, D. S. (1986). "Aquatic invading species", in *The Ecology of Biological Invasions* (Eds R. Groom and J. Burdon), pp. 34–53, Australian Academy of Science, Canberra.

Arthington, A., Conrick, D. L., Connell, D. W., and Outridge, P. M. (1982). *The Ecology of a Polluted Urban Creek, Australian Water Resources Council Technical Paper No. 68*, Australian Government Publishing Service, Canberra.

Bird, J. F. (1980). "Geomorphological implications of flood control measures, Lang Lang River, Victoria", *Australian Geographical Studies*, **18**, 169–183.

Bird, J. F. (1982). "Channel incision at Eaglehawk Creek, Gippsland, Victoria, Australia", *Proceedings of the Royal Society of Victoria*, **94**, 11–22.

Bishop, K. A., and Bell, J. D. (1978). "Observations on the fish fauna below Tallowa Dam (Shoalhaven River, N.S.W.) during river flow stoppages", *Australian Journal of Marine and Freshwater Research*, **29**, 543–549.

Blyth, J. D., Doeg, T. J., and St Clair, R. M. (1984). "Response of the macroinvertebrate fauna of the Mitta Mitta River, Victoria, to the construction and operation of Dartmouth Dam. I. ·Construction and initial filling period", *Occasional Papers of the Museum of Victoria*, **1**, 83–100.

Boulton, A. J., and Suter, P. J. (1986). "Ecology of temporary streams—an Australian perspective", in *Limnology in Australia* (Eds P. De Deckker and W. D. Williams), pp. 313–327, CSIRO and W. Junk, Melbourne and Dordrecht.

Bycroft, B. M., Coller, B. A. W., Deacon, G. B., Coleman, D. J., and Lake, P. S. (1982). "Mercury contamination of the Lerderderg River, Victoria, Australia, from an abandoned gold field", *Environmental Pollution Series A*, **28**, 135–147.

Cadwallader, P. L. (1978). "Some causes of the decline in range and abundance of native fish in the Murray–Darling River system", *Proceedings of the Royal Society of Victoria*, **90**, 211–224.

Cadwallader, P. L. (1986). "Flow regulation in the Murray River system and its effect on the native fish fauna", in *Stream Protection: the Management of Rivers for Instream Uses* (Ed. I. C. Campbell), pp. 115–133, Water Studies Centre, Chisholm Institute of Technology, East Caulfield, Victoria.

Campbell, I. C. (1978). "A biological investigation of an organically polluted urban stream in Victoria", *Australian Journal of Marine and Freshwater Research*, **29**, 245–291.

Campbell, I. C., and Doeg, T. (1989). "Impact of timber harvesting and production on streams: a review", *Australian Journal of Marine and Freshwater Research*, **40**, 519–539.

Chessman, B. C., Robinson, D. P., and Hortle, K. G. (1987). "Changes in the riffle macroinvertebrate fauna of the Tanjil River, southeastern Australia, during construction of Blue Rock Dam", *Regulated Rivers*, **1**, 317–329.

Coleman, D. (1978). *Downstream effects of the Gordon Dam, Lower Gordon River Scientific Survey No. 10*, Hydroelectric Commission of Tasmania, Hobart.

Cosser, P. R. (1988). "Macroinvertebrate community structure and chemistry of an organically polluted creek in south-east Queensland", *Australian Journal of Marine and Freshwater Research*, **39**, 671–683.

Department of Resources and Energy (1983). *Water 2000: A Perspective on Australia's Water Resources to the Year 2000*, Australian Government Publishing Service, Canberra.

Department of Water Resources and Rural Water Commission (1987a). *Western Port Rivers Management Study 2nd Interim Report: Analysis and Appraisal*, Dandenong Valley Authority, Dandenong, Victoria.

Department of Water Resources and Rural Water Commission (1987b). *Western Port Rivers Management Study 3rd Interim Report: Activity Plan*, Dandenong Valley Authority, Dandenong, Victoria.

Department of Water Resources Victoria (1989a). *Water Victoria: a Resource Handbook*, Department of Water Resources Victoria, Melbourne.

Department of Water Resources Victoria (1989b). *Water Victoria: an Environmental Handbook*, Department of Water Resources Victoria, Melbourne.

Dexter, B. D. (1973). "River red gum forests, to flood or not to flood?", *Victorian Resources*, **15**, 20–23.

Dexter, B. D. (1978). "Silviculture of the river red gum forest of the central Murray floodplain", *Proceedings of the Royal Society of Victoria*, **93**, 175–191.

Doeg, T. J. (1984). "Response of the macroinvertebrate fauna of the Mitta Mitta River, Victoria, to the construction and operation of Dartmouth Dam. 2. Irrigation release", *Occasional Papers of the Museum of Victoria*, **1**, 101–108.

Fletcher, A. R. (1979). *Effects of* Salmo trutta *on* Galaxias olidus *and macroinvertebrates in stream communities*, MSc thesis, Monash University, Clayton, Victoria.

Fletcher, A. R. (1986). "Effects of introduced fish in Australia", in *Limnology in Australia* (Eds P. De Deckker and W. D. Williams), pp. 231–238, CSIRO and W. Junk, Melbourne and Dordrecht.

Furse, M. T., Moss, D., Wright, J. F. and Armitage, P. D. (1984). "The influence of seasonal and taxonomic factors on the ordination and classification of running-water sites in Great Britain and the prediction of their macro-invertebrate communities", *Freshwater Biology*, **14**, 257–280.

Harris, J. H. (1986). "Fish passage in Australia", in *Stream Protection. The Management of Rivers for Instream Uses* (Ed. I. C. Campbell), pp. 135–141, Water Studies Centre, Chisholm Institute of Technology, Caulfield East, Victoria.

Helman, P. (1981). "Wild and scenic rivers. A preliminary study of New South Wales", *New South Wales National Parks and Wildlife Service Occasional Paper No. 2*, National Parks and Wildlife Service of New South Wales, Sydney.

Hillman, T. J. (1986). "Billabongs", in *Limnology in Australia* (Eds P. De Deckker and W. D. Williams), pp. 457–470, CSIRO and W. Junk, Melbourne and Dordrecht.

Hortle, K., and Lake, P. S. (1982). "Macroinvertebrate assemblages in channelized and unchannelized section of the Bunyip River, Victoria", *Australian Journal of Marine and Freshwater Research*, **33**, 1071–1082.

Hortle, K., and Lake, P. S. (1983). "Fish of channelized and unchannelized sections of the Bunyip River, Victoria", *Australian Journal of Marine and Freshwater Research*, **34**, 441–450.

Jackson, P. D. and Williams, W. D. (1980). "Effects of brown trout, *Salmo trutta* Linnaeus, on the distribution of some native fishes in three areas of southern Victoria, Australia", *Australian Journal of Marine and Freshwater Research*, **31**, 61–67.

Jolly, V. H., and Chapman, M. A. (1966). "A preliminary study of effects of pollution on Farmer's Creek and Cox's River, New South Wales", *Hydrobiologia*, **27**, 160–192.

Lake, P. S. (1978). "On the conservation of rivers in Australia", *Newsletter of the Australian Society for Limnology*, **16**, 24–28.

Lake, P. S., and Marchant, R. (1990). "Australian upland streams: ecological degradation and possible restoration", *Proceedings of the Ecological Society of Australia*, **16**, 79–91.

Lake, P. S., Coleman, D., Mills, B., and Norris, R. (1977). "A reconnaissance of pollution of the King River in the Comstock-Crotty area, western Tasmania", in *Landscape and Man* (Eds J. B. Kirkpatrick and M. Banks), pp. 157–174, Royal Society of Tasmania, Hobart.

Macmillan, L. (1990). *Conservation Value and Status of Victorian Rivers. Part II. East Gippsland Rivers*, Faculty of Environmental Design and Construction, Royal Melbourne Institute of Technology, Melbourne.

Macmillan, L., and Kunert, C. (1990a). *Conservation Value and Status of Victorian Rivers. Part III. The Wimmera River and its Catchment*, Faculty of Environmental Design and Construction, Royal Melbourne Institute of Technology, Melbourne.

Macmillan, L., and Kunert, C. (1990b). *Conservation Value and Status of Victorian Rivers. Part I. Methodology*, Faculty of Environmental Design and Construction, Royal Melbourne Institute of Technology, Melbourne.

Macmillan, L. A., Kunert, C., and Blakers, M. (1987). *Nature Conservation Value and Status of Rivers in the south-western region, Victoria. Report to the Victorian Department of Water*

Resources, Department of Planning, Policy and Landscape, Royal Melbourne Institute of Technology, Melbourne.

Marchant, R. (1989). "Changes in the benthic invertebrate communities of the Thomson river, south-eastern Australia, after dam construction", *Regulated Rivers*, **4**, 71–88.

Meredith, C., Goss, H., and Seymour, S. (1989). *Nature Conservation Values of the Rivers and Catchments of Gippsland*. *Report No. 44, Water Resource Management Report Series*, Department of Water Resources Victoria, Melbourne.

Mitchell, P. (1990). *The Environmental Condition of Victorian Streams*, Department of Water Resources Victoria, Melbourne.

Nicholas, W. L., and Thomas, M. (1978). *Biological Release and Recycling of Toxic Metals from Lake and River Sediments*. *Australian Water Resources Council Technical Paper No. 33*, Australian Government Publishing Service, Canberra.

Norris, R. H. (1986). "Mine waste pollution of the Molonglo River, New South Wales and the Australian Capital Territory: effectiveness of remedial works at Captains Flat", *Australian Journal of Marine and Freshwater Research*, **37**, 147–157.

Office of the Commissioner for the Environment (1989). *State of the Environment Report 1988. Victoria's Inland Waters*, Office of the Commissioner for the Environment, Melbourne.

Peck, A. J., Thomas, J. F., and Williamson, D. R. (1983). *Effects of man on salinity in Australia. Water 2000 Consultants Report No. 8*, Australian Government Publishing Service, Canberra.

Pressey, R. L. (1986). *Wetlands of the River Murray below Lake Hume. River Murray Commission Report 86/1*, River Murray Commission, Canberra.

Rapport, D. J., Regier, H. A., and Hutchinson, T. C. (1985). "Ecosystem behavior under stress", *American Naturalist*, **125**, 617–640.

Richardson, B. A. (1985). "The impact of forest road construction on the benthic invertebrate and fish fauna of a coastal stream in southern New South Wales", *Bulletin of the Australian Society for Limnology*, **10**, 65–88.

Room, P. M. (1990). "Ecology of a simple plant–herbivore system: biological control of *Salvinia*", *Trends in Ecology and Evolution*, **5**, 74–79.

Seymour, B. S. (1987). *Assessment of the Conservation Values of the Rivers and Streams in the Western Port Region*, Dandenong Valley Authority, Dandenong, Victoria, Australia.

Smith, D. I., and Finlayson, B. (1988). Water in Australia: its role in environmental degradation", in *Land, Water and People. Geographical Essays in Australian Resource Management* (Eds R. L. Heathcote and J. A. Mabbutt), pp. 7–48, Allen and Unwin, Sydney.

Smith, R. E. W., and Pearson, R. G. (1987). "The macro-invertebrate communities of temporary pools in an intermittent stream in tropical Queensland", *Hydrobiologia*, **150**, 45–61.

Standing Consultative Committee on River Improvement (1983). *The State of the Rivers*, Standing Consultative Committee on River Improvement, Melbourne.

Strom, H. G. (1962). *River Improvement and Drainage in Australia and New Zealand*, State Rivers and Water Supply Commission Victoria, Melbourne.

Walker, K. F. (1979). "Regulated streams in Australia: the Murray–Darling system", in *The Ecology of Regulated Streams* (Eds J. V. Ward and J. A. Stanford), pp. 143–163, Plenum Press, New York.

Walker, K. F. (1986). "The Murray–Darling River System", in *The Ecology of River Systems* (Eds B. R. Davies and K. F. Walker), pp. 631–659, W. Junk, Dordrecht.

Weatherley, A. H., Beevers, J. R., and Lake, P. S. (1967). "The ecology of a zinc polluted river", in *Australian Inland Waters and their Fauna: Eleven Studies* (Ed. A. H. Weatherley), pp. 252–278, Australian National University Press, Canberra.

Williams, W. D. (1987). "Salinization of rivers and streams: an important environmental hazard", *Ambio*, **16**, 180–186.

Wright, J. F., Moss, D., Armitage, P. D., and Furse, M. T. (1984). "A preliminary classification of running-water in Great Britain based on macro-invertebrate species and the prediction of community type using environmental data", *Freshwater Biology*, **14**, 221–256.

6

The Rivers of Northern Trinidad: Conservation of Fish Communities for Research

B. H. SEGHERS

Animal Behaviour Research Group, Department of Zoology, University of Oxford, Oxford OX1 3PS, UK

INTRODUCTION

All rivers, no matter how remote, have been impacted in some way by man's global influence on the biosphere. Conservation strategies are constrained by our limited resources, energy, and especially the time available for action. This chapter presents the case for conserving a group of small rivers in the Northern Range mountains of the island of Trinidad in the West Indies (Figure 6.1). These rivers have become a focal point for a growing number of biologists investigating evolutionary processes.

The potential of these rivers as a "natural laboratory" for evolution was first discovered by C. P. Haskins in 1936 (Haskins, pers. comm. 1990). He found several geographically isolated populations of a freshwater fish, the guppy (*Poecilia reticulata*), which differed in colour polymorphism. Some of this geographic variation was correlated with differences in predation pressure from other fish species (Haskins et al, 1961). This discovery and subsequent research by numerous workers have provided one of the best examples of microevolution in natural populations. In these populations we may in fact be witnessing the early stages of speciation (Endler, 1989).

This chapter evaluates the scientific importance of these rivers and their fish communities and reveals the difficulty in conserving aquatic communities which are of great academic interest but have no direct commercial value. Detailed descriptions of these rivers are given by Haskins et al (1961), Seghers (1973), Liley and Seghers (1975), and Endler (1978). For a review of the guppy as a model for evolutionary studies in genetics, behaviour, and ecology, see Schröder (1983).

THE IMPORTANCE OF THE RIVERS AND FISH COMMUNITIES

The rivers of the Northern Range are important for many reasons, not the least of which is the supply of water for domestic use (Granger, 1982). Here we will attempt to document their importance as a scientific resource. There are many indicators that one

River Conservation and Management. Edited by P. J. Boon, P. Calow, and G. E. Petts
© 1992 John Wiley & Sons Ltd

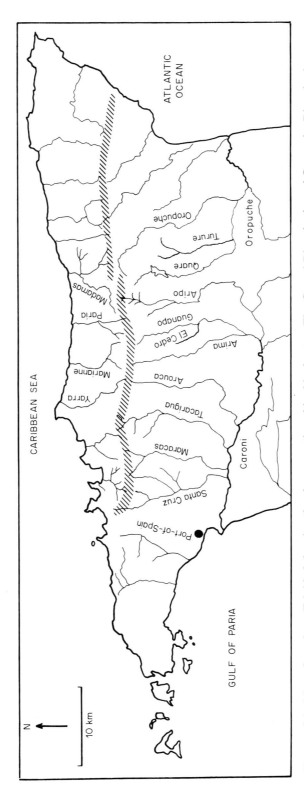

FIGURE 6.1. Map of northern Trinidad showing the rivers mentioned in this chapter. The Caroni River basin and Oropuche River basin are shown in large letters. The slanted lines indicate the location of the Northern Range mountains

can employ to show that the predator–prey system discovered by Haskins has received wide international attention as one of the best natural testing grounds for evolutionary theory. This is apparent by the accelerating number of publications and research theses on these fish, especially in the past decade, and the breadth of topics that have been investigated (Table 6.1). Research-granting agencies in North America and Europe continue to fund new work on this important system, so that over 40 workers from these areas have now carried out research on Trinidad guppies.

TABLE 6.1. Number of publications dealing with Trinidad guppy populations appearing in primary research journals or books (to mid-1990)

Journal	Number
Evolution	11
Animal Behaviour	6
Nature	5
Behavioural Ecology and Sociobiology	5
Ethology	3
Behaviour	2
Proceedings of the National Academy of Sciences	2
Canadian Journal of Zoology	2
Environmental Biology of Fishes	2
Heredity	1
American Zoologist	1
Berichte des naturwissenschaftlichen-medizinischen Vereinigung Innsbruck	1
Copeia	1
Ecology	1
Oecologia	1
American Naturalist	1
Science	1
Chapters in books	4
Total	50

An analysis of 56 publications and theses reveals that the major research has been on colour polymorphism and sexual selection (36%), anti-predator behaviour (21%), evolution of life histories (14%), and variation in courtship behaviour (11%). Other topics (18%) include studies on feeding, respiration, parasites, isolating mechanisms, and biochemical genetics.

One of the new areas that is certain to gain momentum is the use of biochemical genetics to unravel the history and evolutionary dynamics of these populations. Recent work by Carvalho et al (1991, Figure 6.2) and Fajen (1990), studying allozyme variation and mitochondrial DNA (mtDNA) sequencing, respectively, has revealed the presence of very high levels of genetic differentiation, both within and among drainage basins. This has important implications for the conduct of future research on these fish.

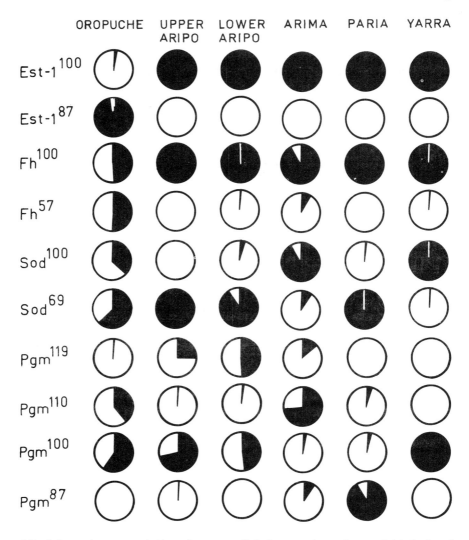

FIGURE 6.2. Schematic representation of average allele frequencies at four variable loci coding for allozymes. Populations of guppies from six rivers were surveyed

THREATS TO THE RIVERS AND FISH POPULATIONS

Over the 23 years that I have been a periodic visitor to Trinidad I have observed a steady deterioration in the quality of rivers, in particular those in the Port-of-Spain to Arima corridor. Over the past century major impacts on river ecology have proceeded east-wards from Port-of-Spain (population 110 000) to encompass most of the Caroni drainage and part of the Oropuche drainage. In recent years it has become increasingly difficult to find undisturbed sites where one can be reasonably confident that the fish community is in equilibrium and the variation in guppy populations reflects adaptations on an evolutionary time scale.

TABLE 6.2. Examples of environmental impacts on the major rivers used for research. From Endler (1986) and personal observations, 1967–1990

Caroni Drainage Basin

Santa Cruz	farming, siltation, pollution, overfishing
Maracas	pollution, overfishing
Tacarigua	pollution, overfishing
Arouca	pollution, overfishing
Arima	pollution, serious siltation, overfishing
El Cedro	farming, pollution
Guanapo	quarrying, water pumping
Aripo	logging, farming, siltation, water pumping, pollution, overfishing

Oropuche Drainage Basin

Quare	headwaters dammed, *Tilapia* introduced
Turure	logging, siltation, inter-basin fish transfer
Oropuche	logging, water pumping

North slope rivers

Yarra	minor impacts
Marianne	minor impacts
Paria	minor impacts
Madamas	minor impacts

For river locations refer to Figure 6.1

At present, the main undisturbed rivers are located in the north-east part of the island, which is isolated from the rest of Trinidad by the Northern Range mountains. These rise to almost 1000 m and form a major barrier to fish dispersal between the south- and north-flowing rivers.

The threats to the rivers and their fauna are not unique to Trinidad but are common to most developing nations: logging, "slash-and-burn" agriculture, erosion, quarrying (siltation), dams, water removal, chemical pollution, disposal of animal waste, introduction of exotic species, and overfishing.

Endler (1986) in a review of the distribution and abundance of fishes and crustaceans of the Northern Range made extensive comments on the health of many of these rivers over the period 1974 to 1985. He considered overfishing with spearguns and nets to be the single most important factor in the destruction of the fish community. Table 6.2 summarizes the environmental impacts on the major rivers used for research.

CONSERVATION MEASURES

Trinidad has a variety of regulations and legislation concerning forests, rivers, and fish and wildlife. The difficulty in conserving freshwater fish populations is the absence of co-ordination among government agencies with interests in these resources (H. Nelson, pers. comm.). For example, the Forestry Division deals with forest reserves, logging, and wildlife but this does not include fish. Fish come under the jurisdiction of the Fisheries Division, but the focus of its effort is on commercially important marine species and the few species of freshwater fish that are exported for the aquarium trade (Kenny and Bacon, 1981). Finally, water management is the responsibility of the Water and Sewerage Authority (WASA) (Millette, 1981). To conserve fish communities in forest rivers obviously requires the combined attention of all three agencies. Hopefully, we may one day see an integrated approach to conservation similar to that of the UK (Ratcliffe, 1986).

Trinidad does have a system of forest and game reserves dating back to 1902 (Ramdial, 1971), and recently a very ambitious proposal for a system of national parks, conservation reserves, and scientific reserves has been developed. Most of this plan remains to be implemented, but it is hoped that some of the fish communities of special concern to researchers in the Northern Range might be part of either the Aripo Savannas Scientific Reserve, the Madamas and Matura National Parks, and the Valencia Nature Conservation Reserve.

There is now a need for those interested in fish communities to lobby for the establishment of Scientific Reserves which include rivers with high scientific value. This should ideally include rivers from both the Caroni and Oropuche basins and several isolated north slope rivers. In the Caroni and Oropuche systems this should include stretches of river that have populations of guppies subjected to heavy predation from characin and cichlid fish predators, and those that are relatively free of predation. The latter will be easier to conserve since they occur mainly at higher elevations in less-disturbed areas. The main concern is for the well-being of sites containing the pike cichlid, *Crenicichla alta*. Undisturbed sites with this important predator are now rare in the Caroni system but there are still some good populations in the Oropuche system.

As indicated in Table 6.2, the rivers of the north slope have experienced only minor impacts and are likely to remain in reasonable condition for the immediate future. Since, however, they do not contain the main predators of the Caroni and Oropuche system, they are less useful for within-river comparative studies of adaptations to low and high predation conditions. Rivers with waterfalls which serve as barriers to the upstream movement of predators are extremely important as "natural experiments" and should be given special protection.

A CODE OF ETHICS FOR RESEARCH

It is ironic that one of the threats to the fish populations should come from the very scientists who are studying these rivers. The interest in these populations has accelerated greatly in the past decade and it is now not uncommon to have 15 to 20 foreign biologists working on these fish each year. Each research group usually works quite independently and its impact on the system may only become apparent some months or years later when data and ideas are exchanged at scientific meetings or in published papers.

Of particular concern is the problem of intra- and inter-basin transfer of guppies and their predators. This can be a powerful research tool, as Endler (1980) and Reznick et al (1990) have demonstrated. Experimental transplants of populations from high-predation to low-predation sites, and vice versa, have provided some of the best evidence for the role of predators in the evolution of prey morphology and life histories. This success, however, should not serve as a *carte blanche* for everyone to move fish about, especially since an interest in biochemical genetics has only recently emerged. It would clearly be disastrous if some student spent years sequencing mtDNA with the aim of reconstructing evolutionary events over thousands and millions of years, only to discover that the fish under study had recently been transferred from some unrelated distant gene pool! The possibility of outbreeding depression resulting from indiscriminate hybridization between genetically discrete sub-populations should also be considered (Vrijenhoek, 1989).

Although there are hundreds of interesting research sites in Trinidad, only a few are relatively undisturbed *and* contain guppies with very distinct phenotypes. Obviously, these have received the greatest attention in the past and will continue to be the focus of future work. This is especially true of the high carotenoid populations of the north slope rivers, where males exhibit large orange and red spots. Much has yet to be learned about these fish and they may prove to be valuable in testing aspects of the Hamilton–Zuk hypothesis on the role of parasitism in the evolution of secondary sexual characteristics (Hamilton and Zuk, 1982; Endler and Lyles, 1989).

In the early days of research on these populations (Seghers, 1973) I made some suggestions for future research. One of these was to stock the Paria River with *Crenicichla alta* and monitor the subsequent evolution (if any) in colouration, behaviour, and life history traits. Fortunately, this experiment was never done and the Paria fish, in their natural state, have continued to provide valuable material for testing hypotheses. I would now disapprove of any inter-basin transfer of guppies or predators. If a strong case could be made for such work, the entire research community should be alerted so that an inter-disciplinary team could gather the maximum information possible. This assumes that we know what the important evolutionary questions will be in the next few decades, and as we do not, it is better to err on the side of conservation.

There is some feeling among guppy biologists working in Trinidad that we are in a race with population explosion and general environmental degradation, and that these rivers will be useless for many research questions in less than a decade. This philosophy advocates that the large experimental perturbations be done as soon as possible while we still have some viable populations to play with. I do not support this view and still retain some optimism that a few key sites can be protected in their quasi-natural condition and that these populations may continue to provide rewarding research opportunities long after the current researchers have retired or moved on to greener pastures.

In this chapter I have emphasized the threats to unique guppy populations. These were discovered because the male phenotypes are so distinct that they caught the attention of C. P. Haskins. However, this does not mean that the other 35 species of freshwater fish in Trinidad do not also have interesting evolutionary stories to tell. For example, some work on *Rivulus hartii* (Seghers, 1978; Fraser and Gilliam, 1987) and several species of characins (Ali, 1990) has shown that population differences are also prevalent in these species. For this reason, inter-population transfer of fish should be discouraged.

EDUCATION AND SOCIO-ECONOMICS

When rivers die, more than just invertebrates and fish perish—the whole catchment is affected. This fact should be part of any environmental education programme. In the long run it may be more effective than any protestations on behalf of some tiny fish that excites only those in ivory towers. If Trinidadians can be made aware that healthy rivers equate with healthy rain forests and bird populations, river conservation may command more attention.

It is now accepted that conservation, especially in developing nations, is predominantly a question of socio-economics (McNeely, 1988). This surely applies to Trinidad, and it is here that some considerable leverage exists. As Trinidad struggles with high unemployment and massive foreign debt there have been concerted efforts to promote tourism using large glossy posters and brochures. These are not all simply promotions of secluded palm-lined beaches but also feature forest birds, butterflies, and small rivers with tumbling waterfalls and crystal-clear pools. Most of these rivers will contain guppies and other fish species. Therefore, in promoting riverside recreation as a tourist attraction (and thus indirectly a source of foreign currency), the quality of the rivers may well gain some attention. People do not enjoy bathing in, or picnicking by, a river full of detergent bottles and foam, rusting automobiles, dead animals, and filamentous algae.

What do concerned Trinidadians think? In a recent survey of 34 Trinidad naturalists by *Naturalist* magazine (June, 1988), almost everyone emphasized the importance of early environmental education in schools and the increased use of the media, especially television, in promoting the awareness of conservation in the population at large. The urgent need for an *enforced* land-use plan was also stressed. Surprisingly, only one respondent mentioned rivers or fish for special protection; the majority were mainly concerned with the conservation of swamps, coral reefs, sea turtles, birds, and mammals.

One naturalist summarized the situation succinctly: "Environmental degradation will continue as long as our economic and development planning ignore ecological principles." This echoed the view of the former Conservator of Forests for Trinidad and Tobago when he referred to "... a myopic generation overpowered by materialistic values" (Ramdial, 1971).

CONCLUSION: A FOUR-PRONGED PLAN OF ACTION FOR CONSERVATION

The conservation of Trinidad's rivers and fish communities will require the effort and co-operation of many persons and agencies in Trinidad and abroad. A four-pronged attack is required:

(1) Develop local and international awareness of the importance of these rivers to Trinidad and the world's scientific community.
(2) Develop and implement an environmental education programme that emphasizes the importance of maintaining natural areas for research and education.
(3) Urge the government of Trinidad and Tobago to strive for effective inter-agency co-ordination of environmental management, with special reference to the conservation of unique riverine fish communities. This should include the establishment of scientific reserves for several key rivers and enforcement to prevent (a) overfishing, (b) the introduction of exotic species, and (c) unauthorized inter-basin transfer of fish.
(4) Develop a code of ethics within the research community that promotes co-operation among scientists internationally and in Trinidad. This code should be based on the principle of conserving the natural genetic resources of the fish populations.

ACKNOWLEDGEMENTS

I have discussed the problems and future of Trinidad's rivers and fish populations with many people and especially wish to thank the following for their information and insights: F. Breden, J. A. Endler, D. F. Fraser, J. F. Gilliam, C. P. Haskins, J. S. Kenny, N. R. Liley, A. E. Magurran, J. L. Price, J. D. Reynolds, and D. A. Reznick. Not all of them may agree with my analysis and I accept full responsibility for the views expressed herein.

REFERENCES

Ali, N. (1990). *Affinities of some freshwater fishes from Trinidad*. MPhil thesis, University of the West Indies, St Augustine, Trinidad.

Carvalho, G. R., Shaw, P. H., Magurran, A. E., and B. H. Seghers. (1991). "Marked genetic divergence revealed by allozymes among populations of the guppy, *Poecilia reticulata* (Poeciliidae) in Trinidad", *Biological Journal of the Linnean Society*, **42**, 389–405.

Endler, J. A. (1978). "A predator's view of animal color patterns", *Evolutionary Biology*, **11**, 319–364.

Endler, J. A. (1980). "Natural selection on color patterns in *Poecilia reticulata*", *Evolution*, **34**, 76–91.

Endler, J. A. (1986). *A Preliminary Report on the Distribution and Abundance of Fishes and Crustaceans of the Northern Range Mountains, Trinidad*, unpublished manuscript.

Endler, J. A. (1989). "Conceptual and other problems in speciation", in *Speciation and its Consequences* (Eds D. Otte and J. A. Endler), pp. 625–648, Sinauer Associates, Sunderland, Massachusetts.

Endler, J. A., and Lyles, A. M. (1989). "Bright ideas about parasites", *Trends in Ecology and Evolution*, **4**, 246–248.

Fajen, A. (1990). *Geographic variation in mtDNA polymorphisms in the Trinidad guppy*, MS thesis, University of Missouri, Columbia.

Fraser, D. F., and Gilliam, J. F. (1987). "Feeding under predation hazard: response of the guppy and Hart's rivulus from sites with contrasting hazard", *Behavioral Ecology and Sociobiology*, **21**, 203–209.

Granger, O. E. (1982). "Climatic fluctuations in Trinidad, West Indies and their implications for water resource planning", *Caribbean Journal of Science*, **17**, 173–201.

Hamilton, W. D., and Zuk, M. (1982). "Heritable true fitness and bright birds: a role for parasites?" *Science*, **218**, 384–387.

Haskins, C. P., Haskins, E. F., McLaughlin, J. J. A., and Hewitt, R. E. (1961). "Polymorphism and population structure in *Lebistes reticulatus*, a population study", in *Vertebrate Speciation* (Ed. W. F. Blair), pp. 320–395, University of Texas Press, Austin.

Kenny, J. S., and Bacon, P. R. (1981). "Aquatic resources", in *The Natural Resources of Trinidad and Tobago* (Eds St G. C. Cooper and P. R. Bacon), pp. 112–144, Edward Arnold, London.

Liley, N. R., and Seghers, B. H. (1975). "Factors affecting the morphology and behaviour of guppies in Trinidad", in *Function and Evolution in Behaviour* (Eds G. P. Baerends, C. Beer, and A. Manning), pp. 92–118, Clarendon Press, Oxford.

McNeely, J. A. (1988). *Economics and Biological Diversity: Developing and Using Economic Incentives to Conserve Biological Resources*, International Union for Conservation of Nature and Natural Resources, Gland.

Millette, E. D. (1981). "Water", in *The Natural Resources of Trinidad and Tobago* (Eds St G. C. Cooper and P. R. Bacon), pp. 52–61, Edward Arnold, London.

Ramdial, B. S. (1971). "The importance of forest reserves and game sanctuaries in Trinidad and Tobago", *The Trinidad Field Naturalists' Club Journal*, 26–37.

Ratcliffe, D. A. (1986). "Selection of important areas for wildlife conservation in Great Britain: the Nature Conservancy Council's approach", in *Wildlife Conservation Evaluation* (Ed. M. B. Usher), pp. 135–159, Chapman and Hall, London.

Reznick, D. A., Bryga, H., and Endler, J. A. (1990). "Experimentally induced life-history evolution in a natural population", *Nature*, **346**, 357–359.

Schröder, J. H. (1983). "The guppy (*Poecilia reticulata* Peters) as a model for evolutionary studies in genetics, behaviour, and ecology", *Berichte des naturwissenschaftlichen-medizinischen Vereinigung Innsbruck*, **70**, 249–279.

Seghers, B. H. (1973). *An analysis of geographic variation in the antipredator adaptations of the guppy, Poecilia reticulata*, PhD thesis, University of British Columbia, Vancouver.

Seghers, B. H. (1978). "Feeding behavior and terrestrial locomotion in the cyprinodontid fish, *Rivulus hartii* (Boulenger)", *Verhandlungen der Internationale Vereinigung für theoretische und angewandte Limnologie*, **20**, 2055–2059.

Vrijenhoek, R. C. (1989). "Population genetics and conservation", in *Conservation for the Twenty-first Century* (Eds D. Western and M. C. Pearl), pp. 89–98, Oxford University Press, Oxford.

SECTION II

RIVER CLASSIFICATION AND THE ASSESSMENT OF CONSERVATION POTENTIAL

Landsat thematic mapper image (Bands 3, 4 and 5) of the River Tyne, north-east England. This technique is valuable in classifying and assessing rivers in terms of catchment land use. (Image processed by National Remote Sensing Centre (NRSC), Farnborough, Hampshire, UK)

7

General Principles of Classification and the Assessment of Conservation Potential in Rivers

R. J. NAIMAN, D. G. LONZARICH, T. J. BEECHIE, and S. C. RALPH

Center for Streamside Studies, AR-10, University of Washington, Seattle, WA 98195 USA

INTRODUCTION

Classification systems have been used for centuries to organize information about ecological systems by scientists and resource managers. Yet the classification of fluvial systems remains in a formative stage because running waters have become recognized only recently as ecological systems in their own right (Vannote et al, 1980), because of the dynamic changes that occur over broad spatial and temporal scales (Salo, 1990), and because classification systems only reflect the current state of knowledge on river function (Frissell et al, 1986). Most attention remains focused on conceptual and regional approaches to stream classification rather than on general approaches applicable across contrasting ecoregions.

The lack of a globally effective stream classification system becomes particularly vexing when attempting to develop and apply conservation management over broad geographic areas. Assessment of conservation potential, defined here as the ecological potential of a stream and its sensitivity to natural and human disturbance, is dependent on the type of stream under consideration. Each stream type possesses a set of characteristics (e.g. system structure, complexity, biogeochemistry, resistance and resilience to change, and productivity) which are related to the local climate, geology, and disturbance regime. These fundamental relationships are essential to the development and application of management prescriptions.

The term "classification" implies that sets of observations or characteristics can be organized into meaningful groups based on measures of similarity or difference (Gauch, 1982). Implicit in this is that relatively distinct boundaries exist and that these may be identified by a set of discrete variables. However, the classification of streams is complicated by both longitudinal and lateral linkages, by changes that occur in the physical features over time, and by boundaries between apparent patches that are often indistinct (Naiman et al, 1988; Pringle et al, 1988; Décamps and Naiman, 1989). Geomorphic and ecological characteristics of streams vary spatially from headwater to

River Conservation and Management. Edited by P. J. Boon, P. Calow, and G. E. Petts
© 1992 John Wiley & Sons Ltd

the sea (Langbein and Leopold, 1966; Vannote et al, 1980), as well as temporally in response to disturbance patterns (Wissmar and Swanson, 1990). Connectivity and variability are fundamental for the long-term maintenance and vitality of stream systems, and become essential but complicating factors in developing an enduring classification scheme.

In this chapter we review the fundamental principles of stream classification through an analysis of conceptual approaches previously used to develop several contrasting classification schemes. Historic and extant classification systems have been based on a variety of spatial scales, from channel units to ecoregions, and have incorporated several combinations of physical and biological components of importance into riverine systems. We evaluate the fundamental approaches to stream classification for their usefulness in understanding stream structure and dynamics, for assessing conservation potential, and for developing management strategies.

STREAM CLASSIFICATION

Historical concepts

The history of stream classification has been reviewed comprehensively by Macan (1961), Illies and Botosaneanu (1963), Hawkes (1975), and Wasson (1989). Rather than summarize these reviews, we address instead the dominant conceptual themes of these early efforts (Figure 7.1). One of the original whole-river schemes was developed for New Jersey (USA) rivers (Davis, 1890). Davis classified streams as young, mature, or old on the basis of observed erosional patterns. Shelford (1911) later attempted to produce a biological classification scheme for whole rivers in Michigan, USA, based on his idea of succession. However, due to longitudinal differences in physical and biological characteristics, whole-stream classification has been of little use (Hawkes, 1975). In contrast, basin-wide drainage measures such as stream order, linkage number, and drainage density have served as simplistic but useful classification systems (Horton, 1945; Strahler, 1957, Vannote et al, 1980).

While early attempts at classifying whole rivers were generally unsuccessful, classification of river segments have had a long and useful history. Many became important tools—if only locally adapted—during the early part of the century (Hawkes, 1975). Early classifications were generally based on perceived patterns of biotic zonation using one or more species of fish or invertebrates as indicators of segment types (Carpenter, 1928; Ricker, 1934; Huet, 1954). In addition, numerous specialists of certain groups of lotic invertebrates also utilized their data to propose organizational patterns (e.g. Plecoptera, Ephemeroptera, Trichoptera—Macan, 1961; Illies and Botosaneanu, 1963). The biotic zonation patterns were generally correlated with gradient or some abiotic feature such as temperature or water chemistry (Hawkes, 1975), although Huet (1954) also recognized the importance of larger spatial scales by incorporating valley form into his scheme.

In spite of widespread recognition of distinct biotic zones along rivers, there were many early critics (Funk and Campbell, 1953; Macan, 1961; Backiel, 1964). Because key

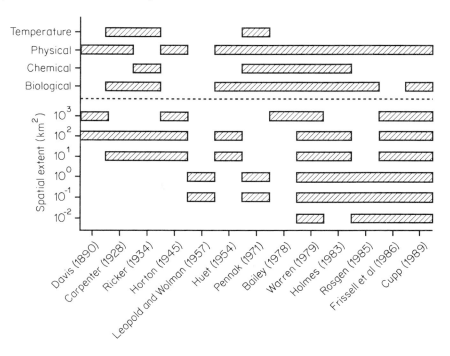

FIGURE 7.1. Conceptual overview of the history of stream classification, the key variables used, and the spatial scale addressed

physical parameters often changed gradually along the stream continuum (e.g. slope and width), it should be expected that species composition would change in a similar manner.

The classification system developed by Illies (1961) was one of the first aimed at classifying rivers worldwide. The system divided stream segments into eight zones based on such physico-chemical variables as water temperature, water velocity, substrate, and altitude (Illies and Botosaneanu, 1963). The zones defined in this system overlapped closely with other biological zonation schemes, but the widespread utility of Illies' classification was that it did not rely on biotic features specific to a zoogeographic region (Harrison, 1965).

There were several general limitations to these historic systems. For the biotic zonation schemes, the reliance on species as indicators of biotic zones meant that they were only valid in basins of similar zoogeographic, geologic, and climatic history. Despite relating physical factors to biotic patterns, these systems failed to construct a conceptual framework for stream classification that could transcend regions. Finally, for both physical and biological zonation systems there were no features relating geologic and climatic processes, which regulate the physical features of streams, to the classification system. Therefore, these efforts were ineffective at relating watershed scale processes to dynamic changes in channel features (Wissmar and Swanson, 1990; Salo, 1990). The application of landscape ecology concepts to rivers has been suggested recently as a useful approach to overcome this difficulty (Décamps, 1984; Ward and Stanford, 1987).

Recent concepts

Ideally, a classification scheme should be based on a hierarchical ranking of linkages between the geologic and climatic settings, the stream habitat features and the biota. These—the geomorphic and climatic processes that shape the abiotic and biotic features of streams—provide a conceptual and practical foundation for understanding the structure and processes of fluvial systems. Furthermore, an understanding of process allows streams to be viewed in a larger spatial and temporal perspective, and to infer the direction and magnitude of potential changes due to natural and human disturbances. An enduring stream classification system, based on patterns and processes and how they are expressed at different temporal and spatial scales (Frissell et al, 1986), should be of fundamental value in assessing conservation potential.

The conservation potential of individual stream classification units can be evaluated by the ultimate and proximate controls on system characteristics (Figure 7.2). As used here, these terms generally correspond to higher and lower levels of a hierarchical ranking of controlling factors. Ultimate controls refer to a set of factors that are acting over large areas (>1 km^2), are stable over long time scales (centuries to millennia), and shape the range of conditions in a drainage network. These include physical characteristics such as regional geology and climate, and biotic characteristics such as zoogeography (Moyle and Li, 1979; Briggs et al, 1990). Proximate controls refer to local geomorphic and biotic processes important at small scales ($<10^2$ m^2) which can change stream characteristics over relatively short time periods (decades or less). Proximate controls are a function of the ultimate factors and include such physical processes as discharge, temperatures, hillslope erosion, channel migration, and sediment transport, and the biotic processes of reproduction, competition, disease, and predation; all of which may be influenced by an equally diverse array of human impacts. Within this conceptual framework, management strategies to effectively maintain important physical and ecological structures may be tailored to local conditions.

The full range of ultimate and proximate controls must be used for effective stream classification. If a stream type is defined only by a limited range of controls then

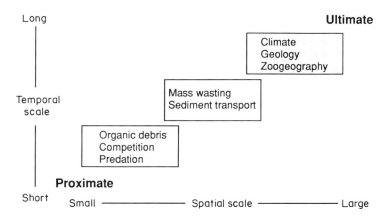

FIGURE 7.2. Proximate and ultimate controlling factors in determining stream characteristics and their relation to spatial and temporal scales

management tools or prescriptions may be too broad or too specific to be effective. For example, low-gradient tributaries traversing a floodplain may be expected to have similar physical features in widely separated geographic regions (shaped by ultimate controls), but because of the location of each tributary within a watershed, they may be regulated by a different combination of factors (proximate controls). A floodplain tributary emerging from a steep, bed-rock channel may be subject to a variety of high energy disturbances such as debris torrents and floods, whereas a floodplain tributary emerging from low foothills with high water storage capacity will be exposed to a different array of disturbances. Additionally, the effect of various land-use practices (such as timber harvest) will be expressed differently in each setting.

Frissell et al (1986) discuss this topic utilizing ideas from hierarchy theory (Allen and Starr, 1982), and construct a continuum of habitat sensitivity to disturbance and recovery time (Figure 7.3). In their scenario, microhabitats are most susceptible to disturbance and river landscapes the least. Furthermore, events that affect smaller-scale habitat characteristics may not affect larger-scale system characteristics, whereas large disturbances can directly influence smaller-scale features of streams. For example, on a small spatial scale, deposition at one habitat site may be accompanied by scouring at another site nearby, and the reach or segment does not appear to change significantly. In contrast, a large-scale disturbance, such as a debris flood, is initiated at the segment level and reflected in all lower levels of the hierarchy (reach, habitat, microhabitat). On a temporal scale, siltation of microhabitats may disturb the biotic community over the short term. However, if the disturbance is of limited scope and intensity, the system may recover quickly to pre-disturbance levels (Niemi et al, 1990).

Tailoring innovative conservation strategies to stream types implies that the classification system includes the physical and biotic characteristics of the stream, as well as the disturbance regime. A successful classification system should be able to categorize the types and frequencies of disturbance that may impact the stream and predict adjustments

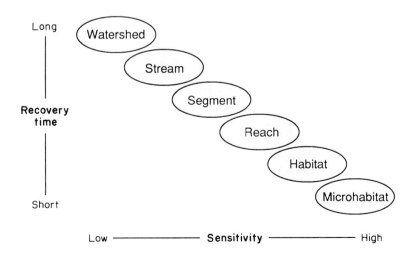

FIGURE 7.3. Relation between recovery time and sensitivity to disturbance for different spatial scales associated with stream systems. See Table 7.1 for definition of spatial scales

in the physical and biotic characteristics. Furthermore, understanding the disturbance processes will assist scientists and managers in assessing impacts of land-use practices.

CLASSIFICATION OF PHYSICAL WATERSHED FEATURES

River classification based on geomorphic characteristics came into prominence in the 1940s (Horton, 1945; Leopold and Wolman, 1957). This has become important to fisheries biologists and land managers since geomorphic patterns are strongly linked to patterns of species distribution and abundance (Huet, 1954; Bisson et al, 1988; Morin and Naiman, 1990). Almost all classification schemes based on physical habitat features have been founded on the perception that stream units (i.e. segment, reach, channel, riffle/pool) are discrete, and can therefore be delineated. However, this has been frequently challenged (Backiel, 1964; Vannote et al, 1980; Cushing et al, 1983).

Despite gradations in physical characteristics that do exist (e.g. stream width, depth, velocity), dramatic and abrupt physical changes are also found (Frissell et al, 1986; Naiman et al, 1988; Kellerhals and Church, 1989). For example, Frissell et al (1986) defined longitudinal boundaries of segment types by easily measured tributary junctions, major waterfalls, or other structural discontinuities, while reaches were defined less clearly by changes in channel gradient. The scope of the issue or nature of the question being considered should then determine the appropriate scale(s) of resolution.

Single-scale classification

Perceived patterns in drainage networks led to the development of the stream order concept (Horton, 1945; Strahler, 1957). Within geographic regions, this system has been correlated with physical and biotic features of streams (Sheldon, 1968; Platts, 1979; Minshall et al, 1983; Naiman, 1983; Naiman et al, 1987; Morin and Naiman, 1990). However, it is much less reliable at predicting patterns and behaviour of stream characteristics across regions, or at micro-scales within regions. For example, major differences in stream size (Minshall et al, 1985) and response to disturbance (Resh et al, 1988) can be encountered for streams of the same order between regions due to variability in geology and hydrology. More importantly, stream order by itself provides little information on processes controlling longitudinal and lateral patterns, and therefore makes predictions of response to both natural and human disturbance imprecise (Naiman et al, 1987). In spite of its almost universal usage in the United States, the value of the stream order classification scheme is only as an indicator of relative biotic and stream segment characteristics and position within a given drainage network. When properly used, however, it can be valuable as an accounting tool in categorizing biological and physical data.

Other more recent approaches to classification include large-scale schemes developed recently for their potential usefulness to regional water resource and fisheries managers. Bailey (1978) defined 11 ecoregions that were intended to delineate large areas ($>10^3$ km^2) of the United States based on climate, physiography, and vegetation. These were chosen because they were thought to be most important in stratifying in-channel features (Rohm et al, 1987). The system has now been tested successfully in at least three areas (the upper Midwest, Arkansas, and Oregon, USA) with respect to chemical characteristics and fish species distribution (Larsen et al, 1986; Whittier et al, 1988). Rohm et al (1987) were able to categorize fish assemblage, physical habitat (e.g. percentage riffle, pool), and water chemistry (e.g. alkalinity, conductivity) patterns into six previously defined ecoregions (Omernik, 1987).

The ecoregion concept is gaining wide acceptance for grouping of streams where large-scale resolution is required (e.g. Rohm et al, 1987). It provides a less costly alternative to labour- and data-intensive classification schemes based on smaller-scale variables since it enables managers to predict physical and biological characteristics based on location. However, it is less useful to land managers operating within the boundaries of single ecoregions because of local variations in geology, discharge, gradient, and channel form.

Other physical methods have been based on actual measurements of channel morphology and water chemistry, and subsequent cluster analysis of measured variables (Pennak, 1971; Cushing et al, 1983). Although such approaches demand intensive field investigation and testing, they are potentially more valuable than *a priori* concepts. Specifically, identifiable patterns are generally based on factors which are ecologically important across different types of drainage basins within a broad geographic region (e.g. channel form, substrate, discharge).

Hierarchical classification

A pervasive theme in recently developed stream classification systems in North America has been a hierarchical perspective that links large regional scales (ecoregions) with small microhabitat scales (Table 7.1). This approach is necessitated by the fact that stream processes operate over 16 orders of magnitude (10^{-7}–10^{8}m spatially and 10^{-8}–10^{7}yr temporally—Minshall, 1988). Several conceptual classification systems have been developed using spatially nested landscape features to account for this broad range (Warren, 1979; Frissell et al, 1986; Cupp, 1989a). The value of hierarchical stream classification is greatest when broadly applied (e.g. global, national, regional scales—Frissell et al, 1986). However, the approach is flexible enough to be modified for regional purposes. Furthermore, the relative importance of controlling factors change with the spatial scale, and it is important to understand the relative roles of these factors in determining the long-term and short-term behaviour of streams. Finally, a hierarchical approach requires fewer variables at any one level for classification. Within most limited geographic regions, managers and scientists need only one or two spatio-temporal scales to classify streams (Table 7.2).

One of the first hierarchical classification systems was developed by Warren (1979). He described 11 levels (ranging from regional ($>10^2$ km^2) to microhabitat (<1 m^2)) defined by five variables (substrate, climate, water chemistry, biota, and culture). Warren did not propose a concrete classification system, but his contribution to the conceptual evolution of stream classification is worth noting because he presented an explicit theoretical structure for a complex, hierarchical system. He stressed the importance of assessing the potential (i.e. all possible developmental states and performances that a system may exhibit while still maintaining its integrity as a coherent unit) of a stream rather than its current condition. Evaluating potential states for a system assists in distinguishing natural variability from human disturbance.

Frissell et al (1986) extended Warren's approach by incorporating spatially nested levels of resolution (e.g. watershed, stream, valley segment, reach, pool/riffle, and

TABLE 7.1. Some events or processes controlling stream habitat on different spatio-temporal scales

System level	Linear spatial scale[a] (m)	Evolutionary events[b]	Developmental processes[c]	Time scale of continuous potential persistence[a] (yr)
Stream system	10^3	Tectonic uplift, subsidence; catastrophic volcanism; sea level changes; glaciation, climate shifts	Planation; denudation; drainage network development	10^6–10^5
Segment system	10^2	Minor glaciation, volcanism; earthquakes; very large landslides; alluvial or colluvial valley infilling	Migration of tributary junctions and bedrock nick-points; channel floor downwearing; development of new first-order channels	10^4–10^3
Reach system	10^1	Debris torrents; landslides; log input or washout; channel shifts, cutoffs; channelization, diversion or damming by man	Aggradation/degradation associated with large sediment-storing structures; bank erosion; riparian vegetation succession	10^2–10^1
Pool/riffle system	10^0	Input or washout of wood, boulders, etc.; small bank failures; flood scour or deposition; thalweg shifts; numerous human activities	Small-scale lateral or elevational changes in bedforms; minor bedload resorting	10^1–10^0
Microhabitat system	10^{-1}	Annual sediment, organic matter transport; scour of stationary substrates; seasonal macrophyte growth and cropping	Seasonal depth, velocity changes; accumulation of fines; microbial breakdown of organics; periphyton growth	10^0–10^{-1}

(Reproduced by permission from Frissell et al, 1986)
[a]Space and time scales indicated are appropriate for a second- or third-order mountain stream
[b]Evolutionary events change potential capacity; that is, extrinsic forces that create and destroy systems at that scale
[c]Developmental processes are intrinsic, progressive changes following a system's genesis in an evolutionary event

microhabitat) (Table 7.2, Figure 7.4). An important conceptual advancement, this system addresses form or pattern within each hierarchical level, as well as origins and processes of development. Nawa et al (1990) used this approach to show that fish species composition, and the sensitivity of channels to disturbance, varied between different valley segment types.

Other significant hierarchical classification systems operating at broad scales of resolution include that of Lotspeich (1980) and Brussock et al (1985). Brussock et al (1985)

TABLE 7.2. Habitat spatial boundaries, conformant with the temporal scales of Table 7.1

System level	Capacity time scale[a] (yr)	Vertical boundaries[b]	Longitudinal boundaries[c]	Lateral boundaries[d]	Linear spatial scale[a] (m)
Stream system	10^6–10^5	Total initial basin relief; sea level or other base level	Drainage divides and sea coast, or chosen catchment area	Drainage divides; bedrock faults, joints controlling ridge valley development	10^3
Segment system	10^4–10^3	Bedrock elevation; tributary junction or falls elevation	Tributary junctions; major falls, bedrock lithological or structural discontinuities	Valley sideslopes or bedrock out-crops controlling lateral migration	10^2
Reach system	10^2–10^1	Bedrock surface; relief of major sediment-storing structures	Slope breaks; structures capable of withstanding < 50 year flood	Local sideslopes or erosion-resistant banks; 50-year floodplain margins	10^1
Pool/riffle system	10^1–10^0	Depth of bedload subject to transport in < 10-year flood; top of water surface	Water surface and bed profile slope breaks; location of genetic structures	Mean annual flood channel; mid-channel bars; other flow-splitting obstructions	10^0
Microhabitat system	10^0–10^{-1}	Depth to particles immovable in mean annual flood; water surface	Zones of differing substrate type, size, arrangement; water depth, velocity	Same as longitudinal	10^{-1}

(Reproduced by permission from Frissell et al, 1986)
[a]Scaled to second- or third-order mountain stream
[b]Vertical dimension refers to upper and lower surfaces
[c]Longitudinal dimension refers to upstream–downstream extent
[d]Lateral dimension refers to cross-channel or equivalent horizontal extent

developed a hierarchical system for large rivers based primarily on predictable patterns of variation in channel-form. Channel-form is an important parameter because it overlays in-channel features (e.g. relief, lithology, and discharge) controlling the physical state of the stream (e.g. temperature, depth, substrate, and velocity) which, in turn, influence the character of biotic resources. Variations in channel-form are believed to be related to lithology, gradient, and climate (state factors) as they act on substrate particle size, bed load, and competence. Brussock and his colleagues examined streams throughout the United States and described seven regions based on differences in state factors. They related channel-form to community structure, and confirmed much of the earlier work of L. B. Leopold, that stream channel-form can be predicted along the length of the river within geographic regions (Leopold et al, 1964).

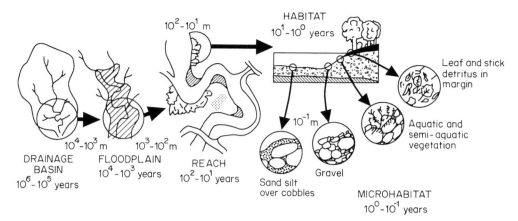

FIGURE 7.4. Hierarchical organizations of a stream system and its habitat sub-systems. Linear spatial scale, approximated to second- or third-order mountain stream, is indicated (adapted from Frissell et al, 1986)

In western North America, two hierarchical classification systems are gaining wide usage among managers (Rosgen, 1985; Cupp, 1989a,b). Cupp (1989a) adapted the hierarchical concept of Frissell et al (1986) to small forested streams in Washington State, USA, using eight hierarchical levels ranging from ecoregion to microhabitat. This system was later modified for use by the Timber, Fish and Wildlife (TFW) Program of Washington, using only the segment level of the hierarchical classification (Cupp, 1989b). Valley segments are distinguished by average channel gradient and valley form (Table 7.3, Figure 7.5). Initial field tests of this system have shown that stream segment types are correlated with habitat units (Beechie and Sibley, 1990). Rosgen (1985) developed a classification system based on geomorphic and in-channel characteristics on a narrow spatial scale of 10^1–10^3 m². The system is characterized by features that include channel gradient, sinuosity, width/depth ratio, bed material, entrenchment, channel confinement, soil erodibility, and stability. It also includes sub-types that are characterized by riparian vegetation, channel width, organic debris, flow regime, meander patterns, depositional features, and sediment supply that may change over short temporal scales. Rosgen's stream-type classification system has been used widely in the western United States for more than ten years for site-specific riparian forest and fisheries management, and for predicting geomorphic and hydrologic processes.

Although the classification systems developed by Cupp (1989a,b) and Rosgen (1985) are based on geomorphic and geologic landscape features, they illustrate two fundamentally different approaches in classification. Rosgen's system is based on present stream characteristics (e.g. channel width, sinuosity). Cupp's system is based on the presumed potential states of the stream (i.e. all possible natural states that may occur in stream features within given segment types). Therefore, Rosgen's method is responsive to the effects of natural and human-induced disturbance as manifested by variations in width–depth ratio or changes in riparian vegetation (i.e. floods, debris flows), whereas Cupp's approach is responsive to disturbances only at the large segment scale, or to severe small-scale disturbances that cause channel features to deviate outside some predicted range or alter the mean state of the system.

103

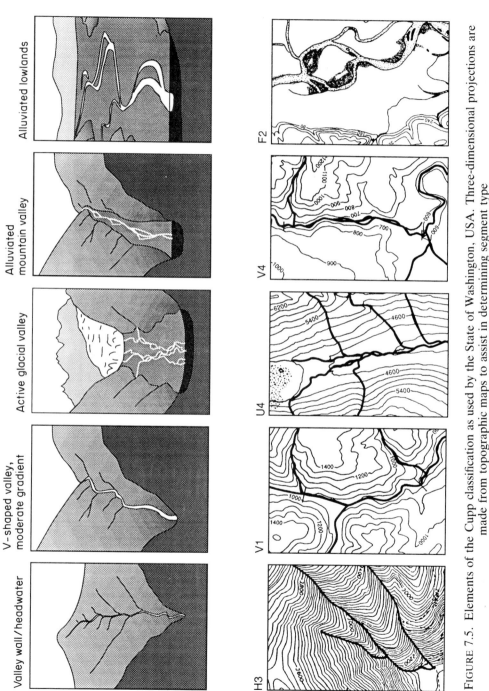

FIGURE 7.5. Elements of the Cupp classification as used by the State of Washington, USA. Three-dimensional projections are made from topographic maps to assist in determining segment type

TABLE 7.3. Valley bottom and sideslope geomorphic characteristics used to identify 18 valley segment types in forested lands of Washington, USA

Valley segment type[a]	Valley bottom gradient[b]	Sideslope gradient[c]	Valley bottom width[d]	Channel patterns	Stream order[e]	Landform and geomorphic features
F1 Estuarine delta	≤ 0.5%	< 5%	> 5X	Unconstrained; highly sinuous; often braided	Any	Occur at mouth of streams on estuarine flats in and just above zone of tidal influence
F2 Alluviated lowlands	≤ 1%	> 5%	> 5X	Unconstrained; highly sinuous	Any	Wide floodplains typically formed by present or historic large rivers within flat to gently rolling lowland landforms; sloughs, oxbows, and abandoned channels commonly associated with mainstream rivers
F3 Wide mainstream valley	≤ 2%	< 5%	> 5X	Unconstrained; moderate to high sinuosity; braids common	Any	Wide valley floors bounded by mountain slopes; generally associated with mainstream rivers and the tributary streams flowing through the valley floor; sloughs and abandoned channels common
F4 Wide mainstream valley	≤ 1–3%	≤ 10%	> 3X	Variable; generally unconstrained	1–4	Generally occur where tributary streams enter low gradient valley floors; ancient or active alluvial/colluvial fan deposition overlying floodplains of larger, low-gradient stream segments; stream may actively downcut through deep alluvial fan deposition

TABLE 7.3. (*continued*)

Valley segment type[a]	Valley bottom gradient[b]	Sideslope gradient[c]	Valley bottom width[d]	Channel patterns	Stream order[e]	Landform and geomorphic features
F5 Gently sloping plateaux and terraces	≤ 2%	< 10%	1–2X	Moderately constrained; low to moderate sinuosity	1–3	Drainage ways shallowly incised into flat to gently sloping landscape; narrow active floodplains; typically associated with small streams in lowlands, cryic uplands or volcanic flanks
M1 Moderate sloping plateaux and terraces	2–5%	< 10–30%	< 2X	Constrained; infrequent meanders	1–4	Constrained, narrow floodplains bounded by moderate gradient sideslopes; typically found in lowlands and foothills, but may occur on broken mountain slopes and volcano flanks
M2 Alluviated, moderate slope bound	≤ 2%	< 5%, gradually increase to 30%	2–4X	Unconstrained; moderate to high sinuosity	1–4	Active floodplains and alluvial terraces bounded by moderate gradient hillslopes; typically found in lowlands and foothills, but may occur on broken mountain slopes and volcano flanks
V1 V-shaped, moderate-gradient bottom	2–6%	30–70%	< 2X	Constrained	≥ 2	Deeply incised drainage ways with steep competent sideslopes; very common in uplifted mountainous topography; less commonly associated with marine or glacial outwash terraces in lowlands and foothills

TABLE 7.3. (*continued*)

Valley segment type[a]	Valley bottom gradient[b]	Sideslope gradient[c]	Valley bottom width[d]	Channel patterns	Stream order[e]	Landform and geomorphic features
V2 V-shaped high-gradient bottom	6–11%	30–70%	< 2X	Constrained	≥ 2	Same as above, but valley bottom longitudinal profile steep with pronounced stair-step characteristics
V3 V-shaped, bedrock canyon	3–11%	70% +	< 2X	Highly constrained	≥ 2	Canyon-like stream corridors with frequent bedrock outcrops; frequently stair-stepped profile; generally associated with folded, faulted or volcanic landforms
V4 Alluviated mountain valley	1–4%	Channel adjacent slopes < 10%; increase to 30% +	2–4X	Unconstrained; high sinuosity with braids and side-channels common	25	Deeply incised drainage ways with relatively wide floodplains; distinguished as "alluvial flats" in otherwise steeply dissected mountainous terrain
U1 U-shaped trough	< 3%	< 5%; gradually increases to 30% +	> 4X	Unconstrained; moderate to high sinuosity; side channels and braids common	1–4	Drainage ways in mid to upper watersheds with history of glaciation, resulting in U-shaped profile; valley bottom typically composed of glacial drift deposits overlain with more recent alluvial material adjacent to channel

TABLE 7.3. (*continued*)

Valley segment type[a]	Valley bottom gradient[b]	Sideslope gradient[c]	Valley bottom width[d]	Channel patterns	Stream order[e]	Landform and geomorphic features
U2 Incised U-shaped valley, moderate-gradient bottom	2–5%	Steep channel adjacent slopes, decreases to < 30%, then increases to > 30%	< 2X	Moderately constrained by unconsolidated material; infrequent short flats with braids and meanders	2–5	Channel downcuts through deep valley bottom glacial till, colluvium, or coarse glacio-fluvial deposits; cross-sectional profile variable, but generally weakly U-shaped with active channel vertically incised into valley fill deposits; immediate side-slopes composed of unconsolidated and often unsorted coarse-grained deposits
U3 Incised U-shaped valley, high-gradient bottom	6–11%	Steep channel adjacent slopes, decreases to < 30%, then increases to > 30%	< 2X	Moderately constrained by unconsolidated material; infrequent short flats with braids and meanders	2–5	Channel downcuts through deep valley bottom glacial till, colluvium, or coarse glacio-fluvial deposits; cross-sectional profile variable, but generally weakly U-shaped with active channel vertically incised into valley fill deposits; immediate side-slopes composed of unconsolidated and often unsorted coarse-grained deposits
U4 Active glacial out-wash valley	1–7%	Initially < 5%, increasing to > 60%	< 4X	Unconstrained; highly sinuous and braided	1–3	Stream corridors directly below active alpine glaciers; channel braiding and shifting common; active channel nearly as wide as valley bottom

TABLE 7.3. (*continued*)

Valley segment type[a]	Valley bottom gradient[b]	Sideslope gradient[c]	Valley bottom width[d]	Channel patterns	Stream order[e]	Landform and geomorphic features
H1 Moderate-gradient valley wall/head-water	3–6%	> 30%	< 2X	Constrained	1–2	Small drainage ways with channels slightly to moderately entren-ched into mountain toe-slopes or head-water basins
H2 High-gradient valley wall/head-water	6–11%	> 30%	< 2X	Constrained; stair-stepped	1–2	Small drainage ways with channels moderately entren-ched into high gradient mountain slopes or headwater basins; bedrock exposures and out-crops common; localized alluvial/ colluvial terrace deposition
H3 Very high-gradient valley wall/head-water	11% +	> 60%	< 2X	Constrained; stair-stepped	1–2	Small drainage ways with channels moderately entren-ched into high gradient mountain slopes or headwater basins; bedrock exposures and out-crops common; localized alluvial/ colluvial terrace deposition

[a]Valley segment type names include alphanumeric mapping codes in italic (from Cupp, 1989a,b)
[b]Valley bottom gradient is measured in length of *ca.* 300 m (1000 ft) or more
[c]Sideslope gradient characterizes the hillslopes within 1000 horizontal and *ca.* 100 m (300 ft) vertical distance from the active channel
[d]Valley bottom width is a ratio of the valley bottom width to active channel width
[e]Stream order as defined by Strahler (1957)

There is considerable disagreement about whether the principal units of classification should be temporally stable (e.g. valley segment) or dynamic (e.g. stream types) (Table 7.4). Arguments for temporal stability suggest that a reach, once classified, is of little management value if it changes naturally over the time scale of land-use practices (Frissell et al, 1986). In contrast, a dynamic classification based on smaller, more dynamic units provides a more accurate description of present conditions in the reach (e.g. active

TABLE 7.4. Summary of contemporary hierarchical and single spatial scale stream classification

	Advantages	Disadvantages
Hierarchical (e.g. Frissell et al, 1986)	Useful at several scales, highly adaptable, can describe both temporally stable and temporally unstable units	Complex, labour intensive
Basin scale (e.g. Lotspeich, 1980; Bailey, 1978)	Temporally stable (> 10 yr). Geographically defined, correlated with zoogeographic boundaries	Limited utility for managers, low resolution, not easily defined *a priori*, does not provide information on individual streams
Valley segments (e.g. Cupp, 1989b)	Temporally stable (> 10 yr), specific to a portion of stream, relatively distinct boundaries	Does not describe stream characteristics
Channel form (e.g. Brussock et al, 1985; Rosgen, 1985; Kellerhals and Church, 1989)	Stream-specific, provides detailed description of stream reach. Temporally unstable (< 10 yr), i.e. responds to disturbance	Not linked to hillslope processes, boundaries relatively indistinct

channel width, riffle/pool ratio). We suggest that both scales are necessary for assessing conservation potential from the perspective of disturbance.

CLASSIFICATION COUPLING BIOLOGICAL AND PHYSICAL FEATURES

Coupling biotic resources with the physical features of the watershed has practical value in assessing the conservation potential of rivers. Existing systems have been based on patterns of species distribution, community structure, and biotic function. Biotic communities serve as integrators of ecological conditions expressed over different time and space scales and, therefore, can be sensitive indicators of environmental vitality. Most classification systems have been based on fish (e.g. Huet, 1954; Karr, 1981) or invertebrate assemblages (e.g. Illies and Botosaneanu, 1963; Cummins, 1974; Wright et al, 1984). However, several recent systems have been based on patterns of riparian vegetation (Harris, 1988) and aquatic plants (Holmes, 1989). In general, all biotic classification schemes assume a predictable relationship between the stream biota and geomorphic and hydrologic controlling factors acting on the system.

Vertebrate community classification

Fish have formed the basis for stream classification systems for several biological and political reasons. Hawkes (1975) argued that fish probably best reflect the general ecological conditions of rivers because they are presumed to be at the top of the aquatic food chain. In addition, because many commercial, recreational, and endangered fish species inhabit rivers, there has been continued need to categorize and manage their habitat. Fisheries managers and scientists have the growing responsibility of identifying fish community associations, their ecological requirements, and designing suitable ways of maintaining their integrity in the face of continued habitat deterioration (Schiemer et al, in press). Despite the merits of this type of classification, there are limitations that may often impede widespread application.

Stream classification systems have often related instream and larger-scale watershed features (e.g. drainage basin, channel morphology) to the conservation and management of stream fisheries (Fausch et al, 1988) (Table 7.5). In general, models of this type usually sacrifice precision for generality, and assume that fish populations are limited by habitat rather than interspecific competition, extrinsic factors (e.g. fishing mortality) or natural disturbance (Fausch et al, 1988). Although there is inherent value in using sensitive fisheries species in stream habitat models, individual species can often show high yearly variability in production independent of physical habitat conditions (Hall and Knight, 1981). In contrast, the entire fish community may provide a more accurate indication of habitat conditions, especially if community parameters are more stable over

limitations

TABLE 7.5. Summary of characteristics used in habitat-based
models

Drainage basin
Drainage density
Stream order
Mean basin elevation
Total stream length
Stream gradient

Channel morphometry and flow
Stream discharge
Width
Depth
Mean velocity
Wetted area
Pool volume
Gradient
Habitat types

Habitat structure, biological,
physical and chemical
Cover for fish
Streambank stability
Depth and velocity preference
Invertebrate drift abundance
Substrate
Temperature
Water chemistry

(Reproduced by permission from
Fausch et al. 1988)

time than population parameters, and relate predictably to habitat features (e.g. complexity, size) and habitat change (Gorman and Karr, 1978; Berkman and Rabeni, 1987; Hughes et al, 1987) (Table 7.6).

Ultimately, zoogeographic factors restrict the geographic scope of classification schemes based on the structure of fish assemblages. However, spatial variability in physical and biotic factors shaping community dynamics can also limit geographic scope. Environmental disturbance regimes vary with climate and geology (Resh et al, 1988). In regions where seasonal flow patterns are predictable, communities may be persistent and resilient (Moyle and Vondracek, 1985). In contrast, regions with highly variable and unpredictable flow patterns (e.g. drainages of south-western United States), communities can exhibit sharp temporal fluctuations in structure (Matthews, 1982). Furthermore, within climatic regions, the influence of floods can vary depending on channel form and substrate (Resh et al, 1988).

Biotic factors can further confound species–habitat relationships. In stream segments where competition and predation are important factors, fluctuations or shifts in physico-chemical conditions manifested in the channel can alter the intensity and direction of competitive and predator–prey interactions (Fraser and Cerri, 1982; Reeves et al, 1987).

Variability in productivity between drainages may also contribute to patterns of diversity seen for given streams (Bunn and Davies, 1990; Morin and Naiman, 1990). Finally, there are various human activities which can produce major alterations in fish community composition (e.g. species introductions, chemical pollution, harvest) without altering physical habitat structure.

Many recent investigations have examined spatial patterns, both within and between basins, of functional characteristics in fish communities (Gorman and Karr, 1978; Moyle and Li, 1979; Schlosser, 1982, 1987; Berkman and Rabeni, 1987). Moyle and Li (1979) speculated that, while species composition may often be unstable, there may be stability in trophic structure in given habitat settings. Furthermore, Schlosser (1987) hypothesized that there is a predictable longitudinal pattern in characteristics of fish communities (e.g. trophic diversity, demography, seasonal stability) in warm-water streams.

A commonly used fish community evaluation and classification scheme for lotic systems in North America is the Index of Biotic Integrity (IBI), which incorporates both

TABLE 7.6. Advantages and disadvantages of using fish populations and communities for stream classification

---

Advantages
Relationship between community function and habitat quality
Predictable response to habitat change
Community attributes are integrators of local and upstream habitat quality
Species are indicators of stream function (e.g. trophic guilds)
Coupling of biotic resources to physical habitat

Disadvantages
Variability in species composition across zoogeographic regions
Structure can vary between drainages due to differences in biotic (e.g. competition, recruitment) and abiotic (e.g. flow) controls
Intensive sampling effort often required; difficulty in quantitatively sampling large rivers

---

TABLE 7.7. Fish community variables used in the
Index of Biotic Integrity

Species composition and richness
Number of species
Presence of intolerant species
Species richness and composition of Darters[a]
Species richness and composition of Catastomids[a]
Species richness and composition of Sunfish[a]
Proportion of green sunfish[a]
Proportion of hybrids[a]

Ecological factors
Number of individuals in sample
Proportion of omnivores
Proportion of insectivorous cyprinids
Proportion of top carnivores

(Adapted from Karr, 1981)
[a]Modified or deleted in different zoogeographic regions

structural and functional components of stream fish communities to assess the environmental quality of stream segments (Karr, 1981) (Table 7.7). The method was developed in the mid-western United States but has been successfully adapted to different geographic regions of the United States (Fausch et al, 1984; Leonard and Orth, 1986). One advantage of the IBI is that population and community attributes are easy to measure (Fausch et al, 1984). However, it does not directly consider in-channel physical factors or extrinsic physical factors which influence community structure, although the fundamental premise of the IBI is that a range of physical features (e.g. channel morphology, flow) control the structural and functional attributes of communities (I. J. Schlosser, pers. comm.). Indicator species used as metrics have been selected because, through their life-history strategies, they are indicators of physical/chemical habitat conditions. Steedman (1988) found that the IBI was very responsive to large-scale patterns of land use in watersheds of southern Ontario, Canada.

The literature on the ecology of stream fish communities is replete with empirical support for stochastic and deterministic structure (Grossman et al, 1982; Moyle and Vondracek, 1985; Matthews, 1986), as well as strong (Gorman and Karr, 1978) and weak species–habitat relationships (Schlosser, 1982). Such disparity is ultimately a consequence of the physico-chemical features of the drainage basin (i.e. geology, climate), channel (i.e. substrate, depth/width ratio), and habitats (i.e. depth, velocity, large organic debris). These are the primary determinants of the physical template influencing the life history attributes, population dynamics, and community structure and function of stream fishes (I. J. Schlosser, pers. comm.).

For both theoretical and management purposes, it is particularly important to characterize community patterns and controlling processes under different physical conditions. Zalewski and Naiman (1985) speculated that the relative importance of biotic and abiotic controls over fish community characteristics vary along a continuum from upstream to the mouth. Poff and Ward (1989) described a conceptual model relating factors of community regulation to characteristics of the flow regime for different regions of the United States. Site-specific management can be applied on the basis of such an understanding. For example, management of fisheries resources would be most effective in reaches where fishes are regulated by biotic factors. This is true partly because communities regulated by abiotic factors, such as floods or drought, have probably evolved life-history strategies to cope with habitat disturbances (Resh et al, 1988). Furthermore, competitive hierarchies may change in communities regulated by biotic factors, thereby altering overall community structure.

Invertebrate community classification

Classification schemes based on patterns in benthic invertebrate community structure also have been an important tool in assessing river water quality and disturbance (e.g. Plafkin et al, 1989; Wright et al, 1989). Hawkes (1975) discussed the value of developing biotic classification schemes which couple the macroinvertebrate distribution with physico-chemical stream features. Because they exhibit diverse life-history strategies, macroinvertebrates are good indicators of both short- and long-term change, as well as local and large-scale disturbances (Minshall, 1988). However, factors which limit the utility of fish classification (e.g. zoogeography, disturbance regimes, biotic interactions, and productivity) can also restrict the strength of invertebrate-based classification systems by altering species–habitat relationships.

In Britain, invertebrate assemblages have formed the basis for the classification of unpolluted rivers and have been used to develop procedures for predicting faunal assemblages at given sites from a small set of physico-chemical variables (Wright et al, 1989). The invertebrate classification system was developed following an intensive biological and physico-chemical survey of rivers throughout Britain (Wright et al, 1984). Environmental variables measured in this programme were those suspected of playing major roles in determining the distribution of the invertebrate fauna, and those which were altered by chemical and thermal pollution and river regulation (e.g. water quality, temperature and flow—Armitage, 1984). The predictive model developed from this classification system was valuable in detecting environmental stress and identifying species-rich communities, both important elements in assessing conservation potential (Wright et al, 1989). This type of predictive system, coupling the invertebrate classification scheme to environmental variables, is largely successful because it employs a small set of variables regulating invertebrate distribution which change with direct impacts on water quality. However, the ability to link this approach to larger landscape features of the watershed (e.g. hierarchical classification) is diminished because the human-induced alterations are considered to be on water quality and in-channel (on-site) physical features rather than larger-scale physical habitat, even though the impacts are often directly on the physical habitat. The potential drawbacks to this approach are that larger-scale geologic features can influence water quality changes (Armitage, 1984) and the initial demand for exhaustive field monitoring of invertebrate assemblages or in-channel physico-chemical variables to establish such a system.

Other classification systems explicitly assess the conservation value of rivers in Britain based on invertebrate species richness, rarity, and frequency of occurrence, and their relation to physico-chemical parameters (Jenkins et al, 1984; Wright et al, 1988, 1989, in press; Armitage, 1989). Jenkins et al (1984) found that sites with the greatest habitat diversity had the greatest conservation value. Furthermore, they found that altitude, width, pH, and water hardness could be used in place of intensive biological surveys to establish the conservation value of a site. Such a system may have general utility in assessing conservation value, since the biotic variables used were independent of taxonomy, the correlated physical variables were easily measured, and the physical variables respond in a predictable manner to watershed disturbance. Again, while such systems are valuable in assessing resource value of stream sites, they are not directly coupled to larger-scale landscape features, and therefore fall short of completely assessing the sensitivity of stream sites to human disturbance.

For two decades there has been an emphasis on organizing species into ecologically meaningful trophic guilds, and elucidating changes in the functional role of assemblages along the length of rivers (Cummins, 1974). This approach takes advantage of changes in trophic diversity that occur naturally along the longitudinal profile of rivers. Vannote et al (1980) predicted that structure and function of invertebrate assemblages in streams would change along a continuum from headwaters to the mouth in response to longitudinal gradients in the relative contribution of externally and internally derived energy inputs. Brussock et al (1985) further related longitudinal gradients in channel form to invertebrate community structure and function for different ecoregions of the United States. This hierarchical classification suggested that geomorphic shifts along the stream continuum can differ sharply between regions and further refined the expectations of the River Continuum Concept (Minshall et al, 1985). Like fish community classification schemes, the value of classifying streams by invertebrate functional groups is the independence from taxonomic structure, thereby enabling comparisons of different basins over larger regions. Minshall (1988), however, argued against relying on such a trophic group classification, using evidence of Hawkins et al (1982), who were unable to find shifts in functional groups in habitats degraded by logging. An added drawback to such a classification is the difficulty of categorizing diverse species into realistic functional feeding groups for all life-history stages.

Plant classification

Various classification systems based on riparian vegetation patterns have also been developed (Harris, 1988; Swanson et al, 1988; Baker, 1989). This has considerable potential in assessing the conservation value of rivers because riparian forests are active boundaries at the interface between upland and aquatic systems, and therefore may be sensitive indicators of environmental vitality and change (Naiman et al, 1988, 1989; Swanson et al, 1988; Naiman and Décamps, 1990), and because riparian forests play an important role in shaping the physical and biotic characteristics of the streams (e.g. stabilizing the channel, buffering floods, shading the stream channel) (Swanson et al, 1982; Gregory et al, in press; Naiman and Décamps, 1990; Naiman, 1990).

The fundamental classification unit of riparian zones is the community type. This is defined either by present vegetative composition or potential climax vegetation (Swanson et al, 1988). Inferences can be drawn regarding environmental gradients and successional relations between community types. Stratification of community types can be based on overstorey or understorey vegetation. The understorey (herbs and shrubs), because of their higher turnover rate, are better indicators of current soil and hydrologic conditions, whereas the canopy is a better integrator of longer temporal patterns. As with other biotic classification systems, the most valuable riparian classification schemes centre on relationships to physical factors associated with the river landscape.

Many authors have addressed the need for ranking riparian zones with respect to conservation value or ecological potential (Slater et al, 1987; Harris, 1988; Swanson et al, 1988; Baker, 1989). Slater et al (1987) used species richness, rarity, and frequency of occurrence to formulate the conservation value of different stream segments. Although these biotic variables were independent of taxonomic structure, the value of the system was diminished by the absence of a relationship between riparian habitat variables and the aquatic biota.

Harris (1988) classified riparian vegetation (i.e. species composition) in relation to six geomorphic valley types in the Sierra Nevada mountains of California, USA. He further noted the importance of incorporating emerging concepts from landscape ecology (e.g. Forman and Godron, 1986; Naiman et al, 1988, 1989) and hierarchical relationships of different landscape elements towards developing an enduring classification system. Specifically, this included defining the proper scale to delimit classification units for ecological and management purposes (i.e. stream segment) and addressing the importance of larger-scale factors in determining smaller-scale patterns. His geomorphic-vegetative units differed in their sensitivity to management, yet were judged to be useful for purposes of resource inventory, detailed ecological studies, and prediction of human-induced alterations. Although Harris suggested several reasons for the valley form–vegetation relationships, he acknowledged that processes governing the observed patterns were beyond the scope of his study.

The classification system described by Harris meets the need of coupling different landscape processes to biotic resources, and predicting sensitivity of stream segments to disturbance. However, the link between riparian vegetation and instream resources can only be weakly inferred.

In the late 1970s efforts were undertaken in Britain to classify rivers from the distribution of aquatic plant assemblages to assess river conservation potential (Holmes, 1989). The basis for this system was that plants integrated short- and long-term conditions in the river, and that they play an important role in the ecology of stream fish and invertebrates as food and shelter. The initial aim of this study was to conduct extensive surveys of rivers throughout Britain. This included complete documentation of plant species diversity and habitat variables. A computer-aided classification system was constructed which stratified rivers and river segments hierarchically. The attempt was valuable largely because rivers in Britain reportedly do not exhibit the typical longitudinal shifts in physical features, being more geomorphically homogeneous along their length (Holmes, 1989).

An evaluation of the biological–physical approach

The importance of biologically based stream classification systems in assessing the conservation value of rivers may be diminished by the fact that such approaches often demand, at least initially, intensive efforts to measure and monitor community characteristics. This is especially true for invertebrates; somewhat less so for fish and riparian vegetation. Furthermore, species–habitat relationships are often confounded by such factors as zoogeography, disturbance, biotic interactions, and productivity. Zoogeographic history is especially important for fishes, less so for vegetation and invertebrates. If biotic classification systems are to have broad application, they must be related to physical features of the landscape in order to make inferences on the effects of land-use disturbances. In this regard Harris (1988) comes closest to accomplishing this objective. Yet disturbances to different landscape elements (e.g. habitat, riparian zone, hillslope) can produce similar impacts on the stream biota. In the absence of information on the cause of stream degradation, and the linkage between the physical and biotic components of the system, it is difficult to gauge the recovery potential of the stream biota (Niemi et al, 1990).

CONSERVATION POTENTIAL BASED ON STREAM CLASSIFICATION

Although the number and diversity of specific classification systems for streams are large, there appears to be a consensus developing on the fundamental attributes of an enduring classification system. These attributes relate to the ability to encompass broad spatial and temporal scales, to integrate structural and functional characteristics under various disturbance regimes, to convey information about underlying mechanisms controlling instream features, and to accomplish this at low cost and at a high level of uniform understanding among resource managers (Figure 7.6). No existing classification system adequately meets all of the model attributes. However, the concepts advanced by Frissell et al (1986) and Cupp (1989a) come closest to meeting these attributes, and are currently being used to address a wide variety of stream-related conservation issues in the north-western United States. Acceptance of two fundamental tenets are implicit in using the approach of these authors: physical structure can be related to biotic and physical functions in the channel, and characteristics of the riparian forest are integrative measures of in-channel dynamics. We recognize that both tenets require further documentation.

The Cupp classification system is currently being applied to seven forested ecoregions of Washington State. Streams are delineated into their component valley segments based upon combinations of five diagnostic features (Figure 7.5). Within the identified valley segments, standardized methods are employed to identify the spatial array and physical dimensions of 14 habitat units (Bisson et al, 1982; Sullivan, 1986) and key channel geometric and bed substrate measurements (Table 7.3). This information is coupled with data on the status and trends in anadromous fish habitat in response to man-induced disturbance associated with timber harvest. This approach yields important information to public and private resource managers which guides them in assessing the potential risks associated with various management actions (Bisson et al, 1988; Beechie and Sibley, 1990; Conquest et al, in press).

Perhaps most importantly, the Cupp classification system has been useful in making resource managers in the north-western United States aware of the diversity of stream types within the region and the need for a variety of management prescriptions for habitat protection and conservation. This is especially important in a region with approximately 20–25 major types of stream segments, and where nearly 80% of the ancient forests have been cut in the last century to sustain a US $9.0 billion yr^{-1} forest products industry employing nearly 60 000 people. The classification system allows

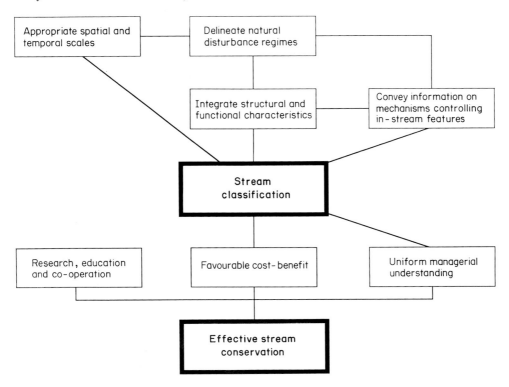

FIGURE 7.6. Relations between essential elements of an ideal stream classification system. All components are required to assess conservation potential based on stream classification

resource managers and scientists to consider alternative forestry practices (e.g. silvicultural techniques, cutting patterns) that are tailored to specific stream and valley bottom configurations rather than using narrowly defined techniques and regulations applied across a few stream sizes and types (Figure 7.6). For example, in Oregon (USA) J. R. Sedell and his colleagues (pers. comm.) have shown that streams with relatively unconstrained channels (e.g. wide valley floor, open riparian canopy, multiple secondary channels) have a greater water residence time, algal biomass, detrital and nutrient retention, and salmonid density than relatively constrained channels. These unconstrained channels are focal points in the drainage network for aquatic productivity and wildlife habitat and therefore require special management attention. Simple prescriptive management, such as riparian zones of fixed width, is less effective than management techniques adapted to local topography and natural disturbance regimes.

This has been effectively demonstrated by Benda et al (in press), who showed how the zonation of geomorphic surfaces in a 260 km^2 montane valley could be used to focus attention on streams where salmonid habitat value was highest. The valley was stratified at a large scale (>50 km^2) by geologic structure and associated geomorphology, and at a smaller scale (<10 km^2) by older lacustrine clay terraces and the more recent floodplain of the main river. Additionally, they quantified differences in the habitat characteristics (channel width, large organic debris, and spawning gravel) of streams on the various geomorphic surfaces. The valley was then partitioned into areas of high and low risk based on the physical habitat characteristics of the streams.

These are only two examples of an emerging perspective for stream and riparian management which uses classification as a basis for designing new approaches for forestry. The placement of logging access roads, decisions on when, where, and how much tree harvest should occur, development of silvicultural restoration techniques and of system models all require adherence to stream type. The most effective stream and riparian models include aquatic and terrestrial disturbance regimes, unique species mixtures, spatial and temporal heterogeneity, and microclimate gradients—all of which vary by stream type. Further, emerging silvicultural techniques for riparian tree species account for genetic vitality, stand development, and system complexity—factors that are specific to stream types. These considerations are essential before new harvest schedules can be developed and implemented.

The search for an ideal classification system is not complete. The fundamental principles of an ideal system are reasonably well articulated. However, it will be necessary for resource managers in specific ecoregions to adapt guiding principles to specific situations using an adaptive management approach (Holling, 1978). The task is difficult and requires a holistic, long-term perspective but, once in place, it provides a solid foundation for making resource decisions that will affect environmental vitality for decades.

ACKNOWLEDGEMENTS

Comments by P. A. Bisson, H. Décamps, I. J. Schlosser, and J. A. Stanford substantially improved the manuscript. The preparation of this chapter was supported by the Washington State Timber/Fish/Wildlife Agreement, a University of Washington Graduate Fellowship, the Center for Streamside Studies and the US Forest Service. This is contribution No. 55 from the University of Washington's Center for Streamside Studies.

REFERENCES

Allen, T. F. H., and Starr, T. (1982). *Hierarchy Perspectives for Ecological Complexity*. University of Chicago Press, Chicago, Illinois.
Armitage, P. D. (1984). "Environmental changes induced by stream regulation and their effect on lotic macroinvertebrate communities", in *Regulated Rivers* (Eds A. Lillehammer and S. J. Saltveit), pp. 139–65, Oslo Universitetsforlaget.
Armitage, P. D. (1989). "The application of a classification and prediction technique based on macroinvertebrates to assess the effects of river regulation", in *Alternatives in Regulated River Management* (Eds J. A. Gore and G. E. Petts), pp. 267–294, CRC Press, Boca Raton, Florida.
Backiel, T. (1964). "On the fish populations in small streams", *Verhandlungen der Internationalen Vereinigung für theoretische und angewandte Limnologie*, **15**, 529–534.
Bailey, R. G. (1978). "Description of ecoregions of the United States", Intermountain Region, United States Forest Service, Ogden, Utah.
Baker, W. L. (1989). "Classification of the riparian vegetation of the montane and subalpine zones in western Colorado", *Great Basin Naturalist*, **9**, 214–228.
Beechie, T. J., and Sibley, T. H. (1990). "Evaluation of the TFW stream classification system on South Fork Stillaguamish streams", The State of Washington Water Research Center, Project No. A-164-WASH, Seattle, Washington.
Benda, L., Beechie, T. J., Johnson, A., and Wissmar, R. C. (in press). "The geomorphic structure

of salmonid habitats in a recently deglaciated river basin, Washington State", *Canadian Journal of Fisheries and Aquatic Sciences*.

Berkman, H. E., and Rabeni, C. F. (1987). "Effect of siltation on stream fish communities", *Environmental Biology of Fishes*, **18**, 285–294.

Bisson, P. A., Nielsen, J. L., Palmason, R. A., and Grove, L. E. (1982). "A system of naming habitat types in small streams, with examples of habitat utilization by salmonids during low streamflow", in *Acquisition and Utilization of Aquatic Habitat Inventory Information. Proceedings (28–30 October 1981)* (Ed. Neil B. Armantrout), pp. 62–73, Western Division of the American Fisheries Society, Portland, Oregon.

Bisson, P. A., Sullivan, K., and Nielsen, J. L. (1988). "Channel hydraulics, habitat use, and body form of juvenile coho salmon, steelhead, and cutthroat trout in streams", *Transactions of the American Fisheries Society*, **117**, 262–273.

Briggs, B. J. F., Duncan, M. J., Jowett, I. G., Quinn, J. M., Hickey, C. W., Davies-Collwy, R. J., and Close, M. E. (1990). "Ecological characterisation, classification, and modelling of New Zealand rivers: An introduction and synthesis", *New Zealand Journal of Marine and Freshwater Research*, **24**, 277–304.

Brussock, P. P., Brown, A. V., and Dixon, J. C. (1985). "Channel form and stream ecosystem models", *Water Resources Bulletin*, **21**, 859–866.

Bunn, S. E., and Davies, P. M. (1990). "Why is the stream fauna of south-western Australia so impoverished?" *Hydrobiologia*, **194**, 169–176.

Carpenter, K. E. (1928). *Life in Inland Waters*, Macmillan, New York.

Conquest, L. L., Ralph, S. C., and Naiman, R. J. (in press). "Implementation of large-scale stream monitoring efforts: sampling design and data analysis issues", in *Biological Monitoring of Freshwater Ecosystems* (Ed. S. Loeb), Academic Press, New York.

Cummins, K. W. (1974). "Structure and function of stream ecosystems", *BioScience*, **24**, 631–641.

Cupp, C. E. (1989a). *Identifying spatial variability of stream characteristics through classification*, MS thesis, University of Washington, Seattle.

Cupp, C. E. (1989b). "Stream corridor classification for forested lands of Washington", Washington Forest Protection Association, Olympia, Washington.

Cushing, C. E., McIntire, C. D., Cummins, K. W., Minshall, G. W., Petersen, R. C., Sedell, J. R., and Vannote, R. L. (1983). "Relationship among chemical, physical and biological indices along river continua based on multivariate analyses", *Archiv für Hydrobiologie*, **98**, 317–326.

Davis, W. M. (1890). "The rivers of northern New Jersey, with note on the classification of rivers in general", *National Geographic Magazine*, **2**, 82–110.

Décamps, H. (1984). "Towards a landscape ecology of river valleys", in *Trends in Ecological Research for the 1980's* (Eds J. H. Cooley and F. G. Golley), pp. 163–178, Plenum Press, New York.

Décamps, H., and Naiman, R. J. (1989). "L'Ecologie des fleuves", *La Recherche*, **20**, 310–318.

Fausch, K. D., Hawkes, C. L., and Parsons, M. G. (1988). "Models that predict standing crop of stream fish from habitat variables: 1950–85", United States Forest Service, Pacific Northwest Field Station, General Technical Report PNW-GTR 213, Portland, Oregon.

Fausch, K. D., Karr, J. R., and Yant, P. R. (1984). "Regional application of an index of biotic integrity based on stream fish communities", *Transactions of the American Fisheries Society*, **113**, 39–55.

Forman, R. T., and Godron, M. (1986). *Landscape Ecology*, John Wiley, New York.

Fraser, D. F., and Cerri, R. D. (1982). "Experimental evaluation of predator–prey relationships in a patchy environment: consequences for habitat use in minnows", *Ecology*, **63**, 307–313.

Frissell, C. A., Liss, W. J., Warren, C. E., and Hurley, M. D. (1986). "A hierarchical framework for stream classification: viewing streams in a watershed context", *Environmental Management*, **10**, 199–214.

Funk, J. L., and Campbell, R. S. (1953). "The population of larger river fishes in Black River, Missouri", *University of Missouri Studies*, **26**, 69–82.

Gauch, H. G. (1982). *Multivariate Analysis in Community Ecology*. Cambridge University Press, Cambridge.

Gorman, O. T., and Karr, J. R. (1978). "Habitat structure and stream fish communities", *Ecology*, **59**, 507–515.

Gregory, S. V., Swanson, F. J., and McKee, W. A. (in press). "An ecosystem perspective of riparian zones", *BioScience.*

Grossman, G. D., Moyle, P. B., and Whittaker, J. O. (1982). "Stochasticity in structural and functional characteristics in an Indiana stream fish assemblage: a test of community theory", *American Naturalist*, **120**, 423–454.

Hall, J.D., and Knight, N. J. (1981). "Natural variation in abundance of salmonid populations in streams and its implication for design of impact studies", Report No. EPA-600/S3-81-021, United States Environmental Protection Agency, Corvallis, Oregon.

Harris, R. R. (1988). "Associations between stream valley geomorphology and riparian vegetation as a basis for landscape analysis in eastern Sierra Nevada, California, USA", *Environmental Management*, **12**, 219–228.

Harrison, A. D. (1965). "River zonation in southern Africa", *Archiv für Hydrobiologie*, **61**, 380–386.

√ Hawkes, H. A. (1975). "River zonation and classification", in *River Ecology* (Ed. B. A. Whitton), pp. 312–374, Blackwell, London.

Hawkins, C. P., Murphy, M. L., and Anderson, N. H. (1982). "Effects of canopy, substrate, composition, and gradients on the structure of macroinvertebrate communities in four Oregon streams", *Ecology*, **62**, 387–397.

Holling, C. S. (Ed.) (1978). *Adaptive Environmental Assessment and Management*, John Wiley, New York.

Holmes, N. T. H. (1989). "British rivers: A working classification", *British Wildlife*, **1**, 20–36.

Horton, R. E. (1945). "Erosional development of streams and their drainage basins: hydrophysical approach to quantitative morphology", *Geological Society of America Bulletin*, **56**, 275–370.

Huet, M. (1954). "Biologie, profils en long et en travers des eaux courantes", *Bulletin Français de Pisciculture*, **175**, 41–53.

Hughes, R. M., Rexstad, R. M., and Bond, E. (1987). "The relationship of aquatic ecoregions, river basins, and physiographic provinces to the ichthyogeographic regions in Oregon", *Copeia*, **1987**, 423–432.

Illies, J. (1961). "Versuch einer allgemein biozonotischen Gliederung der Fliessgewasser", *Verhandlungen der Internationalen Vereinigung für theoretische und angewandte Limnologie*, **13**, 834–844.

Illies, J., and Botosaneanu, L. (1963). "Problèmes et méthodes de la classification et de la zonation écologique des eaux courantes considerées surtout du point de vue faunistique", *Mitteilungen der Internationalen Vereinigung für theoretische und angewandte Limnologie*, **12**, 1–57.

Jenkins, R. A., Wade, K. R., and Pugh, E. (1984). "Macroinvertebrate–habitat relationships in the River Teifi catchment and the significance to conservation", *Freshwater Biology*, **14**, 23–42.

Karr, J. R. (1981). "Assessment of biotic integrity using fish communities", *Fisheries*, **6**, 21–26.

Kellerhals, R., and Church, M. (1989). "The morphology of large rivers: characterization and management", in Proceedings of the International Large River Symposium (D. P. Dodge, Ed) pp. 31–48. *Canadian Special Publication of Fisheries and Aquatic Sciences*, **106**.

Langbein, W. B., and Leopold, L. B. (1966). "River meanders—theory of minimum variance", Professional Paper, United States Geological Survey, 422H. Washington, DC.

Larsen, D. P., Omernik, J. M., Hughes, R. M., Dudley, D. R., Rohm, C. M., Whittier, T. R., Kinney, A. J., and Gallant, A. L. (1986). "The correspondence between spatial patterns in fish assemblages in Ohio streams and aquatic ecoregions", *Environmental Management*, **10**, 815–828.

Leonard, P. M., and Orth, D. J. (1986). "Application and testing of an index of biotic integrity in small, coolwater streams", *Transactions of the American Fisheries Society*, **115**, 401–414.

Leopold, L. B., and Wolman, M. G. (1957). "River channel patterns: braided, meandering and straight", Professional Paper 282-B, United States Geological Survey, Washington, DC.

Leopold, L. D., Wolman, M. G., and Miller, J. P. (1964). *Fluvial Processes in Geomorphology*, W. H. Freeman, San Francisco.

Lotspeich, F. B. (1980). "Watersheds as the basic ecosystem: this conceptual framework provides a basis for a natural classification system", *Natural Resources Bulletin*, **16**, 581–586.

Macan, T. T. (1961). "A review of running water studies", *Verhandlungen. der Internationalen Vereinigung für theoretische und angewandte Limnologie*, **14**, 587–662.

Matthews, W. J. (1982). "Small fish community structure in Ozark streams: structured assembly patterns or random abundance of species", *American Midland Naturalist*, **107**, 42–54.

Matthews, W. J. (1986). "Fish community structure in a temperate stream: stability, persistence and a catastrophic flood", *Copeia*, **1986**, 388–397.

Minshall, G. W. (1988). "Stream ecosystem theory: A global perspective", *Journal of the North American Benthological Society*, **7**, 263–288.

Minshall, G. W., Petersen, R. C., Cummins, K. W., Bott, T. L., Sedell, J. R., Cushing, C. E., and Vannote, R. L. (1983). "Interbiome comparison of stream ecosystem dynamics", *Ecological Monographs*, **53**, 1–25.

Minshall, G. W., Cummins, K. W., Petersen, R. C., Cushing, C. E., Burns, D. A., Sedell, J. R., and Vannote, R. L. (1985). "Developments in stream ecosystem theory", *Canadian Journal of Fisheries and Aquatic Sciences*, **42**, 1045–1055.

Morin, R., and Naiman, R. J. (1990). "The relation of stream order to fish community dynamics in boreal forest watersheds", *Polskie Archiwum Hydrobiologii*, **37**, 135–150.

Moyle, P. B., and Li, H. W. (1979). "Community ecology and predator–prey relationships in warmwater streams", in *Predator–Prey Systems in Fisheries Management* (Eds R. H. Stroud and H. E. Clepper), pp. 171–181, Sport Fishing Institute, Washington, DC.

Moyle, P. B., and Vondracek, B. (1985). "Persistence and structure of the fish assemblage in a small California stream", *Ecology*, **66**, 1–13.

Naiman, R. J. (1983). "The annual pattern and spatial distribution of aquatic oxygen metabolism in boreal forest watersheds", *Ecological Monographs*, **53**, 73–94.

Naiman, R. J. (1990). "Influence of forests on streams", in 1991 *McGraw-Hill Yearbook of Science and Technology*, pp. 151–153. McGraw-Hill, New York.

Naiman, R. J., and Décamps, H. (Eds) (1990). *The Ecology and Management of Aquatic–Terrestrial Ecotones*. UNESCO, Paris, and The Parthenon Publishing Group, Carnforth.

Naiman, R. J., Décamps, H., Pastor, J., and Johnston, C. A. (1988). "The potential importance of boundaries to fluvial ecosystems", *Journal of the North American Benthological Society*, **7**, 289–306.

Naiman, R. J., Décamps, H., and Fournier, F. (1989). "The role of land/inland water ecotones in landscape management and restoration: A proposal for collaborative research", Man and the Biosphere Programme, MAB Digest 4, UNESCO, Paris.

Naiman, R. J., Melillo, J. M., Lock, M. A., Ford, T. E., and Reice, S. R. (1987). "Longitudinal gradients of ecosystem processes and community structure in a subarctic river continuum", *Ecology*, **68**, 1139–1156.

Nawa, R. K., Frissell, C. A., and Liss, W. J. (1990). "Life history and persistence of anadromous fish stocks in relation to stream habitats and watershed classification", *Annual Progress Report. Oregon Department of Fish and Wildlife*, Portland, Oregon.

Niemi, G. J., DeVore, P., Detenbeck, N., Taylor, D., Lima, A., Pastor, J., Yount, J. D., and Naiman, R. J. (1990). "An overview of case studies on recovery of aquatic systems from disturbance", *Journal of Environmental Management*, **14**, 571–587.

Omernik, J. M. (1987). "Ecoregions of the conterminous United States", *Annals of the Association of American Geographers*, **77**, 118–125.

Pennak, R. W. (1971). "Towards a classification of lotic habitats", *Hydrobiologia*, **38**, 321–334.

Plafkin, J. L., Barbour, M. T., Porter, K. D., Gross, S. K., and Hughes, R. M. (1989). "Rapid bioassessment protocols for use in streams and rivers: Benthic macroinvertebrates and fish. Report No. EPA/444/3-87-025", United States Environmental Protection Agency, Washington, DC.

Platts, W. S. (1979). "Relationships among stream order, fish populations, and aquatic geomorphology in an Idaho river drainage", *Fisheries*, **4**, 5–9.

Poff, N. L., and Ward, J. V. (1989). "Implications of stream flow variability and predictability for lotic community structure: A regional analysis for streamflow patterns", *Canadian Journal of Fisheries and Aquatic Sciences*, **48**, 1805–1818.

Pringle, C. M., Naiman, R. J., Bretschko, G., Viarr, J. R., Osgood, M. W., Webster, J. R., Welcomme, R. L., and Winterbourn, M. J. (1988). "Patch dynamics in lotic systems: the stream as a mosaic", *Journal of the North American Benthological Society*, **7**, 503–524.

Reeves, G. H., Everest, F. H., and Hall, J. D. (1987). "Interactions between the redside shiner

(*Richardsonius balteatus*) and the steelhead trout (*Salmo gairdneri*) in western Oregon: influence of water temperature", *Canadian Journal of Fisheries and Aquatic Sciences*, **44**, 1603–1613.

Resh, V. H., Brown, A. V., Covich, A. P., Gurtz, M. E., Li, H. W., Minshall, G. W., Reice, S. R., Sheldon, A. L., Wallace, J. B., and Wissmar, R. C. (1988). "The role of disturbance in stream ecology", *Journal of the North American Benthological Society*, **7**, 433–455.

Ricker, W. E. (1934). "An ecological classification of certain Ontario streams", *Publications of the Academy of Natural Sciences of Philadelphia*, **101**, 277–341.

Rohm, C. M., Giese, J. W., and Bennett, C. G. (1987). "Evaluation of an aquatic ecoregion classification of streams in Arkansas", *Journal of Freshwater Ecology*, **4**, 127–139.

Rosgen, D. L. (1985). "A stream classification system", in *Riparian Ecosystems and Their Management: Reconciling Conflicting Uses* (Eds R. R. Johnson, C. D. Zeibell, D. R. Patton, P. F. Pfolliott, and R. H. Hamre), pp. 91–95, United States Forest Service, General Technical Report M-120, Rocky Mountain Forest and Range Experimental Station, Fort Collins, Colorado.

Salo, J. (1990). "External processes influencing origin and maintenance of inland water–land ecotones", in *The Ecology and Management of Aquatic–Terrestrial Ecotones* (Eds R. J. Naiman and H. Décamps), pp. 37–64, UNESCO, Paris, and The Parthenon Press Publishing Group, Carnforth.

Schiemer, F., Spindler, T., Wintersberger, H., Schneider, A., and Chovance, A. (in press). "Indicators for the ecological status of large rivers", *Verhandlungen der Internationalen Vereinigung für theoretische und angewandte Limnologie*.

Schlosser, I. J. (1982). "Fish community structure and function along two habitat gradients in a headwater stream", *Ecological Monographs*, **52**, 395–414.

Schlosser, I. J. (1987). "A conceptual framework for fish communities in small warmwater streams", in *Community and Evolutionary Ecology of North American Stream Fishes* (Eds W. J. Matthews and D. C. Heins), pp. 17–24, University of Oklahoma Press, Norman, Oklahoma.

Sheldon, A. L. (1968). "Species diversity and longitudinal succession in stream fishes", *Ecology*, **49**, 193–198.

Shelford, V. E. (1911). "Ecological succession I. Stream fishes and method of physiographic analysis", *Biological Bulletin*, **21**, 9–35.

Slater, F. M., Curry, P., and Chadwell, C. (1987). "A practical approach to the examination of the conservation status of vegetation in river corridors in Wales", *Biological Conservation*, **40**, 53–68.

Steedman, R. J. (1988). "Modification and assessment of an index of biotic integrity to quantify stream quality in southern Ontario", *Canadian Journal of Fisheries and Aquatic Sciences*, **45**, 492–501.

Strahler, A. N. (1957). "Quantitative analysis of watershed geomorphology", *American Geophysical Union Transactions*, **38**, 913–920.

Sullivan, K. (1986). *Hydraulics and fish habitat in relation to channel morphology*, PhD dissertation, Johns Hopkins University, Baltimore, Maryland.

Swanson, F. J., Gregory, S. V., Sedell, J. R., and Campbell, A. G. (1982). "Land–water interactions: the riparian zone", in *Analysis of Coniferous Forest Ecosystems in the Western United States* (Ed. R. L. Edmonds), pp. 267–291, US/IBP Synthesis Series 14, Hutchinson Ross, Stroudsburg, Pennsylvania.

Swanson, S., Miles, R., Leonard, S., and Genz, K. (1988). "Classifying rangeland riparian areas: the Nevada Task Force approach", *Journal of Soil and Water Conservation*, **43**, 259–263.

Vannote, R. L., Minshall, G. W., Cummins, K. W., and Sedell, J. R. (1980). "The river continuum concept", *Canadian Journal of Fisheries and Aquatic Sciences*, **37**, 130–137.

Ward, J. V., and Stanford, J. A. (1987). "The ecology of regulated streams: past accomplishments and directions for future research", in *Regulated Streams: Advances in Ecology* (Eds J. F. Craig and J. B. Kemper), pp. 391–409, Plenum Press, New York.

Warren, C. E. (1979). "Toward classification and rationale for watershed management and stream protection", Report No. EPA-600/3-79-059. United States Environmental Protection Agency, Corvallis, Oregon.

Wasson, J. G. (1989). "Éléments pour une typologie fonctionelle des eaux courantes: 1. Revue critique de quelques approches existantes", *Bulletin d'Ecologie*, **20**, 109–127.

Whittier, T. R., Hughes, R. M., and Larsen, D. P. (1988). "Correspondence between ecoregions and spatial patterns in stream ecosystems in Oregon", *Canadian Journal of Fisheries and Aquatic Sciences*, **45**, 1264–1278.

Wissmar, R. C., and Swanson, F. J. (1990). "Landscape disturbances and lotic ecotones", in *The Ecology and Management of Aquatic–Terrestrial Ecotones* (Eds R. J. Naiman and H. Décamps), pp. 65–89, UNESCO, Paris, and The Parthenon Publishing Group, Carnforth.

Wright, J. F., Moss, D., Armitage, P. D., and Furse, M. T. (1984). "A preliminary classification of running water sites in Great Britain based on macro-invertebrate species and the prediction of community type using environmental data", *Freshwater Biology*, **14**, 221–256.

Wright, J. F., Armitage, P. D., Furse, M. T., and Moss, D. (1988). "A new approach to the biological surveillance of river quality using macroinvertebrates", *Verhandlungen der Internationalen Vereinigung für theoretische und angewandte Limnologie*, **23**, 1548–1552.

Wright, J. F., Armitage, P. D., Furse, M. T., and Moss, D. (1989). "Prediction of invertebrate communities using stream measurements", *Regulated Rivers: Research and Management*, **4**, 147–155.

Wright, J. F., Furse, M. T., Armitage, P. D., and Moss, D. (in press). "New procedures for evaluating the conservation interest and pollution status of British rivers based on macroinvertebrate fauna", *Verhandlungen der Internationalen Vereinigung für theoretische und angewandte Limnologie*.

Zalewski, M., and Naiman, R. J. (1985). "The regulation of fish communities by a continuum of abiotic–biotic factors", in *Habitat Modification and Freshwater Fisheries* (Ed. J. S. Alabaster), pp. 3–9, Butterworths, London.

8

Catchment Characteristics and River Ecosystems

K. W. CUMMINS

Department of Biological Sciences, University of Pittsburgh, Pittsburgh, PA 15260, USA

INTRODUCTION

State of knowledge of running-water ecosystems

Running-water ecology has made significant strides in the last 15 years. Perusal of limnology texts published before 1970 will confirm the previous "poor sister" status of lotic ecology. Freshwater science was largely lentic–chemical and planktonic, and the latter was largely non-microbial. Running-water ecology had a fishery perspective in the 1960s, and in the early 1970s it was preoccupied with water quality concerns. Hynes' (1970) landmark book on running-water ecology initiated the present era of greater recognition of lotic studies. Since then, some major paradigms have been developed and there has been an explosion of publications, as exemplified by the extremely large running-water component of the International Society of Theoretical and Applied Limnology. The frontiers of stream ecology for the 1990s, the "decade of the environment", are likely to be the same as for all ecology: global (and regional) climate change, loss of biodiversity, and the release of genetically engineered organisms. Of course, all these so-called "great issues" are interrelated.

Certainly, the present focus by many running-water ecologists on the riparian zone, the stream/river land–water interface, will provide data on systems that are very sensitive to large-scale climate changes. Broadly defined, the riparian zone encompasses everything from the briefly captured upper stream banks during spates to broad floodplains inundated for whole seasons. The riparian zone is the focal point for land–water interactions in the catchment. Root development at the margin of streams and rivers and large fallen trees strongly influence channel structure and patterns and localized velocity of flow (e.g. Cummins et al, 1984; Sedell and Frogatt, 1984). Plant litter, coarse particulate organic matter (CPOM), and detritivores, dissolved (DOM) and fine particulate organic matter (FPOM) from this interface zone are important sources of reduced carbon compounds that fuel the energy requirements of the lotic biota. Furthermore, in the headwaters and along braided river channels riparian shading is usually the limiting control of instream photosynthesis. Perhaps the most fundamental feature of the

River Conservation and Management. Edited by P. J. Boon, P. Calow, and G. E. Petts
© 1992 John Wiley & Sons Ltd

biological organization of running-water ecosystems concerns the predictable shift in the availability and use of the basic nutrient pools—organic matter of terrestrial origin (allochthonous sources) and aquatic photosynthesis (autochthonous sources). This notion, which is embodied in the River Continuum Concept (RCC), could provide a major underlying organizing principle in the conservation and management of running waters in the face of regional climate change superimposed on anthropogenic alterations in land use that vary significantly in space and time.

In many cases, the causative agent in climate change is, and will be, vegetation alteration and removal. Often the areas most affected will be riparian corridors and floodplains. Most of the basic lotic ecosystem paradigms, such as the RCC (e.g. Vannote et al, 1980), include riparian influences on stream/river systems as a basic tenet. The analyses of these influences is being greatly enhanced by remote sensing techniques. The major breakthrough involves translation and extrapolation from the scale of stream and river reach, where intensive on-the-ground measurements are made, to the catchment scale which can now be remotely sensed, by satellite or near-ground flight techniques, and broadly characterized. Information gained from intensive small-scale studies scaled up to broad area and regional scales through the use of remote sensing and Geographic Information System (GIS) analyses is to date the most promising tool for stream/river management and conservation.

An increased scale of spatial analysis is not all that is required. Reference of present measurements (for example, of stream flow) to the historical record adds the critical temporal perspective that is essential for evaluating extant conditions and for the prediction of future trends in a catchment. With paradigms such as the RCC as organizing principles and expanded spatial and temporal analyses, one would predict much greater success in the practice of conservation and management of waterways.

Many other areas of lotic research potentially bear significantly on the future of our understanding of basic running-water ecosystem structure and function at various spatial and temporal scales, including the level of entire catchments, and, therefore, on our ability to conserve and manage streams and rivers. Examples include organic budgets described in great detail (e.g. Naiman et al, 1987; Petersen et al, 1989; Meyer and Edwards, 1990) which have shown the importance of assessing the microbial activity of differing particle sizes separately (e.g. Sinsabaugh and Likens, 1990), the importance of both the upper bank and floodplain (riparian zone) as sources and sinks for organics (e.g. Smock, 1990), and the significance of geomorphic retention debris jams which are highly active aerobic sites (e.g. Hedin, 1990). Because ammonia is a preferred nitrogen source for many micro-organisms, it is likely that anaerobic–aerobic interfaces are sites of intense biological activity (e.g. Cummins, 1988). Although running waters are considered as basically aerobic systems, anaerobic microsites abound—for example, the digestive tracts of the invertebrates (e.g. Martin et al, 1980).

Experimental manipulations of particulate organics have allowed dissection of component processes. The best example is the research of Wallace and co-workers (e.g. Cuffney et al, 1990) in which invertebrate populations were manipulated with the biocide methoxychlor, resulting in significant reductions in leaf litter processing and transport of fine particulate organic matter (FPOM). From these, and a host of other excellent studies, it has become clear that dissolved (DOM) and fine (FPOM) organics abound in running waters all along the catchment network, and their continual sources are the upper bank riparian zone in the headwaters and the floodplains downriver, which, as Smock (1990) points out, serve as local "headwaters". Furthermore, invertebrates make both a qualitative *and* quantitative difference in organic matter dynamics.

Other areas of active lotic research are: plant–herbivore and predator–prey interactions, previously primarily the domain of terrestrial and marine inter-tidal ecologists, referred to respectively as "bottom-up" and "top-down" regulation of community dynamics; population isolation theory, or island biogeography, which has been applied to the "geomorphic islands", such as individual rocks, that exist in stream habitats; and the realm of hydraulics, extending from individual behaviour to community organization. In the area of plant–herbivore interactions, recent evidence indicates that the levels of impact of invertebrates on running-water vascular plants (hydrophytes) may be similar to that observed in terrestrial systems (e.g. Sand-Jensen and Madsen, 1989) and plant chemical defences also operate in aquatic systems (e.g. Newman et al, 1990).

It should be obvious from the above that the field is as active and vital as any in ecology, rich with theory and testable hypotheses. Clearly, all this research activity holds promise for enhancement of practices used in the conservation and management of running waters, such as riparian habitat restoration.

Streams versus rivers

There is considerable confusion and ambiguity concerning the terms "stream" and "river" on both sides of the Atlantic and elsewhere. The size of a body of running water is often described by stream order (e.g. Strahler, 1957) or drainage (catchment) area (Hughes and Omernik, 1981). In general, the popular conception is that a system of orders one to three or four is a stream, and orders larger than this are rivers (or greater or less than $10 \, km^2$ catchment area as the approximate dividing point). Although catchment area generally may be a good predictor of stream size (width and discharge), stream order is most useful in describing the relative position of the channel in question in the whole drainage (catchment) network. That is, first-order streams may differ in gradient, bankfull width, lithology, and other characteristics, but they all share the common feature of being the uppermost portion of their respective drainage net. This means that these "distributaries" will be characterized by the maximum interface between the landscape through which they flow and their instream biology. This interface is mediated through the riparian zone, the ribbon of vegetation that tracks streams worldwide.

The arrogance and myth of management

The concept of "management" is one of the more arrogant human notions. The best management usually involves minimizing human influence—that is, the least "management" possible (e.g. McPhee, 1989). Such non-management reliance on natural processes is a strategy followed to some degree in the world's national parks. It seems clear that the only "management" required to perpetuate natural biological communities is the "management" of human populations. When human cultures fluctuated around a quasi-equilibrium of birth and death rates, that balance was part and parcel of overall ecosystem equilibrium. However, at present the norm is to manage individual non-human species. Most often, this means enhancement of a given species, frequently an alien (exotic) one, in the short run with little or no information on either the short- or long-term impact on ecosystem cohabitants. Few (if any) cases can be documented in which this type of "management" has had a positive effect on (that is, contributed to the continuance of) resident species assemblages. An example is the worldwide distribution of rainbow trout, *Oncorhynchus mykiss* (e.g. MacCrimmon, 1971; Petersen et al, 1987). Furthermore, a great deal of present "management" is restoration effort; namely, the attempt to repair damage of former management programmes, or lack of them.

As long as management is directed totally toward perceived human requirements of the moment, and focused on single species, frequently aliens, it is unlikely to play any useful role in the long-term perpetuation of natural running-water ecosystems. Because the management field has such a poor record of achievement, it is both surprising and disappointing that, even now, so little basic science has enjoyed technological transfer to management strategies. This is a situation that would never be tolerated in the health professions, for example.

BASIC PARADIGMS IN THE STUDY OF LOTIC SYSTEMS

The River Continuum Concept

A hallmark of running-water ecology of the last two decades has been its highly (and fairly unique) interdisciplinary character. There have been important interactions between biological stream ecologists and hydrologists, geomorphologists, and terrestrial botanists. These interdisciplinary interactions brought increased attention by lotic biologists on greater spatial and temporal scales and terrestrial–aquatic interactions. Biological communities were viewed as deterministic systems having evolved toward the most probable conditions of channel pattern and flow. The catchment (watershed) became the basic unit in lotic ecology and running waters were no longer viewed merely as pipes exporting materials away from leaky soils and plants. The aquatic–terrestrial ecotone, the riparian zone, has served as a major focal point for the interactions between the diverse disciplines that constitute modern running-water ecology. It was from this new interdisciplinary character of lotic ecology that the RCC grew (Vannote et al, 1980; Minshall et al, 1983, 1985; Cummins et al, 1984; Cummins, 1988). A feature of the RCC is the integration of ranges of temporal (e.g. flood frequency) and spatial (e.g. habitat patches, stream reaches, or entire catchments) scales, leading to a broadly applicable paradigm. The RCC simply proposes that lotic organisms have evolved to be in concert with the most probable set of physical conditions that are generally predictable from basic geomorphology. Downstream reaches (higher orders) depend upon a certain degree of upstream (lower orders) inefficiency (see nutrient spiralling, below).

Thus, in the headwaters, major carbon inputs are from the riparian zone; in the mid-sized rivers, associated with reduced bank shading but reasonable water clarity, internal primary production becomes a more dominant source of reduced carbon compounds, and in the larger rivers of the lower basin the accumulated loading from the tributary network, and periodically inundated floodplain, become the major carbon sources.

As a major tenet of the RCC, the invertebrates were selected as a group that could be used to analyse basic patterns of running-water ecosystem structure and function. This view links the invertebrate associations along the continuum, from small headwater streams to large rivers, to the basic nutrient pools that also shift along that continuum (e.g. Cummins and Klug, 1979; Minshall et al, 1983). This notion that the organic resources available to invertebrates along the continuum reflect primarily the inputs and influences of the landscapes (terrestrial biomes) through which the waters flow (e.g. Hynes 1975; Corkum, 1989) is a key part of the RCC. The relationship between detrital and algal food resources and the invertebrate functional feeding groups that use these resources has been viewed as a major feature of the RCC (Figure 8.1; Cummins, 1973; Cummins and Klug, 1979; Merritt and Cummins, 1984; Cummins and Wilzbach, 1985). Because detritus is such an important energy source in stream ecosystem dynamics, it is clear that micro-organisms play a pivotal role in the processing of organic carbon in running waters (e.g. Cummins, 1974). In recent years, an ever-increasing number of techniques has been applied to the measurement of microbial activity in lotic systems (e.g. Riemann and Bell, 1990).

Local modifiers, such as inputs from tributaries of much lower order than the receiving river, or man-made impoundments, require special interpretation (e.g. Minshall et al, 1985; Ward and Stanford, 1987; Ward, 1989). Certainly, the historical record indicates that man-made alterations of running-water systems have been highly pervasive

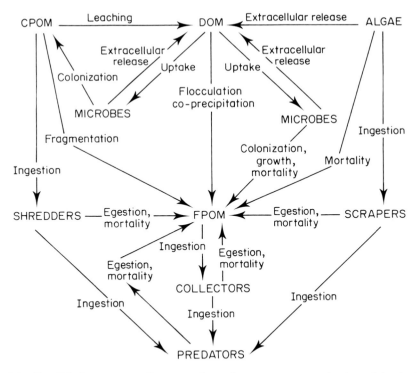

FIGURE 8.1. Simplified summary diagram of nutrient resource pools, invertebrate functional feeding groups, and microbe state variables, and the transfer functions between them. CPOM- =Coarse Particulate Organic Matter (>1 mm); FPOM=Fine Particulate Organic Matter (1 mm > 0.45 μm); DOM=Dissolved Organic M,atter (<0.45 μm); Algae=primary producers

modifiers. For example, many temperate headwater streams were originally less canopy-closed due to beaver activity, and medium and large river channels much more braided, and therefore more directly influenced by riparian vegetation (e.g. Cummins et al, 1984; Sedell and Frogatt, 1984).

Other paradigms

Many other paradigms in running-water ecology have been proposed and are currently being tested, such as hydraulic controls (e.g. Statzner and Higler, 1986) and other aspects of patch dynamics (e.g. Townsend, 1989), and resource (nutrient) spiralling (e.g. Elwood et al, 1983). The concept of resource spiralling has been used to modify models of freshwater nutrient cycling which were developed for lentic (standing) waters to account for the continual downstream movement of nutrients. Thus, the closed cycles of lentic systems become open spirals through downstream displacement. At the same velocity of flow, the tightness of the spirals reflects the rapidity of nutrient turnover when two reaches are compared. Such calculations of spiral length should become standard procedure in lotic studies allowing comparison of nutrient dynamics under a range of flow regimes. Such a comparative base should be of significant use in the conservation and management of running-water ecosystems.

Patterns and characteristics of flow have been suggested as major integrators of species distributions in running waters of all sizes (e.g. orders) worldwide (e.g. Statzner and Higler, 1986; Davis and Barmuta, 1989). The flow is normally characterized by some combination of the Reynolds number, giving information on laminar/turbulent flow, and the Froude number, characterizing flows from tranquil (sub-critical flow) to shooting rapids (super-critical flow). Flow environments have been measured in detail in the immediate region of stream organisms using new technologies, and data collected on their mechanisms for maintaining and changing position, and feeding (e.g. Nowell and Jumars, 1984). The general aspects of this special view of patch dynamics form a basic paradigm of running-water ecology that has been extant for some time, embodied in the "erosion–deposition (riffle–pool) concept" (e.g. Moon, 1939). Stream organisms, such as invertebrates, can be classified according to their adaptations for interacting with flowing-water environments (Merritt and Cummins, 1984). For example, clinging and swimming can be adaptations to erosional microhabitats, sprawling and climbing to depositional ones, and surface skating and burrowing can be adaptations to either. Every major stream invertebrate group has representatives in more than one of these categories, and the two major hydraulic habitats are found in all sizes of streams and rivers, often only centimetres apart. Certainly, hydraulic control is a general paradigm of patch dynamics in running waters, but it can be overridden by a number of factors. For example, if erosional substrates (e.g. cobbles) are placed in depositional habitats, they will be colonized in the short term by riffle clingers, until they become silted over. More specifically, the leaf litter-feeding caddis fly (*Hydatophylax*) that occurs in the western United States can be found in the autumn–winter period in a range of stream sizes (orders 1–5), in both erosional and depositional hydraulic habitats, and in a wide variety of geomorphic settings. The major controlling parameter in this case is the presence of deciduous leaf litter, usually alder (*Alnus*). The pattern is easily discernible in the conifer-dominated streams of the region. Thus, in some instances, the character of the riparian setting is at least as powerful an organizer as local hydraulics (e.g. Cummins et al, 1989). Nevertheless, programmes for the conservation and management of running waters must consider both the patterns of patch dynamics of substrate and flow operating as local mosaics, as well as broader-scale controls such as composition of the riparian vegetation that can transcend local geology and stream order.

A pressing need on the agenda of lotic ecology is the integration of the major running-water paradigms. This is particularly important, since there is presently disagreement about the relatedness and generality of all the major paradigms. For example, Pringle et al (1988) concluded that the concepts of patch dynamics could be usefully integrated into the major paradigms such as the RCC and nutrient spiralling, while Townsend (1989) suggested that the RCC is not generally applicable but patterns of patch dynamics might be.

SPATIAL AND TEMPORAL PERSPECTIVES

Spatial scale

New techniques and insights into spatial and temporal scaling provide the potential for major changes in our views of running-water ecosystems. The information and insights achievable within the general context of remote sensing constitute a major exciting, promising, and relevant frontier. Remote sensing should be considered at both the macro- and the micro-scales. The macro-scale for lotic ecology means stream and river reaches up to entire basins, of special interest being channel form and associated (riparian) vegetation. At the micro-scale organisms can be remotely sensed in concealed locations.

At the macro-scale of spatial perspective, the extent and composition of the riparian component of running-water ecosystems is a powerful organizer of the structural and functional characteristics of running-water communities. As discussed above, channel geomorphology and hydraulics provide basic constraints, or boundary conditions, but the stream-side vegetation can often override or modify these. An example at a small scale can be found in a study conducted on two second-order streams in the Oregon Cascades (Cummins and Gregory, unpublished). The streams are in the same basin and the study reaches are within several kilometres of each other and have similar gradient, substrate, and channel morphology, the major structural difference being reduced large woody debris in one. These very similar streams differ in their riparian vegetation—one is an alder regrowth (20 years), the other a coniferous old growth (400 years). The evidence is convincing that the very significant differences in detrital dynamics and litter-consuming (or shredder) invertebrate associations observed are directly related to this riparian vegetational difference—the timing of the inputs and the turnover times of the litter once it is entrained in the streams. This and other examples suggest that the shredder–litter connection is a useful tool for analysing community organization of small to medium-sized streams and rivers (Cummins et al, 1989). For such analyses, the riparian vegetation needs to be categorized on the basis of the timing of input and turnover of its derived litter. A related point, the current fervour in establishing ecoregions based primarily on upland vegetation, seems likely to be of limited use to stream ecology, for which the important units are basins and the riparian/floodplain vegetation.

Spatial analyses can be made from a range of types of remotely sensed data. Once remotely sensed spatial data have been taken (for example, with satellite or fixed-wing aircraft infra-red photos), they can be digitized and manipulated using GIS. With appropriate seasonal checking for ground truth, the digitizing process can produce data sets suitable for detailed analysis of riparian–stream ecosystems, including analyses of riparian litter inputs categorized by processing (turnover) times of the litter once it is entrained in the streams.

Remote sensing at the micro-scale to provide information on stream organisms in concealed locations and at night provides the basis for behavioural observations that permit the analyses of the use of space, time budgets, interactions, etc. In a general sense, underwater cinematography or video-taping, or the same through microscope devices, are examples of remote micro-sensing, but the most promising is the use of fibre-optic devices for conducting light (e.g. infra-red) to an area and conducting the image back. Such remote sensing techniques have been used by Wilzbach and co-workers (Wilzbach et al, 1988; Wilzbach, 1990) in studies of the behaviour of stream invertebrates. This technique should also provide new insights into the generality of invertebrate distributions in the hyporheic (sediment interstices) zones of running waters (e.g. Williams, 1989).

As stated above, techniques of remote sensing that make it possible to move from one spatial scale to another constitute probably the most powerful tools available for innovations in the conservation and management of stream and river systems; that is, integration of detailed data gathered at various micro-scales with the range of macro-scales of increasing catchment size that normally constitute the units of conservation and management.

Temporal scale

Temporal perspective at the macro-scale requires attention to the historical record for any reach, sub-basin, or entire catchment. This should be a basic initial step in field studies; however, it is still not a routine part of the procedures of lotic ecology. All study sites should contain several monumented (benchmarked) channel cross-section locations and at least one monumented photographic site. In the future such benchmark locations will be more precisely located using satellite-related global positioning equipment. These established locations allow cross-sections to be re-surveyed and photographs re-taken periodically at fixed points (elevation and compass positions). Until it becomes routine to frame conservation and management strategies within the context of an adequate temporal perspective we can expect little enduring success in these efforts.

There are long historical data sets of flow records (hydrographs) for many rivers and streams. Those taken by the US Geological Survey are tabulated on the basis of the Water Year—1 October to 30 September. Thermal, illumination, and detrital input schedules should be kept on the same calendar basis as the discharge records. In order to correspond with such things as life-history cycles, the beginning and end of these annual periods need to be adjusted for latitudinal and altitudinal differences.

As an example, the accumulated temperature (the temperature year) for the water year 1987–1988 in a second-order Appalachian mountain stream in the eastern United States was about 2600 degree-days (the average temperature each day summed over the year). The accumulated temperatures for the autumn–winter and spring–summer invertebrate generation periods were each about 1300 degree-days. This matched fairly well with most of the species present, and served as a suitable time schedule for detrital inputs. Thus, for study reaches, sub-basins and entire catchments, categorized by riparian "ecoregions" ("riparioregions"), we need monumented channel cross-section and photo sites that are re-surveyed each time data are collected and an historical perspective foundation for long-term programmes of data collection for the water, thermal, light, and detrital years. Particularly important will be the calculation of recurrence intervals (that is, the probability of occurrence in any given year—e.g. Morisawa, 1968), once the record is long enough, for each of these parameters so that study sites can be placed within the context of such historical perspective. Further, detailed, local ground truth data should be used to extend the spatial scale of the information to the appropriate basin scale. Within such a context, long-term adjustments of the populations of lotic organisms to most probable conditions should be discernible. Such analyses, of course, have important implications for the patterns of biodiversity in lotic ecosystems. If the least disturbed watersheds (perhaps to be defined as the least changed from the aboriginal condition) are identified as reference sites within basins or riparian ecoregions ("riparioregions"), spatial and temporal patterns of change can be plotted, and perhaps predicted.

THE FUTURE OF LOTIC ECOLOGY IN THE 1990s

The field of stream ecology has been in an exponential phase since the early 1970s, as indicated by papers published and research funds awarded. The field has been thoroughly emancipated from the status of fishery vehicle and poor sister of limnology to a highly interdisciplinary area of inquiry. The thrust of work on running waters has continued to be three-pronged—fisheries, water quality, and general ecological theory—but the last decade has been more productive for the latter than the first two. The integration of these three areas remains a goal for the future—technological transfer from theory to the applied fields of fisheries and water quality. Integration should be possible because if basic stream ecology has a single hallmark it has been its unprecedented success at interdisciplinary integration (geomorphology, hydrology, microbiology and biochemistry, etc.). However, the trend is still away from such integration. The partitioning of many national and international meetings of lotic ecologists remains indicative: fewer papers on fish, separate sessions on water quality, and an ever-increasing diversification of "basic" ecology (population–community–ecosystem dynamics—structure and function). In the United States at least, mission-oriented agencies, such as the Environmental Protection Agency, continue to define their granting priorities to carefully avoid basic running-water ecology. However, as I have attempted to show in this chapter, basic ecological concepts and procedures of lotic ecology would not be merely helpful to the field of conservation and management of streams and rivers, but rather are the essential basis for sound and successful strategies of the future.

REFERENCES

Corkum, L. D. (1989). "Patterns of benthic invertebrate assemblages in rivers of northwestern North America", *Freshwater Biology*, **21**, 191–205.

Cuffney, T. F., Wallace, J. B., and Lugthart, G. J. (1990). "Experimental evidence quantifying the role of benthic invertebrates in organic matter dynamics of headwater streams", *Freshwater Biology*, **23**, 281–289.

Cummins, K. W. (1973). "Trophic relations of aquatic insects", *Annual Review of Entomology*, **18**, 183–206.

Cummins, K. W. (1974). "The structure and function of stream ecosystems", *BioScience*, **24**, 631–641.

Cummins, K. W. (1988). "The study of stream ecosystems: a functional view", in *Ecosystem Processes* (Eds L. R. Pomeroy and J. J. Alberts), pp. 240–245, Springer-Verlag, New York.

Cummins, K. W., and Klug, M. J. (1979). "Feeding ecology of stream invertebrates", *Annual Review of Ecology and Systematics*, **10**, 147–172.

Cummins, K. W., Minshall, G. W., Sedell, J. R., Cushing, C. E., and Petersen, R. C. (1984). "Stream ecosystem theory", *Verhandlungen der Internationalen Vereinigung für theoretische und angewandte Limnologie*, **22**, 1818–1827.

Cummins, K. W., and Wilzbach, M. A. (1985). "Field procedures for the analysis of functional feeding groups in stream ecosystems", Pymatuning Laboratory of Ecology, University of Pittsburgh.

Cummins, K. W., Wilzbach, M. A., Gates, D. M., Perry, J. B., and Taliaferro, W. B. (1989). "Shredders and riparian vegetation", *BioScience*, **39**, 24–30.

Davis, J. A., and Barmuta, L. A. (1989). "An ecologically useful classification of mean and near-bed flows in streams and rivers", *Freshwater Biology*, **21**, 271–282.

Elwood, J. W., Newbold, J. D., O'Neill, R. V., and VanWinkle, W. (1983). "Resource spiralling: an operational paradigm for analyzing lotic ecosystems", in *Dynamics of Lotic Ecosystems* (Eds T. D. Fontaine and S. M. Bartell), pp. 3–27, Ann Arbor, Michigan.

Hedin, L. O. (1990). "Factors controlling sediment community respiration in woodland stream ecosystems", *Oikos*, **57**, 94–105.

Hughes, R. M., and Omernik, J. M. (1981). "Use and misuse of the terms watershed and stream order", in *The Warm Water Streams Symposium* (Ed. L. A. Krumholz), pp. 320–326, American Fisheries Society.

Hynes, H. B. N. (1970). *The Ecology of Running Waters*, University of Toronto Press, Toronto.

Hynes, H. B. N. (1975). "The stream and its valley", *Verhandlungen der Internationalen Vereingung für theoretische und angewandte Limnologie*, **19**, 1–15.

MacCrimmon, H. R. (1971). "World distribution of rainbow trout (*Salmo gairdneri*)", *Journal of the Fisheries Research Board of Canada*, **28**, 663–704.

Martin, M. M., Martin, J. S., Kukor, J. J., and Merritt, R. W. (1980). "The digestion of protein and carbohydrate by the stream detritivore, *Tipula abdominalis* (Diptera, Tipulidae)", *Oecologia*, **46**, 360–364.

McPhee, J. (1989). *The Control of Nature*. Farrar Straus Giroux, New York.

Merritt, R. W., and Cummins, K. W. (Eds) (1984). *An Introduction to the Aquatic Insects of North America*, Kendall/Hunt, Dubuque.

Meyer, J. L., and Edwards, R. T. (1990). "Ecosystem metabolism and turnover of organic carbon along a blackwater river continuum", *Ecology*, **71**, 668–677.

Minshall, G. W., Petersen, R. C., Cummins, K. W., Bott, T. L., Sedell, J. R., Cushing, C. E., and Vannote, R. L. (1983). "Interbiome comparison of stream ecosystem dynamics", *Ecological Monographs*, **53**, 1–25.

Minshall, G. W., Cummins, K. W., Petersen, R. C., Cushing, C. E., Bruns, D. A., Sedell, J. R., and Vannote, R. L. (1985). "Developments in stream ecosystem theory", *Canadian Journal of Fisheries and Aquatic Sciences*, **42**, 1045–1055.

Moon, H. P. (1939). "Aspects of the ecology of aquatic insects", *Transactions of the British Entomological Society*, **6**, 39–49.

Morisawa, M. (1968). *Streams: their Dynamics and Morphology*. McGraw-Hill, New York.

Naiman, R. J., Melillo, J. M., Lock, M. A., Ford, T. E., and Reice, S. R. (1987). "Longitudinal patterns of ecosystem processes and community structure in a subarctic river continuum", *Ecology*, **68**, 1139–1156.

Newman, R. M., Kerfoot, W. C., and Hanscom, Z. (1990). "Watercress and amphiphods: potential chemical defense in a spring-stream macrophyte", *Journal of Chemical Ecology*, **16**, 245–259.

Nowell, A. R. M., and Jumars, P. A. (1984). "Flow environments of aquatic benthos", *Annual Review of Ecology and Systematics*, **15**, 303–328.

Petersen, R. C., Jr, Madsen, B. L., Wilzbach, M. A., Magadza, C. H. D., Paarlberg, A., Kullberg, A., and Cummins, K. W. (1987). "Stream management: emerging global similarities", *Ambio*, **16**, 166–179.

Petersen, R. C., Cummins, K. W., and Ward, G. M. (1989). "Microbial animal processing of detritus in a woodland stream", *Ecological Monographs*, **59**, 21–39.

Pringle, C. M., Naiman, R. J., Bretschko, G., Karr, J. R., Oswood, M. W., Webster, J. R., Welcomme, R. L., and Winterbourn, M. J. (1988). "Patch dynamics in lotic systems: the stream as a mosaic", *Journal of the North American Benthological Society*, **7**, 503–524.

Riemann, B., and Bell, R. T. (1990). "Advances in estimating bacterial biomass and growth in aquatic systems", *Archiv für Hydrobiologie*, **118**, 385–402.

Sand-Jensen, K., and Madsen, T. V. (1989). "Invertebrates graze submerged rooted macrophytes in lowland streams", *Oikos*, **55**, 420–425.

Sedell, J. R., and Frogatt, J. L. (1984). "The importance of stream-side forests to large rivers: the isolation of the Willamette River, Oregon, USA, from its floodplain", *Verhandlungen der Internationalen Vereinigung für theoretische und angewandte Limnologie*, **22**, 1828–1834.

Sinsabaugh, R. L., and Likens, A. E. (1990). "Enzymic and chemical analysis of particulate organic matter from a boreal river", *Freshwater Biology*, **23**, 301–309.

Smock, L. A. (1990). "Spatial and temporal variation in organic matter storage in low gradient, headwater streams", *Archiv für Hydrobiologie*, **118**, 169–184.

Statzner, B., and Higler, B. (1986). "Stream hydraulics as a major determinant of benthic invertebrate zonation patterns", *Freshwater Biology*, **16**, 127–139.

Strahler, H. N. (1957). "Quantitative analysis of watershed geomorphology", *American Geophysical Union Transactions*, **33**, 913–920.

Townsend, C. R. (1989). "The patch dynamics concept of stream community ecology", *Journal of the North American Benthological Society*, **8**, 36–50.

Vannotte, R. L., Minshall, G. W., Cummins, K. W., Sedell, J. R., and Cushing, C. E. (1980). "The river continuum concept", *Canadian Journal of Fisheries and Aquatic Sciences*, **37**, 370–377.

Ward, J. V. (1989). "Riverine–wetland interactions", in *Freshwater Wetlands and Wildlife* (Eds R. R. Sharitz and J. W. Gibbons), pp. 385–400, US Department of Energy Symposium Series 61, Conference 8603101, US Dept of Energy, Office of Science and Technology Information, Oak Ridge, Tennessee.

Ward, J. V., and Stanford, J. A. (1987). "The ecology of regulated streams: past accomplishments and future directions", in *Regulated Streams: Advances in Ecology* (Eds J. F. Craig and J. B. Kemper), pp. 391–409, Plenum Press, New York.

Williams, D. D. (1989). "Towards a biological and chemical definition of the hyporheic zone of two Canadian Rivers", *Freshwater Biology*, **22**, 189–208.

Wilzbach, M. A. (1990). "Non-concordance of drift and benthic activity in *Baetis*", *Limnology and Oceanography*, **135**, 945–952.

Wilzbach, M. A., Cummins, K. W., and Knapp, R. (1988). "Towards a functional classification of stream invertebrate drift", *Verhandlungen der Internationalen Vereinigung für theoretische und angewandte Limnologie*, **23**, 1244–1264.

9

Anticipating the Consequences of River Management for the Conservation of Macroinvertebrates

J. F. WRIGHT, J. H. BLACKBURN, D. F. WESTLAKE, M. T. FURSE, and P. D. ARMITAGE

Institute of Freshwater Ecology, The River Laboratory, East Stoke, Wareham, Dorset BH20 6BB

INTRODUCTION

In Britain, the Nature Conservancy Council (NCC) has the task of selecting a national series of flowing waters for notification as Sites of Special Scientific Interest (SSSIs). The NCC uses a classification of river types based on aquatic and marginal wetland vegetation as a basis for SSSI selection. (Holmes, 1989; Nature Conservancy Council, 1989). When macrophyte surveys indicate that a river or section of river is of potential interest, the initial assessment is normally supplemented with a broad habitat survey (Nature Conservancy Council, 1985) together with further studies to determine the value of the river corridor for invertebrates, fish, birds, and mammals.

In future, a running-water site classification based on the macroinvertebrate fauna of 438 unpolluted sites on almost 80 river systems throughout Britain (Wright et al, 1989), which has been developed by the Institute of Freshwater Ecology (IFE), will offer a further zoological component for the process of site selection.

An ability to place sites within a national classification using the macroinvertebrate fauna is only one of two features in an IFE computer software package called RIVPACS (River Invertebrate Prediction and Classification System). The other feature is a technique that uses the physico-chemical attributes of a site to predict the macroinvertebrate community to be expected in the absence of environmental stress. This "target" community can then be compared with the observed fauna, to establish whether the site has an unusually rich community. Comparison of the fauna at the site under examination with the original 438-site database enables rare and infrequent taxa to be highlighted (Wright et al, in press). These techniques should help to define both the rivers and individual sites which are of high conservation interest with respect to their macroinvertebrates. However, it should be emphasized that RIVPACS has been developed using a

River Conservation and Management. Edited by P. J. Boon, P. Calow, and G. E. Petts
© 1992 John Wiley & Sons Ltd

timed pond-net sampling technique which includes all available habitats at a site, in order to provide a single listing of the species present. Thus no information is available on the habitat preferences of the individual species. For conservation purposes, this information is critical because river management can affect the range of habitats within an important site and result in the loss of species which have a restricted habitat or other specialized requirements.

Studies on the invertebrate fauna of contrasting macrophytes and other substrata in running waters have a long history (Percival and Whitehead, 1929; Whitehead, 1935) and since then, many ecological studies have added to this knowledge. Most researchers focus on the abiotic and biotic factors that influence the occurrence of species and species assemblages in an attempt to provide some understanding of the patterns observed in fresh water (e.g. Hildrew and Townsend, 1987). The importance of this approach cannot be underestimated, but at the same time detailed information on the invertebrate assemblages of contrasting habitats on a range of river systems must be available to ensure that management practices do not destroy both their conservation and scientific interest. Although non-macrophyte substrata, followed by submerged and floating macrophytes, have received most attention to date, more recently there has been a growing awareness of the importance of marginal areas, including emergent vegetation (Jenkins et al, 1984; Ormerod, 1988) as a refuge for macroinvertebrates.

Information on the habitat preferences of macroinvertebrates is particularly relevant at lowland sites where management in the form of channelization (Brookes et al, 1983) and maintenance work (Coles et al, 1989) is widespread and the control of submerged and emergent vegetation is frequently undertaken in summer (Westlake and Dawson, 1982).

In this chapter we report on a sampling programme to document the fauna of lowland rivers in summer. Information on the macroinvertebrates of a wide range of macrophyte and non-macrophyte habitats is being processed individually to provide the necessary database. A major objective is to combine current ability to predict the fauna of a site from environmental variables with detailed information on the habitat preferences of the fauna. In this way, it should be possible to anticipate the likely consequences for the fauna of management practices which alter the range of available habitat types.

SAMPLING PROGRAMME

Seventy-six lowland sites were selected for study from the 438 sites available in the national classification based on the macroinvertebrate fauna. Sites were chosen from each lowland classification group to ensure that a broad range of lowland sites was included. Since it was essential to acquire comparable information on the habitat preferences of invertebrates on a wide range of macrophytes, emphasis was given to sites known to support a high species richness and percentage cover of macrophytes.

The 76 sites encompassed 32 river systems in nine different regions of the National Rivers Authority (NRA). Sixty-six sites were within the Wessex (17), Southern (13), Thames (9), Anglian (17), and Severn–Trent (10) regions of the NRA which are typically lowland. The remaining 10 sites were in the South-West (1), Welsh (3), North-West (3) and Yorkshire (3) regions. A full list of the river and site names can be obtained from the authors.

Each site was visited once between late June and early August in 1988 or 1989. The sampling site was defined as a 100 m length of river and a species list of submerged, floating, and emergent macrophytes was accumulated by observation from the bank, wading, and the use of a grapnel, as necessary. An estimate of the percentage cover of submerged plus floating macrophytes, emergent macrophytes, and other substrata was then obtained by visual assessment of each 10 m interval along the length of the study site.

Twelve macroinvertebrate samples were taken, each one of 15 s duration, using a standard FBA pond-net (mesh size 0.9 mm). Choice of habitats broadly reflected the percentage cover data for macrophytes and other substrata, but was biased in favour of sampling a wider range of macrophytes, in preference to non-macrophyte substrata (e.g. gravel/pebbles, sand, silt, etc.) because of the need for comprehensive information on the macroinvertebrate assemblages of the macrophytes. In sampling a given macrophyte, the 15 s sample included sweep-netting through both the macrophyte and the underlying substratum in which it was rooted. This strategy was adopted because the presence of the macrophyte affects the underlying substratum and this has relevance to the macroinvertebrate fauna, both as habitat and as a food resource. Currently, six macroinvertebrate samples are being processed per site, and these have been chosen to reflect the habitat types with the greatest cover at each site. Identifications are to species level, where adequate keys exist, except in the case of Oligochaeta, Sphaeriidae, Hydracarina, and Chironomidae, which are not being identified further. Early results are being presented at family level in order to demonstrate some major features of the data set.

RESULTS

Estimates of the percentage cover of each major habitat category on each 100 m site in midsummer revealed that the submerged plus floating macrophyte category had the highest cover at 41 sites, a further 29 sites had highest cover of non-macrophyte substrata, and emergent vegetation formed the highest percentage cover at just six sites. The cover data in each of these three broad categories were then examined in relation to distance downstream (Figure 9.1). As expected, the mean percentage cover of emergent macrophytes was highest in the smallest streams and there was a progressive decrease downstream as river widths increased. In contrast, mean percentage cover of submerged plus floating macrophytes increased downstream from a low level in small streams, where shading from both emergent macrophytes and in some cases overhanging trees may have had a negative influence. After a mean percentage cover in excess of 60% between 20 and 30 km there was some evidence of a decrease in the mean proportion of submerged and floating macrophytes, possibly due to deep water, high turbidity, and other disturbances. As a consequence of these changes in the macrophyte categories, non-macrophyte substrata typically contributed *ca.* 50% of the stream bed at sites close to the source before decreasing in the middle reaches and then increasing again at sites greater than 50 km downstream.

During the study, 107 species of submerged, floating, and emergent macrophytes were identified. They comprised 94 angiosperms together with a small number of macroscopic algae, liverworts, mosses, and vascular cryptogams. Just over 20 of these macrophytes were found at 20 or more of the 76 study sites.

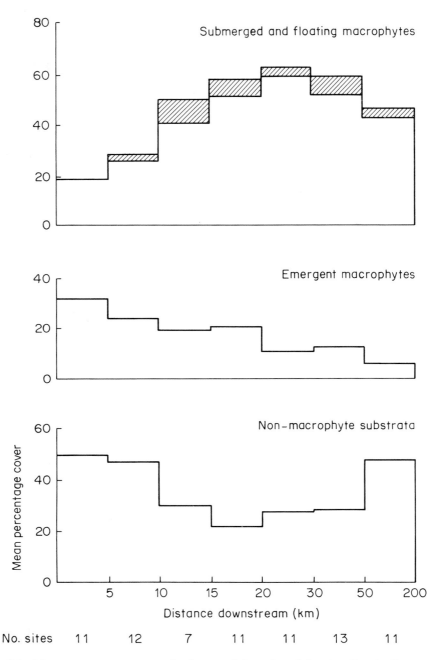

FIGURE 9.1. Mean percentage cover of submerged (open) and floating (hatched) macrophyte, emergent macrophyte and non-macrophyte substrata for the 76 study sites when grouped in relation to their distance downstream

Changes in the mean number of macrophytes per site in relation to distance down-stream are shown in Figure 9.2(a). Macrophyte species richness (angiosperms plus additional taxa) was lowest close to the source (0–5 km), rose in the 5–10 km category before stabilizing at a mean of *ca.* 15 angiosperm taxa per 100 m site further downstream.

Although data at the equivalent taxonomic level are not yet available for the macroin-vertebrate fauna, information on the mean number of families of macroinvertebrates per site after the processing of six samples at 65 sites is presented in Figure 9.2(b). Sites close to the source (0–5 km) support, on average, a smaller number of families than those further downstream, where the mean number of families per site is typically between 30

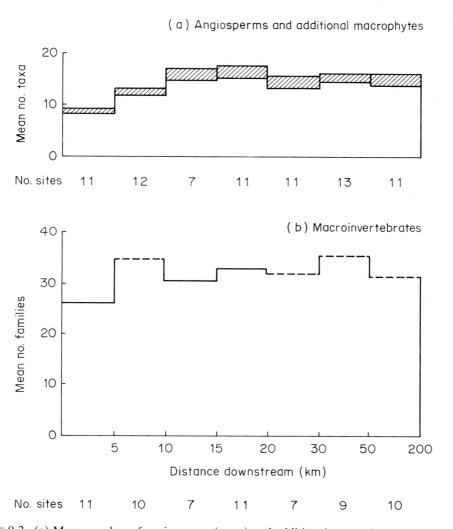

FIGURE 9.2. (a) Mean number of angiosperms (open) and additional macrophyte taxa (hatched) per 100 m site in relation to distance downstream. (b) Mean number of families of macroinverte-brates per site (based on 6×15 s samples) for 65 of the 76 sites in relation to distance downstream. Dashed sections of histogram indicate additional site data required

and 35. Closer examination of both family and species composition at several sites close to the source suggests that they may be subject to environmental stress, such as organic enrichment, resulting in loss of taxon richness. Once macroinvertebrate sample processing is complete, data from all sites will be examined critically to look for evidence of environmental stress. The extent to which lower macroinvertebrate and also lower macrophyte richness is a normal feature of unstressed headwater streams may then be clarified.

The number of macrophyte taxa present at a site may not be as critical to invertebrate richness as the area occupied by particular habitat categories (e.g. submerged, floating, and emergent macrophytes, non-macrophyte substrata) or specific habitat types. For example, there is a positive relationship between the percentage of emergent vegetation at a site over the range 0–25% cover and macroinvertebrate richness at the family level (Figure 9.3). Exceptions to this overall trend are a few sites which are more than 20 km downstream and which have a very low percentage of emergent vegetation yet retain high macroinvertebrate richness. Some of these sites are wide shallow chalk streams with managed banks, while others are large rivers in which the percentage cover by emergent vegetation is inevitably very low by virtue of the width of the river.

However, a high-percentage emergent vegetation alone is no guarantee of high invertebrate richness, and for sites with >25% emergent vegetation the relationship shown in Figure 9.3 is less consistent. In particular, at some sites 0–5 km from the source, where a high percentage of emergent vegetation is frequent (Figure 9.1) low family richness has been recorded. This could be due to the habitat and resource limitations of the sites or a result of imposed environmental stress.

The number of samples processed for the three major habitat categories after examination of 65 sites is given in Table 9.1. More samples have been processed for submerged and floating macrophytes (179) than for emergent macrophytes (105) or non-macrophyte substrata (106). The proportion of samples in these three habitat categories varies downstream but broadly reflects the percentage cover data downstream (Figure 9.1). The number of occasions on which a habitat category had the highest (or joint highest) family richness at a site is also shown in Table 9.1. After allowing for the relative number of samples taken, it is apparent that there was strong over-representation of emergent macrophytes among the most taxon-rich samples. In contrast, there was slight under-

TABLE 9.1. Macroinvertebrate family richness based on data for 65 sites (i.e. 390 samples)

	Non-macrophyte substrata	Submerged and floating macrophytes	Emergent macrophytes	Totals
No. of samples	106 (27.2%)	179 (45.9%)	105 (26.9%)	390 (100%)
Most family-rich sample(s) per site	3 (4%)	25 (33.3%)	47 (62.7%)	75 (100%)

A comparison between the number and percentage of samples from each major habitat category and the number (and percentage) of occasions on which each habitat category provides the most family-rich sample for each site. Joint richest family assemblages on different habitat categories both count, and therefore $n=75$ for 65 sites

representation of submerged plus floating macrophytes, and strong under-representation of non-macrophyte substrata.

A total of 26 different habitat types supported the highest (or joint highest) number of families at one or more sites (Table 9.2). The number of samples processed for these 26 habitat types is also given to indicate their relative importance in the sampling programme. In total, they represent 281 of the 390 samples processed to date.

Of the non-macrophyte habitats sampled, only gravel/pebbles (2 mm/64 mm) held the richest (or joint richest) assemblage of families at a site, and this only rarely in view of the large number of samples processed. In contrast, 11 submerged and floating

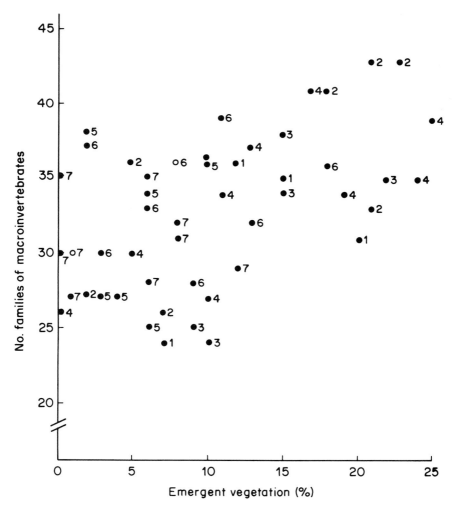

FIGURE 9.3. Scatter diagram of the number of families of macroinvertebrates per site in relation to the percentage of emergent vegetation for 49 sites with 0–25% emergent vegetation. Numbers indicate distance categories downstream: 1 (0–5 km); 2 (> 5–10); 3 (> 10–15); 4 (> 15–20); 5 (> 20–30); 6 (> 30–50); 7 (> 50)

macrophytes are listed, the most notable being *Ranunculus* spp., together with *Myriophyllum* spp., *Callitriche* spp., and *Nuphar lutea*. However, 14 emergent macrophytes are featured in the list, including tall emergents and species with a low growth form. The importance of several of the tall emergents, including *Phalaris arundinacea*, *Sparganium erectum*, and *Glyceria* spp., as a refuge for a wide range of macroinvertebrates at all locations downstream is clearly apparent.

Although the taxonomic composition of the invertebrate assemblages at lowland sites varies downstream, the major habitat categories still provide conditions which differ in

TABLE 9.2. The 26 different habitat types which provided samples with the highest (or joint highest) number of macroinvertebrate families at one or more of the 65 sites

Major habitat category and habitat type	Number of samples	Distance downstream in km (no. sites per category)						
		0–5 (11)	>5–10 (10)	>10–15 (7)	>15–20 (11)	>20–30 (7)	>30–50 (9)	>50 (10)
NON-MACROPHYTES								
Gravel/pebbles	47		1	1				1
SUBMERGED AND FLOATING MACROPHYTES								
Berula erecta	4		1					
Callitriche spp.	19	1	1			1		
Elodea spp.	12						1	
Fontinalis antipyretica	4		1					
Myriophyllum spp.	14		1			1		1
Nuphar lutea	20				1		1	2
Oenanthe fluviatilis	2						1	
Potamogeton lucens	1							1
Potamogeton perfoliatus	5							1
Ranunculus spp.	42		1	1	1		1	3
Sparganium emersum	16				1		1	
EMERGENT MACROPHYTES								
Acorus calamus	2						1	1
Agrostis stolonifera	2	1						1
Apium nodiflorum	7	2						
Epilobium hirsutum	2	1			1			
Glyceria spp.	17	2	1		1	1	2	1
Myosotis spp.	3	1			1			
Nasturtium officinale agg.	11		1			1		
Oenanthe crocata	1	1						
Phalaris arundinacea	21	1	2	3	3	2	2	1
Scirpus lacustris	3			1	1			
Sparganium erectum	21	2		1	1		1	1
Veronica beccabunga	2				1		1	
Veronica anagallis-aquatica	2					1		
Unident. Gramineae	1	1						

The total number of samples processed on each habitat is given together with the number of locations in each downstream category at which the habitat had the most family-rich sample at a site

TABLE 9.3. Mean number of families of macroinvertebrates for selected habitat types in relation to distance downstream

Distance downstream (km)	Gravel/pebbles	*Ranunculus* spp.	*Phalaris arundinacea*
0–5	13.0 (10)	15.0 (1)	19.0 (1)
>5–10	16.9 (13)	25.0 (5)	23.4 (5)
>10–15	15.5 (4)	16.0 (6)	24.0 (3)
>15–20	16.3 (3)	20.2 (10)	25.0 (5)
>20–30	14.7 (3)	18.2 (5)	20.0 (3)
>30–50	13.9 (7)	19.0 (8)	27.5 (2)
>50	16.0 (7)	16.6 (7)	24.0 (2)

(Number of samples given in parentheses)

their ability to sustain a range of macroinvertebrates. Using habitat types which are common at most locations downstream (gravel/pebbles, *Ranunculus* and *Phalaris*) the basic tendency for emergents to support more families of macroinvertebrates than submerged macrophytes, which in turn support more than gravel/pebbles, remains clear (Table 9.3).

DISCUSSION

During the early 1980s there was a growing recognition that taxonomic survey work was required on many of Britain's rivers if their scientific interest was to be maintained, while necessary management operations continued. Although many surveys of plants, invertebrates, fish, birds, and mammals were already in progress, particularly on rivers of high conservation interest, there was a need for a less intensive method for general use within the water industry (Brooker, 1982; Eckstein, 1984). The habitat survey approach proposed by the NCC (1985) is now being used extensively to document the wildlife potential of sections of river prior to management operations (Coles et al, 1989). As a result, information is available on the macrophytes and other features of the river corridor which are likely to increase the wildlife potential of the river. Advice can be offered on sensitive management techniques, and follow-up surveys can determine whether the range of habitats has been sustained or enhanced following river management.

The thinking behind this method is that by safeguarding or increasing the range of habitats along a section of river the richness of the invertebrate and vertebrate fauna can be maintained (Marshall and Westlake, 1978). There is much to recommend this approach, for it sets down a low-cost method with widespread application which provides basic information on those rivers and sites where detailed surveys of the flora and fauna cannot be justified. The habitat survey approach would, however, benefit from access to information on the invertebrate assemblages on the macrophyte and non-macrophyte habitat types. This would give a wider and firmer scientific basis on which to undertake river management while maintaining conservation interest.

Tokeshi and Pinder (1985) state that only a small minority of freshwater invertebrates consume living macrophyte tissue and thus, unlike terrestrial species, they are generally free from obligate associations with plants based on chemical and nutritional compatibility. Nevertheless, submerged, floating, and emergent plants provide contrasting refuges for many invertebrates which can then exploit a variety of food resources, including epiphytic algae, trapped allochthonous material, and decaying macrophytes.

Numerous published studies on British rivers provide data on differences in the macroinvertebrate fauna over a limited range of macrophytes and non-macrophyte substrata (e.g. Wright et al, 1983; Jenkins et al, 1984; Ormerod, 1988). However, an extensive survey of many habitat types at a large number of sites is required to determine whether macroinvertebrates show consistent patterns in their habitat preferences which can be used for their conservation.

Each habitat type must be readily recognizable if the results from the present study are to have application at further lowland sites. Thus the habitats were defined by taxonomic criteria (species and genera of macrophytes) and by substratum particle size in the case of the non-macrophyte habitats. It is self-evident that the structure of (and food resources within) each of these habitats will show some variation between sampling units and that each habitat type will undergo change in its structure and/or food resources over a 12-month period.

On completion of sample processing, it will be possible to determine whether the factors which favour the occurrence of particular macroinvertebrates and which influence species richness best relate to individual habitat types, growth forms within habitat categories (i.e. fine-leaved submerged macrophytes, tall emergent macrophytes, etc), or to the broader habitat categories (submerged and floating macrophytes, emergent macrophytes, and non-macrophyte substrata).

The preliminary results reinforce the generally held view that submerged and floating macrophytes have a more taxon-rich fauna than non-macrophyte substrata. Of greater interest are the strong indications that emergent macrophytes are frequently the most taxon-rich habitats not only in small streams but also in the middle reaches and in larger rivers. They must therefore be given critical attention when assessing the conservation value of lowland running-water sites.

Investigations on several upland rivers in Wales, including the Teifi (Jenkins et al, 1984) and Wye (Ormerod, 1988), have also produced evidence that river margins support distinct assemblages of macroinvertebrates. In a further study on the Upper Twyi, Rutt et al (1989) hypothesized that acidic moorland streams, which currently support characteristic invertebrate taxa in marginal vegetation, might lose this habitat and its associated invertebrate assemblage following conifer afforestation due to increased shading and the greater erosive power of forested catchments.

In this study the positive relationship between the percentage cover of emergent vegetation and macroinvertebrate family richness (Figure 9.3) is an early indicator that over-zealous removal of marginal vegetation during river-maintenance operations could have deleterious effects on the invertebrate assemblages. Smith et al (1990), who examined non-macrophyte substrata in the River Welland in lowland England, found evidence of loss of macroinvertebrate family richness as a result of canalization and dredging operations. Their approach was to determine the family richness of riffles, pools, and runs, and by recommending the reinstatement of the pool–riffle system in future engineering operations, enhance the physical features of the river bed which promote higher macroinvertebrate biomass and family richness.

The extensive nature of the present study, both in terms of sites and habitats surveyed, meant that sampling had to be confined to midsummer only. The major advantage of this was that all macrophyte habitats were well developed and colonized by the macroinvertebrate fauna. At the same time, the strongly seasonal nature of plant growth serves as a reminder that the results represent a snapshot in time. The changes in the availability and importance of some habitats through the year and the influence of other seasonally varying environmental factors can also exert profound effects on the distribution and abundance of the invertebrate fauna.

In a wide-ranging discussion of habitats, Southwood (1977) suggested that there were at least eight quantitative characters of natural habitats which are relevant to the organisms which exploit them. However, he proposed that these characters could be condensed into two axes, which were durational stability (spatial heterogeneity against time) and resource level and constancy (temporal heterogeneity). More recently, stream ecologists have been considering the importance of disturbance in shaping benthic communities, and the location of refugia from which macroinvertebrates can colonize temporary habitats (Hildrew and Townsend, 1987; Resh et al, 1988; Townsend, 1989). These ideas are likely to have widespread application in explaining the underlying causes of the differences in the habitat preferences which are starting to emerge from this study.

Although most marginal macrophytes exhibit spring growth and autumn dieback, many of the taller perennial emergent species still provide year-round habitat and food resources for the macroinvertebrate fauna. Winter frosts and floods affect both the quantity and quality of emergent macrophytes, but their marginal location out of the main current and sturdy root systems suggest that they are likely to be valuable refugia for a variety of macroinvertebrates. In contrast, many submerged and floating macrophytes provide a spectacular volume of new habitat with plentiful food resources in the form of epiphytic algae and detritus for a more limited period of the year. Typically, these habitats are exploited by a wide range of species, some of which occur in great abundance. Non-macrophyte habitats, from coarse substrata to silt, vary in area through the year, not only as a consequence of the growth and recession of macrophytes but also through the direct effect of seasonal changes in the flow regime. They appear to offer a less diverse habitat with more limited food resources for exploitation, compared to macrophytes. This, coupled with their seasonal instability, may be responsible for their restricted macroinvertebrate assemblages.

Once processing of the macroinvertebrate samples is complete, comparison of the detailed species composition of the fauna over the full range of habitats can begin. The primary aim of the study is to link information on the habitat preferences of the macroinvertebrate fauna to faunal predictions obtained using RIVPACS in order to offer a practical method of influencing river management procedures to retain high conservation interest. However, it is clear that the data are also relevant to a consideration of basic questions on the importance of habitat structure, food resources, and stability/ disturbance as factors affecting the macroinvertebrate assemblages of contrasting habitats.

ACKNOWLEDGEMENTS

This study was commissioned by the Nature Conservancy Council. Additional funding has been provided by the Natural Environment Research Council in the current financial year. We are grateful to both organizations and in particular to Dr P. J. Boon, the NCC nominated officer, for his interest in the project. We would also like to thank Mrs J. Winder who drew the figures and Mrs D. Morton who typed the manuscript.

REFERENCES

Brooker, M. P. (1982). *Conservation of Wildlife in River Corridors. Part 1. Methods of Survey and Classification*, Welsh Water Authority, Brecon, Wales.

Brookes, A., Gregory, K. J., and Dawson, F. H. (1983). "An assessment of river channelization in England and Wales", *The Science of the Total Environment*, **27**, 97–111.

Coles, T. F., Southey, J. M., Forbes, I., and Clough, T. (1989). "River wildlife databases and their value for sensitive environmental management", *Regulated Rivers: Research and Management*, **4**, 179–189.

Eckstein, M. I. (1984). *Resources Evaluation and Conservation Studies within River Corridors*, Water Research Centre, Medmenham, Marlow, Bucks.

Hildrew, A. G., and Townsend, C. R. (1987). "Organization in freshwater benthic communities", in *Organization of Communities. The 27th Symposium of The British Ecological Society* (Eds J. H. R. Gee and P. S. Giller), pp. 347–371, Blackwell Scientific Publications, Oxford.

Holmes, N. T. H. (1989). "British rivers. A working classification", *British Wildlife*, **1**, 20–36.

Jenkins, R. A., Wade, K. R., and Pugh, E. (1984). "Macroinvertebrate habitat relationships in the Teifi catchment and the significance to conservation", *Freshwater Biology*, **14**, 23–42.

Marshall, E. J. P., and Westlake, D. F. (1978). "Recent studies on the role of aquatic macrophytes in their ecosystem", *Proceedings of the EWRS 5th Symposium on Aquatic Weeds*, pp. 43–51.

Nature Conservancy Council (1985). *Surveys of Wildlife in River Corridors—Draft Methodology*, Peterborough.

Nature Conservancy Council (1989). *Guidelines for Selection of Biological SSSIs*, Peterborough.

Ormerod, S. J. (1988). "The micro-distribution of aquatic macroinvertebrates in the Wye River system: the result of abiotic or biotic factors?" *Freshwater Biology*, **20**, 241–247.

Percival, E., and Whitehead, H. (1929). "A quantitative study of the fauna of some types of stream-bed", *Journal of Ecology*, **17**, 282–314.

Resh, V. H., Brown, A. V., Covich, A. P., Gurtz, M. E., Li, H. W., Minshall, G. W., Reice, S. R., Sheldon, A. L., Wallace, J. B., and Wissmar, R. C. (1988). "The role of disturbance in stream ecology", *Journal of the North American Benthological Society*, **7**, 433–455.

Rutt, G. P., Weatherley, N. S., and Ormerod, S. J. (1989). "Microhabitat availability in Welsh moorland and forest streams as a determinant of macroinvertebrate distribution", *Freshwater Biology*, **22**, 247–261.

Smith, C. D., Harper, D. M., and Barham, P. J. (1990). "Engineering operations and invertebrates: linking hydrology with ecology", *Regulated Rivers: Research and Management*, **5**, 89–96.

Southwood, T. R. E. (1977). "Habitat, the templet for ecological strategies?" *Journal of Animal Ecology*, **46**, 337–365.

Tokeshi, M., and Pinder, L. C. V. (1985). "Microhabitats of stream invertebrates on two submersed macrophytes with contrasting leaf morphology", *Holarctic Ecology*, **8**, 313–319.

Townsend, C. R. (1989). "The patch dynamics concept of stream community ecology", *Journal of the North American Benthological Society*, **8**, 36–50.

Westlake, D. F., and Dawson, F. H. (1982). "Thirty years of weed cutting on a chalk stream", *Proceedings of the EWRS 6th Symposium on Aquatic Weeds*, 132–140.

Whitehead, H. (1935). "An ecological study of the invertebrate fauna of a chalk stream near Great Driffield, Yorkshire", *Journal of Animal Ecology*, **4**, 58–78.

Wright, J. F., Hiley, P. D., Cameron, A. C., Wigham, M. E., and Berrie, A. D. (1983). "A quantitative study of the macroinvertebrate fauna of five biotopes in the River Lambourn, Berkshire, England", *Archiv für Hydrobiologie*, **96**, 271–292.

Wright, J. F., Armitage, P. D., Furse, M. T., and Moss, D. (1989). "Prediction of invertebrate communities using stream measurements", *Regulated Rivers: Research and Management*, **4**, 147–155.

Wright, J. F., Furse, M. T., Armitage, P. D., and Moss, D. (in press). "New procedures for evaluating the conservation interest and pollution status of British rivers based on the macroinvertebrate fauna", *Verhandlungen der Internationalen Vereinigung für theoretische und angewandte Limnologie*, **24**.

10

Use of a Geographic Information System in the Conservation of Rivers in Virginia, USA

P. L. ANGERMEIER

US Fish and Wildlife Service, Virginia Cooperative Fish and Wildlife Research Unit, Department of Fisheries and Wildlife Sciences, Virginia Polytechnic Institute and State University, Blacksburg, VA 24061-0321, USA

and

A. BAILEY

Center for the Management, Utilization, and Protection of Water Resources, Tennessee Technological University, Box 5033, Cookeville, TN 38505, USA

INTRODUCTION

Streams and rivers serve numerous consumptive (e.g. irrigation, waste disposal, fishery production) and non-consumptive (e.g. aesthetic, ecological, scientific) functions in modern societies. Conservation becomes necessary when some functions (typically, consumptive) diminish the quality or availability of others (typically, non-consumptive). Because biotic components of riverine systems are perhaps the most sensitive to human uses, conservation of rare wild populations is frequently an important management issue. Management agencies may be concerned with conserving riverine biota to protect either consumptive (e.g. fishery) or non-consumptive (e.g. ecological) functions (Angermeier et al, 1991). Major threats to biodiversity include instream (e.g. impoundments, effluents, exotic species) and offstream (e.g. diversions, landscape alteration) disturbances (Angermeier et al, 1986; Sheldon, 1988; Moyle and Williams, in press).

Conservation efforts for aquatic species, notably fishes and mussels, are widespread throughout the United States by both state and federal agencies. About 350 species of freshwater fishes are protected legally over part or all of their geographic ranges in the United States and Canada (Johnson, 1987). From October 1988 until September 1989, direct expenditure by US agencies on 114 federally protected fish and mussel species totalled about US $6 million (US Fish and Wildlife Service, 1990). However, current

River Conservation and Management. Edited by P. J. Boon, P. Calow, and G. E. Petts
© 1992 John Wiley & Sons Ltd

conservation efforts appear inadequate to preserve aquatic biodiversity in the long term. For example, at least 34 of North America's rare fishes suffered declines in population status from 1979 to 1989, while only seven improved in status (Williams et al, 1989). Thus, if biological conservation goals are to be achieved, management agencies must increase the effectiveness of their conservation programmes. Improvements in conservation efficacy may require significant shifts in the value perspectives and management approaches of traditional fisheries science (Higgs, 1987).

Temporal and spatial dynamics of riverine species are determined by relationships among numerous instream, riparian, and watershed processes. Consequently, effective management of rare species may require detailed information on a host of environmental variables over a broad array of temporal and spatial scales. In particular, managers of biodiversity need to know (1) where biota of concern are, (2) where physical, chemical, or biological threats to biota occur, and (3) the extent to which known threats will adversely affect biota. Data may be assimilated for temporal and spatial scales relevant to individuals, populations, species, communities, ecosystems, or landscapes (Noss, 1987; Scott et al, 1987). Given this information, managers can develop cost-effective strategies to minimize further losses of biodiversity or to restore ecological integrity to degraded systems.

The great volumes and diversity of data required to manage biodiversity effectively necessitate the use of computer-assisted analytical tools. Geographic information systems (GISs) are sophisticated computer tools increasingly being applied to conservation problems associated with large spatial scales (US Environmental Protection Agency, 1987). Distinctive capabilities of a GIS include (1) storage, retrieval, updating, and display of existing map data, (2) analyses of spatial relationships among maps, and (3) display of analytical results as tables or new maps. Because a GIS facilitates rapid analysis of large sets of spatial data, appropriate management decisions may be made much faster with GIS than with traditional mapping technology. Previous work (Brown et al, 1988) indicates that GIS technology is useful in addressing management issues at spatial scales of watersheds and river basins, which correspond to scales of ecosystem and landscape phenomena in riverine systems.

The Clinch River basin (CRB) in Virginia and Tennessee is an excellent system for illustrating the application of a GIS to the conservation of aquatic biota. The CRB is part of the Tennessee River basin, which supports one of the richest fish and mussel faunas of any temperate system in the world. The CRB itself supports approximately 118 fish and 47 mussel species, many of which are rare or endemic. Major impacts on the aquatic fauna, including impoundments, introduced species, toxic spills, mining, and agriculture, have caused significant reductions in the abundance and/or geographic range of numerous species (Ahlstedt, 1984; Jenkinson and Ahlstedt, 1988a,b; Neves and Angermeier, 1990). Consequently, the CRB is currently being targeted for protection and restoration of its aquatic communities by state and federal management agencies. This chapter presents a basin-level approach to the conservation of riverine biodiversity. Specific objectives include (1) describing components of a GIS developed for riverine systems in Virginia, USA; (2) illustrating conservation applications of the GIS in the CRB; and (3) identifying additional potential applications relevant to conservation of riverine systems.

MATERIALS AND METHODS

Data sources

The River Reach File of the United States Environmental Protection Agency (Whitworth and Horak, 1985) provided the framework for geographic cross-referencing of all data. This file comprises data on a series of stream reaches, each with upstream and downstream endpoint co-ordinates (latitude and longitude) that typically occur at stream confluences, mouths, or other significant hydrographic locations. Each reach is identified by a unique hierarchical code that specifies region, sub-region, river basin, and sub-basin. The original River Reach File identified approximately 500 reaches in Virginia. We developed a more comprehensive database by identifying all stream reaches at least fourth-order in size, as determined from United States Geological Survey (USGS) Topographic Maps (1 : 24 000 scale). New reaches were added to our River Reach File according to conventional protocol.

The USGS Hydrologic Unit Map of Virginia (1 : 500 000 scale) was digitized to provide a base map of hydrography, river basin boundaries, and state border for the River Reach File. Information on land use was taken from USGS Land Use and Land Cover Maps (1 : 250 000 scale), which distinguish wetlands, forest, urban, agricultural, and barren (mined) lands. Other geographic information was obtained from USGS Topographic Maps and various state and federal agencies, including the Virginia Water Control Board (VWCB); the Virginia Department of Mines, Minerals and Energy; the Virginia Department of Conservation and Recreation; the Virginia Department of Game and Inland Fisheries; the United States Forest Service (USFS); and the United States Soil Conservation Service (USSCS).

Information on the distribution and status of rare fishes and mussels was obtained from a recent compilation of rare species of Virginia (McDonald and Woodward, in press). All fish and mussel species designated in that volume as "threatened" or "endangered" in Virginia were included in our analyses. This list of species included all federally protected species and many species not currently protected by Virginia agencies. In addition, the database contained records of about 3000 fish collections made by various fisheries scientists and managers throughout Virginia since 1960. All fish collections and known locations of rare species were registered to particular stream reaches for analysis and display.

Hardware and software

The GIS described here is based on ARC/INFO software running on a DEC Micro-VAX II minicomputer and on PC ARC/INFO running on an IBM AT personal computer. The bulk of the data were manipulated in an Advanced Revelation (AREV) software system, which allowed more efficient storage and retrieval of data than did INFO. Data were transferred as needed from AREV to ARC/INFO in ASCII text files for purposes of spatial analyses and display.

GIS structure and procedures

The textual database for our GIS comprised two major files, the Reach file and the Fish Collection file. The Reach file contained records for about 4000 stream reaches state-wide, and 150 reaches in the CRB of Virginia. Geographic information was compiled for each reach in 35 data fields (see the Appendix).

Fish collections and other biological data (see the Appendix) were compiled for reaches as available. Collections were known from about 33% of all reaches statewide and 36% of those within the CRB of Virginia. Cross-referencing among files permitted the database to be queried by county, stream name, reach, collection, or species of interest.

The cartographic database for our GIS comprised numerous coverages, including (1) state and county boundaries, (2) hydrologic unit boundaries, (3) hydrography (reaches), (4) soil associations, (5) land use, (6) public lands, (7) active mines, (8) permitted discharges and intakes, (9) stream gauges, and (10) water quality monitoring sites. The unique reach codes were used to relate all data files to the hydrographic coverage.

Land use along streams was analysed by defining a 1 km "buffer" on both sides of each reach, then computing land use within the buffer. For reaches supporting rare species, the buffer was also searched for coal mines and municipal/industrial outfalls.

RESULTS AND DISCUSSION

Eighteen fish and 33 mussel species were designated in McDonald and Woodward (in press) as threatened or endangered in Virginia waters, including four fish and 12 mussel species that are protected federally. Although these rare species occur in 245 stream reaches throughout Virginia (Figure 10.1), the number of species in need of protection from both faunal groups is greatest in the CRB (Figure 10.2). Although it contributes less than 8% of Virginia's land area, the CRB supports 50% of the fish species and 79% of the mussel species in need of conservation, as well as an exceptional diversity of species that are not currently in need of protection. These patterns indicate that the CRB clearly should be the focal point of programmes aimed at conserving aquatic biota in Virginia.

Major threats to the aquatic fauna of the CRB include landscape-level disturbances due to coal mining, agriculture, and urbanization, as well as point-source pollution from industrial and municipal effluents. Analyses of spatial relationships between threats and the biota can help prioritize conservation efforts. For example, agriculture, which occupies 30.7% of the land area in the CRB, represents the most extensive disturbance and the greatest potential for non-point-source pollution. Land use along stream reaches supporting rare species is generally not significantly different (t-test; $P > 0.05$) from land use along other reaches. This suggests that if land use adversely affects aquatic biota, its effects operate at large spatial scales rather than locally, and management solutions to these effects should focus on large-scale processes. Although only 2.1% of the CRB in Virginia is in urban land use, 4.9% of the land within 1 km of streams is urban. The proximity of urban development to streams increases the probability of adverse impacts on aquatic biota. Indeed, reaches supporting rare fishes in the CRB of Virginia are less urbanized (t-test; $P < 0.05$) than other reaches (1.4% cf. 5.6%). Assuming that rare fishes

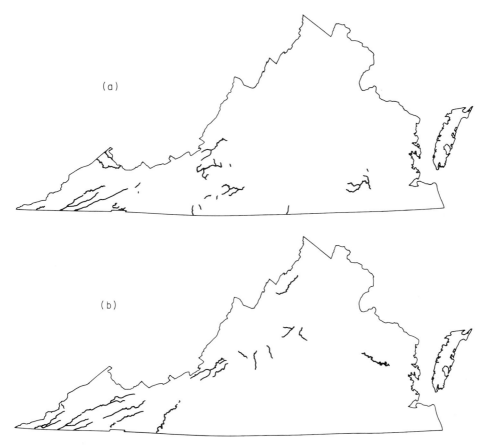

FIGURE 10.1. Plots of Virginia stream reaches known to support at least one of the (a) 18 fish, and (b) 33 mussel species designated as "threatened" or "endangered" in McDonald and Woodward (in press)

were historically more widespread, this pattern suggests that urban development may be instrumental in reducing species ranges, and perhaps should be studied more rigorously.

Numerous potential sources of point-source pollution also occur in the CRB. For example, coal mining is a prominent land use in certain portions of the CRB, and at least 12 active mines are located within 1 km of stream reaches supporting rare species. Indirect effects of coal mining may include stream acidification and deposition of coal particles in stream channels. In addition, 11 of the 48 industrial or municipal effuents legally discharged into the CRB enter reaches that support rare aquatic species. Monitoring of water quality in these and adjacent reaches should continue or be increased to ensure that further degradation of the biota does not occur.

The extent of preserves and public lands and waters is inadequate to protect aquatic biodiversity in the CRB. Less than 10% of the CRB is publicly owned, and virtually none of that land includes or is adjacent to reaches supporting rare aquatic species (Figure 10.3). Over 90% of the publicly owned land belongs to the USFS, which manages land

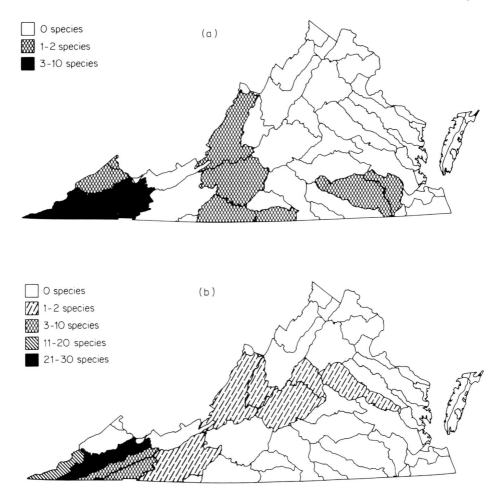

FIGURE 10.2. Plots of the USGS Hydrologic Unit Map of Virginia, illustrating the distribution of (a) fish and (b) mussel species designated as "threatened" or "endangered" in McDonald and Woodward (in press). The Clinch River basin comprises the two sub-basins with at least 11 threatened or endangered mussel species

for multiple uses (including timber production and mining), and not specifically for the preservation of biodiversity. Other public lands and waters are typically too small to provide significant protection to the biota (Figure 10.3). Consequently, the diverse aquatic biota of the CRB lies largely outside any protective land or water ownership, thereby representing a "gap" (Burley, 1988) in the conservation network. Once such gaps are identified, the next step in the conservation process is to establish priorities for action, such as land acquisition or implementation of management practices.

Although public ownership of land parcels and stream segments contributes to conservation goals, the large size of the CRB makes it unlikely that a significant portion will be acquired for a network of preserves. Alternatively, a comprehensive basin-wide management plan should be developed to protect streams over the long term from impacts of mining, agriculture, and urbanization. Such a plan should integrate and expand existing conservation activities, which include (1) state and federal protection of 14 fish and mussel species; (2) implementation of recovery plans for federally protected species; (3) reclamation of mined lands; (4) exclusion of livestock from streams; and (5) research on the mechanisms of impact on aquatic populations. Other activities that may facilitate preservation of the CRB biota include (1) development and application of environmentally sound technology for coal production; (2) strict enforcement of pollution regulations for industries and municipalities; (3) development and implementation of "best management systems" (Karr and Schlosser, 1978); and (4) programmes to educate citizens and landowners regarding conservation of riverine resources.

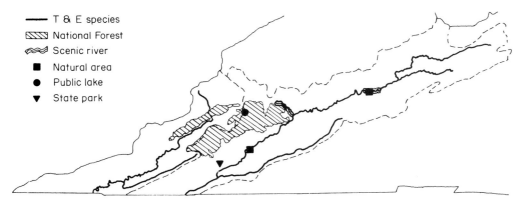

FIGURE 10.3. Plot of the Clinch River basin, illustrating spatial relationships between public lands and protected areas, and stream reaches supporting rare fish or mussel species. (T & E= threatened and endangered)

GIS capabilities are likely to become increasingly important to the management of systems as large as (or larger than) the CRB. A GIS can help managers visualize spatial variation in physical features such as elevation, temperature, stream gradient, soil or geologic formations, physiography, and land use. Such information is useful in understanding spatial and temporal patterns of biological attributes such as species richness, guild composition, and size structure, as well as how those patterns are affected by human activities. Integrating knowledge of spatial relationships among ecological processes, human uses of natural resources, and environmental threats is critical to effectively designing protective preserves (McDowall, 1984; Maitland, 1985; Moyle and Sato, in press) or focusing other conservation strategies. However, GIS technology must not be expected to solve conservation problems. The primary function of GIS is to analyse and present information quickly and efficiently. Effective management still depends entirely on sound decisions by informed managers.

APPENDIX

Titles and descriptions of selected data fields included in the database of the GIS. Geographic data were compiled for each reach, whereas biological data were compiled as available.

Field	*Description*
Geographic data	
COUNTY	County(ies) traversed by reach
DOWN.ELEV	Elevation of downstream endpoint of reach
DOWN.LAT	Latitude (degrees, minutes, seconds) of downstream endpoint of reach
DOWN.LONG	Longitude (degrees, minutes, seconds) of downstream endpoint of reach
DOWN.ORDER	Stream order(s) of other reach(es) confluent with the downstream endpoint of reach
DOWN.REACH	REACH.ID of the receiving reach
DRAINAGE	Major river basin containing reach
GRADIENT	Computed as $\dfrac{\text{UP.ELEV-DOWN.ELEV}}{\text{REACH.LENGTH}}$
HU.CODE	Code identifying river sub-basin; taken from USGS Hydrologic Unit Map
%AGRIC	Percentage of land along reach in agricultural use
%BARREN	Percentage of land along reach that is barren
%FOREST	Percentage of land along reach that is forest
%URBAN	Percentage of land along reach in urban use
%WETLAND	Percentage of land along reach that is wetland
QUADRANGLE	USGS quadrangle(s) (1 : 24 000 scale) traversed by reach
REACH.ID	Unique numerical code for reach; concatenation of HU.CODE and REACH.NO
REACH.LENGTH	Channel length of reach, as measured on USGS 1 : 24 000 scale maps
REACH.NO	Code identifying reach within its Hydrologic Unit
REACH.ORDER	Stream order of reach
ROADS.CROSSING	Number of roads crossing or ending at reach
SINUOSITY	Computed as $\dfrac{\text{REACH.LENGTH}}{\text{STRAIGHT.LENGTH}}$
SOIL.ASSOC	Predominant soil association traversed by reach, as indicated on USSCS 1 : 1 500 000 scale map
STRAIGHT.LENGTH	Linear distance between upstream and downstream endpoints of reach
STREAM.NAME	Name of stream comprising reach, as indicated on USGS 1 : 24 000 scale maps
VWCB.LAT	Latitude (degrees, minutes, seconds) of VWCB water quality monitoring site
VWCB.LONG	Longitude (degrees, minutes, seconds) of VWCB water quality monitoring site
VWCB.STA.NO	Code identifying station number of VWCB water quality monitoring site
UP.ELEV	Elevation of upstream endpoint of reach
UP.LAT	Latitude (degrees, minutes, seconds) of upstream endpoint of reach
UP.LONG	Longitude (degrees, minutes, seconds) of upstream endpoint of reach
UP.ORDER	Stream order(s) of outer reach(es) confluent with the upstream endpoint of reach

Field	Description
UP.REACH	REACH.ID(s) of other reach(es) entering reach
USGS.LAT	Latitude (degrees, minutes, seconds) of USGS flow gauge
USGS.LONG	Longitude (degrees, minutes, seconds) of USGS flow gauge
USGS.STA.NO	Code identifying station number of USGS flow gauge

Biological data

Field	Description
COLLECT.DATE	Date on which fish collection was made
COLLECT.ELEV	Elevation of fish collection site, as measured on USGS 1 : 24 000 scale topographic maps
COLLECT.LONG	Longitude (degrees, minutes, seconds) of fish collection site
COLLECT.NO	Code identifying fish collection
COLLECTOR	Person or agency making collection
COMMON.NAME	Professionally accepted common name of fish species
COUNT	Number of individuals of a given fish species in the collection
DIADROMY	Status of fish species with respect to diadromy (e.g. anadromous, catadromous)
GAME.STATUS	Status of species with respect to value as gamefish (e.g. low, high)
GENUS	Taxonomic genus of a fish species
HABITAT.TYPE	Type of habitat from which fish collection was made (e.g. pool, riffle)
POP.STATUS	Status of fish species with respect to legal protection (e.g. state endangered, federally threatened)
SAMPLE.EFFORT	Measure of sampling effort expended in making fish collection
SAMPLE.GEAR	Type of gear used to collect fish
SPECIES	Specific epithet of taxonomic name of fish species
FISH.CODE	Unique four-letter acronym for fish species

ACKNOWLEDGEMENTS

D. D. Magoulick assisted us with data analysis and map development. E. D. Rockwell made useful comments on an earlier draft of this chapter.

REFERENCES

Ahlstedt, S. A. (1984). *Twentieth century changes in the freshwater mussel fauna of the Clinch River (Tennessee and Virginia)*, MS thesis, University of Tennessee, Knoxville.
Angermeier, P. L., Neves, R. J., and Karr, J. R. (1986). "Nongame perspectives in aquatic resource management", in *Management of Nongame Wildlife in the Midwest: A Developing Art* (Eds J. B. Hale, L. B. Best, and R. L. Clawson), pp. 43–57, North Central Section of The Wildlife Society, Bethesda, Maryland.
Angermeier, P. L., Neves, R. J., and Nielsen, L. A. (1991). "Assessing stream values: perspectives of aquatic resource professionals", *North American Journal of Fisheries Management*, **11**, 1–10.
Brown, R. T., O'Bara, C. J., Bailey, A. G., Choate-Taylor, K., Robinet-Clark, Y., Harper, D. W., George, D. B., and Gordon, J. A. (1988). *Clinch and Powell River Basins Data Integration: GIS Data Base and Watershed Model*, Center for the Management, Utilization and Protection of Water Resources, Tennessee Technological University, Cookeville.
Burley, F. W. (1988). "Monitoring biological diversity for setting priorities in conservation", in *BioDiversity* (Ed. E. O. Wilson), pp. 227–230, National Academy Press, Washington, DC.
Higgs, E. S. (1987). "Changing value perspectives in natural resource allocation: from market to ecosystem", *Transactions of the American Fisheries Society*, **116**, 525–531.

Jenkinson, J. J. and Ahlstedt, S. A. (1988a). *Quantitative Reassessment of the Freshwater Mussel Fauna in the Clinch River, Tennessee and Virginia*, Tennessee Valley Authority, Knoxville, Tennessee.

Jenkinson, J. J. and Ahlstedt, S. A. (1988b). *Quantitative Reassessment of the Freshwater Mussel Fauna in the Powell River, Tennessee and Virginia*, Tennessee Valley Authority, Knoxville, Tennessee.

Johnson, J. E. (1987). *Protected Fishes of the United States and Canada*, American Fisheries Society, Bethesda, Maryland.

Karr, J. R. and Schlosser, I. J. (1978). "Water resources and the land–water interface", *Science*, **201**, 229–234.

Maitland, P. S. (1985). "Criteria for the selection of important sites for freshwater fish in the British Isles', *Biological Conservation*, **31**, 335–353.

McDonald, J. N. and Woodward, S. L. (Eds) (in press). *Virginia's Endangered Species*, McDonald and Woodward Publishing Company, Blacksburg, Virginia.

McDowall, R. M. (1984). "Designing reserves for freshwater fish in New Zealand", *Journal of the Royal Society of New Zealand*, **14**, 17–27.

Moyle, P. B. and Sato, G. M. (in press). "On the design of preserves to protect native fishes", in *Battle Against Extinction: Native Fish Management in the American West* (Eds W. L. Minckley and J. E. Deacon), University of Arizona Press, Tucson.

Moyle, P. B. and Williams, J. E. (in press). "Biodiversity loss in the temperate zone: decline of the native fish fauna of California", *Conservation Biology*.

Neves, R. J. and Angermeier, P. L. (1990). "Habitat alteration and its effects on native fishes in the upper Tennessee River system, east-central USA", *Journal of Fish Biology*, **37** (Supplement A), 45–52.

Noss, R. F. (1987). "From plant communities to landscapes in conservation inventories: a look at The Nature Conservancy (USA)", *Biological Conservation*, **41**, 11–37.

Scott, J. M., Csuti, B., Jacobi, J. D., and Estes, J. E. (1987). "Species richness: a geographic approach to protecting future biological diversity", *BioScience*, **37**, 782–788.

Sheldon, A. L. (1988). "Conservation of stream fishes: patterns of diversity, rarity, and risk", *Conservation Biology*, **2**, 149–156.

United States Environmental Protection Agency (1987). Proceedings of the January 1986 Environmental Protection Agency Workshop and GIS for Environmental Protection, USEPA, Las Vegas, Nevada.

United States Fish and Wildlife Service (1990). *Federal and State Endangered Species Expenditures: Fiscal Year 1989*, Washington, DC.

Whitworth, M. R., and Horak, G. C. (1985). *Guidelines for Implementing Natural Resource Information Systems: The River Reach Fisheries Information System*, Biological Report 85(8), Western Energy and Land Use Team, US Fish and Wildlife Service, Fort Collins, Colorado.

Williams, J. E., Johnson, J. E., Hendrickson, D. A., Contreras-Balderas, S., Williams, J. D., Navarro-Mendoza, M., McAllister, D. E., and Deacon, J. E. (1989). "Fishes of North America endangered, threatened, or of special concern: 1989", *Fisheries*, **14**, 2–20.

11

Non-traditional Applications of Instream Flow Techniques for Conserving Habitat of Biota in the Sabie River of Southern Africa

J. A. GORE

The Center for Field Biology, Austin Peay State University, PO Box 4718, Clarksville, TN 37044, USA

J. B. LAYZER

US Fish and Wildlife Service, Tennessee Cooperative Fishery Research Unit, Tennessee Tech University, Cookeville, TN 38505, USA

and

I. A. RUSSELL

South African National Parks Board, Wilderness National Park, PO Box 35, Wilderness 6560, South Africa

INTRODUCTION

The demand for clean potable water is increasing with human population growth. In most cases, this is met by the withdrawal, inter-basin transfer, or impoundment of those riverine ecosystems that remain relatively undisturbed. The alteration of flows to satisfy human needs and subsequent impacts on ecosystem integrity grow in importance as the predictability of the hydrograph declines. Thus, one might expect that the arid and semi-arid river systems of the world will witness the greatest change from the smallest alterations.

The arid and semi-arid river systems are among the least studied yet may constitute the majority of lotic ecosystems on this planet. It is difficult, at this time, to determine if current theories of lotic ecosystem dynamics and derived management practices are applicable to these systems (Williams, 1988). However, these questions must be answered rapidly and best management practices initiated to conserve the fauna and flora of these unique systems. Since many of these regions (sub-Saharan Africa, for example) are also inhabited by the fastest-growing human populations and subject to the most immediate changes in flow and structure, the need for answers to river conservation and management problems will be intensified.

Southern Africa limnologists and hydrologists have lately become concerned about the viability of their river ecosystems and have established working groups to assess the techniques available to predict and evaluate minimum flow needs (Ferrar, 1989; Bruwer, in press). No formal decisions have been made, but sentiment leans towards models that are based on the response of aquatic organisms to changes in river flow. Gore (1989a) suggested some priorities for establishing minimum flows in that region and stated that minimum flow requirements for biota are only part of a package of management decisions which must be made to properly maintain ecosystem integrity. No single model can answer all user-related changes to a single river ecosystem.

The Instream Flow Incremental Methodology (IFIM) (Bovee, 1982) is one technique to predict minimum flows to protect biota when water quality considerations are not a concern or have been ameliorated by other management practices. IFIM is a set of techniques that assesses the flow patterns of typical stream reaches and attempts to correlate these patterns with the hydraulic preferences (that is, preferences for velocity, depth, substrate, and cover (both riparian and as hydraulic refugia)) of target species of concern. IFIM is based on the assumption that biota in running water have their distribution and certain phases of their life cycles controlled by the hydraulic conditions of the running-water environment. Statzner et al (1988) support this view and suggest that changes in flow patterns (i.e. hydraulic heterogeneity) are a major template controlling zonation of lotic biota. The essence of IFIM is contained within the Physical Habitat Simulation (PHABSIM) (Milhous et al, 1989, provide information on the latest version), a set of sub-routines to manipulate, calibrate, and correlate field-measured hydraulic and biological information into a prediction of available habitat over a range of discharges. The field effort requires, at a minimum, selection of transects across a typical stream reach so that the most upstream and most downstream transects cross hydraulic controls. At each transect, measurements of mean water column velocity (and often surface and near-substrate velocities), depth, substrate character, and presence of overhead cover are recorded at frequent intervals (called cells) (a minimum of 20 measurements). The cell-by-cell data are used in hydraulic simulations to predict changes in these parameters at other discharges and water surface elevations. Nestler et al (1989) provided a review of this technique.

PHABSIM combines these hydraulic predictions with preference data (suitability curves) for target species to predict the available habitat (expressed as weighted usable area (WUA), weighted usable volume (WUV), or weighted usable bottom area (WUBA), as appropriate) at critical flow levels. Bovee (1986) and Gore (1989b) have proposed various methods to acquire and calculate suitability curves for fish, benthos, and other instream uses (i.e. wading, recreational boating, etc.). The inflection point on the curve of habitat availability (where habitat values decline rapidly with decreasing discharge) is usually considered to be the point of minimum acceptable flow to maintain the integrity of the target species population or life-stage. Although there have been a number of criticisms about the ability of PHABSIM to predict density and biomass (Mathur et al, 1985; Scott and Shirvell, 1987; Shirvell, 1989), Gore and Nestler (1988) point out that the appropriate application of this management tool is to advise stream managers on appropriate flow releases rather than attempting to force the model to become an ecological predictor of changes in density and community dynamics.

During research investigations into the application of IFIM to southern African rivers, we attempted to use IFIM to assess minimum flows on the Sabie River in Kruger National Park, South Africa. Traditional uses of IFIM target one or two fish species of concern. However, this study was initiated to determine if IFIM could be used as one of many management tools to maintain the highest possible biotic diversity in this river ecosystem. Where fish assemblages are complex, Leonard and Orth (1988) have recommended that habitat guilds are the appropriate target for instream flow management. We chose to examine target species and habitat guilds in an effort to determine flows which provided the greatest amount of usable habitat. Our application of IFIM was both traditional, in which we examined some target fish species of concern (threatened or endangered), and non-traditional in approach. The non-traditional applications included assessment of the riverine requirements of a pool-dwelling large vertebrate (*Hippopotamus amphibius*) and an attempt to determine if management to maintain the highest diversity of hydraulic conditions correlated well with the highest diversity of fish species and met other biotic demands (i.e. riparian vegetation, etc.). Layzer et al (in press) examined the diversity of hydraulic conditions in several river ecosystems and indicated that high diversity of hydraulic conditions is predictable and correlates well with diversity of fish species which have major niche conditions influenced by flow. This application of IFIM may be the most appropriate in rivers where a high degree of endemism requires protection of all species rather than management of a commercial or game fishery.

MATERIALS AND METHODS

Study site

Kruger National Park is located in the north-eastern corner of the Republic of South Africa in the Transvaal Province. It shares northern borders with Zimbabwe and eastern borders with Mozambique (Figure 11.1). Having a total area of 19 485 km^2, Kruger Park is one of the world's major sub-tropical and tropical savannah nature reserves (Paynter and Nussey, 1986). One of the major vulnerabilities of the park is that it is transected by six major river systems whose flows and water quality can be controlled by structures and agencies external to the park. The government of South Africa is conducting ongoing negotiations with Zimbabwe and Mozambique on the best joint utilization of the rivers flowing into Kruger National Park and may include minimum flow agreements (Department of Water Affairs, 1986; Bruwer, in press).

The Sabie River, a type 8 braided channel system (Rogers and van der Zel, 1989), remains one of the least impacted of the major river systems in the park area. However, a regional water supply scheme is presently under construction for the government of Gazankulu which will extract 1.63 million m^3 per annum. Typical of a tropical river

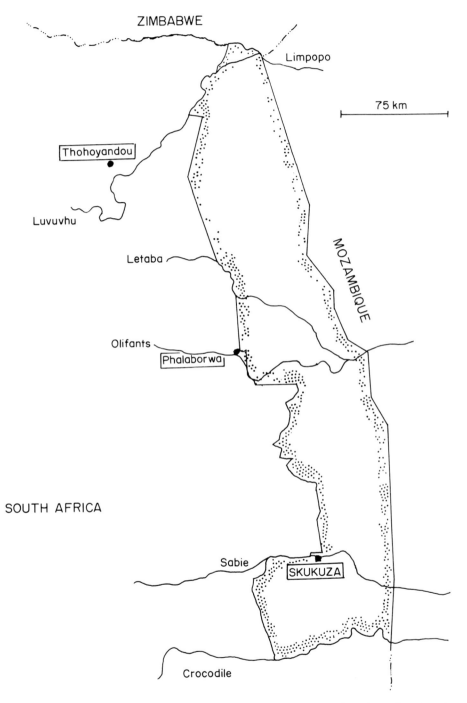

FIGURE 11.1. Generalized map of Kruger National Park showing location of major rivers and village of Skukuza

drainage, the Sabie is slightly alkaline with pH values ranging from 7.6 to 8.3 and water temperatures ranging from 19.3° C in the headwaters to 25° C in the lowland areas (Pienaar, 1978). Substrate varies from large boulders and bedrock in the upper drainage to sand and gravel in large pool areas. Riparian vegetation is typical of the area dominated by *Syzygium guineense*, *Diospyros mespiliformis*, and *Ficus sycomorus* with many beds of *Phragmites mauritianus* lining the river. During the dry season (April to October) the river is relatively clear while the rainy season (November to March) brings turbulent and muddy flows. During our study, in August 1989, flows were low (discharge approximately 4 m^3 s^{-1} (cumecs)) and ideal for assessing minimum flow conditions.

Field methods

Five transects were established at a typical stream reach along the Sabie near the village of Skukuza. The uppermost two transects were across high-gradient riffles with boulder, bedrock, and large cobbled substrates, the next two transects downstream across a deep pool with a sand and gravel substrate, and the most downstream transect across a shallow run (hydraulic control) of gravel and small and medium cobble. Each transect was surveyed according to techniques described by Bovee (1982) and measurements of mean water column velocity, depth, and channel index (Table 11.1) were recorded at intervals of one metre along each transect.

At the Skukuza site (SKU) as well as three other sites located at the western edge of the park (WSS), upstream of Skukuza (AMS), and downstream of Skukuza (BUH),

TABLE 11.1. Substrate/cover code used in the Sabie River study. (The code was entered as three digits in the form "xx.x")

TENS DIGIT	(cover) (visually estimated)
1	<25% Overhead cover
2	25–50% Overhead cover
3	51–75% Overhead cover
4	>75% Overhead cover
ONES DIGIT	(refuge value)
1	No cover
2	Object cover (hydraulic refuge) only
3	Overhead cover only
4	Overhead and object cover
TENTHS DIGIT	(substrate composition) (visual estimate)
1	Fines (sand and smaller)
2	Small gravel (4–25 mm diameter)
3	Medium gravel (25–50 mm)
4	Large gravel (50–75 mm)
5	Small cobble (75–150 mm)
6	Medium cobble (150–225 mm)
7	Large cobble (225–300 mm)
8	Small boulder (300–600 mm)
9	Large boulder (>600 mm)

approximately one day was spent collecting fish by electrofishing and direct observation. For each fish collected and identified, measurements of mean water column velocity, depth, and channel index were recorded. At each of the sites other than SKU, a set of four transects was established at random intervals across the sampling area and at least 50 total measurements of mean water column velocity, depth, and channel index were recorded. These data, plus the normal survey data at SKU, were used to determine the frequency distribution and diversity of these hydraulic parameters at each site. Frequency of capture of fish species was also recorded in order to produce indices of diversity and species richness.

Methods of analysis

As the amount of time available for hydrologic surveys was limited, measurements at Skukuza were only taken for one discharge condition. Water surface elevations for a range of discharges between 1.7 and 8.27 m^3 s^{-1} were predicted and calibrated by application of the MANSQ sub-routine of PHABSIM. Hydraulic simulations of velocity and depth conditions for each water surface elevation were predicted through IFG4.

Although as many as 19 species of fish were captured at some sites, only three species were collected in sufficient numbers to warrant calculation of Class III preference curves. These fish were the bow-stripe barb (*Barbus viviparus*), the lowveld large-mouth (*Serranochromis meridianus*), and the bearded or lowveld catlet (*Chiloglanis swierstrai*). In addition, after interviews with Park biologists, a set of Class I curves for the hippopotamus (*Hippopotamus amphibius*) were also produced for prediction of available habitat. We predicted available habitat as weighted usable area (WUA) over the range of discharges for individual transects (by HABTAE) and the entire surveyed reach (by HABTAT) at the Skukuza site.

Those species most sensitive to changes in water velocity are likely to be first affected by reductions in flow (Bovee, 1982; Statzner et al, 1988). We chose, then, to examine the diversity of velocities available at each discharge simulated at each site and attempt a correlation with species diversity and richness. This correlation suggested that a plot of diversity of velocities against the range of discharges of concern would also provide another discharge for management consideration; that is, the discharge or range of discharges at which the highest diversity of velocities are maintained at the reference site. The analysis of diversity of velocities and discharge was accomplished through simulation by IFG4 from our calibration set. Velocities were converted to frequency histograms at intervals of 3 cm s^{-1} of velocity and diversity of velocities calculated with the Shannon index (Pielou, 1975).

RESULTS

Habitat suitability curves for the target species are listed in the Appendix. Among the fish species, both *Serranochromis* juveniles and *Barbus viviparus* were pool-dwellers with *B. viviparus* being slightly more tolerant of moderate velocities (up to 60 cm s^{-1}). Both species preferred shallow pools (up to 2.5 m). Substrate preferences were also quite similar with a preference for sand and gravel with significant overhead cover (50–75%

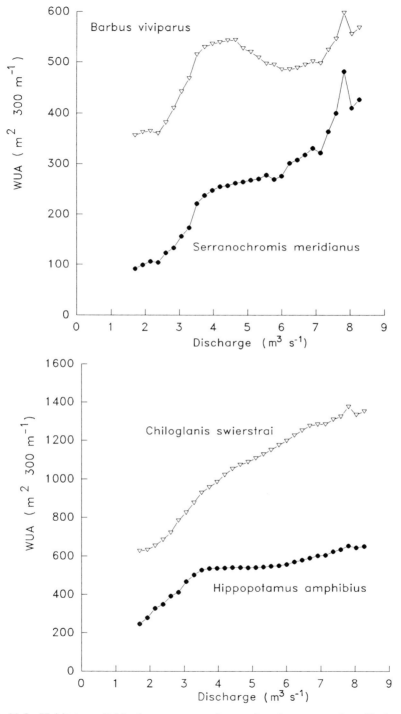

FIGURE 11.2. Habitat available for target species at the site surveyed at Skukuza. Available habitat is expressed as weighted usable area (WUA)

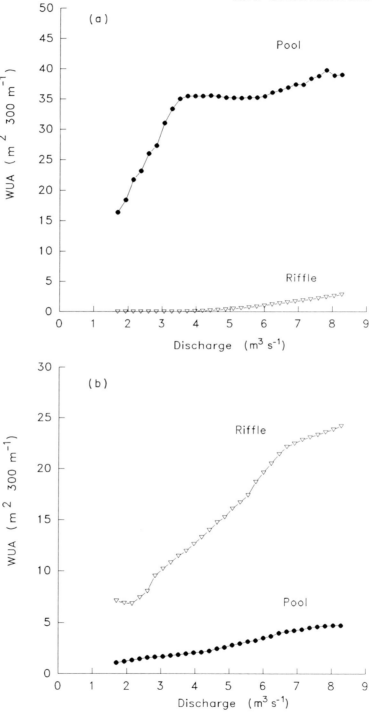

FIGURE 11.3. Available habitat in pools and riffles for (a) pool-dwelling species and (b) riffle-dwelling species. Based upon mean WUA values for all pool transects (solid circles) or all riffle transects (open triangles) for all species within that habitat guild

for *Serranochromis* and over 75% for *Barbus*). Thus, both of these species were classified as pool- and edge-dwelling species. The rock catlet (*Chiloglanis*) appeared to be a typical riffle dweller. Although tolerant of slower speeds and occurring at times in pools, *Chiloglanis* was a riffle dweller found primarily in shallow waters (<50 cm) with velocities between 35 and 150 cm s^{-1} passing over substrates ranging from small to large cobbles and boulders. There was no apparent preference for overhead cover.

Based upon observation and discussion with Park biologists, our *Hippopotamus* curve indicated that velocities up to 60 cm s^{-1} could be easily tolerated but individuals were restricted to a range of depths between 1.5 and 3 m. Preferred substrates ranged from deposited fines to small gravel with equal preference for overhead cover but slightly greater preference for more open water.

The results of the simulations of habitat availability by HABTAT (Figure 11.2) suggest that a minimum flow of 3.5 m^3 s^{-1} will maintain pool-dwelling species like *Barbus viviparus* and *Hippopotamus* while habitat for *Serranochromis meridianus* will be substantially reduced. The riffle dweller (*Chiloglanis*) will lose habitat at a rather steady rate as discharges decline. However, below discharges of 6.5 m^3 s^{-1}, this decline in *Chiloglanis* habitat increases in rate of incremental loss. An evaluation of individual transects, by HABTAE simulation, clarified the point at which minimum discharges might be recommended. An evaluation of pool transects only for pool habitat species (Figure 11.3(a))

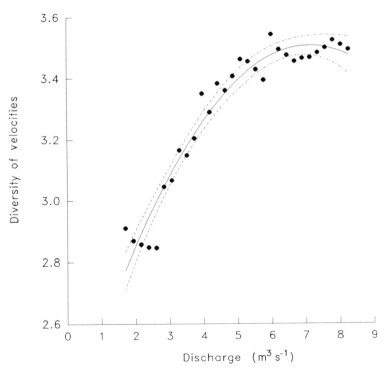

FIGURE 11.4. Regression (with 95% confidence interval (broken lines)) of diversity of predicted velocities and discharges simulated by IFG4 for transects on the Sabie River. Inclusive of the data points: $H_v = 2.24 + 0.35Q - 0.03Q^2$, where H_v is diversity of velocities and Q is discharge ($r^2 = 0.97$)

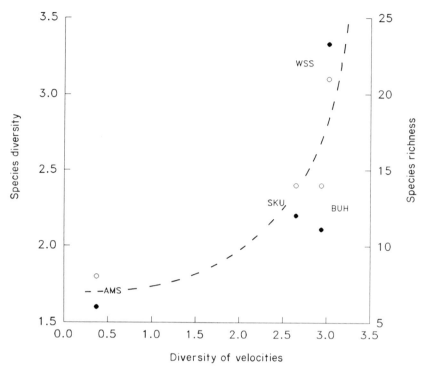

FIGURE 11.5. Relationship (with proposed trend (broken line)) between species diversity (●) and species richness (○) and diversity of velocities at transects on the Sabie River

suggests a minimum flow of 3.5 m³ s⁻¹ while riffle transects, evaluated for riffle dwellers, show the greatest amounts of habitat loss at discharges below 6 m³ s⁻¹ (Figure 11.3(b)).

Correlations between diversity of velocities at all stations and discharge is quite high (Figure 11.4), suggesting that a discharge of 6.5 m³ s⁻¹ or higher will maintain the greatest amount of diverse velocities in a given reach. Although the data points are few, a significant correlation between both diversity and species richness and diversity of velocities is indicated (Figure 11.5). Both richness and species diversity increase rapidly when velocity diversity is above a value of 2.75. A minimum flow to maintain velocity diversity of at least 2.75 is a discharge of 2.5 m³ s⁻¹ at the surveyed station at Skukuza (Figure 11.4).

DISCUSSION AND CONCLUSIONS

Bovee (1982) indicated that riffle-dwelling organisms are the appropriate targets for minimum flow analysis since these will be the first organisms to lose suitable habitat when an area is dewatered. This is borne out on the Sabie, where *Chiloglanis* would probably require a minimum flow of 6 m³ s⁻¹, much higher than the other target species. However, it is interesting to note that unusual depth preferences of pool-dwelling species, such as those of the hippopotamus (where minimum depths are significantly higher than 50 cm), also provide good, sharp indications of minimum allowable flows. This supports conclusions reached by Chutter (1969), who indicated that pool species must also be present to maintain ecosystem integrity and unusual hydraulic requirements might be ignored if concentration is exclusively upon riffle-dwellers. The narrow range of depth preferences for the hippopotamus also indicates that maintaining flows (about 1 m^3 s^{-1}) which simply leave isolated pools is not sufficient to maintain habitat for some pool dwellers. In the case of the hippopotamus, flows which still maintain riffles (albeit at less than minimum available habitat for riffle species) and connect pools along the length of the river must be considered as the minimum for hippopotamus populations.

Our results emphasize the need to establish management goals before field surveys are conducted and preconceived notions regarding discharge patterns and needs are implemented as a portion of a regulated stream programme. Gore and Nestler (1988) and Gore (1989a) have emphasized the need for an interdisciplinary decision prior to the initiation of research on minimum flow reservations. That is, all resource agencies and water-user groups who will either control or derive benefit from the application of new management practices must agree on the goal of the resource management strategy. Are the agencies willing to accept the loss of a certain percentage of habitat or species populations (even whole species populations) in order to provide the greatest benefit to the group of instream users? The tenor of these decisions will create a wide range of allowable minimum flows. On the Sabie River, a realistic minimum discharge (depending upon goal) will range from 2.5 to 6.5 m^3 s^{-1}.

If the goal is simply to preserve the habitat of an endangered fish species (say, *Serranochromis*) the recommended minimum flow might be 3.5 m^3 s^{-1} (Figure 11.2). If that discharge is maintained for most of the year, one might expect greater than a 50% reduction in maintenance habitat available to *Chiloglanis*. That minimum flow would most likely maintain all other fish species except for high-velocity riffle dwellers. Maintenance of flows to provide good habitat for *Chiloglanis*, on the other hand, may be unrealistically high in consideration of demands for irrigation or a drawdown in order to provide particularly high flushing flows. Indeed, if no historical hydrograph has been examined, it may be that some recommended flows are exceeded for such a small portion of the time in any given water year that the recommended flow is absurdly high or impossible to create or maintain. This most often occurs in semi-arid river systems where the floodplain has the potential to provide significant wetted habitat but is only wetted for a small portion of the year.

Although Leonard and Orth (1988) and Bain and Boltz (1989) feel that the habitat guild is the appropriate level of flow indication in most instream flow studies, even these results must be tempered with wise judgement and agreement between stream managers. If the majority of pool dwellers are of particular concern on the Sabie, for example, a minimum discharge of 4 m^3 s^{-1} (Figure 11.3(a)) would be preferred to the minimum of 6.5 m^3 s^{-1} predicted by the riffle curves (Figure 11.3(b)). A 60% loss in habitat potential for riffle dwellers may be considered acceptable if this guarantees preservation of the majority of species of concern, since a greater amount of water will be available for other instream flow uses (irrigation, industry, etc.).

Finally, management to maintain highest diversity of fish species presents yet a third set of management options that must be agreed upon before management of new flow strategies. There is a good correlation between the diversity of hydraulic conditions and fish species diversity (Figure 11.4; Layzer et al, in press). When the object of management will be the maintenance of highest possible diversity of species, regardless of guild membership or conservation status, we suggest that flows which maintain appropriate hydraulic diversities be considered for targets of flow regulation. On the Sabie River, the greatest increases in fish diversity occurred when the diversity of mean velocity conditions was greater than 2.75 (Figure 11.5). This translates, then, to an absolute minimum discharge of $2 \, m^3 \, s^{-1}$, which will maintain a minimum diversity of fish fauna (Figure 11.4). However, a minimum discharge of $3 \, m^3 \, s^{-1}$ increases the diversity of hydraulic conditions (and, therefore, available niche conditions), and should yield a community with higher species diversity. On the Sabie River, the relationship between increased species diversity and hydraulic diversity peaks at approximately $6 \, m^3 \, s^{-1}$. Thus, if such flows could be regulated annually and in consideration of other instream needs, maintenance of flows at or near $6 \, m^3 \, s^{-1}$ should yield a variety of flow habitats to support the highest possible fish diversity. If such flows cannot be managed, the relationships displayed in Figures 11.4 and 11.5 can be used by stream managers to negotiate a minimum flow with the slightest loss of habitat (and presumably species populations) of target species for management.

These sets of curves cannot be considered the final product to be used in negotiating flow reservations. At least one necessary element for maintaining the integrity of the Sabie River ecosystem was not analysed; that is, the fish food source, the macroinvertebrates. Gore (1989b) points out that macroinvertebrates, being less mobile, are likely to have narrower ranges of tolerances to hydraulic change, particularly to changes in velocity (see also discussions by Statzner et al, 1988). Although we did not sample benthic invertebrates in this study, it is necessary to maintain habitat for the food base of insectivorous fish (e.g. *Chiloganis* and *B. viviparus*) in the system. It will be necessary to acquire quantitative samples of benthic macroinvertebrates and develop suitability curves for benthic community diversity (Gore, 1989b, discusses the techniques). However, based upon curves developed for other South African rivers (Arlesa Fouts, University of Tulsa, pers. comm.), we provide a preliminary and speculative curve of available habitat at the Skukuza site on the Sabie River (Figure 11.6). This curve indicates that optimal conditions are maintained between 5 and $7.5 \, m^3 \, s^{-1}$ with a minimum at about $4 \, m^3 \, s^{-1}$. Again, this emphasizes the importance of riffle-dwelling organisms or communities as targets of analysis in minimum-flow prediction. Because there is considerable debate about the transferability of curves from one river system to another (Gore and Nestler, 1988; Bain and Boltz, 1989), these conclusions about benthic distributions must be validated by on-site sampling of benthic organisms.

As in most stream management studies, more field data will increase the reliability of the minimum flow predictions. For example, field-measured water surface elevations at all of the discharges in question as well as calibrated transects at flow conditions will substantially increase the accuracy of the hydraulic simulation. Inclusion of habitat analysis for other trophic levels in the complex food web of the Sabie will ensure that unusual requirements of key species have not been ignored. At a minimum, we feel that suitability curves for benthic community diversity should be produced. We reiterate that these conclusions are only a portion of the data sets which must be considered by stream managers when determining flow regimes to maintain biotic integrity. Among other considerations, instream flow demands for flushing and floodplain spawning as well as

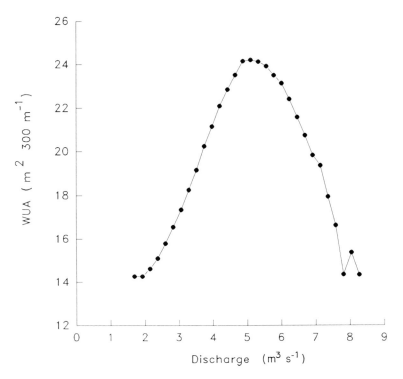

FIGURE 11.6. Speculated relationship between available habitat for diversity of benthic inverte-brates and low flow discharges on the Sabie River. Based upon suitability curves derived from data on rivers in other parts of South Africa

volumetric demands to maintain water quality, riparian vegetation, and industrial, domestic, and agricultural consumption must also be considered. Our study has provided an initial set of discharges for river managers to consider. These can and must be modified as new sets of data on other instream flow demands are considered. Although not a perfect predictor, IFIM remains the best current tool for establishing guidelines to preserve biota of regulated streams.

APPENDIX

Figures 11.A1 and 11.A2 show habitat suitability curves for target species used in IFIM studies of the Sabie River. "Suitability" is defined as the preference (ranging from least to greatest frequency of occurrence) of that species for a physical habitat condition weighted by the frequency of occurrence of all habitat categories in the reach where individuals were sampled. Suitability values range from 0 (unsuitable) to 1 (100% suitable). Thus, if the frequency of occurrence of individuals of a species is identical to the frequency of occurrence of each of the habitat categories (arbitrarily set, usually at increments of 10 cm of depth or 10 cm s^{-1} of velocity), the resulting suitability "curve" would be a horizontal line at a value of 1 (all habitat categories of 100% suitability). Detailed methodologies for determining suitability curves have been described by Gore and Judy (1981) and Bovee (1982).

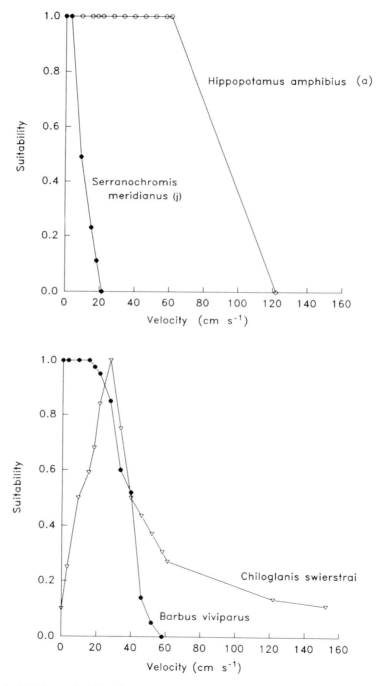

FIGURE 11.A1. Habitat suitability for mean water current velocity for *Hippopotamus amphibius* adults (a) (open circles), *Serranochromis meridianus* juveniles (j) (solid circles, upper plot), *Barbus viviparus* (adults and juveniles) (solid circles, lower plot), and *Chiloglanis swierstrai* (adults and juveniles) (open triangles) collected on the Sabie River, Kruger National Park

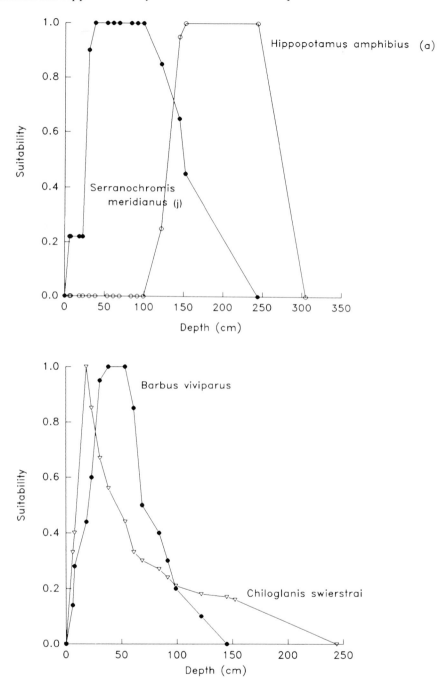

FIGURE 11.A2. Habitat suitability for depth for *Hippopotamus amphibius* adults (a) (open circles), *Serranochromis meridianus* juveniles (j) (solid circles, upper plot), *Barbus viviparus* (adults and juveniles) (solid circles, lower plot), and *Chiloglanis swierstrai* (adults and juveniles) (open triangles) collected on the Sabie River, Kruger National Park

ACKNOWLEDGEMENTS

We thank Mr D. J. Alletson (Natal Parks Board), Mr C. A. Bruwer (Department of Water Affairs), Ms Lesa Fouts (University of Tulsa), and Dr J. M. King (University of Cape Town) for their assistance in field work. We also thank the staff of Kruger National Park for their provision of housing and transportation and particularly Mr Peter Retief for use of computer facilities. Funding for this project was provided through a Fulbright Senior Research Fellowship to JAG as well as project funds from the Foundation for Research Development, Council for Science and Industrial Research, Pretoria.

REFERENCES

Bain, M. B., and Boltz, J. M. (1989). *Regulated streamflow and warmwater stream fish: a general hypothesis and research agenda*, US Fish and Wildlife Service, Biological Report 89(18), Washington, DC.

Bovee, K. D. (1982). "A guide to stream habitat analysis using the instream flow incremental methodology", Instream Flow Information Paper No. 12, US Fish and Wildlife Service, FWS/OBS-82/26, Washington, DC.

Bovee, K. D. (1986). "Development and evaluation of habitat suitability criteria for use in the instream flow incremental methodology", Instream Flow Information Paper No. 21, US Fish and Wildlife Service, Biological Report 86(7), Washington, DC.

Bruwer, C. (Ed.) (in press). *Flow requirements of Kruger National Park rivers, and impact of proposed water resources development. Part I: Water requirements at the critical level*, Department of Water Affairs, Technical Report, Pretoria.

Chutter, F. M. (1969). "The distribution of stream invertebrates in relation to current speed", *Internationale Revue gesamten Hydrobiologie*, **54**, 413–422.

Department of Water Affairs (1986). *Management of the Water Resources of the Republic of South Africa*, The Department of Water Affairs, Pretoria.

Ferrar, A. A. (Ed.) (1989). *Ecological flow requirements for South African rivers*, South African National Science Program, Report Number 162, FRD/CSIR, Pretoria.

Gore, J. A. (1989a). "Setting priorities for minimum flow assessments in Southern Africa", *South African Journal of Science*, **85**, 614–615.

Gore, J. A. (1989b). "Models for predicting benthic macroinvertebrate habitat suitability under regulated flows", in *Alternatives in Regulated River Management* (Eds J. A. Gore and G. E. Petts), pp. 253–265, CRC Press, Boca Raton, Florida.

Gore, J. A., and Judy, R. D., Jr (1981). "Predictive models of benthic macroinvertebrate density for use in instream flow studies and regulated river management", *Canadian Journal of Fisheries and Aquatic Sciences*, **38**, 1363–1370.

Gore, J. A., and Nestler, J. M. (1988). "Instream flow studies in perspective", *Regulated Rivers: Research and Management*, **2**, 93–101.

Layzer, J. B., Russell, I. A., and Gore, J. A. (in press). "Determining instream flows for maintaining habitats of diverse fish assemblages", *Rivers*.

Leonard, P. M., and Orth, D. J. (1988). "Use of habitat guilds of fishes to determine instream flow requirements", *North American Journal of Fisheries Management*, **8**, 399–409.

Mathur, D., Bason, W. H., Purdy, E. J., Jr, and Silver, C. A. (1985). "A critique of the instream flow incremental methodology", *Canadian Journal of Fisheries and Aquatic Science*, **42**, 825–831.

Milhous, R. T., Updike, M. A., and Schneider, D. M. (1989). "Physical Habitat Simulation system reference manual—Version II", Instream Flow Information Paper No. 26, US Fish and Wildlife Service, Biological Report 89(16), Washington, DC.

Nestler, J. M., Milhous, R. T., and Layzer, J. B. (1989). "Instream habitat modeling techniques", in *Alternatives in Regulated River Management* (Eds J. A. Gore and G. E. Petts), pp. 295–315, CRC Press, Boca Raton, Florida.

Paynter, D., and Nussey, W. (1986). *Kruger. Portrait of a National Park*, Southern Book Publ., Johannesburg.

Pielou, E. C. (1975). *Ecological Diversity*, Wiley-Interscience, New York.

Pienaar, U. de V. (1978). *The Freshwater Fishes of the Kruger National Park*, National Parks Board, Pretoria.

Rogers, K. H., and van der Zel, D. W. (1989). "Water quantity requirements of riparian vegetation and floodplains" in *Ecological Flow Requirements for South African Rivers* (Ed. A. A. Ferrar), pp. 94–109, South African National Science Program, Report Number 162, Foundation for Research Development/CSIR, Pretoria.

Scott, D., and Shirvell, C. S. (1987). "A critique of the instream flow incremental methodology with observations on flow determination in New Zealand", in *Regulated Streams: Advances in Ecology* (Eds B. Kemper and J. F. Craig), pp. 27–43, Plenum Press, New York.

Shirvell, C. S. (1989). "Ability of PHABSIM to predict Chinook salmon spawning habitat", *Regulated Rivers*: *Research and Management*, **3**, 277–289.

Statzner, B., Gore, J. A., and Resh, V. H. (1988). "Hydraulic stream ecology: observed patterns and potential applications", *Journal of the North American Benthological Society*, **7**, 307–360.

Williams, W. D. (1988). "Limnological imbalances: an antipodean viewpoint", *Freshwater Biology*, **20**, 407–420.

12

Importance of a Habitat-level Classification System to Design Instream Flow Studies

J. L. KERSHNER

USDA Forest Service, Department of Fisheries and Wildlife, College of Natural Resources, Utah State University, Logan, UT 84322-5210, USA

and

W. M. SNIDER

California Department of Fish and Game, 1416 Ninth Street, Sacramento, CA 95814, USA

INTRODUCTION

Planners of instream flow studies must determine what scale(s) of physical and biological function are needed to make accurate assessments of flow changes on aquatic organisms. In addition, it is often assumed that information gathered at one scale relates to information at other scales. In order to describe these relationships, however, the variables or attributes that make up a particular scale must be defined along with descriptions of how each scale integrates with the others.

Approaches to instream flow studies have used various scales. Planning-level studies at large scales often focus on determining a percentage of annual discharge in a basin (Tennant, 1976) to maintain ecosystem function. However, the majority of instream flow techniques use a hierarchical procedure to categorize stream physical habitat. Information on fish habitat use and life-history requirements are then integrated with the physical information for each scale to determine relationships between flow changes and habitat availability (Waters, 1976; White, 1976; Wesche and Rechard, 1980; Bovee, 1982). Waters (1976) used microhabitat variables to predict how much resting, spawning, and food-producing habitat was needed by various salmonids. Microhabitat measurements along transects of velocity, depth, substrate, and cover were used to quantify habitat for each activity at different flows. Similarly, White (1976) defined microhabitat criteria for

River Conservation and Management. Edited by P. J. Boon, P. Calow, and G. E. Petts
© 1992 John Wiley & Sons Ltd

spawning, rearing, and fish passage and coupled a hydraulic model with these criteria to develop predictions of flow effects on fisheries.

The most widely used instream flow technique in the United States is the Instream Flow Incremental Methodology (IFIM) developed by the US Fish and Wildlife Service (Bovee and Milhous, 1978; Bovee, 1982). Information from this is used in the Physical Habitat Simulation model (PHABSIM) to generate flow/habitat relationships. This combines a physical model of channel and flow conditions with information on species microhabitat use. Traditionally, microhabitat data have been collected by selecting a species/life-stage of interest and gathering sufficient information to describe patterns of habitat use accurately (Bovee and Cochnauer, 1977). Frequency distributions of the range of conditions selected by sampled fish are then calculated to determine the suitability of various microhabitat conditions. These suitability-of-use functions are hydraulic data at different flows to determine a weighted usable area (WUA) of habitat for a particular species and life-stage. This is used to predict the effects of various flow alternatives on habitat availability on the species and life-stage of interest.

Bovee (1982) recommends that the study area be stratified on two scales: (1) study segments (areas that exhibit similar physical character) and (2) study reaches that are selected based on representative characteristics of microhabitat within a segment or based on critical habitat characteristics thought to be important for a particular life-stage of a species. Such a strategy should effectively estimate habitat conditions within the study area. Our experience (Snider et al, 1987) using this approach had left us with a number of questions regarding the integration of information at the different scales. Specifically, we questioned whether representative reaches accurately represented conditions within a given area, and whether microhabitat data gathered in a variety of streams or even different areas of one stream reflected suitable habitat for a particular species or life-stage. While the importance of microhabitat selection to explain fish distribution has been well documented (e.g. Shirvell and Dungey, 1983), fish also appear to select habitat at other scales (channel unit, reach).

For example, in Alaskan streams, Murphy et al (1987) found that channels classified using reach-level characterizations were accurate predictors of some anadromous fish densities. In Oregon, geomorphically unconstrained reaches had larger numbers of juvenile salmonids than constrained reaches (Gordon Reeves, US Forest Service, Corvallis, Oregon, pers. comm.). At the mesohabitat level (e.g. riffles and pools) relationships between fish densities and type of habitat have also been observed. Moore and Gregory (1988) observed higher cutthroat trout fry densities in lateral stream habitats. Both Bisson et al (1988) and Sullivan (1986) describe relationships between individual habitats and their use by coho salmon, steelhead, and cutthroat trout.

Based on our review, we believed that integrating objective reach criteria and a mesohabitat classification into the approach described by Bovee (1982) could enhance the effectiveness of instream flow studies. Similar hierarchies have been used by other workers (Frissell et al, 1986) with success in basin planning applications. Although current methods do use a hierarchical approach to define study sites, the relationships at the mesohabitat scale are not adequately described in these methods. To effectively model the potential effects of flow changes on a given stream site, we believe the following information is necessary: (1) an accurate characterization of channel and habitat characteristics based on objective, repeatable criteria; (2) information on habitat use at each scale; and (3) modelling strategies that effectively combine physical and biological information from the above.

APPROACH

Three units of scale are described in the initial approach (Figure 12.1). These scales—reach, mesohabitat, and microhabitat—were the primary focus of the approach. We initially included stream segments (Bovee, 1982), but felt that the definition was adequate for our purposes and that the questions we had about habitat relationships had primarily centred on these other scales. Several reach-level classifications have been described for streams (Leopold and Wolman, 1957; Rosgen, 1985). We used a system described by Rosgen (1985) which had objective criteria that were easily measured in the field. Five variables were measured to determine discrete reaches: dominant substrate, channel gradient, landform feature, sinuosity, and width/depth ratio.

At the mesohabitat level, individual habitats were classified using a system described by Bisson et al (1982). Twenty-two habitat types were used in this approach. Each habitat unit is based on a set of physical criteria including velocity character, depth profile, location in channel, and forming constraint for pool types (Helm, 1985). Surveyors use illustrated guides to define the habitat, and measure unit length, width, mean depth, and maximum depth.

Microhabitat was quantified as a function of individual mesohabitats. We selected a transect-based approach to determine microhabitat in each mesohabitat. This gave us an accurate assessment of the velocity, depth, substrate, and cover conditions at each unit and information necessary to model habitat/flow relationships.

To determine fish habitat relationships at the various scales, some form of stratified population sampling is necessary. Sampling followed Hankin and Reeves (1988), where

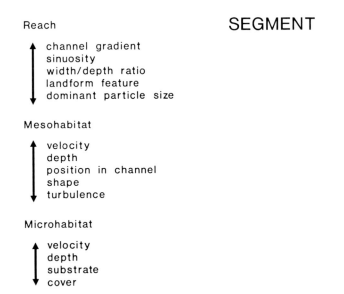

FIGURE 12.1. Proposed habitat hierarchy at the segment scale for designing instream flow studies

fish were sampled using a stratified random sample of habitats in a study area. Fish-distribution information can then be aggregated or disaggregated, depending on the scale of interest. Microhabitat selection by individual fish was determined at the mesohabitat scale and could be aggregated at other scales based on the investigator's approach. Microhabitat observations were made by divers entering each unit at the downstream end and observing the exact position of individual fish. This location was recorded by measuring the length of the fish and noting the exact position in the water column. Measurements of focal depth and velocity, mean column depth and velocity, and cell substrate were noted for each fish (Kershner, 1990).

Study area

The Truckee River is a major river system in east-central California and west-central Nevada. The main Truckee River originates in the Sierra Nevada mountains, flows into Lake Tahoe exiting in the north-west corner of the lake, and flows in a north-easterly direction to its terminus in Pyramid Lake. The Truckee River system has been regulated for over 120 years and provides water for irrigation, municipal and industrial use, and power generation. As the human population of this drainage basin has grown, the Truckee River and its tributaries have been scrutinized for the potential to provide more of the area's water needs.

In July 1986 the California Department of Fish and Game and the US Forest Service agreed to study portions of the basin to quantify instream flow needs for fish in the Truckee and its major tributaries. The following are insights gained while undertaking this study. Our initial approach focused on the two primary sport fish in the study streams, rainbow trout (*Oncorhynchus mykiss*) and brown trout (*Salmo trutta*). For the purposes of this chapter we will focus only on brown trout as the numbers of rainbow trout microhabitat observations over the period were insufficient for a detailed analysis.

Observations of mesohabitat/reach scale relationships

Initially we mapped six streams (third and fourth order) using this approach (Kershner and Snider, in preparation). We chose streams that seemed to represent habitat conditions available throughout the basin. Stream reach types (Table 12.1) in the study streams ranged from high-gradient (Type A), to intermediate-gradient (Type B), to low-gradient (Type C) (Rosgen, 1985). The largest number of stream reaches sampled were

TABLE 12.1. Characteristics of channel reach units

	A type	B type	C type
Gradient	4–10%	1.5–4%	0.1–1%
Sinuosity	1–1.4	1.2–2	1.5–2.5
Width/depth ratio	10 or less	8–20	3–30
Dominant substrate	Silt-bedrock	Silt-bedrock	Silt-bedrock
Landform feature	Variable	Variable	Variable

(Rosgen, 1985)

TABLE 12.2. Mean percentage area, coefficient of variation, and Kruskal–Wallace statistic for each habitat by stream type

	A (N=3)		B (N=11)		C (N=4)		PROB<(CHISQ)
	$\bar{X}$	CV	$\bar{X}$	CV	$\bar{X}$	CV	
Low-gradient riffle	17.8	80	56.1	40.3	71.2	7	0.05[a]
High-gradient riffle	32.3	149	2.9	125	0.4	200	0.23
Cascade	0.3	173	0.1	332	0.2	200	0.5
Backwater	—	—	0.1	332	0.1	200	0.17
Trench pool	2.0	156	0.1	250	—	—	0.1
Plunge pool	8.1	167	2.9	129	0.3	85	0.1
Lateral-scour pool (Tree)	1.9	89	1.6	114	2.1	87	0.76
Lateral-scour pool (Root)	—	—	2.2	100	1.4	65	0.33
Lateral-scour pool (Bedrock)	—	—	2.8	283	—	—	0.56
Dam pool	1.3	141	2.9	111	5.3	117	0.59
Glide	17.7	116	7.3	115	2.9	26	0.22
Run	7.8	78	5.8	84	2.7	58	0.36
Step run	0.9	173	9.2	76	10.1	49	0.07
Main pool	3.3	160	0.2	73	0.4	200	0.44
Edgewater	—	—	—	—	0.1	200	0.17
Channel confluence pool	—	—	0.3	233	0.8	99	0.13
Corner pool	—	—	3.1	141	1.2	105	0.17
Lateral-scour pool (Boulder)	—	—	1.5	193	1.2	148	0.46

(From Kershner and Snider, in preparation)
[a]Significant at 0.05

intermediate-gradient reaches followed by low-gradient and high-gradient ones (Table 12.2).

In Type A reaches high-gradient riffles, cascades, plunge pools, glides, and runs are dominant habitats (Table 12.2). In Type B reaches, low-gradient riffles, lateral-scour pools, dam pools, glides, runs, and step runs dominate, whereas dam pools, lateral-scour pools, low-gradient riffles, and step runs are the major habitats in Type C reaches. Mesohabitat composition showed a weak tendency to vary by stream type. However, it is clear that a high degree of variability existed in the composition of habitats at this scale.

Population response at the mesohabitat level

Initially we chose two streams (Prosser Creek and the Little Truckee River) to study patterns of fish distribution by mesohabitat (Kershner, 1990). Densities of fish were related to mesohabitat, but relationships depended on age class in both streams. Of the initial habitats identified, five were selected to represent the range of habitats available. Brown trout fry show little in the way of a consistent pattern in both the Little Truckee and Prosser Creek (Table 12.3). Brown trout fry in both systems appear to be ubiquitous in many kinds of habitats.

Yearling brown trout were more restrictive in habitat use. In the Little Truckee, more yearling brown trout were associated with lateral-scour pool habitats with some type of

TABLE 12.3. Mean densities (nos m^{-2}) of brown trout in the Little Truckee and Prosser Creek during the Fall of 1987

Habitat type	Fry (<1 year)		Yearling (>1 and <2 years)		Adult (>2 years)	
	No m^{-2}	SE	No m^{-2}	SE	No m^{-2}	SE
Glide						
L. Truckee	0.8	0.5	0.001	0.001	0.0003	0.0003
Prosser	0.06	0.01	0.0003	0.0003	0.004	0.003
Lateral pool						
L. Truckee	0.3	0.1	0.03	0.01	0.06	0.04
Prosser	0.2	0.04	0.007	0.006	0.06	0.02
Main pool						
L. Truckee	0.05	—	0	—	0	—
Prosser	0.4	0.3	0.01	0.01	0.02	0.003
Riffle						
L. Truckee	0.2	0.02	0.001	0.001	0	—
Prosser	0.09	0.01	0.007	0.001	0	0
Run						
L. Truckee	0.4	0.16	0.001	0.001	0.001	0.0008
Prosser	0.08	0.008	0.002	0.001	0.006	0.002
Step run						
L. Truckee	0.4	—	—	—	—	—
Prosser	0.09	0.01	0.003	0.002	0.005	0.004

complex woody cover. In Prosser Creek, observed patterns were similar, although densities in main pools were higher relative to those in the Little Truckee.

Adult brown trout showed a distinct preference for lateral habitats with complex woody debris. Comparisons of the density of fish to percentage habitat area available showed that over 90% of the adult brown trout were found in less than 2% of total habitat available. Winter distributions of brown trout showed similar patterns (J. L. Kershner, unpublished data).

Microhabitat choice by mesohabitat

Mesohabitat location may play a role in microhabitat selection (Kershner, 1990). We examined the two most common components of microhabitat selection to illustrate differences by mesohabitat. Adult brown trout in the Little Truckee exhibited strong relationships to lateral pool habitats and most of the observations from the study were collected at those sites. Focal depth (distance from the bottom) ranged from 0.03 m to 0.2 m (Figure 12.2) while focal velocity showed a consistent pattern of selection from 0.03 m s^{-1} to 0.2 m s^{-1} and then a marked jump at 0.33 m s^{-1} (Figure 12.3).

Yearling brown trout were more abundant in other habitats and patterns in distribution begin to emerge. The dominant focal velocity selected in glides is 0.06 m s^{-1} (Figure 12.3). In lateral pools, two sharp peaks emerge at 0.17 m s^{-1} and 0.3 m s^{-1}. Runs showed bi-modal peaks at 0.27 and 0.33 m s^{-1}. Frequency of focal depths was fairly consistent in lateral pools between 0.03 m and 0.13 m (Figure 12.2). Frequencies declined as depth increased. A shift in use of focal depth occurred in runs. Greater focal depths were selected at higher frequencies (0.13–0.23 m) in runs. Selection of focal depths in main pools peaked at 0.03 m and declined to zero, while depths of 0.3 m were most selected in glides (Figure 12.2).

Brown trout fry were observed in far higher numbers than other life-stages. Focal depths between 0.03 and 0.06 m were selected more frequently in most habitats (Figure 12.2). A second peak of use occurred in lateral pools at 0.17 m and two isolated observations occurred in main pools and lateral pools at 0.3 m and 0.33 m, respectively. Frequencies of focal velocities varied widely among habitats (Figure 12.3). Glide focal velocity use peaked at 0.03 m s^{-1} and declined rapidly. Lateral pool use initially peaked at 0.1 m s^{-1}, declined and showed a second spike at 0.3 m s^{-1}. Riffle use remained fairly constant through a range of flows between 0.03 and 0.33 m s^{-1}. Run use varied widely through a range of velocities.

Application to PHABSIM

We used the PHABSIM system developed by the US Fish and Wildlife Service to determine habitat area available at different stream flows (Bovee and Milhous, 1978). All habitats were modelled at flows of 0.9, 2.8, and $5.7 \text{ m}^3 \text{ s}^{-1}$, which were flows most commonly available during different periods of instream flow regulation. Cross-section data for each habitat were collected at all three stream flows. We collected full sets of mean cell velocities, cell depths, and water surface elevations at $0.9 \text{ m}^3 \text{ s}^{-1}$ as well as water surface elevations at the other flows. Stream discharges were modelled using the IFG4 hydraulic simulation routine (Milhous et al, 1989). We used the WSEI4S subroutine to input water surface elevations from the three flow sets to determine stage–discharge relationships and added these to our IFG4 hydraulic model. Weighted usable area (WUA) was calculated using the HABTAT routine (Milhous et al, 1989).

We examined three different approaches for modelling habitat in the Little Truckee. First, we selected representative reaches based on a randomly selected reach in the same stream type without mesohabitat stratification. We then coupled this hydraulic model with microhabitat use criteria for brown trout from eastern California streams (Smith, 1988). We felt these criteria were probably the best set of data available considering their geographic proximity and we had used these curves in previous studies (Snider et al, 1987). The second approach coupled the same representative reach with brown trout suitability-of-use criteria derived from microhabitat observations on the Little Truckee. This information was aggregated from microhabitat to reach, disregarding patterns observed at the mesohabitat scale. For the third approach, we combined mesohabitats by the percentage of each type found in the study area. We constructed a representative habitat approach based on weighting each habitat by the proportion in which they were represented. We developed suitability-of-use curves based on microhabitat variables present in each mesohabitat and combined these curves with the representative habitat model.

Brown trout fry exhibited similar trends in WUA for all three approaches (Figure 12.4). They were found in a variety of mesohabitats utilizing a wide range of microhabitat conditions. Since these fish exhibited flexible microhabitat strategies, we expected

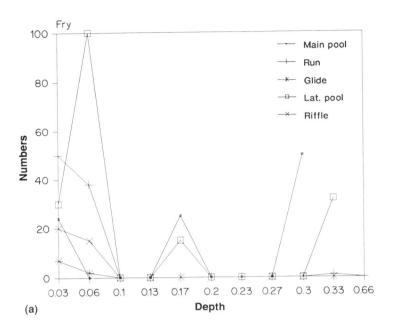

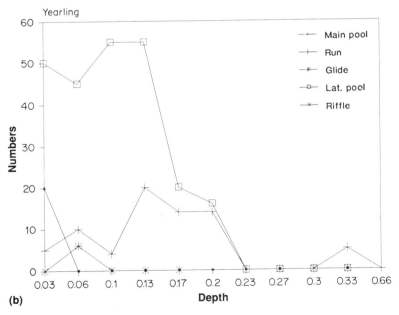

FIGURE 12.2. Observed frequencies of focal depths (m) for brown trout (all life-stages) in the Little Truckee

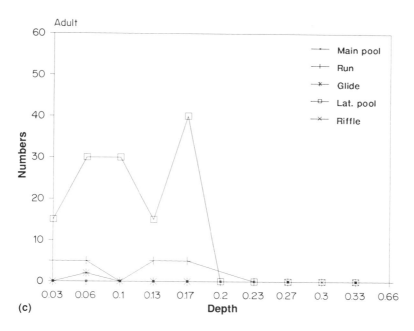

FIGURE 12.2. (*continued*)

them to be able to take advantage of expanding habitat conditions throughout the stream in a full range of mesohabitats. All three approaches reflect increasing habitat available as discharge increases.

Abundance of WUA for yearling brown trout differ markedly depending on the model used. For representative reaches using the East side criteria, WUA increases with discharge through the full range of flows. WUA also increases in the representative reach using suitability criteria generated for the reach, but there are visible differences in WUA (Figure 12.4). The representative habitat approach based on the habitat use criteria shows a slight increase of WUA at $2.8 \, \mathrm{m^3 \, s^{-1}}$ followed by a decline to almost the original value at $5.7 \, \mathrm{m^3 \, s^{-1}}$ (almost no change). Yearling brown trout in the Little Truckee appeared to exhibit strong habitat fidelity to lateral scour habitats in our survey. While corresponding increases in densities through other habitats did occur in autumn 1988, a sixfold increase in density in lateral-scour pools was also noted. Our suspicions were that yearling brown trout may be responding to the cover component of these lateral-scour habitats, and that changes in microhabitat variables as discharge increased would primarily show up as increased WUA when these larger-scale habitat conditions were met.

Adult brown trout showed distinct differences in WUA based on the approach (Figure 12.4). Using the East side criteria WUA showed an increasing trend in habitat for adults. Habitat for adults using the Little Truckee curves and the representative reach showed not only less habitat than the East side WUA but also little increase in habitat as discharge increases. WUA using the representative habitat approach showed virtually no

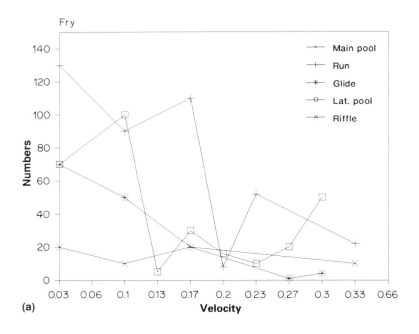

(a)

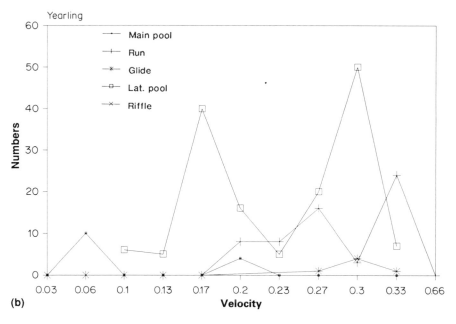

(b)

FIGURE 12.3. Observed frequencies of focal velocities (m s^{-1}) for brown trout (all life-stages) in the Little Truckee

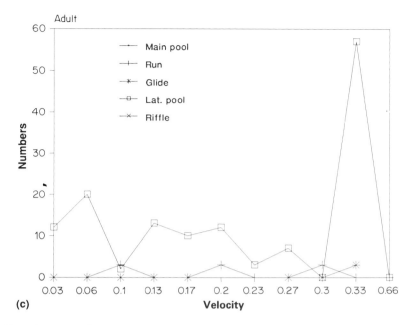

FIGURE 12.3. (*continued*)

change as discharge increases. As with yearlings, adult brown trout showed a strong fidelity to lateral-scour habitats with woody cover. At this range of discharges strong differences in WUA would only be detected as more of the mesohabitat conditions that had suitable microhabitat were available. A small number of microhabitat observations (<20) in lateral-scour habitats at flows of 5.7 and 6.5 m^3 s^{-1} indicated that adult brown trout maintained their position in the mesohabitat even as focal velocity increased (J. Kershner and W. Snider, unpublished data). Heggenes (1988) reported that increases in discharge from four to a hundred times the background flow did not displace brown trout longer than 67 mm FL.

DISCUSSION

Stratification of streams into different habitat scales is a valid approach to design instream flow studies. While certain large-scale watershed variables are not addressed (e.g. water quality, temperature) in this classification, we believe that habitat stratification is a useful way to classify streams after some of these larger issues have been considered. We would recommend this approach only after a thorough pre-project analysis is completed (Bovee, 1982) as other larger-scale factors may play an important role in determining fish position in streams (Baltz et al, 1987). Based on our observations, relationships at the reach scale, even when objective criteria are used, may exhibit a high degree of variability. We believe that to maximize the benefits of this approach, some form of mesohabitat stratification must be attempted in order to facilitate aggregation or disaggregation at other scales.

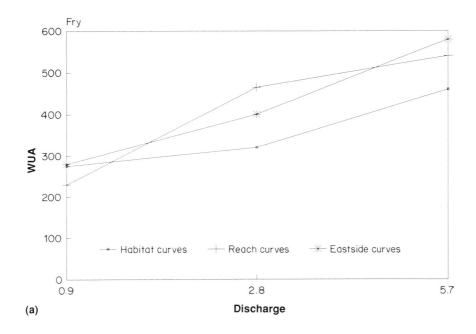

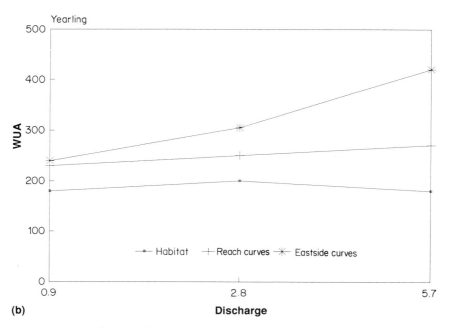

FIGURE 12.4. WUA ($m^2\ 100\,m^{-1}$) for brown trout (all life-stages) using three approaches for habitat characterization and microhabitat suitability

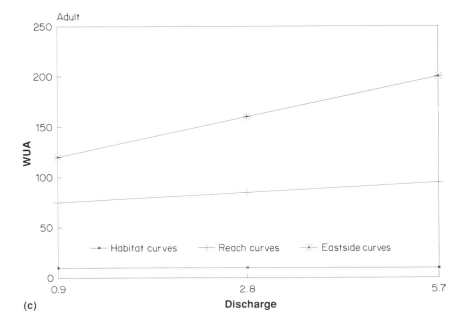

FIGURE 12.4. (*continued*)

Mesohabitat stratification is receiving more attention as a method to relate stream geomorphic characteristics to biological processes. Unfortunately, like all classifications, it is being viewed as a panacea by some (Hawkins et al, in preparation). One of the problems with using this classification is that the original set of habitats was described in small streams (less than fourth order). While the classification has worked reasonably well in basins up to fourth order, relationships in larger watersheds have not been well documented. We are attempting to determine whether the same types of habitat patterns we see in the smaller tributaries are also exhibited in the mainstem Truckee River.

Criticisms of instream flow models, particularly the PHABSIM models, have often centred on the use of species/life-stage criteria (Bovee and Cochnauer, 1977) generated externally to the study area. Gore and Nestler (1988) recommend that site-specific criteria be developed locally and include depth-velocity dependent functions. While we support this recommendation, an added step of identifying the fish habitat relationships at the mesohabitat scale may also be useful. For species/life-stages using a wide range of both mesohabitat and microhabitat conditions, use of external habitat criteria may show similar trends. Species or life-stages that have more specific needs may require the added resolution of first identifying what types of habitats are important and then how microhabitat may be different. At the same time, hydraulic models based on these relationships can determine when specific habitats no longer exhibit the microhabitat characteristics necessary to support the organism(s) of interest.

Our simulations of WUA were run using the HABTAT simulation procedure of the PHABSIM system. While the HABTAT routine has been widely used, other simulations have been developed (Milhous et al, 1989) which may add resolution to the procedure we describe. In particular, the HABTAE simulation calculates WUA or WUV (volume) for each cross-section measured. This routine gives the user the capability of aggregating or disaggregating cross-sections to reflect habitat conditions. It would be particularly useful if the user is interested in habitat volumes given changes in flow.

In the case of adult brown trout, lateral habitats with complex woody debris appear to be important. Habitat versus discharge models may be highly inaccurate where these relationships are not considered. In the Little Truckee, this complexity certainly influences microhabitat choice and may dominate other considerations. While we do not recommend wholesale introductions of woody debris as a substitute for adequate flows, we do feel that considerations of meso-level habitat use may be appropriate when developing flow recommendations and mitigation strategies.

Instream flow determinations require a complex series of steps to determine the flow needs of aquatic organisms. Often managers are faced with a limited time schedule and limited funds to carry out such studies. We believe that habitat-level classifications may aid in determining where instream flow studies should be conducted within the project area and provide insights as to which scale(s) may be important when developing such studies.

REFERENCES

Baltz, D. M., Vondracek, B., Brown, L. R., and Moyle, P. B. (1987). "Influence of temperature on microhabitat choice by fishes in a California stream", *Transactions of the American Fisheries Society*, **116**, 12–20.

Bisson, P. A., Nielsen, J. L., Palmason, R. A., and Grove, L. E. (1982). "A system of naming habitat types in small streams, with examples of habitat utilization by salmonids during low streamflow", in *Acquisition and utilization of aquatic habitat inventory information*, American Fisheries Society, Western Division, Bethesda, Maryland.

Bisson, P. A., Sullivan, K., and Nielsen, J. L. (1988). "Channel hydraulics, habitat use, and body form of juvenile coho salmon, steelhead, and cutthroat trout in streams", *Transactions of the American Fisheries Society*, **117**, 262–273.

Bovee, K. D., (1982). "A guide to stream habitat analysis using the instream flow incremental methodology", Instream Flow Information Paper No. 12, USDI Fish and Wildlife Service, Office of Biological Services. FWS/OBS-82/86.

Bovee, K. D., and Cochnauer, T. (1977). "Development and evaluation of weighted criteria, probability-of-use curves for instream flow assessments: fisheries", Instream Flow Information Paper No. 3, USDI Fish and Wildlife Service, FWS/OBS-77/63.

Bovee, K. D., and Milhous, R. T. (1978). "Hydraulic simulation in instream flow studies: theory and techniques", Instream Flow Information Paper 5, USDI Fish and Wildlife Service, FWS/OBS-78/33.

Frissell, C. A., Liss, W. J., Warren, C. E., and Hurley, M. D. (1986). "A hierarchical framework for stream classification: viewing streams in a water-shed context", *Environmental Management*, **10**, 199–214.

Gore, J. A., and Nestler, J. M. (1988). "Instream flow studies in perspective", *Regulated Rivers*: *Research and Management*, **2**, 93–101.

Hankin, D. G., and Reeves, G. H. (1988). "Estimating total fish abundance and total habitat area in small stream based on visual estimation methods", *Canadian Journal of Fisheries and Aquatic Sciences*, **45**, 834–844.

Hawkins, C. P., Kershner, J. L., Bisson, P. A., Bryant, M., Decker, L. M., Gregory, S. V., McCullough, D., Overton, K., Reeves, G. H., Steedman, R., and Young, M. (in preparation). "Recommendations for a system of stream habitat classification."

Heggenes, J. (1988). "Effects of short-term flow fluctuations on displacement of, and habitual use by, brown trout in a small stream", *Transactions of the American Fisheries Society*, **117**, 336–344.

Helm, W. T. (Ed.) (1985). *Glossary of Stream Habitat Terms*, American Fisheries Society, Western Division, Habitat Inventory Committee.

Kershner, J. L. (1990). *Physical habitat factors influencing the distribution and abundance of fish in the Little Truckee river system*, PhD dissertation (draft), University of California, Davis.

Kershner, J. L., and Snider, W. M. (in preparation). "Observations of habitat use and the relationship to brown trout and rainbow trout distribution in the Little Truckee River", Utah State University, Logan, Utah.

Leopold, L. B., and Wolman, M. G. (1957). "River channel patterns, braided, meandering, and straight", *US Geological Survey Professional Paper* 282-B.

Milhous, R. T., Updike, M. A., and Schneider, D. M. (1989). "Physical habitat simulation system reference manual—Version II", Instream Flow Information Paper No. 26, USDI Fish and Wildlife Service, Biological Report 89(16).

Moore, K. M. S., and Gregory, S. V. (1988). "Summer habitat utilization and ecology of cutthroat trout fry (*Salmo clarki*) in Cascade Mountain streams", *Canadian Journal of Fisheries and Aquatic Sciences*, **45**, 1921–1930.

Murphy, M. L., Lorenz, J. M., Heifetz, J., Thedinga, J. F., Koski, K. V., and Johnson, S. W. (1987). "The relationship between stream classification, fish, and habitat in southeast Alaska", USDA Forest Service, General Technical Report R10-MB-10.

Rosgen, D. L. (1985). "A stream classification system", in *Proceedings of the Symposium on Riparian Ecosystems and their Management: Reconciling Conflicting Uses* (Ed. R. Hamre), pp. 91–95, USDA Forest Service, General Technical Report RM-120, Tucson, Arizona.

Shirvell, C. S., and Dungey, R. G. (1983). "Microhabitats chosen by brown trout for feeding and spawning in rivers", *Transactions of the American Fisheries Society*, **112**, 355–367.

Smith, G. E. (1988). "Selection and use of cover by salmonids in eastern Sierra streams: implications for data partitioning", in *Proceedings of a Workshop on the Development and Evaluation of Habitat Suitability Criteria*, USDI Fish and Wildlife Service, Biological Report 88(11), 73–90.

Snider, W. M., Kershner, J. L., and Smith, G. E. (1987). "Instream flow requirements of selected salmonid resources, Lake Tahoe Basin", Department of Fish and Game, Stream Evaluation Report 87-1.

Sullivan, K. (1986). *Hydraulics and fish habitat in relation to channel morphology*, PhD dissertation, Johns Hopkins University, Baltimore, Maryland.

Tennant, D. L. (1976). "Instream flow requirements for fish, wildlife, recreation, and related environmental resources", in *Proceedings of a Symposium and Specialty Conference on Instream Flow Needs* (Eds J. F. Orsborn and C. H. Allmann), pp. 359–373, American Fisheries Society, Bethesda, Maryland.

Waters, B. F. (1976). "A methodology for evaluating the effects of different stream flows on salmonid habitat", in *Proceedings of a Symposium and Specialty Conference on Instream Flow Needs* (Eds J. F. Orsborn and C. H. Allmann), pp. 254–256, American Fisheries Society, Bethesda, Maryland.

Wesche, T. A., and Rechard, P. A. (1980). "A summary of instream flow methods for fisheries and related research needs", *Bulletin 9*, Eisenhower Consortium for Western Environmental Forestry Research.

White, R. G. (1976). "A methodology for recommending stream resource maintenance flows for large rivers", in *Proceedings of a Symposium and Specialty Conference on Instream Flow Needs* (Eds J. F. Orsborn and C. H. Allmann), pp. 376–399, American Fisheries Society, Bethesda, Maryland.

13

Assessing the Natural Value of New Zealand Rivers

K. J. COLLIER and R. H. S. McCOLL

Department of Conservation, PO Box 10–420, Wellington, New Zealand

INTRODUCTION

Human-induced changes to the natural environment of New Zealand, especially to the lowlands, have been particularly significant since the acceleration of European colonization in the last 150 years. Continuing demands on natural resources have led to growing concern that some types of indigenous ecosystems are not represented in the existing protected areas network which predominantly consists of high country reserves (Figure 13.1). This concern led to legislative recognition that the network should ensure "as far as possible, the survival of all indigenous species of flora and fauna, both rare and commonplace, in their natural communities and habitats, and the preservation of representative samples of all classes of natural ecosystems and landscape which in the aggregate originally gave New Zealand its own recognizable character".

An outcome of this was the Protected Natural Areas Programme (PNAP), which seeks to establish a network of reserves that includes adequate examples of all types of ecosystems (Myers et al, 1987). A programme has also been set up that identifies mainly palustrine wetlands that are of representative and ecological importance (Simpson, 1985). The Department of Conservation (DoC) is responsible for administering these programmes, and is currently developing a network of marine protected areas.

Freshwater ecosystems have received comparatively little attention and remain under-represented in the New Zealand protected areas network (McColl, 1987). Insufficient recognition has been given to the international importance of the native aquatic biota, or to the diverse range of freshwater ecosystems found in New Zealand. Furthermore, modern criteria such as representativeness, diversity, and rarity that can be used to describe natural value (as embodied in the quotation above) have not been adequately interpreted for freshwater ecosystems, making assessment difficult.

In this chapter we describe significant features of New Zealand's running-water ecosystems, review anthropogenic changes that have affected the natural character of streams and rivers, and discuss the application of modern criteria for assessing their natural value with a view to identifying and prioritizing natural riverine areas for

River Conservation and Management. Edited by P. J. Boon, P. Calow, and G. E. Petts
© 1992 John Wiley & Sons Ltd

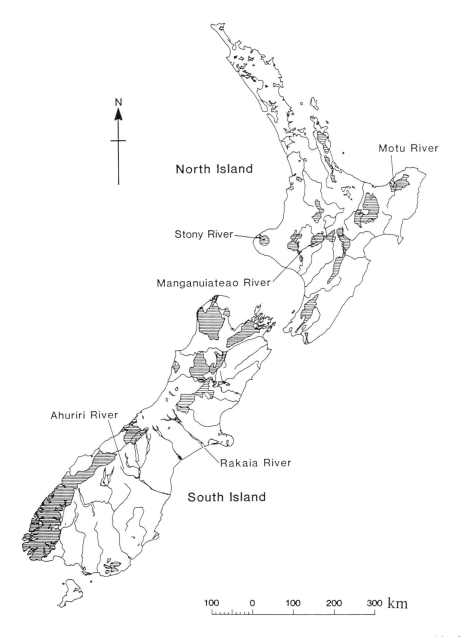

FIGURE 13.1 Map of New Zealand showing protected areas (hatched). Rivers covered by Water Conservation Orders at the time of writing are named

protection. We view rivers from a catchment perspective whereby natural value reflects not only the wetted channel and the aquatic biota therein but also the integrity of adjacent floodplains, wetlands, and terrestrial vegetation.

CHARACTERISTICS OF NEW ZEALAND RIVERS

Description of riverscape

The main islands of New Zealand span 13° of latitude, but the dominion also includes part of Antarctica and over 500 offshore islands that range from the sub-tropical Kermadec Islands at 29° S to the sub-antarctic Campbell Islands at 53° S. Several aquatic invertebrate species are restricted to some of the more distant island groups (McLellan, 1973), but little else is known of the running-water habitats on most offshore islands.

Rivers and streams are abundant on the main islands because of frequent rainfall and the presence of extensive and highly dissected mountain ranges in many areas. No point is further than 130 km from the sea and consequently river systems are short (only four exceed 250 km in length) compared with many in mainland Europe, Asia and America (Higler, 1988; *NZ Official Year Book*, 1988/89). Nevertheless, the range of river types on the main islands is very diverse, reflecting the geologically young and active nature of the landscape.

Several North Island rivers flow down the slopes of dormant volcanoes or drain their extensive ash deposits, and some active volcanic centres give rise to geothermally influenced streams with unusual water chemistries and biological communities (Vincent and Forsyth, 1987). In the South Island, geothermally influenced waters occur mostly along the Alpine Fault which marks the junction of the Indian–Australian and Pacific Plates and gives rise to the axial ranges of the Southern Alps.

Shingle washed into watercourses from the Southern Alps and some North Island mountains is deposited on the eastern lowlands to form large braided rivers (Figure 13.2(a)), examples of which are found in few other places around the world. On the west of the South Island, some large glaciers terminate near the coast and give rise to short and turbid rivers with low summer water temperatures and little aquatic life (Figure 13.2(b)). Naturally acidic, brown-water streams with distinctive microbial communities and epilithon (stone surface organic layers) emanate from wetlands on lowlands of the South Island's west coast (Collier and Winterbourn, 1987, 1990).

Streams with shifting, sandy substrates are common in the north of the South Island, and streams with limestone bedrock and substantial subterranean flows also occur there and at several places in the North Island (e.g. Collier and Wakelin, 1990). Spring- and lake-fed streams are found in many parts of the country and these exhibit varying degrees of constancy of flow and temperature (Figure 13.2(c)). Waikoropupu Springs in the north of the South Island is one of the largest cold springs in the world and supports impressive growths of native macrophytes (Coffey and Clayton, 1988).

In parts of the northern North Island, streams flow through kauri forest (dominated by *Agathis australis*) which is comparable in community structure to lowland tropical rain forest (Towns, 1979). Elsewhere in the North Island and in the South Island, native forest consists predominantly of beech (*Nothofagus* spp.) and mixed podocarp species.

(a)

(b)

(c)

FIGURE 13.2. Examples of different types of rivers that are found in New Zealand. (a) Large river with braided channel; (b) short turbid river fed by glacial meltwater; (c) lake-fed stream with relatively constant flow

Like the northern kauri forests, these are evergreen and provide year-round shade and inputs of leaf litter to the streams that flow beneath their canopies. Approximately 14% of New Zealand is in the alpine zone, and consequently many river catchments extend into subalpine scrub, tussock grassland and scree (Molloy, 1980; Winterbourn, 1987). Mountain streams are typically turbulent and fast-flowing with unstable beds and poor debris-retention characteristics (Winterbourn et al, 1981).

The native biota of New Zealand rivers

The main islands of New Zealand became separated from Gondwanaland about 80 million years ago and the subsequent long isolation has resulted in a very high degree of endemism in the biota. About 90% of the arthropod species are endemic to New Zealand (Kuschel, 1975), as are a similar proportion of the freshwater fish species (McDowall, 1990). However, the diversity of aquatic invertebrate, plant, and fish communities is generally low in New Zealand compared with many lotic (running-water) ecosystems overseas, and, for fish at least, this is thought to reflect the long isolation and tectonic instability of the country (Winterbourn et al, 1981; Coffey and Clayton, 1988; McDowall, 1990).

In pre-human times, the vascular plant and bryophyte communities of New Zealand streams are thought to have consisted predominantly of species adapted to the heavily

FIGURE 13.3. The blue duck (centre) is playing an increasingly important role in river conservation in New Zealand. Pairs occupy territories mostly on undisturbed, fast-flowing rivers

shaded conditions provided by native forest cover (Howard-Williams et al, 1987). Unlike all other significant land masses, emergent flood-resistant plants (rheophytes) are absent from our streams. Similarly, several groups of invertebrates that are common elsewhere are poorly represented in New Zealand running waters. These include several families of Trichoptera and Ephemeroptera, and the Megaloptera, Odonata, Gastropoda, and Crustacea (Winterbourn et al, 1981). The native freshwater fish fauna is also comparatively sparse, with approximately half of the 27 species belonging to the Southern Hemisphere family Galaxiidae (McDowall, 1990). A previously widespread and abundant species of native fish (*Prototroctes oxyrhynchus*) has become extinct since the arrival of Europeans, but the precise reasons for this are unclear.

One species of endemic frog (*Leiopelma hochstetteri*), now confined to the northern half of the North Island, is often closely associated with mountain streams, and an extinct species of stream-dwelling frog (*Leiopelma waitomoensis*) is thought to have occurred in parts of the North Island (Worthy, 1987). New Zealand has no native aquatic mammals, but many species of native birds utilize rivers and their associated floodplains and wetlands as breeding and feeding habitat (Hughey, 1987). The species most closely associated with rivers is the blue duck (*Hymenolaimus malacorhynchos*) (Figure 13.3), which lives year-round on single-channel, fast-flowing rivers, and was once widespread throughout most of the country. Braided rivers are used as seasonal breeding and feeding habitat by several species of Charadriiformes such as the wrybill (*Anarhynchus frontalis*) and black stilt (*Himantopus novaezealandiae*), whereas single-channel, slow-flowing lowland rivers provide feeding habitat for species such as shags (Hughey, 1987).

Anthropogenic changes to the riverscape

Since the arrival of humans in New Zealand approximately 90% of natural wetlands have been drained or otherwise lost (Howard-Williams et al, 1987), and unmodified indigenous forest cover has been reduced from 78% to about 22% of land surface area (Molloy, 1980). Loss of native forest has been particularly pronounced on the lowlands, where it now represents only 15% of its pre-human extent (Anon., 1989), and deciduous Northern Hemisphere willow species (mainly *Salix fragilis*) are now the typical riparian tree (Johnson and Brooke, 1989). Consequently, no rivers in the North Island or on the east of the South Island now exist with catchments that are wholly unmodified from the headwaters to the sea, and only about 11 rivers in these areas have more than half their catchments in unmodified native vegetation.

Removal of native forest along streams and rivers has proved detrimental to the shade-adapted aquatic flora which could not compete with those adventive colonists that are tolerant of high light levels (Howard-Williams et al, 1987). As a result, the macrophyte flora of most of New Zealand's lowland streams is characterized by adventive species such as watercress (*Nasturtium* spp.), sweet grass (*Glyceria* spp.), and starwort (*Callitriche stagnalis*). Clearance of native vegetation from catchments is also thought to have contributed to the decline in distribution of blue duck (Kear, 1972), and to have caused changes in the structure of native fish communities (Hanchet, 1990). In contrast, some aquatic invertebrate communities appear comparatively resilient to removal of riparian vegetation, suggesting adaptability to different food resources and environmental conditions (Winterbourn, 1986; Collier et al, 1989).

Soil erosion, wetland drainage, and river channelization have greatly modified habitat in some rivers (McColl and Ward, 1987), whereas nutrient enrichment from agriculture and other sources has altered the composition and structure of aquatic invertebrate communities in some areas (e.g. Stark, 1985). Construction of dams and abstraction of water have caused problems at a number of sites for some of the 17 native fish species that normally require access to and from the sea to complete their life-cycles. Predation and competition by exotic fishes has also been implicated as a factor that has detrimentally affected native fisheries and some species of aquatic invertebrates (McDowall, 1987; Glova, 1989; Townsend et al, 1990).

Twenty species of exotic fishes (including seven species of salmonids) have been introduced into New Zealand waterways, although most of these have localized distributions at present (McDowall, 1990). Many of the salmonids provide important recreational fisheries, and strong runs of quinnat salmon (*Oncorhynchus tshawytscha*) have become established in braided rivers of the South Island. Brown trout (*Salmo trutta*) and rainbow trout (*Oncorhynchus mykiss*) have become widespread in the high-quality waters of many New Zealand rivers, and they form the basis of an important sports fishery. Several species of freshwater snail (three species of *Lymnaea*, *Planorbarius corneus*, and *Physa acuta*) have also been introduced to New Zealand waters, mostly from aquaria, although *Limnaea stagnalis* was introduced intentionally to provide food for trout (Forsyth and Lewis, 1987). *Physa acuta* is now widely distributed in New Zealand, and in some places is thought to have replaced the endemic snail, *Physastra variabilis*.

ASSESSMENT AND PROTECTION OF NATURAL VALUE

Approaches to assessment

Although biological communities composed of a mixture of indigenous and exotic species may be more diverse than those that occur naturally, they do not represent the situation that *"originally* gave New Zealand its own recognizable character". Nevertheless, as in most countries, physically unmodified ecosystems that have been biologically modified through human activity require careful conservation to ensure that species diversity and ecosystem integrity are maintained. The evolutionary endpoints that mixed communities attain in New Zealand are of considerable scientific interest, and examples may warrant protection on those grounds in the future.

A more pertinent goal of natural area protection should be to ensure the survival of pure examples (where possible) of indigenous communities in unmodified rivers. Indigenous communities occur most frequently away from populated areas where species introductions often originate, and on sections of river above natural barriers (e.g. waterfalls) that can inhibit the dispersal of some exotic species.

The survival of predominantly indigenous communities could be achieved by the preservation of wholly unmodified river catchments or the protection of remnants of riverine ecosystems that retain their natural character within partly modified catchments.

Protection from the headwaters to the sea is particularly desirable, as this would ensure that examples of rivers displaying the full sequence of lotic succession are included in the protected areas network. However, wholly unmodified river catchments are now found only on the west of the South Island, and thus it would not be possible to achieve regional representativeness of physically intact catchments without some form of restoration programme.

Many unmodified catchments on the west of the South Island are already included in existing protected areas (Figure 13.1), but the status of exotic species in these systems is not well documented. Unmodified whole catchments that are not protected need to be inventoried and any threats to their natural integrity identified and contained. Management of rivers at the catchment level and as entities from the source to the sea is a more feasible option in New Zealand than in many other countries because of the relatively short lengths of most rivers, and because rivers generally do not cross regional (or national) boundaries.

Assessing remnants of river ecosystems

Protection of representative remnants of riverine ecosystems that retain their natural character requires a protocol for identification and evaluation of sites. The most feasible means of achieving this is to expand the New Zealand Protected Natural Areas Programme (PNAP) so that the evaluation of running water ecosystems can be linked to future PNA surveys. The underlying principles and mechanisms to achieve this are already in place. Furthermore, the PNAP criteria for natural area assessment are compatible with criteria recently recommended by the New Zealand Limnological Society for assessing the value of aquatic reserves. The latter criteria are:

- Ecological representativeness or rare type of ecosystem
- Degree of modification
- Diversity and pattern
- Rarity and unique features or species
- Long-term viability.

These criteria are also compatible with those employed by other assessment systems in New Zealand, and with criteria used in evaluations of freshwater ecosystems overseas (e.g. Morgan, 1982; Blyth, 1983; Newbold et al, 1983). We have been examining the use of quantitative descriptors to assess these criteria, and have devised a preliminary list for consideration in assessing degree of modification (Table 13.1), diversity and pattern (Table 13.2(a)), and rarity and unique features or species (Table 13.2(b)).

The scale and accuracy at which assessment of riverine areas is carried out will largely be dictated by available resources. A system based mainly on physical features of rivers would be easiest to achieve, and could be augmented with information from local sources and national databases (currently available for freshwater fishes and blue duck) on the status of exotic species and of rare or endangered native species. Thus, most of the descriptors in Tables 13.1 and 13.2 are based on physical attributes of rivers that can be derived from maps, aerial photographs, or local knowledge.

TABLE 13.1. List of physical descriptors that are being considered for assessing degree of modification

---

Catchment in native vegetation (%) (+)
Length lined by native vegetation (%) (+)
Length lined by non-production woodland (%) (+)
Length fenced (%) (+)
No. natural barriers to exotic fish movement (+)
Distance of first natural barrier from headwaters (+)
Road distance to nearest town (+)
Road distance to nearest city (+)
Catchment in production forest (%) (−)
Catchment in improved pasture (%) (−)
Length channelized (%) (−)
No. open-cast mines in catchment (−)
No. road and rail bridges (−)
No. unbridged road crossings (−)
No. water-abstraction points (−)
Baseflow abstracted (%) (−)
No. downstream weirs (−)
No. downstream dams (−)
Length with regulated flow (%) (−)
No. point-source discharges (−)
Baseflow that is waste discharge (%) (−)
No. known exotic aquatic species (−)
Density of goats in catchment (−)
Degree of native species exploitation (−)

Signs indicate whether a high value for a descriptor is likely to have a positive (+) or negative (−) effect on a river

Assessing representativeness

Representativeness refers to the degree to which a system of reserves represents the range of variation found within a region (Austin and Margules, 1986), and this concept underpins the PNAP (Kelly and Park, 1986). Its assessment requires some form of classification system whereby sites are grouped into classes with similar attributes for subsequent evaluation, and clearly defined boundaries that delineate regions within which representativeness can be appraised.

The ecological region and district framework (McEwen, 1987) forms the yardstick against which representativeness is assessed in PNAP. However, these divisions are unsuitable for rivers, as they are based solely on topographical and botanical features of the land, and sometimes use rivers as convenient boundaries. A system of freshwater ecoregions is being developed for New Zealand (Biggs et al, 1990) based on physical and biological data from a nationwide river survey. Such a system should provide an alternative mechanism for interpreting representativeness of rivers in New Zealand, although the accuracy and level of resolution it provides for conservation assessment purposes remains to be tested.

Several classification schemes for New Zealand rivers have been proposed, but none is adequate for conservation assessment. In a survey of the geomorphological charac-

TABLE 13.2. List of descriptors that are being considered for assessing (a) diversity and pattern, and (b) rarity and unique features or species

---

Criterion
  Descriptor

(a) *Diversity and pattern*
   No. stream orders
   Altitudinal range
   No. riparian vegetation types
   No. rock types
   No. associated wetlands, lakes, tarns
   No. discontinuities (e.g. confluences, waterfalls)
   No. hydraulic transition zones (*sensu* Statzner and Higler, 1986)
   No. unmodified interconnecting headwater catchments
   No. tributaries with low degree of modification
   No. pool/riffle sequences per km
   No. cascades per km
   Substrate heterogeneity
   Substrate stability
   Cover for fish (%)
   Cover by native aquatic plants (%)
   No. aquatic plant types

(b) *Rarity and unique features or species*
   No. large waterfalls
   No. unusual rock types
   No. unusual riparian vegetation types
   No. unusual geological formations
   Length of river or river segment
   No. known rare or endangered species

---

teristics of river channels in New Zealand, Mosley (1987) could distinguish only four clear types, and suggested that river characterization rather than classification would be a more appropriate means of describing rivers for management purposes. Descriptors such as amount of rainfall, mean gradient, channel morphology, dominant geology, main vegetation type, and origin of flow could be useful in physically characterizing rivers for conservation assessment purposes. Recent work suggests that origin of flow might provide useful dichotomies for a biologically meaningful classification of New Zealand rivers. Biggs and Close (1989) found that periphyton biomass in gravel-bed rivers of the South Island was regulated to a large extent by hydrological factors that reflected mountain, foothill, or lowland (spring-fed) sources.

Long-term viability

This criterion reflects the potential effectiveness of an area as a conservation unit, and is mainly a function of fragility and size. Fragility is a subjective measure of the sensitivity of a system to environmental change (Usher, 1986). Stream and rivers fed by mountain run-off are likely to have low fragility as repeated large spates may place natural limits on the flora and fauna that can colonize them. This scenario has been suggested for invertebrates in small streams of Westland (Winterbourn et al, 1988) and for periphyton in some Canterbury rivers (Biggs and Close, 1989). Other factors that could influence the fragility of a river include the extent of erosion-prone land in the catchment, the width, vigour, and density of riparian vegetation, the proximity of suitable areas (particularly upstream) for recolonization following a perturbation, and the importance of a site for sensitive biological processes such as native fish spawning. Similarly, a site may be more fragile if its biological integrity is dependent on the passage of migrating fishes through downstream stretches that are not managed with fish passage in mind (McDowall, 1984).

The minimum desirable size of a reserve can be determined by the space required by the top predator to maintain a viable population (Usher, 1986), and in New Zealand we are investigating the utility of blue duck to assess this. Recent genetic work has indicated that there is a naturally high degree of in-breeding in blue duck populations (Triggs et al, in press), and the minimum number required for the establishment of new populations is considered to be 20 territorial pairs (Williams, 1988). On present knowledge, this equates to 15–20 km of continuous habitat (including tributaries), and thus 15 km could be used as a minimum desirable length for riverine reserves in New Zealand. Clearly, this will not be achievable in many lowland areas, and some undisturbed sites will not represent suitable blue duck habitat, but it is nevertheless a useful target size.

Prioritizing sites for protection

The need for representativeness makes the implementation of a riverine extension of the PNAP a matter of urgency, and means that a rapid method of prioritizing sites for natural area selection is required (Figure 13.4). As the key criterion in PNAP, representativeness can be used initially to divide sites into classes, thereby ensuring that a range of river types and habitats is represented in subsequent stages of the evaluation (Kelly and Park, 1986; Margules, 1986). Threshold descriptors could then be invoked to remove from immediate consideration sites that do not meet one or more minimum standards (Figure 13.4). Minimum standards would be key descriptors of degree of modification and could include the presence of a continuous strip of riparian native vegetation, and the absence of unnatural downstream barriers to native fish migration (see Table 13.1). Minimum desirable size could also be used as a threshold descriptor in some regions, although it should not be applied too stringently.

Thus, a priority list of sites in each representative class would be compiled, and could then be evaluated further to assess other aspects of degree of modification, diversity and pattern, and rarity and unique features or species (Figure 13.4). If no sites within a representative class meet minimum standards, the least-modified sites could be further evaluated if they are considered to have high potential value.

Assessment of degree of modification, diversity and pattern, and rarity and unique features or species would be carried out initially from maps, aerial photographs, and databases, and sites with relatively high ranks could then be visited to confirm evaluations and carry out further assessment (Figure 13.4). Fragility and the pragmatic criteria (*sensu* Margules, 1986) of threat and "protectability" would be assessed last. Threat

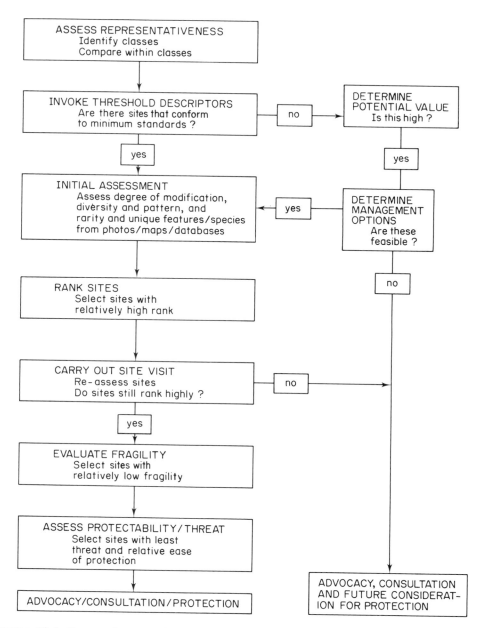

FIGURE 13.4. Proposed protocol for prioritizing sites for protection when assessing the natural value of New Zealand rivers. Classes for assessment of representativeness and minimum standards for threshold descriptors have yet to be determined

reflects the likelihood that future human activities could impinge upon the natural value of a river, whereas protectability is largely dictated by riparian land tenure and conflict of use.

Protection mechanisms

Historically, the protection of rivers in their natural state in New Zealand has been brought about by their inclusion in parks and reserves on Crown land, although this need not necessarily protect the quality of the water or the flow regime. Several statutes administered by DoC could be used to protect natural aquatic values. These include Faunistic Reserves, which can protect unique or pristine populations of aquatic species, and Ecological Areas, which can protect representative ecosystems and rare plant and animal communities, including those on a river bed. DoC also has jurisdiction over strips of land (3–20 m wide) alongside rivers that flow through land currently or previously owned by the Crown, providing a useful tool for maintaining or enhancing the natural integrity of rivers.

In 1981 the amenity value provided by rivers in their natural state was recognized by an amendment to the Soil and Water Conservation Act (Wild and Scenic Rivers Legislation), which made it possible to apply for Water Conservation Orders (WCO). To qualify for a WCO, it must be proved that a river has regionally or nationally outstanding wild, scenic, or other natural characteristics, or outstanding recreational, fisheries, wildlife, scientific, or other features. Under current legislation, WCOs protect only the water and not the channel or catchment, although the presence of a surrounding undisturbed catchment can increase the eligibility of a river for a WCO. At the time of writing, only five WCOs have been gazetted for rivers (Figure 13.1), although several others are pending or under appeal.

New Zealand's environmental legislation is currently under review with the aim of integrating the laws pertaining to natural resource management in an efficient manner. Under the new legislation, minimum water quality standards will be revised and become applicable to all waters, and it will be possible to classify waters at higher standards to protect special ecosystems, fisheries, and spawning areas. There will also be closer integration between land and water management, and catchment management plans devised by Regional Councils will be given statutory backing. Although Faunistic Reserves and Ecological Areas will be unaffected by the new legislation, the principal mechanism for environmental protection of rivers is likely to remain the WCO. It will become possible to use WCOs that can protect water flow and quality in association with Heritage Orders that give protection to the land and the river channel, so that the unit of water management could become the whole catchment.

Recently, an assessment of streams on the Coromandel Peninsula of the North Island's east coast, as part of the PNAP, identified several sites of high natural value, and representative examples of these have been recommended for protection. Where high-value sites occur on private land, implementation of protected status can be pursued through advocacy and negotiation. Consultation and collaboration between private land owners, Regional Councils, developers, and conservation advocates has been a feature of at least two recent conflicts of interest involving freshwater sites in New Zealand. The successful resolution of these conflicts by consultation is an encouraging sign for future issues that threaten the conservation values of rivers.

Discussion and consensus among interested parties and experts are considered essential features in the evolution of a natural areas assessment system for New Zealand rivers. In addition, endorsement is required from central, regional, and district government to ensure that protection recommendations are implemented. Identification of riverine areas with high natural value is the first step towards increasing the representation of rivers in the protected areas network. Now we are at the stage of determining an appropriate scale and classification system for assessing representativeness, and setting levels for threshold descriptors.

ACKNOWLEDGEMENTS

Members of the New Zealand Limnological Society have battled with some of the issues addressed in this chapter, and we acknowledge the ideas stimulated by those discussions. Important individual contributions to the interpretation of criteria for assessing the natural value of New Zealand rivers have been made by Robert McDowall and Stella Penny. Comments on draft manuscripts were kindly made by Barry Biggs, Department of Scientific and Industrial Research, Bob Zuur, Ministry for the Environment, Gordon Glova, Ministry of Agriculture and Fisheries, and Paula Warren, Philip Simpson, Martin Cawthorn, Jan Heine, and Mick Clout, Department of Conservation.

REFERENCES

Anon. (1989). "A national policy for indigenous forests", A discussion paper prepared by a working party convened by the Secretary for the Environment, Ministry for the Environment, Wellington.

Austin, M. P., and Margules, C. R. (1986). "Assessing representativeness", in *Wildlife Conservation Evaluation* (Ed. M. B. Usher), pp. 45–67, Chapman and Hall, London.

Biggs, B. J. F., and Close, M. E. (1989). "Periphyton biomass dynamics in gravel bed rivers: the relative effects of flows and nutrients", *Freshwater Biology*, **22**, 209–231.

Biggs, B. J. F., Duncan, M. J., Jowett, I. G., Quinn, J. M., Hickey, C. W., Davies-Colley, R. J., and Close, M. E. (1990). "Ecological characterisation, classification and modelling of New Zealand rivers: An introduction and synthesis", *New Zealand Journal of Marine and Freshwater Research*, **24**, 277–304.

Blyth, J. D. (1983). "Rapid stream survey to assess conservation value and habitats available for invertebrates", in *Survey Methods for Nature Conservation*, Vol. 1 (Eds K. Meyers, C. R. Margules and I. Musto), pp. 343–375, Proceedings of a workshop held at Adelaide University, 31 August–2 September 1983.

Coffey, B. T., and Clayton, J. S. (1988). *New Zealand waterplants: a guide to plants found in New Zealand freshwaters*, Ruakura Agricultural Centre, Hamilton.

Collier, K. J., and Wakelin, M. (1990). *Invertebrate fauna and ecological value of Ohutu Stream, Ruahine Ranges*, Science and Research Internal Report No. 81, Department of Conservation, Wellington.

Collier, K. J., and Winterbourn, M. J. (1987). "Breakdown of kamahi leaves in four South Westland streams", *Mauri Ora*, **14**, 33–42.

Collier, K. J., and Winterbourn, M. J. (1990). "Structure of epilithon in some acidic and circumneutral South Westland streams", *New Zealand Natural Sciences*, **17**, 1–11.

Collier, K. J., Winterbourn, M. J., and Jackson, R. J. (1989). "Impacts of wetland afforestation on the distribution of benthic invertebrates in acid streams of Westland, New Zealand", *New Zealand Journal of Marine and Freshwater Research*, **23**, 479–490.

Forsyth, D. J., and Lewis, M. H. (1987). "The invertebrates", in *Inland Waters of New Zealand* (Ed. A. B. Viner), pp. 265–290, DSIR Bulletin 241, DSIR, Wellington.

Glova, G. (1989). "Native and salmonid fishes: are they compatible", *Freshwater Catch*, **40**, 12–13.

Hanchet, S. M. (1990). "Effect of land use on the distribution and abundance of native fish in tributaries of the Waikato River in the Hakarimata Range, North Island, New Zealand", *New Zealand Journal of Marine and Freshwater Research*, **24**, 159–171.

Higler, L. W. G. (1988). *A worldwide surface water classification system*, UNESCO, Paris.

Howard-Williams, C., Clayton, J. S., Coffey, B. T., and Johnstone, I. M. (1987). "Macrophyte invasions", in *Inland Waters of New Zealand* (Ed. A. B. Viner), pp. 307–332, DSIR Bulletin 241, DSIR, Wellington.

Hughey, K. F. D. (1987). "Wetland birds", in *Aquatic Biology and Hydroelectric Power Development* (Ed. P. R. Henriques), pp. 264–276, Oxford University Press, Auckland.

Johnson, P. N., and Brooke, P. A. (1989). *Wetland plants in New Zealand*, DSIR Information Series No. 167, DSIR, Wellington.

Kear, J. (1972). "The Blue Duck of New Zealand", *The Living Bird*, **11**, 175–192.

Kelly, G. C., and Park, G. N. (1986). *The New Zealand Protected Natural Areas Programme, a scientific focus*, New Zealand Biological Resources Centre Publication No. 4, DSIR, Wellington.

Kuschel, G. (1975). *Biogeography and Ecology in New Zealand*, W. Junk, The Hague.

Margules, C. R. (1986). "Conservation evaluation in practice", in *Wildlife Conservation Evaluation* (Ed. M. B. Usher), pp. 297–314, Chapman and Hall, London.

McColl, R. H. S. (1987). "Freshwater and wetland habitats", in *Protected Natural Areas in New Zealand*, pp. 22–28, Royal Society of New Zealand Miscellaneous Series 16.

McColl, R. H. S., and Ward, J. C. (1987). "The use of water resources", in *Inland Waters of New Zealand* (Ed. A. B. Viner), pp. 411–459, DSIR Bulletin 241, DSIR, Wellington.

McDowall, R. M. (1984). "Designing reserves for freshwater fish in New Zealand", *Journal of the Royal Society of New Zealand*, **14**, 17–27.

McDowall, R. M. (1987). "Impacts of exotic fishes on the native fauna", in *Inland Waters of New Zealand* (Ed. A. B. Viner), pp. 441–459, DSIR Bulletin 241, DSIR, Wellington.

McDowall, R. M. (1990). *New Zealand freshwater fishes, a natural history and guide*, Heinemann Reed MAF, Wellington.

McEwen, M. (Ed.) (1987). *Ecological regions and districts of New Zealand*, New Zealand Biological Resources Centre Publication No. 5, Department of Conservation, Wellington.

McLellan, I. D. (1973). "Biogeography of aquatic insects in New Zealand", *The New Zealand Entomologist*, **5**, 247–249.

Molloy, L. F. (1980). *Land alone endures: land use and the role of research*, DSIR Discussion Paper No. 3, DSIR, Wellington.

Morgan, N. C. (1982). "An ecological survey of standing waters in north west Africa: II site descriptions for Tunisia and Algeria", *Biological Conservation*, **24**, 83–113.

Mosley, M. P. (1987). "The classification and characterization of rivers", in *River Channels* (Ed. K. S. Richards), pp. 295–320, Basil Blackwell, Oxford.

Myers, S. C., Park, G. N., and Overmars, F. B. (1987). *A guidebook for the rapid ecological survey of natural areas*, New Zealand Biological Resources Centre Publication No. 6, Department of Conservation, Wellington.

Newbold, C., Purseglove, J., and Holmes, N. (1983). *Nature conservation and river engineering*, Nature Conservancy Council, Peterborough.

New Zealand Official Yearbook (1988/89). 93rd Annual Edition, Department of Statistics, Wellington.

Simpson, P. (1985). "WERI: a plug for protection", *The Landscape*, Autumn, 5–9.

Stark, J. D. (1985). "A macroinvertebrate community index of water quality for stony streams", *Water and Soil Miscellaneous Publication No. 87*, Ministry of Works and Development, Wellington.

Statzner, B., and Higler, B. (1986). "Stream hydraulics as a major determinant of benthic invertebrate zonation patterns", *Freshwater Biology*, **16**, 127–139.

Towns, D. R. (1979). "Composition and zonation of benthic invertebrate communities in a New Zealand kauri forest stream", *Freshwater Biology*, **9**, 251–262.

Townsend, C. R., Crowl, T. A., and Scarsbrook, M. R. (1990). "The effect of introduced trout on predatory stoneflies in New Zealand" (Abstract), *Bulletin of the North American Benthological Society*, **7**, 101.

Triggs, S. J., Williams, M. J., Marshall, S. J., and Chambers, G. K. (in press). "Genetic relationships within a population of Blue Duck (*Hymenolaimus malacorhynchos*)", *Wildfowl*, **42**.

Usher, M. B. (1986). "Wildlife conservation evaluation: attributes, criteria and values", in *Wildlife Conservation Evaluation* (Ed. M. B. Usher), pp. 3–44, Chapman and Hall, London.

Vincent, W. F., and Forsyth, D. J. (1987). "Geothermally influenced waters", in *Inland Waters of New Zealand* (Ed. A. B. Viner), pp. 349–377, DSIR Bulletin 241, DSIR, Wellington.

Williams, M. J. (1988). *Conservation strategy for Blue Duck 1988–1992*, Unpublished internal report, Department of Conservation, Wellington.

Winterbourn, M. J. (1986). "Forestry practices and stream communities with particular reference to New Zealand", in *Stream Protection: The Management of Rivers for Instream Uses* (Ed. I. C. Campbell), pp. 57–73, Water Studies Centre, Chisholm Institute of Technology, Melbourne.

Winterbourn, M. J. (1987). "Invertebrate communities", in *Inland Waters of New Zealand* (Ed. A. B. Viner), pp. 167–190, DSIR Bulletin 241, DSIR, Wellington.

Winterbourn, M. J., Collier, K. J., and Graesser, A. K. (1988). "Ecology of small streams on the west coast of the South Island, New Zealand", *Verhandlungen der Internationalen Vereinigung für theoretische und angewandte Limnologie*, **23**, 1427–1431.

Winterbourn, M. J., Rounick, J. S., and Cowie, B. (1981). "Are New Zealand stream ecosystems really different?" *New Zealand Journal of Marine and Freshwater Research*, **15**, 321–328.

Worthy, T. H. (1987). "Palaeoecological information concerning members of the frog genus *Leiopelma*: Leiopelmatidae in New Zealand, *Journal of the Royal Society of New Zealand*, **17**, 409–420.

14

Alternative Ways of Classifying Rivers in Southern Africa

J. M. KING

Freshwater Research Unit, Zoology Department, University of Cape Town, Rondebosch 7700, South Africa

F. C. DE MOOR

Albany Museum, Grahamstown 6140, South Africa

and

F. M. CHUTTER

Division of Water Technology, Council for Scientific and Industrial Research, Pretoria 0001, South Africa

INTRODUCTION

The human population in South Africa is increasing rapidly, from a present-day figure of 33 million to a projected 88 million by 2050 (J. L. Sadie, Department of Economics, University of Stellenbosch, pers. comm.). Similar trends are apparent in other countries of the sub-continent. This is creating unprecedented demands on the region's water resources. As rivers provide virtually all of this water their characters are changing at an accelerating rate. Wise management of them must be based on a thorough understanding of the kinds of rivers that occur on the sub-continent, so that the numbers of each kind can be determined and, within each group, extrapolations made from known to unknown situations. In this chapter we review past classificatory schemes for the region's rivers and present additional features that might be useful in developing a more comprehensive scheme. We also give details of ways in which the rivers may be losing their regional identities due to human activities.

For the purposes of this chapter, the sub-continent is the area south of the Limpopo River, and includes South Africa, southern Namibia, Lesotho, and Swaziland; most of

River Conservation and Management. Edited by P. J. Boon, P. Calow, and G. E. Petts
© 1992 John Wiley & Sons Ltd

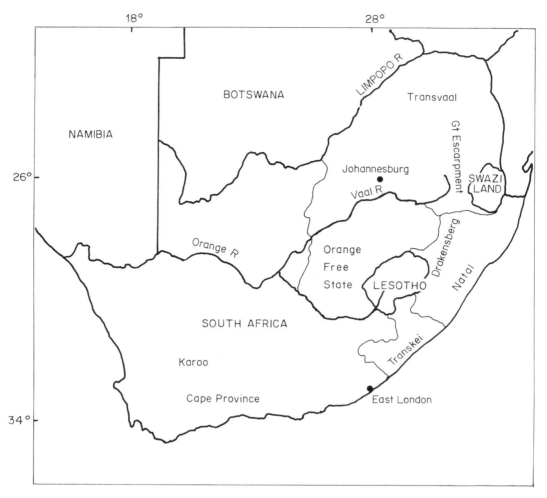

FIGURE 14.1. Southern Africa, showing the location of the major areas referred to in the text

the data presented relate to South Africa. Major areas referred to are shown in
Figure 14.1.

SETTING THE SCENE

Geology and climate

The ecosystems of southern Africa are sculptured by a warm ocean to the east, a cold
ocean to the west, and a landform dominated by a high central plateau (maximum height
3484 m above sea level). Average annual rainfall for South Africa is 497 mm (Department of Water Affairs, 1986), little more than half of the world average of 860 mm.
Sixty-five per cent of South Africa receives less than 500 mm of rain annually, while 21%
receives less than 200 mm.

The combinations of low annual rainfalls with very high potential evaporation rates that can far exceed rainfall result in only 8.6% of rainfall reaching the rivers (Alexander, 1985). This is low compared with other countries with similar annual rainfalls (Canada 65.7%, Australia 9.8%—Braune, 1985) and results in rivers with exceedingly variable flows, variability increasing across the region, in a north-westerly direction, with increasing aridity. The percentage of rainfall appearing as run-off ranges from about 50% in the high-altitude areas of low evaporation (e.g. south-west Cape) to less than 1% in the low-rainfall areas of high evaporation (about one-third of the country). Fully two-thirds of the country's water resources are in the rivers to the east of the Great Escarpment (van Robbroeck, 1977). In general, then, river flow in the north and west tends to be episodic, that further east and south periodic, and that in the east and south-west generally perennial.

One characteristic that is shared by almost all of the rivers is the potential for violence, devastating floods being a common (Kovacs et al, 1985; Perry, 1989) and possibly an increasingly frequent phenomenon (Figure 14.2). Adding extra uncertainty to the general picture is the occurrence of drought conditions, which seem to occur on an approximate 12- or 20-year cycle in different parts of the region (Tyson, 1978), but in a distributionally unpredictable pattern (Zucchini and Adamson, 1984a).

THE AQUATIC ENVIRONMENT

The various river types of the sub-continent have developed upon this climatic and geomorphological foundation, and several attempts have been made to group and describe them, for a variety of purposes.

Geographical classifications

The South African Department of Water Affairs (DWA), which manages the country's water resources, has partitioned South Africa and the countries it encloses into 22 drainage regions (Figure 14.3(a)) for administrative purposes. The contribution of each region to the national mean annual run-off illustrates the uneven distribution of run-off, which is particularly high in the eastern regions and low in the centre, south-east, and west. The Orange River, South Africa's longest river and forming part of its northern border, drains fully 49% of South Africa (DWA regions C and D) while carrying only 23% of its mean annual run-off (Department of Water Affairs, 1986). There are few other rivers of any great length (>300 km) in the sub-continent, the majority arising near the coast.

Noble and Hemens (1978) classified southern African rivers on the basis of environmental factors that determine the structure and productivity of riverine ecosystems. These included the amount of sand and silt in the river bed, the physical nature of the river bed, turbidity, water velocity, temperature fluctuations, and the chemistry (dissolved solids, nutrients) of the river water. The resulting classification, based on the original DWA drainage-region boundaries, divided the sub-continent into seven main

(a)

(b)

FIGURE 14.2. (a) Increasing flood levels on the White Mfolozi River, after the tropical cyclone 'Domoina' struck Natal in January 1984. (b) Equally devastating floods hit the region again three years later (photographs by P. Berridge, KwaZulu Department of Agriculture and Forestry, and released courtesy of South African Department of Water Affairs)

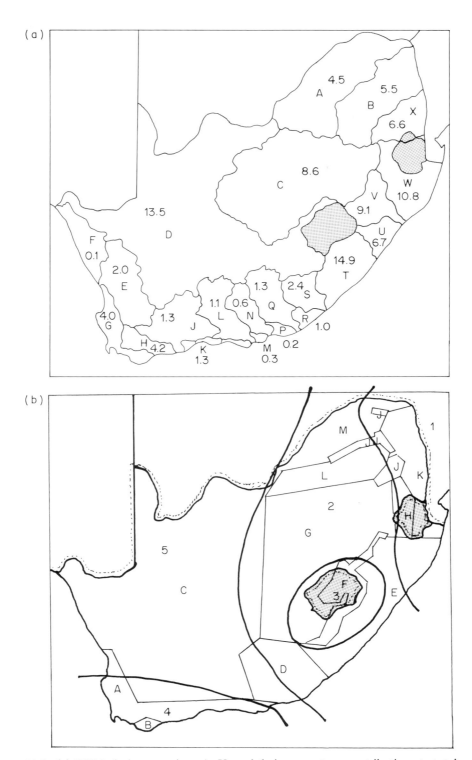

FIGURE 14.3. (a) DWA drainage regions A–X, and their percentage contributions to total mean annual run-off (Values from Noble and Hemens, 1978). (b) Harrison's (1959) 12 hydrobiological regions (A–M) and Allanson et al's (1990) five limnological regions (1–5)

regions of similar rivers. These were the cold, acid rivers of the south-west Cape (DWA regions E, G, H), the clear, brown, acid rivers of the southern Cape (K), the turbid rivers of the southern Karoo, with high levels of dissolved solids (J, L, M, N, P, Q, R), the degrading rivers of the Transkei and Natal (S, T, U, V), the floodplain rivers of the eastern Transvaal escarpment (W, X, A, B), and the turbid Vaal (C) and Orange River system (D, F).

The most recent classification is that of Allanson et al (1990); they did not deal specifically with rivers, but defined five limnological regions in southern Africa, using geomorphological, geochemical, and climatological features (Figure 14.3(b)). Their regions are very similar to the broad climatological regions for fish proposed by Bowmaker et al (1978). Allanson et al's classification has little in common with that based on rivers by Noble and Hemens, the only area delineated in both schemes being the extreme south-western Cape. It is perhaps surprising that Allanson et al did not delineate the high-rainfall, steep-topography area of the eastern Transvaal escarpment as a separate entity. On the other hand, they recognized the intrusion of their arid region 5 to the south-eastern coast, which has not been done in the other classifications.

Harrison (1959) made the first (and, to date, the only) attempt to include biological aspects in a river classification for the region in an internal report of the National Institute for Water Research. His purpose was to delineate areas in which similar riverine invertebrate faunas might be expected to be found. His classification was

FIGURE 14.4. The Doring River in the western Cape drains the semi-arid Karoo (Harrison's region C). It is dry for several months each year, but provides exhilarating white-water rafting for a few weeks each winter (photograph by J. King, University of Cape Town)

therefore based on hydrobiology (specifically of the aquatic macroinvertebrates), physiography, climate, and geology (Figure 14.3(b)). An account of Harrison's ten hydrobiological regions is given by O'Keeffe et al (1989). Briefly, Harrison's classification highlights many of the different features of the rivers of the sub-continent, including the arid and semi-arid interior (C, and G, L and M, respectively) (Figure 14.4), the winter rainfall area of the south-western Cape (A and B) (Figure 14.5), the high-rainfall areas of the Great Escarpment (F, H and J), the major area of floodplains (K), and the short coastal systems of both the arid south-east (D) and the wet east (E) coast (Figure 14.6).

FIGURE 14.5. The Eerste River, in the south-western Cape (Harrison's region A), is typical of the region. Drainage indigenous fynbos vegetation, its high-gradient mountain stream has a boulder-strewn bed, and very pure, lightly stained, acid waters (photograph by J. King, University of Cape Town)

FIGURE 14.6. The Mngazana River in the Transkei flows into the Indian Ocean (Harrison's region E). Its beautiful estuary supports the most southerly major stand of mangrove swamps in Africa (photograph by J. King, University of Cape Town)

Harrison's hydrobiological regions do not coincide with the DWA drainage regions, though each incorporates an alphabetical sequence for identification. Some correlations are apparent with Noble and Hemen's classification, the most obvious difference being Harrison's finer division of the north-east part of the region. Several of Harrison's proposed regions have never been assessed biologically and so the criteria used to separate them need closer attention.

Harrison's most recent account (Harrison, 1978) on the zoogeography of southern African aquatic invertebrates includes (1) a South Temperate Gondwanian fauna, which is now mostly restricted to the south-west Cape and the upper zones of montane rivers and streams elsewhere, and (2) a Pan-Ethiopian Afrotropical fauna, to which most species belong. This latter fauna is sub-divisible into the following groups: widespread, hardy species; tropical or warm stenothermal species; highveld or warm temperate species; cold, stenothermal, montane species; and temporary mountain stream species. From this zoogeography it is not readily evident why Harrison divided regions F + H + J, C + D or G + L + M (Figure 14.3(b)). Consolidation of regions C + D, of J + H + K, and of E + G + L + M would reconcile many of the differences between Harrison's classification and that of Allanson et al while, alternatively, consolidation of H + J + K + L + M would bring closer agreement with Noble and Hemen's classification.

Zonation and biotopes

No classification of rivers can ignore the physical, chemical, and biological changes that occur along the lengths of rivers; rivers are best compared through considering similar zones and biotopes. Noble and Hemens (1978) described how some zones are missing from different kinds of rivers in the sub-continent. The short rivers of the southern Cape, for instance, change abruptly from mountain stream to estuary, while the Karoo rivers have no mountain stream.

Local riverine biotopes may be different from those described for the Holarctic region. For example, the source zones of many rivers consist of bogs and sponges surrounded by flat, open grassland. Where woodlands exist, they are usually evergreen, with year-round inputs of leaf litter. This, combined with the fact that winter and spring are the driest periods of the year for much of the region, influences the dynamics of organic material in the rivers in ways as yet poorly understood (King et al, 1987a, b, 1988). Well-recognized biotopes, such as riffles, pools, and leaf packs, do exist, but there has been no attempt to provide an overview of which are prevalent, or how they might differ in character, across the sub-continent. Such a synthesis could provide a valuable insight into the regional differences that exist between the rivers.

TOWARDS A NEW CLASSIFICATION

There is increasing pressure on local river ecologists to provide guidelines for development and management of the sub-continent's water resources based on sound ecological principles and knowledge. A prerequisite for this is the confirmation (or otherwise) of the hydrobiological/limnological regions already suggested.

At this stage, then, a new look at available information seems appropriate. We outline here three possible ways of using established data (physical, chemical, and biological), to contribute towards both a re-assessment of the hydrobiological regions and a classification of the rivers of southern Africa. Each approach presents a different picture of the kinds of rivers that exist, and different combinations of these and of the earlier classificatory techniques described could be employed by a variety of users for their specific needs.

The physical approach

The Department of Water Affairs holds records of daily stream flow, some of which extend back almost to the beginning of the century, for about 2000 gauging weirs across South Africa. Poff and Ward (1989) recognized such data for North America as "a rich source of information with which to evaluate temporal and spatial patterns of lotic environments across many physiographic and ecographic regions", yet they are largely ignored by river ecologists.

Although no nationwide analysis of stream flow exists, we know that there are widely differing patterns across the sub-continent. These range from the predictable perennial flows of the south-west Cape and Natal, with their respective winter and summer high flows, to the highly unpredictable flows of the rivers of the interior, the north-west and Namibia. Extreme seasonal and annual variability of flow is a feature of most of the

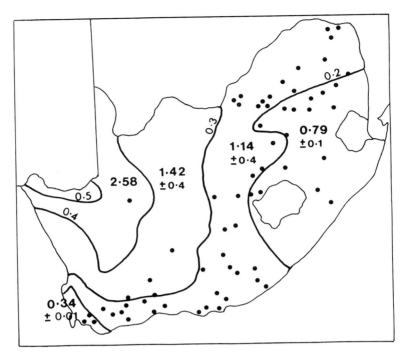

FIGURE 14.7. Means and standard deviations of coefficients of variation of annual stream flow into 67 dams (dots), within regions of similar coefficients of variation of annual rainfall, the latter shown by contours. Data on means and standard deviations of dam inflows from Zucchini and Adamson (1984a). Data on coefficients of variation of annual rainfall from Zucchini and Adamson (1984b)

rivers. Variability in annual flow also increases from east to west (Figure 14.7), with the individual coefficients of variation of annual river flow for those stations shown ranging from 0.33 (predictable: western Cape) to 2.58 (unpredictable: north-west interior), compared to an average of 0.3 for North America and 0.2 for Europe (Braune, 1985).

In work recently started by one of us (JMK) and colleagues, daily flow records for about 200 gauging weirs across South Africa that record near-natural flow are being used to search for and describe the patterns of flow for different regions or different kinds of rivers. Beyond this lies the task of identifying, for each recognized region or river type, that proportion of flow which should be the monthly (or seasonal) minimum recommended flow. This is necessary as a holding action because rapid development of our remaining water resources, together with a poor biological database, means that it will be impossible to apply the sophisticated approach of methodologies such as Instream Flow Incremental Methodology (Bovee, 1982) to more than a small number of the rivers of highest conservation status.

The chemical approach

The major ions in inland waters differ in their proportions in ways that reflect, *inter alia*, the geology, geomorphology, climate, and level of disturbance of the area. Maucha ionic

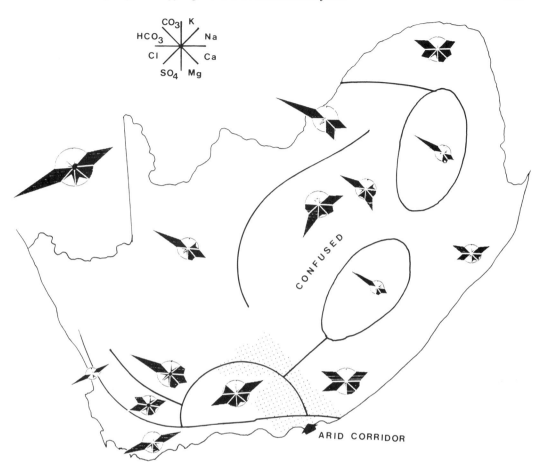

FIGURE 14.8. The pattern of ionic dominance in rivers across the sub-continent, as shown by Maucha ionic diagrams

diagrams (Broch and Yake, 1969) can be used to illustrate these proportions, with the size of the diagrams being directly related to the concentration of salts.

One of us (JMK), with a colleague (J. A. Day, University of Cape Town), recently used the DWA chemical database to analyse the proportions of major ions in about 100 rivers throughout South Africa. Data in the published literature were also used. Though the analysis is far from complete and is presented here in a very simplified form, different patterns of ionic dominance in rivers clearly show across the sub-continent (Figure 14.8). The south-western Cape, to about East London (i.e. DWA regions E, G–K or Harrison's regions A and B), shows dominance by sodium chloride throughout. This may be the result of sea-derived salt being deposited by prevailing south-east winds on highly leached sandstones of the Table Mountain series (J. Willis, Department of Geochemistry, University of Cape Town, pers. comm.). This does not seem to be the full explanation, however, as prevailing onshore winds do not hold throughout that area. A transitional zone occurs north of this, where calcium, magnesium, and bicarbonate share prominence with sodium and chloride; in one area (semi-circle) sulphate also gains prominence. This transitional zone abuts the coast from East London northwards, and extends into the loop of the Limpopo River that forms South Africa's north-eastern border. The south-eastern coastal intrusion of arid conditions incorporated into limnological region 5 by Allanson et al (1990) shows up as relatively large ionic diagrams, indicating high concentrations of salts in both the NaCl-dominated and transitional areas. Zones of very pure water, clearly dominated by calcium, magnesium, and bicarbonate, occur on the mountains in Lesotho and along The Escarpment, while the inland plateau has a similar chemistry, but with higher concentrations of salts and with sodium and sulphate gaining prominence in isolated areas.

The industrial heart of South Africa (around Johannesburg) presents a confused picture of apparently anthropogenically altered water chemistry, with heavy dominance by sulphate in some areas. This could be the result of pyrite decomposition to sulphates, resulting from coal-mining activities, probably aggravated by acid rain due to coal-burning power plants. In Namibia, sodium and chloride dominate, probably because sodium chloride tends to precipitate out last in evaporating water and is typically dominant in temporary waters, salt pans, and other waters in arid areas, overriding any other background ionic dominance.

This simple visual approach seems to have considerable potential, possible applications being to trace the history of increasing pollution of one river using State chemical records, or to search for unusual areas which may have a unique biota, as well as to delineate rivers, or parts of rivers, with a similar ionic composition.

The biological approach

Information on the geographical distribution of the biota is far from comprehensive, but is probably the most useful biological dataset for purposes of river classification. Distributional data on stenotopic species or genera could be used to re-assess the various schemes for dividing the sub-continent into hydrobiological or limnological regions. This approach should highlight areas of similar environmental conditions to which the biota are responding. For instance, the aquatic molluscs *Biomphalaria pfeifferi* and *Gyraulus connollyi* occur in adjacent and clearly defined areas of the sub-continent (Figure 14.9). Brown (1978) stated that the Drakensberg and Lesotho mountains present a barrier to *B. pfeifferi*, but could find no explanation for its absence from a large proportion of the Highveld plateaux of the Transvaal and Orange Free State, where other freshwater snails are plentiful. Its distribution could be partly dictated by biological interactions, but even these would have an environmental foundation, and none of this is reflected in the fact that its distribution stretches over at least seven of Harrison's hydrobiological regions, yet stops in the middle of some of them. Similarly, *G. connollyi* occurs in parts of five of his regions, but seems to be excluded from other parts of them, as shown by its presence at the coast in the south of hydrobiological region E but absence further north-east in region E. Anomalies such as these might be clarified, for instance, by studying Stuckenberg's (1969) map of effective temperatures for the sub-continent. This approach should be used with caution, however, as many species may not be reasonable indicators of different regions, and a community approach may be necessary. Nevertheless, some form of re-assessment of distribution patterns, against a backdrop of the various

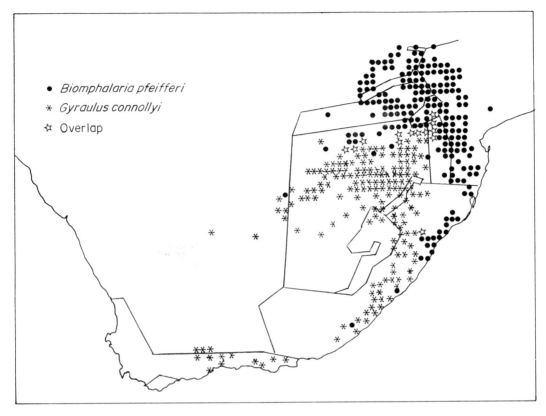

FIGURE 14.9. Distribution of two snail species in the sub-continent, superimposed on Harrison's (1959) hydrobiological regions. Snail distributions after Brown (1978)

environmental conditions and aquatic regions already identified, should be possible and could produce new insights into both the validity of the regions and the conservation status of their rivers.

LOSS OF REGIONAL IDENTITIES

Development of the sub-continent's land and water resources is rapidly changing the character of the rivers, and regional identities may be blurring. Local river ecologists are not focusing on this with a sufficient sense of urgency, and it may soon be too late to record the natural biota of the rivers. The loss of much of our wildlife, including the large riverine vertebrates (hippopotamuses and crocodiles) over almost all of the region means that most rivers had already changed long before scientific studies of them began. Since then, major impacts on the rivers have included increases in silt loads (Rooseboom, 1978; Martin, 1987), salinization and eutrophication (Department of Water Affairs, 1986), the development of land for agriculture and its associated irrigation schemes, the presence of alien aquatic animals (de Moor and Bruton, 1988) and plants, the loss of wetlands (Begg, 1988), the afforestation with alien lumber trees and the replacement of evergreen riparian trees with introduced deciduous ones.

By far the greatest impact, however, must be the regulation of river flow to provide water for human use. In South Africa, the rate of construction of dams increased significantly in the 1950s (Department of Water Affairs, 1986), and is only declining now because most rivers with suitable flows and dam sites have already been dammed. Attention is now turning to the inter-basin transfer of waters from catchments of low demand to ones of high demand. Petitjean and Davies (1988) stated that as the volume of water exported and the distance it is transported increase, so do the likelihood of ecological and environmental changes on both the donor and recipient systems, yet little attention is paid to these aspects of a development. In the only local attempt to assess these impacts, O'Keeffe and de Moor (1988) reported that 46% of the original aquatic invertebrate species had been lost from the Great Fish River, at least partly through imports of water from the Orange River, which changed its flow regime from temporary to semi-permanent.

The 13 inter-basin transfer schemes extant, under construction, or proposed in the sub-continent will transfer 8876×10^6 m^3 of water per annum (Petitjean and Davies, 1988), equivalent to 27% of the total utilizable MAR of South Africa. The most ambitious of these schemes is the Lesotho Highlands Water Project, which will transfer water from Lesotho to the industrial heart of the sub-continent. The monetary cost is expected to be US\$$2.3 \times 10^9$ (Allanson et al, 1990), the ecological consequences are unknown, and at its completion it will become part of a water supply link-up that will stretch across more than one-quarter of South Africa.

CONCLUSION

It is the belief of Allanson et al (1990) that by such wholesale hydrological modifications described above the limnological character of the sub-continent will change. They feel that "understanding the consequences of such changes will be a major part of the limnologist's portfolio during the next 25 years". We agree, and add that verification of its hydrobiological regions and classification of its rivers will be an essential prerequisite to such an understanding.

Assessment of the validity of Harrison's (1959) 12 hydrobiological regions seems the most useful starting point, for their level of resolution is sufficiently fine to allow detection of rivers with obvious physical differences, yet sufficiently coarse to result in a manageable number of regions. Additionally, there are some obvious similarities between his regions and some of the other regional classifications described. However, the important next step remains to be taken. This is the joint recognition by water managers and river ecologists that finances and time should be committed to establishing a sound foundation of river classification, as an aid to the future wise management of the sub-continent's rivers.

ACKNOWLEDGEMENTS

We acknowledge, with many thanks, the very valuable contribution made by Dr Jenny Day, both to the section on ionic diagrams and for her criticisms of the manuscript. We also gratefully acknowledge the contributions of Alison Joubert and Tina Williams toward data collection and analyses, and creation of the figures. Michael Silberbauer wrote the computer program for the mass production of Maucha diagrams. The Department of Water Affairs provided flow and chemical data, and kindly offered some of the photographic slides for the oral presentation. Other photographs were taken directly from its publication *The Water Resources of South Africa*. This chapter was written while the senior author was under contract to the Water Research Commission. The Commission also provided travel funds for oral presentation of this work at the conference in York.

REFERENCES

Alexander, W. J. R. (1985). "Hydrology of low latitude southern hemisphere landmasses", *Hydrobiologia*, **125**, 75–83.

Allanson, B. R., Hart, R. C., O'Keeffe, J. H., and Robarts, R. D. (1990). *Inland Waters of Southern Africa: an Ecological Perspective*. Monographiae Biologicae 64, Kluwer Academic Publishers.

Begg, G. (1988). "The wetlands of Natal (Part 2). The distribution, extent and status of wetlands in the Mfolozi catchment", Natal Town and Regional Planning Report Volume 71, Pietermaritzburg.

Bovee, K. D. (1982). "A guide to stream habitat analysis using the instream flow incremental methodology", Instream Flow Information Paper 12, US Fish and Wildlife Service, FWS/OBS-82/26.

Bowmaker, A. P., Jackson, P. B. N., and Jubb, R. A. (1978). "Freshwater fish", in *Biogeography and Ecology of Southern Africa* (Ed. M. J. A. Werger), pp. 1181–1230, Monographiae Biologicae 31, W. Junk, The Hague.

Braune, E. (1985). "Aridity and hydrological characteristics: Chairman's summary", *Hydrobiologia*, **125**, 131–136.

Broch, E. S., and Yake, W. (1969). "A modification of Maucha's ionic diagram to include ionic concentration", *Limnology and Oceanography*, **14**, 933–935.

Brown, D. S. (1978). "Freshwater molluscs", in *Biogeography and Ecology of Southern Africa* (Ed. M. J. A. Werger), pp. 1153–1180, W. Junk, The Hague.

de Moor, I. J., and Bruton, M. N. (1988). "Atlas of Alien and Translocated Indigenous Aquatic Animals in South Africa", *South African National Scientific Programmes Report, No. 144*. Council for Scientific and Industrial Research, Pretoria.

Department of Water Affairs (1986). *Management of the Water Resources of the Republic of South Africa*, Pretoria.

Harrison, A. D. (1959). "General statement on South African Hydrobiological Regions. Report No. 1, Project 6.8H", Internal report, National Institute for Water Research, Council for Scientific and Industrial Research, Pretoria.

Harrison, A. D. (1978). "Freshwater invertebrates (except molluscs)", in *Biogeography and Ecology of Southern Africa* (Ed. M. J. A. Werger), pp. 1139–1152, Monographiae Biologicae 31, W. Junk, The Hague.

King, J. M., Day, J. A., Davies, B. R., and Henshall-Howard, M. (1987a). "Particulate organic matter in a mountain stream in the south-western Cape, South Africa", *Hydrobiologia*, **154**, 165–187.

King, J. M., Henshall-Howard, M., Day, J. A., and Davies, B. R. (1987b). "Leaf-pack dynamics in a southern African mountain stream", *Freshwater Biology*, **18**, 325–340.

King, J. M., Day, J. A., Hurly, P. R., Henshall-Howard, M., and Davies, B. R. (1988). "Macroinvertebrate communities and environment in a southern African mountain stream", *Canadian Journal of Fisheries and Aquatic Sciences*, **45**, 2168–2181.

Kovacs, Z. P., Du Plessis, D. B., Bracher, P. R., Dunn, P., and Mallory, G. L. C. (1985) *Documentation of the 1984 Domoina Floods*, Department of Water Affairs, Technical Report TR 122, Pretoria.

Martin, A. K. (1987). "Comparison of sedimentation rates in the Natal Valley, south-west Indian Ocean, with modern sediment yields in east coast rivers of South Africa", *South African Journal of Science*, **83**, 716–724.

Noble, R. G., and Hemens, J. (1978). *Inland Water Ecosystems in South Africa—a Review of Research Needs*, South African National Scientific Programmes Report No. 34. Council for Scientific and Industrial Research, Pretoria.

O'Keeffe, J. H., and de Moor, F. C. (1988). "Changes in the physico-chemistry and benthic invertebrates of the Great Fish River, South Africa, following an interbasin transfer of water", *Regulated Rivers: Research and Management*, **2**, 39–55.

O'Keeffe, J. H., Davies, B. R., King, J. M., and Skelton, P. H. (1989). "The conservation status of southern African rivers", in *Biotic Diversity in Southern Africa: concepts and conservation* (Ed. B. J. Huntley), pp. 266–289, Oxford University Press, Cape Town.

Perry, J. E. (1989). "The impact of the September 1987 floods on the estuaries of Natal/Kwazulu; a hydro-photographic perspective", Council for Scientific and Industrial Research, Report 640, Pretoria.

Petitjean, M. O. G., and Davies, B. R. (1988). *A review of the ecological and environmental impacts of inter-basin water transfer schemes in southern Africa, Synthesis (Part I) and international bibliography (Part II)*, Occasional Report No. 38, Ecosystems Programmes, Council for Scientific and Industrial Research, Pretoria.

Poff, N. L., and Ward, J. V. (1989). "Implications of streamflow variability and predictability for lotic community structure: a regional analysis of streamflow patterns", *Canadian Journal of Fisheries and Aquatic Sciences*, **46**, 1805–1818.

Rooseboom, A. (1978). "Sedimentafvoer in Suider-Afrikaanse riviere", *Water Suid Afrika*, **4**, 14–17.

Stuckenberg, B. R. (1969). "Effective temperature as an ecological factor in southern Africa", *Zoologica Africana*, **4**, 145–197.

Tyson, P. D. (1978). "Rainfall changes over South Africa during the period of meteorological record", in *Biogeography and Ecology of Southern Africa* (Ed. M. J. A. Werger), pp. 55–69. W. Junk, The Hague.

Van Robbroeck, T. P. C. (1977). "Inter-basin water transfer in South Africa", Paper presented at the United Nations Water Conference, Mar Del Plata, Argentina, 14–25 March 1977, Document E/Conf. 70 TP223.

Zucchini, W., and Adamson, P. T. (1984a). *The occurrence and severity of droughts in South Africa*, Water Research Commission Report No. 91/1/84, Water Research Commission, Pretoria.

Zucchini, W., and Adamson, P. T. (1984b). *Assessing the risk of deficiencies in streamflow*, Water Research Commission Report No. 91/2/84, Water Research Commission, Pretoria.

SECTION III

RECOVERY AND REHABILITATION

(a) Kammbach. The old channel: straight, geometric cross-section, reinforcement of the channel bed and of the lower banks, agricultural land use up to the edge, no wetland habitats or any woods in the former floodplain

(b) Kammbach. A few months after restoration: silting of the inner bank gives way to spreading vegetation. The ridge between the adjacent still water and the channel should be lowered to improve habitat diversity. (Photographs by Hämmerle, (a) 1986, (b) 1988)

15

Catchment Disturbance and Stream Response: An Overview of Stream Research at Coweeta Hydrologic Laboratory

J. R. WEBSTER

Department of Biology, Virginia Polytechnic Institute and State University, Blacksburg, VA 24061, USA

S. W. GOLLADAY

University of Oklahoma Biological Station, Kingston, OK 73439, USA

E. F. BENFIELD

Department of Biology, Virginia Polytechnic Institute and State University, Blacksburg, VA 24061, USA

J. L. MEYER

Department of Zoology, University of Georgia, Athens, GA 30602, USA

W. T. SWANK

Coweeta Hydrologic Laboratory, 999 Coweeta Lab Rd, Otto, NC 28763, USA

and

J. B. WALLACE

Department of Entomology, University of Georgia, Athens, GA 30602, USA

INTRODUCTION

People interested in stream pollution frequently make a distinction between point-source and non-point-source pollution. Point-source pollution comes out of a pipe; non-point pollution generally enters streams in run-off from surrounding land. It is our contention

River Conservation and Management. Edited by P. J. Boon, P. Calow, and G. E. Petts
© 1992 John Wiley & Sons Ltd

that non-point-source pollution is a major contributor to degradation of water quality and ecosystem integrity in rivers; the direct effects are primarily to small streams and are then transmitted downstream to larger rivers. In this chapter we illustrate how a terrestrial disturbance affects small streams and how these streams respond to and recover from the disturbance.

Small, first-, second-, and third-order streams represent a majority of the shoreline within any drainage network and make up 86% of total stream length in the United States (Leopold et al, 1964). Because these small streams are so closely linked to their catchments (Hynes, 1975; Vannote et al, 1980), terrestrial disturbances, such as logging, can cause severe and long-term disruption, which eventually may impact both local and downstream environments.

While efforts to improve stream quality have generally been directed at point sources, there is fairly wide recognition of the importance of non-point pollution. Non-point-source disturbances cause water quality problems in 38.4% of all stream length in the United States. Specifically, 7.5% of stream length is affected detrimentally by logging and silvicultural practices. Only 12.3% of stream length is affected by point sources (van der Leeden et al, 1990). Put another way, 18% of streams in the United States do not fully support their designated use. In more than one-third of these cases, the reason is non-point-source pollution. Looking specifically at eutrophication caused by nutrient inputs, total discharge of nitrogen from non-point sources in the United States is 4.65×10^6 t yr^{-1} compared to 0.75×10^6 t yr^{-1} from all industrial and municipal sources combined (Moore, 1989). The figures for phosphorus are 1.16 cf. 0.21×10^6 t yr^{-1}, respectively.

Logging has affected nearly all forested areas of North America, and the few remaining areas of old-growth forests are rapidly diminishing. Many streams now classified as undisturbed or reference are probably still responding to past forest disturbances.

Our discussion of how logging affects streams is illustrated with data from Coweeta Hydrologic Laboratory (Figure 15.1). This 2270 ha Forest Service facility in south-western North Carolina, USA, was established in 1934 primarily to study effects of forest land management on the hydrologic cycle (Douglass and Hoover, 1988). For over 20 years Coweeta has been the site of extensive ecological studies, with an emphasis on responses of forests and streams to forestry practices (Swank and Crossley, 1988). The entire basin was selectively logged prior to 1923 and was also affected by chestnut blight in the 1930s (Douglass and Hoover, 1988). Reference catchments are mixed hardwood forests dominated by oaks (*Quercus* spp.), hickories (*Carya* spp.), red maple (*Acer rubrum*), and yellow poplar (*Liriodendron tulipifera*). Catchments 14 and 18 (Figure 15.1) have been used as references for many of our stream studies. Beginning in 1939, selected catchments have been experimentally deforested as part of the long-term goal to understand effects of forest management practices on water yield, water quality, and other forest resources.

Streams draining Catchments 6, 7, 13, and 17 (Figure 15.1) have been intensively studied during the past 20 years to examine effects of forest management practices on stream communities and ecosystem processes. Catchment 6 (C6) is a 8.9 ha area with a complex history of disturbance. In 1942 all riparian vegetation was cut, and in 1958 all marketable timber was removed and the slash was burned. The catchment was fertilized,

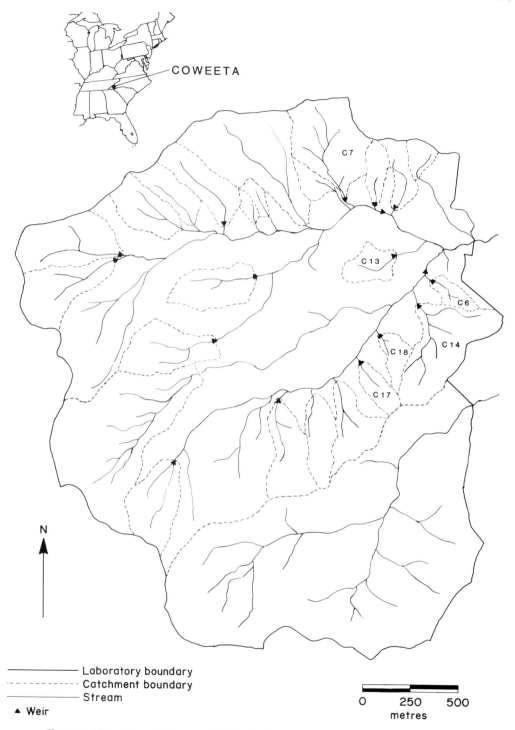

FIGURE 15.1. Map of Coweeta Hydrologic Laboratory, North Carolina, USA

limed, and seeded with grass in 1959. From 1966 to 1968, all vegetation was killed with herbicides. Since 1968 the catchment has undergone natural succession and is now a successional forest dominated by black locust (*Robinia psuedoacacia*) and yellow poplar. C7, a 58.7 ha catchment, was clear-cut in 1977. Regrowth is dominated by hardwood sprouts, herbs, vines, and seedlings. All trees and shrubs were cut on C13 (16.1 ha) in 1939–40 and again in 1962. No products were removed following cutting, and this catchment is presently covered by an intermediate successional forest dominated by yellow poplar and oaks. C17 (13.5 ha) was originally cut in 1942. Regrowth was re-cut annually between 1942 and 1955, and the catchment was planted with white pine (*Pinus strobus*) in 1956. These and other catchments have been described in more detail by Swank and Crossley (1988) and in papers cited in that book.

Streams in the Coweeta basin are all perennial and range from first to fifth order, but most studies have been conducted in first- and second-order streams. The smaller streams are heavily shaded by riparian vegetation and are dependent on allochthonous energy sources. The streams are cool, high gradient, and have very low dissolved ion concentrations. Further descriptions of these streams and reviews of stream research have been published recently (Meyer et al, 1988; Wallace, 1988).

RESULTS

In this chapter we summarize many of the Coweeta studies that have shown (1) how logging directly affects streams and (2) how streams respond to logging, i.e. how processes in streams are modified by logging.

Direct effects of logging on streams

Because evapotranspiration can account for 40–60% of the annual water loss from forested catchments (Kovner, 1956), vegetation is an important regulator of stream flow. Removal of forest vegetation decreases evapotranspiration and increases stream flow (Dunford and Fletcher, 1947; Kovner, 1956; Hewlett and Hibbert, 1961) roughly in proportion to the catchment area cleared (Hewlett and Hibbert, 1961; Hibbert, 1966). The greatest increases in stream flow from disturbed sites have been observed during base flows at the end of the forest growing season when transpiring vegetation would normally deplete most of the water stored in forest soils (Hewlett and Hibbert, 1961). Stream flow may remain elevated for 20 to 30 years following logging, returning to pre-disturbance levels at a rate proportional to forest re-vegetation (Swift and Swank, 1981).

Forest disturbance may also affect patterns of storm run-off. Hewlett and Helvey (1970) reported that storm flow volumes increased 11% and peak discharge increased 7% following forest clearing in a southern Appalachian catchment. Increased storm flows from the disturbed area occurred during all seasons and were attributed to greater soil moisture and lower interception losses, which resulted in more water entering stream source areas (Hewlett and Helvey, 1970).

Headwater streams draining forested areas are typically heavily shaded. Removing overhanging vegetation increases insolation, resulting in increased average stream temperatures, especially during the forest growing season (Swift and Messer, 1971). The duration of stream temperature increase is typically shortlived (less than five years), with temperatures returning to pre-disturbance levels once the canopy closes over the stream (Swift, 1983).

Forest vegetation regulates nutrient inputs to streams by two primary mechanisms: through uptake of nutrients from soil solution and storage in biomass, and by decreasing water movement through soils (Bormann et al, 1969; Vitousek and Reiners, 1975; Vitousek, 1977). Following disturbance, vegetative nutrient uptake is reduced and soil conditions accelerate mineralization of organic matter (Marks and Bormann, 1972; Bormann et al, 1974; Covington, 1981; Binkley, 1984). As a result, concentrations of Ca, K, Na, Mg, and NO_3-N are elevated in stream water, as has been demonstrated at Coweeta (Swank, 1988) and many other sites. Nutrients that are relatively mobile in soil solution or cycle biologically appear to be most affected, and the nitrogen cycle of forested catchments is extremely sensitive to disturbance (Vitousek and Reiners, 1975; Vitousek, 1977; Swank, 1986, 1988; Waide et al, 1988). Concentrations of NO_3-N in streams draining deforested areas usually peak within five years following deforestation (Likens et al, 1970; Brown et al, 1973; Swank, 1988). Coweeta studies show rapid recovery, although concentrations may remain somewhat elevated for 20 or more years (Swank, 1988). As vegetation becomes re-established and nutrients begin to accumulate in biomass, nutrient concentrations in soil solution and stream water decrease (Likens et al, 1970; Brown et al, 1973) and, during intermediate stages of forest succession, may be lower than reference levels (Johnson and Swank, 1973; Vitousek and Reiners, 1975; Vitousek, 1977).

Soil disturbance associated with road building and timber harvest can result in high sediment yields to streams (reviewed by Packer, 1967a,b; Rice et al, 1971; Everest et al, 1987). Soil organic matter, particularly the litter layer, is an important regulator of erodability in forest soils (Bormann et al, 1969). Accumulated litter protects soil from the erosive energy of raindrops, promotes soil particle aggregation, and accelerates rain water percolation. Disturbances that remove the litter layer or compact forest soils promote overland flow and erosion of mineral soil (sediment) into stream channels. Sediment yields decrease as vegetation regrows. However, instream redistribution and transport of sediment may continue for many years (Brown and Krygier, 1971). Coweeta studies of roads and stream sediment were summarized by Swift (1988).

One of the most evident direct effects of logging on forest streams is the reduction in allochthonous inputs. Webster and Waide (1982) reported that autumn leaf inputs to a stream at Coweeta were reduced to less than 2% following logging. Rapid regrowth of successional vegetation returned allochthonous inputs to near-reference levels within 5–10 years (Webster et al, 1990), though quantitative differences in inputs to other disturbed streams were detectable 20 years after disturbance. Data from Coweeta (Table 15.1) indicated that leaf litter fall and total litter fall to disturbed streams were significantly less than to reference streams (*t*-test on means, $\alpha = 0.05$). Wood litter fall (twigs and small branches) was not detectably different. Blow-in, the lateral movement of litter into streams, was also reduced.

In addition to quantitative reduction in litter inputs, there are also major qualitative changes resulting from logging. In the first three years following logging, leaf inputs to Big Hurricane Branch at Coweeta were dominated by herbaceous material and leaves of woody shrubs and rapidly sprouting tree species (Webster et al, 1983). After seven years, qualitative differences were still evident. The relatively refractory leaves of oaks and

TABLE 15.1. Annual litter inputs to streams at Coweeta Hydrologic Laboratory

	Blow-in (g AFDM m^{-1} stream length)			Litter fall (g AFDM m^{-2} stream area)		
	Leaf	Wood	Total	Leaf	Wood	Total
Reference streams						
Grady Branch	79.4 A	7.0 A	87.0 A	470.5 A	123.3 A	669.5 A
Hugh White Creek	64.6 A	3.4 A	70.2 A	409.3 AB	68.0 A	493.7 AB
Disturbed streams						
Sawmill Branch	21.1 B	2.5 A	23.8 B	318.3 B	72.1 A	416.4 BC
Big Hurricane Branch	21.0 B	3.3 A	24.9 B	311.9 B	16.7 B	336.7 C

Entries are means of 10 to 20 collection traps. Means and statistical analyses are based on ln $(x + 1)$ transformed data. Letters represent means that were not significantly different among streams based on analysis of variance followed by a least significant difference test. The Sawmill Branch catchment was originally cut in 1950, but forest regrowth was prevented until 1968. The Big Hurricane Branch catchment was logged in 1977. Data from Webster et al (1990). AFDM = ash free dry mass. Wood includes only twigs and small branches

rhododendron originally accounted for 44% of the leaf input to this stream (Webster and Waide, 1982). In 1983–1984 these species accounted for only 18% of the litter fall, whereas inputs of more labile leaves of herbs and tree species such as birch, maple, dogwood, and willow had increased (Webster et al, 1990). Similar qualitative differences in leaf input to Sawmill Branch were evident more than 15 years after forest succession began, and we anticipate that such differences will probably persist for 50–100 years due to the relatively slow regeneration times of oaks.

Reduced inputs of large woody debris to streams are probably much longer-lasting than reduced leaf inputs. During logging there may be a pulse input of woody material. In the past, general forest management procedures required removal of this material from stream channels; however, this is no longer standard practice in most areas. During subsequent years of forest succession, there is little tree death in the young forest. Limbs and small trees may die as a result of self-thinning, disease, and competitive replacement. However, the time until the forest matures and significant tree mortality occurs may be hundreds of years (Swanson and Lienkaemper, 1978; Likens and Bilby, 1982; Triska et al, 1982).

Stream responses to logging

Accelerated transport of sediment (inorganic particles) and particulate organic matter has been reported in many studies of logging and is usually attributed to increased sediment input associated with forest floor disturbance caused by road construction, road use, and skid trails (e.g. Lieberman and Hoover, 1948; Tebo, 1955; Gurtz et al, 1980; Golladay et al, 1987; Webster et al, 1990). Logging techniques that minimize soil disturbance generate less sediment. Experimental studies in which trees were felled but not removed, thus eliminating most soil disturbance, resulted in no measurable increase in stream turbidity, suggesting little or no increase in sediment transport (Lieberman and Hoover, 1948).

Results from logging Catchment 7 (C7) at Coweeta are fairly typical of clearcut logging in mountainous terrain (Figure 15.2). Three roads were built in this catchment in 1976, and it was logged in 1977 using a cable logging system to minimize soil disturbance. Base-flow sediment transport was elevated for several years but in less than five years had begun dropping and appeared to be rapidly returning to reference levels (Figure 15.2). Other Coweeta studies showed similar results—10 to 20 years after logging, base flow concentrations of particulates were not significantly different from reference levels (Webster and Golladay, 1984; Golladay et al, 1987). However, storm flow transport demonstrates that the effects of forest disturbance are evident for a much longer period (Figure 15.3) (Webster et al, 1990).

Sediments transported in streams contain both organic and inorganic materials. In undisturbed streams at Coweeta, this material is 40–60% inorganic, but when the catchment is logged the inorganic fraction increases more than the organic fraction, resulting in inorganic concentrations over 70% (Webster and Golladay, 1984; Webster et al, 1988). Much of the sediment transport from C7 can be directly attributed to erosion from newly built roads during a storm in 1976 (Swift, 1988). Based on estimates of soil loss from the roads, 80% of the eroded soil remained in the stream channel after 2½ years and was still being exported 8 years later (Swift, 1988). However, data from C13 indicate that not all sediment comes from roads. All trees on this catchment were cut, first in 1939 and again in 1962. The logs were not removed either time—there were no skid trails, no roads, and almost no soil disturbance. Yet annual sediment transport was still well above reference levels in 1984–1985 (Figure 15.3).

Dissolved organic carbon (DOC) may be an important component of stream energetics. Studies at Coweeta have demonstrated that stream microflora remove DOC from the water column and use the more labile components (Meyer et al, 1988). However, based on estimates of annual inputs and outputs, streams at Coweeta are net generators of DOC (Meyer and Tate, 1983). Deforestation decreases export of DOC (Meyer and Tate, 1983) due to decreased inputs from seeps and springs and less leachable benthic organic matter (Meyer et al, 1988).

The effect of forest disturbance on nutrient processing within streams was recently studied by Golladay (1988). His results indicated no differences between disturbed and reference streams in potassium, calcium, or sulphate retention. However, nitrogen and phosphorus were retained less efficiently in streams draining disturbed watersheds than in reference streams. Most nitrogen and phosphorus loss was in association with organic particles. Munn (1989) found that debris dams were major sites of phosphate uptake in an undisturbed Coweeta stream and that phosphate uptake was correlated with benthic organic matter. Hence, as debris dams and benthic organic matter storage change in respect to disturbance, phosphate uptake should change. In another study of forest disturbance and within-stream nutrient dynamics, Webster et al (in press) found no difference between dissolved nitrate and phosphate uptake in reference versus disturbed streams. However, they attributed the lack of difference to a complex of factors that both increased and decreased uptake. Studies by D'Angelo (1990) suggested that physical changes in streams caused by forest disturbance, i.e. elevated temperature, discharge, and water velocity, more significantly affect nutrient dynamics than changes in biotic uptake.

One of the short-term responses to logging is an increase in autochthonous production, i.e. instream primary production. Primary production in Coweeta streams is extremely

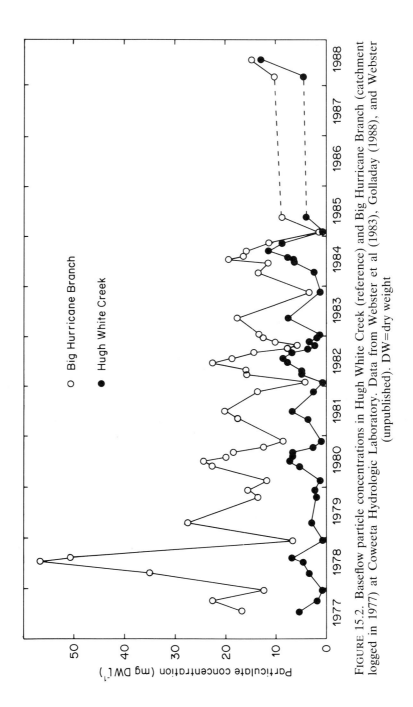

FIGURE 15.2. Baseflow particle concentrations in Hugh White Creek (reference) and Big Hurricane Branch (catchment logged in 1977) at Coweeta Hydrologic Laboratory. Data from Webster et al (1983), Golladay (1988), and Webster (unpublished). DW=dry weight

ANNUAL SEDIMENT TRANSPORT

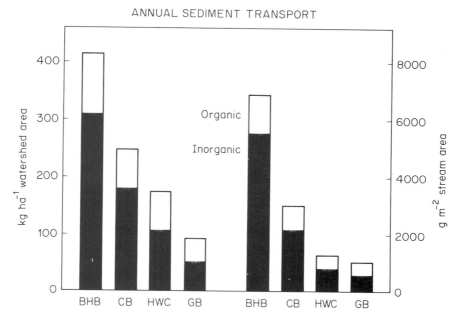

FIGURE 15.3. Annual particle transport in streams at Coweeta Hydrologic Laboratory. Hugh White Creek (HWC) and Grady Branch (GB) drain reference catchments. The Big Hurricane Branch (BHB) catchment was logged in 1977, and trees on the Carpenter Branch (CB) catchment were cut but not removed in 1939 and 1962. The results are based in a computer simulation (Webster et al, 1990) using data from Golladay et al (1987) and Golladay (1988)

low, dominated by diatoms, and limited by light (Hains, 1981; Webster et al, 1983, Lowe et al, 1986). Following logging, filamentous green algae often increase in abundance (Lowe et al, 1986), and there may be significant increase in total primary production (Hains, 1981; Webster et al, 1983). This pulse of autochthonous production can undoubtedly be attributed primarily to the absence of shading, but increased nutrient availability and higher temperatures may also be important in stimulating algal growth. As regrowth of riparian vegetation again shades the stream, primary production returns to low levels (Webster et al, 1983).

Accompanying the shift in the stream energy base, a switch in the dominant benthic invertebrates has been observed in Coweeta streams (Woodall and Wallace, 1972; Gurtz and Wallace, 1984; Wallace and Gurtz, 1986; Wallace, 1988). Shredders, which are dependent on allochthonous inputs, become less important, while production of scrapers and collectors that feed on algae increases. For example, *Baetis* spp. (Ephemeroptera) abundances and production (Wallace and Gurtz, 1986) have been shown to increase following logging. Available evidence strongly suggests that such increases are closely linked with increasing periphyton resources and that species with short generation times, e.g. *Baetis* and many chironomids, respond rapidly following disturbance (Wallace and Gurtz, 1986). Once the canopy closes over the stream reducing light and periphyton production, these species become less important. At Coweeta, five years after logging C7, scraper populations declined from 30% to 13.3% of the total stream macroinvertebrate assemblage (Wallace, 1988). The decline in scrapers was consistent with subsiding autochthonous production. With regrowth of the forest and shading of the stream, leaf litter inputs recovered to 85% of pre-logging levels within seven years (Webster et al, 1990) whereas autochthonous production decreased ten-fold compared to 1977–1978 levels (Webster et al, 1983). As streams return to an allochthonous energy base, shredder production again increases (Haefner and Wallace, 1981).

Transport and accumulation of sediment also influence stream fauna. Tebo (1955) observed significant reductions in densities of macroinvertebrates in a fourth-order stream downstream of the mouth of a smaller logged catchment. Tebo attributed these reductions to accumulated sediments exported from the logged catchment. The downstream sedimentation was ameliorated to some extent by high water during spring, which re-suspended the sediments and transported them further downstream. Gurtz and Wallace (1984) found that the impact of road construction and logging on macroinvertebrate populations in the stream draining C7 at Coweeta was strongly influenced by substrate and geomorphology. Road building and logging resulted in increased concentrations of inorganic and organic seston (Gurtz et al, 1980). Sediment deposition caused a redistribution of stream fauna among substrate types. Accumulation of sediments in depositional habitats such as pools and sandy reaches reduced macroinvertebrate abundances, whereas macroinvertebrates increased in steep-gradient, boulder outcrop habitats (Gurtz and Wallace, 1984).

Effects of logging on leaf breakdown rates in streams are complex. Studies in Big Hurricane Branch (C7) shortly after logging indicated an initial decrease in breakdown rates, apparently because leaves were often buried in sediment (Webster and Waide, 1982). In subsequent years, breakdown rates were higher than before logging and higher than reference stream rates (Table 15.2) (Benfield et al, in press). Meyer and Johnson (1983) also reported accelerated leaf breakdown in a stream draining a logged catch-

TABLE 15.2. Leaf breakdown rates (d^{-1}) in Hugh White Creek (reference) and Big Hurricane Branch (catchment logged in 1977) at Coweeta Hydrologic Laboratory

	1974–1975 pre-logging	1976–1977 during logging	1977–1978	1982–1983	1986–1987
Big Hurricane Branch					
Dogwood	0.0219	0.0134	0.0219	0.0536	0.0237
Red Maple	–	–	–	0.0237	0.0163
White Oak	0.0064	0.0038	0.0090	0.0116	–
Rhododendron	0.0037	0.0011	0.0105	0.0128	0.0090
Hugh White Creek					
Dogwood	–	–	–	0.0297	0.0178
Red Maple	–	–	–	0.0109	0.0102
White Oak	–	–	–	0.0056	–
Rhododendron	–	–	–	0.0047	0.0016

Data from 1974 to 1978 are from Webster and Waide (1982); 1982–1983 data were determined by Golladay and Webster (1988); and 1986–1987 rates are from Benfield et al (in press). Leaf breakdown rates were calculated as the slopes of regression lines relating the logarithm of percentage ash-free dry weight remaining to time

ment. While higher temperatures and nutrients might in part contribute to accelerated breakdown, invertebrate consumption is probably also important. Due to decreased abundance of leaves in disturbed streams, experimentally added leaves are rapidly colonized and consumed by detritivores (Webster and Waide, 1982). Golladay and Webster (1988) reported that small woody debris also breaks down more rapidly following logging, perhaps associated with higher nutrient levels, greater channel instability, and greater invertebrate consumption.

The result of decreased allochthonous leaf inputs, greater particulate organic matter (POM) export, and accelerated leaf breakdown is a decline in the standing crops of benthic organic matter (BOM) in streams. In a study at Coweeta, we found no difference in the mean annual standing crops of fine particulate organic matter (FPOM), but coarse particulate organic matter (CPOM) standing crops were significantly higher in reference streams than in two of the disturbed streams (Table 15.3) (Golladay et al, 1989). The high standing crop of BOM in Carpenter Branch was apparently the result of a rather unusual channel morphology. Large amounts of organic matter accumulated in a long, low gradient, and deeply incised section of this stream.

More recent data comparing three tributary streams draining C7 (logged in 1977) with three reference streams on C14 showed that CPOM was fairly similar in autumn just after leaf fall but that the leaves disappeared much more rapidly from the disturbed streams (Stout, 1990; Figure 15.4). Throughout the summer there was little CPOM available for detritus-feeding invertebrates in streams draining logged areas.

Woody benthic material also declines following forest disturbance (Table 15.3). While slash left in or over the stream may contribute to a short-term increase in woody material (Webster et al, 1983), rapid wood decay (Golladay and Webster, 1988) and the lack of large wood input results in a long-term depletion of wood within stream channels (Golladay et al, 1989). Small wood that enters streams during forest succession is

TABLE 15.3. Benthic organic matter (g AFDM m^{-2}) in Coweeta streams

	FPOM (<1 mm)	CPOM[a] (>1 mm)	Small wood (1–5 cm)	Large wood (>5 cm)	Total BOM	Debris dams (No. per 25 m)
Reference streams						
Grady Branch	147.1	244.0	300.0	4580	5270	0.6
Hugh White Creek	165.8	213.0	311.8	5130	5820	0.4
Disturbed streams						
Sawmill Branch (cleared 1958, regrowth since 1968)	157.0	129.1	78.5	1460	1820	0.0
Big Hurricane Branch (logged, 1977)	112.8	124.2	383.2	2830	3450	0.1
Carpenter Branch (trees felled 1939 and 1962)	386.6	255.2	261.4	230	1130	0.2

Data are arithmetic means reported by Golladay et al (1989). Data are from 1985 to 1986
[a]Includes wood <1 cm

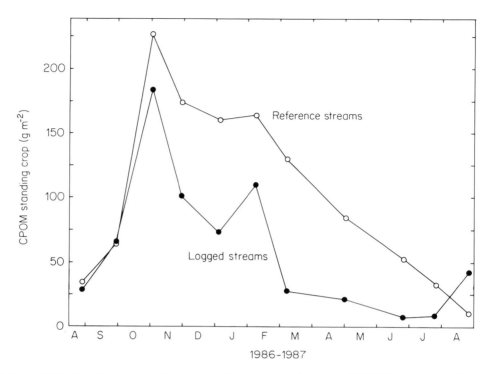

FIGURE 15.4. Standing crops of coarse particulate organic matter (CPOM > 1 mm) in Coweeta streams draining reference and logged (1977) catchments. Each point is the mean of three streams. Each stream value is the mean of five samples. Data from Stout (1990)

generally not large enough to form stable debris dams and also decays rapidly (Likens and Bilby, 1982). Logs of sufficient size to form stable debris dams do not enter the stream until the forest matures.

DISCUSSION

In most studies of forest disturbance, streams and forests have been treated as integrated units (e.g. Likens et al, 1970; Johnson and Swank, 1973; Bormann et al, 1974). While there is no question that streams and the areas they drain are closely linked, the study of catchment units has resulted in the perception of streams as conduits and perhaps obscured differences in the ways forests and streams respond to disturbance. The ability of forests to respond to disturbance is linked to two primary components—living forest vegetation and dead organic matter stored in forest soils (Bormann et al, 1969; Vitousek and Reiners, 1975). Together, vegetation and dead organic matter confer stability to forest ecosystems. Rapid regeneration of vegetation facilitates recovery of ecosystem function while the persistence of soil organic matter minimizes effects of forest disturbance.

Vitousek and Reiners (1975) and Vitousek (1977) extended the concept of forest stability to include changes that occur over succession. They identified three stages that forest ecosystems pass through following disturbance. During the initial stage, or degradation phase, the net organic matter increment of forest ecosystems is negative. The negative increment results from reduced vegetative growth and conditions that favour decomposition in forest soils; net ecosystem production (NEP) is negative and the storage pool of organic matter decreases. During the second (aggradation) phase, the net organic matter increment becomes positive as production of rapidly growing vegetation exceeds ecosystem respiration (NEP>0). Finally, as forests mature, the net organic matter increment becomes zero as vegetative production is balanced by ecosystem respiration (NEP = 0).

Forest disturbance has a greater impact on streams than on forests because of its long-term nature. Cutting and burning are short-term disturbances to forests, and in the absence of further disturbances, forests undergo succession and recovery. Forests recover relatively rapidly because organic matter is internally generated. In contrast, most stream organic matter is derived from external sources and stream net ecosystem production is usually negative (e.g. Fisher and Likens, 1973). Being dependent on imported organic matter, streams cannot fully recover from disturbance until pre-disturbance patterns of organic matter input are re-established (Webster and Patten, 1979; Gurtz et al, 1980; Webster and Swank, 1985).

The sequence of events occurring in Coweeta streams following logging (and perhaps other forest disturbances) conforms quite well to the scenario proposed by Likens and Bilby (1982), Swanson et al (1982), and Likens (1984). There is an initial change from an allochthonous to an autochthonous production base resulting from the opening of the canopy (Period 1 in Figure 15.5). As riparian vegetation regrows, instream primary production decreases as leaf inputs increase (Period 2). Within 10–20 years, leaf inputs quantitatively approach reference levels but differ qualitatively by being more labile than leaf fall in mature forests. Sediment export during these early periods is high, probably resulting from redistribution of material that entered the stream during road building and logging. Benthic organic matter standing stocks are low because of low input and rapid breakdown; hence less DOC is generated by leaching of organic matter stored in the channel. Woody material that existed in the stream prior to logging, and that may have been left in the stream during the logging operation, decays rapidly and is not replaced by the rapidly growing successional forest.

The initial period of autochthonous production and high sediment transport and the following period of decreasing sediment transport with a return to allochthonous production apparently take 20–30 years. Based on very little hard evidence, we suggest that there is a third period during which there is again accelerated sediment loss resulting from poor retention within the stream and erosion of material from within the stream channel (Figure 15.4). Bilby (1981) and Bilby and Likens (1980) demonstrated the importance of woody debris dams to particle retention in streams. Studies in the north-west United States (e.g. Keller and Swanson, 1979; Swanson et al, 1982; Triska et al, 1982; Speaker et al, 1984) also emphasized the role of woody debris dams in streams. Molles (1982) and Trotter (1990) found a similar role for wood in New Mexico streams. We suggest that continued, and perhaps increased, sediment export 20–30 years after logging is associated with the loss of debris dams. Observations of two Coweeta streams support this suggestion. Trees on the catchment drained by Carpenter Branch (C13) were felled in 1939 and again in 1962. However, the logs were not removed. There was

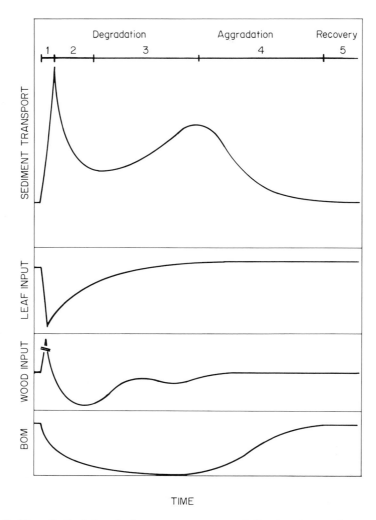

FIGURE 15.5. Hypothetical trends in stream processes following forest disturbance. The five periods of stream response are: (1) high autochthonous production and sediment transport; (2) decreasing sediment transport and return to allochthonous production; (3) minimum retention of benthic organic matter and accelerated sediment loss; (4) aggradation of stream bed material and formation of long-lasting debris dams; and (5) recovery of pre-disturbance conditions

no skidding, and no roads were built in the area. Very little sediment entered the stream as a result of soil surface disturbance (Lieberman and Hoover, 1948). However, annual sediment transport was above reference levels in 1985–1986 (Figure 15.3). At the same time, the amount of wood and the number of debris dams in the stream were both low (Table 15.3). Catchment 6, which is drained by Sawmill Branch, was cleared in 1958. All logs were removed, and the remaining residue was burned. The catchment was planted with grass and maintained in grass from 1959 until 1965. Since 1967 the catchment has reverted to successional vegetation. In a survey of the stream, we found no debris dams (logs with organic debris accumulated upstream, Golladay et al, 1987). Sediment export by this stream continues to be higher than any other stream at Coweeta (Webster and Golladay, 1984; Webster et al, 1988). Active erosion from within the stream channel is evident in both Carpenter Branch and Sawmill Branch.

During this third period, there is also rapid turnover and depletion of particulate organic material. Comparing inputs (Table 15.1) and outputs (Figure 15.3), it is evident that annual export of POM from disturbed streams exceeds inputs. Comparison of the net loss with the standing crop BOM (Table 15.3) shows that benthic material is being rapidly depleted.

The aggradation stage in the post-disturbance history (Period 4 in Figure 15.5) would begin when relatively large logs fall into the channel and form long-lasting debris dams that stabilize sediment movement and begin POM accumulation. Hedin et al (1988) suggested that this may begin about 25 years after disturbance, but at Coweeta this probably does not occur until 50–200 years after logging. The time until the number of debris dams and accumulated BOM reaches pre-disturbance levels may be another 100 years.

There is a major difference between our prediction for the long-term response of Coweeta streams and the recently proposed model for Hubbard Brook (Hedin et al, 1988). The Hubbard Brook model suggests that as soon as debris dams begin to form they act as sinks for sediment, reducing sediment export below pre-disturbance levels. This is a period when the number of debris dams in the streams is minimal and stream bed stability is very low. Since during this period the stream bed itself is the major source of transported sediment (Likens et al, 1970; Likens, 1984), sediment export should be well above pre-disturbance levels. Answers to questions like these concerning long-term responses to disturbance will only come from sustained research efforts in areas where documented disturbance histories already exist.

Several factors might modify the sequence of events illustrated in Figure 15.5. First, the time from logging until Period 3 may be greatly shortened if woody debris is removed from the stream as part of the logging clean-up operation. Historically, wood was considered detrimental in streams, primarily because of possible detrimental effects on salmonids (e.g. Narver, 1971; Bisson et al, 1987), and debris removal was standard procedure (Froehlich, 1973; Bilby, 1984). Second, death of successional vegetation (e.g. pin cherry in north-eastern and black locust in south-eastern United States) may moderate sediment loss during intermediate stages of succession (Likens and Bilby, 1982). Also, the pattern will be affected by the decay characteristics of woody debris. Conifer wood decays much more slowly than hardwoods (e.g. Harmon et al, 1986), and if conifer logs are left in the channel following logging, their decay may be sufficiently slow to retain stream bed stability until the forest matures and tree mortality begins. In a managed forest, the time when significant tree mortality begins to occur (the beginning of Period 4 in Figure 15.5) would indicate a mature forest ready for another rotation of logging. This next period of logging would occur at a time when the lack of debris dams would cause the stream to be most sensitive to further disturbance. The cumulative effects of successive logging would keep the stream in a condition of rapid degradation. Forest management alternatives must be considered with an understanding of both short- and long-term effects on streams and an evaluation of potential cumulative effects of logging rotation intervals.

FIGURE 15.6. Big Hurricane Branch at Coweeta Hydrologic Laboratory. (a) November 1976; (b) the same site in November 1977 after the catchment had been logged. Prior to logging, note the abundance of leaf litter and woody debris. Most of the logs were American chestnut (*Castanea dentata*). After logging, leaf litter was almost absent, there was additional woody debris left from logging, and some of the older wood had been moved. (Pre-logging photograph by M. Gurtz)

Throughout the deciduous forest area of eastern United States, forests are already being logged for the second, third, or fourth time. However, we are not yet seeing the extensive erosion of small stream channels that we would predict based on Figure 15.5. Smock and MacGregor (1988) discussed some of the subtle effects the demise of American chestnut has had on detritus consumers in streams. Perhaps chestnut blight has also had much broader effects on erosion from stream channels. Death of chestnuts, which occurred during the 1930s in the southern Appalachians, added considerable large woody debris to stream channels, providing the channels with a much greater stability and retentiveness than might have been anticipated following the second logging of these forests (Figure 15.6).

In other areas of the United States, the long-term recovery of streams from forest disturbance may be somewhat different. Hedin et al (1988) suggested that sediment export may be minimal during the period of debris dam reformation as sediment is accumulating behind these dams. In another situation, following forest fire in western United States, there is a very rapid decline in stream debris dams as increased run-off from fire-denuded slopes causes severe flooding (Minshall et al, 1989). However, subsequent recovery is very rapid due to the undercutting and blow-down of fire-killed snags.

Downstream effects

While the impact of logging is greatest in small streams actually within logged catchments, some effects are transferred downstream. A drainage network is like a funnel, with headwater streams acting as collectors for downstream reaches.

Increases in base and storm flows resulting from deforestation are generally proportional to area and extent of vegetation removal. While logging one small catchment may cause little change in a large stream, the accumulation of deforested areas within a drainage network may result in significant downstream flooding.

Statzner and Higler (1985) described river systems as being characterized by erosive headwaters, transitional mid-reaches, and accumulative lower reaches. Sediment generated in headwater streams is routed eventually to larger streams. Sediment resulting from catchment disturbance adds to this general pattern, increasing inputs and accelerating erosion within headwater streams. Storms, with flows augmented by reduced forest transpiration and accelerated by the lack of hydraulic retention devices within headwater streams, move the sediment downstream in major pulses. For example, poor land management practices in south-eastern United States have caused massive inputs of sediments to Piedmont rivers, completely changing the structure of these rivers. They are now sediment-laden channels that run red with every storm—very different from the rivers described by Bartram (1791) in his travels through the area.

Various studies have shown that nutrient uptake lengths in headwater streams are very short; that is, headwater streams effectively retain essential nutrients (e.g. Mulholland et al, 1985; Munn, 1989; Webster et al, in press). However, with the possible exception of the loss of gaseous nitrogen (Swank and Caskey, 1982), these nutrients continue their journey downstream, alternating between dissolved and immobilized forms, eventually contributing to the enrichment of downstream systems. In addition to being a source of these nutrients, terrestrial disturbance also accelerates downstream transport because of elevated flows and reduced hydraulic and particulate retention.

Studies at Coweeta have demonstrated that headwater stream fauna are extremely important to the downstream transport of particulate organic material, modifying amounts, timing, and quality (Wallace et al, 1982, 1986; Cuffney et al, 1990; Wallace et al, in review). Continuous measurements of organic particle export from three headwater streams showed that about 36 kg AFDW of FPOM was exported per year for each 100 m reach of headwater stream. Experimental reductions of stream macroinvertebrate communities indicated that feeding by these organisms contributed 56–59% of this export (Cuffney and Wallace, 1989; Wallace et al, in review). Reduced export from these streams has important consequences for downstream communities dependent on upstream sources for organic matter and nutrients. Preservation of faunal diversity and production within headwater streams should be an important consideration in river management (Wallace et al, in review).

Forest management practices in the United States have changed considerably within the past 50 years. Special attention is now paid to soil surface disturbance and to roads, especially where roads cross stream channels. Even more recently, guidelines for woody debris removal have changed in response to concerns over degradation of stream ecosystems. Buffer strips and riparian zone management are integral components of present-day forestry practices and are effective in maintaining fish and macroinvertebrate communities (Burns, 1972; Newbold et al, 1980). However, we feel that additional concern must be placed on the long-term and large-scale aspects of deforestation. The cumulative effects of a mosaic of small-scale logging within a large drainage network have been little studied. Small-stream research is essential for evaluation of cumulative effects of land-use practices from upland areas to downstream river systems. Additionally, the small-scale studies must be considered in the context of the large-scale landscape—the whole drainage basin of the large river.

A practical question is whether it is better to log many small patches over a large basin and have many small streams disturbed a little, or to log some stream catchments intensively. Where even minor disturbance is critical, the latter practice may be better (R. Hauer, pers. comm.). For example, spawning habitat for some upstream migrating fish is destroyed by even small increases in sediment load. Just a little reduction in quality of all headwater streams may mean total loss of critical habitat. While this situation is clearly debatable and in need of further study, it illustrates the need for thinking in terms of large drainage areas. With land ownership seldom following drainage divides, stream management often requires co-operation of many land owners.

ACKNOWLEDGEMENTS

This work was supported by National Science Foundation Grants BSR-8316000 and BSR-8514328. We appreciate comments by J. Melack, B. H. Heede, and E. B. Alexander on an early version of this manuscript. Discussions with G. E. Likens and L. O. Hedin were helpful in formulating our ideas about long-term stream response, and our comments about downstream effects of logging were stimulated by discussion with R. Hauer.

REFERENCES

Bartram, W. (1791). *Travels of William Bartram*, Dover Publications (1928 edition), New York.

Benfield, E. F., Webster, J. R., Golladay, S. W., and Peters, G. T. (in press). "Effects of forest disturbance on leaf breakdown in streams", *Verhandlungen der Internationalen Vereinigung für theoretische und angewandte Limnologie*, **24**.

Bilby, R. E. (1981). "Role of organic debris dams in regulating the export of dissolved and particulate matter from a forested watershed", *Ecology*, **62**, 1234–1243.

Bilby, R. E. (1984). "Removal of woody debris may affect stream channel stability", *Journal of Forestry*, **82**, 609–613.

Bilby, R. E., and Likens, G. E. (1980). "Importance of organic debris dams in the structure and function of stream ecosystems", *Ecology*, **61**, 1107–1113.

Binkley, D. (1984). "Does forest removal increase rates of decomposition and nitrogen release?" *Forest Ecology and Management*, **8**, 229–233.

Bisson, P. A., Bilby, R. E., Bryant, M. D., Dolloff, C. A., Grette, G. B., House, R. A., Murphy, M. L., Koski, K. V., and Sedell, J. R. (1987). "Large woody debris in forested streams in the Pacific Northwest: past, present, and future", in *Streamside Management: Forestry and Fishery Interactions* (Eds E. O. Salo and T. W. Cundy), pp. 143–190, Institute of Forest Resources, University of Washington, Seattle.

Bormann, F. H., Likens, G. E., and Eaton, J. S. (1969). "Biotic regulation of particulate and solution losses from a forest ecosystem", *BioScience*, **19**, 600–611.

Bormann, F. H., Likens, G. E., Siccama, T. G., Pierce, R. S., and Eaton, J. S. (1974). "The export of nutrients and recovery of stable conditions following deforestation at Hubbard Brook", *Ecological Monographs*, **44**, 255–277.

Brown, G. W., Gahler, A. R., and Marston, R. B. (1973). "Nutrient losses after clear-cut logging and slash burning in the Oregon Coast Range", *Water Resources Research*, **9**, 1450–1453.

Brown, G. W., and Krygier, J. T. (1971). "Clear-cut logging and sediment production in the Oregon Coast Range", *Water Resources Research*, **7**, 1189–1199.

Burns, J. W. (1972). "Effects of logging and associated road construction on northern California streams", *Transactions of the American Fisheries Society*, **101**, 1–17.

Covington, W. W. (1981). "Changes in forest floor organic matter and nutrient content following clear cutting in northern hardwoods", *Ecology*, **62**, 41–48.

Cuffney, T. F., and Wallace, J. B. (1989). "Discharge-export relationships in headwater streams: the influence of invertebrate manipulations and drought", *Journal of the North American Benthological Society*, **8**, 331–341.

Cuffney, T. F., Wallace, J. B., and Lugthart, G. J. (1990). "Experimental evidence quantifying the role of benthic invertebrates in organic matter dynamics of headwater streams", *Freshwater Biology*, **23**, 281–299.

D'Angelo, D. J. (1990). *Factors influencing phosphorus retention in streams*, PhD Dissertation, Virginia Polytechnic Institute and State University, Blacksburg, Virginia.

Douglass, J. E., and Hoover, M. D. (1988). "History of Coweeta", in *Forest Hydrology and Ecology at Coweeta* (Eds W. T. Swank and D. A. Crossley, Jr), pp. 17–31, Springer-Verlag, New York.

Dunford, E. G., and Fletcher, P. W. (1947). "Effect of removal of stream-bank vegetation upon water yield", *Transactions of the American Geophysical Union*, **28**, 105–110.

Everest, F. H., Beschta, R. L., Scrivener, J. C., Koski, K. V., Sedell, J. R., and Cederholm, C. J. (1987). "Fine sediment and salmonid production: a paradox", in *Streamside Management: Forestry and Fishery Interaction* (Eds E. O. Salo and T. W. Cundy), pp. 98–142, Institute of Forest Resources, University of Washington, Seattle.

Fisher, S. W., and Likens, G. E. (1973). "Energy flow in Bear Brook, New Hampshire: an integrative approach to stream ecosystem metabolism", *Ecological Monographs*, **43**, 421–439.

Froehlich, H. A. (1973). "Natural and man caused slash in head water streams", *Loggers Handbook*, 33, Pacific Logging Congress, Portland.

Golladay, S. W. (1988). *The effects of forest disturbance on stream stability*, Dissertation. Virginia Polytechnic Institute and State University, Blacksburg, Virginia.

Golladay, S. W., and Webster, J. R. (1988). "Effects of clearcut logging on wood breakdown in Appalachian Mountain streams", *American Midland Naturalist*, **119**, 143–155.

Golladay, S. W., Webster, J. R., and Benfield, E. F. (1987). "Changes in stream morphology and storm transport of organic matter following watershed disturbance", *Journal of the North American Benthological Society*, **6**, 1–11.

Golladay, S. W., Webster, J. R., and Benfield, E. F. (1989). "Effects of forest disturbance on benthic organic matter in streams". *Holarctic Ecology*, **12**, 96–105.

Gurtz, M. E., and Wallace, J. B. (1984). "Substrate-mediated response of stream invertebrates to disturbance", *Ecology*, **65**, 1556–1569.

Gurtz, M. E., Webster, J. R., and Wallace, J. B. (1980). "Seston dynamics in southern Appalachian streams: effects of clear-cutting", *Canadian Journal of Fisheries and Aquatic Sciences*, **37**, 624–631.

Haefner, J. D., and Wallace, J. B. (1981). "Shifts in aquatic insect populations in a first-order southern Appalachian stream following a decade of old field succession", *Canadian Journal of Fisheries and Aquatic Sciences*, **38**, 353–359.

Hains, J. J. Jr (1981). *The response of stream flora to watershed perturbation*, Masters thesis, Clemson University, Clemson, South Carolina.

Harmon, M. E., Franklin, J. F., Swanson, F. J., Sollins, P., Lattin, J. D., Anderson, N. H., Gregory, S. V., Cline, S. P., Aumen, N. G., Sedell, J. R., Cromack, K., Lienkaemper, G. W., and Cummins, K. W. (1986). "Ecology of coarse woody debris in temperate ecosystems", *Advances in Ecological Research*, **15**, 133–302.

Hedin, L. O., Mayer, M. L., and Likens, G. E. (1988). "The effect of deforestation on organic debris dams", *Verhandlungen der Internationalen Vereinigung für theoretische und angewandte Limnologie*, **23**, 1135–1141.

Hewlett, J. D., and Helvey, J. D. (1970). "Effects of forest clear-felling on the storm hydrograph", *Water Resources Research*, **6**, 768–782.

Hewlett, J. D., and Hibbert, A. R. (1961). "Increases in water yield after several types of forest cutting", *Quarterly Bulletin of the International Association of Scientific Hydrology*, **6**, 5–16.

Hibbert, A. R. (1966). "Forest treatment effects on water yield", in *Proceedings of a National Science Foundation Advanced Science Seminar, International Symposium on Forest Hydrology*, pp. 527–543, Pergamon Press, New York.

Hynes, H. B. N. (1975). "The stream and its valley", *Verhandlungen der Internationalen Vereinigung für theoretische und angewandte Limnologie*, **19**, 1–15.

Johnson, P. L., and Swank, W. T. (1973). "Studies of cation budgets in the southern Appalachians on four experimental watersheds with contrasting vegetation", *Ecology*, **54**, 70–80.

Keller, E. A., and Swanson, F. J. (1979). "Effects of large organic material on channel form and fluvial processes", *Earth Surface Processes*, **4**, 361–380.

Kovner, J. L. (1956). "Evapotranspiration and water yields following forest cutting and natural regrowth", *Proceedings of the Society of American Foresters*, pp. 106–110.

Leopold, L. B., Wolman, M. G., and Miller, T. P. (1964). *Fluvial Processes in Geomorphology*, W. H. Freeman and Company, San Francisco.

Lieberman, J. A., and Hoover, M. D. (1948). "The effect of uncontrolled logging on stream turbidity", *Water and Sewage Works*, **95**, 255–258.

Likens, G. E. (1984). "Beyond the shoreline: A watershed-ecosystem approach", *Verhandlungen der Internationalen Vereinigung für theoretische und angewandte Limnologie*, **22**, 1–22.

Likens, G. E., and Bilby, R. E. (1982). "Development, maintenance and role of organic debris dams in New England streams", in *Sediment Budgets and Routing in Forested Drainage Basins* (Eds F. J. Swanson, R. J. Janda, T. Dunne, and D. N. Swanston), pp. 122–128, USDA Forest Service General Technical Report PNW-141, Portland, Oregon.

Likens, G. E., Bormann, F. H., Johnson, N. M., Fisher, D. W., and Pierce, R. S. (1970). "The effects of forest cutting and herbicide treatment on nutrient budgets in the Hubbard Brook watershed-ecosystem", *Ecological Monographs*, **40**, 23–47.

Lowe, R. L., Golladay, S. W., and Webster, J. R. (1986). "Periphyton response to nutrient manipulation in streams draining clearcut and forested watersheds", *Journal of the North American Benthological Society*, **5**, 221–229.

Marks, P. L., and Bormann, F. H. (1972). "Revegetation following forest cutting—mechanisms for return to steady state nutrient cycling", *Science*, **176**, 914–915.

Meyer, J. L., and Johnson, C. (1983). "The influence of elevated nitrate concentration on rate of leaf decomposition in a stream", *Freshwater Biology*, **13**, 177–183.

Meyer, J. L., and Tate, C. M. (1983). "The effects of watershed disturbance on dissolved organic carbon dynamics of a stream", *Ecology*, **64**, 33–44.

Meyer, J. L., Tate, C. M., Edward, R. T., and Crocker, M. T. (1988). "The trophic significance of dissolved organic carbon in streams", in *Forest Hydrology and Ecology at Coweeta* (Eds W. T. Swank and D. A. Crossley, Jr), pp. 269–278, Springer-Verlag, New York.

Minshall, G. W., Brock, J. T., and Varley, J. D. (1989). "Wildfires and Yellowstone's stream ecosystems", *Bioscience*, **39**, 707–715.

Molles, M. C., Jr (1982). "Trichopteran communities of streams associated with aspen and conifer forests: long-term structural change", *Ecology*, **63**, 1–6.

Moore, J. W. (1989). *Balancing the Needs of Water Use*, Springer-Verlag, New York.

Mulholland, P. J., Newbold, J. D., Elwood, J. W., and Webster, J. R. (1985). "Phosphorus spiralling in a woodland stream: seasonal variations", *Ecology*, **66**, 1012–1023.

Munn, N. N. (1989). *The role of stream substrate and local geomorphology in the retention of nutrients in headwater streams*, PhD dissertation, University of Georgia, Athens, Georgia.

Narver, D. W. (1971). "Effects of logging debris on fish production", in *Forest Land Uses and Stream Environment* (Eds J. T. Krygier and J. D. Hall), pp. 100–111, Oregon State University, Corvallis, Oregon.

Newbold, J. D., Erman, D. C., and Roby, K. B. (1980). "Effects of logging on macroinvertebrates in streams with and without buffer strips", *Canadian Journal of Fisheries and Aquatic Sciences*, **37**, 1076–1085.

Packer, P. E. (1967a). "Forest treatment effects on water quality", in *Forest Hydrology* (Eds W. E. Sopper and H. W. Lull), pp. 687–699, Pergamon Press, Oxford.

Packer, P. E. (1967b). "Criteria for designing and locating logging roads to control sediment", *Forest Science*, **13**, 2–18.

Rice, R. M., Rothacher, J. S., and Megahan, W. F. (1971). "Erosional consequences of timber harvesting: an appraisal", in *Watersheds in Transition* (Eds S. C. Csallany, T. G. McLaughlin, and W. T. Striffer), pp. 321–329, American Water Resources Association, Urbana, Illinois.

Smock, L. A., and MacGregor, C. A. (1988). "Impact of American chestnut blight on aquatic shredding macroinvertebrates", *Journal of the North American Benthological Society*, **7**, 212–221.

Speaker, R., Moore, K., and Gregory, S. (1984). "Analysis of the process of retention of organic matter in stream ecosystems", *Verhandlungen der Internationalen Vereinigung für theoretische und angewandte Limnologie*, **22**, 1835–1841.

Statzner, B. H., and Higler, B. (1985). "Questions and comments on the river continuum concept", *Canadian Journal of Fisheries and Aquatic Sciences*, **42**, 1038–1044.

Stout, B. M. (1990). *Effect of forest disturbance on leaf quality and shredder production in streams*, PhD dissertation, Virginia Polytechnic Institute and State University, Blacksburg, Virginia.

Swank, W. T. (1986). "Biological control of solute losses from forest ecosystems", in *Solute Processes* (Ed. S. T. Trudgill), pp. 85–139, John Wiley, New York.

Swank, W. T. (1988). "Stream chemistry responses to disturbance", in *Forest Ecology and Hydrology at Coweeta* (Eds W. T. Swank and D. A. Crossley, Jr), pp. 339–357, Springer-Verlag, New York.

Swank, W. T., and Caskey, W. H. (1982). "Nitrate depletion in a second-order mountain stream", *Journal of Environmental Quality*, **11**, 581–584.

Swank, W. T., and Crossley, D. A. (Eds) (1988). *Forest Hydrology and Ecology at Coweeta*, Springer-Verlag, New York.

Swanson, F. J., Gregory, S. V., Sedell, J. R., and Campbell, A. G. (1982). "Land–water interactions: the riparian zone", in *Analysis of Coniferous Forest Ecosystems in the Western United States* (Ed. R. L. Edmonds), pp. 233–266, Hutchinson Ross, Stroudsburg, Pennsylvania.

Swanson, F. J., and Lienkaemper, G. W. (1978). "Physical consequences of large organic debris in

Pacific Northwest streams", USDA Forest Service Technical Report PNW-69. Portland, Oregon.

Swift, L. W., Jr (1983). "Duration of stream temperature increases following forest cutting in the southern Appalachian mountains", *International Symposium on Hydrometeorology*, pp. 273–275.

Swift, L. W., Jr (1988). "Forest access roads: design, maintenance, and soil loss", in *Forest Hydrology and Ecology at Coweeta* (Eds W. T. Swank and D. A. Crossley, Jr), pp. 313–324, Springer-Verlag, New York.

Swift, L. W. Jr, and Messer, J. B. (1971). "Forest cuttings raise temperatures of small streams in the southern Appalachians", *Journal of Soil and Water Conservation*, **26**, 111–116.

Swift, L. W., Jr, and Swank, W. T. (1981). "Long term responses of streamflow following clearcutting and regrowth", *Hydrological Sciences Bulletin*, **26**, 245–256.

Tebo, L. B., Jr (1955). "Effects of siltation, resulting from improper logging, on the bottom fauna of a small trout stream in the southern Appalachians", *The Progressive Fish-Culturist*, **17**, 64–70.

Triska, F. J., Sedell, J. R., and Gregory, S. V. (1982). "Coniferous forest streams", in *Analysis of Coniferous Forest Ecosystems in the Western United States* (Ed. R. L. Edmonds), pp. 292–332, Hutchinson Ross, Stroudsburg, Pennsylvania.

Trotter, E. (1990). "Woody debris, forest-stream succession, and catchment geomorphology", *Journal of the North American Benthological Society*, **9**, 141–156.

van der Leeden, F., Troise, F. L., and Todd, D. K. (1990). *The Water Encyclopedia*, Lewis Publishers, Chelsea, Michigan.

Vannote, R. L., Minshall, G. W., Cummins, K. W., Sedell, J. R., and Cushing, C. E. (1980). "The river continuum concept", *Canadian Journal of Fisheries and Aquatic Sciences*, **37**, 130–137.

Vitousek, P. M. (1977). "The regulation of element concentrations in mountain streams in the northeastern United States", *Ecological Monographs*, **47**, 65–87.

Vitousek, P. M., and Reiners, W. A. (1975). "Ecosystem succession and nutrient retention: a hypothesis", *BioScience*, **25**, 376–381.

Waide, J. B., Caskey, W. H., Todd, R. L., and Boring, L. R. (1988). "Changes in soil nitrogen pools and transformations following forest clearcutting", in *Forest Hydrology and Ecology at Coweeta* (Eds W. T. Swank and D. A. Crossley, Jr), pp. 221–232, Springer-Verlag, New York.

Wallace, J. B. (1988). "Aquatic invertebrate research", in *Forest Hydrology and Ecology at Coweeta* (Eds W. T. Swank and D. A. Crossley, Jr), pp. 257–268, Springer-Verlag, New York.

Wallace, J. B., and Gurtz, M. E. (1986). "Response of *Baetis* mayflies (Ephemeroptera) to catchment logging", *American Midland Naturalist*, **115**, 25–41.

Wallace, J. B., Webster, J. R., and Cuffney, T. F. (1982). "Stream detritus dynamics: regulation by invertebrate consumers", *Oecologia*, **53**, 197–200.

Wallace, J. B., Vogel, D. S., and Cuffney, T. F. (1986). "Recovery of a headwater stream from an insecticide-induced community disturbance", *Journal of the North American Benthological Society*, **5**, 115–126.

Wallace, J. B., Cuffney, T. F., Webster, J. R., Lugthart, J. G., Chung, K., and Goldowitz, B. S. (in review). "A five-year study of export of fine organic particles from headwater streams: effects of season, extreme discharges, and invertebrate manipulation."

Webster, J. R., Benfield, E. F., Golladay, S. W., Kazmierczak, R. F., Jr, Perry, W. B., and Peters, G. T. (1988). "Effects of watershed disturbance on stream seston characteristics", *Forest Ecology and Hydrology at Coweeta* (Eds W. T. Swank and D. A. Crossley, Jr). pp. 279–294, Springer-Verlag, New York.

Webster, J. R., D'Angelo, D. J., and Peters, G. T. (in press). "Nitrate and phosphate uptake in streams at Coweeta Hydrologic Laboratory", *Verhandlungen der Internationalen Vereinigung für theoretische und angewandte Limnologie*, **24**.

Webster, J. R., and Golladay, S. W. (1984). "Seston transport in streams at Coweeta Hydrologic Laboratory, North Carolina, U.S.A.", *Verhandlungen der Internationalen Vereinigung für theoretische und angewandte Limnologie*, **22**, 1911–1919.

Webster, J. R., Golladay, S. W., Benfield, E. F., Peters, G. T., and D'Angelo, D. J. (1990). "Effects of watershed disturbance on particulate organic matter budgets of small streams", *Journal of the North American Benthological Society*, **9**, 120–140.

Webster, J. R., Gurtz, M. E., Hains, J. J., Meyer, J. L., Swank, W. T., Waide, J. B., and Wallace, J. B. (1983). "Stability of stream ecosystems", in *Stream Ecology* (Eds J. R. Barnes and G. W. Minshall), pp. 355–395, Plenum Press, New York.

Webster, J. R., and Patten, B. E. (1979). "Effects of watershed perturbation on stream potassium and calcium dynamics", Ecological Monographs, **49**, 51–72.

Webster, J. R., and Swank, W. T. (1985). "Stream research at Coweeta Hydrologic Laboratory", in *Proceedings of Speciality Conference Hydraulics and Hydrology in the Small Computer Age*, pp. 868–873, Hydraulics Division, ASCE, Lake Buena Vista, Florida.

Webster, J. R., and Waide, J. B. (1982). "Effects of forest clearcutting on leaf breakdown in a southern Appalachian stream", *Freshwater Biology*, **12**, 331–344.

Woodall, W. R., Jr, and Wallace, J. B. (1972). "The benthic fauna of four small southern Appalachian streams", *American Midland Naturalist*, **88**, 393–407.

16

Vegetation and River Channel Process Interactions

K. J. GREGORY

*Department of Geography, University of Southampton,
Southampton SO9 5NH, UK*

INTRODUCTION

Vegetation influence upon river channels was more significant in the past than today because many more stream channels were bordered by woodland, and there were no regular maintenance programmes which affected channel morphology. Nevertheless, vegetation influences are still significant, particularly in relation to interactions with processes in small channels, and should be a consideration in the conservation and management of rivers.

There is a comparatively small research literature on fluvial geomorphology devoted to the influence of vegetation on river behaviour, and Hickin (1984) noted that fluvial geomorphology had not coped well with processes that were not easily quantifiable and physically or statistically manipulable. He suggested that vegetation exerts a significant control over fluvial processes and morphology through the five mechanisms of flow resistance, bank strength, bar sedimentation, the formation of log jams, and the occurrence of concave bank bench deposition. Several writers have suggested that the influence of vegetation upon channel morphology and process has to be visualized in the context of drainage basin processes, and Gregory and Gurnell (1988) distinguished the morphological influences as including those upon the overall channel morphology, the detailed features of river channels, and the overall channel roughness. Particular aspects of vegetation influence that have been documented include the detailed character of vegetation (e.g. Haslam and Wolseley, 1981), effects of the pattern of vegetation types upon fluvial morphology (Hupp and Osterkamp, 1985; Hupp, 1988), the influence of different types of woodland on channel form (e.g. Murgatroyd and Ternan, 1983), the pattern of relationships throughout river corridors (e.g. Slater et al, 1987), and the roughness of vegetated watercourses which has been documented generally (e.g. Dawson and Charlton, 1988) and has warranted studies of particular aspects (e.g. Dawson, 1986; Watson, 1987). This chapter addresses two particular aspects of the interaction between vegetation and river channel processes. The first is concerned with the influence of in-channel organic accumulations and the second with indicators of channel change

River Conservation and Management. Edited by P. J. Boon, P. Calow, and G. E. Petts
© 1992 John Wiley & Sons Ltd

which are provided by particular vegetation characteristics. Both aspects are analysed with reference to data from a long-term experiment in the New Forest in southern England.

SIGNIFICANCE OF CHANNEL ORGANIC DEBRIS ACCUMULATIONS FOR RIVER CHANNEL PROCESSES

Although several aspects of vegetation–channel interactions have been analysed, it is necessary to consider the within-channel organic debris in relation to the morphology and the processes operating in the river channel. This is because such in-channel debris is an important ingredient in the interaction between vegetation and river channel form and process. Such in-channel debris has been treated as coarse woody debris (CWD) from the ecological point of view by Harmon et al (1986) and by contributions in Barnes and Wayne Marshall (1984). The geomorphological significance of in-channel debris was first demonstrated in the specific investigation of the Sleepers River, Vermont, by Zimmerman et al (1967). Since their significant study, subsequent specific investigations have demonstrated the influence that in-channel organic accumulations can exercise. These influences can, first, affect the morphology of the channel, including the pool–riffle sequence (Keller and Tally, 1979; Sedell et al, 1988; Robison and Beschta, 1990), the roughness of the channel, the bank stability, and the exact location of river channel change. Channel changes, particularly involving the development of cut-offs and changes of channel pattern, can be influenced by coarse debris as shown by Keller and Swanson (1979) and Hickin (1984). Second, debris accumulations are also a significant influence upon stream channel processes because they affect the routing of discharge, especially of peak discharges along the channel (Gurnell and Gregory, 1984), as well as the routing of sediment and sediment storage along the channel (Heede, 1981; Harmon et al, 1986) by inducing localized storage upstream of the debris dams. A particular consequence for stream channel processes is that organic accumulations affect the distribution of erosion (Mosley, 1981) and of potential energy along the stream channel (Marston, 1982). The third influence of organic debris is on river ecology, because debris accumulations affect the diversity of instream habitats (Swanson and Lienkaemper, 1978) and the magnitude of fish populations (Sedell et al, 1988).

Such influences of organic debris accumulations on channel morphology, process, and ecology could lead to the assumption that organic debris accumulations influence channel dynamics but are themselves fairly static. It is therefore necessary to know of the permanence of debris dams, which involves knowledge of the budget of accumulation, storage, and decay and of changes which can occur. Along the Highland Water in the New Forest (UK) it was shown that about a third of the dams changed in some way during a 12-month period (Gregory et al, 1985), and in California it has been demonstrated that there can be a 65% redistribution of the material constituting dams in six years (Lienkaemper and Swanson, 1987). However, in other areas studies have shown that the residence time of material can be much longer, and one investigation (Sedell et al, 1988) has indicated a residence time as great as 200 years. It is necessary to have some idea of the geomorphologically based budget for organic debris dam accumulation and decay, and Harmon et al (1986) have provided a summary of available research results while Cummins et al (1983) reviewed the problems confronting the evaluation of organic matter budgets for stream ecosystems.

CONSEQUENCES OF ORGANIC DEBRIS REMOVAL

An opportunity to investigate the budget of organic debris accumulation and the consequences of debris removal was provided in the drainage basin of the Highland Water, New Forest. This is a portion of the Lymington drainage basin with an area of 11.4 km^2 and has been monitored for 12 years. In an earlier investigation of the debris dams throughout the main channel of the Highland Water a distinction was proposed between active, complete, and partial debris dams (Gregory et al, 1985). Active dams present a complete barrier across the channel and induce a step in the long profile, complete dams are complete across the channel but do not produce a step, and partial dams do not cross the channel completely. When the first survey was undertaken in 1982–1983 there were 287 dams, but a subsequent survey demonstrated that 36% of these had changed in some way, either in character or in precise location, in the succeeding 12 months. A particularly severe storm on 16 October 1987 led to considerable blow-down of trees and debris in the stream channel, which further augmented the pattern of debris accumulations (Figures 16.1(a) and (b)).

As a consequence of the build-up of organic debris the Forestry Commission removed a considerable number of the debris dams between November and December 1989. This clearing was undertaken because of pressure from a fishing club to allow fish to have access to the headwaters for spawning. The removal operations were conducted carefully in a way that minimized direct modification of the channel. Although only 44% of the original dams were removed, this included more than 80% of the complete and active ones which were most significant in obstructing the channel, and it involved removal of at least 70% of the wood debris from the channel. The distribution of the dams removed is indicated by comparing Figure 16.1(c) with Figure 16.1(b). Subsequently, on 25 January 1990 a storm similar to that of October 1987 was accompanied by maximum gusts of 93 knots (172 km h^{-1}), and this led to further blow-down. As a consequence, 25 deciduous and 11 coniferous trees blew down and were placed across the Highland Water stream channel, thus increasing the organic debris significantly very soon after the clearance at the end of 1989.

A further complete re-survey of the dams has been undertaken, was completed in July 1990, and is illustrated in Figure 16.1(d). This shows the great build-up of partial dams, many of which are very small, and their survival partly reflects the paucity of peak discharges from January to July 1990.

The database from this sequence provides an opportunity to develop preliminary estimates for the budget of debris dam accumulation and for the changes consequent upon the removal of the dams. To attempt such a preliminary budget for the Highland Water as a stream typical of southern Britain, the major components of the budget were identified (Figure 16.2) and as many values as possible for each of the components shown in Figure 16.2 were derived from the published literature. The components are of three major types relating to input, storage, and output. To estimate input, six main tree types were distinguished from the New Forest stock maps and the average annual wood and litter fall for each type was estimated. The proportion of wood and leaf fall was estimated

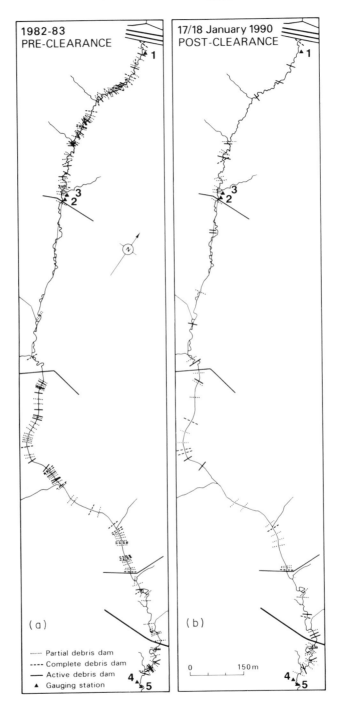

FIGURE 16.1. The Highland Water above Millyford gauging stations. The distribution of debris
accumulation is shown on four occasions and gauging stations are numbered 1 to 5, including the
Millyford gauging stations, which are 4 and 5

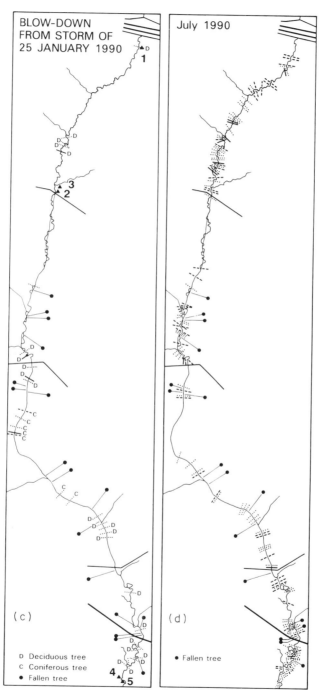

FIGURE 16.1. *(continued)*

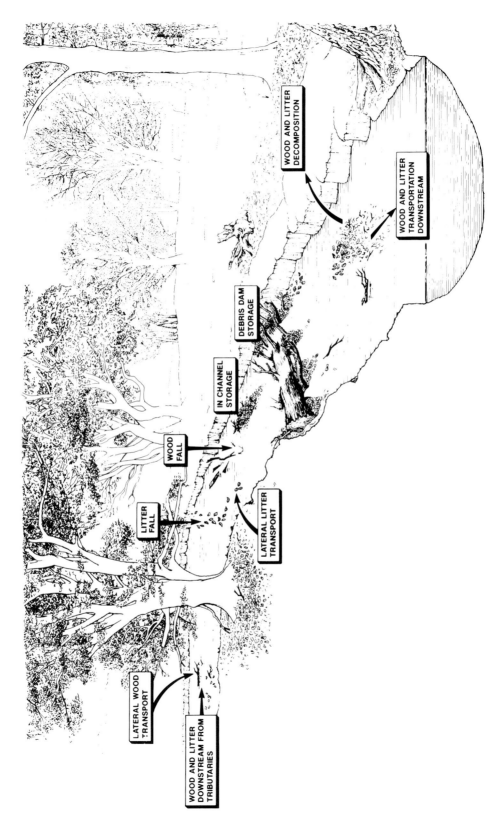

FIGURE 16.2. A diagrammatic representation of the input, storage, and output components involved in the generation of debris dams

TABLE 16.1. Estimated annual budget for debris dam accumulation in Highland Water (tonnes)

Input

	Wood	Litter
Direct fall	4.6±1.2	10.8±2.7
Wind blow	1.2±0.3	2.7±0.8
Lateral transport	1.2±0.3	2.7±0.7
TOTAL	7.0±1.5	16.2±4.2

Storage

	1982–1983	Post-1990 clearance	Input from January storm 1990
Debris dams: Active	2.75	1.29	42.8
Complete	0.83	0.15	
Partial	0.70	0.13	
TOTAL	4.28	1.58	

Output

Decomposition	0.45	10.4
Transport	2.45±0.6	5.8±1.5

(Error values are based on average values quoted in literature as explained in text)

according to the indications given by Bray and Gorham (1964) and Lousier and Parkinson (1976) and approximate proportions of 70% litter and 30% wood were adopted. Supplementary estimates were also made of the material transported downstream and along tributaries, and although this depends upon the sequence of flow events it was possible to derive approximate estimates for lateral transport.

The second major group of components relates to the debris at present resident in the channel, and calculations were made initially in relation to the amount of material in the dams shown on Figure 16.1(a) prior to clearance. This was based upon a reconnaissance survey of nine dams comprising three active, three complete, and three partial dams, and distinction was made between those near the headwaters and the larger ones downstream. These reconnaissance surveys were used to indicate the total mass of wood in all the dams of the main channel, which involved estimating the volume of debris in each type of dam and using an average wood density of 0.5 g cm^{-3} as employed by Keller and Tally (1979). Bilby and Likens (1980) concluded that between 58% and 75% of organic debris in their channels studied was located in dams. However, because of the definition of partial dams in this study it was concluded that a much lower proportion (not more than 10%) was appropriate here, and so this ingredient is not included in Table 16.1.

Output from the system of debris dams is in many ways the most difficult to estimate. There are few clear indications provided in the published literature, although Anderson and Sedell (1979) estimated that some 60–70% of the annual inputs are retained for sufficient time to be biologically utilized by stream macro- and micro-organisms. For the Highland Water it was assumed that 65% remains and 35% is exported out of the system, but there is a considerable amount of error contingent on this, and so a possible error of 25% is indicated. The two other outputs relate to wood and litter decomposition. Based upon published estimates, it was concluded that 1% of the non-exported wood could decompose each year but that the litter is either transported or decays in approximately one year. Because estimates of input and output are preliminary values and not based upon primary measurements, estimates of error have been attempted for input and output components, and Table 16.1 indicates the provisional budget for the Highland Water corresponding to the general situation depicted in Figure 16.1(a). Table 16.1 also gives an estimate of debris removed by clearance from November to January 1990 (Figure 16.1(b)) and of the additional volume of organic debris, largely in the form of fallen trees, that was introduced in January 1990 following the severe storm (Figure 16.1(c)).

These budgets, although very provisional, probably embrace considerable variance, but they do allow an approximate indication of the time-scale of debris accumulation. Assuming that litter is in approximate balance over a year, the situation prior to clearance in 1989 is indicative of net accumulation but with a total storage which is broadly comparable with the annual input. The pattern of accumulation is obviously significantly affected by storm events such as those in 1987 and 1990. Although the input from the January 1990 storm (Table 16.1) is estimated from the total volume of trees over the channel so that only 30–40% of the material is directly above the channel, the storm input could be well in excess of storage before clearance. The amount of input of coarse woody debris from the 1990 event is greater than the volume of material removed by clearance, when at least 70% of the total channel debris was removed and some sections of the channel were cleared completely. Perhaps most significant is that the budget estimates (Table 16.1) indicate that the time scale for replenishment of the debris dams may be comparatively short, so that even without the incidence of extreme storm events such as January 1990 a significant amount of replenishment could occur from deciduous woodland in a period of 5–10 years.

The major initial consequence of the removal of large debris accumulations along a channel such as Highland Water is the modification of the routing of peak discharges along the main channel. It has previously been demonstrated (Gregory et al, 1985) that whereas the low and medium flood peaks were significantly influenced by debris accumulations, the highest flood peaks effectively drowned out some of the dams and so were not significantly affected. Therefore when large numbers of debris dams are present the travel times of low and medium discharge hydrographs are much greater than those of the higher peak discharges. Because five continuously recording gauging stations have been maintained along the main channel for 10 years it has been possible to investigate how flood peaks are modified during routing of specific storm events. A simple way of comparing the situation before debris dam removal with that afterwards is to plot the travel times between gauging stations for particular hydrographs, and an example of this is shown in Figure 16.3. This indicates the travel times between gauging stations 2 and 5 (Figure 16.1) for three time periods and was based upon analysis of simple unambiguous hydrographs, excluding compound hydrographs which reflected spatial and temporal variations in precipitation. The plot demonstrates (Figure 16.3) that whereas prior to debris dam removal corresponding to the situation in Figure 16.1(a) the travel times could be as great as 90–100 min and occasionally greater than 200 min (varying according to peak discharge of the flood event), after the removal of the dams the travel times were greatly reduced and did not extend over such a great range. The average velocity between the two gauging stations for lower peak discharge is now two to three times the average prior to clearance. The blow-down following the storm in January 1990 has not

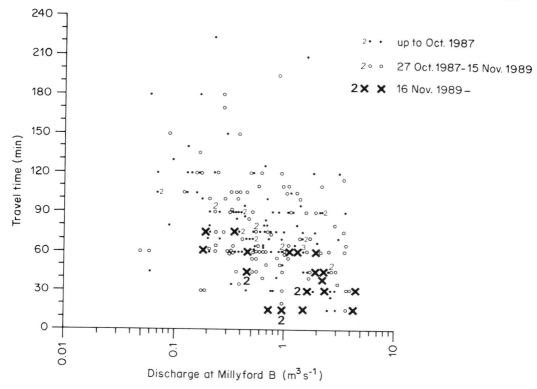

FIGURE 16.3. Travel times for the routing of flood peaks from gauging station 2 to gauging station 5, plotted against peak discharge at gauging station 5, to compare the situation before and after debris dam removal. The hydrographs analysed for the period since 16 November 1989 have low travel time values and averages are given in the text

yet had a signficant influence upon travel times because the trees blown down across the channel will not begin to constitute complete or active dams until later in the year, when additional debris has accumulated.

It is not as easy to demonstrate the significance of debris removal for sediment transport, but after debris removal at the end of 1989 there were clear indications of increased sediment movement along the channel, of decreased sediment storage, of a reduction in the clarity of the pool–riffle sequence, and of an increase in localized bank erosion. Such increased erosion is being monitored at a particular site which has been surveyed several times since 1983 (Gregory and Gurnell, 1988). This is now showing signs of bank erosion on both sides of the channel, an increase in the channel width–depth ratio, and the mobilization of considerable amounts of fine sediment, thus reducing the diversity of instream habitats.

VEGETATION INDICATORS OF RIVER CHANNEL ADJUSTMENTS

Along channels such as the Highland Water organic debris dams affect river channel morphology, process, and ecology. Changes of the dams may occur either due to direct intervention or they may occur naturally more frequently than might be anticipated.

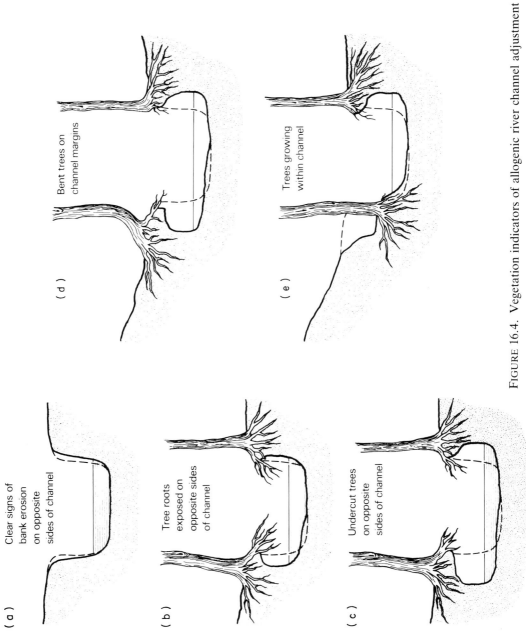

FIGURE 16.4. Vegetation indicators of allogenic river channel adjustment

(a) Clear signs of bank erosion on opposite sides of channel

(b) Tree roots exposed on opposite sides of channel

(c) Undercut trees on opposite sides of channel

(d) Bent trees on channel margins

(e) Trees growing within channel

Such natural changes are superimposed upon an annual cycle, whereby in the autumn and winter dams in temperate deciduous woodlands are augmented by new organic debris, and may also be modified, destroyed, or moved by the winter peak discharges. As a consequence of the adjustments of dam character and position there can be effects on channel morphology, but there are also indications along the Highland Water that the channel is enlarging (Gurnell and Gregory, 1984). To detect such enlargement it is possible to use criteria based on the characteristics of the riparian vegetation. If a channel bank is being actively eroded then it may have indications of vegetation-free bank surfaces (Figure 16.4(a)), exposed tree roots (Figure 16.4(b)), undercut channel banks (Figure 16.4(c)), trees which are curved and have adjusted as they have been undercut (Figure 16.4(d)), or even trees growing at a low level or in the channel as a consequence of erosion that has taken place (Figure 16.4(e)).

Although on slopes it has sometimes been found that curvature and tilting of tree trunks are the result of responses to physical and physiological conditions unrelated to soil creep, and perhaps more associated with shade tolerance and availability of light, (Phipps, 1974), where deformed trees occur extensively along stream channels it seems that they may reflect a response to bank erosion. If such criteria (Figure 16.4) are indicative of bank erosion then they could be manifestations of autogenic channel adjustment if they are restricted to one of the channel banks, because translation of the channel could involve bank erosion on one side and deposition on the other. However, if these features occur on facing sides of the stream channel then this may indicate allogenic channel adjustment involving a change in morphology. The criteria summarized diagrammatically in Figure 16.4 suggest how channel cross-sections with such indicators on facing sides may provide evidence of river channel adjustment by enlargement.

Employing these criteria, the channel adjustment has been mapped throughout the main channel of the Highland Water, and this produces the distribution of channel adjustment indicated in Figure 16.5. Eroding reaches were delimited only when there was convincing evidence on both sides of the channel that enlargement of the channel was occurring. The distribution of definite enlargement, covering some 34% of the channel as mapped in 1983–1984, is substantial, and could indicate that enlargement is taking place along all sections of the channel, although it is definitely recorded in the areas shown in Figure 16.5. Alternatively, it may be that the reaches which are undergoing adjustments according to the criteria shown in Figure 16.4 alternate either with reaches which are comparatively stable or with those that are changing autogenically.

Specific reasons for channel change along the Highland Water include an increase in peak discharge near the head of the catchment following the installation of extensive road drainage with road improvements in 1980, the consequences of a major channelization scheme undertaken in 1967, subsequent channel maintenance which has affected the channel of the Highland Water, together with the annual changes associated with dams of coarse organic debris. At some locations the changes and subsequent removal of debris dams has led to channel enlargement and bank erosion, and at other locations general observation and repeated surveys of monumented channel cross-sections have indicated that such channel enlargement has occurred. Vegetation indicators such as those shown in Figure 16.4 are therefore potentially useful in demonstrating the enlarging reaches along small and medium-sized stream channels. From reconnaissance

266

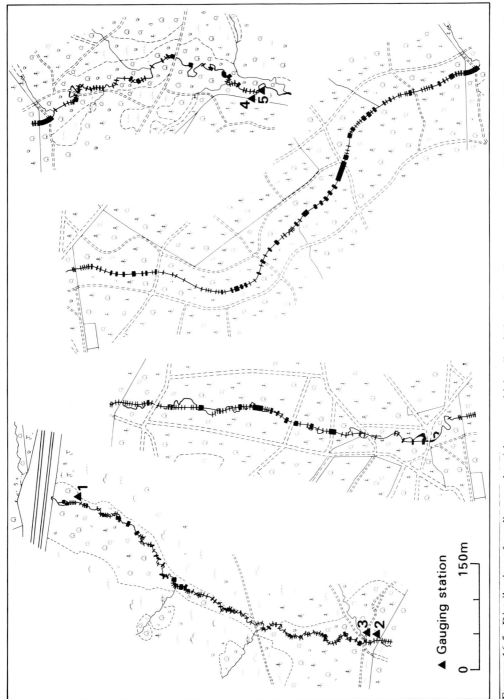

FIGURE 16.5. Distribution of eroding reaches (shown as thicker lines) throughout the main channel of the Highland Water employing the criteria indicated in Figure 16.1. The reach of the Highland Water corresponds to that shown in Figure 16.4. The position of the five gauging stations is indicated

▲ Gauging station

0   150m

inspection it seems that not all stream channels with riparian woodland in southern England show such clear signs of channel enlargement. However, where indications do exist then removal of the in-channel debris or modification of the riparian trees could lead to comparatively rapid bank erosion and further channel adjustments.

THE MANAGEMENT IMPLICATIONS OF ORGANIC DEBRIS REMOVAL

Organic debris accumulations therefore play a significant role by affecting the morphology and processes of small and medium-sized river channels. The dynamics of such accumulations in temperate areas is such that they change quite frequently, and seasonal changes, changes due to large discharges, and additional inputs due to severe storms can give substantial alterations in the biofluvial system. It appears that rates of change will vary according to the type of woodland, and in the basin studied in the New Forest changes in organic debris accumulations occur quite rapidly. The distribution of organic accumulations can influence the distribution of river channel erosion and deposition, and vegetation indicators can be employed to determine the distribution of channel enlargement along channels which are changing. Where there are indications of channel enlargement then it is imperative that channel management be undertaken cautiously. The deliberate removal of debris dams can induce average channel velocities double those that existed prior to removal, and the pattern of channel erosion can be altered with significant changes in the diversity of flow habitats within the channel.

There are significant implications for the management and conservation of river channels, particularly because of the need to be aware of both short- and medium-term dynamics and to maintain habitat diversity. There is a continuing need to achieve a better understanding of the role of coarse woody debris and its dynamics (Harmon et al, 1986), and to retain a diversity of flow habitats (Keller and Tally, 1979) which is assisted by the way in which wood debris maintains the importance of pools (Sedell et al, 1988). It was suggested by Swanson et al (1984), that these features depend to a considerable degree upon the residence time of debris in the channel, and need to be viewed in relation to the budget of debris accumulation. In the Highland Water the recent removal of the majority of organic debris accumulations has followed a tradition of complete clearance of sections of the channel. However, it is desirable to devise a management strategy which does not involve the removal of all the accumulations within a channel, but rather classifies the accumulations and removes them selectively to optimize the retention of habitat diversity. This can be achieved in some areas by developing use of streamside management units (Swanson et al, 1984) as an integral part of the management strategy. Strategies for such management units could be designed in relation to the dynamic pattern of input, storage, and output of debris, and could be achieved by seeking to minimize the changes to stream power along the channel.

The significance of riparian vegetation in maintaining channel stability and in reducing bank erosion is well known, and provides an input to channel management and river conservation. The in-channel organic debris is also an important influence upon the morphology, process, and ecology of woodland river channels, and the interaction of these components is responsible for the varied pattern of habitat diversity which exists and which management practices should seek to maintain as completely as possible. In forested temperate areas, especially deciduous ones, it is important that management strategies should be designed to accept that organic accumulations are an integral part of the system. It should also be recognized that it is necessary to avoid extensive removal of dams because of the immediate increase in flood discharges and channel velocities (which lead to channel adjustments and reduce the diversity of environments), and that selective and frequent maintenance is compatible with the minimization of river channel change.

ACKNOWLEDGEMENTS

The assistance of Mr C. T. Hill, Mr N. M. Harris, Mr K. Hewston, and Mr S. Tooth in data collection is gratefully acknowledged.

REFERENCES

Anderson, N. H., and Sedell, J. R. (1979). "Detritus processing by macroinvertebrates in stream ecosystems", *Annual Review of Entomology*, **24**, 351–377.
Barnes, J. R., and Wayne Marshall, E. (Eds) (1984). *Stream Ecology. Application and Testing of General Ecological Theory*, Plenum Press, New York.
Bilby, R. E., and Likens, G. E. (1980). "Importance of organic debris dams in the structure and function of stream ecosystems", *Ecology*, **61**, 1107–1113.
Bray, J. R., and Gorham, E., (1964). "Litter production in the forests of the world", *Advances in Ecological Research*, **2**, 101–157.
Cummins, K. W., Sedell, J. R., Swanson, F. J., Minshall, G. W., Fischer, S. G., Cushing, C. E., Peterson, R. C., and Vannote, R. I. (1983). "Organic matter budgets for stream ecosystems: Problems in their evaluation", in *Stream Ecology, Application and Testing of General Ecological Theory* (Eds J. R. Barnes and G. W. Minshall), pp. 299–353, Plenum Press, New York.
Dawson, F. H. (1986). "Light reduction techniques for aquatic plant control", in *Lake and Reservoir Management*, Vol. II, pp. 258–262, Proceedings of the 5th annual conference of the North American Lake Management Society, 13–16 November 1985, Geneva, Wisconsin. North American Lake Management Society, Washington, DC.
Dawson, F. H., and Charlton, F. G. (1988). "Bibliography on the hydraulic resistance of roughness of vegetated watercourses", *Freshwater Biological Association Occasional Publication* No. 25, Freshwater Biological Association, Ambleside.
Gregory, K. J., Gurnell, A. M., and Hill, C. T. (1985). "The permanence of debris dams related to river channel processes", *Hydrological Sciences Journal*, **30**, 371–381.
Gregory, K. J., and Gurnell, A. M. (1988). "Vegetation and river channel form and process", in *Biogeomorphology* (Ed. H. A. Viles), pp. 11–42, Blackwell, Oxford.
Gurnell, A. M., and Gregory, K. J., (1984). "The influence of vegetation on stream channel processes", in *Catchment Experiments in Geomorphology* (Eds T. P. Burt and D. E. Walling), pp. 515–535, Geobooks, Norwich.
Harmon, M. E., Franklin, J. F., Swanson, F. J., Sollins, P., Gregory, S. V., Lattin, J. D., Anderson, N. H., Cline, S. P., Aumen, N. G., Sedell, J. R., Lienkaemper, G. W., Cromack, K., and Cummins, K. W. (1986). "Ecology of coarse woody debris in temperate ecosystems", *Advances in Ecological Research*, **15**, 133–302.
Haslam, S. M., and Wolseley, P. A. (1981). *River Vegetation: Its identification, assessment and management*, Cambridge University Press, Cambridge.
Heede, B. M. (1981). "Dynamics of selected mountain streams in the western United States of America", *Zeitschrift für Geomorphologie*, **25**, 17–32.
Hickin, E. J. (1984). "Vegetation and river channel dynamics", *Canadian Geographer*, **28**, 111–126.
Hupp, C. R. (1988). "Plant ecological aspects of flood geomorphology and palaeoflood history", in *Flood Geomorphology* (Eds V. R. Baker, R. C. Kochel, and P. C. Patton), pp. 335–356, Wiley, Interscience, New York.
Hupp, C. R., and Osterkamp, W. R. (1985). "Bottomland vegetation distribution along Passage Creek, Virginia in relation to fluvial landforms", *Ecology*, **66**, 670–681.

Keller, E. A., and Swanson, F. J. (1979). "Effects of large organic material on channel form and fluvial processes", *Earth Surface Processes*, **4**, 361–380.

Keller, E. A., and Tally, T. (1979). "Effects of large organic debris on channel form and fluvial processes in the coastal Redwood environment", in *Adjustments of the Fluvial System* (Eds D. D. Rhodes and G. P. Williams), pp. 169–197, Kendall Hunt, Debuque, Iowa.

Lienkaemper, G. W., and Swanson, F. J. (1987). "Dynamics of large woody debris in streams in old-growth Redwood fir forests", *Canadian Journal of Forest Research*, **17**, 150–156.

Lousier, W. D., and Parkinson, D. (1976). "Litter decomposition in a cool temperate deciduous forest", *Canadian Journal of Botany*, **54**, 419–436.

Marston, R. A. (1982). "The geomorphic significance of log steps in forest streams", *Annals of the Association of American Geographers*, **72**, 99–108.

Mosley, P. M. (1981). "The influence of organic debris on channel morphology and bedload transport in a New Zealand Forest stream", *Earth Surface Processes and Landforms*, **6**, 571–579.

Murgatroyd, A. L., and Ternan, J. L. (1983). "The impact of afforestation on stream bank erosion and channel form", *Earth Surface Processes and Landforms*, **8**, 357–369.

Phipps, R. L. (1974). "The soil creep-curved tree fallacy", *Journal of Research US Geological Survey*, **2**, 371–377.

Robison, E. G., and Beschta, R. L. (1990). "Coarse woody debris and channel morphology interactions for undisturbed streams in South East Alaska, USA", *Earth Surface Processes and Landforms*, **15**, 149–156.

Sedell, J. R., Bisson, P. A., Swanson, F. J., and Gregory, S. V. (1988). "What we know about large trees that fall into streams and rivers", in *From the Forest to the Sea: A story of fallen trees* (Eds C. Maser, R. F. Tarrant, J. M. Trappe, and J. F. Franklin), pp. 47–81, USDA Forest Service, General Technical Report–PNW 229.

Slater, F., Curry, P., and Chadwell, C. (1987). "A practical approach to the evaluation of the conservation status of vegetation in river corridors in Wales", *Biological Conservation*, **40**, 53–68.

Swanson, F. J., and Lienkaemper, G. W. (1978). "Physical consequences of large organic debris in Pacific North West streams", *USDA Forest Service, General Technical Report* PNW–69, 1–13.

Swanson, F. J., Bryant, M. D., Lienkaemper, G. W., and Sedell, J. R. (1984). "Organic debris in small streams, Prince of Wales Island, South East Alaska", *US Department of Agriculture* GTR, PNW, 166.

Watson, D. (1987). "Hydraulic effects of aquatic weeds in UK rivers", *Regulated Rivers: Research and Management*, **1**, 211–227.

Zimmerman, R. C., Goodlet, J. C., and Comer, G. H. (1967). "The influence of vegetation on channel form of small streams", *International Association of Scientific Hydrology: Symposium on River Morphology*, Publication 75, 255–275.

17

Effects of Weirs on the Littoral Environment of the River Murray, South Australia

K. F. WALKER, M. C. THOMS, and F. SHELDON

River Murray Laboratory,
Department of Zoology, University of Adelaide,
Adelaide, South Australia 5000

INTRODUCTION

In planning for conservation, rivers are often regarded as corridors through the landscape. This highlights the longitudinal dimension of river ecosystems, but may conceal the importance of lateral, vertical, and temporal perspectives (e.g. Ward, 1989 and Chapter 2, this volume). In the case of floodplain rivers, lateral linkages may be as necessary for the integrity of the corridor as the downstream passage of water and matter.

Lateral linkages between rivers and riparian land, or between rivers and floodplains, involve transfers of matter and energy along gradients that may include disjunctions or "boundaries." These are transitional zones, but with their own unique features (Naiman et al, 1988). For example:

- Enhanced species diversity (residents and visitors);
- Exchanges of matter and energy between adjacent areas;
- Refuges and other resources for species from these areas; and
- Pathways for dispersal and migration.

This concept is important for river conservation because boundaries are part of the structural and functional integrity of river corridors, and because they are highly vulnerable to disturbance (cf. Resh et al, 1988).

Aquatic river-edge environments are outstanding examples of ecological boundaries, although they have received remarkably little attention from lotic ecologists. The term "littoral" is applicable (e.g. Fisher and La Voy, 1972; Nilsson, 1984), although it is normally used for lakes and marine environments. The riverine littoral zone provides comparatively calm water and stable sediments, with habitat structure conferred by rocks, snags, plants, and bank irregularities. It is influenced also by temporal patterns of disturbance, especially changes in water level.

River Conservation and Management. Edited by P. J. Boon, P. Calow, and G. E. Petts
© 1992 John Wiley & Sons Ltd

In this chapter we describe the littoral zone of the River Murray in South Australia, with particular regard for the effects of high turbidity and the impact of water-level changes associated with a series of weirs. We suggest that this zone has special significance for the ecology of the Murray, and that the concept of a littoral boundary may be important for conservation and management of rivers elsewhere in the world.

ENVIRONMENTAL SETTING

The Murray–Darling system is one of the great river systems of the world (Figure 17.1). The lengths of the principal rivers (5300 km) confer fourth rank among global systems, although the discharge is small (annual mean 318.2 m^3 s^{-1}) even by Australian standards. The Murray rises in the Snowy Mountains and flows north-west as the border between New South Wales and Victoria. For most of its length (2560 km) it flows across dry alluvial plains, gathering tributaries from distant highlands. The Darling (2740 km) flows across semi-desert to meet the Murray at Wentworth, 830 river-km from the sea. Beyond the confluence, the "lower" Murray receives no major tributary inflows (Figure 17.2).

The Murray and Darling are rivers of quite different character, each with a strong influence on the lower reaches. This is shown by comparisons of flow, turbidity, and floodplain communities:

FIGURE 17.1. An aerial view of the River Murray, South Australia, upstream of the limestone gorge, showing typical billabongs (oxbows)

(1) *Flow regime*: Flows in the Murray above the Darling confluence (e.g. Murray at Euston, near Merbein: mean 271 m^3 s^{-1} range 7.4–3495 m^3 s^{-1}) are sustained mainly by high-catchment precipitation in winter and spring, whereas the Darling is fed by unreliable summer monsoons and its flows are more erratic (Darling at Burtundy: 59, 0.0–913). The regime of the lower Murray reflects this variability (Murray at Blanchetown: 318.2, 19.6–1562) (Walker, 1986). During a typical irrigation season (November to May), flows in the Murray at Wentworth are maintained at 2000 ML

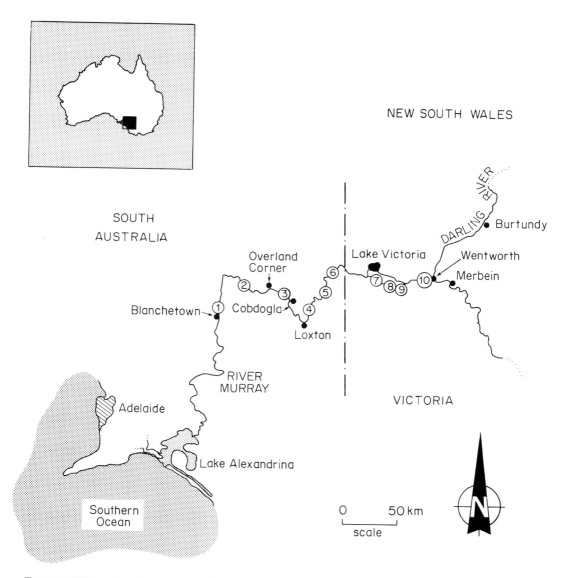

FIGURE 17.2. A sketch map of the lower River Murray showing Locks 1–10 and places mentioned in the text

FIGURE 17.3. The confluence of the River Murray and the Darling River at Wentworth, New South Wales. The highly turbid flows from the Darling have profound effects on the lower Murray environment

day^{-1}, then augmented to 7000 ML day^{-1} by diversions from Lake Victoria (Figure 17.2) before entering South Australia (Mackay et al, 1988). Lake Victoria (680 GL) impounds water diverted from the Menindee Lakes complex (1680 GL) on the Darling. In summer and autumn, therefore, water in the lower Murray is typically a 5:2 mix of Darling and Murray water.

(2) *Turbidity regime*: The Darling is laden with fine clay suspensoids (Woodyer, 1978) and the Murray is comparatively clear, so that there is a striking contrast in turbidity at the confluence (Figure 17.3). Although bank erosion probably has contributed significant amounts of suspended sediment to the lower river for many years (cf. Thoms and Walker, in press a,b), the regime changed with the advent of the Menindee Lakes storage in 1968. Regulated inflows from Lake Victoria now maintain highly turbid flows through spring and summer, although patterns are obscured by variations in flow and salinity (Mackay et al, 1988). In the Darling at Burtundy in 1978–1986 the mean turbidity was 109 NTU (range 10–500, $n = 410$), compared with 29 NTU (3.5–122, 399) in the Murray at Merbein (Mackay et al, 1988). The Darling's effect was evident in the Murray at Overland Corner, far below the confluence, where the average was 82 NTU (15–380, 387). In 1987 Secchi disk transparencies in this area averaged 340 mm (150–610, 39; Lloyd et al, in press); thus little light penetrates below 500 mm.

FIGURE 17.4. The River Murray near Chowilla, South Australia, showing the limestone cliffs typical of the lowermost reaches

(3) *Floodplain communities*: The middle Murray has a broad floodplain (1–20 km) with extensive forests and wetlands (e.g. Dexter et al, 1986; Pressey, 1986). In contrast, the Darling flows in a 10 m deep channel and its discharge is too low and irregular to sustain floodplain communities. The ecological significance of the Murray's wetlands is apparent in the composition of the riverine biota (Walker, 1986).

Below the Darling junction the Murray enters the "Riverland" region of South Australia, and after 500 km turns south toward Lake Alexandrina and the sea (Figure 17.2). In the Riverland the floodplain is broad (4–9 km), with extensive irrigation development, but downstream it is restricted (1–2 km) to a limestone gorge (Figure 17.4). The lower river has been influenced by Tertiary marine incursions and adjustments related to changes in sea level (Twidale et al, 1978).

The Riverland climate is "semi-arid steppe" or *Bsk* in the Köppen classification. At Loxton (Figure 17.2) the mean annual rainfall and evaporation are 278 and 2250 mm, respectively, and mean daily temperature ranges are from 14.7–31.4°C in January to 3.8–15.5°C in July (Kernich, 1984). The riverbank soils are saline grey clays with poor physical properties (e.g. low infiltration rates, low hydraulic conductivities, and high bulk densities), but on the higher terraces sand is mixed with the clay and quality is improved (Cole, 1978). The riparian vegetation grades from lignum (*Muehlenbeckia cunninghamii*) in frequently flooded areas to red gum (*Eucalyptus camaldulensis*) on the riverbanks and black box (*E. largiflorens*) and cooba (*Acacia stenophylla*) on higher ground. The regional vegetation is adversely affected by agriculture and flow regulation (Margules and Partners et al, 1990). There are also severe problems of salinization caused by relictual marine salt and exacerbated by irrigation and the hydraulic effects of weirs (Selby, 1981; Morton and Cunningham, 1985). The mean salinity of the Murray at Overland Corner in 1978–1986 was 370 mg l^{-1} (range 146–723, $n = 396$; after Mackay et al, 1988).

EFFECTS OF WEIR OPERATIONS

Water level regime

Flows in the Murray–Darling system are regulated by several dams, mainly on tributaries to the Murray. By interstate agreement South Australia receives a minimum annual "entitlement" flow of 1850 GL, but the actual average is about 6650 GL (Jacobs, 1989). Water is diverted from the river for irrigation and rural and urban supplies. In general, regulation has altered the seasonal pattern of flows, the frequency and magnitude of floods, and the form of the stage hydrograph (Baker and Wright, 1978; Jacobs, 1989;

FIGURE 17.5. Lock 6, near Renmark, South Australia

Thoms and Walker, 1989). The effects include changes in sediment transport (Thoms and Walker, in press a) and degradation of river and floodplain communities (Walker, 1985).

Flows in the lower Murray are further regulated by a series of 10 weirs (Figure 17.5), extending from Blanchetown (Lock 1) to Wentworth (Lock 10) (Figure 17.2). The weirs (with adjacent locks) were built in 1922–1935 to serve riverboat transport, but they now provide supplementary flow control and maintain levels for irrigation pumps. The weirs are 84–169 m long and the pools are 29–88 km long, with capacities of 13–64 GL. The change in level across each weir is about 3 m.

Each weir incorporates a navigable pass, with 1 m² wooden Boulé panels supported by needle beams and trestles, and a sluice section with bays of 400 mm deep concrete "stop logs". During "high rivers" the panels and stop logs are removed using a mobile crane, and in floods the trestles are folded against the base of the weir. At other times, the lockmaster will manipulate the panels and stop logs in an endeavour to keep the water level within 50 mm (sic) of a designated "pool level".

The effect of weir operations is to maintain a steady upper-pool level except when flows exceed storage capacity. In the river below the weir, however, water levels may vary erratically.

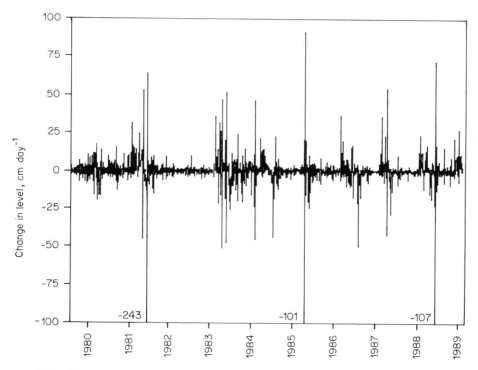

FIGURE 17.6. Changes in water level in the lower pool of the weir at Lock 3, Overland Corner, from January 1980 to June 1989

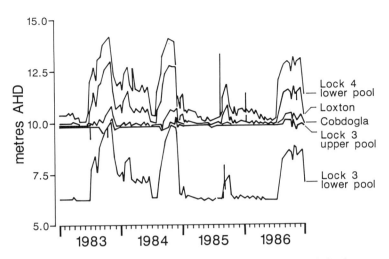

FIGURE 17.7. A progression along the River Murray showing water levels in the years 1983 to 1986 immediately below Lock 4 (Bookpurnong), 27 km below Lock 4 (Loxton), 71 km below Lock 4 (Cobdogla) and at sites immediately above and below Lock 3, 85 km below Lock 4. (AHD, Australian Height Datum)

Figure 17.6 shows water-level changes in the lower pool of Lock 3 (Overland Corner) during 1980–1989. In this period daily rises and falls of ±200 mm were commonplace and changes of more than ±500 mm occurred about once a year. Falls of more than 1 m were recorded on 20 November 1981 (−2.43 m), 7 September 1985 (−1.01 m), and 26 October 1988 (−1.07 m).

Figure 17.7 is a sequence showing river levels at stations from Lock 4 (Bookpurnong) to Lock 3, a distance of 85 river-km, in 1983–1986. Fluctuations below Lock 4 are transferred downriver, although their magnitude is diminished in the approach to Lock 3. The sequence is then reset, beginning a new progression downstream to Lock 2 (Waikerie). Thus, there are gradients of water-level changes between the weirs.

Figure 17.8 shows river levels at the site of Lock 3 in 1921–1929. The completion of the weir in 1925 is signalled by the separation of upper and lower pool levels. From the few prior data, it seems that the river now is subject to more short-term variation than it was before regulation. Apart from this, no special importance is attached to changes on a daily basis as opposed to any other unit of time. Indeed, for some kinds of physical or biological effects it may be more appropriate to consider rises or falls over two or more consecutive days.

Physical environment

Channel morphology

The Murray has a low gradient, reflecting its long geological history (e.g. Walker, 1986; Thoms and Walker, in press b). Below the Darling junction the average channel slope is

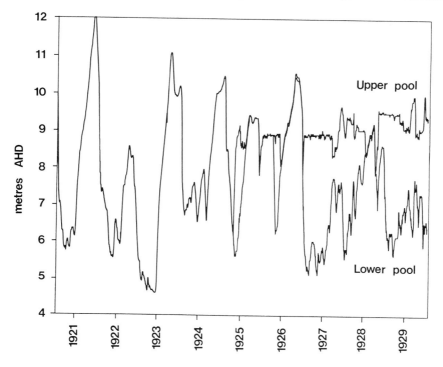

FIGURE 17.8. Water levels in the River Murray at Overland Corner between 1921 and 1929. Construction of Lock 3 was completed in 1925. (AHD, Australian Height Datum)

55 mm km^{-1}, and water takes two weeks to travel from the junction to the sea (830 km). Estimates of specific stream power (related to discharge, channel slope, and width) are 0.44–5.62 J s^{-1} m^{-2}, typical of stable, inactive, meandering rivers (cf. Ferguson, 1981). Channel stability is promoted also by the cohesive nature of the riverbank sediment (12–41% silt and clay).

Patterns of water and sediment transport changed, however, with construction of the weirs (Thoms and Walker, 1989, in press b). The river channel now is undergoing a series of adjustments involving erosion of sediment below each weir and deposition behind the next weir. The adjustments are variously advanced, reflecting the position of each weir in the downstream sequence. Ratios of width/depth have increased by up to 23% in some reaches and decreased by up to 22% in others. Whereas the unregulated Murray had a compound channel, with benches reflecting adjustments to extreme flows, the benches now are mostly eroded (Thoms and Walker, in press b). Where they are preserved, the uppermost benches are part of the littoral zone in the regulated river.

Figure 17.9 shows measurements of bank erosion at stations between Locks 2 and 4 (153 river-km) during 1988–1989. For 1988 the aggregate loss was 800 000 tonnes of bank material, and for 1989 the aggregate was 1.04 million tonnes. Most of these losses occurred following rapid falls in water level. Over a week in September 1988, and again

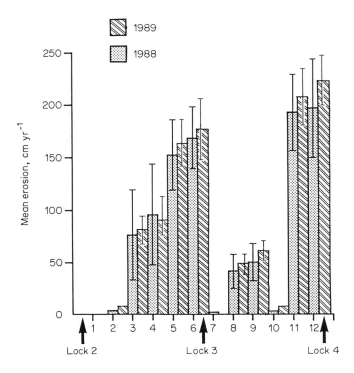

FIGURE 17.9. Bank erosion at 12 sites on the Murray between Locks 2 and 4 in 1988 and 1989. Each bar represents the mean bank retreat (with associated standard error) relative to 10 survey markers

over a week in October 1989, the river fell 2.5 m and 2.6 m, respectively. On each occasion the banks remained saturated and large sections slid into the river.

The bank slope at most sites has increased by erosion; for example, bank slopes immediately below Lock 4 increased from 65° to 72° in 1988 and from 72° to 81° in 1989. The increased slope and general morphology of the banks suggest that abrupt block failure (Thorne and Tovey, 1980) is the mechanism of erosion. This is promoted by rapid falls in water level rather than scouring by high discharges. The effect of the smaller, more frequent changes in level associated with routine weir operations may be to undermine the toe of the bank so that it is vulnerable to larger falls.

Groundwater dynamics

Along the banks in some areas (e.g. Locks 2–3) there are saline groundwater seepages with patches of efflorescing salt, usually devoid of littoral plants. In some areas, depending on regional hydraulic gradients, the groundwater rises with water in the river channel during high flows, and flows toward the channel when the river falls. If the fall is rapid and substantial the groundwater may entrain saline water from deep aquifers, adding to bank instability and boosting salinity levels in the river. According to Barnett (1989), substantial reductions in saline recharge could be achieved by reducing the rate of drawdown during the recession of floods. The effects on recharge of smaller variations in water level are not known.

Biological environment

Habitat patchiness

The exposed, sandy sediments of the open channel offer refuge for little more than sparse populations of chironomids and oligochaetes. Exposed riverbanks also are poor habitats. Instead, the main sanctuaries are scattered "patches" in the littoral zone, including exposed tree roots, limestone rubble, water plants, and snags. These patches are resources (e.g. shelter, food and oviposition, spawning or nesting sites) for many organisms associated with the river and its floodplain. The biological diversity associated with these areas, especially the plants and snags, suggests that patchiness (Pringle et al, 1988) is a vital part of the Murray ecosystem.

Littoral plants

Aquatic and semi-aquatic plants are a conspicuous feature of the littoral zone. They trap and consolidate sediments and so promote the development of benthos; they provide a substratum for Aufwuchs and a source of invertebrates and algae for the riverine plankton (Shiel and Walker, 1984; Sullivan et al, 1988). The plants are also a refuge for fish, amphibians, reptiles, birds, and mammals (Walker, 1986).

Figure 17.10 shows the distributions and abundances of common littoral plants recorded in a survey between Locks 2 and 4 (153 km) in February 1988. The ubiquitous species are common reeds (*Phragmites australis*), spiny sedge (*Cyperus gymnocaulos*), common couch (*Cynodon dactylon*), saltwater couch (*Paspalum vaginatum*), curly pondweed (*Potamogeton crispus*), and ribbonweed (*Vallisneria* sp.). The distributions of several other species are correlated with gradients in the erosive power of the water (Thoms and Walker, in press b; cf. Roberts and Ludwig, in press). For example, some plants (e.g. red water milfoil, *Myriophyllum verrucosum*) favour lower-pool environments where the dominant regime is erosional. Others are most frequent in depositional upper-pool environments (e.g. broadleaf cumbungi, *Typha orientalis*), although these sites are limited because the banks of the weir pools are choked by willows (*Salix babylonica*). Other plants are too rare or patchily distributed to be categorized in this way.

At the pool levels typical of spring–summer the littoral zone has three parts:

• *Upper littoral*: The uppermost 0.5 m, equivalent to the euphotic zone and subject to daily fluctuations, depending on proximity to weirs. The vegetation includes semi-aquatic (e.g. sedges) and emergent species (e.g. reeds).
• *Middle littoral*: From 0.5 to 2 m, characterized by submerged plants including *Potamogeton*, *Myriophyllum*, and *Vallisneria*.

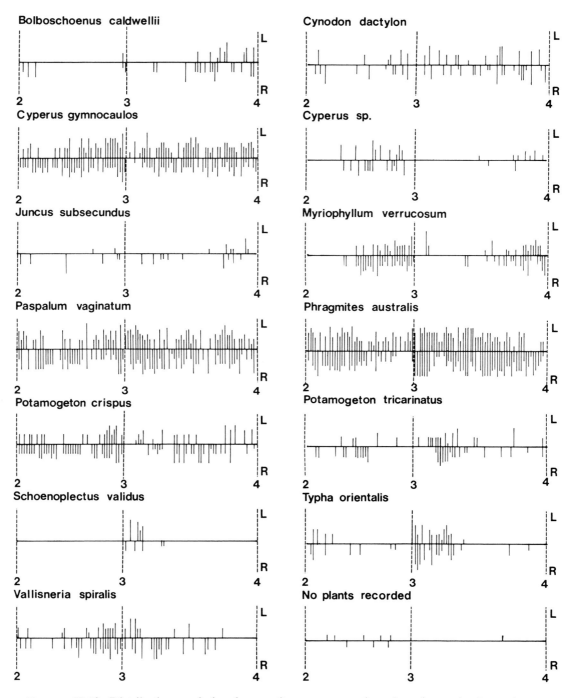

FIGURE 17.10. Distributions and abundances of common aquatic and semi-aquatic plants along the River Murray between Locks 2 and 4, February 1988. Transects were surveyed at 1 km intervals, and the abundance of plant species on each bank was recorded on a scale of 0–5 (0= absent; 5=extremely abundant)

• *Lower littoral*: From 2 to 4 m, without plants. This stratum is best represented by river mussels (see *Macroinvertebrates*), with snags as an important microhabitat.

Figure 17.11 shows the zonation typical of sites in the lower, middle, and upper weir pools. The composition of the strata varies with distance between weirs, reflecting tolerances to flooding and drying, different bank slopes, and other expressions of the gradient of water level changes.

Snags

Red-gum snags are another prominent littoral feature, derived from trees undermined by bank erosion (Figure 17.12) and branches lost to storm damage or osmotic stress in hot weather (Lloyd et al, in press). Snags lying across the path of the current provide sheltered pockets for littoral plants. Like the plants, snags are a haven for fish and invertebrates; they also provide roosts for water birds, feeding sites for water rats, and basking sites for tortoises (Walker, 1986). The "habitat value" of a snag may be influenced by its location (eroding/depositing bank), configuration (few/many branches), structural complexity (smooth/pitted), the proportion below the surface, and its orientation relative to the current (Lloyd et al, in press). O'Connor (1991) has demonstrated a relationship between structural complexity and numbers of macroinvertebrate species in a stream in the Victorian catchment of the Murray.

Snags in the Murray have long been regarded as undesirable because they are hazards for boats and supposedly encourage localized erosion and retard the flow of water for irrigation. De-snagging operations were once prevalent but have been scaled down in recent years, partly because there is more awareness of the environmental value of snags.

The number of red-gum snags in the river may have been increased by bank erosion. A census over an 8.8 km reach below Lock 3 in October 1987 indicated 27 snags km^{-1} (Lloyd et al, in press). This was a conservative estimate, based only on snags visible above the surface. Many of these were groups of trees undermined by bank erosion (Figure 17.13).

In the upper littoral zone (<50 cm) there are sparse algal growths on snags and other submerged surfaces. In deeper water, where there is little or no light, most of the biomass associated with snags is fungi and nematodes. Little is yet known of this community but in Lake Alexandrina, near the Murray mouth, Nicholas et al (in press) recorded nematode densities of 10 000 m^{-2}, including the scavenging genera *Eutobrilus* and *Tripyla* and the predatory *Enoploides* and *Mesacanthion*.

Macroinvertebrates

Following an extensive 5-year sampling program, Bennison et al (1989) suggested that the macroinvertebrate fauna of the lower Murray is depauperate compared to other parts of the river. The claim was based on numbers of organisms rather than taxa (three stations on the lower river yielded 85–104 taxa, compared with 87–139 taxa at comparable stations elsewhere). The evidence is equivocal, however, because the stations may not have been representative. Another difficulty is that the samples were from mesh-bag "artificial substrates", and downstream changes in faunal composition could merely

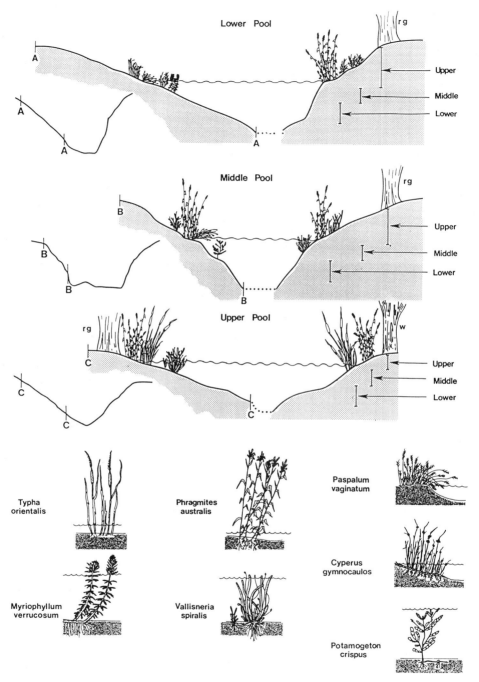

FIGURE 17.11. Typical zonations of aquatic and semi-aquatic plants in the lower, middle and upper pools of the River Murray between two weirs (e.g. Locks 2–4). At each site a typical profile is shown (left), and zonations are shown for depositional and eroding banks. Red gums (rg) are common on the riverbank except in the upper pools, where weeping willows (w) predominate

FIGURE 17.12. Part of the Murray littoral zone in South Australia, showing emergent plants and red-gum snags. This is below the weir at Lock 3, where the magnitude of water level fluctuations is greatest

reflect the propensities of different species to colonize the samplers. Nevertheless, taking account of supplementary net samples, the survey showed a clear qualitative change in the lower Murray: there is a proportionate decrease in insects and an increase in crustaceans. This is in general keeping with the River Continuum Concept (Vannote et al, 1980).

Table 17.1 lists macroinvertebrates typical of the littoral zone of the lower Murray (see also Boulton and Lloyd, in press, for data on the fauna of floodplain wetlands). The common insects include chironomids, caddis flies, and mayflies, with some typically lacustrine forms (e.g. *Cloeon*), and common crustaceans include prawns, shrimps, and the crayfish or "yabbie", *Cherax destructor* (Parastacidae). The yabbie is typical of lentic environments and streams but appears to have extended its range to the littoral zone and weir pools of the lower river. The Murray crayfish (*Euastacus armatus*) (Parastacidae), a once-common riverine species, is on the verge of local extinction (Walker, 1985, 1986).

A similar change has occurred among the freshwater mussels (Hyriidae) (Walker, 1981). The river mussel (*Alathyria jacksoni*) requires a relatively strong current, and although it is still common in middle- and lower-pool environments, its range has been fragmented by weir construction. The floodplain mussel (*Velesunio ambiguus*) is typical of billabongs and other floodplain wetlands, but is now common in parts of the main channel where there is shelter from the current. In lower-pool environments the floodplain mussel congregates in the middle littoral (0.5–2 m) and the river mussel in the

FIGURE 17.13. The exposed roots of a river red gum indicate bank erosion along the River Murray, South Australia

lower littoral zone (2–4 m), often along the edge of a bench. *V. ambiguus* is tolerant of oxygen depletion and dehydration but absent from fast-flowing water, probably because it is a comparatively weak burrower. *A. jacksoni* may be excluded from floodplain wetlands by its inability to tolerate low oxygen (Sheldon and Walker, 1989), and from the middle and upper littoral zone by its lack of mobility and vulnerability to dehydration. For the mussels, as for the crayfish, much of the evidence to implicate the weirs in changed distribution is circumstantial because there are so few historical data.

Gastropods are now rare in the lower Murray, but have been common in the past. Museum records and scattered shells (especially *Plotiopsis balonnensis* (Thiaridae) and *Vivipara sublineata* (Viviparidae)) on the riverbanks and in aboriginal shell middens show that prior to regulation the lower Murray supported about 15 species (cf. Smith, 1978). Over the past decade there have been isolated records of *Glyptophysa cosmeta* and *Gyraulus meridionalis* (Planorbidae), *Posticobia* sp. (Hydrobiidae), *P. balonnensis*, and *V. sublineata*. *Potamopyrgus niger* (Hydrobiidae) was widespread in 1980–1985 but not in 1987–1989 (cf. Bennison et al, 1989; Lloyd et al, in press). Two species which have persisted, albeit in small numbers, are the ancylid *Ferrissia petterdi* and an introduced planorbid, *Physa* sp. Faced with changeable water levels, *Physa* may gain some advantage from its ability to float freely. *F. petterdi* may also have some defence if, like others of its genus, it is drought resistant (Richardot, 1977).

TABLE 17.1. Some common macroinvertebrates from the littoral zone of the Murray between Locks 2–4, South Australia

Annelida		
Oligochaeta		Tubificidae
Mollusca		
Bivalvia	Corbiculidae	*Corbiculina australis*
	Hyriidae	*Alathyria jacksoni*
		Velesunio ambiguus
	Sphaeriidae	*Sphaerium* sp.
Gastropoda	Ancylidae	*Ferrissia petterdi*
	Planorbidae	*Physa* sp.
Arthropoda		
Arachnida	Pisauridae	*Dolomedes* sp.
	Tetragnathidae	*Tetragnatha* sp.
Crustacea	Cladocera	*Alona* sp.
		Biapertura sp.
		Chydorus sp.
		Ilyocryptus sp.
		Macrothrix sp.
	Copepoda	*Calamoecia ampulla*
		Eucyclops sp.
	Amphipoda	*Afrochiltonia* sp.
	Decapoda	*Caridina mccullochi*
		Cherax destructor
		Paratya australiensis
		Macrobrachium australiense
	Ostracoda	*Limnocythere* sp.
Insecta	Diptera	Ceratopogonidae
		Chironomus cloacalis
		Cladotanytarsus sp.
		Cricotopus sp.
		Cryptochironomus sp.
		Kiefferulus intertinctus
		Pentaneura sp.
		Polypedilum sp.
		Procladius paludicola
		Simulium sp.
		Tanytarsus spp.
	Ephemeroptera	*Atalophlebia* sp.
		Cloeon sp.
		Tasmanocoenis spp.
	Hemiptera	*Limnogonus* sp.
		Micronecta spp.
	Odonata	*Austroagrion watsoni*
	Trichoptera	*Ecnomus* spp.
		Oecetis sp.
		Triplectides spp.

(Lloyd et al, in press)

Fish

Native fish populations throughout the Murray have declined since regulation began (Cadwallader, 1986) and in the lower river several species, commercial and otherwise, are approaching local extinction. The probable causes of the decline include habitat changes, interactions with exotic fish, and fishing methods. Common carp (*Cyprinus carpio*) are popularly assumed to have had adverse effects since they became widespread in the early 1970s (cf. Fletcher et al, 1985). Flow regulation is significant because floods enhance spawning and recruitment in several species, and suitable floods now are less frequent and less prolonged. The weirs complement the effects of regulation through dams; in particular, rapid changes in water level are likely to degrade the littoral zone as a resource for fish.

The littoral zone is an avenue for fish migration. The lower Murray supports a small "Reach Fishery" which employs drum nets to intercept fish moving upstream along the banks (Walker, 1983). In recent years the catch has included Murray cod (*Maccullochella peeli*), callop (*Macquaria ambigua*), silver perch (*Bidyanus bidyanus*), and the exotic common carp and European perch (*Perca fluviatilis*). The weir at Lock 6 includes a crude fish passage, but its value is uncertain (Mallen-Cooper, 1989). Littoral areas are also a nursery for several species, including bony bream (*Nematalosa erebi*; Puckridge and Walker, 1990). They harbour more small fish species than floodplain wetlands, and are particularly favoured by smelt (*Retropinna semoni*) and bigheaded gudgeon (*Philypnodon grandiceps*; Lloyd and Walker, 1986).

DISCUSSION

The perception of a river as a corridor highlights the vulnerability of river ecosystems to fragmentation caused by unsympathetic land- or water-management. This is especially so for semi-arid rivers like the Murray, because the river–floodplain corridor is so unlike the surrounding landscape. The littoral boundary is a key part of the corridor, being a zone of concentrated physical and biological diversity and a resource for both riverine and riparian communities. If the littoral zone is disturbed, the ecosystem may undergo radical changes.

The Murray is free of many of the pollution hazards that afflict large rivers in other parts of the world, but it has been changed profoundly in the last 70 years. An artificial pattern of summer-irrigation flows has overtaken, but not entirely subdued, an ancient regime prone to erratic droughts and floods. The environmental impact of this change may owe as much to weirs as to dams. Although the effects of individual weirs are more localized, their impact is extended by the concentration of 10 weirs over 830 river-km. Thus, weirs have transformed the lower Murray into a chain of cascading pools, and initiated a series of biological and physical adjustments that is not yet complete.

The weirs have supplanted most of the former riverine environment with pool habitats, and the distributions of river and floodplain (lacustrine) species have altered accordingly. This is shown by changes in the distributions of crayfish and freshwater mussels. Further, the decline of the Murray's native fish is most advanced in South Australia. In general, weir operations appear to have reinforced and extended the changes imposed by dams in other parts of the system.

The decline of gastropods is not documented and, as with all biological problems pertaining to the Murray, there are few historical data. Some possible factors include salinity, pesticides, predation, and habitat destruction by carp and alienation of flood-plain wetlands by flow regulation. None of these should be discounted, but perhaps the best working hypothesis is to relate the decline to turbidity and water level changes. High turbidities inhibit plant growth through shading and siltation. Under these conditions the superimposition of frequent, rapid changes in water level represents a major disturbance for plants, including the periphyton that the snails require for food and habitat. The snails are slow-moving and, with few exceptions, are not able to compensate for rapid changes in water level. The patchy spatial and temporal distribution of the various species suggests that they are responding to local changes in the availability of food or other resources (cf. Lodge and Kelly, 1985). Under these circumstances there is a likelihood of more regional extinctions.

The Murray's compound channel is a relict of the pre-regulation regime and a significant part of the littoral zone in the modern river. Benches are no longer apparent below the weirs, where they have been eroded, and they are no longer active in the weir pools. They are reasonably well preserved, however, in middle-pool environments, and provide a stable, sheltered, shallow area for the development of littoral plant and animal communities.

The relationships between these communities and the gradients of disturbance be-tween weirs are poorly understood. The nature of the gradients—and the barriers represented by the weirs themselves—suggest that the continuity of the littoral zone has been interrupted. This may be a fundamental reason for the general decline of the native ecosystem. Clearly, there are many opportunities for research.

Given the importance of the Murray as a resource, the managing authorities make a surprisingly small commitment to environmental research. As the references in this chapter will show, much of the archival literature now is published by government departments, but most is in the nature of surveys and reviews rather than scientific research. The view of management appears to be that the basic problems are well known and that the priorities are problems of a social, political, and administrative nature. A priority for environmental scientists, therefore, must be to prosecute the case for strategic research.

A strong case already exists for operational changes to offset the effects of turbidity and water level fluctuations. Turbidity reductions may require changes in the mix of Darling and Murray water used in irrigation flows. In weir management an option may be to relax the 50 mm tolerance that, apparently for reasons of tradition, governs the target levels for the weir pools. Clearly, given the interaction between turbidity and water level changes, an integrated approach is required.

ACKNOWLEDGEMENTS

This chapter is based partly on work supported by the Australian Water Research Advisory Council (AWRAC Project 86/40). River stage data were obtained in microfiche from the Engineering and Water Supply Department, South Australia. We are grateful to Mr A. F. Close, Murray–Darling Basin Commission, for supply of discharge data, and Professor W. D. Williams, University of Adelaide, for comments on a draft manuscript.

REFERENCES

Baker, B. W., and Wright, G. L. (1978). "The Murray Valley: its hydrologic regime and the effects of water development on the river", *Proceedings of the Royal Society of Victoria*, **90**, 103–110.

Barnett, S. (1989). *The hydrogeology of the Murray Basin in South Australia, with special reference to the alluvium of the River Murray floodplain*, MSc thesis, School of Earth Sciences, Flinders University of South Australia.

Bennison, G. L., Hillman, T. J., and Suter, P. J. (1989). "Macro-invertebrates of the River Murray (survey and monitoring: 1980–1985)", *Water Quality Report 3*, Murray–Darling Basin Commission, Canberra.

Boulton, A. J., and Lloyd, L. N. (in press). Macroinvertebrate assemblages in floodplain habitats of the River Murray, South Australia", *Regulated Rivers: Research and Management*.

Cadwallader, P. L. (1986). "Fish of the Murray–Darling system", in *The Ecology of River Systems* (Eds B. R. Davies and K. F. Walker), pp. 679–694, W. Junk, Dordrecht.

Cole, P. J. (1978). "Soils and land use of the River Murray valley in South Australia", *Proceedings of the Royal Society of Victoria*, **90**, 167–176.

Dexter, B. D., Rose, H. J., and Davies, N. (1986). "River regulation and associated forest management problems in the River Murray red gum forests", *Australian Forestry*, **49**, 16–27.

Ferguson, R. I. (1981). "Channel form and channel changes", in *British Rivers* (Ed. J. Lewin), pp. 90–125, Allen & Unwin, London.

Fisher, S. G., and La Voy, A. (1972). "Differences in littoral fauna due to fluctuating water levels below a hydroelectric dam", *Journal of the Fisheries Research Board of Canada*, **29**, 1472–1476.

Fletcher, A. R., Morison, A. K., and Hume, D. J. (1985). "Effects of carp, *Cyprinus carpio* L., on communities of aquatic vegetation and turbidity of waterbodies in the lower Goulburn River basin", *Australian Journal of Marine and Freshwater Research*, **36**, 311–327.

Jacobs, T. A. (1989). "Regulation of the Murray–Darling system", in *Proceedings of the Workshop on Native Fish Management* (Ed. B. Lawrence), pp. 55–96. Murray–Darling Basin Commission, Canberra.

Kernich, A. M. (1984). "The climate of the River Murray and environs, South Australia", Department of Agriculture, South Australia, River Murray Irrigation and Salinity Investigation Program Technical Paper 11.

Lloyd, L. N., and Walker, K. F. (1986). "Distribution and conservation status of small freshwater fish in the River Murray, South Australia", *Transactions of the Royal Society of South Australia*, **106**, 49–57.

Lloyd, L. N., Walker, K. F., and Hillman, T. J. (in press). *Environmental significance of snags in the River Murray*, Completion Report, Australian Water Research Advisory Council, Project 85/45, Department of Primary Industries and Energy, Canberra.

Lodge, D. M., and Kelly, P. (1985). "Habitat disturbance and the stability of freshwater gastropod populations", *Oecologia (Berlin)*, **68**, 111–117.

Mackay, N. J., Hillman, T. J., and Rolls, J. (1988). "Water quality of the River Murray. Review of monitoring, 1978 to 1986", *Water Quality Report 3*, Murray–Darling Basin Commission, Canberra.

Mallen-Cooper, M. (1989). "Fish passage in the Murray–Darling Basin", in *Proceedings of the Workshop on Native Fish Management* (Ed. B. Lawrence), pp. 123–135, Murray–Darling Basin Commission, Canberra.

Margules and Partners, Smith, P., Smith, J., and Department of Conservation, Forests and Lands, Victoria (1990). *Riparian Vegetation of the River Murray*, Murray–Darling Basin Commission, Canberra.

Morton, R., and Cunningham, R. B. (1985). "Longitudinal profile of trends in salinity in the River Murray", *Australian Journal of Soil Research*, **23**, 1–13.

Naiman, R. J., Décamps, H., Pastor, J., and Johnston, C. A. (1988). "The potential importance of boundaries to fluvial ecosystems", *Journal of the North American Benthological Society*, **7**, 289–306.

Nicholas, W. L., Bird, A. F., Beech, T. A., and Stewart, A. C. (in press). "The nematode fauna of the Murray River estuary: the effects of the barrages across its mouth", *Hydrobiologia*.

Nilsson, C. (1984). "Effect of stream regulation on riparian vegetation", in *Regulated Rivers* (Eds A. Lillehammer and S. Saltveit), pp. 93–106, Universitetsforlaget, Oslo.

O'Connor, N. A. (1991). "The effects of habitat complexity on the macroinvertebrates colonising wood substrates in a lowland stream", *Oecologia (Berlin)*, **85**, 504–512.

Pressey, R. L. (1986). *Wetlands of the River Murray below Lake Hume*, River Murray Commission, Canberra, Environmental Report 86/1.

Pringle, C. M., Naiman, R. J., Bretschko, G., Karr, J. R., Oswood, M. W., Webster, J. R., Welcomme, R. L., and Winterbourn, M. J. (1988). "Patch dynamics in lotic systems: the stream as a mosaic", *Journal of the North American Benthological Society*, **7**, 503–524.

Puckridge, J. T., and Walker, K. F. (1990). "Reproductive biology and larval development of a gizzard shad, *Nematalosa erebi* (Günther) (Dorosomatinae: Teleostei), in the River Murray, South Australia", *Australian Journal of Marine and Freshwater Research*, **41**, 695–712.

Resh, V. H., Brown, A. V., Covich, A. P., Gurtz, M. E., Li, H. W., Minshall, G. W., Reice, S. R., Sheldon, A. L., Wallace, J. B., and Wissmar, R. C. (1988). "The role of disturbance in stream ecology", *Journal of the North American Benthological Society*, **7**, 433–455.

Richardot, M. (1977). "Ecological factors inducing aestivation in the freshwater limpet *Ferrissia wauteri* (Basommatophora: Ancylidae), I. Oxygen content, organic matter content and pH of the water", *Malacological Reviews*, **10**, 7–13.

Roberts, J., and Ludwig, J. A. (in press). "Riparian vegetation along current-exposure gradients in floodplain wetlands of the River Murray, Australia", *Journal of Ecology*.

Selby, J. (1981). "A salty problem for the River Murray", *New Scientist*, **90**, 842–844.

Sheldon, F., and Walker, K. F. (1989). "Effects of hypoxia on oxygen consumption by two species of freshwater mussel (Unionacea: Hyriidae) from the River Murray", *Australian Journal of Marine and Freshwater Research*, **40**, 491–499.

Shiel, R. J., and Walker, K. F. (1984). "Zooplankton of regulated and unregulated streams: the Murray–Darling river system, Australia", in *Regulated Rivers* (Eds A. Lillehammer and S. Saltveit), pp. 263–270, Universitetsforlaget, Oslo.

Smith, B. J. (1978). "Molluscs of the Murray–Darling river system", *Proceedings of the Royal Society of Victoria*, **90**, 203–209.

Sullivan, C., Saunders, J., and Welsh, D. (1988). "Phytoplankton of the River Murray, 1980–1985", *Water Quality Report 2*, Murray–Darling Basin Commission, Canberra.

Thoms, M. C., and Walker, K. F. (1989). "Preliminary observations of the environmental effects of flow regulation on the River Murray, South Australia", *South Australian Geographical Journal*, **89**, 1–14.

Thoms, M. C., and Walker, K. F. (in press a). "Sediment transport in a regulated semi-arid river: the River Murray, Australia", *Canadian Journal of Fisheries and Aquatic Sciences*.

Thoms, M. C., and Walker, K. F. (in press b) "Channel changes related to low-level weirs on the River Murray, South Australia", in *Lowland Floodplain Rivers: Geomorphological Perspectives* (Eds P. A. Carling and G. E. Petts), British Geomorphological Research Group Symposia Series, John Wiley, Chichester.

Thorne, C. R., and Tovey, N. K. (1980). "Stability of composite river banks", *Earth Surface Processes and Landforms*, **6**, 469–484.

Twidale, C. R., Lindsay, J. M., and Bourne, J. A. (1978). "Age and origin of the Murray River and gorge in South Australia", *Proceedings of the Royal Society of Victoria*, **90**, 27–42.

Vannote, R. L., Minshall, G. W., Cummins, K. W., Sedell, J. R., and Cushing, C. E. (1980). "The river continuum concept", *Canadian Journal of Fisheries and Aquatic Sciences*, **37**, 130–137.

Walker, K. F. (1981). *Ecology of freshwater mussels in the River Murray*, Australian Water Resources Council Technical Paper 63.

Walker, K. F. (1983). "Impact of Murray–Darling Basin development on fish and fisheries", *FAO Fisheries Reports*, **288**, 139–149.

Walker, K. F. (1985). "A review of the ecological effects of river regulation in Australia", *Hydrobiologia*, **125**, 111–129.

Walker, K. F. (1986). "The Murray–Darling river system", in *The Ecology of River Systems* (Eds B. R. Davies and K. F. Walker), pp. 631–659, W. Junk, Dordrecht.

Ward, J. V. (1989). "The four-dimensional nature of lotic ecosystems", *Journal of the North American Benthological Society*, **8**, 2–9.

Woodyer, K. D. (1978). "Sediment regime of the Darling River", *Proceedings of the Royal Society of Victoria*, **90**, 139–147.

18

A Building-block Model for Stream Restoration

R. C. PETERSEN, L. B.-M. PETERSEN and J. LACOURSIÉRE

Stream and Benthic Ecology Group,
Limnology Institute, University of Lund,
Box 65, 221 00 Lund, Sweden

INTRODUCTION

In agricultural areas, farmers and government authorities have become concerned about the loss of nutrients to the sea, and the deterioration of surface water quality by non-point-source pollution. This awareness comes from information which shows that agricultural lands are releasing large amounts of nutrients, such as nitrogen, compared to forested undisturbed watersheds (Table 18.1). While there may be a general consensus of opinion that something has to be done, there has been little organization of what can be done and how to do it. This is in conflict with the rather large database that exists on the basic and applied ecology of running waters (e.g. Hynes, 1967, 1970; Fontain and Bartell, 1983; Resh and Rosenberg, 1984), their associated freshwater wetlands (e.g. Good et al, 1978; Brinson et al, 1981; Howard-Williams, 1985; Mitsch and Gosselink, 1986) and the effect of various restoration measures (e.g. Gore, 1985; Cairns, 1988).

This chapter describes eight restoration measures which can be used to redesign small streams in agricultural areas to decrease the transport of nutrients to surface waters and to restore the animal and plant life along and within stream channels. Each measure has its own environmental benefit, cost, and land-use needs. Since each stream is different, the restoration measures can be viewed as "building blocks", which may be put together in various ways, leaving out or using this or that measure, depending on the stream.

While the orientation of this chapter, and the measures described, are to address the problems of lowland agricultural streams, the building-block approach can be used to restore any stream and should be viewed as a general strategy to provide landowners and government authorities with solutions. It is also a way to explain in simple language what can be done to improve the condition of our streams. Other restoration measures specific for regional problems and topography can be added. The list of building blocks discussed here is by no means exhaustive or final.

River Conservation and Management. Edited by P. J. Boon, P. Calow, and G. E. Petts
© 1992 John Wiley & Sons Ltd

TABLE 18.1. Comparison of nitrogen leakage from forested and agricultural catchments

Type	Country	kg N km^{-2} yr^{-1}	Reference
Forested	USA	127	Bormann et al (1968)
		103	Taylor et al (1971)
Agricultural	Finland	1700	Jaakola (1984)
	Sweden	1700	Rosswall and Paustian (1984)
		2700	Rosswall and Paustian (1984)
		2100	Rosswall and Paustian (1984)
		800	Rosswall and Paustian (1984)
		3600	Bergström (1987)
	Denmark	3200	Jensen (1976)
	USA	3430	Jackson et al (1973)
		2600	Groffman et al (1986)
		1500	Groffman et al (1986)
		2513	Yates and Sheridan (1983)

The present condition of streams in the agricultural landscape

The present condition of most streams in agricultural areas has been reduced to a drainage ditch with minimal self-cleaning capacity and nature conservation value (Figure 18.1(a)). During the beginning of this century, many lowland areas were drained to increase the area for agriculture. This was done by straightening and deepening the stream channel giving the typical channelized stream of lowland agricultural areas. This resulted in four physical changes: (1) a loss of stream length, (2) a loss of riffles and pools, (3) a loss of riparian floodplains and wetlands, and (4) a loss of vegetation along the stream.

All four physical alterations changed both the hydraulics and biology of the stream. The loss of stream length occurred as meanders were removed, which caused a shortening of water-retention time, and a decrease in hydraulic energy dissipation. More energy, therefore, was available for bank erosion and sediment transport (Dunne and Leopold, 1978). The increased sediment transport resulted in increased channel instability, bed degradation, changed channel pattern, and sedimentation of downstream ponds or reservoirs. Biological degradation took place because of habitat loss. Due to a shortening of stream length, water was transported faster to the sea, the self-cleaning capacity was reduced, and nutrient transport to the sea was increased.

The loss of riffle and pool associations removed areas of hydraulic head conservation within pools, and energy dissipation within riffles. This sequential storage and dissipation was one way that streams attain hydraulic balance with their kinetic energy, and a stable hydraulic configuration within the channel. Loss of riffles and pools resulted in a stream bottom that was homogeneous, thus reducing habitat for macroinvertebrates and both habitat and spawning grounds for fish.

The loss of riparian floodplains and wetlands resulted in a decrease in the water table and an increase in run-off (Wolf, 1956). It also caused a reduction in the biodiversity of flora and fauna and the loss of the self-cleaning capacity of these wetlands (Mitsch and Gosselink, 1986). Moreover, drainage of marshes and wetlands resulted in an increase in

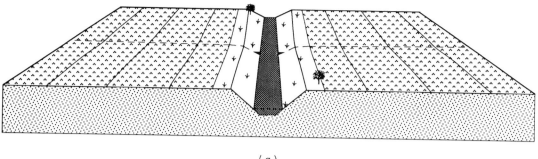

(a)

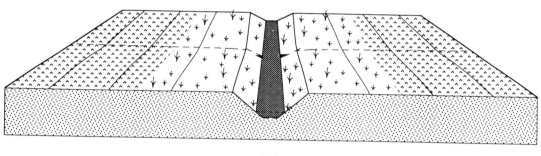

(b)

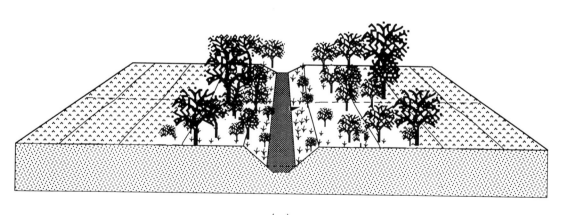

(c)

FIGURE 18.1. (a) The channelized streams of agricultural areas have been deepened and straightened to allow drainage of the surrounding landscape. (b) The first and most important restoration
measure is to set aside land along the stream channel to act as a buffer strip between the land and
the running water. (c) In order to stabilize the channel banks and to provide vegetation for nutrient
retention and wildlife, the buffer strip should be replanted with quick-growing native riparian plant
species

flood peaks. This loss in discharge buffering capacity means that more water more rapidly enters the channel system, which again increases erosion, nutrient transport, and sediment load. The importance of short-term discharge events in the calculation of nutrient budgets for small catchments cannnot be underestimated. In one study, reported in Petersen et al (1987), a 24-hour nutrient surge was recorded in a small agricultural brook in western Denmark that was equivalent to 10 years' base flow of organic material, one half-year of nitrogen, and 30 years of phosphorus.

The loss of vegetation along the stream caused an increase in sediment yield to the channel system by gravitational downslope movement, gullying, and sideslope failures (Dunne and Leopold, 1978). The removal of stream-side vegetation also increased solar radiation, which stimulated aquatic macrophytes within the channel. In both England and Denmark weed cutting in streams is a common practice to prevent flooding where the riparian vegetation has been removed (Dawson and Kern-Hansen, 1979).

All the changes in stream channel configuration were made to remove water more efficiently from potential agricultural lands; channelized streams were a correct engineering solution to society's need for more land to produce food. However, while channelized streams remove water, they do not take advantage of the ability of streams to retain and reduce nutrients leaking from agricultural fields, nor are they designed to conserve and protect wildlife and habitat. It is for these goals, as well as water removal, that the following building-block model of stream re-engineering is proposed.

RESTORATION MEASURES

Buffer strips

The strip of land between the stream channel and the surrounding landscape is sometimes referred to by different names such as the riparian zone or buffer strip. If the strip is wider it may come under the name of riparian wetland, stream valley, and floodplain. When referring to an entire catchment and long lengths of channel the term "corridor" is sometimes used (Décamps et al, 1987; Chauvet, 1988). The different names apply to differences in width, flooding conditions, soil conditions, and geomorphology, but conceptually these terms all refer to the same piece of land—the interface area between the channel and the terrestrial landscape.

In this chapter we use the term "buffer strip" to highlight the idea that the riparian zone acts as a buffer between agricultural fields and the stream channel, and recommend that the first and most important restoration measure is to set aside 10 m wide strips on each side of the channel (Figure 18.1(b). This buffering capacity occurs as dissolved and particulate nutrients are precipitated, flocculated, adsorbed abiotically, or consumed or converted biologically by the plant and microbial communities of the strip. In addition to nutrient reduction processes, the buffer strip and its vegetation stabilizes the banks along the stream and creates a complex habitat which traps and retains sediments coming from the fields. It is for this reason that the first step in any stream-restoration programme must be to protect and set aside land along the length of the stream. If the natural functions of a small stream are to be restored and maintained, then it is a waste of time to make changes in the channel without protecting the channel banks and the riparian area.

The ability of narrow strips of riparian land to retain and reduce nutrient concentrations has been well documented. A summary of some of the available literature gives a

TABLE 18.2. Percentage reduction in nitrogen by buffer strips of different widths (either width below ground or surface flow)

Width (m)	Initial concentration (mg N l^{-1})	Reduction (%)	Reference
Subsurface flow			
30	5.2	100	Pinay and Décamps (1988)
25		68	Lowrance et al (1984)
19	7.4	93	Peterjohn and Correll (1984)
50	6.8	99	Peterjohn and Correll (1984)
Surface flow			
30	175.2	98	Doyle et al (1977)
30	69.3	98	Doyle et al (1977)
30	47.0	98	Doyle et al (1977)
50	4.5	78	Peterjohn and Correll (1984)

range from 68% to 100% reduction in nutrient concentration, depending on the initial concentration and factors such as width and soil type (Table 18.2). In the study by Peterjohn and Correll (1984), a 50 m wide riparian forest separating agricultural fields from a stream removed 89% of the nitrogen and 80% of the phosphorus that entered it. The study estimated that there was a net removal of 11 kg ha yr^{-1} of particulate organic nitrogen, 0.83 kg ha yr^{-1} of dissolved ammonium nitrogen, 47.2 kg ha yr^{-1} of nitrate nitrogen, and 3.0 kg ha yr^{-1} of particulate phosphorus.

While there is clear evidence that agricultural lands are releasing nutrients and the riparian buffer strips retain and reduce nitrogen and phosphorus, there is no such evidence that constructing buffer strips will effectively reduce nitrogen loss from agricultural catchments. There is, however, circumstantial evidence that they will. For example, it is well known that there is good agreement between the amount of nitrogen loss to surface waters and the percentage of the catchment in row crop agriculture. This relationship can be seen when the percentage agriculture of five Swedish catchments is plotted against their annual nitrogen load (Figure 18.2). Since nitrogen loss should be a constant per unit area, there should be a linear relationship between load and percentage in row crops. However, a curvilinear, exponential model seems to best fit the data and even has a y-intercept of 230 kg N km^{-2} yr^{-1}, which compares favourably with the loss of nitrogen from forested catchments (Table 18.1).

A field study of the five catchments shows that stream riparian areas are not disturbed unless a large proportion of the catchment is devoted to agriculture. In catchments with a small percentage of agriculture, most is restricted to the flat areas and the riparian areas are not disturbed. As the land devoted to agriculture increases, i.e. ploughing closer to the stream, there is a much higher rate of loss of riparian stream-side vegetation. In catchments totally devoted to agriculture not only are the riparian buffer strips, and wetlands, removed but the stream itself may be buried beneath the ground. The self-cleaning capacity, not to mention the nature conservation value, is therefore highly reduced.

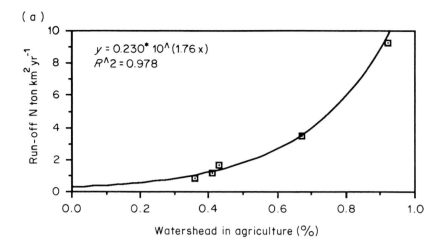

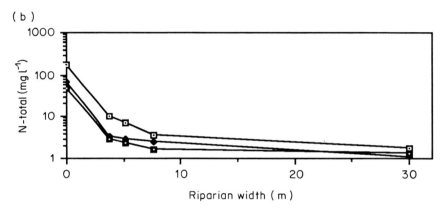

FIGURE 18.2. (a) Nitrogen run-off from five agricultural catchments plotted against percentage watershed in row crops (graph based on data in Ryding, 1984). (b) Reduction in total nitrogen in 30 m of riparian buffer strip in three experiments starting at three different initial levels. Reduction is curvilinear with most reduction occurring when concentrations are high. (Graph based on data in Doyle et al. 1977)

While there is clear evidence that buffer strips reduce nutrients, it is not clear how wide buffer strips should be. The values will most likely be different if the target is nutrient reduction in surface or sub-surface run-off, fish or bird community protection, or biodiversity conservation. Doyle et al (1977) have looked at nitrogen reduction in surface run-off at 4, 8, 15, and 30 m using three different initial nitrate concentrations (Figure 18.2(b)). For all three initial concentrations, there was a curvilinear reduction in nitrate which levels off at 10 m. In a study carried out in south Sweden, 90% of the initial phosphorus concentration was removed after 8 m passing over a grass buffer strip (L. Petersen, unpublished).

When considering bird species conservation, it is already fairly well established that the present "agrobusiness" landscape results in impoverished bird populations. In a large-scale mapping and habitat analysis of bird populations using infra-red aerial photography in southern Sweden, Robertson et al (1990) concluded that a relatively cheap and effective conservation measure for bird populations "would be to leave strips of scrub or deciduous woodland along the boundaries of the arable fields". Usually, these areas between fields are removed in modern farming. The riparian corridor along streams is another of these habitats that are lost and would be relatively cheap to restore for bird conservation.

While the details of the width of the buffer strip required for reducing nutrient leakage from agricultural fields, for conserving stream habitat, and for conserving bird populations requires additional work, it is fairly clear that care should be taken to have a riparian width that allows several trees, rather than one, to dominate the buffer strip. A "one-tree wide" buffer strip will favour raptors, thus reducing bird populations. A "five-tree" buffer strip which is about 10 m wide will provide the appropriate habitat complexity to protect this diversity. Therefore, based on both nutrient reduction and habitat considerations, buffer strips at least 10 m wide on each side of the stream can be suggested as a restoration goal.

Revegetation

Once the buffer strip is set aside, it will revegetate naturally or it can be replanted (Figure 18.1(c)). Replanting with native species of riparian woody trees and shrubs will speed up the process of colonization as well as reducing erosion of sediment into the channel.

There is a significant difference in the role of the riparian vegetation, depending on which tree species is used. *Alnus*, the common riparian tree in southern Sweden, is a non-leguminous angiosperm that possesses an endophytic actinomycetal fungus in root nodules that is able to fix nitrogen up to a rate of 225 kg N ha^{-1} yr^{-1} or 22.5 g N m^{-2} yr^{-1} (Wetzel, 1975). In areas that are nitrogen-poor, and where the riparian vegetation has been removed, *Alnus* may act as a significant nitrogen source for streams and lakes (Dugdale and Dugdale, 1961). In contrast, aspen (*Populus tremuloides*) has been shown to minimize nitrogen loss to streams in New Mexico (Gosz, 1978). The actual uptake of nitrogen for the above-ground portion of an aspen community in New Mexico was about 89 kg N ha^{-1} yr^{-1} or 8.9 g N m^{-2} yr^{-1}.

These differences in vegetation are especially important when the riparian zone along a stream is being used to absorb nutrients from agricultural land. Riparian vegetation has been reported to reduce the loss of nitrate (Verry and Timmons, 1982; Lowrance et al, 1983, 1984) and phosphate from agricultural lands and to improve water quality. Lowrance et al (1984) reports that a riparian zone received 50 kg N ha^{-1}; of these 10 kg came from nitrogen fixation by *Alnus* and *Myrica* with the other 40 kg coming from mixed row crops. Thirty kg were lost by denitrification within the riparian zone, the remainder becoming tied up in wood or lost to the stream.

It is advised that the buffer strip be planted with a fast-growing woody shrub. This can be alder, willow, or hybrid aspen. Broader buffer strips could be used for growing energy forests. Without planting, the buffer strips will re-seed naturally with annual plants and could take up to seven years for the complete effect to be seen.

Horseshoe wetlands

As mentioned above, in many areas in northern Europe and temperate North America, agricultural lands were created from wetlands by lowering the stream channel. To aid drainage, most of these lands have been underlain by drainage tiles. These carry drain water directly to the stream, and in effect create numerous point-sources for nutrients.

One solution to this agricultural point-source pollution is to create mini-wetlands at the mouth of each drain tile before it enters the stream (Figure 18.3). These can be called riparian wetland horseshoes, and are a restoration measure and manipulation which will reduce the nutrient load to the stream. They are semi-circular-shaped excavations dug into the buffer strip to expose each drainage tile and allow the water it is carrying to flow over an 8 m stretch of wetland. These excavations will create mini-wetlands, and will reduce both nitrogen and phosphorus from each point source. The excavation will be dug 8 m deep into the buffer strip, allowing the water from the tiles to flow over a grassy, shrub section before entering the stream.

The creation of horseshoes can be linked to several other problems. One objection by landowners to buffer strips is that the roots of the woody vegetation will penetrate and clog drain tiles as they pass under the buffer strip. If a buffer strip is to be established, then each drain tile end has to be replaced by a solid pipe. Instead of replacing the pipe a horseshoe can be constructed.

Although each horseshoe is small, their large number along the length of a stream will have a large impact on nitrogen load. This will occur during the late fall and early spring when drain tiles are flowing. This will be important, since it is during peak run-off periods that most of the nitrogen and phosphorus leaves the catchment (Petersen et al, 1987).

Each horseshoe should be at least 10 m wide and 8 m deep as shown in Figure 18.3. This leaves a 2 m strip between the field and the horseshoe. A small dirt lip will be installed to prevent direct run-off from the field. This will give approximately 80 m^2 of

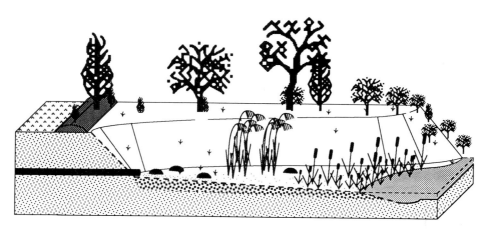

FIGURE 18.3. Basic schematic of a riparian wetland horseshoe which will receive water from the drain-tile system and act as a zone of nutrient retention

stream bank wetland, which is in direct contact and at the same level as the stream. Using values for wetland uptake of nitrogen of 750 kg ha^{-1} yr^{-1} (a conservative estimate) this would give the horseshoe a nitrogen reduction value of 4 kg horseshoe^{-1} yr^{-1}.

Side-slope reduction

One of the major sources of sediment and phosphorus to streams is the small-scale land failures that periodically occur along the length of a channelized stream. This can be so frequent that the channel has to be re-dug every few years to maintain flow. A simple recommendation then is to reduce the stream channel side slope from the present 50% (i.e. 1:2) to a minimum of 25% (1:4) (Figures 18.4 and 18.5(a)). Again, this restoration measure will be most effective when the buffer strip has already been purchased.

Channel slope reduction will have several benefits. First, the reduced bank slope will lower the frequency of bank failure and the amount of soil entering directly into the channel. Second, it will increase the width of the stream channel creating an area that will function like a floodplain. This will allow the stream to dissipate its energy by expanding on to the floodplain during peak flow, and not be eroding the channel walls. Expansion on to the floodplain will reduce velocity and sediment transport ability. Sediment will, therefore, be deposited on the channel slopes and not in downstream receiving waters.

Meander valley

Once floodplains are in place, the channel will revert to its natural tendency to develop meanders. In order to save time and reduce the amount of sediment that the stream will have to move in order to come into equilibrium, the channel should be meandering (Figures 18.4 and 18.5(b)).

Re-configuration of the channel path can be set following established hydrological concepts (Brookes, 1984), or it may be copied from historical records. The stream itelf will assist in this process. A meandering channel by definition is one that has a channel length at least 1.5 times the length of the down-valley distance, where an absolutely straight channel has a channel length of 1.00 (Leopold et al, 1964). In a meandering channel, flow patterns alternately transport sediment from the concave bank and deposit it near the convex bank. This erosional and depositional process is the way the stream dissipates its energy, and because this process is the most probable physical state for channel form in a homogeneous soil matrix, the meander frequency averages five to seven channel widths.

In comparison with the habitat conditions prevailing within a straight channel, a meandering channel is physically far more diverse and can therefore sustain more complex faunal and floral communities, which in turn are an integral component of the self-cleaning ability of a stream system. Since many stream processes can be quantified on a length basis, the longer the channel, and the longer the time the water spends in contact with the channel, the greater its nutrient retention and spiralling properties (Elwood et al, 1981; Newbold et al, 1982).

302

FIGURE 18.4. Restoration of an agricultural stream in southern Sweden. Meanders have been replaced (foreground) and side-slope reduced (background) (photograph by L. Petersen)

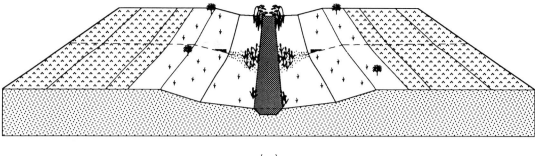

(a)

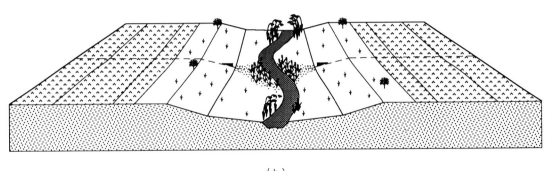

(b)

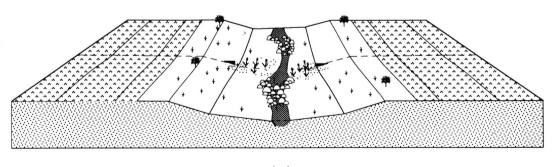

(c)

FIGURE 18.5. (a) Though a relatively expensive measure, reducing the side-slope of a channelized stream will reduce erosion and limit phosphorus addition to the stream. (b) Once the side-slope has been reduced or where the channel depth allows it, the stream can be made to meander. (c) In streams with coarser sediments, series of riffles and pools can be constructed of rocks and gravel placed in the channel, to bring the stream into equilibrium with its load

Riffle–pools

With a steeper channel energy gradient, and coarser sediments, the stream will form naturally alternating shallow and deep sections, referred to as riffles and pools. Essentially these are meanders turned 90°, since both riffles and pools, and meanders, minimize the variance in bed shear and friction (Curry, 1972). Therefore, riffles and pools should be used as a restoration building block, where those sections of stream that have a steep gradient and coarse stream sediments exist (Figure 18.5(c)).

The physical dimensions of riffle–pool associations are again determined by the hydrology, and as with meander frequency should be designed to have one pair, a riffle and a pool, at a downstream distance of five to seven times the stream width (Leopold et al, 1964). For a stream 1 m wide a riffle–pool pair should occur every 5–7 m. Again based on empirical hydrological evidence, the riffles should be about 3 m long followed by a 2 m long pool. Actual spacing is not critical since the stream will readjust the rocky sediments itself during floods.

Alternating riffle–pool sequences are an important aspect of restoring the within-channel habitat of small streams. In addition to stimulating re-oxygenation of the water by increased turbulence in riffle sections, the clean rocky substrate is a prime habitat for many aquatic invertebrates and a feeding ground for fish. The pools are refuge areas for fish as well as storage areas for organic material that is slowly released into the stream.

Riparian wetlands/swamp forest

Along many channelized agricultural streams there are areas which are seasonally difficult for the farmer to plough due to excess water. These swamp areas are usually former wetlands or swamp forests, and if able to be reclaimed will enhance both wildlife conservation and nutrient-retention ability (Figure 18.6(a)).

There is considerable interest in using wetlands as cost-effective nutrient-reduction systems. In studies in Sweden, where there is a need to reduce the nitrogen load to the Baltic Sea by 50%, Rosenberg et al (1990, Table 18.2) have estimated that the cost for reducing each kg of nitrogen entering the Baltic would be US$ 0.6 for coastal wetland restoration, US$ 1.9–53.4 for remedial agricultural measures, and US$ 15.6–31.2 for a 75% reduction in municipal wastewater. The reduction, however, may not be due to denitrification—real nitrogen loss—but may be more of a change in the temporal pattern of nitrogen uptake by wetlands. Howard-Williams (1985) has suggested that true nitrogen reduction through denitrification may be a minor and overestimated function, while the change in temporal pattern of nitrogen flow through a wetland may be the more important function.

In terms of a restoration building block, it can be suggested that instead of establishing wetlands at the freshwater/marine interface it could be more effective to establish wetlands and swamp forests all along the riparian corridor. The reduction in nutrients would occur at the source. It may still be effective to restore estuarine wetlands but, given the magnitude of the problem, a corridor may be more effective and have considerably greater overall benefits.

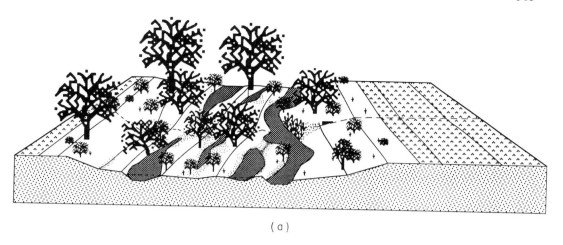

(a)

(b)

FIGURE 18.6. (a) Where the topography allows it, larger extensions of the channel can be restored to swamp forest and wetland areas. These areas will function to both reduce sediments and for nature conservation. (b) Channel or side-channel ponds are a desirable way to retain water for irrigation, provide habitat, and retain nutrients within the catchment

Ponds

Small ponds created within the meander valley or created as an extension of the horseshoe wetland are an economical and multi-use restoration measure (Figure 18.6(b)). Their uses include water retention for later use for irrigation, crayfish growing, or as a fish pond. In Sweden crayfish production is a particular favourite of farmers with ponds on their lands (Furst and Andersson, 1988). Usually the ponds are created off-channel and not placed on the stream itself.

While using ponds for intensive aquaculture is not recommended and may cause more nutrient problems, a typical small channel pond when not used for aquaculture will retain organic material and nitrogen, and with sediment processes nitrogen reduction can be achieved. Regardless, the many uses of ponds, both for recreation and nature conservation, make them a recommended building block for restoring small agricultural streams.

REDUCTION OF NUTRIENT LOSS FROM CATCHMENTS WITH RESTORED STREAMS

At present there are no studies of the nutrient-reduction ability of small catchments that have had the entire length of their streams restored by means of riparian wetlands, buffer strips, or reconfigured channels. Therefore, it is not known what the exact decrease in nitrogen loss will be following restoration.

However, we do know that the nutrient reduction ability of a stream is dependent on its length, physical complexity, and integrity of its riparian buffer strip (Petersen et al, 1987). Howard-Williams (1985) has summarized the nitrogen reduction values for natural streams and wetlands. If we use a median spiralling coefficient of 0.02 m h^{-1} calculated from Howard-Williams (1985) and an average base flow concentration of 5 g NO_3-N m^{-3}, then 16 g NO_3-N m^{-2} week^{-1} could be converted to nitrous oxide and dinitrogen. Today, a typical channelized stream has an average drainage density of 1 km km^{-2}. With restoration we can assume that the channel length will increase. Regardless, even without an increase in the channel length, a fully restored stream channel in 1 km^2 of agricultural land will have a nitrogen-processing ability of 803 kg NO_3-N yr^{-1}. Given that agricultural lands are leaking a median of 2500 kg N km^{-2} yr^{-1} (Table 18.1) the nitrogen-reduction capacity of fully functioning stream channels is about 30%.

ECONOMICS OF STREAM RESTORATION

The economics of stream restoration is an important consideration when deciding to restore lowland streams. For buffer strips the value of the farmland in terms of the market price and its profitability has to be compared to financial work that the corridor can perform. In southern Sweden, good agricultural land will vary in price from US$ 3000 to US$ 5000 per hectare. Petersen et al (1987) have estimated the cost of treating a combination of municipal and light industry sewage as US$ 25 per kg nutrient (phosphorus and nitrogen combined). This is the price that society has said it is willing to pay for nutrient reduction. If we use the reported values for nutrient reduction in buffer strips and multiply this by the value of each kg, then the land has an exchange value of US$ 1370–2195 ha^{-1} yr^{-1}. The net economic benefit of setting aside 10 m buffer strips can therefore be realized in 2–3 years.

Re-channelizing lowland stream beds to their former meander configuration has been done in Germany, Austria, and Denmark. The cost will depend on the size of the channel and the amount of soil that has to be removed. For example, in Denmark the Gelsø, a 4 m wide agricultural river, was increased from a length of 1340 m to 1720 m at a total cost of US$ 210 000 (Erik Pedersen, Søderjyllands Amt., pers. comm.). Most of the cost was to place the channel back to its former meanders. In Germany, where there are many stream-restoration projects under way, to meander 0.9 km of a small stream, 5 m wide, costs approximately US$ 250 000 (Otto, 1988). In Essen, Germany, a summary of 14 stream-restoration projects carried out since 1983 had a range of 50 to 1000 DM m^{-1} of watercourse length and/or 6 to 60 DM m^{-2} riparian bank surface (Londong and Stecker, 1986). Similar reconstructions with similar prices have been carried out in Austria.

After the cost of setting aside the land which should be viewed as a base cost, it is up to the individual restoration programme which measure to use. Each will have its own additional cost. For example, the cost of replanting the buffer strips will vary from one country to another, but in Sweden revegetation costs about US$ 2500 km^{-1} of stream bank. The construction of a horseshoe which consists of just removing 50 m^3 of soil and filling in with a layer of rock and gravel should cost about US$ 250 per horseshoe. Building several in one day would keep the cost down.

The cost of the measure should be compared to the existing maintenance costs of channelized streams. For example, in Sweden channelized streams in sandy soil areas have to be re-dredged every three years at a cost of US$ 5000–10 000 km^{-1}. To reduce the side-slope angle from 80° to 45° in a 5 m wide strip along the channel will require about 10 000 m^3 of soil to be redistributed. If the main cost is only for the earth-moving device, it will cost about US$ 40 000 km^{-1} to change. Considering that this will significantly reduce the need for channel dredging as well as reducing the phosphorus contribution, side-slope reduction is a cost-effective restoration measure.

CONCLUSION

The purpose of this chapter has been to outline an approach for restoring the quality of small watercourses now being used as drainage ditches. We suggested that, as drainage ditches, these small streams were well engineered for removing water. This water-removal function was appropriate a century ago when the groundwater and the marine environment were not overloaded, and more land was needed for agriculture, but this engineering has turned out to be a clear case of not thinking of sustainable development.

The large percentage of the landscape devoted to modern agricultural practices, the loss of the self-cleaning capacity of streams, and removal of riparian wetlands has now resulted in an overload of freshwater systems, the groundwater and the sea with nutrients. For the marine environment, this is leading to the wholesale death of entire ecosystems (Nixon, 1990). In addition, the amount of land needed for crop production is now less than 25 years ago, and in fact too much food production is occurring in northern Europe. For this reason, it is time to start thinking about how to restore our streams. This reversal has to occur at the local and individual level and is already happening in many areas throughout Sweden, Denmark and Germany, but there is still a need for solutions to the problems in the form of new ideas, approaches, and technology.

The building blocks described should be viewed as a series of suggestions to land-owners and regional authorities on how to solve these problems. The foundation for this approach is to re-establish and then protect the riparian area. Once this is set aside, additional building blocks can be selected and added according to local needs. For this reason, the presentation in this chapter has been written in a format intended to be easily read. However, these suggestions are based on sound ecological principles and an understanding of the social and economic constraints placed on ecosystem restoration.

ACKNOWLEDGEMENTS

We wish to thank the help by two young scientists; Bobby, who loaned us his LEGO® building blocks, and Linnea, who helped with the computer graphics. The computer graphics were done by

J. Lacoursière after sketches by RCP. This research was supported by grants from the Swedish Environmental Protection Board (SNV), the Swedish Council for Forest and Agricultural Research (SJFR), and the Swedish Council for Planning and Co-ordination of Research (FRN) and as part of the Unesco MAB Ecotone Programme.

REFERENCES

Bergström, L. (1987). "Nitrate leaching and drainage from annual and perennial crops in tile-drained plots and lysimeters", *Journal of Environmental Quality*, **16**, 11–18.

Bormann, F. H., Likens, G. E., Fisher, D. W., and Pierce, R. S. (1968). "Nutrient loss accelerated by clear-cutting of a forest ecosystem", *Science*, **159**, 882–884.

Brinson, M. M., Lugo, A. E., and Brown, S. (1981). "Primary productivity, decomposition and consumer activity in freshwater wetlands", *Annual Review of Ecology and Systematics*, **12**, 123–161.

Brookes, A. (1984). "Recommendations bearing on the sinuosity of Danish stream channels: Consequences of realignment, spatial extent of natural channels, processes and techniques of natural and induced restoration", National Agency of Environmental Protection, Freshwater Laboratory, Silkeborg.

Cairns, J., Jr (Ed.) (1988). *Rehabilitating Damaged Ecosystems*, CRC Press, Boca Raton, Florida.

Chauvet, E. R. (1988). "Influence of the environment on willow leaf litter decomposition in the alluvial corridor of the Garonne", *Archiv für Hydrobiologie*, **112**, 371–386.

Curry, R. R. (1972). "Rivers—A geomorphic and chemical overview", in *River Ecology and Man* (Eds D. J. Allee, H. B. N. Hynes, S. Neff, P. Ruggles, W. C. Starrett, R. Stroud, and T. P. Vande Sande), pp. 9–32, Academic Press, New York.

Dawson, F. H., and Kern-Hansen, U. (1979). "The effect of natural and artificial shade on the macrophytes of lowland streams and the use of shade as a management technique", *Internationale Revue der gesamten Hydrobiologie*, **64**, 437–455.

Décamps, H., Joachim, J., and Lauga, J. (1987). "The importance for birds of the riparian woodlands with the alluvial corridor of the River Garonne, S. W. France", *Regulated Rivers: Research and Management*, **1**, 301–316.

Doyle, R. C., Stanton, G. C., and Wolf, D. C. (1977). "Effectiveness of forest and grass buffer strips in improving the water quality of manure polluted runoff", *American Society of Agricultural Engineers*, paper no. 77-2501.

Dugdale, R. C., and Dugdale, V. C. (1961). "Sources of phosphorus and nitrogen for lakes on Afognak Island", *Limnology and Oceanography*, **6**, 13–23.

Dunne, T., and Leopold, L. B. (1978). *Water in Environmental Planning*, Freeman and Company, New York.

Elwood, J. W., Newbold, J. D., O'Neill, R. V., Stark, R. W., and Singley, P. T. (1981). "The role of microbes associated with organic and inorganic substrates in phosphorus spiralling in a woodland stream", *Verhandlungen der Internationalen Vereinigung für theoretische und angewandte Limnologie*, **21**, 850–856.

Fontaine, T. D., and Bartell, S. M. (Eds) (1983). *Dynamics of Lotic Ecosystems*, Ann Arbor Science, Ann Arbor, Michigan.

Furst, M., and Andersson, B. O. (1988). "Restoration of the crayfish fishery in Lake Hjälmaren", Institute of Freshwater Research of the Swedish National Board of Fisheries, Drottningholm.

Good, R. E., Whigham, D. F., and Simpson, R. L. (Eds) (1978). *Freshwater Wetlands: Ecological Processes and Management Potential*, Academic Press, New York.

Gore, J. A. (1985). *The Restoration of Rivers and Streams*, Butterworths, Boston.

Gosz, J. R. (1978). "Nitrogen inputs to stream water from forest along an elevational gradient in New Mexico", *Water Research*, **12**, 725–734.

Groffman, P. M., House, G. J., Hendrix, P. F., Scott, D. E. and Crossley, D. A. Jr (1986). "Nitrogen cycling as affected by interactions of components in a Georgia Piedmont agroecosystem", *Ecology*, **67**, 80–87.

Howard-Williams, C. (1985). "Cycling and retention of nitrogen and phosphorus in wetlands: a theoretical and applied perspective", *Freshwater Biology*, **15**, 391–431.

Hynes, H. B. N. (1967). "The stream and its valley", *Verhandlungen der Internationalen Vereinigung für theoretische und angewandte Limnologie*, **22**, 876–894.

Hynes, H. B. N. (1970). *The Ecology of Running Waters*, Liverpool University Press, Liverpool.

Jaakola, A. (1984). "Leaching losses of nitrogen from a clay soil under grass and cereal crops in Finland", *Plant and Soil*, **76**, 59–66.

Jackson, W. A., Asmussen, L. E., Hauser, E. W., and White, A. W. (1973). "Nitrate in surface and subsurface flow from a small agricultural watershed", *Journal of Environmental Quality*, **2**, 480–482.

Jensen, H. E. (1976). "Nitrogen movement and leaching in soil", *Nordic Hydrology*, **7**, 19–30.

Loepold, L. B., Wolman, M. G., and Miller, J. P. (1964). *Fluvial Processes in Geomorphology*, Freeman and Company, New York.

Longdong, D., Stecker, A. (1986). "The cost of renaturalizing brooks in the administrative area of the Emscher and Lippeverband", *Wasser und Boden*, **38**, 392–398.

Lowrance, R. R., Todd, R. T., and Asmussen, L. E. (1983). "Waterborne nutrient budgets for the riparian zone of an agricultural watershed", *Agriculture, Ecosystems and Environment*, **10**, 371–384.

Lowrance, R. R., Todd, R., Fail, J., Hendrickson, O., Leonard, R., and Asmussen, L. (1984). "Riparian forest as nutrient filters in agricultural watersheds", *BioScience*, **34**, 374–377.

Mitsch, W. J., and Gosselink, J. G. (1986). *Wetlands*, Van Nostrand Reinhold, New York.

Newbold, J. D., O'Neill, R. V., Elwood, J. W., and van Winkle, W. (1982). "Nutrient spiralling in streams: Implications for nutrient limitation and invertebrate activity", *American Naturalist*, **120**, 628–652.

Nixon, S. W. (1990). "Marine eutrophication: A growing international problem", *Ambio*, **19**, 102–108.

Otto, A. (1988). "*Naturnaher Wasserbau, Modell Holzbach*", AID-Schriftenreihe des Ministeriums für Ernährung, Landwirtschaft und Forsten, Bundesanstalt für Gewässerkunde, Koblenz.

Peterjohn, W. T., and Correll, D. L. (1984). "Nutrient dynamics in an agricultural watershed: Observations on the role of a riparian forest", *Ecology*, **65**, 1466–1475.

Petersen, R. C., Madsen, B. L., Wilzbach, M. A., Magadza, C. H. D., Paarlberg, A., Kullberg, A., and Cummins, K. W. (1987). "Stream management. Emerging global similarities", *Ambio*, **6**, 166–179.

Pinay, G., and Décamps, H. (1988). "The role of riparian woods in regulating nitrogen fluxes between the alluvial aquifer and surface water: A conceptual model", *Regulated Rivers: Research and Management*, **2**, 507–516.

Resh, V. H., and Rosenberg, D. M. (Eds) (1984) *The Ecology of Aquatic Insects*, Praeger, New York.

Robertson, J. G., Eknert, M. B., and Ihse, M. (1990). "Habitat analysis from infra-red aerial photographs and the conservation of birds in Swedish Agricultural Landscapes", *Ambio*, **19**, 195–203.

Rosenberg, R., Elmgren, R., Fleischer, S., Johnsson, P., Persson, G., and Dahlin, H. (1990). "Marine eutrophication case studies in Sweden", *Ambio*, **19**, 123–125.

Rosswall, T., and Paustian, K. (1984). "Cycling of nitrogen in modern agricultural systems", *Plant and Soil*, **76**, 3–21.

Ryding, S. O. (1984). "Trender i Ringsjöns näringstillförsel och vattenkvalitet 1975–1983", Mimeograph, Institute of Limnology, Uppsala.

Taylor, A. W., Edwards, W. M., and Simpson, E. C. (1971). "Nutrients in stream draining woodland and farmland near Coshocton, Ohio", *Water Research*, **7**, 81–89.

Verry, E. S., and Timmons, D. R. (1982). "Waterborne nutrient flow through an upland-peatland watershed in Minnesota", *Ecology*, **63**, 1456–1467.

Wetzel, R. G. (1975). *Limnology*, W. B. Sanders, Philadelphia.

Wolf, P. (1956). "Utdikad civilisation", *Skrifter utgivna av Svenska Lax-och Laxöringsföreningen VII*, Malmö.

Yates, P., and Sheridan, J. M. (1983). "Estimating the effectiveness of vegetated floodplains/wetlands as nitrate–nitrite and orthophosphorus filters", *Agriculture, Ecosystem and Environment*, **9**, 303–314.

19

Habitats as the Building Blocks for River Conservation Assessment

D. M. HARPER, C. D. SMITH,

Department of Zoology, University of Leicester, University Road, Leicester LE1 7RH, UK

and

P. J. BARHAM

National Rivers Authority, Bromholme Lane, Brampton, Huntingdon PE18 8NE, UK

INTRODUCTION

Accurate and concise conservation recommendations are needed by river managers in Britain for several reasons. A series of Acts of Parliament and parliamentary Select Committees have given the river authorities (Regional Water Authorities and their successor since 1989, the National Rivers Authority (NRA)) increasingly stronger duties and powers to promote nature conservation (Hellawell, 1988; Anon., 1989). This requires information about conservation priorities and methods. Public opinion is increasingly unsympathetic towards development works such as river engineering which do not harmonize with the environment (Williams and Bowers, 1987). Many river engineers share this opinion and require information to become good conservationists. Engineers are re-discovering that river management which encourages natural development of the river can be economic in capital and maintenance, and an ecological input to the planning stage of river works is now regularly sought (Gardiner, 1988).

Conservation information comes in different forms, and is used for varied purposes. On a large scale (e.g. countrywide) it is necessary for biologists to build up databases on species and communities so that information about their distribution and abundance (or rarity) can be considered in plans for any particular site or river. On a smaller scale (e.g. single catchment) precise information is required from surveys which can be incorporated into detailed site plans or maintenance schedules (Ash and Woodcock, 1988). In between these two scales is information which leads to "codes of practice"—the general ecological education of people whose work has an impact upon the river environment (Andrews and Williams, 1988).

River Conservation and Management. Edited by P. J. Boon, P. Calow, and G. E. Petts
© 1992 John Wiley & Sons Ltd

The large-scale databases existing in Britain are fairly good: national recording and mapping schemes for plants, birds and mammals, and a survey scheme for aquatic invertebrates give us adequate information about rarity values of species and their associations in communities (Wright et al, 1989). The main drawbacks of national databases are that they are expensive to create and maintain and they lack the precise definition required for individual rivers. The latter criticism is mitigated where they confer a predictive ability. Large-scale programmes have the vital function of allowing any detailed study to be viewed in a broader geographical context.

At the level of individual rivers and their catchments, knowledge is more patchy, and surveys generally focus upon limited aspects of the riverine environment. The most comprehensive biological study of the River Teifi in Wales took about 2700 man-days to complete, covered mammals, birds, fish, invertebrates, and aquatic plants, but only recorded the frequency of occurrence of physical habitats (Brooker, 1982, 1983). The "River Corridor Survey" methodology (NCC, 1985) used widely by the NRA usually only considers plant habitats, and limited physical features (Coles et al, 1989). The large body of information about invertebrates and fish which has been collected for water quality and fisheries management is often difficult to collate. Geomorphological assessments consider a range of channel characteristics, but discuss the direct biological implications of channel design briefly, if at all (Brookes, in press).

In an attempt to bridge the gap between biological and geomorphological surveys, we describe a study which focused upon the habitats of the river channel. These are structured by the geomorphology of the river but themselves influence the composition and conservation value of the aquatic biological community. We have shown that, for an individual river, information about the mechanisms which determine the riffle–pool system, meandering, etc. and their appropriate nature at a site would enable these features to be retained (or re-created), and with them, their biological communities (Smith et al, 1990).

Division of the riverine environment into separate habitats (a "top-down" approach) is usually done intuitively, from a knowledge of natural history. This does not compromise the usual aim of obtaining a full species list, but may fail to recognize habitats of true conservation value. To assemble a list of habitats from the requirements of individual species (a "bottom-up" approach) is presently impractical. We sought to classify habitats according to observed species distributions—a "top-down" approach, but free from the problem of subjectivity. This offers to further our ability to make use of habitats as the true "building blocks of river conservation".

Macroinvertebrates were chosen as a model for study. They contribute significantly to riverine species diversity and act as the main pathway between primary production and many fish species. They also play a key role in many practical schemes for water quality indication. Despite their importance, through practical difficulties the macroinvertebrates are seldom considered explicitly in impact assessment of river management works.

The objectives were:

(1) To characterize the macroinvertebrate species assemblage associated with a large number of intuitive "potential habitats". It was postulated that some of the potential habitats would support similar macroinvertebrate species—these groups, or "functional habitats", would be determined by multivariate analysis of the data.

(2) To repeat the study in a different catchment, to find out how the list of functional habitats responded to changes in species and potential habitats.
(3) To test the assumed causal relationship between species richness and habitat richness. In a channel which lacks a known set of functional habitats there should be a predictable set of absent species if the assumption is valid.

STUDY SITES

Three lowland streams in the East Midlands of England were chosen to pursue the three objectives. A 5 km length of the River Welland (catchment *ca* 470 km^2 at the study site) was used for the first phase of the study. It is a physically diverse clay stream with considerable cultural eutrophication. In other respects the chemical water quality is good and it supports a diverse fauna and flora, although local rarities were eliminated during an arterial drainage scheme in 1969 (Messenger, 1971).

The River Wissey, which was used in the second phase, is of similar size to the first stream. There is a high groundwater contribution to discharge in the chalk catchment and consequently it is a less eutrophic stream than the Welland, also with less tendency for spates. Results of biological monitoring by the National Rivers Authority showed that the macroinvertebrate community was different from that of the River Welland.

The River Kym was used for the third phase of the study. It is a clay stream like the River Welland but the flow and depth are dominated by "ponding" due to a succession of bridge foundations and a gauging station weir. The catchment area—and therefore discharge—is less than that of the Welland, but through past dredging the size of the channel is similar. Habitats associated with fast, shallow water and coarse substrate were absent in the 5 km length studied.

METHODS

Indicator species analysis has been widely used for the multivariate analysis of species assemblages, using the TWINSPAN program (Hill, 1979). Dichotomous division of a set of samples on the basis of species composition (via ordination) progresses until a predefined group size or level of division is reached, irrespective of the absolute difference between samples at each level. Most applications have sought to explain species composition in terms of measured environmental variables, using techniques such as multiple discriminant analysis. A "stopping-point" for the classification is found where further division cannot be explained in terms of the chosen variables. Further differences between samples may be due to complex effects of a wider range of variables and species interaction, or to sampling error.

Our requirement was to find the point at which sampling error took precedence, since all controls of species composition were important (though we did not seek to identify them). Between three and five samples were taken from examples of each potential habitat. For each branch of the classification, the last level at which replicates remained together was considered to constitute one functional habitat in respect of the macroinvertebrate community (Figure 19.1). In this way the appropriate stopping-points were decided directly from the data, rather than from the judgement of the investigator. The maximum level of division was made large enough, at 10 for the Welland and 8 for the

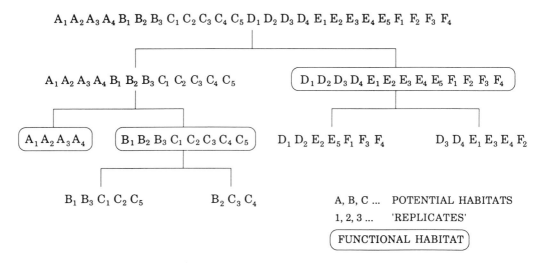

FIGURE 19.1. Method of determining functional habitats from classification of potential habitat replicates. Where replicates from a potential habitat become separated, this indicates the "parent group" to be a functional habitat

Wissey, to reach a stopping-point on each branch of the classification. Pseudospecies cut levels were 0, 10, 100, 1000. Otherwise, the defaults were adopted for options provided by TWINSPAN.

On the River Welland, 181 samples were taken from 42 potential habitats during August 1988; and on the River Wissey, 95 samples from 19 potential habitats during August 1989. The lower number of potential habitats on the Wissey was due in part to a lesser number of macrophyte species and in part to a less pronounced riffle–pool sequence, so more uniform flow. Several sampling methods were employed, but with a view to providing results equivalent at the intended TWINSPAN pseudospecies categories of 0–9, 10–99, 100–999, 1000+.

Single samples were taken from 26 potential habitats on the River Kym during August 1989, using the same sampling methods as on the other rivers. Indicator species analysis was not prescribed for this part of the study and so replication was unnecessary.

Samples were stored in a cold room at 4°C and live-sorted within 36 h of collection (usually within 12 h), with sub-sampling of groups represented by more than 100 individuals. Further identification was carried out in most cases to species, with the most frequent exceptions being Hydracarina (no further), Chironominae and Tanypodinae (to genus), and several other groups of Diptera (e.g. Ceratopogonidae and Tipulidae, no further). Nymphs of Hemiptera and larvae of some Coleoptera were often also left at a higher taxonomic level than the adults. The Welland, Wissey, and Kym samples contained 142, 122 and 105 taxa, respectively, from a total of 190 taxa.

RESULTS

The indicator species analysis was applied to data obtained from the River Welland and the River Wissey, to determine the list of functional habitats for each river (Figure 19.2). Classification of the River Welland samples suggested 20 functional habitats from the 42

FIGURE 19.2. Potential habitats sampled on the River Welland and River Wissey, with the functional habitats derived from classification using TWINSPAN

TABLE 19.1. Species absent from one river (Welland or Kym) but present in at least five samples from the other river

---

Absent from River Kym

Simulium (Simulium) ornatum Meigen
S. (Simulium) erythrocephalum DeGeer
S. (Wilhelmia) equinum L.
S. (Eusimulium) angustipes Edwards
Ephemerella ignita (Poda)
Baetis scambus Eaton
B. vernus Curtis
B. rhodani (Pictet)

Hydropsyche contubernalis McLachlan
H. pellucidula (Curtis)
H. angustipennis (Curtis)
H. siltalai Döhler
Leuctra geniculata (Stephens)
Theodoxus fluviatilis (L.)
Ancylus fluviatilis Muller
Elmis aenea (Muller)
Limnius volckmari (Panzer)

Absent from River Welland

Phryganea grandis L.
Acroloxus lacustris (L.)

Platycnemis pennipes (Pallas)

Chironomidae and Oligochaeta not included

potential habitats sampled. Common sense dictated that some be disregarded or merged; for example, the samples from shoots of emergent macrophyte species formed a functional habitat, as did their roots, but clearly these cannot arise separately and so should be grouped as "emergent macrophytes". This line of reasoning produced a shorter list of 16 habitats.

From the 19 potential habitats studied on the River Wissey, 12 functional habitats were suggested by TWINSPAN, and the set was reduced to nine through the consideration previously described. The potential habitats sorted to form functional habitats which were largely a sub-set of those identified on the River Welland, in spite of differences in macroinvertebrate species composition and dominance.

The species found in the Rivers Welland and Kym were similar in many respects, as expected from two neighbouring clay streams. The major habitat difference between the streams was the absence of riffle flow, substrate, and associated macrophytes on the Kym. The main difference between the macroinvertebrate communities of the two rivers was absence of a set of species on the Kym which were common on the Welland, though a small number of species were unique to the Kym (Table 19.1).

All the species restricted to the Welland were most abundant in habitats defined by more rapid flow and coarse substrate, although they also occurred in some habitats which were present on the Kym. Of the species which were found only on the River Kym, at least *Phryganea grandis* and *Acroloxus lacustris* are characteristic of still and slowly flowing water. The Kym is effectively a series of long pools, and for its channel size has a small catchment, which must reduce the severity of flood events.

DISCUSSION

Throughout the practice of nature conservation, habitat is established as a most sensitive and urgent issue. The conservation of "high-profile" riverine bird and mammal species has always considered habitat to be of prime importance, along with protection from immediate sources of damage such as pollution, hunting, and trapping (Holmes, 1986). The River Corridor survey methodology and its derivatives involve vascular plants as target species, in their own right and as indicators of overall river condition. A high proportion of practical recommendations for macrophyte conservation address habitat requirements, more or less explicitly.

The conservation of river macroinvertebrates does not receive attention commensurate with their large contribution to aquatic biodiversity. The reasons for this are understandable. They are prized by few as an amenity; they are more difficult to identify than plants, birds, and mammals; the requirements of fewer species are reliably known; and specific recommendations for their conservation are difficult to construct in lay terms. The solution to the first problem lies in education for natural awareness and conscience. The other difficulties are reduced if habitats can be made a target for conservation effort.

Multivariate analysis using TWINSPAN identified a list of habitats with distinct macroinvertebrate species complements on two rivers, from more extensive lists of "potential habitats". Improvements to sewage-treatment facilities on the upper Welland have encouraged the presence of pollution-intolerant species only in recent years, while the spring-fed Wissey has a history of high water quality. The Wissey has also been subject to less physical disturbance in terms of both severity and frequency than the Welland. One might then have expected the River Wissey to support more species with narrow habitat-specificity; and that this would lead to further division of habitat groups such as "emergent macrophytes". That this did not occur supports the practical application of functional habitats as conservation units. At least within the environmental range of the two study rivers, functional habitats are "portable" between catchments; therefore their use on a new river does not require that costly basic research is repeated. The study rivers encompass only a part of the variety of rivers even within the UK and so further work would be needed to identify habitats objectively for other river types. As a strategy for use in other climatic zones (e.g. alpine, semi-arid) the classification procedure would remain valid, with the main priority being to reduce the cost of its use.

Some qualifications before the practical application of a functional habitat set are indicated from the lists of "preferential species" reported by TWINSPAN for each dichotomy. For example, replicate samples from *Potamogeton lucens* separated together from the main body of submerged plant samples, and strict interpretation to the classification regards it as a functional habitat. However, the habitat contribution of *P. lucens* to the macroinvertebrate community lies wholly "within" that of the other submerged plants, since the separation is based entirely on absence of species from *P. lucens*. At a basic level the corresponding objective for macroinvertebrate conservation might read "the presence of at least one submerged macrophyte is important, preferably not *P. lucens* alone". The explanation for *P. lucens* may be unusually simple, since the leaves become inhospitably chalk-encrusted in calcareous rivers, but we need not have known this to use the information.

"Common sense" was used in producing a final list of functional habitats for the rivers. This operated in comparing habitats for practical purposes (e.g. merging shoots and roots of the same plants) and in comparing species preferences (e.g. recognizing *P. lucens* as a special case). The objectivity of the technique is compromised through such use of judgement—while sometimes necessary, such changes to the classification should be made with caution.

The basis of habitat conservation as a tool is the assumption that species richness follows from habitat richness, subject to limits imposed by chemical water quality. There are three possible approaches to study the effect of habitat composition on the community. Habitat availability could be manipulated experimentally—this would be costly and results long in coming. The effects of habitat enhancement work can be monitored—audit surveys are now frequently implemented on recent projects. The comparison of the Rivers Welland and Kym studied effects of long-standing habitat "damage" on macroinvertebrate species richness.

Most differences in macroinvertebrate species composition accorded with the absence of a set of habitats from the ponded River Kym. The results emphasized that within the set of habitats in which a species is observed there is a smaller set which must be represented for the species to succeed. Although we can see that the species absent from the Kym are normally most abundant in habitats absent from the Kym, they were also present to some degree in "Kym habitats" on the Welland. The hidden requirements could be for egg-laying sites, or requirements of a specific life-stage, or even features on a wider spatial/temporal scale. In consequence, distribution of a species among habitats should be viewed carefully—the presence of species A in habitat X may be dependent upon the availability of habitat Y.

Attention to the shortfalls in habitat availability, probably during channel maintenance, can be predicted to have a beneficial effect on species richness. While naturalness is an important objective for conservation, the status of a stretch of river can be considered in the context of the whole river. The flow at some sites on the River Welland is impounded, but the intermittent artificial ponding enhances overall habitat diversity of the catchment and adds to the visual amenity and fisheries value.

The use of habitats as the building blocks of river conservation addresses biological diversity as a prime conservation objective. On the majority of rivers in the East Midlands of England this is a relevant, productive approach, since site uniqueness and species rarity have previously been compromised by a long history of unsympathetic management. Current, more enlightened management practices—including the encouragement of habitat diversity—will produce rivers in which rarities and sites of special interest occur once more. This priority is valid throughout many managed lowland rivers in the UK and elsewhere, though clearly where "rarity value" is already high the need to consider local requirements of important individual species remains.

ACKNOWLEDGEMENTS

The study described here was funded by the National Rivers Authority (Anglian Region). The chapter is published with the permission of the Regional Manager, although the opinions stated here are the authors' own. Fieldwork and sorting was carried out with the assistance of Dr Andrew Smart and students of the Department of Zoology, University of Leicester.

REFERENCES

Andrews, J. H., and Williams, G. (1988). "The development of wildlife conservation on rivers", *Royal Society for the Protection of Birds Conservation Review*, **2**, 78–80.

Anon. (1989). *The Water Act*, HMSO, London.

Ash, J. R. V., and Woodcock, E. P. (1988). "The operational use of river corridor surveys in river management", *Journal of the Institute of Water and Environmental Management*, **2**, 423–428.

Brooker, M. P. (1982). *Conservation of Wildlife in River Corridors. Part 1. Methods of Survey and Classification*, Welsh Water Authority, Brecon.

Brooker, M. P. (1983). *Conservation of Wildlife in River Corridors. Part 2. Scientific Assessment*, Welsh Water Authority, Brecon.

Brookes, A. (in press). "Geomorphological assessment in river management", Paper presented to the Engineering Section of the Institution of Water and Environmental Management, 19 January 1990.

Coles, T. F., Southey, J. M., Forbes, I., and Clough, T. (1989). "River wildlife databases and their value for sensitive environmental management", *Regulated Rivers: Research and Management*, **4**, 179–189.

Gardiner, J. L. (1988). "Environmentally sound river engineering: examples from the Thames catchment", *Regulated Rivers: Research and Management*, **2**, 445–469.

Hellawell, J. M. (1988). "River regulation and nature conservation", *Regulated Rivers: Research and Management*, **2**, 425–443.

Hill, M. O. (1979). "TWINSPAN—A FORTRAN program for arranging multivariate data in an ordered two-way table by classification of the individuals and attributes", *Ecology & Systematics*, Cornell University, Ithaca, New York.

Holmes, N. T. H. (1986). *Wildlife Surveys of Rivers in Relation to River Management* (ER 1292-M), Water Research Centre, Medmenham.

Messenger, G. (1971). *Flora of Rutland*, Leicester Museums, Leicester.

NCC (1985). *Surveys of Wildlife in River Corridors: draft methodology*, Nature Conservancy Council, Peterborough.

Smith, C. D., Harper, D. M., and Barham, P. J. (1990). "Engineering operations and invertebrates: linking hydrology with ecology", *Regulated Rivers: Research and Management*, **5**, 89–96.

Williams, G., and Bowers, J. K. (1987). "Land drainage and birds in England and Wales", *Royal Society for the Protection of Birds Conservation Review*, **1**, 25–30.

Wright, J. F., Armitage, P. D., Furse, M. T., and Moss, D. (1989). "Prediction of invertebrate communities using stream measurements", *Regulated Rivers: Research and Management*, **4**, 147–155.

20

Rehabilitation of Streams in South-west Germany

K. KERN

*Universität Karlsruhe, Institut für Wasserbau und Kulturtechnik,
Department of Environmental River Engineering, Kaiserstr. 12,
D-7500 Karlsruhe 1, Germany*

INTRODUCTION

Stream regulation in south-west Germany dates back to the Roman occupation. Natural river systems in the Upper Rhine Valley were altered mainly for strategic reasons. Medieval water mills, timber-floating, and irrigation of meadows changed smaller streams as well throughout the country. Clearing of woodland for cultivation caused significant soil erosion in upper watersheds and corresponding sedimentation in downstream floodplains. This led to increased deposition on floodplains (amounting to several metres in many cases), influencing stream morphology, especially in loess areas.

Considerable changes in flow systems have occurred in the last 150 years. Modification of the River Rhine and River Neckar for flood protection and navigation led to an intensified use of the floodplains. Many flood channels and numerous drainage ditches were built to increase the area available for agriculture. In many cases roads and railway tracks were placed on the floodplains, often accompanied by straightening of rivers and streams. Prospering industries and spreading settlements in the twentieth century produced a growing amount of wastewater, causing severe pollution in the rivers and streams, especially by the 1950s and early 1960s. Major efforts in the 1960s and 1970s in wastewater treatment led to a significant improvement in water quality in the last decade. At present, 92% of all residents in the state of Baden-Württemberg (Figure 20.1) are connected to one of the 1260 treatment plants purifying the wastewater down to an average biological oxygen demand of 15 mg l^{-1} (compared with 68 mg l^{-1} in 1975). As a result, stream-water quality has improved considerably. Two-thirds of the rivers and streams in the state of Baden-Württemberg are unpolluted or less polluted in 1990, as the statistics of 400 sampling sites reveal (Figure 20.2) (Braukmann, 1991).

With the improvement of water quality, public interest began to focus on the structural defects and poor aesthetics of channelized rivers and streams. In 1985 the state water authorities started a programme for the rehabilitation of 15 sections of small streams all

---

River Conservation and Management. Edited by P. J. Boon, P. Calow, and G. E. Petts
© 1992 John Wiley & Sons Ltd

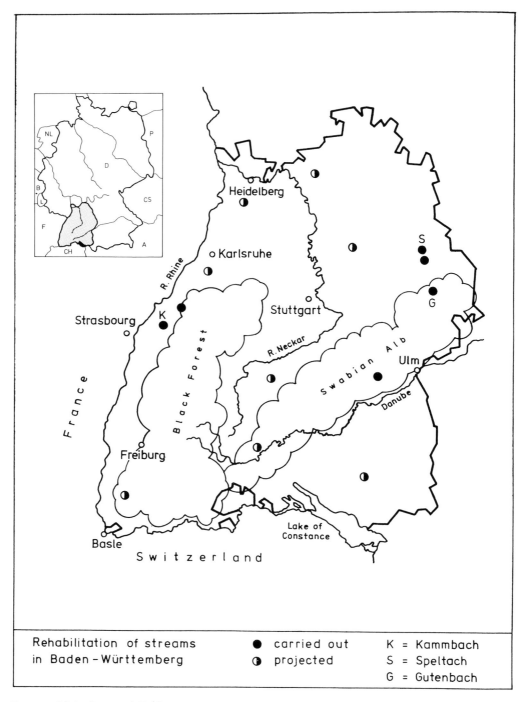

FIGURE 20.1. State of Baden-Württemberg (Germany): location of streams covered by the rehabilitation pilot programme

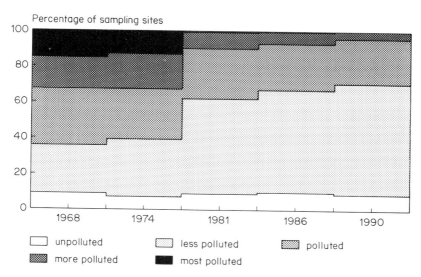

FIGURE 20.2. Development of river and stream pollution in the state of Baden-Württemberg based on saprobic analysis of 400 sampling sites (reproduced from Braukmann, 1991, by permission)

over the state. The objectives based on scientific support of the University of Karlsruhe are to:

- Optimize (interdisciplinary) planning;
- Learn how to rehabilitate different stream types;
- Learn how to restore streams efficiently with minimal effort;
- Optimize the ecological monitoring; and
- Spread the idea.

By 1990 either pre-planning or final planning has been completed on eight projects and five have been realized completely or in parts. Two projects have been cancelled, one because of water-quality problems, the other due to restrictions in a nature reserve.

The following statements are closely related to the experiences which were made in this programme and to a nationwide survey by the author (Kern and Nadolny, 1986).

PLANNING STEPS

Testing feasibility

The successful rehabilitation of channelized watercourses needs an intensive interdisciplinary planning process. Before starting, the feasibility of the project has to be investigated.

Evaluation and plausibility

The ecological systems along a stream should be examined very carefully. It is necessary to repair damage *from the source to the mouth*, including tributaries. It does not make sense to spend a lot of money for the restoration of a 500 m section which is followed by a 300 m closed conduit that hinders the migration of fish and other species, although there are many examples of such projects.

Water quality

The required minimum standard should be "less polluted" according to many limnologists. In general practice no project proposal will be rejected, when it is classified "polluted" on the scale commonly used in Germany. Nevertheless, it is necessary in all cases to look for pollution sources in order to improve water quality. *The expectation of self-purification in a rehabilitated stream must never be a substitute for further efforts in pollution control.*

Legal aspects and ownership

Without additional area ecological re-development is limited to a few improvements on a very small scale. *Stream bed habitats can only develop when lateral movements of the channel can be allowed*, and bank erosion is no longer regarded as flood damage. In addition, existing water rights might prevent effective rehabilitation measures.

Objectives

The main objective of stream rehabilitation is the conservation of nature. Wetlands are the most endangered habitats in Germany. The majority of all species which are endangered or already extinct in the state of Baden-Württemberg depend on wetland areas. Typical river-bed and floodplain habitats must be developed by structural measures and extensive maintenance.

Many rehabilitation projects are initiated in the name of landscape improvement. The demand for recreation will influence the project planning, especially in the vicinity of settlements. The specific objectives of a project are to be defined at an early stage. Rehabilitation of river-bed morphology could be emphasized as well as restoration of floodplain structures and habitats. Sometimes the improvement of drop structures to facilitate migration of aquatic fauna is the main issue (Gebler, 1991).

Participants

On the employer's side all institutions which are directly involved should be represented: (community) administration, nature conservation and water authorities, farmers' administration, fisheries, etc. On the consultant's side a range of specialists should be involved, including civil engineers, landscape engineers, biologists, sedimentologists, or geographers, depending on the specific requirements.

Data collection

Rehabilitation must be based on a thorough knowledge of the stream history and its present condition. There are five key topics. First, land use must be considered, including historical land use and former floodplain extent, present land use and future prospects, flood protection, and flood-protection requirements. Second, floodplain habitats must be assessed: valuable habitats—oxbows, depressions, forested wetlands, etc.; ecological evaluations: soil properties, groundwater influence and detrimental impacts such as deposits or dredging, ecological development, survey of flora and fauna. Third, channel morphology and stream type must be described, attention being given to the present state of stream bed and stream bank, sediment transport, stability of stream bed, natural stream type and its properties, historical changes of stream bed. Fourth, there must be consideration of hydrological and hydraulic data. Due attention must be given to possible changes in discharge related to land use or stream management, historical and present bankfull discharge, and hydraulic evaluation of morphological stability under present conditions. Finally, limnological investigations are required. These must include chemical and physical properties, saprobidy, possible pollution sources and a survey of fauna, including endangered species of fish, molluscs, and insects; sources of recolonization, prospects of rehabilitation.

A comprehensive analysis of the information obtained is essential for the development of the so-called "Leitbild" as a guide towards the final rehabilitation concept.

The Leitbild concept

The Leitbild is a description of the desirable stream properties regarding only the natural potential, not considering the economic or political aspects that influence the realization of a scheme (Figure 20.3). It is based on three elements:

(1) Natural stream properties (stream pattern, morphodynamics, floodplain morphology, natural flow dynamics and flooding, potential vegetation, etc.);
(2) Irreversible changes of abiotic and biotic factors (e.g. changes of the run-off regime or sediment transport, dredging of alluvial sediments in the floodplain, extinct species, etc.);
(3) Aspects of cultural ecology; specific traditional stages of land use caused an increase of species which are endangered by modern agriculture.

From the Leitbild towards the final rehabilitation concept, which can be carried out, two more steps have to be taken. The Leitbild of the stream system represents the *ideal solution* not taking into account conditions of today: present land use, water rights, flood-protection requirements, etc. Only in very few cases is it possible to carry out the Leitbild draft without major concessions. Normally, numerous restrictions are imposed on the project, preventing an "ideal" solution. Therefore it is up to the planners to decide which parts and aspects of the project are essential to the ecological rehabilitation. This represents the *optimal solution* under present conditions. This preliminary design may be based on several alternative drafts with different ecological and economic effects.

The optimal solution will have to be discussed with all participants, including the public. Usually only minor alterations are imposed by the legal procedure which follows the internal vote in the working group. The final project design may be called the *feasible solution*. The final outline includes the engineering draft with all morphological changes,

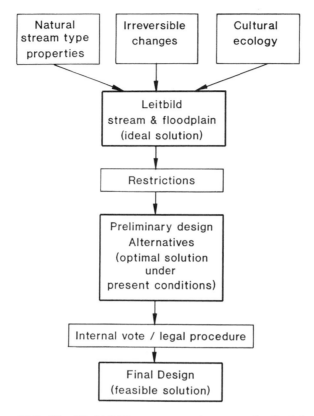

FIGURE 20.3. The "Leitbild"– concept and steps to the final design

structural works, and the hydraulic design of the channel, floodplain discharge capacity as well as stability considerations. Planting schemes, bank-protection works (where necessary), and rules for future maintenance are included along with probable costs of the project. Further ecological aspects, such as water quality improvement and protection of endangered habitats and species, are integrated into the project design.

PROJECT EXAMPLES

Kammbach (lowland stream)

The Kammbach (see data in Table 20.1 and the plates on p. 230) was channelized in 1961 as part of a large land-reclamation project in the Upper Rhine Valley. The discharge is limited to 4 m³ s⁻¹ by a railroad-crossing culvert and the bed was reinforced with dry-laid stones without regard to well-known tendencies to silt up. Maintenance included not only cutting the prospering water plants in the sun-exposed channel but also dredging out the silt and sand that diminishes the flow capacity.

Homogeneous flow velocities, regular interferences (by maintenance), and considerable pollution degraded the ecological value of the channelized stream. Figure 20.4

TABLE 20.1. Data for the Kammbach stream

Location:	Upper Rhine Valley near Strasbourg (Figure 20.1)
Altitude:	141 m
Catchment area:	16 km^2
Mean annual discharge:	0.13 m^3 s^{-1}
Design flood:	4 m^3 s^{-1}
Geology of watershed:	Sandstone, loess
Geology of project area:	Alluvial sediments of Upper Rhine Valley
Soil type in floodplain:	Sandy clay, pseudo gley
Land use in floodplain:	Agriculture—70% arable, 30% pastureland
Channel morphology:	Straight trapezoidal channel, width: 6.5 m, channel bed and lower banks lined with dry-laid stones
Sediments:	Silty sand, small gravel
Slope:	0.07–0.10%
Water quality:	Polluted (Pollution class III)
Rehabilitated stretch:	1.7 km (in 1988)

shows the former impoverished, and the potential restored, community of fish (Ness, 1989). The former fish community was well adjusted to the degraded habitat without suffering too much from the poor water quality. The potential fish community was evaluated according to the expected evolution of stream morphology, including riparian trees rooting at the stream banks as might develop in 15 or 20 years after rehabilitation.

Little information was available on the former stream pattern since the 1961 regulation was not the first interference. Based on the morphological stream type, the Kammbach was expected to meander. The projection had to take into account the controlled discharge which is considerably smaller than the natural flood flow. In addition, man-made siltation of the channel bed had to be considered in the rehabilitation concept.

Pollution problems have not been discussed as intensively as they should have been. Fertilizer run-off from maize growing all along the channel banks is believed to influence water quality, since the pollution index is getting worse along the Kammbach.

There is a sediment trap located at the beginning of the rehabilitated section which is supposed to retain sand and silt to delay downstream sedimentation. The course of the stream shows slight bends, but no meanders. Below the sediment trap an artificial oxbow is attached to the new stream. In a broader section an island is dividing the stream flow. The width of the cross-section varies between 10 and 30 m compared to the constant 8 m of the former channel. On both sides a strip of land has been taken out of production, in an attempt to reduce nutrient and pesticide infiltration. The costs amounted to 140 DM m^{-1}, not including the purchase of land.

Critical review

One benefit of the scheme was to maintain large open areas giving way to succession, and no reinforcements were brought into the new channel. However, more attention should have been paid to pollution problems; the height of the "islands" and "peninsulas" prevents frequent flooding (and the development of more wetland vegetation); more trees should have been planted along the new stream; and siltation can only be

Fish community Kammbach stream	Before rehab.			Potential		
	juvenile	sub-adult	adult	juvenile	sub-adult	adult
Noemacheilus barbatulus	×	×	×	×	×	×
Gasterosteus aculeatus	×	×	×	×	×	×
Anguilla anguilla		×			×	×
Gobio gobio	×	×	×	×	×	×
Phoxinus phoxinus			×	×	×	×
Rhodeus sericeus amarus			×	×	×	×
Leuciscus cephalus	×	×			×	×
Rutilus rutilus		×				
Misgurnus fossilis				×	×	×

FIGURE 20.4. Fish community before rehabilitation (in 1987) and predicted (potential) fish population after full recovery of the Kammbach (re-drawn after Ness, 1989)

partially controlled by the sediment trap. If severe problems arise, a second or third sediment trap upstream may be required.

Speltach (upland stream)

The Speltach (see data in Table 20) was channelized in the 1930s for the purpose of agricultural improvement. The former meanders were cut and the length of the stream course shortened by an average of 7%. Simultaneously, the bankfull discharge was increased to 13 m³ s⁻¹. Hence every other year the floodplain along the stream was inundated. The channel included a few drop structures which did not prevent slight bed erosion amounting to 40 cm within 50 years. Local bank erosion broadened the channel from an original average of 6 m up to 12 m in some sections.

A study of sediment yield of the watershed (Briem and Kern, 1989) revealed that in this special case the Keuper formations mainly produce dissolved and silty materials, and there is a natural lack of coarse sediments. Drilling showed that the floodplain has risen several metres since early settlements. The evidence consisted of pieces of pottery that were found underneath a 3 m layer of homogeneous clay. Coarse material could not be found anywhere in the sediments of the floodplain. Nevertheless, the present channel, as well as the former stream, is running over old layers of clay. Hydraulic calculations show that the shear stress is high enough to transport all coarse materials in the channel, causing abrasion of the cohesive clay. How, then, could the stream bed follow the rising

TABLE 20.2. Data for the Speltach stream

Location:	Hilly region northeast of Stuttgart (Figure 20.1)
Altitude:	410–420 m
Catchment area:	35 km^2
Mean annual discharge:	0.32 m^3 s^{-1}
Mean annual flood:	11.9 m^3 s^{-1}
10-year flood:	21 m^3 s^{-1}
Geology of watershed:	Keuper formations
Geology of project area:	Alluvial sediments of the Keuper (clay)
Soil type in floodplain:	Pseudo gley-pelasol, clay soil
Land use in floodplain:	Agriculture—30% arable, 70% pastureland
Channel morphology:	Straight earth channel with severe bank erosion in some sections
Sediments:	Clay bed, partially covered with layers of gravel
Slope:	0.24–0.30%
Water quality:	Less polluted (Pollution class II)
Rehabilitated section:	2 km (in 1989)

floodplain level? The most likely answer is "by meandering". The geomorphological study proposed that the stream should be allowed to meander wherever possible and that stream bed confining techniques should be used on sections with higher slopes.

A few trees and bushes shaded small sections of the water surface. Some drop structures had caused large scour-holes downstream and backwater effects upstream. Stream banks of some sections were covered with sedges. The aquatic habitat was dominated by homogeneous flow conditions with constant depths and widths, interrupted by backwater areas with greater depths and lower velocities. Figure 20.5 shows the fish community before rehabilitation in a backwater area compared to the expected fish community in the rehabilitated stream. With a *successful* rehabilitation the number of fish species is expected to *decrease* by 50% due to altered flow conditions (Ness, 1989)!

Only a small strip of land was available along the channel for the prospective 4.6 km section to be rehabilitated. The channel rehabilitation has been divided into three groups according to stream bank stability and bed erosion:

No erosion:	Only planting trees above average water level.
Mild erosion:	Regrading of the stream banks and planting several rows of trees. Changing the vertical drop structures into inclined ones to help fish migration.
Severe erosion:	Broadening the channel without fixing the mid-channel bed. Single rocks and small islands are to increase turbulence and the variety of habitats. Armouring with rockfill in some heavily damaged sections. Regrading of the stream banks and planting several rows of trees.
Sedges:	No measures.

A 5 m riparian strip of land borders the rehabilitated section on both sides. The costs amounted to 150 DM m^{-1}, not including the purchase of land.

Fish community Speltach stream	Before rehab.			Potential		
	juvenile	sub-adult	adult	juvenile	sub-adult	adult
Salmo trutta f. *fario*			×			×
Gasterosteus aculeatus	×	×	×			
Phoxinus phoxinus	×	×	×	×	×	×
Noemacheilus barbatulus	×	×	×	×	×	×
Leuciscus cephalus		×				×
Rutilus rutilus		×	×			
Cyprinus carpio			×			
Anguilla anguilla			×			
Tinca tinca			×			
Leuciscus idus			×			
Gobio gobio				×	×	×

FIGURE 20.5 Fish community before rehabilitation (in 1988) in backwater area of the Speltach and predicted (potential) population after full recovery (re-drawn after Ness, 1989)

Critical review

In the long term, meandering is essential to stabilize the Speltach and more land should be reclaimed from the farmers. Since the cohesive clay of the floodplain is resistant to bank erosion, meanders should be reconstructed immediately, otherwise it might take hundreds of years until meandering effectively starts shaping the aquatic habitat. In addition, the mature trees will stabilize the straight channel form. Furthermore, the suspended load can be expected to accumulate on the regraded stream banks, reshaping the stream bed into the old channel form.

Gutenbach (suburban mountain stream)

The Gutenbach (see data in Table 20.3) was channelized and heavily armoured with pavement including the lower banks in 1969 (Figure 20.6). At that time it was running through a narrow valley in the vicinity of Oberkochen. The city of Oberkochen has since spread and the pastureland of the valley was to be turned into a new residential area. Since the course of the channel was unfavourable to the development of the settlement, it was decided to relocate the stream entirely.

TABLE 20.3. Data for the Gutenbach stream

Location:	City of Oberkochen, mountainous region east of Stuttgart (Figure 20.1)
Altitude:	502–512 m
Catchment area:	12 km^2
50 year flood:	15 m^3 s^{-1}
Geology of watershed:	Jurassic karst topography
Geology of project area:	Alluvial sediments (clay) mixed with eroded material from the hillsides
Land use in floodplain:	Pastureland converted to a new residential area
Channel morphology:	Straight trapezoidal channel, almost completely paved
Slope:	1.45%
Water quality:	Unpolluted (Pollution class I)
Rehabilitated stretch:	0.84 km (in 1987)

FIGURE 20.6. The channelized Gutenbach as a pure technical solution in the late 1960s (photograph by Konold, 1984)

FIGURE 20.7. The morphological diversity of the stream, only two years after restoration, was sustained by a heavy flood occurring immediately after construction (photograph by Czerniak, 1989)

Only the first 200 m followed the old stream bed. The rest of the watercourse was laid from one side of the valley to the other crossing the residential area after 300 m.

The width of the channel varies from 7 to 23 m, including a narrow floodplain. The reinforcement of the channel bed was reduced to a small amount of rockfill with Jurassic stones. A few unprofessionally constructed drop structures were washed away by a bankfull flood that occurred immediately after completion of the earthworks. Due to this event, the morphology of the new watercourse has changed into a natural shape (Figure 20.7). The places endangered by erosion could easily be identified and only local reinforcements were brought into the stream bed. Nevertheless, morphological changes have to be watched carefully, since there are signs of erosion. The costs just for the stream works amounted to 240 DM m^{-1}.

MONITORING PROGRAMME

In order to control the results of the restoration efforts, a monitoring programme was established covering stream bed morphology, limnology, vegetation, and faunal groups. The monitoring was not implemented as a scientific research programme but as a device to improve further restoration projects. For all projects field observations of the original status were made.

Daily variations of temperature, oxygen, pH, and conductivity were recorded in each project. In addition, single values of ion parameters (PO_4, SO_3, NO_2, NO_3, NH_4, Cl) and hardness were measured. Invertebrates were also examined in order to assess water quality. Fish populations were assessed (Ness, 1991) and samples of (immobile) Coleoptera were evaluated using the method of Buck and Konzelmann (1985).

Riparian vegetation communities were mapped as well as in the floodplain based on methods of Ellenberg (1978), Braun-Blanquet (1964), and others. "Eco-morphological" evaluation of the channel bed was undertaken using a seven-step classification by Werth (1987) that includes stream pattern and riparian condition, variability of flow, and riparian woods. It is also intended to observe changes in the stream pattern after reshaping the channel bed. This would involve three or four field observations over a 10-year period after structural restoration. As yet there are no precise results, but three tendencies are clear:

(1) Rapid morphological changes can be expected in the first years after completion (sometimes with undesired effects);
(2) Vegetation can be dominated by exotic species suppressing domestic potential natural vegetation; and
(3) The fish population will not significantly change in the early years.

Establishing the monitoring programme proved to be difficult due to conflicting methods and approaches, mainly concerning fauna, limnology and vegetation. Best results were obtained when one experienced person was commissioned to do the monitoring for all projects in each specialist area.

PRELIMINARY GUIDELINES

Successful rehabilitation of stream habitats can be achieved in many cases. The following three rules should be obeyed:

(1) *Rehabilitation must include the floodplain*: Especially for lowland streams, frequent inundation of the floodplain is essential for the development of specific habitats. Therefore, bankfull discharges have to be lowered to natural conditions, which in many cases correspond to three or four times the average flow. In areas where natural inundation must be confined to a certain extent, an artificial secondary floodplain system may be constructed (Figure 20.8). Since the evolution of a natural floodplain morphology in alluvial streams takes hundreds of years (and we do not have the patience) the rehabilitated floodplain system must be reshaped by man. In those cases where alluvial soil textures are irreversibly destroyed, i.e. by dredging, the rehabilitation of the floodplain ecosystem is limited to a certain extent.

(2) *Rehabilitation of the stream bed must make use of flow dynamics*: The stream pattern fitting best to the actual flow dynamics and sediment transport can only be shaped by the inherent stream forces. Artificial shaping may start the rehabilitation process, but can never be a substitute. In cases of severe bed erosion due to higher bankfull discharges or higher gradients, artificial armouring by stream bed reinforcements combined with drop structures is imperative. In these cases full rehabilitation can only be achieved by controlling the causes of primary erosion.

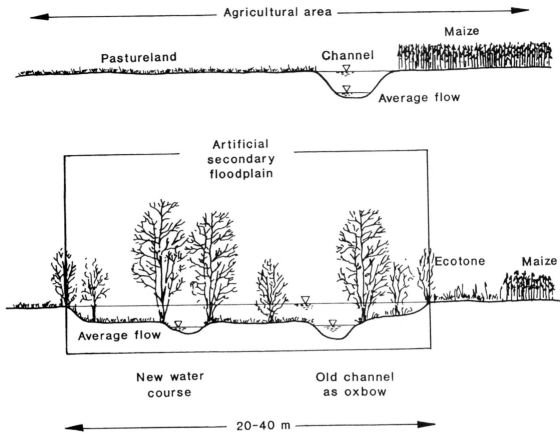

FIGURE 20.8. Artificial secondary floodplain ecosystem in an agricultural area

(3) *Rehabilitation of streams must include water quality*: The improvement of water quality must be the first step in any rehabilitation concept. The structural rehabilitation of "most polluted" rivers and streams is a waste of tax-payers' money.

CONCLUSIONS

None of us really knows how to rehabilitate rivers and streams; we know too little about natural flow systems. The morphology of alluvial rivers has been the favourite study area of generations of geographers and engineers, and still is. But what do we know about the morphology of small alluvial streams? What of non-alluvial systems?

The development of rehabilitated streams should be watched carefully and the results should be reviewed critically. None of the projects which the author has seen so far (Kern and Nadolny, 1986) is fulfilling all criteria proposed above. Many projects are suffering from too much bank protection, too little space for development, and too much civil and landscape engineering. *The pleasant appearance of a rehabilitated stream must not deceive us about the deficiencies of the inherent ecosystem.*

ACKNOWLEDGEMENTS

I am grateful to Professor Larsen for presenting this work at the conference in York (September, 1990), and Professor Petts and Dr Carling for carefully reviewing the manuscript.

REFERENCES

Braukmann, U. (1991). "Limnologische Untersuchungen bei naturgemäßer Gewässergestaltung", in *Beiträge zur naturnahen Umgestaltung von Fließgewässern*, Institut für Wasserbau und Kulturtechnik, Proc. No. 180, pp. 177–195, University of Karlsruhe.
Braun-Blanquet, J. (1964). *Planzensoziologie*, 3rd edn. Springer-Verlag, New York.
Briem, E., and Kern, K. (1989). *Untersuchungen zur Beurteilung der Geschiebehaushalts der Speltach*, University of Karlsruhe, FRG, unpublished report.
Buck, H., and Konzelmann, E. (1985). "Vergleichende koleopterologische Untersuchungen zur Differenzierung edaphischer Biotope", in *Ökologische Untersuchungen an der ausgebauten Murr* (Ed. Landesanstalt für Unweltschutz Baden-Württemberg), Vol. 1, pp. 195–310, Karlsruhe.
Ellenberg, H. (1978). *Vegetation Mitteleuropas mit den Alpen in ökologischer Sicht*, Ulmer Verlag, Stuttgart.
Gebler, R. (1991). "Naturgemäße Bauweisen von Sohlenstufen", in *Beiträge zur naturnahen Umgestaltung von Fließgewässern*, Institut für Wasserbau und Kulturtechnik, Proc. No. 180, pp. 235–281. University of Karlsruhe.
Kern, K., and Nadolny, J. (1986). *Naturnahe Umgestaltung ausgebauter Fließgewässer— Projektstudie*, Institut für Wasserbau und Kulturtechnik, Proc. No. 175, University of Karlsruhe.
Ness, A. (1989). *Pilotprojekt "Naturnahe Umgestaltung ausgebauter Fließgewässer in Baden-Württemberg"—Untersuchungen zur Fischfauna*, Report for Ministerium für Umwelt Baden-Württemberg, p. 218. FRG, unpublished, Heidelberg.
Ness, A. (1991). "Interpretation von Untersuchungen der Fischfauna", in *Beiträge zur naturnahen Umgestaltung von Fließgewässern*, Institut für Wasserbau und Kulturtechnik, Proc. No. 180, pp. 186–222. University of Karlsruhe.
Werth, W. (1987). *Ökomorphologische Gewässerbewertung in Oberösterreich (Gewässerzustandskartierung)*, pp. 122–128, Österreichische Wasserwirtschaft, 5/6.

21

Recovery and Restoration of Some Engineered British River Channels

A. BROOKES

Technical Services, National Rivers Authority, Thames Region, Kings Meadow House, Kings Meadow Road, Reading, Berkshire RG1 8DQ, UK

INTRODUCTION

Channel modification for various purposes has been both widespread and intensive in England and Wales. Lamplugh, in 1914, showed how small streams had been aligned to run parallel with straight fence-lines along old field systems, either for convenience of cultivation or as boundaries between individual farms. Larger watercourses were diverted or impounded over short lengths for irrigation of water meadows, to feed ornamental lakes, or more often to provide power for small water mills. Within cities and towns, streams have often been confined within a conduit. Most recently larger rivers have been modified for the purposes of navigation, to achieve the engineering objectives of flood alleviation and agricultural drainage or straightened adjacent to roads and railways (Brookes et al, 1983).

The Land Drainage Improvement Works (Assessment of Environmental Effects) Regulations 1988, otherwise known as Statutory Instrument 1217 (MAFF/WO, 1988), has placed an obligation on drainage bodies in England and Wales to decide whether proposed drainage improvements are likely to have significant environmental effects (National Rivers Authority, 1990). Section 8 of the Water Act 1989 relates to general environmental duties of drainage bodies which include the need "to further the conservation and enhancement of natural beauty and the conservation of flora, fauna and geological or physiographical features of special interest". Such legislation has focused attention on the need to minimize adverse impacts and to ensure appropriate reinstatement and mitigation measures are taken, and to provide enhancement.

Nevertheless there is considerable scope for allowing the recovery, or facilitating restoration, of morphological characteristics to river channels that have already been modified at various dates in the past (Figures 21.1 and 21.2). These include modified channels adjacent to land undergoing a change of use, or flood-alleviation or agricultural schemes that were previously over-designed.

There is an increasing amount of literature on the recovery and restoration of rivers for various purposes (Gore, 1985). Rectifying past mistakes includes re-creating pools and

River Conservation and Management. Edited by P. J. Boon, P. Calow, and G. E. Petts
© 1992 John Wiley & Sons Ltd

FIGURE 21.1. Restoring gravels to a small lowland stream (photograph by A. Brookes)

FIGURE 21.2. Restoring the bends to a lowland stream in southern Jutland, Denmark (straightened course in foreground) (photograph by M. B. Nielsen)

riffles (Keller, 1978), restoring the original courses of straightened reaches (Brookes, 1987a), narrowing over-wide channels, and breaking-out concrete channels and culverts (Thames Water Authority, 1988), in addition to allowing channels to recover naturally. Numerous studies have shown the importance of geomorphology in anticipating hydraulic and ecological stability in river channels. Brookes (1990) attempted to evaluate the success of restoration projects in terms of the energy or stream power of the river occupying the channel. At stream powers of less than 15 W m^{-2} failure resulted from deposition of sediment, while at the highest stream powers instream features were destroyed by erosion. The most successful projects lay in the middle range of stream powers, with a median value of about 35 W m^{-2}, where excessive erosion or deposition is not a problem. The intention of this chapter is to develop the database further by assessing at a total of 60 sites in England and Wales the additional key factors of bed and bank stability and availability of sediment from the upstream catchment. These sites also include a variety of channel types assessed for the nature and significance of natural recovery. Attention is focused on those channel works that involve widening and/or deepening and channel straightening. By allowing natural features such as a pool–riffle sequence, non-uniform channel geometries, and a mixed substrate to re-form, or by facilitating restoration, then biological and aesthetic recovery may follow (Brookes, 1988).

METHOD

Figure 21.3 shows the locations of 60 sites with modified channels at which natural recovery was measured, or at which restoration projects were initiated. Sites were selected to include a variety of physical and hydrological environments and to cover a number of different channel sizes. They have been divided into high-energy rivers (in excess of 35 W m^{-2}) and low-energy rivers (less than 35 W m^{-2}). At each site the nature and magnitude of adjustment was assessed by re-surveying cross-sections and long-profiles taken at the time of the design of the works. In a few instances where sections and plans no longer existed, alternative historical records were consulted, including maps and aerial and ground photographs.

CHANNEL MODIFICATION INVOLVING WIDENING AND/OR DEEPENING

Adjustments of channel morphology have been observed in reaches which have been widened and/or deepened. For example, a reach of the River Tame near Birmingham, widened for flood-alleviation purposes in 1930, reverted to a more natural width in less than 30 years in the absence of maintenance (Nixon, 1966). This is attributed to the enlarged reach being in equilibrium with the design flow event while out of equilibrium with the normal range of flows. Widening of a channel reduces the stream power per unit bed area, thereby decreasing the sediment discharge. Thus low flows which tend to predominate for most of the time deposit sediment, which may subsequently become stabilized by vegetation to form more permanent morphological features. Reaches which have been deepened may act as sediment traps (Griggs and Paris, 1982; Newson, 1986). Sediment accumulations may have to be regularly removed from channels which have been substantially widened and/or deepened (Hydraulics Research Ltd, 1987).

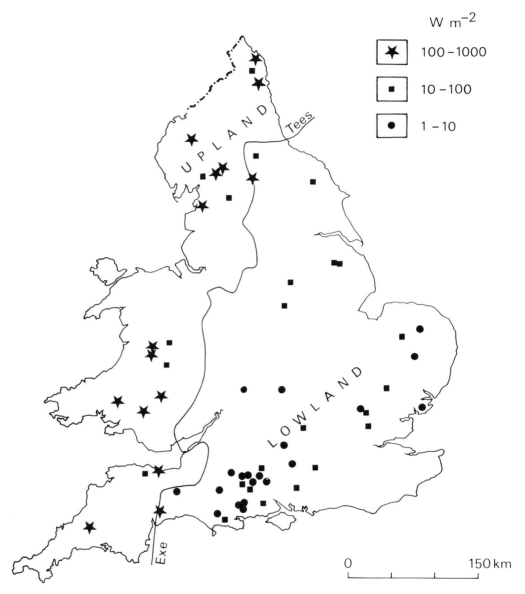

FIGURE 21.3. Location of study sites in England and Wales

Natural recovery processes

High-stream power sites

The majority of high-energy rivers studied had mobile gravel-bed channels and, therefore, a supply of sediment from upstream. The principal adjustment process for the reaches which had been deepened was to infill with gravel (Table 21.1). One of the problems of lowering the bed level in a channel is that a nickpoint or break of slope is

TABLE 21.1. Examples of adjustment in resectioned reaches of high-energy rivers

River/county	Drainage area (km^2)	Date of works	Date of survey	Reduced capacity (%) average/(maximum)	Maintenance requirement
Ithon (Powys)	195	1968	1981	12 (22)	Frequent
Caldew (Cumbria)	41	1949	1982	35 (60)	Infrequent
Lynher (Cornwall)	26	1964	1981	8 (12)	None
Lune (Westmorland)	16	1968	1982	1 (11)	Negligible
Waren Burn (Northumbria)	26	1949	1981	9 (11)	None
Aln (Northumbria)	107	1947	1981	4 (20)	None
Pickering (Yorkshire)	72	1962	1982	3 (10)	None
Clow Beck (Co. Durham)	27	1964	1982	4 (8)	None
Severn (Powys)	460	1974	1982	5 (15)	Infrequent

created which then migrates upstream as material is drawn into the deepened reach to achieve a new equilibrium profile. On the River Ithon a drop weir had been installed at the upstream end to counter this problem, while on the River Caldew a gravel trap had been constructed. However, despite these engineering structures, infilling by gravel of the excavated reaches still occurred. For the River Ithon gravel shoals and point bars tended to re-develop at the same locations existing prior to construction, despite regular maintenance. By contrast, the River Lune in Westmorland, which was resectioned in 1970 over a distance of nearly 2.5 km, had not been adversely affected by gravel infilling. Although infilling had occurred at Newbiggin, at the upstream limit of the works, locally reducing the capacity by 11%, the capacity of the whole scheme had been reduced by less than 1%. This can be related to the fact that the enlarged reach is very long in relation to the drainage area (16 km^2) and that the upstream source area for gravel is therefore limited.

Bank slumping had occurred at most of the sites, but since this is more a function of bank stability than fluvial erosion, and did not significantly reduce the width of widened channels, it is not considered here as a recovery process.

In sections of the Waren Burn in Northumbria, where the channel had been widened in 1949 by 30%, deposits of coarse sand had accumulated to form a bench, narrowing the low-flow channel to approximately the original natural width. In general, high-energy rivers with erodible bed materials re-formed pools where the flow lines converged on the outside of a bend. However, in no instance was the re-formed pool–riffle sequence as well defined as that existing prior to the works or in adjacent reaches.

Low-stream power sites

For lowland rivers which had been widened it was found that deposits of silt formed benches which reduced the low-flow width. This was evident for works carried out on the Rivers Cherwell in Oxfordshire and Isle in Somerset. Figure 21.4 depicts recovery of the River Cherwell over a period of 14 years since widening in 1967. Three types of bench were distinguished: the first (1) was a more permanent feature incorporating silts and sands to a maximum depth of 2.0 m, being stabilized by typical bank vegetation. The fine sands included in the upper layers of these benches contained fragments of wood and were probably flood deposits. At the inner edge of these deposits a second bench feature (2) contained almost exclusively silt and was stabilized by grass. Finally, at the margin of these stabilized benches ephemeral silt deposits were located, supporting reed species during the summer but re-worked during peak winter discharges (Figure 21.4: 3a, 3b). These three features appear to represent the progressive narrowing of the low-flow channel over time. Although it is difficult to pin-point the sediment sources for deposition features such as these, observation at several sites suggests that they may in part be derived from eroding agricultural catchments, from eroding tributaries with steeper slopes, and from sewage-treatment works.

A further type of adjustment was the deposition of silt in excavated pools in schemes on the Little Ouse in Suffolk, the Holland Brook in Essex, and the River Bourne in Hampshire, where works were completed in 1967, 1962, and 1960, respectively. These deposits generally formed below low-water level and were unstable during periods of high flow. Deposits accumulated in less than one year in a deepened reach of the Broughton Brook in Hampshire, a chalk stream with a seasonally high sediment load.

Pronounced pools were not observed in any of the resectioned reaches. Shallow pools were observed on the outside of bends where flow lines typically converge and cause scour. These probably developed where the bed was unstable immediately following excavation, allowing materials to be redistributed.

Restoration procedures

Clearly, restoration of a widened or deepened reach needs to consider potential natural recovery processes, which depend not only on the energy of the river but also on the availability of sediment. For example, installing a deflector or hurdle in a low-energy river with a high silt load could be used to enhance the development of a berm if correctly sited. A recent restoration project carried out in the River Thames catchment is outlined below to highlight the use of geomorphological design criteria.

343

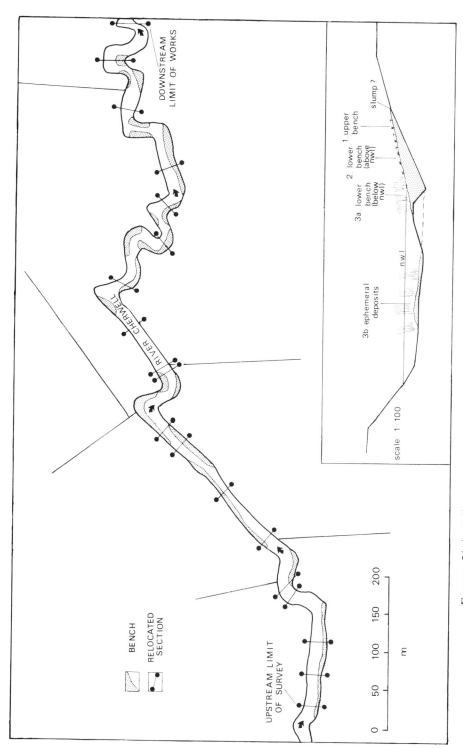

FIGURE 21.4. Adjustments within the widened reach of the River Cherwell, Oxfordshire

River Lyde

The River Lyde at Newnham in Hampshire is a medium-sized chalk stream with natural widths ranging between 4 m and 6 m. The stream bed is stable, composed predominantly of a layer of medium to coarse gravels. A total length of 1.3 km below Newnham Lane Bridge was considered for restoration in 1987, although it was decided that the first 80 m of channel below the bridge would benefit most. This length had probably been subject to a heavy maintenance dredge during the past 10–20 years, the spoil being spread along the left bank. The reach had an artificial width of about 9 m compared to natural widths of 5–6 m in adjacent reaches, and was over-deep. The specific stream power of the river at this point was only 22 W m^{-2} and the bed and banks were inherently stable. The low slope and flow velocities in this reach had induced sedimentation and the dominance of emergent plants such as bulrush (*Schoenoplectus lacustris*). However, because most of the sediment load is trapped immediately upstream in the backwater at Lyde Mill, natural recovery is inevitably slow. To improve the morphological variability of the reach it was decided that the channel could be narrowed to an optimum width of 5–6 m by regrading of the centre and leaving a 3–4 m remnant of the existing channel as a berm at a higher level. Adjacent reaches were identified as having the ideal natural symmetry and substrate which should be emulated. Placement of gravels was also recommended following regrading.

CHANNEL MODIFICATION BY STRAIGHTENING

Generally, cut-offs in non-erodible channels have no morphological effect, while those in erodible channels undergo long-term adjustment. Straightening reduces the high stage flow resistance through the removal of bend resistance. Eliminating bends also increases the slope by providing a shorter channel path. An increase of slope enables the transport of more sediment than is supplied from the upstream end of the channelized reach, and the difference is obtained from the bed, causing degradation which progresses upstream as a nickpoint (Parker and Andres, 1976). Straightened reaches of high-energy streams remain very unstable with limited formation of pools and riffles; more typically unstable sand or gravel bars form. Meander growth may occur very rarely in straightened channels such as the River Ystwyth in mid-Wales (Lewin, 1976). Studies have suggested that adjustments such as these may take from 30 years to more than of 1000 years (De Vries, 1975).

Natural recovery processes

Meander growth was observed on the River Severn at Llandinam in mid-Wales, a gravel-bed river, realigned during construction of a railway in the early 1850s (Figure 21.5). By comparing maps and aerial photographs of various dates with the original meandering channel of 1846 and the straightened course of 1857, progressive recovery is depicted over a period of 125 years. By 1982 the channel had almost recovered its original slope by re-meandering in the absence of substantial bank-protection measures. Significant stages of meander development occur during peak flows and the location of pools and riffles varies with this adjustment. By contrast, the River Lune at Kelleth in Westmorland,

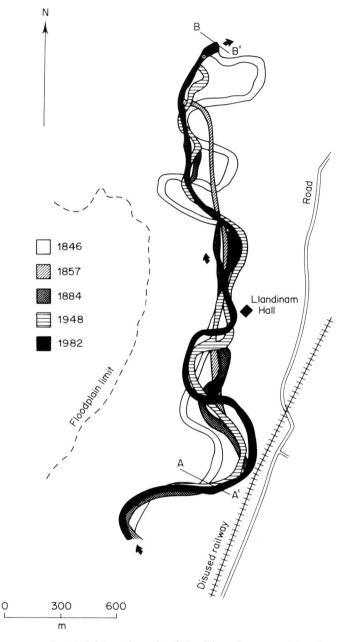

FIGURE 21.5. Recovery of a straightened reach of the River Severn at Llandinam, mid-Wales

realigned over a distance of 1.5 km in 1975, had not adjusted because the channel was cut into bedrock and the banks were restrained by gabions.

Instability is common in channels which have been realigned in erodible earth channels. Even for the River Roding in Essex, a moderate-energy river, a reach straightened in glacial cobbles was observed to become unstable during flood flows.

Low-stream power sites

Adjustments are more limited in low-energy environments. The principal effect on two realigned reaches of the River Allen at Witchampton in Dorset, which underwent a flood-alleviation scheme in 1963, was that the straightened reaches were over-deepened and served as silt traps for ephemeral deposits moving from upstream.

Restoration procedures

Given that few straightened river channels appear to have recovered naturally, then there is considerable scope for restoration. Reinstatement of bends is now common practice along straightened watercourses in Denmark (Figure 21.2) (cf. Brookes, 1987a), although virtually untried in England and Wales. The principal concern is not one of channel stability, since re-introduction of bends reduces the slope and hence the potential for erosion, but rather is related to the issues of land ownership and land-take involved. Restoration techniques can perhaps be applied more widely to straightened lengths of channel, although given the types of natural adjustment in such channels there is the need for appropriate design. Straightening a channel increases the slope and hence the potential for erosion, especially where the river has sufficient power to erode and where the bank materials are weakly cohesive. Potential instability within straightened reaches means that the success of restored features such as a gravel substrate, or a more appropriate channel width, depends on the detailed design.

Scotsgrove Brook

The Scotsgrove Brook, a lowland clay stream near Thame in Oxfordshire, underwent an agricultural drainage scheme between 1978 and 1982 (Thames Water Authority, 1987). The scheme had significant short-term impacts on the instream and marginal flora and fauna, while morphologically the stream had been slow to recover over the past decade. To rectify these problems, a total sum of £25 000 was allocated in 1988 by the drainage body (Thames Water Authority) for environmental improvement.

These monies were targeted at the lowest reach of the Scotsgrove Brook, the worst affected by the scheme. This reach extended upstream from the junction with the River Thame, for a distance of 400 m, and was straightened with a uniform cross-section and lack of morphological diversity and landscaping (Figure 21.6). Straightening the channel had more than doubled the natural slope, giving an average specific stream power of 80 W m^{-2}, which exceeds the threshold of 35 W m^{-2} (Brooks, 1990). Although the silty-clay bank material was cohesive the bed was relatively unstable, deposits above the armoured layer being transient. Indeed, an attempt by fisheries staff to install pools and riffles immediately following the works had not been successful. The restoration works carried out during September 1989 were therefore designed to be stable.

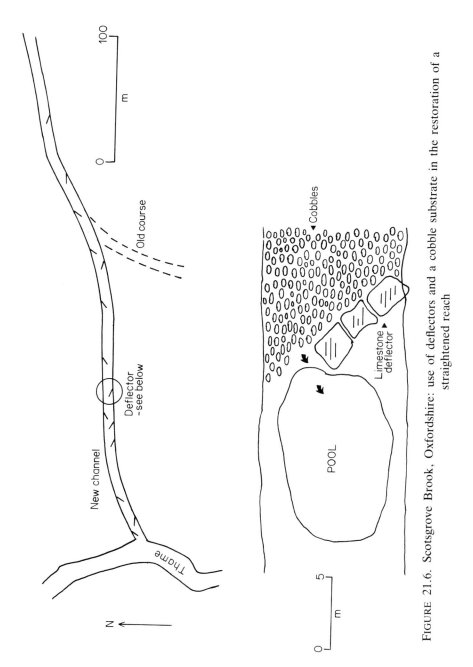

FIGURE 21.6. Scotsgrove Brook, Oxfordshire: use of deflectors and a cobble substrate in the restoration of a straightened reach

To compensate for the uniform cross-section of the channel, deflectors were constructed at intervals (Figure 21.6). These were intended to create a more sinuous low-flow path within the channel, the deflectors alternating from side to side. In natural lowland rivers pools generally correspond to the outside of a bend where the flow lines converge. In a straightened channel such as the Scotsgrove Brook the absence of bends means that the flow lines have to be converged artificially if a pool is to be maintained. The shear stress exerted on the bed of the channel at bankfull flow was calculated to be approximately 47 N m^{-3}. This value exceeds the maximum unit tractive force value required for the design of a stable channel in coarse gravel with water transporting colloidal silts (32 N m^{-3}) (see Webber, 1971). Given the potential for erosion of reinstated materials, the deflectors were constructed of large limestone blocks (*ca* 0.75 × 0.75 × 0.75 m). Three blocks placed closely together formed a deflector of about 2.25 m length (Figure 21.6).

The deflectors were intended to converge the flow lines, thereby encouraging scour of ephemeral silt deposits at low flow. Immediately downstream from each deflector a pool of approximately 3 m length and 0.7 m depth was excavated. Behind each deflector limestone cobbles were placed to form a new stable riffle area (Figure 21.6). The pools, riffles, and deflectors have remained stable over the past year, which has included a number of bankfull flows moving through the channel.

This example is based on a straightened clay stream which is relatively stable. Even in this environment, it is recommended that over-design by choosing larger materials is sensible. Clearly, extreme caution should be exerted in higher-energy rivers where even large limestone blocks, or boulders not fixed into the bed of the channel, are likely to be eroded.

DISCUSSION AND RECOMMENDATIONS

Channel maintenance offsets stream recovery, while lack of such maintenance permits gradual stream recovery. The nature and rate of adjustment following channel works depends not only on the available energy or stream power but also on the sediment supply from the catchment upstream or from channel erosion. The plan shape of a modified reach is also important: even in relatively low-energy rivers a bend may cause the flow lines to converge locally and scour a shallow pool.

A variety of morphological adjustments have been identified for modified reaches of high-energy gravel-bed rivers over periods of up to 125 years. In particular, the process of infilling by gravel drawn from upstream was responsible for reducing the capacity of many of the enlarged channels. Use of allowable mean velocity as an engineering design criterion in gravel-bed rivers means that, while erosion may be prevented in most cases, no attention is paid to deposition. Clearly, sediment-laden streams will deposit if maximum velocities are insufficient to keep the sediment in motion. However, the maximum average value obtained for the reduction of the enlarged capacity by adjustment was 35% for the River Caldew (in a period of 35 years), and at the majority of sites the value was less than 12%. This relatively small amount of adjustment could be attributed to a number of factors, including an insufficient source area for gravel above the scheme, associated structural works to prevent infill, or channel maintenance. Shoals and shallow pools developed as reaches infilled.

The reduction of the enlarged channel capacity at resectioned lowland sites was also insignificant, with a maximum value of 9% being obtained for the River Cherwell in Oxfordshire in the absence of regular maintenance over a period of 14 years. In view of these findings, it is concluded that the modified channels studied were not significantly affected by morphological adjustment and that this is, therefore, unlikely to have a major impact on the conveyance of flood flows or arterial drainage. By undertaking further hydraulic modelling studies the significance of re-formed deposits on flood flows could be calculated for these channels. It is recommended that these types of recovery be allowed to continue, where hydraulic performance is not endangered, until a new equilibrium is attained. Where a widened reach adjusts by sediment deposition then this may be beneficial to both the flora and fauna by creating a more natural low-flow width (e.g. Brookes, 1987b). Maintenance or management plans should be drawn up to protect such features where feasible. In exceptional circumstances, where a straightened channel has naturally regained its original sinuosity, a corridor could be designated to accommodate that adjustment.

Channel recovery occurs across a wide range of stream powers in England and Wales. Lack of natural adjustment at low-stream power sites means that restoration of morpho-

TABLE 21.2. Channel modification involving resectioning (widening and/or deepening)

	Sediment available	None or limited sediment supply
High energy 35–1000 W m^{-2} (H)	Adjustment by deposition in over-wide trapezoidal section (especially silt and/or sand) Deepened reach may function as trap for sediment moving from upstream (e.g. gravel). This may follow bank slumping Convergence of flow on bend may re-form pool and asymmetrical cross-section	No or limited recovery of over-wide section. Pools typically poorly developed Severe slumping of banks in over-deep reach Caution with restoration (e.g. new substrate or deflectors used to narrow channel likely to wash out if channel is self-adjusting)
Low energy under 35 W m^{-2} (L)	Over-wide trapezoid typically narrows to more natural low-flow width; may have sinuous path. The benches formed by deposition typically become stabilized with vegetation; in chalk streams these deposits may be ephemeral Limited/no development of pools, especially if bed is immobile (e.g. stable segregated bed) Deflectors/reinstated substrate could be buried by sediment	Little or no natural recovery Intervention required to restore more natural morphology (e.g. channel narrowing; placement of substrate). Risk of failure is low, although still needs adequate design

TABLE 21.3. Channel modification, involving realignment by cutting off bends

	Erodible channel	Non-erodible channel
High energy 35–1000 W m^{-2} (H)	Exceptionally, the channel may attempt to regain the former sinuosity (very high energy)	Limited recovery (especially in bedrock). Chalk or clay may inhibit adjustment
	More typically, a nickpoint migrates upstream, causing erosion of bed and collapse of banks. Bed may become armoured with cobbles or gravels: energy then expended by eroding laterally	Measures to mitigate adverse impacts of straightened reach (e.g. restoration of substrate; pools/ riffles) have high risk of failure unless adequately sized and located
	Pool–riffle sequence unstable and ill-defined in straight reach	
	Restoring bends will reduce slope and minimize instability; careful design required. Measures to mitigate adverse effects of straight reach have high risk of failure through erosion	
Low energy under 35 W m^{-2} (L)	Limited adjustment; possibly some downcutting but no real evidence of bank slumping	Inability to recover naturally; straightened reach may be subject to siltation (e.g. chalk or clay streams)
	Bends could be restored with low risk of instability through erosion	Mitigation of straightened reach (e.g. new substrate) or restored bends may fail from siltation

logical features may be required. It is essential to establish for each individual stream the restoration design which is hydraulically and biologically appropriate. Some indication of the physical constraints which have determined the success or failure of restoration designs can be obtained from projects already implemented in similar environments. As yet, there are relatively few documented examples, and it is difficult to make accurate predictions and recommendations. Nevertheless, by following preliminary guidance such as that given in Tables 21.2 and 21.3 for reaches which have been resectioned or straightened it is suggested that some of the worst pitfalls can be overcome. Particular problems arise when attempting to enhance a straightened reach of channel through re-introduction of substrate or channel narrowing. Even in lowland clay rivers, the potential for scour in straightened reaches means that materials must be appropriately sized and located.

There is considerable scope for restoring the morphological characteristics of modified rivers in England and Wales given the extent of man's impact. Morphological assessment of an entire catchment such as the River Stort in Hertfordshire/Essex can prioritize those lengths of channel which could benefit from restoration or natural recovery (Brookes, in press). The Thames Region of the National Rivers Authority is already making recommendations for channel restoration to developers and landowners requiring Land Drainage Consent. For example, if it is proposed to relocate a straightened watercourse as part of a commercial or industrial development then it may be possible to re-create a more natural course, which could also become a feature of that development. However, monies could also be allocated solely for the purpose of drainage bodies restoring watercourses.

Objective data on restoration projects still need to be collected if more accurate ways of predicting performance of planned schemes are to be developed. The first edition of the Royal Society for the Protection of Birds *Rivers and Wildlife Handbook* (Lewis and Williams, 1984) provided a compilation of data on selected projects but did not evaluate channel stability. There is a need to take measurements from various sites with the objective of building up a national database. The basic data which are required for an assessment of stability include the bankfull dimensions of the channel under consideration, the slope, the local geology and soil type, observations on sediment sources, together with an evaluation of the success or failure of a project. These data can then be used in hydraulic calculations to determine channel stability.

ACKNOWLEDGEMENTS

The views expressed in this chapter are those of the author and not necessarily those of the National Rivers Authority. Much of the background data were collected under a Natural Environment Research Council studentship, held at the University of Southampton and Freshwater Biological Association (1980–1983). Further data were collected during tenure of a University College of Wales Research Fellowship at Aberystwyth (1984–1986). The proposals for restoring the Scotsgrove Brook and River Lyde were undertaken while at the National Rivers Authority (Thames Region) and its immediate predecessor, the Thames Water Authority (1986–1990).

REFERENCES

Brookes, A. (1987a). "Restoring the sinuosity of artificially straightened stream channels", *Environmental Geology and Water Science*, **10**, 33–41.

Brookes, A. (1987b). "Recovery and adjustment of aquatic vegetation within channelization works in England and Wales", *Journal of Environmental Management*, **24**, 365–382.

Brookes, A. (1988). *Channelized Rivers: Perspectives for Environmental Management*, John Wiley, Chichester.

Brookes, A. (1990). "Restoration and enhancement of engineered river channels: some European experiences", *Regulated Rivers: Research and Management*, **5**, 45–56.

Brookes, A. (in press). "Geomorphological assessment in river planning and management in the Thames Region of the National Rivers Authority", *Journal of the Institution of Water and Environmental Management*.

Brookes, A., Gregory, K. J., and Dawson, F. H. (1983). "An assessment of river channelization in England and Wales", *The Science of the Total Environment*, **27**, 97–112.

De Vries, M. (1975). *A morphological time scale for rivers*, Delft Hydraulics Laboratory Publication, No. 147.

Gore, J. A. (Ed.) (1985). *The Restoration of Rivers and Streams: Theories and Experience*, Butterworths/Ann Arbor, Michigan.

Griggs, G. B., and Paris, L. (1982). "Flood control failure: San Lorenzo River, California", *Environmental Management*, **6**, 407–419.

Hydraulics Research Ltd (1987). *Morphological effects of river works: a review of current practice*, Report for the Ministry of Agriculture, Fisheries and Food, Hydraulics Research Report No. SR116, Wallingford.

Keller, E. A. (1978). "Pools, riffles and channelization", *Environmental Geology*, **2**, 119–127.

Lamplugh, G. W. (1914). "Taming of streams", *Geographical Journal*, **43**, 651–656.

Lewin, J. (1976). "Initiation of bedforms and meanders in coarse-grained sediment", *Bulletin of the Geological Society of America*, **87**, 281–285.

Lewis, G., and Williams, G. (Eds) (1984). *Rivers and Wildlife Handbook: a guide to practices which further the conservation of wildlife on rivers*, Royal Society for the Protection of Birds, Bedfordshire, and the Royal Society for Nature Conservation, Lincoln.

Ministry of Agriculture, Fisheries and Food/Welsh Office (1988). *The Land Drainage Improvement Works (Assessment of Environmental Effects) Regulations 1988. Statutory Instrument 1217*, HMSO, London.

National Rivers Authority (1990). *Environmental Assessment Guidelines: a procedure for ensuring environmental factors are taken into account in the design and implementation of land drainage improvement works*, NRA, Thames Region, Reading.

Newson, M. D., (1986). "River basin engineering—fluvial geomorphology", *Journal of the Institution of Water Engineers and Scientists*, **40**, 307–324.

Nixon, M. (1966). "Flood regulation and river training", in *River Engineering and Water Conservation Works* (Ed. R. B. Thorn), pp. 293–297, Butterworths, London.

Parker, G., and Andres, D. (1976). "Detrimental effects of river channelization", *Proceedings of Conference Rivers '76, American Society of Civil Engineers*, pp. 1248–1266.

Thames Water Authority (1987). *Scotsgrove Brook Channel Improvement Scheme: A post-project appraisal*, Final Report, Reading.

Thames Water Authority (1988). *Ravensbourne Catchment Study: Sundridge Park*, London.

Webber, N. B. (1971). *Fluid Mechanics for Civil Engineers*, Chapman and Hall, London.

22

Restoration of Salmonid Rivers in Finland

E. JUTILA

*Finnish Game and Fisheries Institute, Fisheries Division,
PO Box 202, SF-00151 Helsinki, Finland*

INTRODUCTION

A great majority of Finland's territory belongs to the catchment area of the Baltic Sea. Nearly all the rivers along the coast of the Baltic Sea once had important stocks of salmonid fish, but now most of them have been destroyed by human activities: pollution, the development of hydroelectric power, over-exploitation of the natural stocks, etc. The decline of wild stocks of Baltic salmon is particularly alarming. The proportion of wild smolt of the total smolt production of the Baltic Sea was in 1989 estimated to be less than 10%; over 90% of the smolts were hatchery reared (Christensen and Larsson, 1979; Anon, 1990).

There are over 60 rivers flowing from Finland into the northern parts of the Baltic Sea and almost all of them, in former times, supported their own stocks of migratory fish, among which the salmon (*Salmo salar*), sea trout (*Salmo trutta* m. *trutta*), river-spawning whitefish (*Coregonus lavaretus*), grayling (*Thymallus thymallus*), and river lamprey (*Lampetra fluviatilis*) were especially valuable (Figure 22.1). Correspondingly, the inland waters had numerous stocks of lake trout (*Salmo trutta* m. *lacustris*), whitefish, and grayling, and at least in the Lake Saimaa area, landlocked salmon (*Salmo salar* m. *sebago*) (Christensen and Larsson, 1979; Ikonen, 1984).

Environmental changes caused by human activities, especially during this century, have nevertheless destroyed or severely damaged most of these stocks. The damming of rivers for hydroelectric power has had the most serious consequences for migratory fish, with nearly all Finland's major salmon rivers flowing into the Baltic Sea having been harnessed for this purpose during the last 50 years. In addition, industrial and municipal effluents have caused pollution problems in many important salmon rivers such as the Kokemäenjoki and the Kymijoki.

Extensive damage has likewise been caused to migratory fish stocks by the dredging of rivers and brooks. This was first done in order to facilitate boat traffic, and later, during this century, increasingly for timber-floating. In the 1950s and 1960s, in particular,

River Conservation and Management. Edited by P. J. Boon, P. Calow, and G. E. Petts
© 1992 John Wiley & Sons Ltd

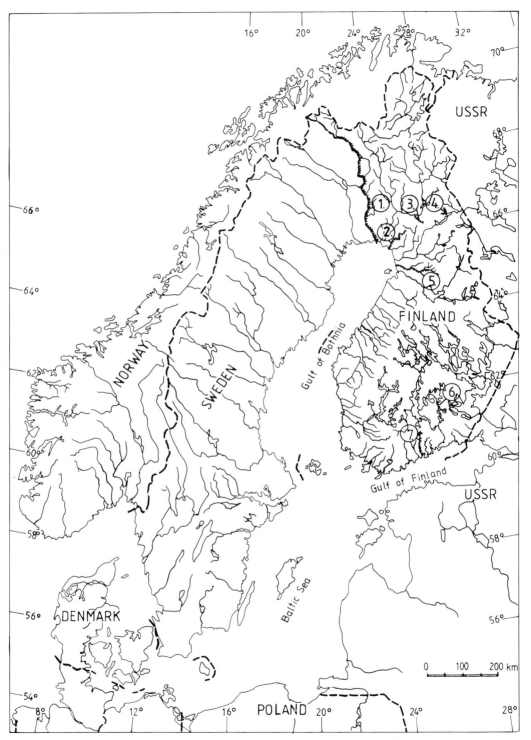

FIGURE 22.1. Finnish salmonid rivers enhanced by restoration and stocking with salmon and trout parr, studied by electric fishing. 1=River Tornionjoki, 2=River Simojoki, 3=River Kuohunkijoki, 4=River Piispajoki, 5=River Kiiminkijoki, 6=Rapid of Puuskankoski, and 7=River Vantaanjoki

almost all flowing waters, especially in northern and eastern Finland, were dredged thoroughly using bulldozers (Jutila, 1985). According to Lammassaari (1990), the total length of the timber-floating routes in rivers at that time was 40 000 km, about a quarter of which was dredged by bulldozers. The extensive use of rivers for timber-floating is typical for northern lowland forest areas, and equally extensive effects for salmonid rivers can only be found in northern Sweden and north-western parts of the Soviet Union. Finally, natural stocks in the last remaining Baltic salmon and sea trout rivers have weakened since the 1970s because of overfishing in the sea (Jutila and Pruuki, 1988).

METHODS FOR ENHANCING SALMON AND TROUT STOCKS

There are several ways to enhance impoverished migratory fish stocks, including regulation of fishing, stocking with smolt, construction of fish-ways, and water-pollution control (e.g. Mills, 1989). Two methods are considered here: restoration of dredged rapids for spawning and nursery areas, and stocking of the rapids with parr. In Finland these two methods have been increasingly used because of the extensive damage caused by dredging, and because most of the natural salmon and trout stocks are weak or have died out.

Interest in habitat modification in dredged rapids has been aroused again because timber-floating has now ceased in almost all the Finnish rivers, leaving a large number of dredged rivers and rapids suitable for enhancement or restocking with salmon and trout. The Finnish water legislation also obliges the water authorities to make good the damage caused to valuable fish stocks and fishing operations by dredging. There are now several plans under way for the restoration of rivers, and over 50 separate stretches of rapids or whole rivers have already been restored during the last 10 years. In recent years a total of about 4–5 million FIM (US\$ 1 million) has been spent annually on restoring the Finnish rivers. Widespread use has been made of stocking with salmon and trout parr for this purpose, and according to the fish-farming statistics, a total of over 5×10^6 newly hatched fry of salmonid fish were stocked in Finland in 1986, and the corresponding number of older parr of these species amounted to nearly 1.2×10^6.

Restoration of dredged rapids

Effects of dredging on fish habitats and stocks

Dredging of rapids reduces and spoils the spawning and nursery areas of salmonid fish in many ways. The pushing of stones from the rapids on to the banks and the closing of side channels with stones turns the rapids into smoothly flowing channels. This radically reduces the nursery areas in the rapids and leaves a deep, narrow channel which is usually unfavourable for parr and smolt production. Electrofishing carried out in the River Simojoki in northern Finland, for example, has shown the mean population density of salmon parr at sampling sites in dredged rapids (1–4 parr per 100 m^2) to be only about one-third of that in the natural rapids (6–9 parr per 100 m^2) (Toivonen and Jutila, 1982; Jutila, 1985) (Table 22.1).

The transformation of rapids into deep, narrow channels lowers the natural level of the water, thus leaving a great deal of the area along the banks dry during low-water periods.

TABLE 22.1. Population densities of salmon and trout parr in some restored Finnish rivers

River	Years	Species	Mean population density (parr per 100 m²)			Reference
			Undisturbed areas	Dredged areas	Restored areas	
Simojoki	1972–1976	Salmon	6.4–9.1	0.7–3.6	[a]	⎫ Toivonen and
Simojoki	1977–1980	Salmon	[b]	[a]	4.7– 9.7[b]	⎬ Jutila (1982)
Piispajoki	1979–1985	Trout	–	–	8.8–31.3[c]	⎫ Jokikokko
Piispajoki	1986–1988	Trout	–	–	0.0– 6.2[c]	⎬ (1987, 1989)
Puuskankoski	1978–1985	Trout	–	0.0–0.5	4.3–12.7	Jutila (1987b)

[a]Restoration of dredged rapids in 1976
[b]Includes both undisturbed and restored areas
[c]Stocking with brown trout fry in 1978–1985, no stocking since 1986

Erosion washes the fine bottom material suitable for spawning out from the rapids into the pools, which may silt up. In winter, slushy ice fills the dredged rapids, which increases the spawning mortality and also drives the fish away. The dredging of rapids also reduces oxygenation, accentuates fluctuations in flow, and reduces the quantity and quality of the aquatic vegetation and prey available to the fish. The structures provided for timber-floating hinder fish migration and make fishing in the river difficult (Jutila, 1985).

Restoration of spawning areas

The natural structure of the bottom is usually seriously impaired in dredged rapids. The first stage in supporting the whole reproduction cycle from egg to smolt in a stretch of rapids is to ensure the adequacy of the spawning grounds, often by improving old silted-up or eroded areas, or constructing new spawning beds. Raking the gravel may be effective if some of the original gravel material is still left on the bottom. Old spawning areas have usually been improved by digging holes and ridges in the silted-up substrates which consist of coarse gravel and small stones.

The spawning grounds of salmon and trout have often been almost totally destroyed in dredged rivers, e.g. in the River Kuohunkijoki in northern Finland, studied by Kännö (1987), where no natural reproduction of brown trout has been observed since restoration, due to the lack of spawning grounds. If no natural spawning grounds are available or are heavily eroded, they have been constructed by introducing new material into the rapids. Screened gravel or cobbles of diameters between 5 and 50 mm have been used for this purpose. The thickness of the new spawning ground layer is usually 20–40 cm. New spawning grounds are normally located in water depths of 30–60 cm during the spawning season and have water velocities ranging from 0.4 to 0.8 m s^{-1}. Spawning beds are provided in several locations within the rapids, especially near the upper and lower ends. This pattern corresponds to observations made in natural spawning beds and nursery areas of young salmon and trout parr (e.g. Smith, 1973; Hermansen and Krog, 1985; Heggberget et al, 1988).

Restoration of nursery areas of salmon and trout

A particular focus of interest in the restoration of rapids is the nursery areas of the parr. Restoration involves moving stones from the banks back to the middle of the channel and the re-opening of closed side channels to redirect water to these areas. Several types of construction have been used in the middle channel. When restoration operations began in the late 1970s and early 1980s, the dredged middle channel was only made narrower, to allow timber-floating in future, but this gave rather poor results, especially in typical rivers with few lakes and major fluctuations in flow.

Electrofishing in the River Simojoki showed that only about half of the damage caused by dredging had been rectified, due to insufficient restoration of the deep middle channel (Jutila, 1987a). The real increase in nursery areas has been a restricted one because water is still conducted only into the deep middle channel during low-water periods and the shallow bank areas remain dry. Now a narrow middle channel is left mainly in the larger rivers or stretches of rapids to meet the demands of boat traffic or canoeing.

Other methods for restoring nursery areas are being increasingly favoured. In order to return the whole area of the rapids to parr and smolt production, stones and boulders have been spread evenly over the entire middle channel, and stream deflectors, constructed of stones, have been used to direct the water near the banks. Stones have been placed as low thresholds to raise the water surface in the rapids, to slow down the stream in the middle channel, and to create more variable habitats for various sizes of parr and smolt. Hollows have been dug and boulders have been put into the rapids as aids to the ascending, resting, and overwintering larger fish.

At least in small rivers, the use of stone thresholds has proved to be an effective means of restoration. Kännö (1987) has observed highest densities of grayling, (6–14 fry per 100 m^2 in rapids on the River Kuohunkijoki restored in the form of stone thresholds and small pools, where the corresponding densities in rapids which had been restored by distributing single stones and boulders evenly over the middle channel were only 2–3 grayling fry 100 m^2.

In some cases special areas have been restored for rod and line fishing by constructing resting places for the ascending fish, removing bushes, and arranging sites for open fires along the banks of the rapids.

Stocking of rapids with parr

Stocking objectives

Hatchery-reared parr have been used in recent years for the stocking and restocking of salmonid rivers in connection with restoration. Stocking with various sizes of parr is necessary in order to start smolt production in the rapids immediately after restoration, i.e. to prevent cyprinids and predatory fish from occupying the new bottom habitats. Moreover, stocking has to be continued for at least 3–5 years after restoration to ensure the commencement of natural reproduction in the rapids. Primarily for genetic reasons, stocking with 1-year-old parr has been favoured, because these remain in the rapids for 1–3 years before smolt migration.

Stocking with parr has also been increasingly used to strengthen endangered salmon and trout stocks. The last remaining natural stocks of Baltic salmon and sea trout have declined severely since the 1970s due to intensive sea fishing, and the landlocked salmon of Lake Saimaa are practically totally dependent on stocking with hatchery-reared smolt.

Stocking practice

Stocking with 1-year-old salmon and trout parr normally takes place at the beginning of the growing season, in May–June. Stocking densities in the rapids vary from one river to another, e.g. the mean figure in the River Simojoki has varied between 10 and 30 1-year-old salmon parr per 100 m^2 (Jutila and Pruuki, 1988), while the experiments performed in the River Kiiminkijoki have employed stocking densities of 1-year-old parr of 1–80 salmon per 100 m^2 and about 35 trout per 100 m^2. Stocking experiments have also been carried out in the Rivers Vantaanjoki and Kiiminkijoki with newly hatched salmon and trout fry and with 1-summer-old salmon and trout parr (Ikonen et al, 1987; Niemitalo and Pasanen, 1989).

RESULTS AND DISCUSSION

Restoration of rapids

The results of restoration depend on the care taken in both planning and executing the work. The results are also closely dependent on the management of the migratory fish stocks. Stocking with parr and smolt is usually necessary to enhance salmon and trout stocks. In rivers with natural salmon and trout stocks, parr occupy the restored areas of the rapids fairly soon after restoration; e.g. 1-summer-old salmon parr were observed in restored rapids during the next summer in the River Simojoki. Insufficient restoration can nevertheless still lead to lower densities than in natural rapids (Jutila, 1987a).

According to Kännö (1987), restoration of the River Kuohunkijoki increased the total area of rapids by about 30% as compared with the dredged situation. The biomass of fish in the rapids decreased at first due to the restoration work, but increased after two years. Stocking with brown trout parr increased the numbers of brown trout to the extent that it was the most common fish species four years after restoration. Natural reproduction of grayling in the river was observed from the third year onwards.

The results of restoration are affected not only by the state of the river but also by the circumstances during the feeding migration of the smolts. In the River Piispajoki, which flows into the regulated Lake Kiantajärvi, stocking with newly hatched brown trout fry resulted in densities from 9 to 31 parr per 100 m^2 in the restored rapids (Jokikokko, 1987), but once stocking ceased, no natural spawning of brown trout was observed (Table 22.1). One probable reason for this may be the wide range of regulation of the water level in the lake, which may indirectly affect the survival of the brown trout from smolt to spawning fish (Jokikokko, 1989).

Some rapids have also been restored with special regard to sport fishing, releasing older fish into them as well as parr. Population densities and catches of brown trout were studied in the rapid of Puuskankoski in southern Finland before and after restoration. It was shown that there was no natural reproduction of brown trout before restoration, but it started soon after restoration and stocking with parr, smolt, and adults. The upper part of the rapid was left dredged, and no natural reproduction had been observed there in the course of over 10 years. Annual catches of brown trout have averaged 100–200 kg (140–240 fish) in the restored part of the rapid (Jutila, 1987b), especially due to the introduction of adult fish.

Results of the restoration works in the Finnish northern lowland rivers are most comparable to those in Swedish rivers flowing into the northern part of the Baltic Sea. According to Karlström (1977), the population density of trout was 0.9 parr per 100 m^2 in the dredged rapids of the River Skellefte älv, while undisturbed areas had 5.5 parr per 100 m^2. The restoration of dredged rapids resulted in the rise of parr densities to the same level as observed in undisturbed areas.

Stocking with parr

As a result of stocking the Rivers Simojoki and Tornionjoki with 1-year-old salmon parr, the mean population densities have been 13–20 parr per 100 m^2 in the Simojoki, and 6–9 parr per 100 m^2 in the Tornionjoki, which exceed the parr densities observed in unstocked rapids (Table 22.2). From the River Simojoki 20–25% of the stocked parr have been shown to have migrated into the sea as smolts. In the River Tornionjoki the proportion of stocked, fin-clipped salmon in different age groups in the catch samples has been 13% on average, indicating that 10–20% of the stocked parr survived to smolt size (Jutila and Pruuki, 1988).

The effects of parr stocking on the characteristics of the salmon and trout stocks depend on factors such as the brood stock and growth in the hatchery. In the River Tornionjoki no differences were observed between the stocked salmon and salmon of

TABLE 22.2. Annual mean population densities of salmon and trout parr in August in some Finnish rivers stocked with fry and 1-year-old parr in May–June

River	Years	Species	Mean population density (parr per 100 m^2)		Reference
			Stocked in spring	Observed in autumn	
Simojoki	1984–1986	Salmon	11–29 (1-yr)	13–20	Jutila and Pruuki (1988)
Tornionjoki	1980–1986	Salmon	[a] (1-yr)	6–9	Jutila and Pruuki (1988)
Kiiminkijoki	1985–1988	Salmon	345[b] (fry)	4[b]	Niemitalo and Pasanen (1989)
Kiiminkijoki	1985–1988	Salmon	1–80 (1-yr)	31[b]	Niemitalo and Pasanen (1989)
Kiiminkijoki	1985–1988	Trout	220[b] (fry)	16[b]	Niemitalo and Pasanen (1989)
Kiiminkijoki	1985–1988	Trout	36[b] (1-yr)	16[b]	Niemitalo and Pasanen (1989)
Vantaanjoki	1984–1986	Salmon	110–209 (fry)	21–36	Ikonen et al (1987)
Vantaanjoki	1983–1986	Trout	106–1531 (fry)	2–183	Ikonen et al (1987)

[a]Exact stocking densities not known
[b]Mean density for the whole period

natural origin in the sex composition of the catch, the number of years spent in the river before migrating to the sea, or catching areas in the river. In the River Simojoki, however, the average smolt age has dropped by one year and the average size of smolt has decreased by 1–2 cm. This is probably due to the more rapid growth of parr in the hatchery during their first year as compared with that of natural parr in the river itself (Jutila and Pruuki, 1988).

Comparison of the economic results of the stocking of the Rivers Simojoki and Tornionjoki has shown this method to be a viable one, and it is likely that the quality of the smolt produced by stocking a river with 1-year-old parr is better than by hatchery-reared smolt, and corresponds fairly well to that of natural smolt (Jutila and Pruuki, 1988).

Niemitalo and Pasanen (1989) have studied parr densities of salmon and trout in a stretch of rapids on the River Kiiminkijoki into which fry and parr of salmon and trout had been released. Electrofishing experiments carried out in the late summer showed the mean densities of salmon to be about 4 1-summer-old parr per 100 m², and about 31 2-summer-old parr per 100 m². The corresponding densities of trout were about 16 1-summer-old parr per 100 m² and also about 16 2-summer-old parr per 100 m². Stocking with newly hatched salmon fry have thus given rather poor results, but results have been better for trout fry and for parr of both salmon and trout.

Ikonen et al (1987) present results of the stocking of the River Vantaanjoki in southern Finland with salmon and trout fry. The densities obtained were 21–36 parr per 100 m² on average for salmon and 2–183 parr per 100 m² for trout. Ikonen et al (1987) estimate that it is possible to create trout densities of 30 parr per 100 m² in this manner.

The results of stocking with fry and parr in the Finnish rivers are similar to those of the stocking experiments in Swedish rivers. In Sweden, the data of Karlström (1984) from the Rivers Byske and Öre indicate that densities from 6 to 9 parr per 100 m² may be obtained in areas stocked with 1+-year-old parr. In the River Mörrum, densities of 41–65 parr per 100 m² have been obtained by releasing salmon fingerlings into the rapids (Karlström, 1977).

Stocking with salmon and trout parr in the northern Finnish rivers resulted in higher population densities of parr than observed in some unstocked rivers in northern Sweden (1–5 parr per 100 m² for salmon, 1–6 parr per 100 m² for trout—Karlström, 1977), and similar or lower densities than in northern Norway (15–20 parr per 100 m²—Power, 1973; 8–30 parr per 100 m²—Heggberget, 1984). In the southern Finnish rivers the corresponding densities have been lower than observed in some rivers in southern Sweden (26–155 parr per 100 m² for salmon, 5–27 parr per 100 m² for trout—Karlström, 1977), in southern Norway (15–115 parr per 100 m²—Saltveit and Styrvold, 1984), and in Scotland (234 parr per 100 m² for salmon, 131 parr per 100 m² for trout—Egglishaw and Shackley, 1977). Compared with other northern Baltic and Scandinavian rivers, the enhancement of salmonid rivers in Finland has given promising results.

REFERENCES

Anon. (1990). *Report of Baltic Salmon and Trout Assessment Working Group*, ICES, Doc. C.M. 1990/Assess:21 (mimeo).

Christensen, O., and Larsson, P. -O. (Eds) (1979). *Review of Baltic salmon research. A synopsis compiled by the Baltic Salmon Working Group*, ICES, Cooperative Research Report 89.

Egglishaw, H. J., and Shackley, P. E. (1977). "Growth, survival and production of juvenile salmon and trout in a Scottish stream", *Journal of Fish Biology*, **11**, 647–672.

Heggberget, T. G. (1984). "Populations of presmolt Atlantic salmon (*Salmo salar L.*) and brown trout (*Salmo trutta L.*) before and after hydroelectric development and building of weirs in the River Skjoma, North Norway", in *Regulated Rivers* (Eds A. Lillehammer and S. J. Saltveit), pp. 293–308. Universitetsforlaget As. Oslo-Bergen-Stavanger-Tromsö.

Heggberget, T. G., Haukebö, T., Mork, J., and Ståhl, G. (1988). "Temporal and spatial segregation of spawning in sympatric populations of Atlantic salmon, *Salmo salar* L., and brown trout, *Salmo trutta* L.", *Journal of Fish Biology*, **33**, 347–356.

Hermansen, H., and Krog, G. (1985). "A review of brown trout (*Salmo trutta*) spawning beds, indicating methods for their re-establishment in Danish lowland rivers", in *Habitat Modification and Freshwater Fisheries* (Ed. J. S. Alabaster), pp. 116–123, Butterworths, London.

Ikonen, E. (1984). "Migratory fish stocks and fishery management in regulated Finnish rivers flowing into the Baltic Sea", in *Regulated Rivers* (Eds A. Lillehammer and S. J. Saltveit), pp. 437–451. Universitetsforlaget As. Oslo-Bergen-Stavanger-Tromsö.

Ikonen, E., Ahlfors, P., Mikkola, J., and Saura, A. (1987). "The enhancement of sea trout and salmon in the Vantaanjoki River watercourse", (in Finnish), Finnish Game and Fisheries Research Institute, *Monistettuja julkaisuja*, **62**, 1–106, Helsinki.

Jokikokko, E. (1987). "The density of brown trout parr in the restored Piispajoki and Mustajoki Rivers in 1978–1985" (in Finnish), Finnish Game and Fisheries Research Institute, *Monistettuja julkaisuja*, **71**, 133–166, Helsinki.

Jokikokko, E. (1989). "The density of brown trout parr in the restored Piispajoki and Mustajoki Rivers in 1986–1988" (in Finnish), *Suomen kalastuslehti*, **96**, 340–343.

Jutila, E. (1985). "Dredging of rapids for timber-floating in Finland and its effects on river-spawning fish stocks", in *Habitat Modification and Freshwater Fisheries* (Ed. J. A. Alabaster), pp. 104–108, Butterworths, London.

Jutila, E. (1987a). "The development of salmon smolt production and catches in the Simojoki River after restoration work in 1982–1985" (in Finnish), Finnish Game and Fisheries Research Institute, *Monistettuja julkaisuja*, **71**, 47–96, Helsinki.

Jutila, E. (1987b). "Smolt production, fishery and catches of brown trout in the Puuskankoski Rapid after restoration in 1978–1985" (in Finnish), Finnish Game and Fisheries Research Institute, *Monistettuja julkaisuja*, **71**, 167–206, Helsinki.

Jutila, E., and Pruuki, V. (1988). "The enhancement of the salmon stocks in the Simojoki and Tornionjoki Rivers by stocking parr in the rapids", *Aqua Fennica*, **18**, 93–99.

Kännö, S. (1987). "The development of the fish stocks in the Kuohunkijoki River after the restoring of the rapids" (in Finnish), Finnish Game and Fisheries Research Institute, *Monistettuja julkaisuja*, **71**, 97–132, Helsinki.

Karlström, Ö. (1977). "Habitat selection and population densities of salmon (*Salmo salar* L.) and trout (*Salmo trutta* L.) parr in Swedish rivers with some reference to human activities", *Acta Universitatis Upsaliensis*, **404**, 1–72.

Karlström, Ö. (1984). *Reproduction conditions in the natural salmon rivers in northern Sweden* (in Swedish), Fiskeriintendenten, Övre norra distriktet (mimeo).

Lammassaari, V. (1990). "Floating and its effects on watercourses" (in Finnish with English summary), *Vesi-ja ympäristöhallinnon julkaisuja—sarja* A Nr 54, Helsinki.

Mills, D. (1989). *Ecology and Management of Atlantic Salmon*, Chapman and Hall, London.

Niemitalo, V., and Pasanen, P. (1989). "On the management of the salmon and sea trout stocks in the Kiiminkijoki River" (in Finnish), *Suomen kalastuslehti*, **96**, 289–292.

Power, G. (1973). "Estimates of age, growth, standing crop and production of salmonids in some North Norwegian rivers and streams", *Report of the Institute for Freshwater Research, Drottningholm*, **53**, 78–111.

Saltveit, S. J., and Styrvold, J. O. (1984). "Density of juvenile Atlantic salmon (*Salmo salar L.*) and brown trout (*Salmo trutta L.*) in two Norwegian regulated rivers", in *Regulated Rivers* (Eds

A. Lillehammer and S. J. Saltveit), pp. 309–319, Universitetsforlaget As. Oslo-Bergen-Stavanger-Tromsö.

Smith, A. K. (1973). "Development and application of spawning velocity and depth criteria for Oregon salmonids", *Transactions of the American Fisheries Society*, **2**, 312–316.

Toivonen, J., and Jutila, E. (1982). *Report on parr population densities, tagging experiments and river catches of the salmon stock of the River Simojoki in 1972–1980*, ICES Doc. C.M. 1982/M:40 (mimeo).

23

Strategies for Conservation of a Danubian Fish Fauna*

F. SCHIEMER

Department of Limnology, University of Vienna, Althanstr. 14,
A 1090 Vienna, Austria

and

H. WAIDBACHER

Department of Hydrobiology, University of Agriculture, Feistmantelstr. 4,
A 1180 Vienna, Austria

INTRODUCTION

The conservation of the free-flowing sections of the Austrian Danube received considerable public attention in the mid-1980s, when the ecological impacts of a planned large hydropower dam east of Vienna near the Czechoslovakian border were discussed. The project was stopped at the last moment because of the strong public opposition and the results of ecological impact studies. Ecological studies on the riparian biota were therefore intensified, and a proposal was made to establish an "Alluvial Zone National Park".

Studies on the fish fauna were initiated in 1983 in order to analyse possible ecological consequences of hydropower dams, and were later continued in order to develop guidelines for improved ecological management and criteria for a National Park. In order to achieve these goals it is necessary to define evaluation criteria for the structural quality of rivers. Such criteria must be based on a sound knowledge of the autecological requirements of characteristic species associations with reference to the original conditions. It became apparent that fish communities are good indicators for habitat structure as well as for the ecological integrity of large river systems because of the complex habitat requirements of many fish species in the course of their life cycles.

---

*This chapter is dedicated to Professor A. Ruttner-Kolisko on the occasion of her 80th birthday.

River Conservation and Management. Edited by P. J. Boon, P. Calow, and G. E. Petts
© 1992 John Wiley & Sons Ltd

ENVIRONMENTAL STATUS OF THE DANUBE IN AUSTRIA

The Danube flows over nearly 3000 km from its origin in the Black Forest in south-western Germany to its Delta in the Black Sea, passing through Europe in a west-to-east direction. The Austrian stretch of 350 km length belongs to the uppermost of three geographically well-separated sections. This upper part extends from the river's source to the Austrian/Czechoslovakian border ("Devin Gate"). The Austrian part is topographically well defined by its steepness (average slope 0.43‰) and high bedload transport. The discharge increases considerably mainly due to large tributaries from the Alps, especially the Inn, Traun, and Enns. The morphological condition of the river alternates between canyons with narrow riparian zones in the upstream sections to a braided course with large alluvial areas, especially in the plains in the eastern part of Austria. Figure 23.1 shows the braided river course near Vienna in the last century, illustrating the obviously rich ecological structure with gradients of current velocity, substrate, and riparian vegetation.

During the last hundred years these ecological conditions have been considerably changed by river regulation and damming. The main regulation started in the second half of the nineteenth century, and resulted in considerable changes due to a straightening and enforcement of one main channel and an abandonment of side channels. This had major effects on:

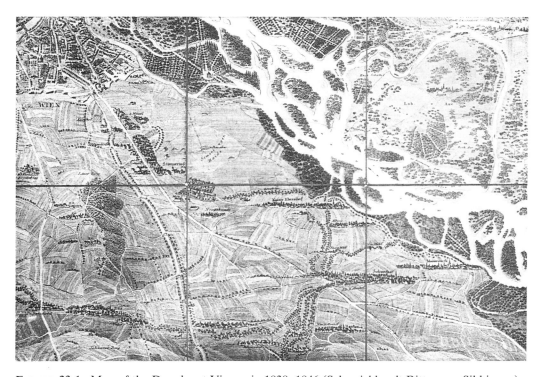

FIGURE 23.1. Map of the Danube at Vienna in 1830–1846 (Schweickhardt Ritter von Sikkingen)

(1) The ecological conditions of the river itself (increase of flow velocity, bedload erosion, and deepening of the river bed;
(2) The exchange conditions between river and riparian zone; and
(3) The relative proportion of alluvial habitat types.

The Austrian part of the Danube has a high potential for hydroelectrical power production due to its high discharge and steep slope. Construction of base-load hydro-power dams started in 1954 with the ultimate goal of forming a continuous chain of impoundments along the Austrian river section. At present, eight out of the 11 planned dams have been completed and only two stretches of free flow still remain (Figure 23.2).

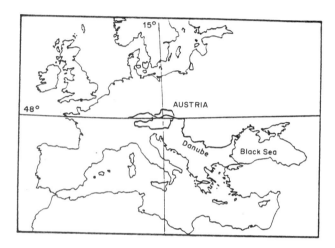

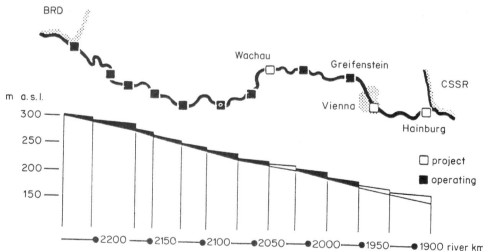

FIGURE 23.2. The Austrian part of the Danube with the locations of hydroelectric power plants. The inserted map outlines the course of the Danube river and the location of Austria (reproduced by permission from Schiemer and Spindler, 1989)

The construction of impoundments resulted in severe ecological degradation due to an almost complete disconnection between river and lateral backwaters, the monotonous shoreline constructions, and a stabilized water level. The characteristic limnological features of these impoundments are short retention times, low water temperatures, sedimentation of fine particles near the weirs, reduction of littoral gravel banks in the uppermost sections of the impoundments, low levels of plankton and high levels of zoobenthos in the fine sediment depositions.

Another major change occurred with regard to pollution, which has increased especially since the 1950s but became more controlled during the 1980s. There is good evidence that habitat structure has a greater effect on the fish populations in the Danube below Vienna than do the present pollution levels; therefore pollution is not addressed in this chapter.

FISH FAUNA

The fish fauna of the Austrian Danube is characterized by its large number of species (Jungwirth, 1984; Schiemer and Spindler, 1989). This species richness is explainable by the zoogeographical significance of the Danube as a major migration route for a diverse Central Asian and Ponto-Caspian fauna (Banarescu, 1960; Balon et al, 1986). From an ecological point of view, this diversity is due to the intersection of rhithral conditions in the canyons and epipotamal conditions with a still-existing habitat diversity in the alluvial plains. The fauna in the upstream canyon zones still contains characteristic rhithral elements such as *Salmo trutta* m. *fario*, *Thymallus thymallus*, and *Phoxinus phoxinus*, although they have become less prominent in the impounded areas due to the interruptions between the Danube and its main tributaries.

Fifty-seven species have been recorded during the recent surveys, 52 of which are autochthonous or long-term established elements. A few of them are influenced by stocking programmes (e.g. *Esox lucius*, *Stizostedion lucioperca*). The majority, however, are based on natural reproduction.

Comparing the present species lists with the historical records, we find that most of the original fauna is still present. Only the large anadromous Acipenseridae, seasonal immigrants from the Black Sea (*Huso huso*, *Acipenser güldenstädti*, *Acipenser stellatus*, *Acipenser nudiventris*), had strongly declined in the last century due to overfishing, and have completely disappeared since their migration route was blocked by the construction of large dams at the "Iron Gate" (Yugoslavia/Romania).

There are practically no records on the population structure prior to river regulation. However, it is evident from habitat changes that rheophilic species must have declined in favour of the eurytopic and limnophilic groups. This is shown by the fact that most of the riverine species found in the Danube are in the "Red Lists" of endangered taxa (Table 23.1) (Lelek, 1980). Several of these species appear to have declined during the last decades, indicating that the conditions for sustaining a characteristic riverine fish fauna in the Danube are critical.

THE STRUCTURE OF THE FISH COMMUNITY IN THE FREE-FLOWING SECTION DOWNSTREAM FROM VIENNA

Figure 23.3 shows the faunistic composition at eight locations belonging to three habitat types, (1) the inshore zone of the river itself, (2) backwaters with open connections to the

TABLE 23.1. List of fish species of the Austrian Danube encountered during recent surveys and their state of endangeredness

Rheophilic	Eurytopic	Limnophilic
A		
(1) *Acipenser ruthenus*	(3) *(Anguilla anguilla)*	(1) *Leucaspius delineatus*
(2) *Salmo trutta f.f.* ●	(3) *Esox lucius*	(3) *Scardinius erythrophthalamus*
(1) *Hucho hucho*	(3) *Rutilus rutilus*	(1) *Rhodeus sericeus amarus*
(3) *(Oncorhynchus mykiss)*	(3) *Alburnus alburnus*	(3) *Carassius carassius*
(3) *Thymallus thymallus*	(3) *Blicca bjoerkna*	(3) *Tinca tinca*
(2) *Chondrostoma nasus*	(3) *Abramis brama*	(1) *Misgurnus fossilis*
(2) *Barbus barbus*	(3) *Carassius auratus gibelio*	(2) *Stizostedion volgensis*
(1) *Rutilus pigus virgo*	(3) *Perca fluviatilis*	(3) *(Gasterosteus aculeatus)*
(1) *Rutilus frisii meidingeri*	(3) *Stizostedion lucioperca*	
(2) *Leuciscus leuciscus*	(3) *Proterorhinus marmoratus*	
(3) *Leuciscus cephalus*	(1) *Silurus glanis*	
(1) *Vimba vimba*	(3) *Gymnocephalus cernua*	
(1) *Phoxinus phoxinus*	(1) *Cyprinus carpio* ■	
(1) *Gobio kessleri*		
(3) *Gobio albipinnatus*		
(1) *Gobio uranoscopus*		
(2) *Noemacheilus barbatulus*	() introduced before 1900	
(1) *Alburnoides bipunctatus*	(1) endangered species	
(3) *Cottus gobio*	(2) vulnerable species	
(1) *Gymnocephalus baloni*	(3) presently not endangered	
(2) *Gymnocephalus schräetzer*	A all stages of life history are confined to the	
(2) *Zingel zingel*	main river	
(1) *Zingel streber*	B some stages of life history are confined to	
	well connected anabranches or tributaries	
B	● autochthonous populations endangered	
(1) *Leuciscus idus*	■ wild form of carp	
(1) *Abramis sapa*		
(1) *Abramis ballerus*		
(3) *Pelecus cultratus*		
(2) *Aspius aspius*		
(1) *Cobitis taenia*		
(3) *Gobio gobio*		
(1) *Lota lota*		
31 Species	13 Species	8 Species
24 endangered/vulnerable	2 endangered/vulnerable	4 endangered/vulnerable

Among the rheophilic species two groups are distinguished: (A) all stages of life history confined to the main river; (B) some stages confined to backwaters or tributaries

river, and (3) disconnected backwaters, which are flooded only during flood events at intervals of 5–10 years. Three ecological guilds of species are distinguished in accordance with the grouping given in Table 23.1.

The faunal composition in the main river channel is dominated, both in terms of species numbers and numerical composition, by the endangered rheophilic group. The percentage contribution of eurytopic forms, e.g. roach (*Rutilus rutilus*) and bream (*Abramis brama*), lies between 20% and 30%.

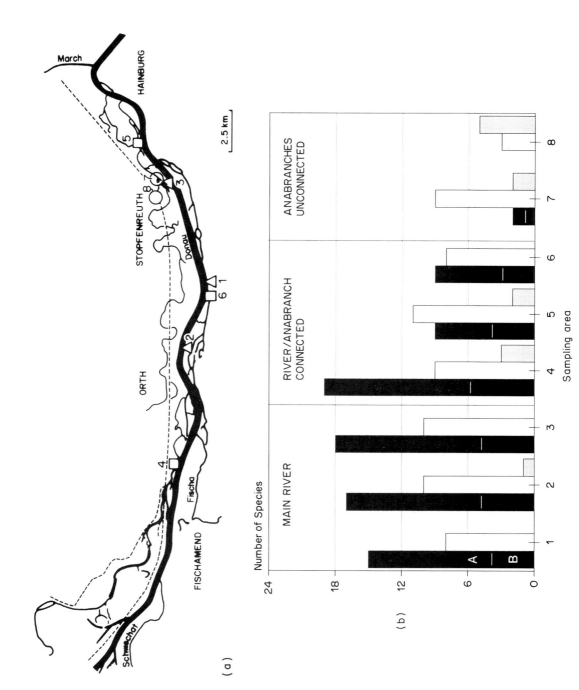

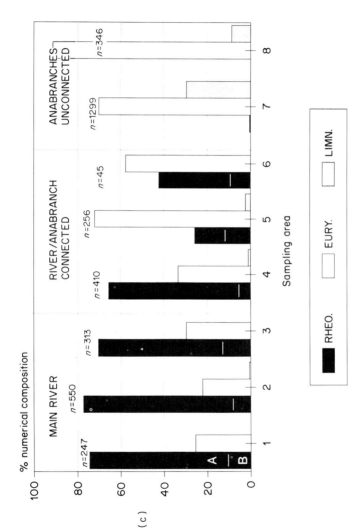

FIGURE 23.3. Composition of the fish fauna in different habitats downstream from Vienna. (For (b) and (c), the letters A and B represent two groups of rheophilous species—see Table 23.1). (a) River system with the position of the sampling areas. Triangles (1, 2, 3): in main river; squares (4, 5, 6): in backwaters with open connections to the river; circles (7, 8): in disconnected backwaters. (b) Number of species of different ecological guilds (see Table 23.1.). (c) Proportion of rheophilic, eurytopic, and limnophilic fish in the total catch (E-boat fishing, long-lining); *n*=number of fish collected

(a)

(b)

FIGURE 23.4. (a) Backwater connected to the River Danube. Such lateral connections are important to many riverine species as feeding grounds or as winter and flood refuge. (b) Backwater disconnected from the River Danube. These areas are characterized by a high cover of macrophytes, and their fish fauna comprise eurytopic and limnophilic species (photographs by F. Schiemer)

Backwaters connected to the river (Figure 23.4(a)) show a diverse fauna, including a large number of rheophilic species. Locations 4, 5 and 6 in Figure 23.3 are ranked according to decreasing connectivity. Location 4 represents a backwater with a constantly deep and wide opening to the river even at low water levels, whereas in Locations 5 and 6 migrations of fish are reduced below mean water levels by levees or narrow openings. In accordance with these exchange conditions for the fish fauna, the significance of riverine species is distinctly higher in Location 4. Detailed studies on the seasonal occurrence of fish in connected side-arms have shown that these lateral connections are particularly important for many riverine species as feeding grounds for some and as winter and flood refuge for others.

As was stressed by Antipa (1910) this lateral integrity of the alluvial system also enhances its general fish productivity. At present in the 50 km stretch of the Austrian Danube below Vienna only six backwaters exist which have open connections to the river. In the disconnected backwaters (Figure 23.4(b)), with generally high cover of macrophytes and accumulation of soft sediments, eurytopic species such as roach, bream, and silver bream (*Blicca bjoerkna*), prevail, but limnophilic (and polythermic) forms (tench (*Tinca tinca*); rudd (*Scardinius erythrophthalmus*); crucian carp (*Carassius carassius*)) are also well represented (Schiemer, 1985).

The most significant ecological features for an endangered riverine fauna are, however, the specific requirements for the larval and juvenile stages. Detailed studies on the distribution pattern of fish fry in various habitat types in the Danube and its backwaters downstream of Vienna (Table 23.2) provide clear evidence that many of the rheophilic species during their early life-phase are bound to the inshore zone of the river itself. The lowest population density of the 0+ age class and lowest species diversity are found along the linear, artificial shorelines (rip-rap—Figure 23.5(a)). A high diversity and a large number of fry of endangered species are restricted to small bays and shallow sloping gravel banks of the river shore (Figure 23.5(b)). Riverine shoreline structure is thus a decisive characteristic for the existence or the disappearance of a highly specific Danubian fish fauna.

The ecological quality of the existing inshore zones of the Danube can be evaluated on the basis of the ecological requirements of riverine fish species in the course of their early ontogenetic development. In a recent study of the free-flowing Danube between Vienna and the Czechoslovakian border, only 18 zones of 1–2 km length were identified which form potential fish nurseries. The structural properties of these 18 zones (e.g. littoral development at mean water level) correlates closely with the diversity and number of fry species. Of these 18 zones, only six provide high-quality conditions for the recruitment of riverine fish. They represent approximately 15% of the total shore length. Sixty per cent are linear embankments constructed of rip-rap and are practically devoid of fry (Schiemer et al, in press).

It is likely that the present shore structure is inadequate for long-term maintenance of the characteristic fish associations. This idea is supported by the decline of formerly common species which has been observed in recent years.

TABLE 23.2. Composition of the fish fry fauna in five habitat types. Results from surveys in 1985 and 1986 downstream of Vienna

Habitat type	n	Species number	Rheophilic	Eurytopic	Limnophilic	Endangered	Diversity
Disconnected backwaters	3043	17	3 (0.2%)	9 (54.6%)	5 (45.2%)	3	2.12
Connected backwaters	3237	9	3 (3.9%)	6 (96.1%)		2	1.42
River shore, sheltered bay	2437	14	8 (62.1%)	6 (37.9%)		5	2.34
River shore, gravel bank	1046	17	12 (73.4%)	5 (26.6%)		9	2.85
River shore, rip-rap	46	3	1 (8.1%)	2 (91.9%)			0.49

Indicated are: number of individuals analysed, number of species, number of species in each ecological guild (rheophilic, eurytopic, limnophilic) and their percentage contribution to the population, number of endangered species and Shannon–Weaver diversity index

FIGURE 23.5. (a) Linear, artificial shoreline (rip-rap) of the River Danube. This represents approximately 60% of the total shore length of the free-flowing Austrian Danube below Vienna. Such areas are practically devoid of fish fry. (b) A diversified shoreline structure on the River Daunube—an essential requirement for a diverse fish fauna (photographs by F. Schiemer)

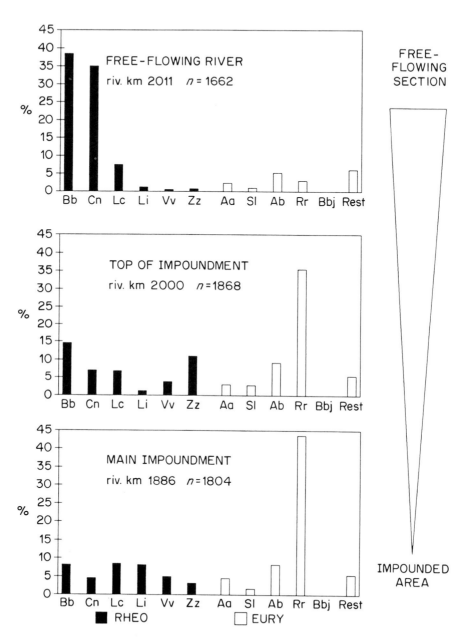

FIGURE 23.7. Faunal composition in a longitudinal transect from the free-flowing river ("Wachau") to the impoundment "Althenwörth". Results from E-boat fishing and long-lining. (Abbreviations of species as in Figure 23.6)

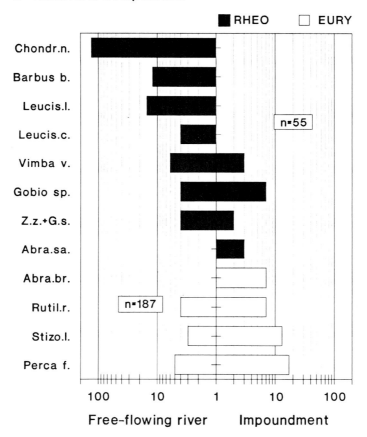

FIGURE 23.8. Numerical composition of fish fry in the inshore zone of the free-flowing upstream zone ("Wachau") and the impounded downstream areas ("Althenwörth"). Total catch from four shore-seining operations, July and August 1989

lateral gradients of the former braided-river situation. Under the present conditions within impoundments the different velocity preferences are expressed in a longitudinal sequence of the three species from the topset to the barrage in impounded zones (e.g. "Altenwörth"—Zauner, in preparation). Further studies are necessary, especially on the requirements for reproduction and for early development, to determine whether the present conditions are sufficient for a long-term maintenance of viable populations.

In summary, the fish fauna of the impoundments is generally impoverished with a distinct predominance of habitat generalists and low densities of riverine species. Within the latter guild the relative proportion is changing from nase and barbel to chubb and possibly *L. idus* and *V. vimba*. The development of limnophilic (polythermic) elements, e.g. tench (*Tinca tinca*), wels (*Silurus glanis*), or common carp (*Cyprinus carpio*), in the impoundments is restricted by low temperature, low macrophyte cover and possibly the low zooplankton development.

FIGURE 23.9. *Zingel zingel*, one of three species of rheophilic Percidae characteristic of the River Danube (photograph by H. Filka)

SUMMARY OF MAIN HABITAT REQUIREMENTS

Figure 23.10 summarizes some of the main habitat requirements of the fish fauna which will have to be considered in further management procedures. According to the preferred zones of occurrence of the adults (circles) and their spawning and nursery grounds (arrows), five groups of species are distinguished:

(1) Riverine species dependent on the connectivity of the Danube and its tributaries as they require rhithral conditions for spawning and during their early life stages (e.g. *Hucho hucho*, *Lota lota*). *L. lota*, for example, showed a striking decline in population density in impoundments, where upstream migration into the tributaries is blocked;
(2) Riverine species with spawning grounds and nurseries in the inshore zone of the river itself (majority of species, e.g. *Chondrostoma nasus*, *Barbus barbus*, *Gobio* spp., Danube percids, etc.);
(3) Riverine species with a preference for low-flow conditions (e.g. connected backwaters) during certain periods in the adult stage (e.g. as feeding grounds or winter refuge), but spawning grounds and nurseries in the river (e.g. *Abramis ballerus*, *Aspius aspius*);
(4) Eurytopic species ("habitat generalists") found both in the river and various types of stagnant water bodies. Some species such as *Esox lucius* and the wild form of *Cyprinus carpio* require flooded vegetation as spawning areas;

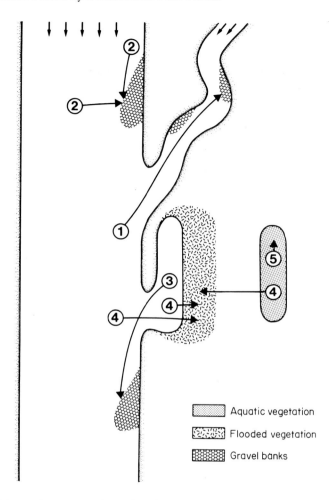

FIGURE 23.10. Schematic presentation of main habitat requirements of five guilds of fish (see text). Circles: preferred habitats of adults; arrows: spawning and nursery sites

(5) Limnophilic species confined to various microhabitats of disconnected former river branches with a strong development of submerged vegetation (see Table 23.1).

CONSERVATION MANAGEMENT

Conservation management must be oriented towards the original ecological situation in the alluvial zones prior to the main river regulation. Therefore the primary goal from a conservation perspective must be the maintenance and improvement of the ecological conditions in the remaining free-flowing sections of the river.

We have identified the reduced inshore structure and the strongly reduced hydrological integration of the river and its alluvial zone at mid-water level as the main ecological shortcomings. Our analysis allows us to define the type of action required for improving the present ecological conditions. The most important recommendations are:

(1) Increase the diversity of the inshore river bed structure (especially at slip-off slopes) by reducing the monotonous steep-sloped rip-raps and enhancing more bed-sediment dynamics within the shallow littoral areas, in order to improve the quality of spawning substrates and nurseries for rheophilic species.
(2) Create larger flooding areas at low flood events to improve the hiding capacity for fish at increased water flow (i.e. reduce population losses, due to high velocity in the channelized Danube) and enhance the spawning capacity for flood-zone spawners.
(3) Re-activate the lateral integration between the river and its abandoned backwaters by upstream connections at mean water level. Such an increased connectivity will not only increase the extent of inshore structure and the habitat diversity with regard to stream velocity and sediments, but will also improve the potential for riverine species with temporal requirements for still-water conditions and the productivity of the fish fauna in general.

Some of the planned measures are indicated in Figure 23.11 for a section of the alluvial zone downstream of Vienna which was recently bought by WWF (Worldwide Fund for Nature).

In the existing impoundments, which obviously have a lower conservation potential, structural properties as well as the integration with tributaries and lateral backwaters require ecological management. The main proposed procedures are:

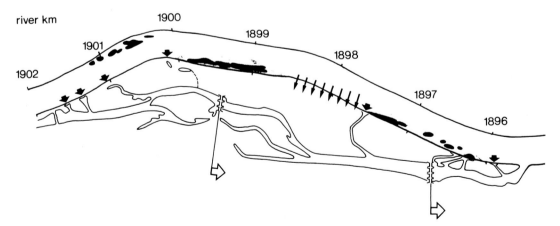

FIGURE 23.11. Illustrated management recommendations for an alluvial zone downstream of Vienna. Indicated is the backwater situation on the right bank between river-km 1896–1902. Recommendations for restructuring: thick black arrows=upstream openings of backwaters at mean water level; thin black arrows=lowering of the embankments; white arrows=reduction of levees in the backwater system to increase hydrological dynamics; grey shading shows enlargement of existing (black) shallow water gravel banks

(1) Restructure the monotonous shorelines using short groynes, wooden structures, blocks, and macroporous rip-raps to improve habitat structure, nursery conditions, and hiding capacity during floods;

(2) Restructure the deeper river bed with artificial reefs to improve hiding capacity for fish, especially during winter and during flood events;

(3) Create large lateral still-water areas by reconstruction of side-dams to enhance conditions (temperature, food supply, and habitat structure), especially for eurytopic and limnophilic species;

(4) Create and enlarge shallow water gravel banks in the uppermost impounded zone to improve spawning grounds and nurseries for endangered rheophilic species;

(5) Reduce barriers between the river and its tributaries to allow the migration of rhithral spawners and increase population exchange;

(6) Connect the river with its lateral backwaters.

Most of these management recommendations, especially those for the free-flowing section, require major changes from an engineering point of view. From an ecological perspective large-scale, long-term experiments will be necessary to evaluate, improve, and consolidate these proposals.

Recently, political decisions have been taken for the establishment of an Alluvial Zone National Park along the free-flowing Danube from Vienna to the Czechoslovakian border. This decision recognizes the international significance of this area as a characteristic element of the Central European landscape and its cultural tradition.

The status of a National Park will establish the legal framework for stopping the economy-oriented utilization of the area (e.g. with regard to forestry or hydropower damming) and should provide the necessary funding to improve the ecological conditions as outlined above with reference to the original situation before river regulation.

ACKNOWLEDGEMENTS

Field data were obtained with the help of many colleagues both from the Department of Limnology, University of Vienna and the Department of Hydrobiology, University of Agriculture, Vienna. We thank Dipl. Ing R. Janisch and "Donaukraft" for allowing us to use stock assessment data from the "Melk" impoundment, T. Spindler, G. Zauner, and H. Wintersperger for analysing the faunistic data, and A. Gunatilaka and G. Imhof for reading the manuscript.

The study was supported by the Austrian Fonds zur Förderung der wissenschaftlichen Forschung, Project No. S-35, MaB—Proj. "Ökosystemstudie Donaustau Altenwörth" and the Österr. Wasserwirtschaftsverband, Proj. "Interdisziplinäre Studie Donau".

REFERENCES

Antipa, G. (1910). *Regiunea inundabila a Dunarii*, Staren ei actvala si mijloacele de a o pue in valcare, Bucharest.

Balon, E. K., Crawford, S. S., and Lelek, A. (1986). "Fish communities of the upper Danube River (Germany, Austria) prior to the new Rhein–Main–Donau connection", *Environmental Biology of Fishes*, **4**, 243–271.

Banarescu, P. (1960). "Einige Fragen zur Herkunft der Süßwasserfischfauna der europäisch-mediterranen Unterregion", *Archiv für Hydrobiologie*, **57**, 16–134.

Jungwirth, M. (1984). "Die fischereilichen Verhältnisse in Laufstauen alpiner Flüsse, aufgezeigt am Beispiel der österreichischen Donau", *Österreichische Wasserwirtschaft*, **36**, 103–110.

Lelek, A. (1980). *Threatened fresh water fishes of Europe*, Council of Europe Nature and Environment Series 18.

Schiemer, F. (1985). "Die Bedeutung von Augewässern als Schutzzonen für die Fischfauna", *Österreichische Wasserwirtschaft*, **37**, 239–245.

Schiemer, F., and Spindler, T. (1989). "Endangered fish species of the Danube river in Austria", *Regulated Rivers: Research and Management*, **4**, 397–407.

Schiemer, F., Spindler, T., Wintersperger, H., Schneider, A., and Chovanec, A. (in press). "Fish fry associations: Important indicators for the ecological status of large rivers", *Verhandlungen der Internationalen Vereinigung für theoretische und angewandte Limnologie*, **24**.

Waidbacher, H. (1989). "Zum Einfluß der Uferstruktur auf Fischbestände—Stauraumgestaltung Altenwörth", *Österreichische Wasserwirtschaft*, **41**, 172–178.

Zauner, G. (in preparation). *Vergleichende Untersuchungen zur Ökologie der drei Donauperciden Schraetzer (G. schraetzer), Zingel (Z. zingel) und Streber (Z. streber) in gestauten und ungestauten Donauabschnitten*, MS thesis, University of Agriculture, Vienna.

SECTION IV
PROTECTING RIVERS—LEGISLATION AND PUBLIC PARTICIPATION

The River Feshie, northern Scotland, at its confluence with the River Spey. (For its significance to this Section see Chapter 2. Photograph P.J. Boon.)

24

River Conservation and Catchment Management: A UK Perspective

M. D. NEWSON

Centre for Land Use and Water Resources Research,
University of Newcastle-Upon-Tyne,
Newcastle-upon-Tyne NE1 7RU, UK

DERIVATION OF PRINCIPLES; CONTINUITY, EQUILIBRIA, CONTROL

During the 1970s and 1980s the general systems approach to science, the driving force in a previous era of scientific ecology (Goldsmith, 1988), became popular among the natural sciences. Physical geography took a leading role in the revival and the river basin became the textbook example of an open system.

Popular concern about environmental quality was growing at the same time, and two aspects of systems thinking—interdependence of constituent parts and time-dependent behaviour—became of day-to-day relevance in many river issues both of conservation and pollution control. A number of popular environmental concerns fit a river basin; for example, the loss of wetlands (NCC, 1984); loss of channel diversity (Newbold et al, 1983), and pollution from diffuse agricultural sources (Headworth, 1989; House of Lords, 1989). These topics clearly relate the land of the river basin to the quantity and quality of the waters within and beyond it. The first principle to grasp in all aspects of river conservation is, therefore, that *land and water are a hydrological continuum and must be managed together.*

To a conservation-oriented readership this may be axiomatic, but to politicians and planners, even those with some formal knowledge of systems science, there is still a problem in laying out the river basin system conceptually to the point where, for example, actions in a remote upland forest are considered of obvious relevance to a town's flood problems hundreds of kilometres downstream.

A further, almost insuperable, problem in educating politicians and planners about the operation of the river basin system is that of time scales. We seek to manage rates of change in nature so as to make them "appropriate", not just to our own perceptions but such that some functions (e.g. diversity, resilience, etc.) are optimized.

The time scales required for comprehensive understanding (and hence rational management) of river basins are so diverse that communications are difficult between the

River Conservation and Management. Edited by P. J. Boon, P. Calow, and G. E. Petts
© 1992 John Wiley & Sons Ltd

relevant disciplines. For example, while the engineer hydrologist operating a flood-warning system works to the hour or minute, a civil engineer constructing a flood-protection scheme for a city may work to a century and the geomorphologist to tens of millennia (Hickin, 1983; Newson, 1986). Conservation research itself often seems incapable of bridging the inevitable gaps between these time and space scales. In relation to national policy making, it is clear that broader activities of classification are an essential input to the selection of sites (e.g. Haslam, 1978; Smith and Lyle, 1979; Holmes, 1983). However, if practised in isolation, there remains a deficit of knowledge in relation to the predictive ability to manage long-term (Hellawell, 1988); sustainability requires predictability and climatic change is making predictability particularly difficult for river systems (Newson and Lewin, 1991).

The second principle worth setting out for river conservation is, therefore, that *we need to understand river phenomena in terms of the equilibrium condition of the site affected and, if possible, of the system as a whole* (Patrick et al, 1982; Lewin et al, 1988). Thus, reaches apparently devastated after an overnight flood or pollution incident have been observed to recover in a year, while the verdict "no effects seen here" nearly always means ". . . yet"! Such misjudgements of equilibrium states pose great difficulties in a rational system of management, be that management for rarity, diversity, or any other conservation criteria (Ratcliffe, 1977).

Are these first two *scientific* principles new to the agenda of river basin management? In the era of prehistory in which rivers were deified, one imagines harmonious, equilibrium relationships typical of primitive societies (McNeely and Pitt, 1984). However, the needs of settled agriculture produced, as long ago as 6000 BC, hydraulic civilizations for whom river manipulation by feats of civil engineering was backed by very strong social structures. There is little evidence to suggest a high degree of environmental understanding or concern in these early river basin cultures; indeed, that on the Indus may have perished as a result of environmental change. It has taken basic scientific guidance from hydrology (as distinct from hydraulic engineering technology) during the last 300 years to enable us, at last, to consider management of the *collecting* processes of the river basin (as distinct from the *distribution* processes of irrigation or water supply). We are now technically equipped to manage river basin systems according to the first two principles above, if we have the collective will so to do.

The third principle of river conservation is, therefore, that *the nature and type of river management systems are critical to conservation*. In the UK we moved to management units coincident with river basin boundaries as late as the 1930s, in support of land drainage—not a notably conservational activity and one bearing the marks of distribution philosophies ("getting the water away"—Newson, 1989) rather than collection. It has had the effect of rendering 35 500 km of river channel in England and Wales under management by structures or regular maintenance (Brookes et al, 1983).

It was the Victorian era of river-borne cholera epidemics (early 1830s, late 1840s—Howe, 1972) which, through forcing municipal suppliers to seek water from the "pure" hills, led to the earliest catchment management schemes. These were very prescriptive of land use and land management; water supply authorities purchased large tracts of the uplands as what we would now call "protection zones" in order to minimize the costs of purification. However, other Victorian pressures on river systems, such as industrial pollution, were not countered in such a fundamental way. Refinement of the common law principle of riparian rights made it possible for those with property and livelihoods affected by upstream changes to take action against the perpetrators. Salmonid fisheries received statutory protection in 1861 but river systems were not protected against biotic damage from pollutants until discharges became controlled through the statutes of 1876, 1951, and 1974. Diffuse, largely agricultural, pollution did not come under (potential) control until the Water Act 1989.

We may conclude from this very brief review that, with the exception of small upland catchments purchased by water suppliers, the joint management of land and water has not been a central feature of UK public policy. Indeed, neither the establishment of land-drainage boards nor of upland catchment management schemes has aimed to be beneficial to conservation. As a consequence, little research has been promoted on river "health", outside the narrow definition of human physical health, and little progress made on institutional controls of river basin activities other than those directly connected with water management. Indeed, water management itself has become a major influence upon river regime and quality (Petts, 1984).

TRANSLATION OF PRINCIPLES INTO POLICY: PROBLEMS OF KNOWLEDGE

If we wish to see the principles of continuity and equilibrium incorporated into river basin management we must interact with public policy. I wish to examine this interface, using our knowledge of the effects of plantation forestry in Britain.

The river system is a transport system for water, sediments, solutes, and biota. Less than 2% of precipitation falls on the network of river channels—the remainder falls on land to initiate a cascade of processes resulting in river channel flows. Early contributions to hydrology recognized the partition of run-off between surface routes and groundwater routes. In humid climates, however, hydrologists have now elaborated a multitude of flow processes and patterns (notably through-flow and the resulting "contributing area" hypothesis—Dunne and Leopold, 1978) which has had a revolutionary effect on our concepts of land/water interactions.

The corollary of these advances in our understanding of the structure and operation of the process cascade is that we have become even more aware of anthropogenic impacts on patterns of run-off, rates of run-off, solids content of run-off, and the dissolved content of run-off.

Prior to this, hydrologists had considered rates of evaporation and transpiration to be the most likely river basin properties to be vulnerable to a cultural influence. Measurement of rainfall and run-off are relatively easy; evapotranspiration measurement is far from easy but, by subtraction, experimental hydrologists quickly established, for example, the impact of forests on annual totals of evapotranspiration (Bates and Henry, 1928, through to Calder and Newson, 1979). The early pieces of field experimentation in hydrology, involving a manipulation of land use, were stimulated by the qualitative studies of conservationists such as Marsh, whose *Man and Nature* (1864) is primarily directed at what we would now call an ecosystems approach to river basins. Forests and water continued as concerns for conservation management (for example, in the career of Aldo Leopold (Tanner, 1987)) and their interaction has come to dominate the hydrologists' research on anthropogenic effects.

The influence of forests on river systems has dominated human perceptions of land/ water interactions. Public policy in France adopted a reforestation campaign in response to the floods of 1875 and 1897—mainly because of the observations of conservationists and geographers, but essentially on the advice of an engineer. In contrast, in Switzerland the disastrous effects of nineteenth-century floods on navigable channels promoted the channelization and canalization of river channels by engineers.

The large volume of published research this century concerning forest influence has had a very variable response from public policy. In the UK the Gathering Grounds Committee (Ministry of Health, 1948) was able to *recommend* afforestation on reservoir catchments, largely for reasons of pollution control, with conifer plantations preventing public access, intensification of livestock farming, and soil erosion. However, for the subsequent 40 years, a succession of papers has revealed the largely damaging effects of plantation conifers in the British uplands on the physical, chemical, and biological habitat of streams (Maitland et al, 1990).

Science seldom acts politically and its methods are put under severe pressure when required to answer policy questions (Collingridge and Reeve, 1986) but we may well ask why hydrology has had relatively little impact in establishing a response to the principle of land/water joint management. The answer has again much to do with scale. The experimental catchment used by hydrologists is seldom larger than 10 km^2. The unconquerable paradox of this situation is that, as measurements become increasingly comprehensive and accurate via spatial reductionism, applicability becomes restricted by inability to extrapolate conclusions. Those conclusions may also be irrelevant to the "normal" unit of land use and land management. While plots and lysimeters of a few hundred square metres are popular with hydrologists (Calder, 1976; Ward and Robinson, 1990) they cannot be treated in the "normal" way by forestry or farming operations. Thus, results from small-scale experiments are greeted by claims that they are unrepresentative. Extrapolations from these experiments become more problematic as their focus moves down the hydrological cascade. Evaporation at canopy level can be extrapolated relatively easily to whole regions whereas processes affecting water quality may be entirely local, much influenced by management practice and therefore rooting research data to the spot (Newson and Calder, 1989).

The example of forestry in the UK, therefore, leads us to the rather cynical view that the prospects for the "hydrologic civilization" are bleak. While recent progress has been made in defining codes of practice for an accommodation between forestry and water interests there is still little power in the hands of river managers or conservationists to allocate the use of land, despite the size and thoroughness of the knowledge base. Consequently, continuity and equilibrium principles are not yet fully underpinning policy. One result is that conservationists experience slow progress in finding support for their view of the river basin system.

PROTECTING RIVER HABITATS

The Land Drainage Act 1930 established basin-wide authorities for the first time, but their attention was restricted solidly to the river channel network and to the "main" elements of that. "Getting the water away" without causing damaging floods is a popular aim for a wetland island under population pressure (Newson, 1989). However, the onslaught of structural and maintenance measures perpetrated by enthusiastic engineers overshot to the point where both drainage and river "training" and "flood proofing" seriously reduced the quality of river systems as ecosystems (Purseglove, 1988). "Relative naturalness" has necessarily become a criterion for conservation (NCC, 1989).

River habitats were included in the first national conservation review (Ratcliffe, 1977), which included a number of large systems; nevertheless, the attention of policy makers was mainly on the spectacular loss of *wetland* habitats (NCC, 1984). The Wildlife and Countryside Act 1981 permitted a more comprehensive approach by the Nature Conservancy Council (NCC) to the notification of Sites of Special Scientific Interest (SSSIs), but progress at survey in relation to river sites has been understandably slow, paralleling the policy opportunities and resources. Delay in obtaining fundamental river controls has produced an opportunity for an accommodating approach by land drainers, aided by new guidance (Water Space Amenity Commission, 1983; Newbold et al, 1983; Lewis and Williams, 1984; Hemphill and Bramley, 1989) and new legislation (MAFF, 1988a, b).

Hellawell (1988) personally bemoaned the lack of a comprehensive approach to site protection and nominated his own reaches; he defended his choice with a reference to the desirability of attaining some form of control over catchments as well as channels:

It has proved impractical, so far, to designate whole catchments in order to afford protection to important sites but mounting pressure on water resources makes this, or an effective alternative, increasingly imperative. Until this problem has been resolved, the few catchments which are virtually unaffected by pollution or environmental manipulation will continue to form our major freshwater wildlife resource (p. 428).

Fortunately, such pleas are being heard now, thanks to changes in the structure of the water industry in England and Wales (which will make it similar to its counterparts in Scotland) and it is to the opportunities provided by the Water Act 1989 (Macrory, 1989; Howarth, 1990) for the operation of our three scientific conservation principles that we now turn.

THE NEXT STEPS: VIA ECOTONES TO THE CATCHMENT

As Machiavelli realized, "men prosper so long as fortune and policy are in accord". At present, in the UK, river conservation has fortune in the form of the belated public realization that the river system does not operate to provide a cheap route for transport, pipeline for water, drain for floods, and tank for pollutants. But is policy in accord? In the UK public policy on the environment is evolving as a compromise between the traditional principles of pollution control: no action without scientific proof; best practicable means of control; polluter pays (DoE, 1988), and the contemporary need for much wider principles: precautionary principle of action; sustainability; public and international accountability.

While these headings still apply mainly to pollution control, they are equally relevant to conservation; a meaningful incorporation of conservation principles into public policy would quickly achieve precautionary action and sustainability (but not necessarily accountability). Thus we may expect to see approaches to river conservation adhere to policies with a more traditional development orientation. Given, in future, a precautionary principle for public action, what are the signs for a marriage of the knowledge base and actions to "promote" nature conservation throughout the river system?

We may summarize recent strategic thinking by many disciplines and interests associated with management of river systems by using the word "extensification". Figure 24.1(a) illustrates the "extensification" of interests by hydrologists, river managers, and conservationists, which is a feature of recent policy developments. Figure 24.1(b) is a development designed to show five scales of management at increasing distances from the channel in a typical valley cross-section. This figure emphasizes an achievable extension of conservation policies beyond the early notion of "buffer zones". Other interests and agencies can provide assistance in dealing with network conditions (e.g. fisheries, recreation), but their need for land "take" is much less than that of conservation and their actions consequently less controversial. The conservation interest expands the channel in conceptual and policy terms, in opposition to its contraction and containment by traditional land drainage policies. It can only do this if "fortune and policy are in accord".

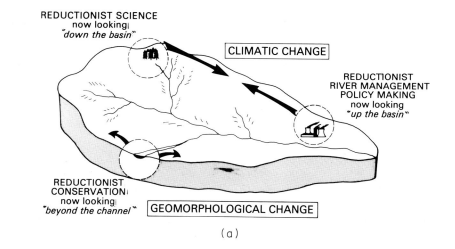

(a)

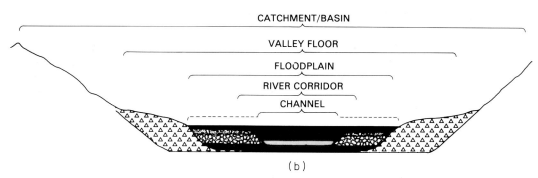

(b)

FIGURE 24.1. (a) Current moves to extend sectional interests in river-basin management. (b) Cross-section of valley to show the zones to which conservation interests should extend from the channel

TABLE 24.1. Extending the conservation interest in rivers

Scale	Justifications	Policy trends
1. Channel	(1) Continuity: linear habitat (2) Diversity of morphology (3) Bio-indicators for human use	Downturn in land-drainage/ benefits of bio-engineering and restoration
2. River corridor	(1) Migration of channel (2) Interaction of biota (3) Habitat: shade, shelter	Less intensive land use bank- side; demands for recreation. Paths. Surveys
3. Floodplain	(1) Natural flood control (2) Groundwater strips nutrients (3) Species of temporary wetlands	Set-aside/use of washlands/ major wetlands for flood control
4. Valley floor	(1) Soligenous mires (2) Landscape value (3) Extended corridors—migration	Valley change surveys— towards landscape protection/ ESAs
5. Catchment	(1) Systematic management (2) Contiguity of corridors (3) Basins—environmental units	Protection zones, controls on urban development; extension SSSI criteria

The knowlege base for an extension of legitimate conservation interest from channels to catchments is summarized in Table 24.1. The broader scientific concept underlying the extension of mere "buffer zones" is that of *ecotones* (Décamps et al, 1990). A recent Man and the Biosphere conference, reported by Décamps and colleagues, concluded that "in riverine landscapes, nutrient and sediment retention efficiency is positively related to the percentage of the landscape that is composed of land/inland water ecotones" (p. 176).

These are defined as including littoral zones, wetlands, groundwater exchange zones, and riparian forests, and their protective influence on neighbouring systems is proportional to the length and shape of the contact zones. There are consequently benefits for environmental management from extending the ecotone concept:

The restoration and creation of land/inland water ecotones will provide for and enhance the economic and social values of landscapes, including landscape quality, recreational use (including tourism), production of resources (such as fish and fibre), waste water management from urban, industrial and agricultural sources and flood control (p. 176).

PROGRESS IN THE UK

The NCC's policy has made an important forward step in the guidelines for selection of biological SSSIs (NCC, 1989). These make no binding prescriptions on the importance of catchment characteristics or protection; the criteria for wetlands and open waters are quite strict on the matter. There are, however, no upstream and downstream buffers and the only lateral extensions occur in the case of "extensive riparian vegetation", "adjacent semi-natural, wet habitat which is intimately linked with the river", and "non-wetland habitats adjacent to the river provided that they contribute significantly to sustaining fauna associated with the river". Interestingly, "marginal vegetation should also be included if it is thought to be important as a nutrient interceptor". In the light of recent French (Pinay and Décamps, 1988) and UK findings (Haycock, pers. comm.) this is perhaps the facilitating clause for an extension to more of the floodplain and valley floor. The vehicle of river corridor surveys, successfully implemented as a protection against damage from land-drainage schemes, should be further empowered for this wider task and technical reviews are already under way.

Both site selection for protection and action against land-drainage schemes have encouraged national river evaluation on the basis of the Holmes' (1983) river classification based on macrophyte communities. With the introduction of the use of invertebrate communities (Armitage et al, 1983) to the selection criteria both the conservation and pollution-control agencies will be using the same classification; this should lead to joint ventures in the extension of SSSIs or to a combination of the "Potentially Damaging Operation" list used to protect SSSIs and the protection zone criteria available to the National Rivers Authority (NRA). As many rivers have the potential to recover from past engineering or pollution damage, national reviews should be continually repeated. Currently, the Clyde River Purification Board in Scotland has applied for four formerly polluted rivers to be reclassified as salmonid rivers.

Many conservationists expressed concern about the recent reorganization of the water industry in England and Wales (Macrory, 1989; Howarth, 1990)—principally because of the privatization of water supply and sewerage. As a result, there has been a change to private, commercial management of substantial areas of "wet estate" , much of it of high conservation value. The privatized water and sewerage authorities have made no significant environmental commitments other than to adopt the traditional standpoint of farmers ("we are naturally in the business of a clean environment" or similar words). However, the corollary of privatization (albeit forced upon the UK by the intervention of the European Community), the establishment of a National Rivers Authority, can now be seen as a positive (or at least potentially positive) gain. Described as "the strongest environmental protection agency in Europe" by its Chairman, as a "guardian of the water environment" by its publicity, and with a land-use expert as its first Chief Executive, there is clearly considerable potential. The Authority has already applied pollution law more stringently and set up the Nitrate Sensitive Areas scheme (MAFF/ DoE, 1990). However, the conservation interest cannot rest: the NRA must derive a proper practical definition of the phrase within the Water Act "to promote the conservation of nature" (see DoE/Welsh Office, 1989). It is worth noting that the government's framework for these duties includes "integrated land use and management plans".

An alarming element of Table 24.1 is the extent to which the identifiable policy trends are reversible; many are *ad hoc*, non-statutory, or are "accommodations" rather than "allocations" (see Newson, 1990). It is therefore important that the NRA's research agenda is substantiated to allow the organization to press for sustainable, scientifically-based improvements to policy. I have already pointed out that only the most comprehensive and long-lasting science in this field has its results incorporated into policy. In this case sustainable also means enforceable: resources will be required to raise river management criteria from those of an era of non-statutory objectives to less accommodating, absolute levels of environmental protection, including the use of biotic indicators.

The river management situation in Britain can no longer be seen in isolation, especially with respect to Europe. Already European Community water quality legislation can be reasonably presented as having touched the UK's environmental conscience over its treatment of rivers and coastal seas. A sequence of Directives has forced the UK to formalize its heavy reliance on the assimilative capacity of the fluvial environment (compared with the European preference for emission standards). This trend continues unabated: the introduction of Environmental Assessment (EA) to UK legislation in July 1988 has had repercussions for all aspects of river basin management (notably drainage), not the least of which is the need in EA for widespread public consultation. Of direct relevance to conservation is the forthcoming "Eutrophication Directive", under which discharges into water bodies "which are found to be eutrophic or which in a short time may become eutrophic" must be reduced (in the case of agriculture) or treated (as in the case of sewage). The Directive is therefore likely to lead to catchment planning of a type above and beyond the delimitation of Nitrate Sensitive Areas. Completely new approaches are likely, such as the creation of land-use zoning in relation to watercourses and water bodies (Newson, 1991).

CONCLUSIONS

Perhaps the greatest challenge to environmental management is that of properly understanding environmental science. Science will continue to underpin management but it is essential to appreciate that environmental science cannot translate directly into action in the same way that, for example, engineering science becomes incorporated into technology. Environmental science deliberately seeks extensive, holistic remedies but carries a risk of uncertainty in its findings. Nevertheless, it can guide precautionary policies if its work is professionally structured. The ability to classify rivers (Armitage et al, 1983; Holmes, 1983) is the essential starting point so that SSSI designations can be considered in relation to these classifications. To date, only a comparatively short length of river has been notified as SSSI in its own right, highlighted by a recent NCC review in which all SSSIs containing running water were classified into four groups (Boon, pers. comm.). The selection of "river SSSIs" needs to become more fully representative, keying to both the desirable and achievable aspects of conservation categories. We need to remember at the same time the considerable capacity of rivers to recover, and the NCC may wish to officially promote recovery by technical means, a very successful process in North America (Gore, 1985) and parts of Europe (Brookes, 1984).

Quite surprisingly, monitoring is once more in vogue and an Environmental Change Network is to be established by the Natural Environment Research Council. Conservationists must resist the temptation to believe that monitoring always yields bad news. If equilibrium concepts are close to a core definition of conservation we need to seek from monitoring a definition of those ecosystems which have the capacity and resilience to permit human exploitation and the return of wastes.

Finally, conservationists must occupy a full, professional, yet distinctive role in the general field of environmental management. Tendencies to exceptionalism and privacy must be cured, if for no other reason, because conservation, especially that of river systems, needs land. The extension of river conservation to corridors, floodplains, valley floors, and catchments will only occur through planning—an essentially public process (Gardiner, 1991), be it via formal Environmental Assessment of projects or the day-to-day consultation protocols of NRA or River Purification Board officers. The criteria for notification of freshwater SSSIs must be reviewed continually in the light of parallel developments in catchment planning and control occurring in the river-basin organizations (Newson, 1991).

One of the compelling public images of the environmental changes now considered likely from global warming is of conservation in the face of rapid environmental change, largely facilitated by corridors for migration (Hobbs et al, 1990) of which river valleys are obvious candidates as "greenways" (Bridgewater and Woodin, 1990).

With the potential for "fortune and policy" to accord being offered to those concerned with river conservation, the message of the NCC's review of the conservation task in Britain (NCC, 1984) remains valid: "for all those who affirm the importance of nature conservation the challenge will be to turn opportunity and intention into achievement" (p. 101).

REFERENCES

Armitage, P. D., Moss, D., Wright, J. F., and Furse, M. T. (1983). "The performance of a new biological water quality score system based on macroinvertebrates over a wide range of unpolluted running-water sites", *Water Research*, **17**, 333–347.

Bates, C. G., and Henry, A. J. (1928). "Forest and streamflow at Wagon Wheel Gap, Colorado", Final Report, *Monthly Weather Review, Suppl.*, **30**.

Bridgewater, P., and Woodin, S. J. (1990). "Global warming and nature conservation", *Land Use Policy*, **7**, 165–168.

Brookes, A. (1984). *Recommendations Bearing On The Sinuosity Of Danish Stream Channels*, National Agency of Environmental Protection, Silkeborg.

Brookes, A., Gregory, K. J., and Dawson, F. H. (1983). "An assessment of river channelization in England and Wales", *Science of the Total Environment*, **27**, 97–112.

Calder, I. R. (1976). "The measurement of water losses from a forested area using a 'natural' lysimeter", *Journal of Hydrology*, **30**, 311–325.

Calder, I. R., and Newson, M. D. (1979). "Land use and upland water resources in Britain—a strategic look", *Water Resources Bulletin*, **15**, 1628–1639.

Collingridge, D., and Reeve, C. (1986). *Science Speaks To Power. The Role Of Experts In Policymaking*, Frances Pinter, London.

Décamps, H., Fournier, F., Naiman, R. J., and Petersen, R. C. (1990). "An international research effort on land/water ecotones in landscape management and restoration", *Ambio*, **19**, 175–176.

Department of the Environment/Welsh Office (1988). *Integrated Pollution Control: A Consultation Paper*, HMSO, London.

Department of the Environment/Welsh Office (1989). *The Water Act 1989. Code Of Practice On Conservation, Access And Recreation*, DoE/Welsh Office, London.

Dunne, T., and Leopold, L. B. (1978). *Water In Environmental Planning*, W. H. Freeman, San Francisco.

Gardiner, J. L. (Ed.) (1991). *River Projects and Conservation: A Manual for Holistic Appraisal*, John Wiley, Chichester.

Goldsmith, E. (1988). "Gaia: some implications for theoretical ecology", in *Gaia—The Thesis*,

The Mechanisms And The Implications (Eds P. Bunyard and E. Goldsmith), pp. 145–164, Wadebridge Ecological Centre, Camelford.

Gore, J. A. (1985). *The Restoration Of Rivers And Streams*, Butterworths, Boston, Massachusetts.

Haslam, S. M. (1978). *River Plants*, Cambridge University Press, Cambridge.

Hellawell, J. M. (1986). *Biological Indicators Of Freshwater Pollution And Environmental Management*, Elsevier, London.

Hellawell, J. M. (1988). "River regulation and nature conservation", *Regulated Rivers: Research and Management*, **2**, 425–443.

Headworth, H. G. (1989). "Contamination of groundwaters from diffuse sources arising from farming activities", *Journal of the Institution of Water and Environmental Management*, **3**, 517–521.

Hemphill, R. W., and Bramley, M. E. (1989). *Protection Of River and Canal Banks: A Guide To Selection and Design*, Butterworths, London.

Hickin, E. J. (1983). "River channel changes: retrospect and prospect", *Special Publications of the International Association of Sedimentology*, **6**, 61–83.

Hobbs, R. J., Saunders, D. A., and Hussey, B. M. T. (1990). "Nature conservation—the role of corridors", *Ambio*, **19**, 94–95.

Holmes, N. T. H. (1983). "Typing British rivers according to their flora", *Focus on Nature Conservation*, **4**, Nature Conservancy Council, London.

Holmes, N. T. H., and Newbold, C. (1984). "River plant communities—reflectors of water and substrate chemistry", *Focus on Nature Conservation*, **9**, Nature Conservancy Council, Shrewsbury.

House of Lords (1989). *Nitrate In Water*, Select Committee on European Communities, 16th Report, HMSO, London.

Howarth, W. (1988). *Water Pollution Law*, Shaw and Sons, London.

Howarth, W. (1990). *The Law Of The National Rivers Authority*, NRA/Centre for Law in Rural Areas, Aberystwyth.

Howe, G. M. (1972). *Man, Environment and Disease In Britain: A Medical Geography*, Penguin Books, Harmondsworth.

Lewin, J., Macklin, M. G., and Newson, M. D. (1988). "Regime theory and environmental change—irreconcilable concepts?" in *International Conference on River Regime* (Ed. W. R. White), pp. 431–445, John Wiley, Chichester.

Lewis, G., and Williams, G. (1984). *Rivers and Wildlife Handbook*, RSPB/RSNC, Sandy, Bedfordshire.

Macrory, R. (1989). *Water Act 1989. Text and Commentary*. Sweet and Maxwell, London.

Maitland, P. S., Newson, M. D., and Best, G. A. (1990). "The impact of afforestation and forestry practice on freshwater habitats", *Focus on Nature Conservation*, **23**, Nature Conservancy Council, Peterborough.

Marsh, G. P. (1864 (1965)). *Man and Nature*, Harvard University Press.

McNeely, J. A., and Pitt, D. (Eds) (1984). *Culture and Conservation: The Human Dimension in Environmental Planning*, Croom Helm, London.

Ministry of Agriculture, Fisheries and Food (1988a). *Conservation Guidelines For Drainage Authorities*, HMSO, London.

Ministry of Agriculture, Fisheries and Food (1988b). Land drainage. The Land Drainage Improvement Works (Assessment Of Environmental Effects) Regulations 1988. *Statutory Instruments* 1217, HMSO, London.

MAFF/DoE (1990). "Water, England and Wales, Agriculture. The Nitrate Sensitive Areas (Designation) Order 1990", *Statutory Instruments* 1013, HMSO, London.

Ministry of Health (1948). *Report Of The Gathering Grounds Committee*, HMSO, London.

Nature Conservancy Council (1984). *Nature Conservation In Britain*, Shrewsbury.

Nature Conservancy Council (1989). *Guidelines For The Selection Of Biological SSSIs*, Peterborough.

Newbold, C., Purseglove, J., and Holmes, N. T. H. (1983). *Nature Conservation and River Engineering*, Nature Conservancy Council, Peterborough.

Newson, M. D. (1986). "River basin engineering—fluvial geomorphology", *Journal of the Institution of Water Engineers and Scientists*, **40**, 307–324.

Newson, M. D. (1989). "Conservation management of peatlands and the drainage threat: hydrology, politics and the ecologist in the UK", in *Peatland Ecosystems and Man: An Impact Assessment* (Ed. P. Hulme), International Peat Society/British Ecological Society.

Newson, M. D. (1990). "Forestry and water—'good practice' and UK catchment policy", *Land Use Policy*, **7**, 53–58.

Newson, M. D. (1991). "Catchment control and planning: emerging patterns of definition, policy and legislation in UK water management", *Land Use Policy*, **8**, 9–15.

Newson, M. D., and Calder, I. R. (1989). "Forests and water resources: problems of prediction on a regional scale", *Philosophical Transactions of the Royal Society of London*, **B324**, 283–298.

Newson, M. D., and Lewin, J. (1991). "Climatic change, river flow extremes and fluvial erosion—scenarios for England and Wales", *Progress in Physical Geography*, **15**, 1–17.

Patrick, D. M., Smith, L. M., and Whitten, C. B. (1982). "Methods for studying accelerated fluvial change", in *Gravel Bed Rivers* (Eds R. D. Hey, J. C. Bathurst, and C. R. Thorne), pp. 783–815, John Wiley, Chichester.

Petts, G. E. (1984). *Impounded Rivers*, John Wiley, Chichester.

Pinay, G., and Décamps, H. (1988). "The role of riparian woods in regulating nitrogen fluxes between the alluvial aquifer and surface water: a conceptual model", *Regulated Rivers: Research and Management*, **2**, 507–516.

Purseglove, J. (1988). *Taming The Flood*, Oxford University Press, Oxford.

Ratcliffe, D. (Ed.) (1977). *A Nature Conservation Review*, Cambridge University Press, Cambridge.

Smith, I., and Lyle, A. (1979). *Distribution Of Freshwaters In Great Britain*, Institute of Terrestrial Ecology, Edinburgh.

Tanner, T. (Ed.) (1987). *Aldo Leopold: The Man and His Legacy*, Soil Conservation Society of America, Iowa.

Ward, R. C., and Robinson, M. (1990). *Principles Of Hydrology*, 3rd edn, McGraw-Hill, Maidenhead.

Water Space Amenity Commission (1983). *Conservation and Land Drainage Guidelines*, London.

25

Catchment Planning: The Way Forward for River Protection in the UK

J. L. GARDINER

National Rivers Authority, Thames Region, Kings Meadow House, Kings Meadow Road, Reading, Berkshire RG1 8DQ, UK

and

L. COLE

Land Use Consultants, 41 Chalton Street, London NW1 1JB

INTRODUCTION

There are many roads of logic that lead to the concept of strategic planning for river catchments. In England and Wales the combination of new legislation (the Water Act 1989) and two drought summers in southern and eastern England (1989 and 1990) have focused public attention on water; particularly water quality and quantity. However, to be effective and sustainable, the environmental protection of water implies not only pollution control but more particularly protection of its total physical environment.

It can be argued that the basis for physical or morphological protection lies in land-use designation (as embodied in English planning legislation), without which no amount of law will avail against indiscriminate use and pollution of land and groundwater. In spite of (or because of) the political role of rivers as natural boundaries, historical accident has done much to destroy rivers and their immediate surrounds. Those with powers to control land use have not been charged with the proper care of rivers (even today, some local authorities in the UK claim to have no responsibility for flood defence), and those who are now sizing up their task as custodians of the water environment recognize both the burden of their inheritance and the inadequacy of their powers in isolation.

With the passing of the Water Act 1989, protection of the water environment has entered a new era; the National Rivers Authority (NRA) has been created as the guardian of the total water environment with a duty under Section 8 of the Act to "further" and "promote the conservation and enhancement of natural beauty and the conservation of flora, fauna and geological or physiographical features of special interest". To fulfil this role the NRA has to meet three fundamental challenges. First, it

River Conservation and Management. Edited by P. J. Boon, P. Calow, and G. E. Petts
© 1992 John Wiley & Sons Ltd

must minimize the environmental impact of its own proposals, primarily in the field of flood defence. Second, it must exercise effective influence over land use. Since World War II, the rapid increase in the use of structural controls in flood defence has made it hard for experienced land drainage engineers to accept that levels of service in flood defence can be best maintained through planning and development control rather than through traditional engineering means. Not only is this method usually better for the environment and more acceptable socially, it can also be far more cost-effective in terms of public investment in both capital works and subsequent channel maintenance—which has been shown to increase as a result of channelization works (Countryside Commission, 1987).

The third challenge offered by the Water Act is for the NRA to promote the direct enhancement of the river environment. In the past, Water Authorities were only required to consider conservation and enhancement when undertaking specific river works, such as river maintenance or flood works. Under the Act, however, the duty to conserve and enhance is untied from all other specific functions. In other words, river enhancements can be carried out in their own right.

With these three challenges in mind, this chapter seeks to outline how catchment and land-use planning can help conserve and enhance the river corridor. But the first question to address is "what is a river corridor"?

A DEFINITION OF RIVER CORRIDORS

A river corridor can be said to comprise a river and adjacent land having an existing or potential value related to the presence of the river. This value will include consideration of recreation, amenity, and nature conservation, among other things.

In engineering terms, a river corridor should perhaps be defined by the 1:100-year floodplain. This can be assessed synthetically by modelling, but in reality would normally only apply to relatively natural rivers in rural areas. A different definition is needed in urban areas, and should be understandable and acceptable to all interested parties.

Clearly, in urban areas one is forced to work within the existing development pattern. However, it can be argued that the basic minimum to be designated as river corridor should be the area of land required for the river to achieve a natural meandering course with associated riparian habitats. This minimum corridor should be designated even if at present it is completely developed, on the basis that future re-development would be obliged to recognize restoration of the river corridor as a conservation principle. Where the river has been straightjacketed as a concrete-lined channel, this minimum corridor could be equivalent to a strip either side of the existing channel, with the width (e.g. a minimum of 50 m) determined by a morphological assessment of the likely meandering pattern of the river unconstrained by concrete. Superimposed on this basic minimum would be a series of objectives which seek to reflect local circumstances:

(1) To retain open land protected by Green Belt or other designations;
(2) To conserve water-table dependent habitats;
(3) To protect open land for flood storage.

By combining these objectives and superimposing them on the basic minimum, a "beaded" river corridor is defined, with a minimum 100 m-wide thread, complemented by beads of open land conserved in accordance with different objectives. These objectives may well dictate an extension of green space beyond either the recognized or morphological floodplain.

THE IMPORTANCE OF RIVER CORRIDORS IN STRATEGIC PLANNING

The aim of promoting the concept of river corridors must be twofold: first, to ensure the protection of their existing value and, second, to provide an incentive to re-form the natural river environment where it has been destroyed by development and/or river works, and where at present the continuity of the natural river corridor has been broken.

Studies have shown that there is a very high correlation between the river corridors of south-east England and existing environmental designations; notably, Sites of Special Scientific Interest (SSSIs), Areas of Outstanding Natural Beauty (AONBs), and Environmentally Sensitive Areas (ESAs). This is perhaps hardly surprising, considering the profound effect that rivers have had in shaping the character of the English landscape and our perception of it. This suggests that river corridors warrant their own statutory designation in recognition of the overriding influence which they have had in creating the value which is only reflected at present in a series of disparate, isolated designations. In other words, current designations fail to recognize rivers as the creative force and single element which frequently binds these high-value designations together. In many circumstances, if the river were to disappear the associated value would be all but lost and the existing statutory designations would no longer be valid. In a few instances in England the entire river from source to mouth is of sufficiently high nature conservation importance to merit notification as an SSSI; for example, the Blythe in Worcestershire, the Itchen in Hampshire, and the Avon in Wiltshire. However, the more usual circumstance these days is to find rivers which have sections that retain a high nature conservation value caught between highly manipulated reaches that have been largely stripped of interest. In these situations the tendency is to recognize the points of specific interest but to ignore the conservation potential of intervening sections. The challenge, therefore, is to recognize that the entire river corridor has existing or potential conservation interest and should be treated as a single unit subject to strict development control with a presumption in favour of conservation, restoration, and public access.

This firm step towards allocation of land use may sound dramatic, but in reality it reflects and supports a growing trend, and can be seen as an insurance policy to facilitate the good work already undertaken by partnerships or achieved in negotiations between the NRA, developers, local authorities and conservation bodies. The general message from developers is that they are quite happy to work within set criteria, but wish to have firm guidance rather than having to reconcile different views from the various authorities.

THREAT TO THE INTEGRITY OF RIVER CORRIDORS

The experience in the NRA Thames Region, particularly on London's rivers, can be regarded as symptomatic of the UK as a whole, if perhaps rather more extreme in some respects owing to the large population served. As such, lessons learned in the highly urbanized London catchments may be transferred to less developed catchments on the basis that "prevention is better than cure". The threats to the integrity of river corridors can be broadly divided into three groups.

Increased risk of flooding can be caused by:

- Loss of floodplain through development and land-raising associated with waste disposal and "agricultural improvements"
- Increased surface water run-off caused by urbanization throughout the catchment

Increased risk of pollution can be caused by:

- Agricultural intensification and afforestation
- Industrialization
- Sewage effluent
- Surface water run-off (from buildings, highways, airports, etc.)
- Lack of dilution because of low flows

Low flows in rivers and falling water tables are associated with:

- Increased abstraction
- Rationalization of sewage works leading to discharge of effluent either further down the catchment or in an entirely different catchment

In the past, the response to these threats has been to find ever more complex engineering solutions which have increasingly divorced rivers from their original natural character. Taking this process to its extreme, rivers may be relegated to open drains sized to cope with major flash floods but normally supporting nothing more than stagnant pools of sewage effluent held between banks of silt washed down by the last flash flood. The alternative to the engineering solution is to understand and respond to the relationship between rivers and their broader environmental context.

THE RELATIONSHIP BETWEEN RIVERS AND THEIR CATCHMENTS

A catchment can be defined as the area drained by a single surface-water system (a river, its tributaries, and related drainage) whose boundaries are defined by topography. This concept is understood by students of geography and hydrology but is all too frequently forgotten in strategic planning, partly because it is the rivers themselves, rather than their catchment boundaries, which have tended to be the physical features used to define local authority areas in the UK.

Rivers under greatest stress are those where development and land uses within the catchment have completely ignored their potential impact on the river system. This is exemplified by the philosophy of flood alleviation adopted by the Greater London Council (GLC) Public Health Department in relation to the River Ravensbourne. The assumption adopted by the GLC when designing its flood-alleviation schemes was that all sites identified for development in the Greater London Development Plan (GLDP) would be fully utilized and would not include any on-site storage of flood waters. To achieve this standard of service, engineering options were largely focused on channel widening and straightening (Cole, 1989). These works were designed to cope with a future 1 in 30-year flood in a fully developed catchment. However, on the Ravensbourne the design standard actually achieved for today's condition has been estimated to be more in the range of 1 in 50 to 1 in 500. The impact of these river works has been profound (London Wildlife Trust, 1985). Out of almost 70 km of total river channel on the Ravensbourne, only about 30% remains in a semi-natural condition, the rest having been canalized or culverted.

Realizing the unacceptability of this type of flood alleviation, Thames Water (now NRA Thames Region), who assumed responsibility for flood alleviation in the London area following the demise of the GLC, altered the design parameters for all the London rivers. In terms of scheme design, a maximum 10% increase in the currently developed area within the catchment has been assumed, rather than development of all areas allocated in the GLDP (LUC and LDP, 1989). The effect of this has been to reduce significantly the assumed rate of flood flows, thereby offering scope for a range of more sensitive engineering options. This example clearly shows the dependence of this approach on forward planning and development control.

THE ROLE OF RIVER CATCHMENT PLANNING

The fundamental aim of river catchment planning is to conserve, enhance, and, where appropriate, restore the total river environment through effective land and resource planning across the total catchment area. As such, it can be regarded as the taproot of sustainable development, a forward planning strategy to be fully integrated with traditional areas, such as transportation, housing, and minerals abstraction/waste disposal, dealt with by local planning authorities.

The purpose of catchment planning is, first and foremost, to understand the catchment in terms of:

• Surface water
• Groundwater
• Land uses and how these assist in either regulating or disrupting the water cycle

With this understanding, catchment planning should then allow clear decisions to be taken on:

• How to manage the existing situation
• How problems should be approached and solved in the future

Instead of relying on structural engineering solutions, catchment planning offers other solutions to river corridor management, not least:

• A change in land-use allocation within the catchment
• A change in permitted development and control of urban run-off within the catchment
• A change in emphasis from structural to non-structural forms of flood alleviation
• A pro-active approach to water quality and pollution control (e.g. using the cleaning effect of natural vegetation and controlling the time of travel of pollutants into the

river system with buffer strips, sacrificial channels and catch-pits integrated with flood-control requirements).

THE FUTURE OFFERED BY RIVER CATCHMENT PLANNING

In New Zealand the Catchment Boards and their equivalent of the UK County Councils have just merged into 14 Regional Councils based on river catchments, with a primary role in integrated, geographic resource management under the enabling Resource Management Bill. The purpose of this massive reorganization is to promote the sustainable management of natural and physical resources, enabling people to meet their present needs without compromising the needs of future generations. One of the principles is:

5(e) The maintenance of the natural, physical, and cultural features which give New Zealand its character, and the protection of them from inappropriate subdivision, use and development including:
(i)   The maintenance of the natural character of the coastal environment and the margins of lakes and rivers; and
(ii) The retention of natural landforms and vegetation; and
(iii) The recognition and protection of heritage values including historic places and waahi tapu (New Zealand Resource Management Bill, 1989)

In the UK such a combination of river catchment-based authorities is not a practicable possibility. However, the same objectives can still be achieved by the local authorities within a single catchment co-ordinating and mutually adopting common catchment plan policies as part of their statutory plans. These policies will have been drawn up by the NRA, in liaison with the local authorities, as part of the catchment plan for the area in question.

If catchment planning becomes an accepted concept throughout all forms of statutory planning, river corridors would then be conserved and restored by:

(1) Direct control over floodplain development and redevelopment;
(2) Development elsewhere in the catchment in sympathy with hydrological controls and the needs of the natural environment;
(3) Restoration of the river corridors themselves as basic natural and amenity resources.

As argued above, river corridor designations should be applied to both existing good river corridor environments requiring conservation and those where major works are required to re-create a river environment with natural river profiles and fringing and aquatic vegetation. In the latter case restoration will be achieved by steering and guiding redevelopment when it occurs within or directly adjacent to the designated corridor. Loss of river corridors has occurred over many years. It is unrealistic, therefore, to imagine that restoration will happen overnight, but it can be potentiated through the planning process, thus forming the backbone of "green chains" throughout urban areas and allowing continuity of wildlife ecosystems from source to sea.

THE THAMES APPROACH

It was to be expected that the highly developed symptoms of stress shown by the water environment in the Thames catchment would lead to calls for concerted action by the NRA. A major effort is needed to control pollution. Public concern, however, which has increased so markedly over the last decade, is directed not only at the apparent quality of the water in the river but also at the appearance (morphology) of the river corridor (House and Gardiner, in press).

Since the mid-1980s, the NRA Thames Region and its predecessor (Rivers Division of Thames Water) has undertaken an unprecedented number of major initiatives, such as studies of the Lower Colne (Gardiner, 1988), alleviation of low flows (Thames Water, 1988), the River Thames Strategic Flood Defence Initiative (Gardiner, 1990a), and dynamic modelling of the Thames from Lechlade to Southend, in all representing well over £100 million of capital investment. At the same time, it has had to deal with a spectacular increase in development—some 70% between 1986 and 1989. This activity has provided a unique opportunity to develop and test theory and methodology and has been condensed into a manual for river projects appraisal (Gardiner, 1991). At the same time, it has become clear that all these projects should have grown from river catchment plans. The recent environmental assessment legislation (MAFF/WO, 1988), together with the evolving concept of sustainable development (Brundtland, 1987), has led to the conclusion that river catchment planning, developed in partnership with local authorities, is the only way forward (Gardiner and Phillips, 1988).

NRA Thames Region, in liaison with local authorities, is now embarking on a programme for the production of catchment management plans for flood defence and the environment in all urban areas. In particular, the recent requirement for Metropolitan Local Authorities to prepare Unitary Development Plans has provided the NRA with the ideal opportunity to introduce a range of draft standard policies for inclusion in these new Statutory Local Plans. The response from local authorities has exceeded expectations; the readiness to join forces appears to flow from the NRA's investment in river modelling and environmental data to support planning decisions, and its desire to conserve river corridors as vital "environmental infrastructure".

The draft policies put forward so far fall broadly under the headings of floodplain protection, catchment planning, and river corridors, and include the following:

Floodplain protection
Policy 1: In the areas at risk from flooding (as defined on the floodplain map held by the NRA) there will be a general presumption against new development or the intensification of existing development.
Policy 2: Appropriate flood protection will generally be required where the redevelopment of existing developed areas is permitted in areas at risk from flooding. The flood-protection requirements for such redevelopments will be defined by the Council in consultation with the NRA.
Catchment planning
Policy 3: Planning permission will not normally be granted for new development of existing urban areas if such development could result in an increased flood risk in areas downstream due to additional surface water run-off. Consequently, the Council will

consult the NRA and adjacent boroughs prior to the granting of planning permission to assess the impact of any proposals on its area which appear likely to have significant surface water run-off consequences.

Policy 4: Where development is permitted which is likely to increase the risk of flooding, it must include appropriate attenuation measures defined by the Council in consultation with the NRA.

Policy 5: The Council will, in consultation with the NRA, seek to ensure that development proposals that require planning permission, and other land-use activities over which the Council has control or influence, do not cause adverse effects on the freshwater fisheries of the district/county/borough.

Policy 6: The Council will not permit any development with a requirement for the abstraction of water from a river, water table, aquifer, or other groundwater source which will have adverse effects on the flow of water to the detriment of water quality, wildlife and amenity.

River corridors

Policy 7: The Council, in consultation with the NRA, will seek to promote river corridors as important areas of open land both within the borough and, where relevant, across the borough boundary by:

(1) Conserving existing areas of value within river corridors and, wherever possible, seeking to restore and enhance the natural elements of the river environment;
(2) Supporting initiatives which will result in improvements to water quality;
(3) Where appropriate, promoting public access in river corridors; and
(4) Identifying appropriate locations for water-related recreation along river corridors.

Policy 8: The Council, in consultation with the NRA, will seek to ensure that all works in, under, over, and adjacent to watercourses are appropriately designed and implemented.

Policy 9: There will be a presumption against any development which will detrimentally affect the character of the district's rivers, river banks, or land in the immediate vicinity of a river, i.e. where the development impinges visually on the riverside landscape. The term "river" includes any adjoining marshland, or other related water feature.

Policy 10: There will be a general presumption against development which would adversely affect the integrity of the tidal defences.

Policy 11: Where development relating to the tidal defences is permitted, the Council will, in consultation with appropriate bodies including the NRA, require appropriate measures to be incorporated to protect the integrity of the defences.

All these policies are supported by reasons, as required of local authority planning. The general interest shown by local authorities in these policies was demonstrated by Chiltern District Council who put forward two of their own policies (Policies 6 and 9 above). In the case of Policy 6, further consideration is now leading to separate policies being formulated on water quality and water resources. It will be noted that the term "river corridors" has already been put forward in these draft policies; the exact definition most appropriate for planning purposes, however, will emerge from discussion—this chapter being a part of that discussion. Nevertheless, in the interim, local authorities are making reference to river corridors in their Unitary Plans. In some instances they have been included as part of a list of statutory and non-statutory designations which the Council is positively seeking to conserve and enhance. Overall, it is not considered appropriate (or possible) to try to perfect standard policies; they will be subject to change to fit local circumstances and as time moves on, but they will be regularly monitored when local authority plans are reviewed every four years or so.

CONCLUSION

The drive towards conservation and restoration of river corridors depends on the success of welding NRA objectives into statutory land-use planning and development control, and realizing them through rigorous monitoring and enforcement. This is provided for under Section 8 of the Water Act and other powers available to the NRA which may be complementary to those of local authorities (Gardiner, 1990b) such as bye-laws, which allow effective enforcement against infilling of the floodplain. It will also depend on developing an accepted methodology which includes environmental assessment of the existing river corridor and its potential, and contingent valuation (public willingness to pay) to justify expenditure on restoration works in the public interest but not part of a development proposal (Gardiner, 1990b); both are currently NRA research and development tasks.

Clearly, river catchment plans will provide a means of identifying, facilitating, and keeping under review potential changes to river corridors. It is to be hoped that rivers will no longer be put through ever more complex and artificial manipulations in response to adverse changes in the catchment. Instead, catchment land use should be planned to ensure the long-term conservation and enhancement of the river environment.

DISCLAIMER

The views expressed in this paper are those of the authors and are not necessarily shared by the National Rivers Authority.

REFERENCES

Brundtland, G. H. (1987). *Our Common Future*, Report of the World Commission on Environment and Development (Chairman: G.H. Brundtland), Oxford University Press, Oxford.
Cole, L. M. (1989). *The Future of Our Rivers: Enhancement or Degradation*, Unpublished centenary lecture presented to the Landscape Institute.
Countryside Commission (1987). *Changing River Landscapes*, CCP238, Countryside Commission, Cheltenham.
Gardiner, J. L. (1988). "Environmentally sound river engineering: examples from the Thames Catchment", *Regulated Rivers: Research and Management*, **1**, 171–184.
Gardiner, J. L. (1990a). "The River Thames Strategic Planning Initiative: Planning, a model influence", in *International Conference on River Flood Hydraulics* (Ed. W. R. White), John Wiley, Chichester.
Gardiner, J. L. (1990b). "River catchment planning for flood defence and the environment", *Journal of the Institution of Water and Environmental Management*, **4**, 442–450.
Gardiner, J. L. (Ed.) (1991). *River Projects and Conservation: A Manual for Holistic Appraisal*, John Wiley, Chichester.

Gardiner, J. L., and Phillips, S. (1988). "Planning for the river catchment", *Planning Magazine*, 798.

House, M. A., and Gardiner, J. L. (in press). "River catchment planning and public perception of river corridors for recreation and amenity: the UK scene", in *Proceedings of the International Symposium on Wetlands and River Corridor Management* (Ed. J. A. Kusler), Association of Wetland Managers, Berne, New York/Omni Press, Madison.

Land Use Consultants in association with Llewelyn-Davies Planning (1988). *Ravensbourne Catchment Planning and Environmental Assessment*, Unpublished report.

London Wildlife Trust (1985). *The Ravensbourne River System—a Survey Report*, London.

Ministry of Agriculture, Fisheries and Food/Welsh Office (1988). *The Land Drainage Improvement Works (Assessment of Environmental Effects) Regulations 1988. Statutory Instrument 1217*, HMSO, London.

Thames Water (1988). *Study of Alleviation of Low River Flows Resulting from Groundwater Abstraction*, Main report (unpublished).

26

Conservation of Rivers in Scotland: Legislative and Organizational Limitations

A. E. BROWN

Nature Conservancy Council for England, Northminster House, Peterborough PE1 1UA, UK

and

D. L. HOWELL

Research and Development, Nature Conservancy Council for Scotland, 2/5 Anderson Place, Edinburgh EH6 5NP, UK

INTRODUCTION

Conserving the wildlife resources of rivers poses some particularly difficult problems because of the dynamic nature of the habitat and the often diverse range of land uses within catchments. Rivers are also exploited in a number of ways, and perhaps the foremost of these in industrialized countries is their use as a disposal route for diluting, dispersing, and degrading waste products.

The basic aims, methods, successes, and failures of nature conservation in Britain are outlined in *Nature Conservation in Great Britain* (Nature Conservancy Council, 1984). The cornerstone of nature conservation in Britain has been, and continues to be, the protection of all major natural and semi-natural habitat types and their associated flora and fauna, through the acquisition and designation of nature reserves and a variety of other site-protection mechanisms. However, it is recognized that in many areas, only a small proportion of the total resources of nature can be protected in this way. Legislation protects 790 000 ha of Scotland (10% of the total area) for the purposes of nature conservation (Nature Conservancy Council data, unpublished), but wildlife in the 90% of Scotland outside protected areas also needs to be safeguarded.

The conservation of wildlife is dependent on the maintenance of appropriate physical and chemical conditions. In Scotland, some of the factors that affect these conditions in rivers are controlled, or are capable of control, by government organizations and agencies, while others are not (Figure 26.1). This chapter focuses on those factors over

River Conservation and Management. Edited by P. J. Boon, P. Calow, and G. E. Petts
© 1992 John Wiley & Sons Ltd

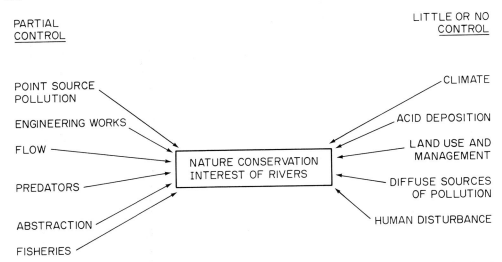

FIGURE 26.1. Some factors affecting the nature conservation interest of rivers in Scotland (adapted from Edwards and Howell, 1989)

which a degree of control is currently possible and explores the ways in which the present organizational and legislative framework limits the extent to which nature conservation interests are served.

In order to simplify a complex topic, only four main aspects are considered: pollution control, abstraction and compensation flows, fisheries, and nature conservation. The chapter is confined to Scotland because there are complex differences in these aspects between Scotland and the rest of Britain.

SCOTTISH RIVER RESOURCES

In Britain standing and running waters cover only 1% of the land area, but throughout much of northern and western Scotland this coverage rises to 5% (Smith and Lyle, 1979) and in some areas such as the Western Isles it is as high as 10% (Waterston et al, 1979). Because of this dense coverage, Scotland contains a high proportion of the freshwater resource of Britain.

Smith and Lyle (1979) estimated from a detailed map study that there are 6628 river systems in Scotland. The geology and geomorphology result in many short rivers (e.g. less than 30 km long) in the west which often descend rapidly to the sea. In the east there are a smaller number of large meandering rivers. Acidic, poorly buffered water predominates in the upper catchments, and lower reaches reflect the nutrient loadings arising from different rock types and land uses.

Sporting interests, tourist authorities, and, to some extent, politicians all promote an image of Scotland's rivers as clear, natural systems of high water quality and high wildlife interest, set in a dramatic and wild landscape. In many areas this is broadly true, but Scottish rivers also suffer from the problems experienced elsewhere in Britain such as pollution from agriculture and sewage (Nature Conservancy Council, 1989a). A number

TABLE 26.1. Water quality classification scheme used in Scotland

Class 1	Rivers unpolluted or recovered from pollution Lengths of river: (a) where the water is clear and which are known to have received no significant polluting discharges; or (b) which, though receiving some pollution, have a BOD normally less than 3 mg l^{-1}, are well oxygenated and are known to have received no significant discharges of toxic materials or of suspended matter which affects the river bed.
Class 2	Rivers of fairly good quality Lengths of river: (a) not in Class 1 on BOD grounds; or (b) which may have a substantially reduced oxygen content; or (c) irrespective of BOD, which are known to have received polluting discharges, possibly containing toxic substances, which cannot be shown either to affect fish or to have been removed by natural processes.
Class 3	Rivers of poor quality Lengths of river: (a) not in Class 4 on BOD grounds; or (b) which may have a dissolved oxygen saturation, below 50% for considerable periods; or (c) containing substances which are suspected of reaching toxic concentrations at times.
Class 4	Grossly polluted rivers Lengths of river: (a) which have an offensive appearance or smell; or (b) which have a BOD of 12 mg l^{-1} or more under normal conditions; or (c) which are completely de-oxygenated at any time; or (d) which contain substances known to reach toxic concentrations at times; or (e) which are known to be incapable of supporting fish life.

of other problems are particularly widespread in Scotland, notably the effects of acidification (UK Acid Waters Review Group, 1988), afforestation and forestry practice (Maitland et al, 1990), fish farming (Institute of Aquaculture et al, 1990) and channel modification, flow control, and catchment transfers as part of the hydro-electricity industry (Hellawell, 1988; Johnson, 1988).

In Scotland a simple water quality classification system has been in use since 1974 (Table 26.1). Using this classification, a comparison of water quality between 1974 and 1985 is possible (Table 26.2). This shows that some deterioration in quality took place between 1974 and 1980, during a period when both private and public expenditure were severely curtailed (Mackay, 1988). However, by 1985, 95.3% of Scottish rivers were classified as Class 1 (Scottish Development Department, 1987) and it is clear that overall there has been a reduction in the lengths of rivers in lower classes. Much of this improvement in the poorest-quality rivers has been achieved in stretches that pass through urban areas (see e.g. Hammerton, 1986) and this progress is largely due to the

TABLE 26.2. Quality of fresh waters in Scotland 1974–1985

Year	Class 1 Length (km)	%	Class 2 Length (km)	%	Class 3 Length (km)	%	Class 4 Length (km)	%
1974	45 503.1	94.8	1852.7	3.9	422.4	0.9	204.7	0.4
1980	45 359.8	94.5	2126.4	4.4	296.9	0.6	199.8	0.4
1985	45 712.4	95.3	1821.7	3.8	283.4	0.6	167.1	0.3
Change 1974/1985	+209.3	+0.5	−31.0	−0.1	−139.0	−0.3	−37.6	−0.1

Data from Scottish Development Department (1976, 1983, 1987)

success of the pollution-control authorities in securing reductions in pollution from sewage works and heavy industry.

These data, however, mask several aspects that are of concern from a nature conservation viewpoint. First, the classification system does allow significant changes in water chemistry to occur—which can have substantial effects on flora and fauna—before a river slips from Class 1 to Class 2. Second, the methods for the survey and the classification were designed and implemented with particular reference to point sources of pollution, so the classification does not easily detect changes arising from diffuse sources of pollution, although these changes can seriously damage river habitats and wildlife (Nature Conservancy Council, 1989a).

The 1974 and 1980 surveys (Scottish Development Department, 1976, 1983) included data on river invertebrates, but this was difficult to present in a suitable summarized format. The 1990 survey is using a new biological classification system ("RIVPACS"), developed by the Institute of Freshwater Ecology, which should enable a clear, easily assimilated summary of the biological condition of rivers in Scotland to be produced.

Nonetheless, many Scottish rivers do retain considerable wildlife interest which has been described by many authors (e.g. Maitland, 1966; Berry and Johnston, 1980; Berry, 1985; Jenkins, 1985; Charter, 1988; Badenoch, 1989) and which is considered to be of national and, in certain aspects, international importance (Nature Conservancy Council, 1990).

PRINCIPAL ORGANIZATIONS AND LEGISLATION

At an international level the European Community has a significant effect on British environmental legislation through the adoption of Directives, which may cover many subjects including water quality, waste disposal, chemical emissions, wildlife protection, and countryside management. A thorough account of the Directives and their effect on UK legislation and practice is provided by Haigh (1989).

In Scotland, regulatory responsibility for rivers is divided between a number of different departments and agencies (Figure 26.2) which have complex working arrangements with central government and with each other. They also operate at very different geographical scales.

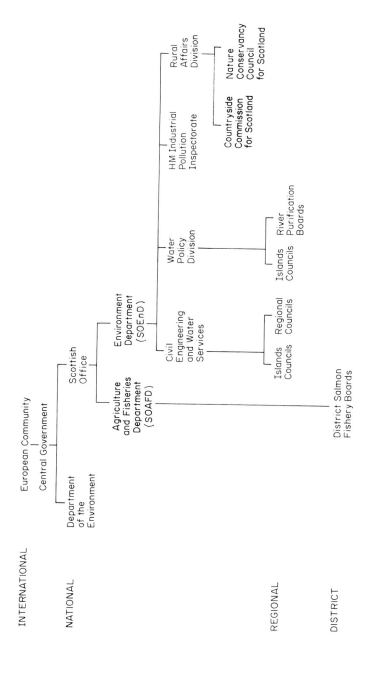

FIGURE 26.2. Principal government organizations involved with rivers in Scotland

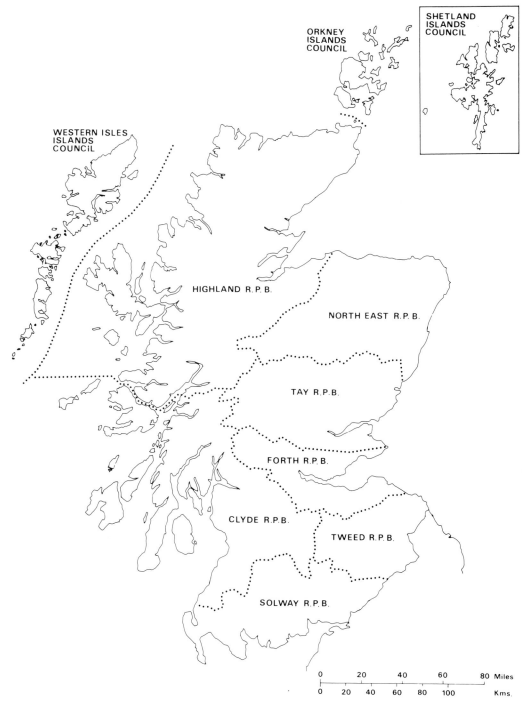

FIGURE 26.3. The Scottish river purification authorities: River Purification Boards (RPBs) and
Islands Councils

The Scottish Office is responsible for most of the policy issues on environmental protection, land use, and development that affect rivers. Within the Scottish Office there are a number of departments and divisions, each responsible for different policy areas. Of particular note is the Water Policy Division of the Environment Department (SOEnD), to which the seven River Purification Boards and three Islands Councils (collectively known as the River Purification Authorities) report. These authorities (Figure 26.3) are responsible for water pollution control in Scotland; the nine Regional Councils and the Islands Councils are responsible for water supply and sewerage. Following the reorganization of the Nature Conservancy Council (see p. 419), advice on nature conservation in Scotland is now provided by the Nature Conservancy Council for Scotland, which reports to the Rural Affairs Division of SOEnD. The main areas of responsibility of government organizations and the principal items of legislation involved are summarized in Table 26.3.

LEGISLATION AND ORGANIZATION

Pollution control

During the reorganization of local government in Scotland in the 1970s it was recognized that there was an advantage in ensuring that the pollution-control functions of the River Purification Boards were kept separate from the sewage-disposal functions of the Regional Councils. Seven new Boards were thus established covering the whole of Scotland except for the Western Isles, Orkney, and Shetland.

Each of the Boards has an appointed board of management, which is essentially a policy-making body. The Boards have one-third of their members representing Regional Councils (often drawn mostly from the water and sewerage committees), one-third representing District Councils, and one-third appointed by the Secretary of State for Scotland. Biologists, chemists, hydrologists, microbiologists, and pollution inspectors are employed to provide the technical support required to fulfil the Boards' pollution-control duties.

Discharge of polluting matter to rivers and other waters is illegal unless it is within the terms of a consent issued by the local Board or Islands Council. The data presented in Table 26.4 illustrate recent variations in compliance performance of discharges consented by the seven Boards. Where consented discharges fail to meet the necessary standards, most Boards adopt a policy of persuasion rather than prosecution in attempting to improve compliance. Indeed, examination of the Boards' annual reports indicates that most prosecutions are for *unconsented* discharges (e.g. spillages and leaks); it is less common for a prosecution to involve failure to comply with a discharge consent.

Where effluents fail to meet consent conditions, the Boards' annual reports often given little indication of either the margin of failure or the severity of any resulting environmental impacts. The Boards also define compliance in a variety of ways, although a standardized approach would make comparisons easier. It is therefore difficult to draw detailed conclusions from the data in Table 26.4, but they do suggest that the "persuasion" philosophy is meeting with mixed success in terms of improving compliance with discharge consent conditions. Unfortunately, Boards may often be reluctant to take legal proceedings because of the costs and staff time involved and the occasional difficulties in

TABLE 26.3. The main government organizations, areas of responsibility, and legislation in Scotland

Topic	Organizations involved	Responsibilities	Principal legislation
Pollution control	Scottish Office Environment Department (Water Policy Division)	Policy on use of water resources, disposal of effluents, protection and monitoring of water quality	Rivers (Prevention of Pollution) (Scotland) Act 1951 Control of Pollution Act 1974 (as amended by the Water Act 1989)
	River Purification Authorities (seven River Purification Boards and three Islands Councils)	Prevention of pollution, control of discharges, monitoring	Control of Pollution Act 1974 (as amended by the Water Act 1989)
	Scottish Office Agriculture and Fisheries Department	Advice and assistance to agriculture on avoiding pollution	Agriculture Act 1986
Abstraction and compensation flows	Landowners	Right to abstract	Common Law
	River Purification Authorities	Partial control over agricultural abstraction	Spray Irrigation (Scotland) Act 1964
	Regional Councils	Provide compensation flows from water supply reservoirs	Water (Scotland) Act 1980

	Hydro-electricity generating companies	Provide compensation flows from impoundments	Electricity (Scotland) Act 1979 Electricity Act 1989
Fisheries	Scottish Office Agriculture and Fisheries Department	Advice on fisheries management (especially economically important species); control of fish diseases	Diseases of Fish Acts 1937, 1983
	District Salmon Fishery Boards	Management of salmon and sea trout fisheries	Salmon Fisheries (Scotland) Acts 1862, 1868 Salmon Act 1986
Nature conservation	Nature Conservancy Council for Scotland	Protection of wildlife, advice and dissemination of knowledge, research	Wildlife and Countryside Act 1981
	All government departments	Required to have regard to nature conservation in the exercise of their functions	Countryside (Scotland) Act 1967

TABLE 26.4. Percentage compliance of discharges with River Purification Board (RPB) consent conditions, 1985–1989

RPB	1985	1986	1987	1988	1989
Sewage effluent					
Clyde	65	57*	56*	56*	60*
Forth	40*	48*	45*	60*	N/A
Highland	67	58	70	N/A	N/A
North East	68	58	65	65	62
Solway	66	66	69	79	75
Tay	61	50	53	67	57
Tweed	61	64	52	59	63
Trade effluent					
Clyde	54	45*	52*	51*	56
Forth	43*	40*	47*	60*	N/A
Highland	76	67	71	N/A	N/A
North East	55	59	72	73	72
Solway	62	48	30	69	65
Tay	30	32	57	58	59
Tweed	55	55	64	66	83

Notes: (1) Percentages are calculated from the number of *samples* complying with consent conditions, except where marked '*', which denotes a percentage calculated from the number of *discharges* complying. Borderline samples are excluded from the definition of compliance, with the exception of the Solway and Forth RPB data from 1988 onwards
(2) N/A—data not presented, or annual report not available at time of writing
(3) Data presented are for discharges to tidal *and* inland waters, since in most cases the statistics provided by the Boards do not distinguish between the two

Source: River Purification Board annual reports

persuading the Procurator Fiscal (who prepares and conducts prosecutions) of the strength of their case (D. Hammerton, pers. comm.). Demonstration of a failure to comply with consent will usually also require supporting evidence of significant environmental damage if a prosecution is to be successful.

The Boards set their budgets and then requisition their expenditure from the Regional Councils which lie within the Boards' areas. The Regional Councils meet these costs through revenue from the local taxation system and from central government grant support. Finding adequate resources in this way can pose particular problems for the Boards when the expenditure of local authorities is under tight constraints.

In October 1988 the Scottish Office embarked on a policy review of the River Purification Boards. The review was to examine the Boards' functions, resources, and relationships with the Scottish Office, their geographical organization and the composition of their management. This exercise provides the Scottish Office with the opportunity to examine some of the issues raised above, and the review team's findings were reported recently (Scottish Development Department, 1990).

The report largely endorses the *status quo*, although a number of changes are suggested. These include a proposal to alter the composition of the Boards' management, so that Secretary of State appointees would constitute 50% of the board personnel, with Regional and District Councils each contributing 25%. This would enable a wider range of interests to be represented than is possible under the present system, particularly in the smaller Boards. One other proposal of particular interest relates to funding arrangements, and suggests that Boards should be able to charge polluters for the costs involved in issuing discharge consents and monitoring compliance with consent conditions. This proposal would provide an additional source of funding for the Boards and is in accordance with the "polluter pays" principle.

At the time of writing, the review team's report had been sent out to interested parties for consultation, but it seems unlikely that the review will result directly in more integration of pollution control with other aspects of water resource management in Scotland. The review team acknowledge in their report that this would require a more substantial and wide-ranging study than the current exercise.

In the outer islands (Shetland, Orkney, and the Western Isles) the separation of pollution control and sewage-disposal functions was considered unnecessary because of the low population densities and generally good water quality. Although they have the same pollution control responsibilities as the River Purification Boards, at the time of writing, the Islands Councils do not directly employ chemists, biologists, or hydrologists in discharging these duties. Instead, they are largely dependent on contracting advice and services from other local authority departments, the mainland Boards, and private laboratories.

The Scottish Office five-yearly water quality surveys do not refer to the outer islands, and the Islands Councils are not required to publish annual reports on their pollution-control activities. Thus it is difficult to obtain information on water quality, pollution incidents, complaints, and consents or to make any comparisons with the mainland Boards, who are required to produce annual reports.

Several authors have drawn attention to the high nature conservation interest of fresh waters on the Scottish islands (Darling and Boyd, 1964; Berry and Johnston, 1980; Berry, 1985). To maintain this interest it is essential that the Islands Councils have the resources necessary to protect water quality and that they are able to respond immediately to water-pollution incidents.

Compensation flows and abstraction

Maintaining the nature conservation interest of rivers requires, among other things, a discharge regime which is as unmodified by human activity as possible. The effects of river regulation, including abstraction and compensation flows, have been reviewed in Petts and Wood (1988). In Scotland, disruption of natural flows is considerable and illustrates major deficiencies in the scope and implementation of legislation.

There are over 100 reservoirs in Scotland, the majority of which were built between 1850 and 1950, for the purposes of potable water supply and hydro-electricity generation. Gustard et al (1987) provided a historical review of compensation flows and surveyed reservoir releases throughout the British Isles. They concluded that the majority of reservoirs were releasing the same compensation flows as when the reservoir was first impounded and that these flows were determined by industrial and political factors that no longer apply. Furthermore, the majority of flows were set when there was little or no hydrometric data available and little knowledge of the impact of impoundments on downstream flora and fauna.

Powers are available to the Secretary of State for Scotland to modify compensation provisions by Order under the Water (Scotland) Act 1980, and the authors consider that all current releases should be reviewed, particularly those from the older reservoirs. This should enable compensation flows to be set at a level more appropriate to the requirements of nature conservation and other relevant interests.

The situation regarding abstraction is of serious concern to environmental bodies, as neither the Secretary of State for Scotland nor the River Purification Authorities have any powers over private rights to abstract water. These rights are covered by common law. As the River Purification Authorities set discharge consents on the basis of available dilution they are faced with an entirely unsatisfactory position: they can control the amount of polluting matter entering a river, but not the amount of water flowing in the channel to dilute and disperse the pollution. Even in unpolluted waters, excessive abstraction can lead to deoxygenation and, ultimately, drying of the river bed (Tay River Purification Board, 1989).

The limited control over agricultural abstraction is confined to spray irrigation, and obtaining an Order under the Spray Irrigation (Scotland) Act 1964 is a complex and time-consuming exercise. In the case of the Order for the West Peffer Burn in East Lothian, the Forth River Purification Board submitted the draft application to the Scottish Development Department in March 1967 but the Order was not granted until November 1973 (Scottish River Purification Boards' Association, 1987). Even allowing for the fact that this was the first Order and that an application for an Order might now only take a year (Sargent, pers. comm.), this may still be too long when the need to control the abstraction may be immediate.

Irrespective of the length of time taken to obtain an Order, there appear to be other difficulties. For example, the development of mobile hose-reel irrigation equipment renders the fixed Orders of the Act inflexible and inadequate (Tay River Purification Board, 1989). The same Board also points out that some agricultural sectors, such as potato growers, rent fields over wide areas, and even if an Order is obtained for a particular catchment they can move production elsewhere and hence transfer the abstraction problem beyond the catchment affected by the Order.

The Scottish River Purification Boards' Association (1987) called for a licensing system for *all* significant abstractions (i.e. not just those for spray irrigation). If fully implemented, such a system would undoubtedly improve the protection of wildlife in the affected rivers.

Fisheries

Fisheries legislation in Scotland is particularly complex, with many Acts dating as far back as the 1800s. Because of the social and economic importance of salmon and trout, much of the legislation refers to these species and little relates to the other fish species that are present.

In recent years concern has grown (e.g. Maitland, 1987, 1989) over the introduction of non-native fish, including farmed fish, into rivers because of the potential for competition with native species, impacts on genetic diversity, and the introduction of fish pathogens.

Where natural populations exist, the introduction of non-native fish species (or fish of non-indigenous stocks) will reduce the nature conservation value of the existing populations. Yet, in the last 200 years, 13 species of fish have been added to the Scottish fauna and many of these are likely to have been the result of deliberate, uncontrolled introductions (Maitland, 1987).

The Scottish Office Agriculture and Fisheries Department (SOAFD) concentrates its freshwater fisheries effort on the economically important species (i.e. salmon and trout). Given the recent spread of non-native fish species, the increase in recreational coarse fishing, and the possible growth in commercial exploitation of species such as eels and arctic charr, it is important that SOAFD broadens its research and advisory activities to ensure that these new developments do not damage existing riverine fish communities.

Management of river fisheries is primarily the responsibility of the District Salmon Fishery Boards, but their remit only extends to salmon and sea trout. Boards have control over the release of these species into their rivers but some parts of Scotland are not covered by the Boards, so in these areas (e.g. the Loch Lomond catchment) there is no control over such releases. The Boards are composed of fishery proprietors along the river, so they have access to a wealth of local knowledge, although in the past they have rarely had the benefit of locally based scientific advice and support (but see below). Their responsibility only for salmon and sea trout also means that the management and conservation of other fish species may be neglected, and they have no powers to prevent introduction of fish not native to their rivers, or even to Scotland (Maitland, 1987).

In order to achieve a more balanced approach to the conservation of salmonid and other fish, a major review of fishery management legislation and practice is required. Control over the introduction of non-native species should be strengthened and the funding, structure, coverage, and responsibilities of the District Salmon Fishery Boards should be examined. Some of these aspects were discussed in detail 25 years ago by the Hunter Committee (Anon, 1965), which was established to review salmon and trout legislation in Scotland. Few of the Committee's recommendations were implemented, but many of them still merit serious consideration.

Nature conservation

In order to balance the foregoing discussion of other organizations and the legislation under which they operate, it is important to consider these aspects directly in relation to nature conservation. Until recently, nature conservation advice in Scotland was provided by the Nature Conservancy Council (NCC), an organization covering the whole of Britain and reporting directly to the Department of the Environment in London (see Figure 26.2). However, recent legislation divided the NCC into three separate country agencies: the Scottish successor agency is the Nature Conservancy Council for Scotland (NCCS), which is 1992 will merge with the Countryside Commission for Scotland (which provides advice on landscape issues and informal countryside recreation). This reorganization of resources in Scotland provides an opportunity to examine how the conservation of rivers can best be carried forward by the new Scottish agency working in association with central government, statutory authorities, and the wider population in Scotland.

Much of the activity of the NCCS centres on the protection of the most valuable sites, designated as Sites of Special Scientific Interest (SSSIs) under the Wildlife and Countriside Act 1981. Only land which is of "special interest" may be notified, and in most cases this excludes notifying the catchment areas of rivers (see Nature Conservancy Council, 1989b for river SSSI selection criteria). Anyone with a legal interest in the river has to be served with the notification papers, and they are then required to consult the NCCS before undertaking any operations that are identified as being potentially damaging. These requirements place a considerable burden on the NCCS to find all the people with legal interests, to discuss the details with them, and then to deal effectively with all the subsequent consultations.

The resources required to notify rivers as SSSIs, together with some concern over the effectiveness of the designation for rivers, have restricted the number actually notified. In addition, more habitat information is undoubtedly required if fresh waters (and rivers in particular) are to feature more strongly in the Scottish SSSI complement, and there are several NCCS-funded surveys and research projects in progress which should begin to fill some of the gaps in our knowledge of natural freshwater communities in Scotland. Information on upland rivers (e.g. those at altitudes greater than 750 m) is particularly scarce, although some headwater catchments receive "incidental" protection through their location within the boundaries of large terrestrial upland SSSIs.

Of the estimated 6628 river systems in Scotland (Smith and Lyle, 1979), only 16 have been notified specifically because of their riverine interest. The last water quality survey of Scotland (Scottish Development Department, 1987) examined nearly 48 000 km of inland waters, but only 400 km of river are notified as SSSI, of which the River Tweed accounts for 345 km. This river was notified under earlier legislation, the National Parks and Access to the Countryside Act 1949, which did not have such onerous consultation requirements and the river has yet to be renotified under the Wildlife and Countryside Act 1981.

Land-use activities (e.g. agriculture, forestry) in river catchments can damage the nature conservation interest of rivers (Nature Conservancy Council, 1989a) but the boundaries of river SSSIs usually exclude the catchment area unless this is itself also of special scientific interest. This means that the designation of rivers as SSSIs may not be as effective a protection measure as it is for other habitat types. Nonetheless, the SSSI "label" still serves a useful function, as it identifies the nature conservation importance of the river and reminds all who have an interest in the river, or the ability to regulate potentially damaging activities, to take account of its nature conservation importance.

Conservation is, of course, a shared responsibility, but this is not always adequately reflected in the legislation. The Countryside (Scotland) Act 1967 states that every government department shall have regard to the "desirability of conserving the natural beauty and amenity of the countryside", and the definition of natural beauty includes the conservation of flora and fauna. This duty is extended by the Agriculture Act 1986 for SOAFD and the Wildlife and Countryside Act 1981, as amended, for the Forestry Commission, such that they are required to achieve a "balance" between their primary activities and nature conservation.

In England and Wales the Water Act 1973 placed a similar duty on Water Authorities to "have regard to the desirability of" conserving natural beauty and of conserving flora and fauna. This was subsequently strengthened by the Wildlife and Countryside Act 1981, so that they are required "to further the conservation and enhancement of natural beauty" and to take account of their actions on such flora and fauna. This represents a significant change, as the emphasis is on a requirement to "further" (i.e. advance) conservation rather than "have regard" to it. More recently, the conservation duties of the new regulatory body in England and Wales, the National Rivers Authority, were further strengthened by the Water Act 1989, which imposes a duty upon the Authority to "promote" (i.e. actively encourage) nature conservation. Unfortunately, none of these provisions apply in Scotland.

It is difficult to assess the extent to which the duty to further conservation in England and Wales has influenced developments. The House of Commons Environment Committee, in their examination of the effectiveness of the Wildlife and Countryside Act (Environment Committee, 1985), considered that the water authorities had performed their conservation duties well, and said that "a great deal of change of attitude is evidently going on". It would seem reasonable to extend this duty to Scotland, and this would do much to ensure that the various authorities with responsibilities for managing river resources are able to take account legitimately of nature conservation and actually undertake work to improve the natural environment.

POSITIVE DEVELOPMENTS AND OPPORTUNITIES

Recent amendments to the Control of Pollution Act 1974, have introduced powers which, if implemented, may considerably improve the ability of regulatory agencies to assist in protecting the nature conservation interest of Scottish rivers. Under Section 30B of the amended Act, a new statutory water quality classification may be introduced. This represents an important opportunity, as the current non-statutory classification is considered to be too insensitive to detect some changes which are ecologically significant. The classification could be improved by introducing criteria relating, for example, to nitrogen, phosphates, and suspended solids. An improved system would enable adverse changes to be detected at an earlier stage and would provide a more accurate measure of ecosystem health.

Section 30C enables the Secretary of State for Scotland to set statutory water quality objectives. These are important, as they determine the kind of standards that are applied when applications to discharge are considered. Typical non-statutory water quality objectives currently include suitability for potable water supply and salmonid fisheries, but not nature conservation. In order to ensure that sufficiently high standards are applied to protect wildlife, nature conservation must be accepted as a legitimate water quality objective in its own right.

The Act provides powers to prohibit or restrict particular activities in a catchment through the designation of "Water Protection Zones", one of the few statutory mechanisms available for controlling pollution from diffuse sources in river catchments. In 1986, the government suggested that these powers, which enable the Secretary of State to make regulations on a site-by-site basis, could be used to prevent pollution affecting nature conservation sites. Such measures are necessary if pollution from, for example, agriculture and forestry is to be reduced. However, they have never been used, possibly because of the large amount of evidence that would be required and the apparent absence of any compensation provisions for those whose activities would be restricted by the regulations.

Under the same Act, the Secretary of State can issue a statutory Code of Good

Agricultural Practice (the current code is non-statutory). Compliance with the Code will no longer be an acceptable defence (as it was previously under this legislation) if pollution is caused by agricultural activity. The existing Code is limited in scope and should be rewritten by pollution-control authorities in liaison with agricultural interests, to take account of new developments such as the forthcoming regulations on storage of silage, slurry, and agricultural fuel oil. The new Code should be more comprehensive and self-contained and should be distributed to all farmers.

Developments of European Community legislation are also encouraging, with new Directives covering sewage disposal, nitrates, phosphates, and wildlife habitats being produced. Although it is often difficult to attribute environmental effects to particular items of legislation, there are few who would disagree that the European Community has been and will continue to be a major driving force behind higher standards and improved protection for the environment.

Public awareness of environmental issues continues to grow, and in Scotland this has included concern for rivers. In recent years several campaigns have taken place or are in progress. In 1988 the "Clean Forth" campaign was launched. The Forth River Purification Board and the Keep Scotland Beautiful organization combined their efforts in a massive clean-up exercise of rivers throughout the Forth catchment. This was followed by an educational programme which began in 1989, and a number of charitable river trusts have now been set up in the area to increase public participation in river habitat improvements. A similar initiative, "Clyde Pride", is planned for the Clyde River Purification Board's area in 1991. In April 1990 Scottish Conservation Projects launched "Operation Brightwater", a three-year campaign which aims to make people more aware of the threats to fresh waters and to encourage practical involvement in conservation. The level of sponsorship and support from private industry and a variety of statutory and voluntary bodies suggests that the campaign will do much to increase the involvement of the public in conservation work.

It has been encouraging in the last 1–2 years to see the statutory fishery authorities appointing biologists under the auspices of fishery trusts and foundations. In particular, the Tweed Foundation is to be applauded for its initiative in employing a biologist to implement a formal fishery Management Plan for the Tweed basin, which includes proposals for managing the entire freshwater fish community. Similar developments are occurring in other parts of the country, and hopefully they will improve the science and practice of fishery management in Scotland and provide a much-needed boost to river conservation.

DISCUSSION

Regulatory control over rivers (and activities that affect rivers) is divided among a number of different departments and agencies. This division of responsibilities is a particular feature of the Scottish system, and is the result of a long historical development of legislation and the adoption of organizational structures intended to meet the particular needs of Scotland. The overall result is in marked contrast to the concept of integrated river basin management that predominated in England and Wales until the privatization of the Water Authorities. Although the post-privatization structure, with its clear separation of sewage treatment and water supply from the regulatory functions, does have some similarities to the situation in Scotland, the wider remit of the National Rivers Authority provides for a more effective integration of functions such as pollution control, abstraction control, fisheries management, and nature conservation, than is yet available in Scotland.

The present legal controls and policies affecting rivers are integrated only in the sense that the Scottish Office retains overall responsibility. While it is perhaps unrealistic and impractical at present to bring into one unit all those authorities that currently have some responsibility for rivers, there is a need for a range of institutional and policy changes to improve the integration of controls over activities affecting water quality, discharge regimes, and the physical structure of river channels.

The principal advantage in Scotland is the central position of the Scottish Office, to which most agencies currently report. It is ideally placed to take a broad overview of environmental issues and to begin to co-ordinate and integrate the activities of each of its departments. Two current government initiatives (the policy review of the River Purification Boards and the proposals for merging the countryside and conservation agencies in Scotland) together provide an important opportunity to re-examine the mechanisms for conserving Scotland's rivers. The Scottish Office is also in a position to promote environmental legislation. In particular, much of the legislation relating to rivers deserves careful review, as important aspects are still not covered adequately. Existing powers need to be fully utilized and new measures should be introduced as new environmental problems arise. There is a need for more emphasis to be placed on an anticipatory and precautionary approach.

Significant improvements in water quality have been achieved in Scottish rivers in recent years, particularly by reducing point-source pollution in urban areas. However, changing land-use practices and intensifying demands on water resources are posing new threats to the outstanding nature conservation interest of Scotland's rivers, particularly in rural areas, where agriculture, forestry, and fish farming are important components of the economy. A more comprehensive and integrated river management framework will be required if these emerging threats are to be addressed more effectively in the future.

ACKNOWLEDGEMENTS

We would like to thank all those who have given freely of their time to inform and advise us on aspects of Scottish administrative systems, laws and organizations. In particular, we would like to thank Dr P. S. Maitland, Mr D. Hammerton (who commented on an earlier draft), Mr D. W. Mackay, and staff at the Nature Conservancy Council, especially Mrs K. E. Sweetman.

REFERENCES

Anon. (1965). *Scottish Salmon and Trout Fisheries: Second Report by the Hunter Committee*, HMSO, Edinburgh.
Badenoch, C. O. (1989). "The conservation of the river", in *Tweed towards 2000—Tweed Foundation Symposium* (Ed. D. Mills), pp. 13–18, Tweed Foundation, Berwick-on-Tweed.
Berry, R. J. (1985). *The Natural History of Orkney*, Collins, London.
Berry, R. J., and Johnston, J. L. (1980). *The Natural History of Shetland*, Collins, London.
Charter, E. (1988). "Vegetation of the waters and wetlands of the Spey Valley", in *Land Use in the River Spey Catchment* (Ed. D. Jenkins), pp. 176–181, Aberdeen Centre for Land Use, Aberdeen.

Darling, F. F., and Boyd, J. M. (1964). *The Highlands and Islands*, Collins, London.

Edwards, R., and Howell, R. (1989). "Welsh rivers and reservoirs: management for wildlife conservation", *Regulated Rivers*, **4**, 213–223.

Environment Committee (1985). *Operation and Effectiveness of Part II of the Wildlife and Countryside Act. Report and Proceedings of the Committee*, HMSO, London.

Gustard, A., Cole, G., Marshall, D., and Bayliss, A. (1987). *A study of compensation flows in the UK*, Report No. 99, Institute of Hydrology, Wallingford.

Haigh, N. (1989). *EEC Environmental Policy and Britain*, Longman, Harlow.

Hammerton, D. (1986). "Cleaning the Clyde—a century of progress?" *Journal of the Operational Research Society*, **37**, 911–921.

Hellawell, J. M. (1988). "River regulation and nature conservation", *Regulated Rivers*, **2**, 425–443.

Institute of Aquaculture, Institute of Freshwater Ecology and Institute of Terrestrial Ecology (1990). *Fish Farming and the Scottish Freshwater Environment*, Contract report to the Nature Conservancy Council, Edinburgh.

Jenkins, D. (Ed.) (1985). *The Biology and Management of the River Dee*, Institute of Terrestrial Ecology, Huntingdon.

Johnson, F. G. (1988). "Hydropower development on rivers in Scotland", *Regulated Rivers*, **2**, 277–292.

Mackay, D. W. (1988). *Nature Conservation and the Work of the River Purification Boards*, Unpublished report to the Nature Conservancy Council, Edinburgh.

Maitland, P. S. (1966). *Studies on Loch Lomond 2: The Fauna of the River Endrick*, Blackie, Glasgow.

Maitland, P. S. (1987). "Fish introductions and translocations—their impact in the British Isles", in *Angling and Wildlife in Fresh Waters*, (Eds P. S. Maitland and A. K. Turner), pp. 57–65, Institute of Terrestrial Ecology, Grange-over-Sands.

Maitland, P. S. (1989). *The Genetic Impact of Farmed Atlantic Salmon on Wild Populations*, Nature Conservancy Council, Edinburgh.

Maitland, P. S., Newson, M. D., and Best, G. A. (1990). *The Impact of Afforestation and Forestry Practice on Freshwater Habitats*, Focus on Nature Conservation, 23. Nature Conservancy Council, Peterborough.

Nature Conservancy Council (1984). *Nature Conservation in Great Britain*, London.

Nature Conservancy Council (1989a). *Royal Commission on Environmental Pollution—Study on Freshwater Quality. Evidence submitted by NCC*, Unpublished report, Peterborough.

Nature Conservancy Council (1989b). *Guidelines for Selection of Biological SSSIs*, Peterborough.

Nature Conservancy Council (1990). *A Brief Assessment of the Nature Conservation Importance of Scottish Freshwaters*, Unpublished report, Edinburgh.

Petts, G. E., and Wood, R. (Eds) (1988). "River regulation in the United Kingdom", *Regulated Rivers*, **2**, 199–477.

Scottish Development Department (1976). *Towards Cleaner Water 1975*, HMSO, Edinburgh.

Scottish Development Department (1983). *Water Pollution Control in Scotland: recent developments*, Edinburgh.

Scottish Development Department (1987). *Water Quality Survey of Scotland, 1985*, HMSO, Edinburgh.

Scottish Development Department (1990). *First Policy Review of the River Purification Boards*, Edinburgh.

Scottish River Purification Boards' Association (1987). *Royal Commission on Environmental Pollution—Study on Freshwater Quality. Evidence submitted by SRPBA: "Freshwater Quality in Scotland"*, Unpublished report, Glasgow.

Smith, I. R., and Lyle, A. A. (1979). *Distribution of Freshwaters in Great Britain*, Institute of Terrestrial Ecology, Cambridge.

Tay River Purification Board (1989). *Tay River Purification Board Annual Report for 1989*, Perth.

United Kingdom Acid Waters Review Group (1988). *Acidity in United Kingdom Fresh Waters*, Second report of the UK Acid Waters Review Group, HMSO, London.

Waterston, A. R., Holden, A. V., Campbell, R. N., and Maitland, P. S. (1979). "The inland waters of the Outer Hebrides", *Proceedings of the Royal Society of Edinburgh*, **77B**, 329–357.

27

The Amenity and Environmental Value of River Corridors in Britain

C. H. GREEN and S. M. TUNSTALL

Flood Hazard Research Centre,
Middlesex Polytechnic, Queensway, Enfield EN3 4SF, UK

INTRODUCTION

This chapter addresses "value" in a broad but essentially economic way by discussing:

- How the public uses river corridors;
- What features people like about river corridors;
- What they want the characteristics of river corridors to be; and
- The resulting economic value of river water quality improvements.

The economic value to individuals of an improvement to a river corridor can be described as the difference between what they would like the river corridor to be and how much they like it now. We will be discussing the results of work undertaken to evaluate the economic benefits of improving river water quality. These results should be viewed within the wider programme of work being undertaken at the Flood Hazard Research Centre on river corridors, including research on public preferences for river corridor features and validation of a scale of perceived water quality (Burrows and House, 1989; House et al, 1990) and studies of public attitudes towards the local environment, flood hazards, and river management schemes (Fordham et al, 1991).

THE ECONOMIC VALUE OF RIVER WATER QUALITY IMPROVEMENTS

Improvements to river water quality potentially yield a range of economic benefits (Fisher and Raucher, 1984). Given that small watercourses predominate in the UK, the main categories of potential user benefits are:

- Increased pleasure to existing visitors to river corridors;
- The gains resulting from additional visits attracted to the site;
- Any additional amenity gain to properties neighbouring the watercourse; and

River Conservation and Management. Edited by P. J. Boon, P. Calow, and G. E. Petts
© 1992 John Wiley & Sons Ltd

● The attraction of inward investment from overseas, or lower development costs compared to the opportunity costs of developing other sites in the UK.

In addition, there has been much speculation in the economic literature (Brookshire et al, 1986) as to the existence of non-use values: i.e. that the public values the preservation of environmental goods such as river corridors for reasons other than the enjoyment they obtain from visiting or living near a river corridor.

PROBLEMS OF ECONOMIC EVALUATION

In economics all values are subjective and it is a convention to refer to anything of which the individual prefers a greater to a lesser amount as a "good". This good may be a commodity but may equally be something as apparently intangible as the attractiveness of a river corridor. If more of the good is provided, then an economic benefit results if any individual prefers more of that good. To estimate this benefit, economics seeks rigorous methods of evaluating the gain in terms of money, and of estimating the number of people who so gain, or equally lose, by a change from one set of characteristics to another in order to estimate the total economic gain or loss. The overall economic value = value per individual × the number of individuals.

Since an individual, or different individuals, may prefer more of a good to less for many different reasons, it is frequently helpful to refer to different categories of benefit such as recreational benefit or non-use benefit, there being as many categories of benefit as individuals have reasons to prefer more to less of the good. In establishing the economic benefits of river water quality improvement, the analyst is faced with four main problems:

(1) What is the good of which they desire more or less?
(2) Who benefits? The definition of that proportion of the population which gains by a change in the availability of some good;
(3) Why do they value that good?
(4) How are valid and reliable measures of the values to be derived?

What?

A good has no economic value unless an individual prefers some quantity of that good over another quantity. That which the individual prefers, however, is not necessarily what the scientist considers preferable. To evaluate water quality, as with any other environmental good (Green, 1980), it is necessary to know first what the individual means by water quality and to measure water quality in those terms. Moreover, unless the individual can perceive the difference between two standards of water quality, he or she will not benefit by an improvement from one to the other. Thus, a measure of perceived water quality is required.

The concept of user-related water quality is not new: in the United States, both Mitchell and Carson (1981) and Smith and Desvousges (1986) used water quality ladders in surveys. The ladders were used to represent a scale of water quality to the respondents, with each rung of the ladder representing a level of water quality. However, these categorical scales were defined solely in terms of fitness for the instream recreational uses of boating, fishing, and swimming. The scales addressed neither the issue of whether water quality could be perceived nor the out-of-stream recreational use of river corridors and non-use values. The concept of perceived water quality is not new either; a number of studies have been undertaken in the United States (Scherer and Coughlin, 1971; Ditton and Goodale, 1973; Kooyoomjian and Clesceri, 1974). However, these concentrated on poor water quality rather than on a perceptual scale which could be tied back to biochemical predictors.

We assumed that casual visitors had only three types of data available to them upon which to base any assessment of water quality: physical indicators, the presence or absence of biological indicators of water quality, and the presence or absence of other users such as fishermen or swimmers who might be assumed to know about the quality of the water. A small exploratory survey of 204 river corridor users was undertaken in 1986 to determine the degree of consensus by visitors on whether the presence or absence of each indicator showed that the water quality was good or bad (Green et al, 1987). On the basis of ecological advice, this scale was then revised to include additional biota which were both sensitive to water quality (for lowland waters) and potentially recognizable by the casual visitor (Green et al, 1989).

In the river corridor users' study the following year, we asked respondents whether or not they had seen any of the items listed, and also a simple question as to their judgements of the water quality at the site they were visiting (Table 27.1). Two Likert scales (Likert, 1932) were derived, one composed of items indicative of poor water quality and the other of items indicative of good water quality. The items included in the two scales are shown in Table 27.1. For each respondent, a score was obtained on each scale by adding up the number of items on the scale perceived to be present or absent. The reliability of the scales was tested using Cronbach's Alpha (Cronbach, 1951), a statistical procedure in which the average correlation of an item with all the other items in the scale is measured. This is taken as an indication of the degree to which the scale is measuring a common entity. The reliabilities of both scales as indicated by the standardized alpha were found to be just satisfactory (Table 27.1).

Scores on the poor water quality scale are significantly but weakly correlated with those on the question concerning perceived water quality:

$$\text{Water quality} = 0.31 \text{ attractive river} - 0.47 \text{ poor water quality}$$
$$(R^2 = 0.44; F = 306.97; p < 0.0001) \tag{27.1}$$

Thus, the more of the items they had seen on their visit, the poorer they were likely to judge the quality of the water. However, the good water quality scale is not significantly correlated with perceived water quality. This tends to suggest that the public has a clear idea of what it means by a polluted river and also of what is an attractive river, but no clear expectation of what is an unpolluted river. This work has subsequently been extended by Burrows and House (1989), House and Sangster (1990), and House et al, (1990).

We proposed the hypothesis that the enjoyment that visitors gain from their visits is unlikely to be wholly dependent upon perceived water quality, but is likely to depend on

TABLE 27.1. Mean scores on perceived water quality[a] when indicators were seen or not seen by river corridor users

Indicators	Item seen Mean	Item seen Std dev	Item seen N	Item not seen Mean	Item not seen Std dev	Item not seen N	Somers' d[b]	Item included in scale[c]
Dead fish on surface of water	0.50	0.94	14	2.52	1.75	819	−0.607	–
Unusual smells	1.13	1.35	186	2.88	1.67	645	−0.488	1
Water unusual colour (e.g. red)	1.29	1.45	185	2.82	1.70	649	−0.422	1
Water appears muddy	1.83	1.54	508	3.50	1.60	325	−0.414	1
Oily look to water	1.19	1.39	159	2.79	1.70	674	−0.408	1
Protruding rubbish, (e.g. bedsteads, trolleys, tyres, bicycles, etc.)	1.81	1.71	405	3.11	1.57	432	−0.398	1
Foam on water	1.34	1.31	193	2.82	1.72	644	−0.388	1
Can see pipes discharging into river	1.58	1.64	168	2.71	1.72	660	−0.309	1
Plants in water appear dirty	1.90	1.69	369	2.99	1.66	448	−0.276	1
Rubbish on banks	1.96	1.70	422	3.01	1.66	412	−0.275	1
Brown 'cotton wool' growing on surface of water	1.33	1.42	39	2.55	1.75	789	−0.258	1
Green scum on water (e.g. algae)	2.05	1.71	347	2.78	1.73	483	−0.187	–
No plants growing in or on surface of water	2.13	1.73	282	2.68	1.75	544	−0.156	–
Columns of midges over water like smoke	1.93	1.57	190	2.65	1.78	642	−0.140	1
Grebe on water	1.49	1.64	37	2.53	1.76	722	−0.087	–
Crowfoot/white lily growing on surface of water	2.06	1.56	53	2.52	1.77	770	−0.058	–
Can see many fish in water	3.46	1.64	115	2.31	1.73	706	0.277	–
Swans on water	2.96	1.41	107	2.41	1.80	729	0.255	2
Adults fishing	3.00	1.65	100	2.41	1.76	737	0.188	2
Canoeists	2.76	1.37	41	2.47	1.78	796	0.188	2
Coots/moorhens on water	2.76	1.63	161	2.39	1.78	662	0.173	2
Can see river bottom	2.74	1.76	457	2.15	1.71	369	0.171	–
Ducks/mallards on water	2.70	1.61	273	2.37	1.82	564	0.169	2
People swimming	2.76	1.26	21	2.48	1.77	815	0.146	–
Many different plants growing in/on river	2.72	1.72	438	2.21	1.69	375	0.091	–
Kingfishers flying over river	2.94	1.78	17	2.47	1.76	818	0.071	–
Dragonflies/damselflies are numerous	2.47	1.69	118	2.48	1.77	716	0.030	2

[a]Perceived water quality rated on a scale from 0 = very polluted to 6 = very clean

[b]Somers' d statistic indicates the strength and direction of the association between the indicators and perceived water quality scores with a range from −1 to +1 with 0 indicating no association. (*SPSS/PC Base Manual*, SPSS, Inc.)

[c]Items included in scale: 1 = poor water quality scale, 2 = good water quality scale. Reliability of scales indicated by standardized alpha = 0.74 and 0.72

other factors such as the overall quality of the river corridor. Thus, we argued that the value of an improvement in river water quality was likely to be lower for a river corridor composed of industrial dereliction than for one where the corridor landscape was seen as attractive. Equally, it may be expected that the enjoyment the visitor gains from one activity will be less affected by perceived water quality than it would be for some other activities.

How?

The only valid and reliable method (Green et al, 1990) which could be used for evaluating both recreational and non-use benefits was the Contingent Valuation Method (CVM). The CVM (Cummings et al, 1986) is essentially the application of social science survey methodologies to the estimation of economic values. In this study we sought to evaluate three different potential benefits from water quality improvements:

(1) The additional enjoyment to existing users;
(2) The increase in amenity enjoyment to residents living near the river coridor;
(3) The overall national non-use value.

Three separate surveys were undertaken to derive these values.

Who?

In order to calculate economic benefits it is necessary to estimate not only the average benefit per individual but also the number of individuals who benefit. We also undertook the three separate surveys to explore the definition of the population who benefit: a survey of 872 river corridor users at 12 sites—the river corridor survey; a survey of 303 residents at nine sites living close to accessible river corridors—the amenity survey; and a survey of 319 residents at seven sites living at least 2 km away from an accessible watercourse—the remote sites survey. Defining the population who benefit is particularly problematic in the case of non-use benefits (Tunstall et al, 1988). Figure 27.1 illustrates the location of sites where interviews were undertaken.

The results from the remote sites survey have been discussed elsewhere (Green et al, 1990). The selection of the 12 sites for the survey of river corridor users was based upon a three-tier stratification of water quality by corridor quality and by type of site. Sites were categorized as having good or bad water quality and good or bad corridor quality. Sites were classified according to their expected usage and location into three site types: town centre sites, local parks, and "honeypot" sites. The honeypot sites, many of which were in country parks, were located outside or on the edge of urban areas and were expected to attract day visitors and visitors from a greater distance than local parks. The nature of activities undertaken at sites of different type was expected to vary and this was indeed the case (Table 27.2).

Honeypot sites and local parks were closer than expected in the activities undertaken. This occurred for two reasons: first, many honeypot sites are used by local residents; second, a number of sites which we anticipated would be used by local residents proved to attract visitors from a much greater distance.

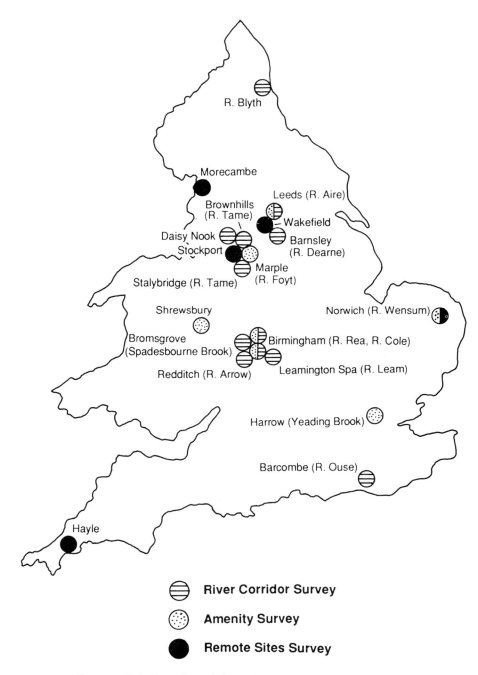

FIGURE 27.1. Location of sites where surveys were undertaken

TABLE 27.2. Percentage of river corridor users giving certain activities as their main reason for being at the river by type of site

Main reason for visit	Town centre (%)	Type of site Local park (%)	Honeypot (%)
Going for a walk for pleasure	24	29	31
Taking the children for a walk	16	16	25
Walking the dog	3	16	23
Passing through	46	17	8
Fishing, boating, birdwatching	–	5	2
Picknicking	2	2	6
Other reasons	9	15	5
Number of cases	176	435	261

Why?

There has been much speculation in the economic literature as to the reasons why the public may value the environment over and above the use value (Brookshire et al, 1986; Madriaga and McConnell, 1987; Tunstall et al, 1988). However, we found that empirical work to test these hypotheses was sparse (Croke et al, 1984). In this study, we discovered that non-use motivations were regarded by respondents as more important reasons for increasing public expenditure on water quality improvements than were use values. Moreover, the most important reason for increasing public expenditure was the moral dimension: "We ought not to pollute" (Green et al, 1987).

In subsequent work, looking more widely at environmental values, we have found that agreement about the importance of environmental conservation tends to be coupled with an orientation towards a moral view of the world rather than a utilitarian one (Green and Tunstall, 1990a).

VISITS TO, AND PREFERENCES FOR, RIVER CORRIDORS

Visiting frequency

Of the households living adjacent to a river corridor, 82% had visited the river corridor; the mean frequency of visiting was 2.6 visits per week and the median frequency once per week. For up to 15 min travel time, the frequency of visiting could be best explained by the following equation:

$$\log_{10} (\text{frequency per year}) = 2.01523 - 0.7780 \log_{10} (\text{travel time})$$
$$(0.06772) \quad (0.11719) \text{ (standard error)} \quad (27.2)$$

This implies that river sites generate rather more local visits than does the average small local park, which typically receives between 0.29 and 0.53 visits per week per adult within the local area (Greater London Council, 1968).

In some instances river corridors attracted visitors from a wider area than had been expected; the mean distance travelled to reach the site was at least 1 mile. In comparison, according to a survey of the use of open space in Liverpool, a small local park (2–100 acres) typically draws its visitors from up to half a mile away and only very attractive small parks draw their visitors from up to a mile away (Balmer, 1973). This suggests either that mobility has increased since the Liverpool survey was undertaken in 1971 or that rivers add significantly to the attractiveness of parks.

Overall, the indications from the surveys are that sites with rivers both attract more frequent visits and those from a greater distance than the evidence on park visiting would lead us to expect.

What do visitors want?

In all three surveys we asked questions about desirable features or improvements to river corridors, and, in the case of people in the user and amenity surveys, their judgements as to the quality of the site at present. In the survey of residents living at least 2 km from a watercourse, respondents were asked to rate a series of features in terms of their desirability (Table 27.3), as we had asked the corridor users in the exploratory study in 1986 (Green et al, 1987). These ratings were then subjected to a principal components analysis followed by an oblimin rotation. Principal components analysis is a statistical technique (Hotelling, 1933; Kendall and Stuart, 1961) which is used when it is hypothesized that correlations between groups of variables occur because these variables depend upon one or more common underlying but unmeasured variables. Here it was applied to the correlation matrix for respondents' ratings of the different features or characteristics of river corridors. Thus, the factors shown in Table 27.3 do not indicate the relative importance of the factors but the degree to which there are differences between respondents in the importance that they give to the characteristics which reflect that component.

Table 27.3 shows that the greatest differences between respondents are in their preferences for children's facilities and that there are relatively small differences between respondents' preferences for convenience. Three of the components—facilities for children, facilities, and places to visit—are themselves strongly correlated. Not surprisingly, families with children are more likely to desire these features. They are less likely to want a rich environment than are the elderly (Green and Tunstall, 1990b). Perhaps more importantly, there were significant differences between the preferences of those who had visited a river corridor in the last six months and those who had not. Those who had were significantly more likely to score higher on the "rich environment" component and lower on both the "places to visit" and "facilities" component, although there were no significant differences for the remaining categories.

Thus, it would appear, first, that there are identifiable groups with different preferences in the population and, second, that current visitors, those who have visited within the last six months and who form the greater proportion of the sample, desire relatively unspoilt, natural river corridors. They find those features which would attract the remainder of the population as positive detractors.

In addition, residents living near to a river corridor were asked to rate their estate or road for its performance on 18 characteristics. By regressing their subsequent judge-

TABLE 27.3. Mean scores on preferences for river corridor features and results of a principal components analysis of preferences for respondents in remote sites survey

Components	Mean score[a]	Percentage of variance explained
Component 1—facilities for children		25.0
Toilets	7.5	
Children's play area	6.4	
Picnicking facilities	6.0	
Component 2—rich environment		12.6
Many birds and insects to be seen/heard	7.6	
Many plants in and around the water	7.5	
Many well-grown trees and plants	8.4	
Component 3—places to visit		11.7
Historic monuments	4.7	
Historic buildings to visit	5.4	
Visitor centre/museum	4.4	
Component 4—convenience		7.5
Toilets	7.5	
Fishing	3.6	
Dry paths	7.0	
Not too many people	7.6	
Easy and cheap to get to	7.7	
Adequate car parking	7.7	
Component 5—facilities		5.7
Adequate car parking	7.7	
Café/restaurant	6.3	
Row boats for hire	4.2	
Motor boat trips	4.4	
Number of cases = 319		Total 62.5

[a]Respondent means exclude those who do not want the particular feature

Preference for features of a river corridor rated on a scale from 0 = no effect upon enjoyment to 10 = add most to enjoyment

ments of attractiveness of their estate or road as a place to live upon these characteristics, we sought to assess which were significant in determining the desirability of the locality. As Figure 27.2 shows, we were successful in accounting for 63% of the differences in respondents' judgements of the overall attractiveness of their road or estate. The most important characteristic to influence the desirability of their locality was the quality of the local environment. Every one standard deviation change in respondents' assessment of the local environment was reflected in a 0.265 standard deviation change in their judgement of the overall desirability of the locality.

Respondents were also asked to rate, in terms of importance, 10 possible disadvantages and four possible advantages of living near a river. In addition, they were asked to

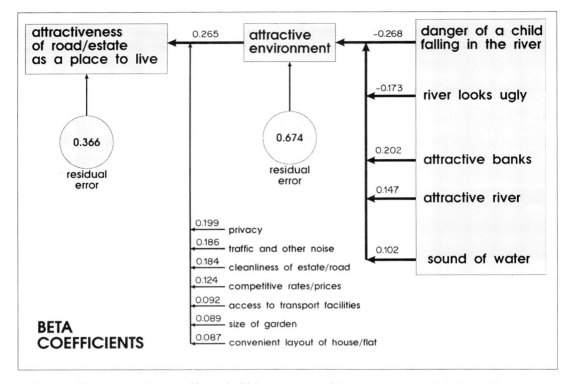

FIGURE 27.2. Determinants of households' assessment of the attractiveness of their road/estate as a place to live. (Beta coefficients are standardized regression coefficients which provide an indication of the relative contribution of the independent variables in determining the dependent variable)

rate the present attractiveness of the river banks, the river itself, the ease of access, and cleanliness of the water. Five of these factors explained a significant proportion of the differences in respondents' assessment of the area's environmental quality as a whole (Figure 27.2). Given that the river corridor in each case comprises only a part of the environment of the estate, the proportion of the variance explained is quite high. There is evidence, therefore, that the perceived quality of the river affects respondents' assessments of the desirability of their neighbourhood quite strongly.

Different areas, however, reported different problems and equally, in response to another question in the interview—differences in the desirability of a number of improvements to the river corridor. The mean scores on desirable improvements and current problems given by people living near the River Severn in Shrewsbury and the Yeading Brook in Harrow are shown in Figures 27.3 and 27.4. In turn, the desired improvements fit the perceived importance of various advantages and disadvantages. The most notable difference between the two areas shown is the relatively strong desire in Shrewsbury for beaches, pubs, and cafés. This seems likely to be a reflection of the different size of the watercourses in the two locations—little more than a brook in the case of the Yeading, while the Severn is a major river.

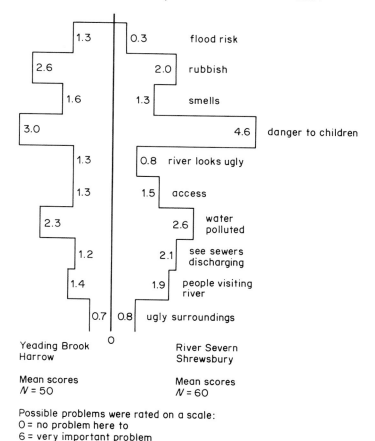

FIGURE 27.3. The importance of possible problems in living near a river: mean scores for the Yeading Brook, Harrow, and River Severn, Shrewsbury

That the public desires, and values, what it regards as environmentally rich river corridors does not necessarily mean that its preferences and perceptions coincide with those of ecologists. It might be that the public's preferences were grounded in a desire for the picturesque or for the conservation of furry mammals. However, there is now some evidence (Green and Tunstall, 1990a) that the preferences of the public and of ecologists are closer than might be anticipated and could be said to be environmentally centred rather than personally oriented. They want what they believe to be environmentally desirable rather than what they, personally, find attractive.

These studies only indicate in general terms the public's preferences; while they show the public's preference for a rich environment, they can provide no indication of what this really means. Recent work (House and Sangster, 1990; House et al, 1990) has provided greater detail on public preferences; for instance, between trees and grass. Similarly, Coker et al (1989) have shown how the economic value of the recreational potential of a possible channel improvement varies with the features the improvement scheme offers.

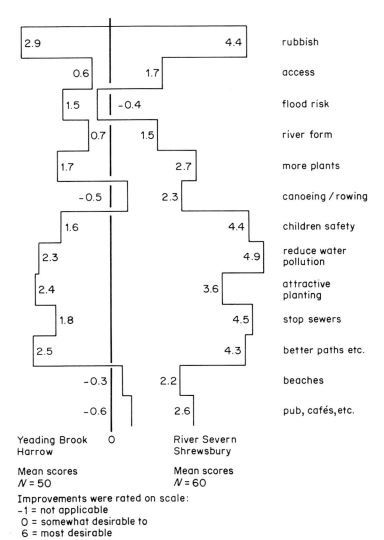

FIGURE 27.4. The improvements to the river desired by residents living near the Yeading Brook, Harrow, and the River Severn, Shrewsbury: mean scores

Values of water quality improvement

Of the residents surveyed living next to a river corridor, 63% stated that they liked living near a river. From a discriminant analysis (Klecka, 1975), which predicted 80% of these responses, the strongest factors associated with this were the following specific advantages of living near a river: the attractiveness of the plants and wildlife in and around the river; the attractiveness of the river corridor as a place to walk or sit; and the sound of water. Liking to live near the river was negatively associated with high scores for the following disadvantages: water pollution, and seeing sewers emptying. Liking decreased

TABLE 27.4. Mean value put on increased enjoyment of living in their home if water quality were improved to three standards

Water quality standard	Arithmetic mean (single sum in £s[a])	Log mean	Log standard deviation
If water quality were good enough:			
For water birds (e.g. swans, coots, ducks, etc.) to use water	546	2.72	0.56
To support many fish (including trout), dragonflies, and to allow many different types of plant to grow both in the water and on the edges	562	2.67	0.54
To be safe for children to paddle or swim	582	2.90	0.40
Number of cases = 78 − 87			

[a] Mean calculated for those who consider their enjoyment would be increased only

with distance from the river and was positively associated with being able to see the river from the respondent's house or garden.

A very similar pattern was associated with judgements by residents that their enjoyment of living in the home would be increased by improvements in river water quality to each of three specified standards. The simple scale of water quality standard used is shown in Table 27.4. When further asked to value this increase in amenity as a lump-sum payment in pounds, the results given in Table 27.4 were obtained. Both the logarithmic and the arithmetic means are given since the former are required for statistical comparisons and the latter values for economic analysis. Differences in the value in pounds that individual respondents placed on this enjoyment (£ enjoy) could be predicted from respondents' assessments of the relative desirability of stopping sewers flowing into the river in relation to their enjoyment of living near a river now (improve):

$$\log (\text{£ enjoy}) = 0.51 \text{ (improve)}$$

$$(R^2 = 0.22; \ F = 8.22; \ df = 1,24; \ p = 0.085)$$

(27.3)

Visitors at the river corridor sites were also asked whether their enjoyment from a visit would be increased if water quality were improved to each of the three specified standards. Over 50% of visitors indicated that it would increase their enjoyment and a similar proportion said they would visit more frequently. The values that they placed upon this increase in enjoyment in pence per visit are given in Table 27.5. In a regression analysis of these values upon the hypothesized explanatory variables, differences between values given by respondents could be explained by differences in the degree to which respondents feel that improvements in water quality would increase their enjoyment, and in their assessment of the overall quality of the river corridor (Green and Tunstall, in press).

A substantial proportion of both visitors and non-visitors to river corridors interviewed in the remote sites survey were willing to pay an increase in water rates (56% and 45%,

TABLE 27.5. Estimated mean value in pence per visit[a] of an improvement in river water quality to three standards offered by river corridor users at different types of site

Water quality standard	Type of site		
	Town centre Pence per visit	Local park Pence per visit	Honeypot Pence per visit
If water quality were good enough:			
For water birds (e.g. swans, coots, ducks, etc.) to use water	37	42	41
To support many fish (including trout), dragonflies, and to allow many different types of plant to grow both in the water and on the edges	42	48	41
To be safe for children to paddle or swim	36	38	45
Number of cases	176	435	261

[a]Mean estimates are averaged across those who would gain extra enjoyment and those who say improvement in river water quality would make no difference to their enjoyment and therefore improvements would have no value for them in pence per visit

respectively) to be spent on improving river water quality. For those willing to pay, the amount that they were willing to pay averaged £13.59 per year for non-users of river corridors and £19.56 per year for users of river corridors (Green et al, 1990).

ECONOMIC VALUE OF RIVER CORRIDORS

While the values of the increases in the enjoyment to the individual visitor are quite small, the numbers of visitors are so great that the resulting benefits are large. For example, the River Bollin in north-west England runs from above Macclesfield through Wilmslow to join the Manchester Ship Canal. Water quality in England and Wales is assessed using the National Water Council classification (NWC, 1977). This consists of five broad categories of water quality (1A, 1B, 2, 3, 4), which are defined in the first instance, in terms of a series of 95 percentile or annual average concentrations of dissolved oxygen, biochemical oxygen demand, and ammonia. The River Bollin above Macclesfield is designated as NWC classes 1A and 1B. However, in Macclesfield there are a large number of storm sewer overflows and the water quality falls to NWC class 3. The effects of the overflows dominate the quality of the river water downstream as far as the outfall of the Macclesfield sewage-treatment works, a distance of 5.9 km. This stretch of river includes the picturesque village of Prestbury, which is not only a relatively wealthy commuter area but also attracts a significant number of tourists. Macclesfield itself is a prosperous town; the Borough Council also has a long-term commitment to open up the Bollin Valley as a recreational and environmental resource and to create a new focus for the town on the river. This emphasis is part of a drive to promote tourism centred upon the industrial heritage of the silk industry in the area.

TABLE 27.6. Calculation of the user benefits of water quality improvements to the River Bollin, Macclesfield (January 1987 prices)

Location	Number of adult visits per year	Benefit per visit (pence)	User benefits (£ per year)
Prestbury	20 000[a]	41	8 200
Riverside Park	200 000[b]– 340 000[c]	48	96 000– 163 000
Superstore store	30 000[d]	42	12 600
Town centre	16 000– 18 000[e]	42	6 700– 7 600
Old Mill site	11 300[c]	48	5 400

Total annual benefits = £129 000–197 000

[a]Estimate given by Prestbury Amenity Society
[b]Estimate given by Macclesfield Borough Council
[c]Estimate derived from equation (27.1)
[d]Based upon estimates of daily vehicle movements given to the Public Inquiry
[e]Estimate based upon visitor count members for the Silk Museum in Macclesfield

The river is accessible to visitors at five main points; Table 27.6 records the estimates of adult visits to these sites and the annual user benefit there. These estimates are somewhat conservative; the estimate for Prestbury omits visits by local residents, and that for the Old Mill site omits visits from areas other than from the new housing development. Overall, the discounted present value of these benefits falls in the range of £2–3 million, assuming that the annual user benefits shown in Table 27.6 accrue over the life of the improvement scheme but are discounted at the Test Discount Rate of 6% per annum.

From the figures given in Table 27.4, amenity benefits to those living near the river add a lump-sum benefit of approximately £110 000. In addition, there are non-use benefits, but we do not consider it possible yet to evaluate these reliably for a specific site (Green and Tunstall, 1990b).

CONCLUSIONS

(1) Water quality is both a final good—an end in its own right, and an intermediary good—a means to an end. The public wants an unpolluted river because pollution is held to be a bad thing in principle which should not occur. Visitors and local residents also want good water quality because they wish to visit or live by a river corridor that supports a wide variety of wildlife.

(2) Overwhelmingly, people want river corridors that are quiet, rich in flora and fauna, form attractive landscapes, but with basic facilities such as toilets and paths. There are signs that for more major rivers, features such as pubs and facilities for children are desired, and families with children are more likely to want such features. In general, however, they are not desired: we suggest that this is because they are seen as likely to attract other visitors. As a caveat, we should note that concerns with

the safety of children and with public health generally come before those for nature conservation and an attractive river environment.

(3) The public has a comparatively clear idea of what it means by a polluted river, but it does not see a river of good quality as unpolluted; rather, such a river will be judged in terms of its attractiveness.

(4) A large proportion of the population is willing to pay increased water rates to achieve water quality improvements. This is less because water quality improvements would increase their enjoyment when visiting rivers than because of the essentially moral concern that we should not cause pollution.

(5) The value of the increase in enjoyment when visiting rivers, as a result of water quality improvements, is quite low for each individual, but because the number of visits is so large the benefits of such improvements can be quite substantial.

(6) River corridors, compared to parks and other open spaces, attract more frequent visits and draw visitors from a wider area.

(7) Proximity to a river corridor can substantially increase the attractiveness of an area as a place to live.

ACKNOWLEDGEMENTS

The research described was undertaken under contract to the Water Research Centre through funding from the Department of the Environment. The views expressed are, however, not necessarily those of either organization.

REFERENCES

Balmer, K. (1973). *Use of Open Space in Liverpool*, Liverpool City Council, Liverpool.

Brookshire, D. S., Eubanks, L. S., and Sorg, C. F. (1986). "Existence values and normative economics: implications for valuing water resources", *Water Resources Research*, **22**, 1509–1518.

Burrows, A., and House, M. A. (1989). "Public perception of water quality and the use of rivers for recreation", in *River Basin Management—V* (Ed. H. Laikari), pp. 371–379, Pergamon Press, Oxford.

Coker, A., Tunstall, S. M., and Penning Rowsell, E. C. (1989). *An Evaluation of the Recreational and Amenity Benefits of a Flood Alleviation Scheme for Maidenhead*, Report to Thames Water, Flood Hazard Research Centre, Enfield.

Croke, K. G., Swartzman, J. D., and Brenniman, G. R. (1984). "The relationship between perceived motivation for water pollution abatement programs and preferred methods for financing such programs", *Journal of Environmental Systems*, **14**, 395–404.

Cronbach, L. J. (1951). "Coefficient alpha and the internal structure of tests", *Psychometrika*, **16**, 177–193.

Cummings, R. G., Brookshire, D. S., and Schulze, W. D. (1986). *Valuing Environmental Goods: an Assessment of the "Contingent Valuation Method"*, Rowman and Allanheld, Totowa, New Jersey.

Ditton, R. B., and Goodale, T. L. (1973). "Water quality perception and the recreational uses of Green Bay, East Michigan", *Water Resources Research*, **9**, 569–579.

Fisher, A., and Raucher, R. (1984). "Intrinsic benefits of improved water quality: conceptual and empirical perspectives", *Advances in Applied Micro-Economics*, **3**, 37–66.

Fordham, M., Tunstall, S. M., and Penning-Rowsell, E. C. (1991). "Choice and preference in the Thames floodplain: the beginnings of a participatory approach?" *Landscape and Urban Planning*, **20**, 183–187.

Greater London Council (1968). *Surveys of the Use of Open Spaces*, Research Paper No. 2, Planning Department, Greater London Council, London.

Green, C. H. (1980). "Revealed preference theory: assumptions and presumptions", in *Society, Technology and Risk Assessment* (Ed. J. Conrad), pp. 49–56, Academic Press, London.

Green, C. H., Suleman, M., and Wood, J. (1987). "Investment appraisal for urban storm drainage", in *Topics in Urban Storm Water Quality, Planning and Management* (Eds W. Gujer and V. Krejci), pp. 351–356, Ecole Polytechnique Fédérale, Lausanne.

Green, C. H., and Tunstall, S. M. (1990a). "Is the economic evaluation of environmental goods possible?" Paper given at Gestion des Risques et environnement, Paris.

Green, C. H., and Tunstall, S. M. (1990b). "Recreational and amenity preferences for river corridors", Flood Hazard Research Centre, Enfield.

Green, C. H. and Tunstall, S. M. (in press). "The benefit of river water quality improvement", *Applied Economics*.

Green, C. H., Tunstall, S. M., and House, M. A. (1989). "Evaluating the benefits of river water quality improvement", in *Impact Forecasting and Assessment: methods, results, experiences* (Eds P. M. van der Staal and F. A. van Vught), pp. 171–180, Delft University Press, Delft.

Green, C. H., Tunstall, S. M., N'Jai, A., and Rogers, A. (1990). "The economic evaluation of environmental goods", *Project Appraisal*, **5**, 70–82.

Hotelling, H. (1933). "Analysis of complex statistical variables into principal components", *Journal of Educational Psychology*, **24**, 417–441.

House, M. A., and Sangster, E. K. (1990). "Public participation in river corridor management', Paper given at IWEM 90, Glasgow.

House, M. A., Hyde, V. M., and Sangster, E. K. (1990). *River Corridor Features: Nature Conservation and Public Perception and Preferences*, Internal Report, Flood Hazard Research Centre, Enfield.

Kendall, M. G., and Stuart, A. (1961). *Advanced Theory of Statistics*, Griffin, London.

Klecka, W. R. (1975). "Discriminant analysis", in *SPSSX: Statistical Package for Social Sciences* (Eds N. H. Nie, C. H. Hull, J. G. Jenkins, K. Steinbrenner, and D. H. Bent), pp. 434–467, McGraw-Hill, New York.

Kooyoomjian, K., and Clesceri, N. (1974). "Perception of water quality by selected respondent groupings in inland water based recreational environments", *Water Resources Bulletin*, **10**, 728–744.

Likert, R. (1932). *A Technique for the Measurement of Attitudes*, Columbia University Press, New York.

Madriaga, B., and McConnell, K. E. (1987). "Exploring existence value", *Water Resources Research*, **22**, 936–942.

Mitchell, R. C., and Carson, R. T. (1981). *An experiment in determining willingness to pay for national water quality improvements*, Report prepared for the US Environmental Protection Agency, Washington, DC.

National Water Council (1977). *Final Report of the Working Party on Consent Conditions for Effluent Discharges to Freshwater Streams*, London.

Scherer, U., and Coughlin, R. (1971). *The influence of water quality in the evaluation of stream sites*, Report No. 27, Regional Science Research Institute, Philadelphia.

Smith, V. K., and Desvousges, W. H. (1986). *Measuring Water Quality Benefits*, Kluwer-Nijhoff, Boston.

SPSS Inc. (1988). *SPSS/PC Base Manual*, p. B103, Chicago.

Tunstall, S. M., Green, C. H., and Lord, J. (1988). *The evaluation of environmental goods by the Contingent Valuation Method*, Flood Hazard Research Centre, Enfield.

28

River Protection in Ontario, Canada: A Case for Holistic Catchment Management

D. P. DODGE and R. M. BIETTE

Ontario Ministry of Natural Resources, Queen's Park, 99 Wellesley Street West, Toronto, Ontario, Canada M7A 1W3

INTRODUCTION

Ontario is the second largest province in Canada (1.06 million km^2) (lat. 42° to 57° N: long. 74° to 95° W), drained by three major catchments: the Winnipeg River to the Arctic Ocean, the Hudson–James Bays system, and the Laurentian Great Lakes through the St Lawrence to the Atlantic Ocean. Major and minor river systems occur in each catchment. There is a total of 250 000 lakes (>1.0 ha), including parts of four of the five Laurentian Great Lakes. The total length of all of the thousands of rivers and streams has not yet been measured. Ontario has a population of 9.6 million but 70% of its people and their impact are concentrated in 10% of its land mass in the south, around the lower Laurentian Great Lakes on the most fertile land and in the areas of longer growing seasons.

This disparity in the distribution of population has combined with two different and rigid attitudes about riverine and associated resource management. In the south, economics drove most municipalities to view waterways as either inconveniences in the way of development or as convenient outlets for storm drainage and other effluents. This approach appears to be an extension of the frontier mentality that wilderness should be conquered and natural systems should be made to conform to a set of ideas and traditions based on those advocated in Europe during the Industrial Revolution (Edwards et al, 1989). In the north, extraction and living off the land were the main principles in resource management. As long as these two pursuits were not disadvantaged, any approach to riverine management would be acceptable (Brousseau and Goodchild, 1989).

Overall, it appeared that society was prepared to allow any damage to the environment to meet economic gain as long as that damage could be repaired. It was part of the cost of doing business; at some later time, enough money might be generated to clean up.

River Conservation and Management. Edited by P. J. Boon, P. Calow, and G. E. Petts
© 1992 John Wiley & Sons Ltd

OWNERSHIP AND RESPONSIBILITY

At least 12 major Acts, administered by as many agencies in the federal, provincial, and municipal governments, can be applied to manage and regulate rivers in Ontario. Canada was created a country by the British North America Act 1867. In 1982 the Constitution Act formally removed the requirement for approval of any Canadian law by the British Parliament. Both Acts divided powers between the federal government and the provinces. In general, ownership and legislative responsibility for most resources, including land and water, were delegated to the provinces. The situation is less clear for fish and their habitats; case law indicates that the provinces own the fish by right of owning the water and therefore can enact law to collect fees for the use of fish. However, the overall well-being of fish (i.e. the need to maintain fish stocks and their habitats for long-term use), and the law to achieve this objective, remain federal responsibilities.

The law is more convoluted for the division of power within the provincial jurisdiction. On the one hand, the Ministry of Natural Resources (MNR) is responsible for managing all the Crown lands and waters (mostly in Northern Ontario), while municipalities administer patented land (mostly in southern Ontario). MNR is also responsible for the management and protection of wetlands and fish habitat, even though by statute the responsibility for the latter is still in federal jurisdiction. To confuse the issue further, another provincial agency administers water quality law and sometimes water quantity management. In addition, quasi-government agencies called conservation authorities (CAs), funded from provincial and municipal taxes, are responsible for the management of flooding and erosion on floodplains of selected catchments.

TABLE 28.1. Degradation since 1850 of riverine habitat for native salmonids (e.g. *Salvelinus fontinalis*) from selected Ontario tributaries to the Laurentian Great Lakes

	Lake Superior	Lake Huron	Lake Erie	Lake Ontario
Total length surveyed (km)	2052	4617	9393	2849
Degraded (%)	39.7	60.7	73.9	84.7
Relative concentration of population and industrialization	1.0	1.6	5.0	8.3

This convoluted network of responsibility and law permitted the continued deterioration in the quality and quantity of riverine environments, uncontrolled development and urban sprawl, and a generation of conflicts out of all proportion to the stakes. Users developed insensitivity for other users. No one appeared to be in charge. The permitting of many uses permanently denied other uses. The entire process seemed to be generated by an anthropocentric and arrogant assumption that humans can alter the natural hydrograph such that all the benefits from a river can be realized and most disadvantages neutralized. This process over the last 100 years has altered the potential of streams so that species of fish disappeared and miles of stream became stormwater and agricultural drains (Table 28.1).

NEW IDEAS CHALLENGE OLD WAYS

Managing by catchment or basin

This concept remains an innovative idea in most jurisdictions in North America, and is not universally accepted in many other parts of the world. The rationale for catchment management is bedded in the idea that a catchment can be an organic unit in itself. Changes in a catchment at one point may have ramifications in other parts of the catchment, spatially and/or temporally removed from the point of original change. However, a catchment or basin does not fit the political idea of how human populations and votes are distributed. Furthermore, management units defined by lines that follow topography are alien to the traditional North American approach that uses straight lines to define political boundaries.

The basin/catchment concept is receiving growing support in Canada (Mitchell and Gardner, 1983) but is not yet as well an established principle as it is in Britain (Craine, 1969). In Ontario the CAs are organized by catchments, but legislation restricts the mandate of a CA to flood and erosion control and the management of the floodplain to achieve that objective. Holistic catchment management is not part of the mandate of CAs.

The ecosystem concept

In the last decade North American conservationists and resource managers have been talking to each other (and themselves) about ecosystems. The concept of a world that is inter-related and, therefore, inter-dependent has received broad general support in both scientific and lay communities, but there have been, and will continue to be, some problems associated with the application of the ecosystem concept. For example, how does one actually *manage* an ecosystem and set milestones to measure results? There is also inertia and scepticism in financial organizations used to rapid and high returns from investments, and there is a reluctance to wait a long time for results.

Another difficulty is the tendency to construct artificial systems, instead of rehabilitating rivers and allowing the re-establishment of natural systems. For example, although managers of the Great Lakes are formally committed to the establishment of self-sufficient fish populations and their habitat (GLFC, 1980), the public likes catching non-native salmon and trout. Thus, issues associated with artificial systems dominate decision making, and incentives to achieve natural and self-sustaining fish communities are weakened. At the same time, the public and management agencies ignore the risks associated with artificial systems, especially their tendency to destabilize very rapidly under stress (Eschenroder, 1989).

Sustainable development

The concept of sustainable development is not new (Brown, 1981) but has won new champions as a result of the recent UN Report (Brundtland, 1987). At a glance, this concept appeared to be ready-made for revitalization of river resource management in Ontario. However, there are some major concerns that "sustainable development" is being embraced without any satisfactory definition of the concept (Rees, 1989). What does "sustainable" mean in a practical sense, and what forms of development would meet the spirit of the definition? Rees (1989) has proposed the following working definition which we believe is applicable to holistic river management.

> Sustainable development is positive socioeconomic change that does not undermine the ecological and social systems upon which communities and society are dependent. Its successful implementation requires integrated policy, planning, and social learning processes; its political viability depends on the full support of the people it affects through their governments, their social institutions, and their private activities.

Clearly, if society undertakes to apply the philosophy of sustainable development, a major shift in the structure of national economies and even a new form of social organization may be necessary.

The concept has other detractors. Sustainable development is viewed by some as a means to do "business as usual, with a treatment plant" (Fox, 1990). Even Gro Halem Brundtland, chairperson of the UN-WCED, sees economic growth as the mainstay of sustainable development whereby wealthy and rich economies will design more environmentally friendly technologies, more profits would be available to invest in the environment, environmental degradation would become environmental aggradation, and renewable resources would be replenished (Brundtland, 1987).

However, economic expansion is inextricably entwined with population growth. Thomas Malthus proposed this relationship 300 years ago. So the question of sustainable development now revolves around the perplexity of reducing the growth of human populations, with all its attendant moral and social issues.

PROBLEMS TO OVERCOME

Ethics and arrogance

North America was explored, settled, and developed by courageous people who accepted the challenge of conquering a wilderness. Unfortunately, this conquering spirit has developed an attitude that feeds on the quick-fix, here-and-now philosophy and ignores the moral issue of society's duty to posterity (Taylor, 1979; Partridge, 1981). Traditionally, the impacts from present-day management have eliminated many options for the future. It is narrow-minded to suppose that science and technology can recover many of these.

Moreover, where lack of data and understanding of the complexities of ecosystems should have induced humble ignorance, respect, and restraint, human arrogance has wreaked havoc on delicate ecosystems and obliterated entire species with their unique genetic codes. This may be the act posterity finds least forgivable.

A question of ownership

Although the Constitution Act 1982 perpetuates the dual roles of federal and provincial governments in the management of riverine systems in Canada, a concern is growing that this duality cannot continue if adequate considerations are going to be made to meet the long-term management goals that society is demanding. It appears that no one is "in charge". Decisions are not being made at a local level but instead by administrations remote from the rivers being managed. Also, there is major duplication of effort and a concomitant waste of time and energy. It is obvious that Ontario must seek constitutional changes to make the province the senior steward of its aquatic resources.

River science

More resources are needed to study and understand how rivers function. The recent International Large Rivers Symposium (Dodge, 1989) showed the high level of interest developing around the world for this specialized science. The conference also demonstrated that research is needed in major areas of river management such as deltaic functions and floodplain dynamics of biotic production (Welcomme et al, 1989). Considerable interest is now growing in the science and technology of rehabilitation of degraded river channels (Brookes, 1989). Research into the human element has lagged behind research into the environmental element. A better understanding of the forces (e.g. motives of people and corporations) behind the causes of environmental problems could have influenced decisions that we now realize have reduced or eliminated many future options (De Groot, 1989).

PROGRESS WITHOUT PERFECTION

Much has gone wrong over the last two centuries, but there have been significant events occurring over the last decade in Ontario that offer reasons for hope that change and enlightenment will soon become part of river resource management.

Managing ecosystems

In spite of many detractors and critics of this principle, Ontario has made the ecosystem concept an integral part of its long-term planning for fisheries resources and environments for both running and standing water. Over the past two years the Strategic Plan for Ontario Fisheries (SPOF II), first developed in 1976, has undergone major review and revision by teams of citizens and public servants (OMNR, 1991a). SPOF II identified three major issues that threaten the long-term sustainability of Ontario's fisheries resources. These were declining aquatic ecosystem health and loss of fish habitat, loss of fish, and shareholder conflicts. To overcome these problems, Ontario is proposing the following goal and objectives:

Goal for Ontario fisheries: Healthy aquatic ecosystems that provide sustainable benefits to satisfy, in part, society's present and future requirements for a high-quality environment, wholesome food, employment and income, recreational activity, and cultural heritage.

Objectives: In order to provide sustainable benefits over the next decade and beyond, the objectives of the Strategic Plan shall be to:

- Protect healthy aquatic ecosystems;
- Rehabilitate degraded aquatic ecosystems; and
- Improve cultural, social, and economic benefits from Ontario's fisheries resource.

Further, SPOF II has recognized certain truths or "guiding principles" that will underpin fisheries and aquatic habitat management:

Sustainable development
- Sustainable development requires that adverse impacts on natural elements, such as air, land, and water, be minimized to ensure the aquatic ecosystem's overall integrity.

Limit to resource
- There is a limit to the natural productive capacity of aquatic ecosystems and, hence, to the amount of fish that can be harvested from them.

Natural reproduction
- Naturally reproducing fish communities, based on native fish populations, provide predictable and sustainable benefits with minimal long-term cost to society.

Knowledge
- Good fisheries management is scientifically based and relies on the acquisition and use of the best available knowledge.

Societal benefits
- Resource management decisions, including allocation, shall be based on the social, cultural, and economic benefits and costs to society, both present and future.

Added to this renewal of fisheries management is a significant declaration by the Ministry of Natural Resources (MNR) that it intends to emphasize conservation of natural resources as a first priority in allocation. Furthermore, any use of a naturally renewable resource must not put at risk the survival and long-term sustainability of that resource. As a result, the value of natural resources has become more apparent to both the public and the political administration (OMNR, 1991b).

Second, MNR wants to build more long-term partnerships with public, business, and industry whereby the costs and profits from enlightened resource management can be shared. MNR anticipates that these partnerships will improve the process of "valuation", where previously the costs of management were not part of the costs of using natural resources. Other areas that will receive increased emphasis include accountability from managers, improving the knowledge base of the resource, and developing criteria to measure progress.

Sharing mandates

Although the Constitution Act 1982 allows for change, the process of delegation from federal to provincial jurisdictions of fish population and habitat management appears not to be a priority at present. Anticipating that shared responsibilities would continue to be the *modus operandi* at least through the early 1990s, Ontario and Canada have formalized their relationship into a Canada–Ontario Fisheries Agreement (COFA). In COFA, both governments have agreed to the basic tenets espoused by SPOF, and have developed a specific Memorandum of Intent (MOI) to deal with the difficult issue of protecting and rehabilitating fish habitat.

Bilateral activities

Two influential agencies, the International Joint Commission (IJC) and the Great Lakes Fishery Commission (GLFC), formed through treaties and conventions between Canada and the United States, have developed proposals for bilateral allocation and management of the Great Lakes that are based on the principle of ecosystem management. Within the IJC arena, the Parties have agreed to develop ecosystem health indicators to aid the evaluation of pollution-control efforts. The first ecosystem indicator, set for Lake Superior, is using the productivity, stability, and self-propagation of lake trout (*Salvelinus naymaycush*) and the crustacean, *Pontoporeia hoyi*, as specific measures of how effective the two countries have been in their investment of resources to clean water and maintain a large oligotrophic water body.

Similarly, the GLFC has provided the impetus for federal, state, and provincial agencies around all five Laurentian Great Lakes to make ecosystem plans involving fish community goals and objectives, and, thus, to move away from the former and narrow scheme whereby agencies planned for single use and single species.

In both cases, the proof of these changes is yet to be measured, but one can say intuitively that any change from managing for single species to managing for ecosystems has to be better, if only to increase the probability that subsequent actions may have positive results.

Involving the public

Ontario has become a strong advocate of public involvement. For both public and resource management agencies, the development of partnerships has not always been a comfortable process, but each group is beginning to see that the advantages outweigh any disadvantages. For the scientist and administrator there may have been a frustrating period in the process when it seemed that the "public" had no sense of the complexities of managing biological systems, and were capable only of demanding a particular point of view in a "me-first" shout. However, once the public understood certain biological concepts, the process accelerated. Scientists also learned to speak simply and clearly, not always an attribute for which the scientific world is famous. For the public, there was a period of frustration because the development of a partnership seemed to take too long, scientific principles appeared to impede rather than assist decisions, and results took a very long time to appear. However, citizens soon learned how to hold their own in debate and not be overawed by scientists. The public also learned that there are limits to a resource, so that not all things can be offered to all people everywhere they want them. This very effective approach to resource planning is now used successfully in Ontario, notably in the environmental assessment process and the development of SPOF II.

Entrepreneurship

Resource management agencies must consider ways and means of involving the private sector in improving river management and conservation. At present, Canadian and Ontario law does not permit delegating the overall responsibility of fish habitat management in particular, and Crown land in general, from government to the private sector. However, many opportunities arise regularly where the desire to make a profit can be turned to the advantage of natural resource management. On the face of it, this statement appears to be heretical, for many of us know that the past attitude of the private sector has been one of the most inhibiting factors preventing the achievement of sustainability. The clue seems to be the need to emphasize profitability. Planck and Trimble (1990) have described a situation for the Grand River in Ontario, which provides an example of this.

A certain area of the floodplain in the Grand River catchment had become degraded by infilling with sorted and poorly sorted gravels and sands. This area is being considered for a housing development. The developer saw a resource in the river floodplain that others had classified as a problem. The draft development plan proposes the removal of the useful materials to re-sculpture the floodplain contours and to accommodate more of the flood design for a 100-year storm event. The unsorted materials would be used to raise the near banks to allow land development. The extracted materials would generate royalties to the Crown, which off-set costs of floodplain management. For the permission to use these "waste" materials, the developer intends to construct fish and wildlife habitats and general recreation areas to specifications provided by natural resource managers. Furthermore, a sense of ownership for this new habitat will be included with material used to advertise the sale of the new homes. Finally, there is an expectation that property values will increase, anticipating that the home-buying public will place an increased value on property associated with areas of natural and re-created habitat.

CONCLUSION

There is a growing feeling of optimism in Ontario that in this decade we will do a better job in protecting and managing rivers. This optimism is based mainly on the will of the public for change and for increasing emphasis on the environment. This willingness to change is demonstrated by the birth of the "greening" movement, more responsible industry, and more responsive governments who are changing direction to integrate natural resource programmes, to emphasize conservation and protection and to use habitat protection law when necessary.

This decade seems to be "turn-around" time. Sensible management of rivers that includes environmental protection—once a radical concept—has become a conservative motto.

ACKNOWLEDGEMENTS

The ideas and concepts in this chapter are more than something that the two authors could generate. The sense of responsibility for an ecosystem started as the brainchild of the late K. H. Loftus, former Director of the Fisheries Branch in Ontario. His forethought generated a movement that is just now beginning to influence how riverine resources are managed in Ontario. The authors respectfully dedicate this chapter to the memory of Ken Loftus.

DISCLAIMER

The views expressed are those of the authors and not necessarily those of the Ontario Ministry of Natural Resources.

REFERENCES

Brookes, A. (1989). "Alternative channelization procedures", in *Alternatives in Regulated River Management* (Eds J. A. Gore and G. E. Petts), CRC Press, Boca Raton, Florida.

Brousseau, C. S., and Goodchild, G. A. (1989). "Fisheries and yields in the Moose River Basin, Ontario", in *Proceedings of the International Large River Symposium* (Ed. D. P. Dodge), pp. 145–158, Canadian Special Publication of Fisheries and Aquatic Sciences, 106.

Brown, L. (1981). *Building a Sustainable Society*, W. W. Norton, New York.

Brundtland, G. H. (1987). *Our Common Future*, Report of the World Commission on Environment and Development (Chairman: G. H. Brundtland), Oxford University Press, Oxford.

Craine, L. E. (1969). *Water Management Innovations in England*, The John Hopkins Press, Baltimore, Maryland.

De Groot, W. T. (1989). "Environmental research in the environmental policy cycle", *Environmental Management*, **13**, 659–662.

Dodge, D. P. (Ed.) (1989). *Proceedings of the International Large River Symposium*, Canadian Special Publication of Fisheries and Aquatic Sciences, 106.

Edwards, C. J., Hudson, P. L., Duffy, W. G., Nepszy, S. J., McNabb, C. D., Haas, R. C., Liston, C. R., Manny, B., and Busch, W. -D. N. (1989). "Hydrological, morphometrical, and biological characteristics of the connecting rivers of the international Great Lakes", in *Proceedings of the International Large River Symposium* (Ed. D. P. Dodge), pp. 240–264, Canadian Special Publication of Fisheries and Aquatic Sciences, **106**.

Eschenroder, R. L. (1989). "A perspective on artificial systems for the Great Lakes", Paper presented at *Wild Trout IV*, Yellowstone Park, Wyoming, USA, 18–19 September 1989.

Fox, J. (1990). "A "sustainable" cure for a suffering planet", *The Financial Post*, 17 July.

Great Lakes Fishery Commission (GLFC) (1980). *A joint strategic plan for management of Great Lakes Fisheries*, GLFC, Ann Arbor, Michigan.

Mitchell, B., and Gardner, J. (Eds) (1983). *River Basin Management: Canadian Experiences*, University of Waterloo, Department of Geography, Waterloo.

Ontario Ministry of Natural Resources (OMNR) (1991a). *Strategic Plan for Ontario Fisheries (SPOF II). An Aquatic Ecosystem Approach to Managing Fisheries*, Queen's Printer, Toronto.

Ontario Ministry of Natural Resources (OMNR) (1991b). *Direction '90s*, Queen's Printer, Toronto.

Partridge, E. (Ed.) (1981). *Responsibilities to Future Generations, Environmental Ethics*, Prometheus Books, Buffalo, New York.

Planck, J., and Trimble, K. (1990). "Willow Run: An integrated planning concept for the Grand River: An environmental analysis", Paper presented at Floodplain Rivers Conference, Baton Rouge, Louisiana, 9–11 April.

Rees, W. E. (1989). "Defining sustainable development", *CHS Research Bulletin*, May, UBC Centre for Human Settlements, University of British Columbia, Vancouver.

Taylor, M. E. (1979). "Ecology and governments in Canada", in *Ecology Versus Politics in Canada* (Ed. W. Leiss), University of Toronto Press, Toronto.

Welcomme, R. L., Ryder, R. A., and Sedell, J. A. (1989). "Dynamics of fish assemblages in river systems—a synthesis", in *Proceedings of the International Large River Symposium* (Ed. D. P. Dodge), pp. 569–577, Canadian Special Publication of Fisheries and Aquatic Sciences, **106**.

29

River Conservation—Future Prospects

R. L. WELCOMME

Food and Agriculture Organization of the United Nations, Fishery Resources and Environment Division, Via delle Terme di Caracalla, 00100 Rome, Italy

INTRODUCTION: CONCEPTS OF CONSERVATION AND USE

The increasing awareness of the various stresses man is placing on this planet has entered public consciousness to such a degree that all sectors of the population in developed countries and many in the developing world now place environmental concerns high on their list of priorities for action. One measure of this is the organization of the United Nations Conference on Environment and Development, which in 1992 will draw participation from the very highest levels of the countries of the world. That matters have reached this stage is the result of a long process from initial discoveries by scientists, through the popularizers of the media, to those who ultimately make the decisions on legislation and funding in our societies. During this process, the nature of conservation itself has been subject to much debate. Initially, the intentions and mechanisms appeared quite simple, with selected wild ecosystem types or species being conserved *in situ* and especially valuable material preserved *ex situ*. It would now appear that these limited aims are insufficient to respond to the needs for conservation under the steadily increasing pressures of today. The creation of natural parks and reserves, while still an acceptable aim for some specific purposes, does not fill the need to maintain environmental quality and genetic diversity over the whole planet, including those areas directly impacted by man. Nor does it incorporate the protection of the genetic diversity created by man through his various strains of crops and domestic animals. This means that management must now incorporate both the *conservation* and the *use* aspects of the resource. Furthermore, it is no longer possible to view the management and conservation of natural resources within the frame of any one use, such as fisheries, recreation, or forestry. Conservationists, as well as resource managers, are therefore obliged to proceed together to define strategies whereby the productivity and diversity of the various biotic systems can be sustained.

River Conservation and Management. Edited by P. J. Boon, P. Calow, and G. E. Petts
© 1992 John Wiley & Sons Ltd

THE BASIN APPROACH

Within this general framework flowing water ecosystems pose special problems relative to other types of system. They exist in a matrix of terrestrial and other aquatic environments which impress upon the river or stream their own characteristics. Any river thus tends to express the sum of the activities occurring within its basin. This effect clearly becomes more severe as stream order increases and problems of conservation of rivers vary greatly according to river size. It is relatively easy to conserve small, low-order streams as part of a more general terrestrial reserve area but it becomes progressively more difficult to maintain larger rivers in an unaltered state without equivalent conservation policies for the basins upstream. River conservation is therefore largely a problem of conservation of catchment areas.

Policies for regulating activities within river basins are very much conditioned by the high economic potential of water and the energy it contains. The nature of the aquatic resource is subjected to impacts from works which modify the morphology of the terrestrial matrix and alter the quantity and timing of the water flow through the system. In addition, discharge and infiltration of pollutants modify the quality of the water, usually to the detriment of the organisms living in it. Particular concern has been expressed on the effects of large dams on the river systems downstream of them. This concern is justified in that the ecology of large floodplain rivers is such that the flood pulse is the main driver of their biotic and abiotic pressures, and suppression of this seasonal event through impoundment radically alters the system. It is clearly naive to think that the exploitation of the rich nutrient, transport, water, and energy resources, which represent the core of the wealth of so many nations, will cease because of the resulting changes to the environment. It is doubtful, therefore, that many pristine large river environments will survive this century and the earlier decades of the next. In Western Europe all large rivers and most smaller ones have been modified (Petts et al, 1989), as have rivers throughout the temperate zones, and similar processes are under way in the tropics. In this context, those concerned with the living natural resources of rivers are rarely fully in control of the systems they purport to manage. The real decisions that affect the overall characteristics of the system are taken in other fora to which they are often not party. Under these circumstances, two strategies are possible. First, managers can work within the context imposed by applying means to mitigate the worst of the impacts. Second, they can seek to become better integrated into the whole decision-making process in order to limit further deterioration and restore already damaged systems.

CONSERVATION NEEDS OF RIVERS

Tools for the management of river systems and their resources under constraints of other uses have been developing over the last few decades. Small temperate streams and rivers have been studied for a considerable time mainly because of their value for sport fisheries and other forms of recreation. Because of their inherent use in their natural state, their relatively low value for other purposes and their large numbers, a greater proportion of low-order, rhithronic watercourses have tended to persist in a less modified condition than higher-order rivers. The many approaches to the study of these systems have led to the elaboration of classification systems providing for zonation within one river or typologies between systems. More recently, the river continuum concept (Vannote et al, 1980) introduced a dynamic element into this description of longitudinal process. It suggested that the lowest-order, headwater streams were dominated by riparian and terrestrial components from which came the initial injection of coarse particulate carbon. In middle-order rivers the processes were considered mainly internal to the channel, the community structure along a channel being conditioned by the serial processing of the allochthonous organic material as it moves downstream. Studies on small rivers have equally resulted in the development of techniques for the estimation of instream flow needs or for the calculation of the quality of individual habitats and streams aimed at providing managers with the information needed to conserve such systems. These are exemplified by several contributions in this volume.

Many of the contributions deal with relatively small systems. It is therefore important to expand somewhat on the special problems of higher-order rivers. Research on large potamonic rivers is a comparatively recent phenomenon, and knowledge of such systems is consequently more restricted. This is due in some measure to the methodological difficulties associated with the study of large rivers, the lack of perceived importance of such waters, and a series of misconceptions as to the nature of the systems in question. Nevertheless, scientists such as Antipa working on the Romanian Danube around the turn of the century (Antipa, 1910) came to appreciate that large rivers consist of two components, the channel and the floodplain, and that processes in unmodified large rivers were determined by the interplay between them. This holistic approach now appears to have been premature in that it did not correspond to the more general perceptions of the functioning of rivers at a time when river channels in the temperate zone were becoming increasingly separated from the lakes and swamps of the floodplain by impoundment and canalization. Although extensive modification of river valleys had occurred during the Middle Ages, Western cultures had tended to avoid extensive building on the floodplains of rivers, at least up to the Renaissance, and the water meadows and residual lowland flood forests were incorporated into the general pattern of natural resource use (Yon and Tendron, 1981). The introduction of new technologies with the Industrial Revolution gave expanded capacity to control floods and shape channels, and led to a rapid occupation of the previously avoided, low-lying lands along the river margins. Increased needs for food, transport, and waste disposal accelerated the rate of modification, and within a couple of centuries the former floodplain of the river was almost disassociated from its channel across much of Europe and North America. Small wonder, therefore, that river biologists tended to interpret river dynamics solely in terms of channel processes and, where considered at all, to classify floodplain lakes together with more classically lentic waters.

Growing concern for the sustainability of the fisheries of large tropical systems had provoked studies on their biology as early as the 1950s. At the same time, the deteriorating state of the large rivers in the temperate zone, due to pollution and the impacts of river-control works, was stimulating work on these systems. The publication of the results of this research and its open discussion in international meetings such as the Large Rivers Symposium held in Ontario, Canada, in 1986 (Dodge, 1989) has encouraged the evolution of concepts and models to explain the functioning of unmodified rivers, as well as to interpret the effects of human interventions.

FIGURE 29.1. The Kilombero floodplain, Tanzania, showing features of undrained plains

Research on tropical rivers rapidly showed the degree of interrelationship between the river channel and the inundated floodplain (Figures 29.1 and 29.2). The dynamics of components of the system as far removed as fish, on the one hand, and carbon and nutrients, on the other, confirmed the intimate relationship between the two components of the system, and it was concluded that the river–floodplain complex was functionally interrelated (Welcomme, 1985). Results of studies in temperate rivers in which some river reaches remained in a relatively unspoilt condition, such as the Atchafalaya (Bryan and Sabins, 1979), Danube (Holcik and Bastl, 1976) and Rhone (Amoros et al, 1982), later confirmed that the conclusions drawn from tropical systems also applied to unmodified temperate rivers. Indeed, large river systems with pronounced flood season-ality seem to behave in a broadly similar manner, irrespective of latitude or continent. The interaction between channel and floodplain is summarized by the flood pulse concept (Junk et al, 1989), which maintains that the productivity of flood systems originates in a moving littoral in which mobilization of nutrients occurs as water invades a transition zone between the terrestrial and aquatic phases of the system. These processes imply a lateral zonation across the floodplain regulated by the extent and duration of flood that is the counterpart to the longitudinal zonation that dominates in smaller streams. The concept also indicates that the same processes govern floodplain functions wherever the plain is situated in the river system. There is now considerable evidence that the phenomena associated with the aquatic–terrestrial transition zone apply equally to many other types of seasonally fluctuating wetlands. The riparian zone, which

(a)

(b)

FIGURE 29.2. The Magdalena floodplain, Colombia, (a) at low water and (b) at high water, showing the variation between the two states

although never directly submerged, has also been shown to play a greater role in regulating the processes of unmodified lower-order streams than thought hitherto. It may be considered that the elucidation of the role of the littoral and riparian ecotones is one of the major conceptual advances in our understanding of rivers, and has had far-reaching implications for planning for river conservation. The major task of river restoration today is to find ways in which this area of complex carbon, nutrient, and biotic interactions can be rehabilitated and re-incorporated into the system as a whole.

It is difficult to foresee any major changes in direction in the technical aspects of conservation of rivers in the next few years. Workers on the *lower-order streams* should concern themselves with *lateral* relationships by continuing to explore the aquatic–terrestrial interface and the origins and fate of allochthonous inputs to the system. Here conservation strategies should aim at maintaining intact, or restoring, the vegetation cover upon which the inputs are based, or, if that is not possible, finding alternative vegetation patterns which fulfil the same function. Strategies for *middle-order rivers* should be aimed at the conservation or maintenance of the *longitudinal* processes. It is in these reaches that the most work appears to have been done, and several techniques for restoration, mainly based on enhancing channel diversity and restoring the riparian strip, have been suggested. Some authors have cast doubt on the potential success of these practices, but, on the whole, the examples given are sufficiently encouraging as to point the way for a larger and more widespread deployment of such techniques. In the *larger potamonic rivers* concerns should centre around the management of the *lateral processes* with the re-incorporation of floodplain features into the system. This is by far the most difficult area, because of the costs and complex land ownership disputes that such actions are likely to generate. Furthermore, knowledge is still lacking on the typologies of floodplains and the factors regulating their relative productivity. For this reason, decisions on how to conserve lowland wetlands associated with rivers are liable to be even more politically aggravated than in other areas.

MOTIVES FOR CONSERVATION

Many objectives for conservation have been cited. These largely represent what may be regarded as the inherent aesthetic and academic values underlying conventional conservation. To these should be added utilitarian values of the aquatic resource such as those produced by fisheries, traditional drawdown agriculture, or floodplain forestry, all of which have the capacity to substantially alter the nature of the system if pursued incorrectly. On the other hand, if adequate management strategies can be defined, such resources can be cropped with a high degree of sustainability and even contribute to the conservation of the resource. This is particularly the case in fisheries, where angling has been one of the major driving forces in the conservation of environmental quality in the north temperate zone. Rivers worldwide provide *ca.* 5×10^6 tons of high-quality animal protein per year in addition to their recreation value, and their fish communities supply seed for further production from aquaculture. However, the dynamics of the complex multi-species fish communities of large rivers are little understood, and increased studies on how best to develop, manage and conserve them are urgently needed.

In the face of the multiple motives for conservation and the rather different endpoints of the various processes, one of the problems besetting any attempt to reach a consensus on how the natural resource should be managed is the lack of a clear, common vision of what is required of the resource. Societies are more often aware of what they do not want than have a clear appreciation of what the endpoint of the conservation process should be. It is doubtful, for instance, that many would want to return to the pristine, wilderness state, nor would they wish to continue with the corrupted state in which most water-courses are found today. Instead, one supposes that in parts of Europe some form of garden-like landscape—often resembling parks designed by Nash, the eighteenth-century British landscape architect—in which natural processes can be allowed to proceed, but with a heavy subsidy from man, is commonly accepted as the most desirable end-state. In North America and Australia there would, perhaps, be a greater tolerance of the wild condition. In the developing world there is an even more severe dichotomy between the ways in which the developed nations would wish to see their natural resources conserved to preserve the wilderness state, and the aspirations of the countries themselves to develop and benefit by these same resources. Attempts at compromise between the various interest groups to satisfy all usually lead to indecisiveness and unsatisfactory solutions for all. This means that the managers are forced into a situation where they will have to adopt a single aim for conservation hopefully based upon the majority view.

THE DECISION-MAKING PROCESS

It is precisely this formulation of the majority view which presents the greatest problems in the conservation, development, and management of rivers, in common with all natural resources today. Many have commented on the need for political will but it is far from clear as to what the origins of such "will" should be, or where it should reside. It is perhaps useful to explore the reasons underlying the difficulties which are experienced in reaching decisions about the disposal of natural resources. Much of the problem comes down to the questions of who has access to the resource, how the various aspects of the resource are allocated among potential users, and who is responsible for making and enforcing these decisions. In this the processes adopted by different societies are apt to vary, and some decisions of other societies may appear puzzling or illogical if the cultural values of the society concerned are not understood. The current reaction in certain quarters to conservation as being an essentially Anglo-Saxon ethic and thus of no validity for other societies is one manifestation of this.

There seem to be two main ways in which human societies perceive their relationship to natural resources which affect not only their general political form but also the time frames under which they operate and their appreciation of risk. At one extreme there is the belief that natural resources are limited and fixed in kind and in quantity. This implies that the resources available to the members of a society are fixed and that increases in the richness of any individual can only be bought at the cost of others. Societies dominated by this attitude tend to view the risks inherent in innovation as unacceptable and to adopt long-term strategies in their interactions with the environment. They either tend to adopt egalitarian structures or to evolve towards a type of feudalism where a privileged class controls almost all the resources. In either case the *status quo* is defended by a rigorous code of behaviour, usually sanctioned by tradition or religion, dissenters from which are treated harshly. Such societies tend to develop functional relationships with their environment through a homogeneous "world view" and generally prove successful in sustaining their resource bases within certain limits on their populations. This manner of viewing the world is particularly common among those countries with strongly rural economies.

A striking example of the management systems that arise within this framework is that of the River Niger. Here a series of ancient and modern cultures have successfully managed a river–floodplain system set in an arid and unproductive landscape for a variety of rural pursuits, including fisheries, cattle rearing, and agriculture through a complex and traditionally based allocation system.

The alternative belief is that the total resources available to society can be increased. Societies with this viewpoint accept the risks of innovation and adopt shorter-term solutions to environmental problems. At their most extreme, they adopt anarchic open-access systems under which all are free to enjoy the benefits of such small portions of the resource as they can garner. As there is no unified belief system it is difficult to reach any form of public consensus on the endpoint of any development policy, and societies operating under these assumptions have proved notoriously inefficient in the management of their natural resource base. Such a conception of nature is typical of urbanized nations, particularly early in their industrialization process, and have resulted, in Europe, in the degradation of most rivers, including the Rhine, and in North America, the Mississippi. While subsistence and artisanal rural societies tend to the resource-limited view, increasing independence from the agricultural base tends to encourage a mix between the two positions. Western societies in particular have oscillated between the two extremes over the last two millennia, but recently the open-resource concept has prevailed and extended to much of the rest of the world. That this situation cannot continue has been a repeated theme among the environmentally concerned which now seems to have gained wider recognition. What is less clear is what forms of mechanism will be necessary to define responsibility and accountability for conservation in the future.

There have been a series of transformations in the role of governing organizations with regard to natural resources which largely correspond to the two views described above. In pre-industrial, rural societies, authority seems to assume a custodianship role, holding the resource in trust for a higher, usually supernatural, authority. Relationships between cause and effect were poorly understood and stemmed from a long-term empiricism codified within the society. At this stage, government, through its various arms, was highly interventionist and largely controlled the allocation of the resources among users and access at the level of the individual, according to rigid religious or traditional precepts. In early industrialized societies interest in the traditional forms of natural resource management lapsed in favour of an unchecked economic expansion, usually at the cost of the natural resource. Where these natural resources were utilized they were subject to similar exploitative patterns as other sectors of the economy, and little control was exercised on the individual user. Although the connection between the increasing industrialized urbanization was recognized, the effects were regarded as an acceptable price to pay for progress. Both these attitudes persist today in various parts of the world, and the differences between them lie at the root of some of the incomprehensions that are experienced in trying to formulate common attitudes towards conservation. In modern post-industrialized societies the scale of environmental degradation has proceeded to the point that it can no longer be tolerated, although a number of opposing views still persist as to how the limited resources available should be deployed. For example, Regier and Bronson (pers. comm.), developing the work of Norton (1989), have distinguished four world views currently held within elements of north temperate societies. These views—exploitist, utilist, integrist, and inherentist—all propose different forms of interaction between society and nature. Here the decision-making authority, be it government or some other delegated body, now appears to act as a referee discerning the consensus of the various interested groups and defining conservation and management policies accordingly. This referee capacity assumes a free flow of information on the effects of the various types of use so that decisions can best reflect the majority common interest.

It is now clear that a single national authority is insufficient by itself to conserve rivers, and that a hierarchical structure of rights and responsibilities is more appropriate to the way the living aquatic world itself is organized. Certain types of decision can only be viewed in a global context, others at a regional, national, or local entity level. In the case of rivers the global context is generally too large, and although some may claim that global climatic changes will eventually affect river systems along with all environments, this level of decision making lies largely outside the scope of the sector. Many river basins are sub-regional, covering the national territories of several countries. Yet others are local in that their whole course is completed within the boundaries of one country. The national level of organization is probably the least relevant for dealing with the problems of river conservation and management at both levels, as very few nations coincide totally with a single river system. As frequently reiterated, the natural management unit is the river basin, but although a number of basin authorities do exist worldwide, they are usually relatively powerless, or are aimed at one particular use such as navigation. Their interests are usually subordinated either to those of their member countries or to the larger state within which they exist. Because many national authorities have some responsibility for water and its use, numerous Acts from diverse sources regulate activities in rivers. Furthermore, legislation from other sectors of the national jurisdiction can also impinge on rivers. Such fragmented regulation systems are frequently insensitive to the variety and differences among catchments, or even to the special needs of the aquatic environment itself.

If rivers are to be conserved and their resources managed constructively, greater efforts have to be made to involve the public directly in the decision-making process. Appropriate mechanisms for action at this level include public workshops and other fora, either for the better education of the population or to reach local decisions on resource allocation. The more informed allocation of the resources among the various users at all levels implies limitations on many activities now taken for granted, such as the rights to abstract water, to discharge noxious wastes, or even to enjoy continued unrestricted access to the recreational facilities a water body might offer. It also implies the need for the assumption of responsibility by the user and his increasing bearing of the real cost of his activities. This process has already led, and will probably lead increasingly in the future, to the criminalization of practices that diverge from what is perceived as the greatest good for the majority. In other words, for effective conservation policies to be pursued it would appear inevitable for there to be a certain reversion to the limited resources view of the world and the associated restrictive moral codes that accompany it.

REFERENCES

Amoros, C. M., Richardot-Coulet, M., and Patou, G. (1982). "Les ensembles fonctionelles des entités écologiques qui traduisent l'évolution de l'hydrosystème en intégrant la géomorphologie et l'anthropisation (example de l'haut Rhône Français)", *Revue de Géographie de Lyon*, **57**, 49–62.

Antipa, G. (1910). *Regiunea inundabila a Dunarii. Starea ei actuala si mijloacele de a o pue in valoare*, Bucharest.

Bryan, C. F., and Sabins, D. S. (1979). "Management implications in water quality and fish standing stock information in the Atchafalaya river basin, Louisiana", in *Proceedings of the Third Coastal Marsh and Estuary Management Symposium* (Eds J. W. Day, D. D. Culley, R. E. Turner, and A. J. Mumphrey), pp. 293–316, Louisiana State University, Baton Rouge.

Dodge, D. P. (Ed.) (1989). *Proceedings of the International Large Rivers Symposium (LARS)*, Canadian Special Publication on Fisheries and Aquatic Sciences 106.

Holcik, J., and Bastl, I. (1976). "Ecological effects of water level fluctuations upon the fish populations of the Danube River floodplain in Czechoslovakia", *Acta Sciencia Naturalis Brno*, **10**, 1–46.

Junk, W. J., Bayley, P. B., and Sparks, R. E. (1989). "The flood-pulse concept in river–floodplain systems", in *Proceedings of the International Large Rivers Symposium (LARS)* (Ed. D. P. Dodge), pp. 110–127, Canadian Special Publication on Fisheries and Aquatic Sciences 106.

Norton, B. G. (1989). "Intergenerational equity and environmental decisions: A model using Rawls' 'veil of ignorance'", *Ecological Economics*, **1**, 137–159.

Petts, G. E., Moller, H., and Roux, A. L. (1989). *Historical Change of Large Alluvial Rivers: Western Europe*, John Wiley, Chichester.

Vannote, R. L., Minshall, G. W., Cummins, K. W., Sedell, J. R., and Cushing, C. E. (1980). "The river continuum concept", *Canadian Journal of Fisheries and Aquatic Sciences*, **37**, 370–377.

Welcomme, R. L. (1985). *River Fisheries*, FAO Fisheries Technical Paper 262.

Yon, D., and Tendron, G. (1981). *Alluvial Forests of Europe*, Council of Europe National Environmental Service 22.

Index